T0186094

Lecture Notes in Computer Science

Lecture Notes in Artificial Intelligence　14175

Founding Editor

Jörg Siekmann

Series Editors

Randy Goebel, *University of Alberta, Edmonton, Canada*
Wolfgang Wahlster, *DFKI, Berlin, Germany*
Zhi-Hua Zhou, *Nanjing University, Nanjing, China*

The series Lecture Notes in Artificial Intelligence (LNAI) was established in 1988 as a topical subseries of LNCS devoted to artificial intelligence.

The series publishes state-of-the-art research results at a high level. As with the LNCS mother series, the mission of the series is to serve the international R & D community by providing an invaluable service, mainly focused on the publication of conference and workshop proceedings and postproceedings.

Gianmarco De Francisci Morales ·
Claudia Perlich · Natali Ruchansky ·
Nicolas Kourtellis · Elena Baralis ·
Francesco Bonchi
Editors

Machine Learning and Knowledge Discovery in Databases

Applied Data Science and Demo Track

European Conference, ECML PKDD 2023
Turin, Italy, September 18–22, 2023
Proceedings, Part VII

Springer

Editors
Gianmarco De Francisci Morales ⓘ
CENTAI
Turin, Italy

Claudia Perlich
NYU and Two Sigma
New York, NY, USA

Natali Ruchansky ⓘ
Netflix
Los Angeles, CA, USA

Nicolas Kourtellis ⓘ
Telefonica Research
Barcelona, Spain

Elena Baralis ⓘ
Politecnico di Torino
Turin, Italy

Francesco Bonchi ⓘ
CENTAI
Turin, Italy

ISSN 0302-9743   ISSN 1611-3349 (electronic)
Lecture Notes in Artificial Intelligence
ISBN 978-3-031-43429-7   ISBN 978-3-031-43430-3 (eBook)
https://doi.org/10.1007/978-3-031-43430-3

LNCS Sublibrary: SL7 – Artificial Intelligence

This Springer imprint is published by the registered company Springer Nature Switzerland AG
The registered company address is: Gewerbestrasse 11, 6330 Cham, Switzerland

Paper in this product is recyclable.

Preface

The 2023 edition of the European Conference on Machine Learning and Principles and Practice of Knowledge Discovery in Databases (ECML PKDD 2023) was held in Turin, Italy, from September 18 to 22, 2023.

The ECML PKDD conference, held annually, acts as a worldwide platform showcasing the latest advancements in machine learning and knowledge discovery in databases, encompassing groundbreaking applications. With a history of successful editions, ECML PKDD has established itself as the leading European machine learning and data mining conference, offering researchers and practitioners an unparalleled opportunity to exchange knowledge and ideas.

The main conference program consisted of presentations of 255 accepted papers and three keynote talks (in order of appearance):

- Max Welling (University of Amsterdam): Neural Wave Representations
- Michael Bronstein (University of Oxford): Physics-Inspired Graph Neural Networks
- Kate Crawford (USC Annenberg): Mapping Generative AI

In addition, there were 30 workshops, 9 combined workshop-tutorials, 5 tutorials, 3 discovery challenges, and 16 demonstrations. Moreover, the PhD Forum provided a friendly environment for junior PhD students to exchange ideas and experiences with peers in an interactive atmosphere and to get constructive feedback from senior researchers. The conference included a Special Day on Artificial Intelligence for Financial Crime Fight to discuss, share, and present recent developments in AI-based financial crime detection.

In recognition of the paramount significance of ethics in machine learning and data mining, we invited the authors to include an ethical statement in their submissions. We encouraged the authors to discuss the ethical implications of their submission, such as those related to the collection and processing of personal data, the inference of personal information, or the potential risks. We are pleased to report that our call for ethical statements was met with an overwhelmingly positive response from the authors.

The ECML PKDD 2023 Organizing Committee supported Diversity and Inclusion by awarding some grants that enable early career researchers to attend the conference, present their research activities, and become part of the ECML PKDD community. A total of 8 grants covering all or part of the registration fee (4 free registrations and 4 with 50% discount) were awarded to individuals who belong to underrepresented communities, based on gender and role/position, to attend the conference and present their research activities. The goal of the grants was to provide financial support to early-career (women) scientists and Master and Ph.D. students from developing countries. The Diversity and Inclusion action also includes the SoBigData Award, fully sponsored by the SoBigData++ Horizon2020 project, which aims to encourage more diverse participation in computer science and machine learning events. The award is intended to cover expenses for transportation and accommodation.

The papers presented during the three main conference days were organized in four different tracks:

- Research Track: research or methodology papers from all areas in machine learning, knowledge discovery, and data mining;
- Applied Data Science Track: papers on novel applications of machine learning, data mining, and knowledge discovery to solve real-world use cases, thereby bridging the gap between practice and current theory;
- Journal Track: papers published in special issues of the journals Machine Learning and Data Mining and Knowledge Discovery;
- Demo Track: short papers introducing new prototypes or fully operational systems that exploit data science techniques and are presented via working demonstrations.

We received 829 submissions for the Research track and 239 for the Applied Data Science Track.

We accepted 196 papers (24%) in the Research Track and 58 (24%) in the Applied Data Science Track. In addition, there were 44 papers from the Journal Track and 16 demo papers (out of 28 submissions).

We want to thank all participants, authors, all chairs, all Program Committee members, area chairs, session chairs, volunteers, co-organizers, and organizers of workshops and tutorials for making ECML PKDD 2023 an outstanding success. Thanks to Springer for their continuous support and Microsoft for allowing us to use their CMT software for conference management and providing support throughout. Special thanks to our sponsors and the ECML PKDD Steering Committee for their support. Finally, we thank the organizing institutions: CENTAI (Italy) and Politecnico di Torino (Italy).

September 2023

Elena Baralis
Francesco Bonchi
Manuel Gomez Rodriguez
Danai Koutra
Claudia Plant
Gianmarco De Francisci Morales
Claudia Perlich

Organization

General Chairs

Elena Baralis   Politecnico di Torino, Italy
Francesco Bonchi   CENTAI, Italy and Eurecat, Spain

Research Track Program Chairs

Manuel Gomez Rodriguez   Max Planck Institute for Software Systems, Germany
Danai Koutra   University of Michigan, USA
Claudia Plant   University of Vienna, Austria

Applied Data Science Track Program Chairs

Gianmarco De Francisci Morales   CENTAI, Italy
Claudia Perlich   NYU and TwoSigma, USA

Journal Track Chairs

Tania Cerquitelli   Politecnico di Torino, Italy
Marcello Restelli   Politecnico di Milano, Italy
Charalampos E. Tsourakakis   Boston University, USA and ISI Foundation, Italy
Fabio Vitale   CENTAI, Italy

Workshop and Tutorial Chairs

Rosa Meo   University of Turin, Italy
Fabrizio Silvestri   Sapienza University of Rome, Italy

Demo Chairs

Nicolas Kourtellis   Telefonica, Spain
Natali Ruchansky   Netflix, USA

Local Chairs

Daniele Apiletti   Politecnico di Torino, Italy
Paolo Bajardi   CENTAI, Italy
Eliana Pastor   Politecnico di Torino, Italy

Discovery Challenge Chairs

Danilo Giordano   Politecnico di Torino, Italy
André Panisson   CENTAI, Italy

PhD Forum Chairs

Yllka Velaj   University of Vienna, Austria
Matteo Riondato   Amherst College, USA

Diversity and Inclusion Chair

Tania Cerquitelli   Politecnico di Torino, Italy

Proceedings Chairs

Eliana Pastor   Politecnico di Torino, Italy
Giulia Preti   CENTAI, Italy

Sponsorship Chairs

Daniele Apiletti   Politecnico di Torino, Italy
Paolo Bajardi   CENTAI, Italy

Web Chair

Alessandro Fiori   Flowygo, Italy

Social Media and Publicity Chair

Flavio Giobergia   Politecnico di Torino, Italy

Online Chairs

Alkis Koudounas   Politecnico di Torino, Italy
Simone Monaco   Politecnico di Torino, Italy

Best Paper Awards Chairs

Peter Flach   University of Bristol, UK
Katharina Morik   TU Dortmund, Germany
Arno Siebes   Utrecht University, The Netherlands

ECML PKDD Steering Committee

Massih-Reza Amini   Université Grenoble Alpes, France
Annalisa Appice   University of Bari, Aldo Moro, Italy
Ira Assent   Aarhus University, Denmark
Tania Cerquitelli   Politecnico di Torino, Italy
Albert Bifet   University of Waikato, New Zealand
Francesco Bonchi   CENTAI, Italy and Eurecat, Spain
Peggy Cellier   INSA Rennes, France
Saso Dzeroski   Jožef Stefan Institute, Slovenia
Tias Guns   KU Leuven, Belgium
Alípio M. G. Jorge   University of Porto, Portugal
Kristian Kersting   TU Darmstadt, Germany
Jefrey Lijffijt   Ghent University, Belgium
Luís Moreira-Matias   Sennder GmbH, Germany
Katharina Morik   TU Dortmund, Germany
Siegfried Nijssen   Université catholique de Louvain, Belgium
Andrea Passerini   University of Trento, Italy

Program Committee

Guest Editorial Board, Journal Track

Marco Cotogni   University of Pavia, Italy
Gabriele D'Acunto   Sapienza University of Rome, Italy
Cassio Fraga Dantas   TETIS, Université Montpellier, INRAE, France
Jérôme Darmont   Université Lumière Lyon 2, France
George Dasoulas   Harvard University, USA
Sébastien Destercke   Université de Technologie de Compiègne, France
Shridhar Devamane   Global Academy of Technology, India
Claudia Diamantini   Università Politecnica delle Marche, Italy
Gianluca Drappo   Politecnico di Milano, Italy
Pedro Ferreira   University of Lisbon, Portugal
Cèsar Ferri   Universitat Politècnica de València, Spain
M. Julia Flores   Universidad de Castilla-La Mancha, Spain
Germain Forestier   University of Haute-Alsace, France
Elisa Fromont   Université de Rennes 1, France
Emanuele Frontoni   University of Macerata, Italy
Esther Galbrun   University of Eastern Finland, Finland
Joao Gama   University of Porto, Portugal
Jose A. Gamez   Universidad de Castilla-La Mancha, Spain
David García Soriano   ISI Foundation, Italy
Paolo Garza   Politecnico di Torino, Italy
Salvatore Greco   Politecnico di Torino, Italy
Riccardo Guidotti   University of Pisa, Italy
Francesco Gullo   UniCredit, Italy
Shahrzad Haddadan   Rutgers Business School, USA
Martin Holena   Czech Academy of Sciences, Czech Republic
Jaakko Hollmén   Stockholm University, Sweden
Dino Ienco   INRAE, France
Georgiana Ifrim   University College Dublin, Ireland
Felix Iglesias   TU Vienna, Austria
Angelo Impedovo   Niuma, Italy
Manfred Jaeger   Aalborg University, Denmark
Szymon Jaroszewicz   Warsaw University of Technology, Poland
Panagiotis Karras   Aarhus University, Denmark
George Katsimpras   National Center for Scientific Research
                                     Demokritos, Greece
Mehdi Kaytoue   Infologic R&D, France
Dragi Kocev   Jožef Stefan Institute, Slovenia
Yun Sing Koh   University of Auckland, New Zealand
Sotiropoulos Konstantinos   Boston University, USA
Lars Kotthoff   University of Wyoming, USA
Alkis Koudounas   Politecnico di Torino, Italy
Tommaso Lanciano   Sapienza University of Rome, Italy

Helge Langseth	Norwegian University of Science and Technology, Norway
Thien Le	MIT, USA
Hsuan-Tien Lin	National Taiwan University, Taiwan
Marco Lippi	University of Modena and Reggio Emilia, Italy
Corrado Loglisci	University of Bari, Aldo Moro, Italy
Manuel López-ibáñez	University of Manchester, UK
Nuno Lourenço	CISUC, Portugal
Claudio Lucchese	Ca' Foscari University of Venice, Italy
Brian Mac Namee	University College Dublin, Ireland
Gjorgji Madjarov	Ss. Cyril and Methodius University in Skopje, North Macedonia
Luigi Malagò	Transylvanian Institute of Neuroscience, Romania
Sagar Malhotra	Fondazione Bruno Kessler, Italy
Fragkiskos Malliaros	CentraleSupélec, Université Paris-Saclay, France
Giuseppe Manco	ICAR-CNR, Italy
Basarab Matei	Sorbonne Université Paris Nord, France
Michael Mathioudakis	University of Helsinki, Finland
Rosa Meo	University of Turin, Italy
Mohamed-Lamine Messai	Université Lumière Lyon 2, France
Sara Migliorini	University of Verona, Italy
Alex Mircoli	Università Politecnica delle Marche, Italy
Atsushi Miyauchi	University of Tokyo, Japan
Simone Monaco	Politecnico di Torino, Italy
Anna Monreale	University of Pisa, Italy
Corrado Monti	CENTAI, Italy
Katharina Morik	TU Dortmund, Germany
Lia Morra	Politecnico di Torino, Italy
Arsenii Mustafin	Boston University, USA
Mirco Mutti	Politecnico di Milano/University of Bologna, Italy
Amedeo Napoli	University of Lorraine, CNRS, LORIA, France
Kleber Oliveira	CENTAI, Italy
Gabriella Olmo	Politecnico di Torino, Italy
Marios Papachristou	Cornell University, USA
Panagiotis Papapetrou	Stockholm University, Sweden
Matteo Papini	Universitat Pompeu Fabra, Spain
Vincenzo Pasquadibisceglie	University of Bari, Aldo Moro, Italy
Eliana Pastor	Politecnico di Torino, Italy
Andrea Paudice	University of Milan, Italy
Charlotte Pelletier	IRISA - Université Bretagne-Sud, France
Ruggero G. Pensa	University of Turin, Italy
Simone Piaggesi	University of Bologna/ISI Foundation, Italy

Area Chairs, Research Track

Fabrizio Angiulli	University of Calabria, Italy
Annalisa Appice	University of Bari, Aldo Moro, Italy
Antonio Artés	Universidad Carlos III de Madrid, Spain
Martin Atzmueller	Osnabrück University, Germany
Christian Böhm	University of Vienna, Austria
Michael R. Berthold	KNIME, Switzerland
Albert Bifet	Université Paris-Saclay, France
Hendrik Blockeel	KU Leuven, Belgium
Ulf Brefeld	Leuphana University, Germany
Paula Brito	INESC TEC - LIAAD/University of Porto, Portugal
Wolfram Burgard	University of Technology Nuremberg, Germany
Seshadhri C.	UCSC, USA
Michelangelo Ceci	University of Bari, Aldo Moro, Italy
Peggy Cellier	IRISA - INSA Rennes, France
Duen Horng Chau	Georgia Institute of Technology, USA
Nicolas Courty	IRISA - Université Bretagne-Sud, France
Bruno Cremilleux	Université de Caen Normandie, France
Jesse Davis	KU Leuven, Belgium
Abir De	IIT Bombay, India
Tom Diethe	AstraZeneca, UK
Yuxiao Dong	Tsinghua University, China
Kurt Driessens	Maastricht University, The Netherlands
Tapio Elomaa	Tampere University, Finland
Johannes Fürnkranz	JKU Linz, Austria
Sophie Fellenz	RPTU Kaiserslautern-Landau, Germany
Elisa Fromont	IRISA/Inria rba - Université de Rennes 1, France
Thomas Gärtner	TU Vienna, Austria
Patrick Gallinari	Criteo AI Lab - Sorbonne Université, France
Joao Gama	INESC TEC - LIAAD, Portugal
Rayid Ghani	Carnegie Mellon University, USA
Aristides Gionis	KTH Royal Institute of Technology, Sweden
Chen Gong	Nanjing University of Science and Technology, China
Francesco Gullo	UniCredit, Italy
Eyke Hüllermeier	LMU Munich, Germany
Junheng Hao	University of California, Los Angeles, USA
José Hernández-Orallo	Universitat Politècnica de Valencia, Spain
Daniel Hernández-Lobato	Universidad Autonoma de Madrid, Spain
Sibylle Hess	TU Eindhoven, The Netherlands

Sriparna Saha   IIT Patna, India
Ute Schmid   University of Bamberg, Germany
Lars Schmidt-Thieme   University of Hildesheim, Germany
Michele Sebag   LISN CNRS, France
Thomas Seidl   LMU Munich, Germany
Junming Shao   University of Electronic Science and Technology
                                     of China, China
Arno Siebes   Utrecht University, The Netherlands
Fabrizio Silvestri   Sapienza University of Rome, Italy
Carlos Soares   University of Porto, Portugal
Christian Sohler   University of Cologne, Germany
Myra Spiliopoulou   Otto-von-Guericke-University Magdeburg,
                                     Germany
Jie Tang   Tsinghua University, China
Nikolaj Tatti   University of Helsinki, Finland
Evimaria Terzi   Boston University, USA
Marc Tommasi   Lille University, France
Heike Trautmann   University of Münster, Germany
Herke van Hoof   University of Amsterdam, The Netherlands
Celine Vens   KU Leuven, Belgium
Christel Vrain   University of Orleans, France
Jilles Vreeken   CISPA Helmholtz Center for Information
                                     Security, Germany
Wei Ye   Tongji University, China
Jing Zhang   Renmin University of China, China
Min-Ling Zhang   Southeast University, China

Area Chairs, Applied Data Science Track

Annalisa Appice   University of Bari, Aldo Moro, Italy
Ira Assent   Aarhus University, Denmark
Martin Atzmueller   Osnabrück University, Germany
Michael R. Berthold   KNIME, Switzerland
Hendrik Blockeel   KU Leuven, Belgium
Michelangelo Ceci   University of Bari, Aldo Moro, Italy
Peggy Cellier   IRISA - INSA Rennes, France
Yi Chang   Jilin University, China
Nicolas Courty   IRISA - UBS, France
Bruno Cremilleux   Université de Caen Normandie, France
Peng Cui   Tsinghua University, China
Anirban Dasgupta   IIT Gandhinagar, India

Tom Diethe	AstraZeneca, UK
Carlotta Domeniconi	George Mason University, USA
Dejing Dou	BCG, USA
Kurt Driessens	Maastricht University, The Netherlands
Johannes Fürnkranz	JKU Linz, Austria
Faisal Farooq	Qatar Computing Research Institute, Qatar
Paolo Frasconi	University of Florence, Italy
Elisa Fromont	IRISA/Inria rba - Université de Rennes 1, France
Glenn Fung	Liberty Mutual, USA
Joao Gama	INESC TEC - LIAAD, Portugal
Jose A. Gamez	Universidad de Castilla-La Mancha, Spain
Rayid Ghani	Carnegie Mellon University, USA
Aristides Gionis	KTH Royal Institute of Technology, Sweden
Sreenivas Gollapudi	Google, USA
Francesco Gullo	UniCredit, Italy
Eyke Hüllermeier	LMU Munich, Germany
Jingrui He	University of Illinois at Urbana-Champaign, USA
Jaakko Hollmén	Aalto University, Finland
Andreas Hotho	University of Würzburg, Germany
Daxin Jiang	Microsoft, Beijing, China
Alipio M. G. Jorge	INESC TEC/University of Porto, Portugal
George Karypis	University of Minnesota, USA
Eamonn Keogh	UC, Riverside, USA
Yun Sing Koh	University of Auckland, New Zealand
Parisa Kordjamshidi	Michigan State University, USA
Lars Kotthoff	University of Wyoming, USA
Nicolas Kourtellis	Telefonica Research, Spain
Stefan Kramer	JGU Mainz, Germany
Balaji Krishnapuram	Pinterest, USA
Niklas Lavesson	Blekinge Institute of Technology, Sweden
Chuan Lei	Amazon Web Services, USA
Marius Lindauer	Leibniz University Hannover, Germany
Patrick Loiseau	Inria, France
Giuseppe Manco	ICAR-CNR, Italy
Gabor Melli	PredictionWorks, USA
Anna Monreale	University of Pisa, Italy
Luis Moreira-Matias	Sennder GmbH, Germany
Nuria Oliver	ELLIS Alicante, Spain
Panagiotis Papapetrou	Stockholm University, Sweden
Mykola Pechenizkiy	TU Eindhoven, The Netherlands
Jian Pei	Simon Fraser University, Canada
Julien Perez	Naver Labs Europe, France

Program Committee, Research Track

Matthias Aßenmacher	LMU Munich, Germany
Sara Abdali	Microsoft, USA
Evrim Acar	Simula Metropolitan Center for Digital Engineering, Norway
Homayun Afrabandpey	Nokia Technologies, Finland
Reza Akbarinia	Inria, France
Cuneyt G. Akcora	University of Manitoba, Canada
Ranya Almohsen	West Virginia University, USA
Thiago Andrade	INESC TEC/University of Porto, Portugal
Jean-Marc Andreoli	Naverlabs Europe, France
Giuseppina Andresini	University of Bari, Aldo Moro, Italy
Alessandro Antonucci	IDSIA, Switzerland
Xiang Ao	Institute of Computing Technology, CAS, China
Héber H. Arcolezi	Inria/École Polytechnique, France
Jerónimo Arenas-García	Universidad Carlos III de Madrid, Spain
Yusuf Arslan	University of Luxembourg, Luxemburg
Ali Ayadi	University of Strasbourg, France
Steve Azzolin	University of Trento, Italy
Pierre-Luc Bacon	Mila, Canada
Bunil K. Balabantaray	NIT Meghalaya, India
Mitra Baratchi	LIACS/Leiden University, The Netherlands
Christian Bauckhage	Fraunhofer IAIS, Germany
Anna Beer	Aarhus University, Denmark
Michael Beigl	Karlsruhe Institute of Technology, Germany
Khalid Benabdeslem	Université de Lyon, Lyon 1, France
Idir Benouaret	Epita Research Laboratory, France
Paul Berg	IRISA, France
Christoph Bergmeir	Monash University, Australia
Gilberto Bernardes	INESC TEC/University of Porto, Portugal
Eva Besada-Portas	Universidad Complutense de Madrid, Spain
Jalaj Bhandari	Columbia University, USA
Asmita Bhat	TU Kaiserslautern, Germany
Monowar Bhuyan	Umeå University, Sweden
Adrien Bibal	University of Colorado Anschutz Medical Campus, USA
Manuele Bicego	University of Verona, Italy
Przemyslaw Biecek	Warsaw University of Technology, Poland
Alexander Binder	University of Oslo, Norway
Livio Bioglio	University of Turin, Italy
Patrick Blöbaum	Amazon Web Services, USA

Thomas Bonald	Télécom Paris, France
Ludovico Boratto	University of Cagliari, Italy
Stefano Bortoli	Huawei Research Center, Germany
Tassadit Bouadi	Université de Rennes 1, France
Ahcène Boubekki	UiT, Arctic University of Norway, Norway
Luc Brogat-Motte	Télécom Paris, France
Jannis Brugger	TU Darmstadt, Germany
Nhat-Tan Bui	University of Science - VNUHCM, Vietnam
Mirko Bunse	TU Dortmund, Germany
John Burden	University of Cambridge, UK
Wolfram Burgard	University of Technology, Germany
Julian Busch	Siemens Technology, Germany
Sebastian Buschjäger	TU Dortmund, Germany
Oswald C.	NIT Trichy, India
Seshadhri C.	UCSC, USA
Xin-Qiang Cai	University of Tokyo, Japan
Zekun Cai	University of Tokyo, Japan
Xiaofeng Cao	University of Technology, Sydney, Australia
Giuseppe Casalicchio	LMU Munich, Germany
Guilherme Cassales	University of Waikato, New Zealand
Oded Cats	TU Delft, The Netherlands
Remy Cazabet	Université de Lyon, Lyon 1, France
Mattia Cerrato	JGU Mainz, Germany
Ricardo Cerri	Federal University of Sao Carlos, Brazil
Prithwish Chakraborty	IBM Research, USA
Harry Kai-Ho Chan	University of Sheffield, UK
Joydeep Chandra	IIT Patna, India
Vaggos Chatziafratis	Stanford University, USA
Zaineb Chelly Dagdia	UVSQ - Université Paris-Saclay, France
Hongyang Chen	Zhejiang Lab, China
Huaming Chen	University of Sydney, Australia
Hung-Hsuan Chen	National Central University, Taiwan
Jin Chen	University of Electronic Science and Technology of China, China
Kuan-Hsun Chen	University of Twente, The Netherlands
Ling Chen	University of Technology, Australia
Lingwei Chen	Wright State University, USA
Minyu Chen	Shanghai Jiaotong University, China
Xi Chen	Ghent University, Belgium
Xiaojun Chen	Institute of Information Engineering, CAS, China
Xuefeng Chen	Chongqing University, China
Ying Chen	RMIT University, Australia

Yueguo Chen	Renmin University of China, China
Yuzhou Chen	Temple University, USA
Zheng Chen	Osaka University, Japan
Ziheng Chen	Walmart, USA
Lu Cheng	University of Illinois, Chicago, USA
Xu Cheng	Shanghai Jiao Tong University, China
Zhiyong Cheng	Shandong Academy of Sciences, China
Yann Chevaleyre	Université Paris Dauphine, France
Chun Wai Chiu	Keele University, UK
Silvia Chiusano	Politecnico di Torino, Italy
Satyendra Singh Chouhan	MNIT Jaipur, India
Hua Chu	Xidian University, China
Sarel Cohen	Academic College of Tel Aviv-Yaffo, Israel
J. Alberto Conejero	Universitat Politècnica de València, Spain
Lidia Contreras-Ochando	Universitat Politècnica de València, Spain
Giorgio Corani	IDSIA, Switzerland
Luca Corbucci	University of Pisa, Italy
Roberto Corizzo	American University, USA
Baris Coskunuzer	University of Texas at Dallas, USA
Fabrizio Costa	Exeter University, UK
Gustavo de Assis Costa	Instituto Federal de Goiás, Brazil
Evan Crothers	University of Ottawa, Canada
Pádraig Cunningham	University College Dublin, Ireland
Jacek Cyranka	University of Warsaw, Poland
Tianxiang Dai	Huawei European Research Institute, Germany
Xuan-Hong Dang	IBM T.J. Watson Research Center, USA
Thi-Bich-Hanh Dao	University of Orleans, France
Debasis Das	Indian Institute of Technology Jodhpur, India
Paul Davidsson	Malmö University, Sweden
Marcilio de Souto	LIFO, University of Orleans, France
Klest Dedja	KU Leuven, Belgium
Elena Demidova	University of Bonn, Germany
Caglar Demir	Paderborn University, Germany
Difan Deng	Leibniz University Hannover, Germany
Laurens Devos	KU Leuven, Belgium
Nicola Di Mauro	University of Bari, Aldo Moro, Italy
Jingtao Ding	Tsinghua University, China
Yao-Xiang Ding	Nanjing University, China
Lamine Diop	EPITA, France
Gillian Dobbie	University of Auckland, New Zealand
Stephan Doerfel	Kiel University of Applied Sciences, Germany
Carola Doerr	Sorbonne Université, France

Nanqing Dong	University of Oxford, UK
Haizhou Du	Shanghai University of Electric Power, China
Qihan Du	Renmin University of China, China
Songlin Du	Southeast University, China
Xin Du	University of Edinburgh, UK
Wouter Duivesteijn	TU Eindhoven, The Netherlands
Inês Dutra	University of Porto, Portugal
Sourav Dutta	Huawei Research Centre, Ireland
Saso Dzeroski	Jožef Stefan Institute, Slovenia
Nabil El Malki	IRIT, France
Mohab Elkaref	IBM Research Europe, UK
Tapio Elomaa	Tampere University, Finland
Dominik M. Endres	University of Marburg, Germany
Georgios Exarchakis	University of Bath, UK
Lukas Faber	ETH Zurich, Switzerland
Samuel G. Fadel	Leuphana University, Germany
Haoyi Fan	Zhengzhou University, China
Zipei Fan	University of Tokyo, Japan
Hadi Fanaee-T	Halmstad University, Sweden
Elaine Ribeiro Faria	UFU, Brazil
Fabio Fassetti	University of Calabria, Italy
Anthony Faustine	ITI/LARSyS - Técnico Lisboa, Portugal
Sophie Fellenz	RPTU Kaiserslautern-Landau, Germany
Wenjie Feng	National University of Singapore, Singapore
Zunlei Feng	Zhejiang University, China
Daniel Fernández-Sánchez	Universidad Autónoma de Madrid, Spain
Luca Ferragina	University of Calabria, Italy
Emilio Ferrara	USC ISI, USA
Cèsar Ferri	Universitat Politècnica València, Spain
Flavio Figueiredo	Universidade Federal de Minas Gerais, Brazil
Lucie Flek	University of Marburg, Germany
Michele Fontana	University of Pisa, Italy
Germain Forestier	University of Haute-Alsace, France
Raphaël Fournier-S'niehotta	CNAM, France
Benoît Frénay	University of Namur, Belgium
Kary Främling	Umeå University, Sweden
Holger Froening	University of Heidelberg, Germany
Fabio Fumarola	Prometeia, Italy
María José Gómez-Silva	Universidad Complutense de Madrid, Spain
Vanessa Gómez-Verdejo	Universidad Carlos III de Madrid, Spain
Pratik Gajane	TU Eindhoven, The Netherlands
Esther Galbrun	University of Eastern Finland, Finland

Claudio Gallicchio	University of Pisa, Italy
Chen Gao	Tsinghua University, China
Shengxiang Gao	Kunming University of Science and Technology, China
Yifeng Gao	University of Texas Rio Grande Valley, USA
Luis Garcia	University of Brasilia, Brazil
Dominique Gay	Université de La Réunion, France
Suyu Ge	University of Illinois at Urbana-Champaign, USA
Zhaocheng Ge	Huazhong University of Science and Technology, China
Alborz Geramifard	Facebook AI, USA
Ahana Ghosh	Max Planck Institute for Software Systems, Germany
Shreya Ghosh	Penn State University, USA
Flavio Giobergia	Politecnico di Torino, Italy
Sarunas Girdzijauskas	KTH Royal Institute of Technology, Sweden
Heitor Murilo Gomes	University of Waikato, Sweden
Wenwen Gong	Tsinghua University, China
Bedartha Goswami	University of Tübingen, Germany
Anastasios Gounaris	Aristotle University of Thessaloniki, Greece
Michael Granitzer	University of Passau, Germany
Derek Greene	University College Dublin, Ireland
Moritz Grosse-Wentrup	University of Vienna, Austria
Marek Grzes	University of Kent, UK
Xinyu Guan	Xian Jiaotong University, China
Massimo Guarascio	ICAR-CNR, Italy
Riccardo Guidotti	University of Pisa, Italy
Lan-Zhe Guo	Nanjing University, China
Lingbing Guo	Zhejiang University, China
Shanqing Guo	Shandong University, China
Karthik S. Gurumoorthy	Walmart, USA
Thomas Guyet	Inria, France
Huong Ha	RMIT University, Australia
Benjamin Halstead	University of Auckland, New Zealand
Massinissa Hamidi	LIPN-UMR CNRS 7030, France
Donghong Han	Northeastern University, USA
Marwan Hassani	TU Eindhoven, The Netherlands
Rima Hazra	Indian Institute of Technology, Kharagpur, India
Mark Heimann	Lawrence Livermore, USA
Cesar Hidalgo	University of Toulouse, France
Martin Holena	Institute of Computer Science, Czech Republic
Mike Holenderski	TU Eindhoven, The Netherlands

Adrian Horzyk	AGH University of Science and Technology, Poland
Shifu Hou	Case Western Reserve University, USA
Hongsheng Hu	CSIRO, Australia
Yaowei Hu	University of Arkansas, USA
Yang Hua	Queen's University Belfast, UK
Chao Huang	University of Hong Kong, China
Guanjie Huang	Penn State University, USA
Hong Huang	Huazhong University of Science and Technology, China
Nina C. Hubig	Clemson University, USA
Dino Ienco	Irstea Institute, France
Angelo Impedovo	Niuma, Italy
Roberto Interdonato	CIRAD, France
Stratis Ioannidis	Northeastern University, USA
Nevo Itzhak	Ben-Gurion University, Israel
Raghav Jain	IIT Patna, India
Kuk Jin Jang	University of Pennsylvania, USA
Szymon Jaroszewicz	Polish Academy of Sciences, Poland
Shaoxiong Ji	University of Helsinki, Finland
Bin-Bin Jia	Lanzhou University of Technology, China
Caiyan Jia	School of Computer and Information Technology, China
Xiuyi Jia	Nanjing University of Science and Technology, China
Nan Jiang	Purdue University, USA
Renhe Jiang	University of Tokyo, Japan
Song Jiang	University of California, Los Angeles, USA
Pengfei Jiao	Hangzhou Dianzi University, China
Di Jin	Amazon, USA
Guangyin Jin	National University of Defense Technology, China
Jiahui Jin	Southeast University, China
Ruoming Jin	Kent State University, USA
Yilun Jin	The Hong Kong University of Science and Technology, Hong Kong
Hugo Jonker	Open University of the Netherlands, The Netherlands
Adan Jose-Garcia	Lille University, France
Marius Köppel	JGU Mainz, Germany
Vana Kalogeraki	Athens University of Economics and Business, Greece
Konstantinos Kalpakis	University of Maryland Baltimore County, USA

Andreas Kaltenbrunner	ISI Foundation, Italy
Shivaram Kalyanakrishnan	IIT Bombay, India
Toshihiro Kamishima	National Institute of Advanced Industrial Science and Technology, Japan
Bo Kang	Ghent University, Belgium
Murat Kantarcioglu	UT Dallas
Thommen Karimpanal George	Deakin University, Australia
Saurav Karmakar	University of Galway, Ireland
Panagiotis Karras	Aarhus University, Denmark
Dimitrios Katsaros	University of Thessaly, Greece
Eamonn Keogh	UC, Riverside, USA
Jaleed Khan	University of Galway, Ireland
Irwin King	Chinese University of Hong Kong, China
Mauritius Klein	LMU Munich, Germany
Tomas Kliegr	Prague University of Economics and Business, Czech Republic
Dmitry Kobak	University of Tübingen, Germany
Dragi Kocev	Jožef Stefan Institute, Slovenia
Lars Kotthoff	University of Wyoming, USA
Anna Krause	University of Würzburg, Germany
Amer Krivosija	TU Dortmund, Germany
Daniel Kudenko	L3S Research Center, Germany
Meelis Kull	University of Tartu, Estonia
Sergey O. Kuznetsov	HSE, Russia
Beatriz López	University of Girona, Spain
Jörg Lücke	University of Oldenburg, Germany
Firas Laakom	Tampere University, Finland
Mateusz Lango	Poznan University of Technology, Poland
Hady Lauw	Singapore Management University, Singapore
Tuan Le	New Mexico State University, USA
Erwan Le Merrer	Inria, France
Thach Le Nguyen	Insight Centre, Ireland
Tai Le Quy	L3S Research Center, Germany
Mustapha Lebbah	UVSQ - Université Paris-Saclay, France
Dongman Lee	KAIST, South Korea
Yeon-Chang Lee	Georgia Institute of Technology, USA
Zed Lee	Stockholm University, Sweden
Mathieu Lefort	Université de Lyon, France
Yunwen Lei	University of Birmingham, UK
Vincent Lemaire	Orange Innovation, France
Daniel Lemire	TÉLUQ University, Canada
Florian Lemmerich	RWTH Aachen University, Germany

Youfang Leng	Renmin University of China, China
Carson K. Leung	University of Manitoba, Canada
Dan Li	Sun Yat-Sen University, China
Gang Li	Deakin University, Australia
Jiaming Li	Huazhong University of Science and Technology, China
Mark Junjie Li	Shenzhen University, China
Nian Li	Tsinghua University, China
Shuai Li	University of Cambridge, UK
Tong Li	Hong Kong University of Science and Technology, China
Xiang Li	East China Normal University, China
Yang Li	University of North Carolina at Chapel Hill, USA
Yingming Li	Zhejiang University, China
Yinsheng Li	Fudan University, China
Yong Li	Huawei European Research Center, Germany
Zhihui Li	University of New South Wales, Australia
Zhixin Li	Guangxi Normal University, China
Defu Lian	University of Science and Technology of China, China
Yuxuan Liang	National University of Singapore, Singapore
Angelica Liguori	University of Calabria, Italy
Nick Lim	University of Waikato, Sweden
Baijiong Lin	The Hong Kong University of Science and Technology, Hong Kong
Piotr Lipinski	University of Wrocław, Poland
Marco Lippi	University of Modena and Reggio Emilia, Italy
Bowen Liu	Stanford University, USA
Chien-Liang Liu	National Chiao Tung University, Taiwan
Fenglin Liu	University of Oxford, UK
Junze Liu	University of California, Irvine, USA
Li Liu	Chongqing University, China
Ninghao Liu	University of Georgia, USA
Shenghua Liu	Institute of Computing Technology, CAS, China
Xiao Fan Liu	City University of Hong Kong, Hong Kong
Xu Liu	National University of Singapore, Singapore
Yang Liu	Institute of Computing Technology, CAS, China
Zihan Liu	Zhejiang University/Westlake University, China
Robert Loftin	TU Delft, The Netherlands
Corrado Loglisci	University of Bari, Aldo Moro, Italy
Mingsheng Long	Tsinghua University, China
Antonio Longa	Fondazione Bruno Kessler, Italy

Grigorios Loukides	King's College London, UK
Tsai-Ching Lu	HRL Laboratories, USA
Zhiwu Lu	Renmin University of China, China
Pedro Henrique Luz de Araujo	University of Vienna, Austria
Marcos M. Raimundo	University of Campinas, Brazil
Maximilian Münch	University of Applied Sciences Würzburg-Schweinfurt, Germany
Fenglong Ma	Pennsylvania State University, USA
Pingchuan Ma	The Hong Kong University of Science and Technology, Hong Kong
Yao Ma	New Jersey Institute of Technology, USA
Brian Mac Namee	University College Dublin, Ireland
Henryk Maciejewski	Wrocław University of Science and Technology, Poland
Ayush Maheshwari	IIT Bombay, India
Ajay A. Mahimkar	AT&T, USA
Ayan Majumdar	Max Planck Institute for Software Systems, Germany
Donato Malerba	University of Bari, Aldo Moro, Italy
Aakarsh Malhotra	IIIT-Delhi, India
Fragkiskos Malliaros	CentraleSupelec, France
Pekka Malo	Aalto University, Finland
Hiroshi Mamitsuka	Kyoto University, Japan/Aalto University, Finland
Domenico Mandaglio	University of Calabria, Italy
Robin Manhaeve	KU Leuven, Belgium
Silviu Maniu	Université Paris-Saclay, France
Cinmayii G. Manliguez	National Sun Yat-Sen University, Taiwan
Naresh Manwani	IIIT Hyderabad, India
Giovanni Luca Marchetti	KTH Royal Institute of Technology, Sweden
Koji Maruhashi	Fujitsu Research, Fujitsu Limited, Japan
Florent Masseglia	Inria, France
Sarah Masud	IIIT-Delhi, India
Timothée Mathieu	Inria, France
Amir Mehrpanah	KTH Royal Institute of Technology, Sweden
Wagner Meira Jr.	Universidade Federal de Minas Gerais, Brazil
Joao Mendes-Moreira	INESC TEC, Portugal
Rui Meng	BNU-HKBU United International College, China
Fabio Mercorio	University of Milan-Bicocca, Italy
Alberto Maria Metelli	Politecnico di Milano, Italy
Carlo Metta	CNR-ISTI, Italy
Paolo Mignone	University of Bari, Aldo Moro, Italy
Tsunenori Mine	Kyushu University, Japan

Nuno Moniz	INESC TEC, Portugal
Pierre Monnin	Université Côte d'Azur, Inria, CNRS, I3S, France
Carlos Monserrat-Aranda	Universitat Politècnica de València, Spain
Raha Moraffah	Arizona State University, USA
Davide Mottin	Aarhus University, Denmark
Hamid Mousavi	University of Oldenburg, Germany
Abdullah Mueen	University of New Mexico, USA
Shamsuddeen Hassan Muhamamd	University of Porto, Portugal
Koyel Mukherjee	Adobe Research, India
Yusuke Mukuta	University of Tokyo, Japan
Pranava Mummoju	University of Vienna, Austria
Taichi Murayama	NAIST, Japan
Ankur Nahar	IIT Jodhpur, India
Felipe Kenji Nakano	KU Leuven, Belgium
Hideki Nakayama	University of Tokyo, Japan
Géraldin Nanfack	University of Namur, Belgium
Mirco Nanni	CNR-ISTI, Italy
Franco Maria Nardini	CNR-ISTI, Italy
Usman Naseem	University of Sydney, Australia
Reza Nasirigerdeh	TU Munich, Germany
Rajashree Nayak	MIT ADT University, India
Benjamin Negrevergne	Université Paris Dauphine, France
Stefan Neumann	KTH Royal Institute of Technology, Sweden
Anna Nguyen	IBM, USA
Shiwen Ni	SIAT, CAS, China
Siegfried Nijssen	Université catholique de Louvain, Belgium
Iasonas Nikolaou	Boston University, USA
Simona Nisticò	University of Calabria, Italy
Hao Niu	KDDI Research, Japan
Mehdi Nourelahi	University of Wyoming, USA
Slawomir Nowaczyk	Halmstad University, Sweden
Eirini Ntoutsi	Bundeswehr University Munich, Germany
Barry O'Sullivan	University College Cork, Ireland
Nastaran Okati	Max Planck Institute for Software Systems, Germany
Tsuyoshi Okita	Kyushu Institute of Technology, Japan
Pablo Olmos	Universidad Carlos III de Madrid, Spain
Luis Antonio Ortega Andrés	Autonomous University of Madrid, Spain
Abdelkader Ouali	Université de Caen Normandie, France
Latifa Oukhellou	IFSTTAR, France
Chun Ouyang	Queensland University of Technology, Australia
Andrei Paleyes	University of Cambridge, UK

Menghai Pan   Visa Research, USA
Shirui Pan   Griffith University, Australia
Apostolos N. Papadopoulos   Aristotle University of Thessaloniki, Greece
Chanyoung Park   KAIST, South Korea
Emilio Parrado-Hernandez   Universidad Carlos III de Madrid, Spain
Vincenzo Pasquadibisceglie   University of Bari, Aldo Moro, Italy
Eliana Pastor   Politecnico di Torino, Italy
Anand Paul   Kyungpook National University, South Korea
Shichao Pei   University of Notre Dame, USA
Yulong Pei   TU Eindhoven, The Netherlands
Leonardo Pellegrina   University of Padua, Italy
Ruggero Pensa   University of Turin, Italy
Fabiola Pereira   UFU, Brazil
Lucas Pereira   ITI/LARSyS - Técnico Lisboa, Portugal
Miquel Perello-Nieto   University of Bristol, UK
Lorenzo Perini   KU Leuven, Belgium
Matej Petkovifá   University of Ljubljana, Slovenia
Lukas Pfahler   TU Dortmund, Germany
Ninh Pham   University of Auckland, New Zealand
Guangyuan Piao   Maynooth University, Ireland
Francesco Piccialli   University of Naples Federico II, Italy
Martin Pilát   Charles University, Czech Republic
Gianvito Pio   University of Bari, Aldo Moro, Italy
Giuseppe Pirrò   Sapienza University of Rome, Italy
Francesco S. Pisani   ICAR-CNR, Italy
Srijith P. K.   IIIT Hyderabad, India
Marc Plantevit   EPITA, France
Mirko Polato   University of Turin, Italy
Axel Polleres   Vienna University of Economics and Business,
                                  Austria
Giovanni Ponti   ENEA, Italy
Paul Prasse   University of Potsdam, Germany
Mahardhika Pratama   University of South Australia, Australia
Philippe Preux   Inria, France
Ricardo B. Prudencio   Universidade Federal de Pernambuco, Brazil
Chiara Pugliese   CNR-ISTI, Italy
Erasmo Purificato   Otto-von-Guericke-University Magdeburg,
                                  Germany
Abdulhakim Qahtan   Utrecht University, The Netherlands
Lianyong Qi   China University of Petroleum, China
Kun Qian   Amazon Web Services, USA
Tieyun Qian   Wuhan University, China

Chuan Qin	BOSS Zhipin, China
Yumou Qiu	Iowa State University, USA
Dimitrios Rafailidis	University of Thessaly, Greece
Edward Raff	Booz Allen Hamilton, USA
Chang Rajani	University of Helsinki, Finland
Herilalaina Rakotoarison	Inria, France
M. José Ramírez-Quintana	Universitat Politècnica de Valencia, Spain
Jan Ramon	Inria, France
Rajeev Rastogi	Amazon, India
Domenico Redavid	University of Bari, Aldo Moro, Italy
Qianqian Ren	Heilongjiang University, China
Salvatore Rinzivillo	CNR-ISTI, Italy
Matteo Riondato	Amherst College, USA
Giuseppe Rizzo	Niuma, Italy
Marko Robnik-Sikonja	University of Ljubljana, Slovenia
Christophe Rodrigues	Pôle Universitaire Léonard de Vinci, France
Federica Rollo	University of Modena and Reggio Emilia, Italy
Luca Romeo	University of Macerata, Italy
Benjamin Roth	University of Vienna, Austria
Céline Rouveirol	LIPN - Université Sorbonne Paris Nord, France
Salvatore Ruggieri	University of Pisa, Italy
Pietro Sabatino	ICAR-CNR, Italy
Luca Sabbioni	Politecnico di Milano, Italy
Tulika Saha	University of Manchester, UK
Pablo Sanchez Martin	Max Planck Institute for Intelligent Systems, Germany
Parinya Sanguansat	Panyapiwat Institute of Management, Thailand
Shreya Saxena	Quantiphi, India
Yücel Saygin	Sabanci Universitesi, Turkey
Patrick Schäfer	Humboldt-Universität zu Berlin, Germany
Kevin Schewior	University of Southern Denmark, Denmark
Rainer Schlosser	Hasso Plattner Institute, Germany
Johannes Schneider	University of Liechtenstein, Liechtenstein
Matthias Schubert	LMU Munich, Germany
Alexander Schulz	CITEC - Bielefeld University, Germany
Andreas Schwung	Fachhoschschule Südwestfalen, Germany
Raquel Sebastião	IEETA/DETI-UA, Portugal
Pierre Senellart	ENS, PSL University, France
Edoardo Serra	Boise State University, USA
Mattia Setzu	University of Pisa, Italy
Ammar Shaker	NEC Laboratories Europe, Germany
Shubhranshu Shekhar	Carnegie Mellon University, USA

Jiaming Shen	Google Research, USA
Qiang Sheng	Institute of Computing Technology, CAS, China
Bin Shi	Xi'an Jiaotong University, China
Jimeng Shi	Florida International University, USA
Laixi Shi	Carnegie Mellon University, USA
Rongye Shi	Columbia University, USA
Harsh Shrivastava	Microsoft Research, USA
Jonathan A. Silva	Universidade Federal de Mato Grosso do Sul, Brazil
Esther-Lydia Silva-Ramírez	Universidad de Cádiz, Spain
Kuldeep Singh	Cerence, Germany
Moshe Sipper	Ben-Gurion University of the Negev, Israel
Andrzej Skowron	University of Warsaw, Poland
Krzysztof Slot	Lodz University of Technology, Poland
Marek Smieja	Jagiellonian University, Poland
Gavin Smith	University of Nottingham, UK
Carlos Soares	University of Porto, Portugal
Cláudia Soares	NOVA LINCS, Portugal
Andy Song	RMIT University, Australia
Dongjin Song	University of Connecticut, USA
Hao Song	Seldon, UK
Jie Song	Zhejiang University, China
Linxin Song	Waseda University, Japan
Liyan Song	Southern University of Science and Technology, China
Zixing Song	Chinese University of Hong Kong, China
Arnaud Soulet	University of Tours, France
Sucheta Soundarajan	Syracuse University, USA
Francesca Spezzano	Boise State University, USA
Myra Spiliopoulou	Otto-von-Guericke-University Magdeburg, Germany
Janusz Starzyk	WSIZ, Poland
Jerzy Stefanowski	Poznan University of Technology, Poland
Julian Stier	University of Passau, Germany
Michiel Stock	Ghent University, Belgium
Eleni Straitouri	Max Planck Institute for Software Systems, Germany
Łukasz Struski	Jagiellonian University, Poland
Jinyan Su	University of Electronic Science and Technology of China, China
David Q. Sun	Apple, USA
Guangzhong Sun	University of Science and Technology of China, China

Joao Vinagre	Joint Research Centre - European Commission, Belgium
Jordi Vitria	Universitat de Barcelona, Spain
Jean-Noël Vittaut	LIP6 - CNRS - Sorbonne Université, France
Marco Viviani	University of Milan-Bicocca, Italy
Paola Vocca	Tor Vergata University of Rome, Italy
Tomasz Walkowiak	Wrocław University of Science and Technology, Poland
Ziwen Wan	University of California, Irvine, USA
Beilun Wang	Southeast University, China
Chuan-Ju Wang	Academia Sinica, Taiwan
Deng-Bao Wang	Southeast University, China
Di Wang	KAUST, Saudi Arabia
Dianhui Wang	La Trobe University, Australia
Hongwei Wang	University of Illinois at Urbana-Champaign, USA
Huandong Wang	Tsinghua University, China
Hui (Wendy) Wang	Stevens Institute of Technology, USA
Jiaqi Wang	Penn State University, USA
Puyu Wang	City University of Hong Kong, China
Qing Wang	Australian National University, Australia
Ruijie Wang	University of Illinois at Urbana-Champaign, USA
Senzhang Wang	Central South University, China
Shuo Wang	University of Birmingham, UK
Suhang Wang	Pennsylvania State University, USA
Wei Wang	Fudan University, China
Wenjie Wang	Shanghai Tech University, China
Yanhao Wang	East China Normal University, China
Yimu Wang	University of Waterloo, Canada
Yue Wang	Microsoft Research, USA
Yue Wang	Waymo, USA
Zhaonan Wang	University of Tokyo, Japan
Zhi Wang	Southwest University, China
Zijie J. Wang	Georgia Tech, USA
Roger Wattenhofer	ETH Zurich, Switzerland
Pascal Weber	University of Vienna, Austria
Jörg Wicker	University of Auckland, New Zealand
Michael Wilbur	Vanderbilt University, USA
Weng-Fai Wong	National University of Singapore, Singapore
Bin Wu	Zhengzhou University, China
Chenwang Wu	University of Science and Technology of China, China

Di Wu	Chongqing Institute of Green and Intelligent Technology, CAS, China
Guoqiang Wu	Shandong University, China
Peng Wu	Shanghai Jiao Tong University, China
Xiaotong Wu	Nanjing Normal University, China
Yongkai Wu	Clemson University, USA
Danyang Xiao	Sun Yat-Sen University, China
Zhiwen Xiao	Southwest Jiaotong University, China
Cheng Xie	Yunnan University, China
Hong Xie	Chongqing Institute of Green and Intelligent Technology, CAS, China
Yaqi Xie	Carnegie Mellon University, USA
Huanlai Xing	Southwest Jiaotong University, China
Ning Xu	Southeast University, China
Xiaolong Xu	Nanjing University of Information Science and Technology, China
Hao Xue	University of New South Wales, Australia
Yexiang Xue	Purdue University, USA
Sangeeta Yadav	Indian Institute of Science, India
Qiao Yan	Shenzhen University, China
Yan Yan	Carleton University, Canada
Yu Yan	People's Public Security University of China, China
Yujun Yan	Dartmouth College, USA
Jie Yang	University of Wollongong, Australia
Shaofu Yang	Southeast University, China
Yang Yang	Nanjing University of Science and Technology, China
Liang Yao	Tencent, China
Muchao Ye	Pennsylvania State University, USA
Michael Yeh	Visa Research, USA
Kalidas Yeturu	Indian Institute of Technology Tirupati, India
Hang Yin	University of Copenhagen, Denmark
Hongwei Yong	Hong Kong Polytechnic University, China
Jaemin Yoo	KAIST, South Korea
Mengbo You	Iwate University, Japan
Hang Yu	Shanghai University, China
Weiren Yu	University of Warwick, UK
Wenjian Yu	Tsinghua University, China
Jidong Yuan	Beijing Jiaotong University, China
Aras Yurtman	KU Leuven, Belgium
Claudius Zelenka	Christian-Albrechts University of Kiel, Germany

Akka Zemmari	University of Bordeaux, France
Bonan Zhang	Princeton University, USA
Chao Zhang	Zhejiang University, China
Chuang Zhang	Nanjing University of Science and Technology, China
Danqing Zhang	Amazon, USA
Guoqiang Zhang	University of Technology, Sydney, Australia
Guoxi Zhang	Kyoto University, Japan
Hao Zhang	Fudan University, China
Junbo Zhang	JD Intelligent Cities Research, China
Le Zhang	Baidu Research, China
Ming Zhang	National Key Laboratory of Science and Technology on Information System Security, China
Qiannan Zhang	KAUST, Saudi Arabia
Tianlin Zhang	University of Manchester, UK
Wenbin Zhang	Michigan Tech, USA
Xiang Zhang	National University of Defense Technology, China
Xiao Zhang	Shandong University, China
Xiaoming Zhang	Beihang University, China
Xinyang Zhang	University of Illinois at Urbana-Champaign, USA
Yaying Zhang	Tongji University, China
Yin Zhang	University of Electronic Science and Technology of China, China
Yongqi Zhang	4Paradigm, China
Zhiwen Zhang	University of Tokyo, Japan
Mia Zhao	Airbnb, USA
Sichen Zhao	RMIT University, Australia
Xiaoting Zhao	Etsy, USA
Tongya Zheng	Zhejiang University, China
Wenhao Zheng	Shopee, Singapore
Yu Zheng	Tsinghua University, China
Yujia Zheng	Carnegie Mellon University, USA
Jiang Zhong	Chongqing University, China
Wei Zhou	School of Cyber Security, CAS, China
Zhengyang Zhou	University of Science and Technology of China, China
Chuang Zhu	Beijing University of Posts and Telecommunications, China
Jing Zhu	University of Michigan, USA
Jinjing Zhu	Hong Kong University of Science and Technology, China

Junxing Zhu	National University of Defense Technology, China
Yanmin Zhu	Shanghai Jiao Tong University, China
Ye Zhu	Deakin University, Australia
Yichen Zhu	Midea Group, China
Zirui Zhuang	Beijing University of Posts and Telecommunications, China
Tommaso Zoppi	University of Florence, Italy
Meiyun Zuo	Renmin University of China, China

Program Committee, Applied Data Science Track

Jussara Almeida	Universidade Federal de Minas Gerais, Brazil
Mozhdeh Ariannezhad	University of Amsterdam, The Netherlands
Renato M. Assuncao	ESRI, USA
Hajer Ayadi	York University, Canada
Ashraf Bah Rabiou	University of Delaware, USA
Amey Barapatre	Microsoft, USA
Patrice Bellot	Aix-Marseille Université - CNRS LSIS, France
Ludovico Boratto	University of Cagliari, Italy
Claudio Borile	CENTAI, Italy
Yi Cai	South China University of Technology, China
Lei Cao	University of Arizona/MIT, USA
Shilei Cao	Tencent, China
Yang Cao	Hokkaido University, Japan
Aniket Chakrabarti	Amazon, USA
Chaochao Chen	Zhejiang University, China
Chung-Chi Chen	National Taiwan University, Taiwan
Meng Chen	Shandong University, China
Ruey-Cheng Chen	Canva, Australia
Tong Chen	University of Queensland, Australia
Yi Chen	NJIT, USA
Zhiyu Chen	Amazon, USA
Wei Cheng	NEC Laboratories America, USA
Lingyang Chu	McMaster University, Canada
Xiaokai Chu	Tencent, China
Zhendong Chu	University of Virginia, USA
Federico Cinus	Sapienza University of Rome/CENTAI, Italy
Francisco Claude-Faust	LinkedIn, USA
Gabriele D'Acunto	Sapienza University of Rome, Italy
Ariyam Das	Google, USA

Jingtao Ding	Tsinghua University, China
Kaize Ding	Arizona State University, USA
Manqing Dong	eBay, Australia
Yushun Dong	University of Virginia, USA
Yingtong Dou	University of Illinois, Chicago, USA
Yixiang Fang	Chinese University of Hong Kong, China
Kaiyu Feng	Beijing Institute of Technology, China
Dayne Freitag	SRI International, USA
Yanjie Fu	University of Central Florida, USA
Matteo Gabburo	University of Trento, Italy
Sabrina Gaito	University of Milan, Italy
Chen Gao	Tsinghua University, China
Liangcai Gao	Peking University, China
Yunjun Gao	Zhejiang University, China
Lluis Garcia-Pueyo	Meta, USA
Mariana-Iuliana Georgescu	University of Bucharest, Romania
Aakash Goel	Amazon, USA
Marcos Goncalves	Universidade Federal de Minas Gerais, Brazil
Francesco Guerra	University of Modena e Reggio Emilia, Italy
Huifeng Guo	Huawei Noah's Ark Lab, China
Ruocheng Guo	ByteDance, China
Zhen Hai	Alibaba DAMO Academy, China
Eui-Hong (Sam) Han	The Washington Post, USA
Jinyoung Han	Sungkyunkwan University, South Korea
Shuchu Han	Stellar Cyber, USA
Dongxiao He	Tianjin University, China
Junyuan Hong	Michigan State University, USA
Yupeng Hou	UC San Diego, USA
Binbin Hu	Ant Group, China
Jun Hu	National University of Singapore, Singapore
Hong Huang	Huazhong University of Science and Technology, China
Xin Huang	Hong Kong Baptist University, China
Yizheng Huang	York University, Canada
Yu Huang	University of Florida, USA
Stratis Ioannidis	Northeastern University, USA
Radu Tudor Ionescu	University of Bucharest, Romania
Murium Iqbal	Etsy, USA
Shoaib Jameel	University of Southampton, UK
Jian Kang	University of Rochester, USA
Pinar Karagoz	METU, Turkey
Praveen C. Kolli	Carnegie Mellon University, USA

Yang Wang   University of Science and Technology of China,
                            China
Zhihong Wang   Tsinghua University, China
Zihan Wang   Shandong University, China
Shi-ting Wen   Ningbo Tech University, China
Song Wen   Rutgers University, USA
Zeyi Wen   Hong Kong University of Science and
                            Technology, China
Fangzhao Wu   Microsoft Research Asia, China
Jun Wu   University of Illinois at Urbana-Champaign, USA
Wentao Wu   Microsoft Research, USA
Yanghua Xiao   Fudan University, China
Haoyi Xiong   Baidu, China
Dongkuan Xu   North Carolina State University, USA
Guandong Xu   University of Technology, Sydney, Australia
Shan Xue   Macquarie University, Australia
Le Yan   Google, USA
De-Nian Yang   Academia Sinica, Taiwan
Fan Yang   Rice University, USA
Yu Yang   City University of Hong Kong, China
Fanghua Ye   University College London, UK
Jianhua Yin   Shandong University, China
Yifang Yin   A*STAR-I2R, Singapore
Changlong Yu   Hong Kong University of Science and
                            Technology, China
Dongxiao Yu   Shandong University, China
Ye Yuan   Beijing Institute of Technology, China
Daochen Zha   Rice University, USA
Feng Zhang   Renmin University of China, China
Mengxuan Zhang   University of North Texas, USA
Xianli Zhang   Xi'an Jiaotong University, China
Xuyun Zhang   Macquarie University, Australia
Chen Zhao   Baylor University, USA
Di Zhao   University of Auckland, New Zealand
Yanchang Zhao   CSIRO, Australia
Kaiping Zheng   National University of Singapore, Singapore
Yong Zheng   Illinois Institute of Technology, USA
Jingbo Zhou   Baidu, China
Ming Zhou   University of Technology, Sydney, Australia
Qinghai Zhou   University of Illinois at Urbana-Champaign, USA
Tian Zhou   Alibaba DAMO Academy, China
Xinyi Zhou   University of Washington, USA

Yucheng Zhou	University of Macau, China
Jiangang Zhu	ByteDance, China
Yongchun Zhu	CAS, China
Ziwei Zhu	George Mason University, USA
Jia Zou	Arizona State University, USA

Program Committee, Demo Track

Ferran Diego	Telefonica Research, Spain
Jan Florjanczyk	Netflix, USA
Mikko Heikkila	Telefonica Research, Spain
Jesus Omaña Iglesias	Telefonica Research, Spain
Nicolas Kourtellis	Telefonica Research, Spain
Eduard Marin	Telefonica Research, Spain
Souneil Park	Telefonica Research, Spain
Aravindh Raman	Telefonica Research, Spain
Ashish Rastogi	Netflix, USA
Natali Ruchansky	Netflix, USA
David Solans	Telefonica Research, Spain

Sponsors

Platinum

Gold

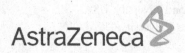

Silver

Bronze

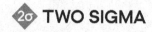

PhD Forum Sponsor

Publishing Partner

Invited Talks Abstracts

Neural Wave Representations

Max Welling

University of Amsterdam, The Netherlands

Abstract. Good neural architectures are rooted in good inductive biases (a.k.a. priors). Equivariance under symmetries is a prime example of a successful physics-inspired prior which sometimes dramatically reduces the number of examples needed to learn predictive models. In this work, we tried to extend this thinking to more flexible priors in the hidden variables of a neural network. In particular, we imposed wavelike dynamics in hidden variables under transformations of the inputs, which relaxes the stricter notion of equivariance. We find that under certain conditions, wavelike dynamics naturally arises in these hidden representations. We formalize this idea in a VAE-over-time architecture where the hidden dynamics is described by a Fokker-Planck (a.k.a. drift-diffusion) equation. This in turn leads to a new definition of a disentangled hidden representation of input states that can easily be manipulated to undergo transformations. I also discussed very preliminary work on how the Schrödinger equation can also be used to move information in the hidden representations.

Biography. Prof. Dr. Max Welling is a research chair in Machine Learning at the University of Amsterdam and a Distinguished Scientist at MSR. He is a fellow at the Canadian Institute for Advanced Research (CIFAR) and the European Lab for Learning and Intelligent Systems (ELLIS) where he also serves on the founding board. His previous appointments include VP at Qualcomm Technologies, professor at UC Irvine, postdoc at the University of Toronto and UCL under the supervision of Prof. Geoffrey Hinton, and postdoc at Caltech under the supervision of Prof. Pietro Perona. He finished his PhD in theoretical high energy physics under the supervision of Nobel laureate Prof. Gerard 't Hooft. Max Welling served as associate editor-in-chief of IEEE TPAMI from 2011–2015, he has served on the advisory board of the NeurIPS Foundation since 2015 and was program chair and general chair of NeurIPS in 2013 and 2014 respectively. He was also program chair of AISTATS in 2009 and ECCV in 2016 and general chair of MIDL in 2018. Max Welling was a recipient of the ECCV Koenderink Prize in 2010 and the ICML Test of Time Award in 2021. He directs the Amsterdam Machine Learning Lab (AMLAB) and co-directs the Qualcomm-UvA deep learning lab (QUVA) and the Bosch-UvA Deep Learning lab (DELTA).

Physics-Inspired Graph Neural Networks

Michael Bronstein

University of Oxford, UK

Abstract. The message-passing paradigm has been the "battle horse" of deep learning on graphs for several years, making graph neural networks a big success in a wide range of applications, from particle physics to protein design. From a theoretical viewpoint, it established the link to the Weisfeiler-Lehman hierarchy, allowing us to analyse the expressive power of GNNs. We argue that the very "node-and-edge"-centric mindset of current graph deep learning schemes may hinder future progress in the field. As an alternative, we propose physics-inspired "continuous" learning models that open up a new trove of tools from the fields of differential geometry, algebraic topology, and differential equations so far largely unexplored in graph ML.

Biography. Michael Bronstein is the DeepMind Professor of AI at the University of Oxford. He was previously a professor at Imperial College London and held visiting appointments at Stanford, MIT, and Harvard, and has also been affiliated with three Institutes for Advanced Study (at TUM as a Rudolf Diesel Fellow (2017–2019), at Harvard as a Radcliffe fellow (2017–2018), and at Princeton as a short-time scholar (2020)). Michael received his PhD from the Technion in 2007. He is the recipient of the Royal Society Wolfson Research Merit Award, Royal Academy of Engineering Silver Medal, five ERC grants, two Google Faculty Research Awards, and two Amazon AWS ML Research Awards. He is a Member of the Academia Europaea, Fellow of the IEEE, IAPR, BCS, and ELLIS, ACM Distinguished Speaker, and World Economic Forum Young Scientist. In addition to his academic career, Michael is a serial entrepreneur and founder of multiple startup companies, including Novafora, Invision (acquired by Intel in 2012), Videocites, and Fabula AI (acquired by Twitter in 2019).

Mapping Generative AI

Kate Crawford

USC Annenberg, USA

Abstract. Training data is foundational to generative AI systems. From Common Crawl's 3.1 billion web pages to LAION-5B's corpus of almost 6 billion image-text pairs, these vast collections – scraped from the internet and treated as "ground truth" – play a critical role in shaping the epistemic boundaries that govern generative AI models. Yet training data is beset with complex social, political, and epistemological challenges. What happens when data is stripped of context, meaning, and provenance? How does training data limit what and how machine learning systems interpret the world? What are the copyright implications of these datasets? And most importantly, what forms of power do these approaches enhance and enable? This keynote is an invitation to reflect on the epistemic foundations of generative AI, and to consider the wide-ranging impacts of the current generative turn.

Biography. Professor Kate Crawford is a leading international scholar of the social implications of artificial intelligence. She is a Research Professor at USC Annenberg in Los Angeles, a Senior Principal Researcher at MSR in New York, an Honorary Professor at the University of Sydney, and the inaugural Visiting Chair for AI and Justice at the École Normale Supérieure in Paris. Her latest book, *Atlas of AI* (Yale, 2021) won the Sally Hacker Prize from the Society for the History of Technology, the ASIS&T Best Information Science Book Award, and was named one of the best books in 2021 by *New Scientist* and the *Financial Times*. Over her twenty-year research career, she has also produced groundbreaking creative collaborations and visual investigations. Her project *Anatomy of an AI System* with Vladan Joler is in the permanent collection of the Museum of Modern Art in New York and the V&A in London, and was awarded with the Design of the Year Award in 2019 and included in the Design of the Decades by the Design Museum of London. Her collaboration with the artist Trevor Paglen, *Excavating AI*, won the Ayrton Prize from the British Society for the History of Science. She has advised policymakers in the United Nations, the White House, and the European Parliament, and she currently leads the Knowing Machines Project, an international research collaboration that investigates the foundations of machine learning.

Contents – Part VII

Demo

Sustainability, Climate, and Environment

Continually Learning Out-of-Distribution Spatiotemporal Data for Robust Energy Forecasting

Arian Prabowo[1][✉][ID], Kaixuan Chen[1], Hao Xue[1][ID], Subbu Sethuvenkatraman[2][ID], and Flora D. Salim[1][ID]

[1] UNSW, Sydney, Australia
{arian.prabowo,kaixuan.chen,hao.xue1,flora.salim}@UNSW.edu.au
[2] CSIRO, Newcastle, Australia
subbu.sethuvenkatraman@csiro.au

Abstract. Forecasting building energy usage is essential for promoting sustainability and reducing waste, as it enables building managers to adjust energy use to improve energy efficiency and reduce costs. This importance is magnified during anomalous periods, such as the COVID-19 pandemic, which have disrupted occupancy patterns and made accurate forecasting more challenging. Forecasting energy usage during anomalous periods is difficult due to changes in occupancy patterns and energy usage behavior. One of the primary reasons for this is the shift in distribution of occupancy patterns, with many people working or learning from home. This has created a need for new forecasting methods that can adapt to changing occupancy patterns. Online learning has emerged as a promising solution to this challenge, as it enables building managers to adapt to changes in occupancy patterns and adjust energy usage accordingly. With online learning, models can be updated incrementally with each new data point, allowing them to learn and adapt in real-time. Continual learning methods offer a powerful solution to address the challenge of catastrophic forgetting in online learning, allowing energy forecasting models to retain valuable insights while accommodating new data and improving generalization in out-of-distribution scenarios. Another solution is to use human mobility data as a proxy for occupancy, leveraging the prevalence of mobile devices to track movement patterns and infer occupancy levels. Human mobility data can be useful in this context as it provides a way to monitor occupancy patterns without relying on traditional sensors or manual data collection methods. We have conducted extensive experiments using data from four buildings to test the efficacy of these approaches. However, deploying these methods in the real world presents several challenges.

Keywords: Forecasting · Energy · Continual Learning · COVID

1 Introduction

Accurate prediction of the electricity demand of buildings is vital for effective and cost-efficient energy management in commercial buildings. It also plays a significant role in

---

The original version of this chapter was revised: the unintentional errors in the table 3 and a small punctuation error in the section 6.3. have been corrected. The correction to this chapter is available at https://doi.org/10.1007/978-3-031-43430-3_34

© The Author(s), under exclusive license to Springer Nature Switzerland AG 2023, corrected publication 2023
G. De Francisci Morales et al. (Eds.): ECML PKDD 2023, LNAI 14175, pp. 3–19, 2023.
https://doi.org/10.1007/978-3-031-43430-3_1

maintaining a balance between electricity supply and demand in modern power grids. However, forecasting energy usage during anomalous periods, such as the COVID-19 pandemic, can be challenging due to changes in occupancy patterns and energy usage behavior. One of the primary reasons for this is the shift in distribution of occupancy patterns, with many people working or learning from home, leading to increased residential occupancy and decreased occupancy in offices, schools, and most retail establishments. Essential retail stores, such as grocery stores and restaurants, might experience a divergence between occupancy and energy usage, as they have fewer dine-in customers but still require energy for food preparation and sales. This has created a need for new forecasting methods that can adapt to changing occupancy patterns.

Online learning has emerged as a promising solution to this challenge, as it enables building managers to adapt to changes in occupancy patterns and adjust energy usage accordingly. With Online learning, models can be updated incrementally with each new data point, allowing them to learn and adapt in real-time [13].

Furthermore, continual learning methods offer an even more powerful solution by addressing the issue of catastrophic forgetting [6, 17]. These methods allow models to retain previously learned information while accommodating new data, preventing the loss of valuable insights and improving generalization in out-of-distribution scenarios. By combining online learning with continual learning techniques, energy forecasting models can achieve robustness, adaptability, and accuracy, making them well-suited for handling the challenges posed by spatiotemporal data with evolving distributions.

Another solution is to use human mobility data as a proxy for occupancy, leveraging the prevalence of mobile devices to track movement patterns and infer occupancy levels. Human mobility data can be useful in this context as it provides a way to monitor occupancy patterns without relying on traditional sensors or manual data collection methods [28].

In this study, we evaluate the effectiveness of mobility data and continual learning for forecasting building energy usage during anomalous periods. We utilized real-world data from Melbourne, Australia, a city that experienced one of the strictest lockdowns globally [4], making it an ideal case for studying energy usage patterns during out-of-distribution periods. We conducted experiments using data from four building complexes to empirically assess the performance of these methods.

2   Related Works

2.1   Energy Prediction in Urban Environments

Electricity demand profiling and forecasting has been a task of importance for many decades. Nevertheless, there exist a limited number of work in literature that investigate how human mobility patterns are directly related to the urban scale energy consumption, both during normal periods as well as adverse/extreme events. Energy modelling in literature is done at different granularities, occupant-level (personal energy footprinting), building-level and city-level. Models used for energy consumption prediction in urban environments are known as Urban Building Energy Models (UBEM). While top-down UBEMs are used for predicting aggregated energy consumption in urban areas using macro-economic variables and other aggregated statistical data, bottom-up UBEMs are more suited for building-level modelling of energy by clustering buildings into groups of similar characteristics [2]. Some examples in this respect are SUNtool, CitySim, UMI, CityBES, TEASER and HUES. Software modelling (simulation-based) is also a heavily used approach for building-wise energy prediction (Eg: EnergyPlus [7]). Due to fine-grain end-user level modelling, bottom-up UBEMs can incorporate inputs of occupant schedules. There also exist occupant-wise personal energy footprinting systems. However, for such occupant-wise energy footprinting, it requires infrastructure related to monitoring systems and sensors for indoor occupant behaviours, which are not always available. Also, due to privacy issues, to perform modelling at end-user level granularity, it can be hard to get access to publicly available data at finer temporal resolutions (both occupancy and energy) [33]. Building-wise energy models also have the same problems. Simulation-based models have complexity issues when scaling to the city level, because they have to build one model per each building. Moreover, simulation-based models contain assumptions about the data which make their outputs less accurate [1]. Consequently, it remains mostly an open research area how to conduct energy forecasting with data distribution shifts.

2.2 Mobility Data as Auxiliary Information in Forecasting

The study of human mobility patterns involves analysing the behaviours and movements of occupants in a particular area in a spatio-temporal context [28]. The amount of information that mobility data encompasses can be huge. The behaviour patterns of humans drive the decision making in many use-cases. Mobility data in particular, can act as a proxy for the dynamic (time varying) human occupancy at various spatial densities (building-wise, city-wise etc.). Thus such data are leveraged extensively for many tasks in urban environments including predicting water demand [31], urban flow forecasting [34], predicting patterns in hospital patient rooms [8], electricity use [12] etc. that depend on human activities.

Especially, during the COVID19 pandemic, mobility data has been quite useful for disease propagation modelling. For example, in the work by [32], those authors have developed a Graph Neural Network (GNN) based deep learning architecture to forecast the daily new COVID19 cases state-wise in United States. The GNN is developed such that each node represents one region and each edge represents the interaction between the two regions in terms of mobility flow. The daily new case counts, death counts and intra-region mobility flow is used as the features of each node whereas the inter-region mobility flow and flow of active cases is used as the edge features. Comparisons against other classical models which do not use mobility data has demonstrated the competitiveness of the developed model.

Nevertheless, as [28] state, the existing studies involving human mobility data lack diversity in the datasets in terms of their social demographics, building types, locations etc. Due to the heterogeneity, sparsity and difficulty in obtaining diverse mobility data, it remains a significant research challenge to incorporate them in modelling techniques [2]. Yet, the lack of extracting valuable information from such real-world data sources remains untapped, with a huge potential of building smarter automated decision making systems for urban planning [28].

2.3 Deep Learning for Forecasting

Deep learning has gained significant popularity in the field of forecasting, with various studies demonstrating its effectiveness in different domains [11]. For instance, it has been widely applied in mobility data forecasting, including road traffic forecasting [24–26], and flight delay forecasting [30]. In the realm of electricity forecasting, Long Short-Term Memory (LSTM) networks have been widely utilized [21]. Another popular deep learning model for electricity load forecasting is Neural basis expansion analysis for interpretable time series forecasting (N-BEATS) [20].

However, one common challenge faced by these deep learning methods is the performance degradation when the data distributions change rapidly, especially during out-of-distribution (OOD) periods. Online learning methods have been proposed to address this issue [14, 16, 18]. However, online learning methods can suffer from catastrophic forgetting, where newly acquired knowledge erases previously learned information [28]. To mitigate this, continual learning methods have been developed, which aim to retain previously learned information while accommodating new data, thereby improving generalization in OOD scenarios.

One approach to continual learning is Experience Replay [6, 17], a technique that re-exposes the model to past experiences to improve learning efficiency and reduce the effects of catastrophic forgetting. Building upon this idea, the Dark Experience Replay++ algorithm [5] utilizes a memory buffer to store past experiences and a deep neural network to learn from them, employing a dual-memory architecture that allows for the storage of both short-term and long-term memories separately. Another approach is the Fast and Slow Network (FSNet) [22], which incorporates a future adaptor and an associative memory module. The future adaptor facilitates quick adaptation to changes in the data distribution, while the associative memory module retains past patterns to prevent catastrophic forgetting. These continual learning methods have shown promise in mitigating catastrophic forgetting and improving generalization in OOD scenarios.

In the context of energy forecasting, the utilization of continual learning techniques holds great potential for addressing the challenges posed by OOD spatiotemporal data. By preserving past knowledge and adapting to new patterns, these methods enable more robust and accurate energy forecasting even during periods of rapid data distribution shifts.

3 Problem Definition

3.1 Time Series Forecasting

Consider a multivariate time series $\mathcal{X} \in \mathbf{R}^{T \times N}$ comprising mobility data, weather data, and the target variable, which is the energy consumption data. The time series consists of T observations and N dimensions. To perform H-timestamps-ahead time series forecasting, a model f takes as input a look-back window of L historical observations $(\mathbf{x}_{t-L+1}, \mathbf{x}_{t-L+2}, ..., \mathbf{x}_t)$ and generates forecasts for H future observations of the target variable y, which corresponds to the energy consumption of a building. We have:

$$f_\omega(\mathbf{x}_{t-L+1}, \mathbf{x}_{t-L+2}, ..., \mathbf{x}_t) = (y_{t+1}, y_{t+2}, ..., y_{t+H}), \tag{1}$$

where ω denotes the parameters in the model.

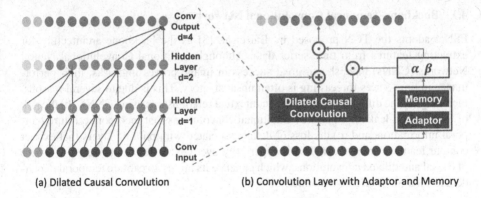

(a) Dilated Causal Convolution   (b) Convolution Layer with Adaptor and Memory

Fig. 1. The convolution architecture in TCN

3.2 Continual Learning for Time Series Forecasting

In a continual learning setting, the conventional machine learning practice of separating data into training and testing sets with a 70% to 30% ratio does not apply, as learning occurs continuously over the entire period. After an initial pre-training phase using a short period of training data, typically the first 3 months, the model continually trains on incoming data and generates predictions for future time windows. Evaluation of the model's performance is commonly done by measuring its accumulated errors throughout the entire learning process [27].

4   Method

Continual learning presents unique challenges that necessitate the development of specialized algorithms and evaluation metrics to address the problem effectively. In this context, a continual learner must strike a balance between retaining previously acquired knowledge while facilitating the learning of new tasks. In time-series forecasting, the challenge lies in balancing the need to learn new temporal dependencies quickly while remembering past patterns, a phenomenon commonly referred to as the stability-plasticity dilemma [9]. Building on the concept of complementary learning systems theory for dual learning systems [15], a Temporal Convolutional Network (TCN) is utilized as the underlying architecture, which is pre-trained to extract temporal features from the training dataset. Subsequently, the convolutional layers of the TCN are customized with a future adaptor and an associative memory module to address the challenges associated with continual learning. The future adaptor facilitates quick adaptation to changes, while the associative memory module is responsible for retaining past patterns to prevent catastrophic forgetting. In this section we describe in detail the architecture of FSNet [22].

4.1 Backbone-Temporal Convolutional Network

FSNet adopts the TCN proposed by Bai et al. [3] as the backbone architecture for extracting features from time series data. Although traditional Convolutional Neural Networks (CNNs) have shown great success in image-processing tasks, their performance in time-series forecasting is often unsatisfactory. This is due to several reasons, including (a) the difficulty of capturing contextual relationships using CNNs, (b) the risk of information leakage caused by traditional convolutions that incorporate future temporal information, and (c) the loss of detail associated with pooling layers that extract contour features. In contrast, TCN's superiority over CNNs can be attributed to its use of causal and dilated convolutions, which enhance its ability to capture temporal dependencies in a more effective manner.

Causal Convolutions. In contrast to traditional CNNs, which may incorporate future temporal information and violate causality, causal convolutions are effective in avoiding data leakage in the future. By only considering information up to and including the current time step, causal convolutions do not alter the order in which data is modelled and are therefore well-suited for temporal data. Specifically, to ensure that the output tensor has the same length as the input tensor, it is necessary to perform zero-padding. When zero-padding is performed only on the left side of the input tensor, causal convolution can be ensured. In Fig. 1(a), zero-padding is shown in light colours on the left side. There is no padding on the right side of the input sequence because the last element of the input sequence is the latest element on which the rightmost output element depends. Regarding the second-to-last output element, its kernel window is shifted one position to the left compared to the last output element. This implies that the second-to-last element's latest dependency on the rightmost side of the input sequence is the second-to-last element. By induction, for each element in the output sequence, its latest dependency in the input sequence has the same index as the element itself.

Dilated Convolutions. Dilated convolution is an important component of TCN because causal convolution can only access the past inputs up to a certain depth, which is determined by the kernel size of the convolutional layer. In a deep network, the receptive field of the last layer may not be large enough to capture long-term dependencies in the input sequence. In dilated convolutions, the dilation factor is used to determine the spacing between the values in the kernel of the dilated convolution. More formally, we have:

$$Conv(\mathbf{x})_i = \sum_{m=0}^{k} w_m \cdot \mathbf{x}_{i-m \times d} \qquad (2)$$

where i represents the i-th element, w denotes the kernel, d is the dilation factor, k is the filter size. Dilation introduces a fixed step between adjacent filter taps. Specifically, if the dilation factor d is set to 1, the dilated convolution reduces to a regular convolution. However, for $d > 1$, the filters are expanded by d units, allowing the network to capture longer-term dependencies in the input sequence. A dilated causal convolution architecture can be seen in Fig. 1(a).

4.2 Fast Adaptation

FSNet modify the convolution layer in TCN to achieve fast adaptation and associative memory. The modified structure is illustrated in Fig. 1(b). In this subsection, we first introduce the fast adaptation module.

In order to enable rapid adaptation to changes in data streams and effective learning with limited data, Sahoo et al. [27] and Phuong and Lampert [23] propose the use of shallower networks and single layers that can quickly adapt to changes in data streams or learn more efficiently with limited data. Instead of limiting the depth of the network, it is more advantageous to enable each layer to adapt independently. In this research, we adopt an independent monitoring and modification approach for each layer to enhance the learning of the current loss. An adaptor is utilized to map the recent gradients of the layer to a smaller, more condensed set of transformation parameters to adapt the backbone. However, the gradient of a single sample can cause significant fluctuation and introduce noise into the adaptation coefficients in continual time-series forecasting. As a solution, we utilize Exponential Moving Average (EMA) gradient to mitigate the noise in online training and capture the temporal information in time series:

$$\hat{g}_l = \gamma \hat{g}_l + (1 - \gamma)\hat{g}_l^t, \tag{3}$$

where $\hat{g}_l^t$ denotes the gradient of the l-th layer at time t, $\hat{g}_l$ denotes the EMA gradient, and γ represents the momentum coefficient. For the sake of brevity, we shall exclude the superscript t in the subsequent sections of this manuscript. We take $\hat{g}_l$ as input and get the adaptation coefficient μ_l:

$$\mu_l = \Omega(\hat{g}_l; \phi_l), \tag{4}$$

where $\Omega(\cdot)$ is the chunking operation in [10] that partitions the gradient into uniformly-sized chunks. These segments are subsequently associated with the adaptation coefficients that are characterized by the trainable parameters ϕ_l. Specifically, the adaptation coefficient μ_l is composed of two components: a weight adaptation coefficient α_l and a feature adaptation coefficient β_l. Then we conduct weight adaptation and feature adaptation. The weight adaptation parameter α_l performs an element-wise multiplication on the corresponding weight of the backbone network, as described in:

$$\tilde{\theta}_l = tile(\alpha_l) \odot \theta_l, \tag{5}$$

where we represent the feature maps of all channels in a TCN as θ_l, while the adapted weights are denoted by $\tilde{\theta}_l$. The weight adaptor is applied per-channel on all filters using the tile function, which repeats a vector along the new axes, as indicated by $tile(\alpha_l)$. Finally, the element-wise multiplication is represented by $\odot$. Likewise, we have:

$$\tilde{h}_l = tile(\beta_l) \odot h_l, \tag{6}$$

where $h_l = \tilde{\theta}_l * \tilde{h}_{l-1}$ is the output feature map.

4.3   Associative Memory

In order to prevent a model from forgetting old patterns during continual learning in the context of time series, it is crucial to preserve the appropriate adaptation coefficients μ, which encapsulate adequate temporal patterns for forecasting. These coefficients reflect the model's prior adaptation to a specific pattern, and thus, retaining and recalling the corresponding μ can facilitate learning when the pattern resurfaces in the future. Consequently, we incorporate an associative memory to store the adaptation coefficients of recurring events encountered during training. This associative memory is denoted as $M_l \in \mathbf{R}^{N \times d}$, where d represents the dimensionality of μ_l and is set to a default value of 64.

Memory Interaction Triggering. To circumvent the computational burden and noise that arises from storing and querying coefficients at each time step, FSNet propose to activate this interaction only when there is a significant change in the representation. The overlap between the current and past representations can be evaluated by taking the dot product of their respective gradients. FSNet leverage an additional EMA gradient $\hat{g}'_l$, with a smaller coefficient γ' compared to the original EMA gradient $\hat{g}_l$, and measure the cosine similarity between them to determine when to trigger the memory. We use a hyper-parameter τ, which we set to 0.7, to ensure that the memory is only activated to recall significant pattern changes that are more likely to recur. The interaction is triggered when $cosine(\hat{g}_l, \hat{g}'_l) < -\tau$.

To guarantee that the present adaptation coefficients account for the entire event, which may extend over an extended period, memory read and write operations are carried out utilizing the adaptation coefficients of the EMA with coefficient γ'. The EMA of μ_l is computed following the same procedure as Eq. 3. In the event that a memory interaction is initiated, the adaptor retrieves the most comparable transformations from the past through an attention-read operation, which involves a weighted sum over the memory items:

$$r_l = softmax(M_l \hat{\mu}_l), \tag{7}$$

$$\tilde{\mu}_l = \sum_{i=1}^{k} TopK(r_l)[i] M_l[i], \tag{8}$$

where $TopK(\cdot)$ selects the top k values from r_l, and $[i]$ means the i-th element. Retrieving the adaptation coefficient from memory enables the model to recall past experiences in adapting to the current pattern and improve its learning in the present. The retrieved coefficient is combined with the current parameters through a weighted sum: $\mu_l = \tau \mu_l + (1 - \tau)\tilde{\mu}_l$. Subsequently, the memory is updated using the updated adaptation coefficient:

$$M_l = \tau M_l + (1 - \tau)\tilde{\mu} \otimes TopK(r_l), \tag{9}$$

where $\otimes$ denotes the outer-product operator. So far, we can effectively incorporate new knowledge into the most pertinent locations, as identified by the top-k attention values of r_l. Since the memory is updated by summation, it can be inferred that the memory μ_l does not increase as learning progresses.

5   Datasets and Contextual Data

This paper is based on two primary data sources: energy usage data and mobility data, as well as two contextual datasets: COVID lockdown dates and temperature data. The statistical summary of the main datasets are provided in Table 1 and visualized in Fig. 2. These datasets were collected from four building complexes in the Melbourne CBD area of Australia between 2018 and 2021.

Table 1 outlines the essential statistical properties of energy usage and mobility data collected from the four building complexes. It is evident from the data that energy usage varies significantly between the buildings, with BC2 having over ten times the average energy usage of BC4. Similarly, the mobility data shows distinct differences, with BC2 having a mean pedestrian count over three times greater than BC4. These differences emphasize the complexity of forecasting for energy usage in different building complexes.

Table 1. The summary statistics of the four datasets, each of which represents an aggregated and anonymized building complex (BC).

		BC1	BC2	BC3	BC4
Temporal	start	2019-01-01	2018-01-01	2018-01-01	2019-07-01
	end	2020-12-31	2020-12-31	2020-12-31	2020-12-31
	num of record	17304	24614	26196	13200
	duration (years)	2.0	3.0	3.0	1.5
	granularity	hourly	hourly	hourly	hourly
Energy (kWh)	mean	207.27	278.17	166.42	26.64
	std	111.59	88.67	66.60	13.21
	min	3.25	1.32	5.38	0.00
	0.25	112.72	203.38	112.62	17.45
	median	169.29	272.68	144.34	21.75
	0.75	297.33	342.10	206.63	31.06
	max	611.67	709.41	371.64	83.01
Mobility (count)	mean	661.4	977.8	804.9	295.8
	std	876.8	936.2	761.4	387.3
	min	0	0	0	0
	0.25	37	149	127	33
	median	209	614	528	135
	0.75	1004	1818	1349	386
	max	6025	5053	3780	2984

It is worth noting that lockdown had a more significant impact on mobility than energy usage, as illustrated in Fig. 2. Additionally, both energy usage and mobility started declining even before the start of lockdown.

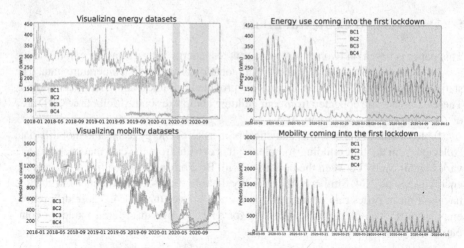

Fig. 2. Visualizing the four datasets and their features, showing the significant changes in distributions due to lockdowns. Plots on the left column are smoothed with a Gaussian filter with sigma = 24 h. Red areas are lockdowns. (Color figure online)

5.1 Energy Usage Data

The energy usage data was collected from the energy suppliers for each building complex and measured the amount of electricity used by the buildings. To protect the privacy of the building owners, operators, and users, the energy usage data from each building was aggregated into complexes and anonymized. Buildings in the same complexes can have different primary use (e.g. residential, office, retails)

5.2 Mobility Data

The mobility data was captured by an automated pedestrian counting system installed by the City of Melbourne http://www.pedestrian.melbourne.vic.gov.au/ [19], and provided information on the movement patterns of individuals in and around each building complex. The system recorded the number of pedestrians passing through a given zone as shown in Fig. 3. As no images were recorded, no individual information was collected. Some sensors were installed as early as 2009, while others were installed as late as 2021. Some devices were moved, removed, and upgraded at various times. Seventy-nine sensors have been installed, and we have chosen four sensors, one for each building complex. We performed manual matching between the complexes and sensors by selecting the sensor that was closest to each building complex.

5.3 COVID Lockdown Dates

We used data on the dates of the COVID lockdowns in Melbourne, one of the strictest in the world. Our datasets coincides with the first lockdown from March 30, 2020 to May 12, 2020 (43 days), and the second lockdown from July 8 to October 27,

Fig. 3. Diagram of automated pedestrian counting system. Obtained from the City of Melbourne website [19].

2020 (111 days). We also divided the time into pre-lockdown and post-lockdown periods, taking the date of the first lockdown (March 30, 2020) as the boundary. We took this information from https://www.abc.net.au/news/2021-10-03/melbourne-longest-lockdown/100510710 [4].

5.4 Temperature Data

Temperature records are extracted from the National Renewable Energy Laboratory (NREL) Asia Pacific Himawari Solar Data [29]. As the building complexes are located in close proximity to one another, we utilized the same temperature data for all of them.

5.5 Dataset Preprocessing

For this study, we have fixed an observation of $L = 24$ h and a forecast horizon size of $H = 24$ h, to mimic a day-ahead forecasting experiment. To accurately link the foot traffic mobility data with the building, we carefully handpicked the pedestrian counting sensor that is located in the immediate vicinity of the building and used its corresponding mobility signal. The energy usage load of the building, the foot traffic volume, and the temperature degree were all aligned based on their timestamps.

6 Experiments and Results

We conducted two sets of experiments to evaluate the effectiveness of our proposed methods for predicting energy usage during anomalous periods. The first set of experiments evaluated the impact of including mobility contextual data in our models. The second set of experiments assessed the importance of continual learning. In addition, we conducted ablation experiments on FSNet to investigate the impact of different components of the model on the overall performance.

6.1 Experimental Setup

The experiments were conducted on a high-performance computing (HPC) node cluster with an Intel(R) Xeon(R) Platinum 8268 CPU @ 2.90GHz and Tesla V100-SXM2. The software specifications included intel-mkl 2020.3.304, nvidia-cublas 11.11.3.6, cudnn 8.1.1-cuda11, fftw3 3.3.8, openmpi 4.1.0, magma 2.6.0, cuda 11.2.2, pytorch 1.9.0, python3 3.9.2, pandas 1.2.4, and numpy 1.20.0.

The data was split into three months for pre-training, three months for validation of the pre-training, and the rest was used for the usual continual learning setup. No hyperparameter tuning was conducted as default settings were used. The loss function used is MSE.

6.2 Mobility

Table 2. Performance comparison between different contextual features. Results are average over 10 runs with different random seed. The standard deviation is shown. The algorithm used was FSNet with continual learning. +M is the improvement of adding mobility over no context, +T is the improvement of adding temperature over no context, T+M is the improvement of adding mobility over temperature only.

(MAE)	dataset	no context	mobilityonly	temp. only	both	+M	+T	T+M
Pre-Lockdown	BC1	0.1591	0.1587	0.1595	0.1516	0.0004	0.0004	0.0079
		±0.0252	±0.0334	±0.0269	±0.0332			
	BC2	0.1711	0.1993	0.1947	0.1708	−0.0282	−0.0236	0.0239
		0.0085	±0.0385	±0.0391	±0.0068			
	BC3	0.2629	0.2866	0.2509	0.2403	−0.0237	0.0120	0.0105
		±0.0373	±0.0534	±0.0262	±0.0095			
	BC4	0.2706	0.2516	0.3142	0.2776	0.0190	−0.0436	0.0366
		±0.0370	±0.0206	±0.1581	±0.0312			
Post-Lockdown	BC1	0.1484	0.1475	0.1434	0.1369	0.0033	0.0041	0.0041
		±0.0318	±0.0464	±0.0283	±0.0355			
	BC2	0.1636	0.1902	0.1849	0.1624	0.0072	−0.0194	0.0053
		±0.0085	±0.0371	±0.0381	±0.0063			
	BC3	0.2418	0.2654	0.2299	0.2198	−0.0014	−0.0251	0.0355
		±0.0374	±0.0537	±0.0252	±0.0089			
	BC4	0.3236	0.2943	0.4134	0.3282	0.0293	−0.1191	0.0852
		±0.0602	±0.0294	±0.3215	±0.0502			

To assess the significance of the mobility context in predicting energy usage during anomalous periods, we performed a contextual feature ablation analysis, comparing pre- and post-lockdown performance. Table 2 presents the results of our experiments. Our findings suggest that the importance of mobility context is unclear in pre-lockdown periods, with mixed improvements observed, and the improvements are small compared to the standard deviations. However, post-lockdown, the importance of mobility context is more pronounced, and the best performance was achieved when both mobility and temperature contexts were utilized. Notably, our analysis revealed that post-lockdown, the improvement brought about by the mobility context is larger than that achieved through temperature alone, as observed in BC1, BC2, and BC4. This could be due to the fact that temperature has a comparatively simple and regular periodic pattern such that deep learning models can deduce them from energy data alone.

6.3 Continual Learning

Table 3. Comparing the performance of different algorithm with or without continual learning (CL). The metric used is MAE. Results are average over 10 runs with different random seed. The standard deviation is shown.

	dataset	FSNet (no CL)	FSNet	TCN (no CL)	OGD	ER	DER++
Pre-Lockdown	BC1	0.3703 ±0.0607	**0.1583** ±0.0280	0.3668 ±0.0379	0.2056 ±0.0413	0.1820 ±0.0217	0.1696 ±0.0130
	BC2	0.6272 ±0.0914	**0.1712** ±0.0063	0.5176 ±0.0607	0.2465 ±0.0105	0.2322 ±0.0056	0.2272 ±0.0062
	BC3	0.6750 ±0.0638	**0.2462** ±0.0151	0.6500 ±0.0698	0.3308 ±0.0812	0.2862 ±0.0432	0.2726 ±0.0334
	BC4	1.0018 ±0.1053	**0.2802** ±0.0312	1.1236 ±0.1040	0.3910 ±0.0520	0.3511 ±0.0323	0.3408 ±0.0210
Post-Lockdown	BC1	0.4537 ±0.0517	**0.1429** ±0.0275	0.4179 ±0.0443	0.1797 ±0.0342	0.1589 ±0.0168	0.1482 ±0.0094
	BC2	0.6506 ±0.0994	**0.1628** ±0.0057	0.5209 ±0.0535	0.2313 ±0.0085	0.2188 ±0.0060	0.2148 ±0.0068
	BC3	0.7168 ±0.0632	**0.2255** ±0.0145	0.7083 ±0.0793	0.3014 ±0.0709	0.2636 ±0.0373	0.2518 ±0.0286
	BC4	1.8415 ±0.2765	**0.3314** ±0.0520	1.8307 ±0.2319	0.4496 ±0.0643	0.4162 ±0.0475	0.4043 ±0.0338

We conducted an experiment to determine the significance of continual learning by comparing the performance of various popular models with and without continual learning.

The models used in the experiment are:

- **FSNet** [22]: Fast and slow network, described in detail in the method section of this paper. In the no CL, version we use the exact same architecture, however we use the traditional offline learning.

- **TCN** [1]: Temporal Convolutional Network, is the offline learning baseline. It modifies the typical CNN using causal and dilated convolution which enhance its ability to capture temporal dependencies more effectively. The next three methods are different continual learning methods that uses TCN as the baseline.
- **OGD**: Ordinary gradient descent, a popular optimization algorithm used in machine learning. It updates the model parameters by taking small steps in the direction of the gradient of the loss function.
- **ER** [6, 17]: Experience Replay, a technique used to re-expose the model to past experiences in order to improve learning efficiency and reduce the effects of catastrophic forgetting.
- **DER++** [5]: Dark Experience Replay++ is an extension of the DER (Deep Experience Replay) algorithm, which uses a memory buffer to store past experiences and a deep neural network to learn from them. DER++ improves upon DER by using a dual-memory architecture, which allows it to store both short-term and long-term memories separately.

Table 3 displays the results, which demonstrate the consistent importance of continual learning in 1both the pre- and post-lockdown periods, with improvements multiple times larger than the standard deviations.

7   Conclusion

In this study, we investigated the impact of mobility contextual data and continual learning on building energy usage forecasting during out-of-distribution periods. We used data from Melbourne, Australia, a city that experienced one of the strictest lockdowns during the COVID-19 pandemic, as a prime example of such periods. Our results indicated that energy usage and mobility patterns vary significantly across different building complexes, highlighting the complexity of energy usage forecasting. We also found that the mobility context had a greater impact than the temperature context in forecasting energy usage during lockdown. We evaluated the importance of continual learning by comparing the performance of several popular models with and without continual learning, including FSNet, OGD, ER, and DER++. The results consistently demonstrated that continual learning is important in both pre- and post-lockdown periods, with significant improvements in performance observed across all models. Our study emphasizes the importance of considering contextual data and implementing continual learning techniques for robust energy usage forecasting in buildings.

Acknowledgment. We highly appreciate Centre for New Energy Technologies (C4NET) and Commonwealth Scientific and Industrial Research Organisation (CSIRO) for their funding support and contributions during the project. We would also like to acknowledge the support of Cisco's National Industry Innovation Network (NIIN) Research Chair Program. This research was undertaken with the assistance of resources and services from the National Computational Infrastructure (NCI), which is supported by the Australian Government. This endeavor would not have been possible without the contribution of Dr. Hansika Hewamalage and Dr. Mashud Rana.

Ethics

Ethical Statement

Data collection: the data used in this paper are a mixture of public and private data. For privacy reasons, the energy usage data cannot be made available publicly. The lockdown dates, and pedestrian data can be access publicly. Lockdown dates is by ABC, an Australian public news service https://www.abc.net.au/news/2021-10-03/melbourne-longest-lockdown/100510710 and the pedestrian data is from City of Melbourne, a municipal government http://www.pedestrian.melbourne.vic.gov.au/.

Statement of Informed Consent: This paper does not contain any studies with human or animal participants. There are no human participants in this paper, and informed consent is not applicable.

Ethical Considerations

There are several ethical considerations related to this paper.

Data Privacy. The use of data from buildings may raise concerns about privacy, particularly if personal data such as occupancy patterns is being collected and analyzed. Although the privacy of individual residents, occupants, and users are protected through the building level aggregations, sensitive information belonging to building managers, operator, and owners might be at risk. To this end, we choose to further aggregate the few buildings into complexes and make it anonymous. Unfortunately, the implication is that we cannot publish the dataset.

Bias and Discrimination. There is a risk that the models used to predict energy usage may be biased against certain groups of people, particularly if the models are trained on data that is not representative of the population as a whole. This could lead to discriminatory outcomes, such as higher energy bills or reduced access to energy for marginalized communities. We do acknowledge that the CBD of Melbourne, Australia is not a representative of energy usage in buildings in general, in CBD around the world, nor Australia. However, our contribution specifically tackle the shift in distributions, albeit only temporally and not spatially. We hope that our contributions will advance the forecasting techniques, even when the distributions in the dataset are not representative.

Environmental Impact. This paper can make buildings more sustainable by improving energy usage forecasting, even during anomalous periods, such as the COVID-19 pandemic. Robust and accurate forecasting enables building managers to optimize energy consumption and reduce costs. By using contextual data, such as human mobility patterns, and continual learning techniques, building energy usage can be predicted more accurately and efficiently, leading to better energy management and reduced waste. This, in turn, can contribute to the overall sustainability of buildings and reduce their impact on the environment.

References

1. Ali, U., et al.: A data-driven approach for multi-scale GIS-based building energy modeling for analysis, planning and support decision making. Appl. Energy **279**, 115834 (2020)
2. Ali, U., Shamsi, M.H., Hoare, C., Mangina, E., O'Donnell, J.: Review of urban building energy modeling (UBEM) approaches, methods and tools using qualitative and quantitative analysis. Energy Build. **246**, 111073 (2021)
3. Bai, S., Kolter, J.Z., Koltun, V.: An empirical evaluation of generic convolutional and recurrent networks for sequence modeling. arXiv preprint arXiv:1803.01271 (2018)
4. Boaz, J.: Melbourne passes buenos aires' world record for time spent in lockdown (2021)
5. Buzzega, P., Boschini, M., Porrello, A., Abati, D., Calderara, S.: Dark experience for general continual learning: a strong, simple baseline. Adv. Neural. Inf. Process. Syst. **33**, 15920–15930 (2020)
6. Chaudhry, A., et al.: On tiny episodic memories in continual learning. arXiv preprint arXiv:1902.10486 (2019)
7. Crawley, D.B., et al.: Energyplus: creating a new-generation building energy simulation program. Energy Build. **33**(4), 319–331 (2001). Special Issue: BUILDING SIMULATION'99
8. Dedesko, S., Stephens, B., Gilbert, J.A., Siegel, J.A.: Methods to assess human occupancy and occupant activity in hospital patient rooms. Build. Environ. **90**, 136–145 (2015)
9. Grossberg, S.: Adaptive resonance theory: how a brain learns to consciously attend, learn, and recognize a changing world. Neural Netw. **37**, 1–47 (2013)
10. Ha, D., Dai, A.M., Le, Q.V.: Hypernetworks. In: International Conference on Learning Representations (2016)
11. Herzen, J., et al.: Darts: user-friendly modern machine learning for time series. J. Mach. Learn. Res. **23**(124), 1–6 (2022)
12. Hewamalage, H., Chen, K., Rana, M., Sethuvenkatraman, S., Xue, H., Salim, F.D.: Human mobility data as proxy for occupancy information in urban building energy modelling. In: 18th Healthy Buildings Europe Conference (2023)
13. Hoi, S.C., Sahoo, D., Lu, J., Zhao, P.: Online learning: a comprehensive survey. Neurocomputing **459**, 249–289 (2021)
14. Kar, P., Li, S., Narasimhan, H., Chawla, S., Sebastiani, F.: Online optimization methods for the quantification problem. In: Proceedings of the 22nd ACM SIGKDD International Conference on Knowledge Discovery and Data Mining, pp. 1625–1634 (2016)
15. Kumaran, D., Hassabis, D., McClelland, J.L.: What learning systems do intelligent agents need? Complementary learning systems theory updated. Trends Cogn. Sci. **20**(7), 512–534 (2016)
16. Li, S.: The art of clustering bandits. Ph.D. thesis, Università degli Studi dell'Insubria (2016)
17. Lin, L.J.: Self-improving reactive agents based on reinforcement learning, planning and teaching. Mach. Learn. **8**, 293–321 (1992)
18. Mahadik, K., Wu, Q., Li, S., Sabne, A.: Fast distributed bandits for online recommendation systems. In: Proceedings of the 34th ACM International Conference on Supercomputing, pp. 1–13 (2020)
19. City of Melbourne: City of Melbourne - pedestrian counting system
20. Oreshkin, B.N., Dudek, G., Pełka, P., Turkina, E.: N-beats neural network for mid-term electricity load forecasting. Appl. Energy **293**, 116918 (2021)
21. Pełka, P., Dudek, G.: Pattern-based long short-term memory for mid-term electrical load forecasting. In: 2020 International Joint Conference on Neural Networks (IJCNN), pp. 1–8. IEEE (2020)
22. Pham, Q., Liu, C., Sahoo, D., Hoi, S.C.: Learning fast and slow for online time series forecasting. arXiv preprint arXiv:2202.11672 (2022)

23. Phuong, M., Lampert, C.H.: Distillation-based training for multi-exit architectures. In: Proceedings of the IEEE/CVF International Conference on Computer Vision, pp. 1355–1364 (2019)
24. Prabowo, A.: Spatiotemporal deep learning. Ph.D. thesis, RMIT University (2022)
25. Prabowo, A., Shao, W., Xue, H., Koniusz, P., Salim, F.D.: Because every sensor is unique, so is every pair: handling dynamicity in traffic forecasting. In: 8th ACM/IEEE Conference on Internet of Things Design and Implementation, IoTDI 2023, pp. 93–104. Association for Computing Machinery, New York (2023). https://doi.org/10.1145/3576842.3582362
26. Prabowo, A., Xue, H., Shao, W., Koniusz, P., Salim, F.D.: Message passing neural networks for traffic forecasting (2023)
27. Sahoo, D., Pham, Q., Lu, J., Hoi, S.C.: Online deep learning: learning deep neural networks on the fly. In: Proceedings of the 27th International Joint Conference on Artificial Intelligence, pp. 2660–2666 (2018)
28. Salim, F.D., et al.: Modelling urban-scale occupant behaviour, mobility, and energy in buildings: a survey. Build. Environ. **183**, 106964 (2020)
29. Sengupta, M., Xie, Y., Lopez, A., Habte, A., Maclaurin, G., Shelby, J.: The national solar radiation data base (NSRDB). Renew. Sustain. Energy Rev. **89**, 51–60 (2018)
30. Shao, W., Prabowo, A., Zhao, S., Koniusz, P., Salim, F.D.: Predicting flight delay with spatio-temporal trajectory convolutional network and airport situational awareness map. Neurocomputing **472**, 280–293 (2022)
31. Smolak, K., et al.: Applying human mobility and water consumption data for short-term water demand forecasting using classical and machine learning models. Urban Water J. **17**(1), 32–42 (2020)
32. Wang, L., et al.: Using mobility data to understand and forecast COVID19 dynamics. medRxiv (2020)
33. Wei, P., Jiang, X.: Data-driven energy and population estimation for real-time city-wide energy footprinting. In: Proceedings of the 6th ACM International Conference on Systems for Energy-Efficient Buildings, Cities, and Transportation, BuildSys 2019, pp. 267–276. Association for Computing Machinery, New York (2019)
34. Xue, H., Salim, F.D.: TERMCast: temporal relation modeling for effective urban flow forecasting. In: Karlapalem, K., et al. (eds.) PAKDD 2021. LNCS (LNAI), vol. 12712, pp. 741–753. Springer, Cham (2021). https://doi.org/10.1007/978-3-030-75762-5_58

Counterfactual Explanations for Remote Sensing Time Series Data: An Application to Land Cover Classification

Cassio F. Dantas[1](✉), Thalita F. Drumond[3], Diego Marcos[2], and Dino Ienco[1]

[1] INRAE, UMR TETIS, University of Montpellier, Montpellier, France
cassio.fraga-dantas@inrae.fr
[2] Inria, UMR TETIS, University of Montpellier, Montpellier, France
[3] EPF Engineering School, Montpellier, France

Abstract. Enhancing the interpretability of AI techniques is paramount for increasing their acceptability, especially in highly interdisciplinary fields such as remote sensing, in which scientists and practitioners with diverse backgrounds work together to monitor the Earth's surface. In this context, counterfactual explanations are an emerging tool to characterize the behaviour of machine learning systems, by providing a post-hoc analysis of a given classification model. Focusing on the important task of land cover classification from remote sensing data, we propose a counterfactual explanation approach called *CFE4SITS* (CounterFactual Explanation for Satellite Image Time Series). One of its distinctive features over existing strategies is the lack of prior assumption on the targeted class for a given counterfactual explanation. This inherent flexibility allows for the automatic discovery of relationship between classes. To assess the quality of the proposed approach, we consider a real-world case study in which we aim to characterize the behavior of a ready-to-use land cover classifier. To this end, we compare *CFE4SITS* to recent time series counterfactual-based strategies and, subsequently, perform an in-depth analysis of its behaviour.

1 Introduction

Raising the acceptability of machine learning techniques is of paramount importance, especially in highly interdisciplinary fields of application like remote sensing in which scientists and practitioners from different background as agronomy, ecology, biodiversity, forestry and data science work together to make value of satellite data to monitor the Earth surface [1]. Like in many application domains [2], deep learning techniques have also gained widespread popularity in the remote sensing community [3] due to impressive results on a variety of remote sensing tasks such as satellite image super-resolution, satellite image restoration, biophysical variables estimation and land cover classification [3], to name a few. Of crucial importance, this last task provides useful knowledge to support many downstream

Code is available at github.com/tanodino/CF_SITS.

G. De Francisci Morales et al. (Eds.): ECML PKDD 2023, LNAI 14175, pp. 20–36, 2023.
https://doi.org/10.1007/978-3-031-43430-3_2

geospatial analyses [4]. Due to the advent of the recent spatial missions [5] like the European Space Agency's Sentinel one, data is systematically made available over any area of the planet's continental surface at high spatial (order of 10 m) and temporal (an acquisition up to every five/six days) resolution. This kind of information can be shaped as Satellite Image Time Series (SITS) and it contains information about the evolution of the Earth surface of a particular study area allowing, for instance, to distinguish vegetated land covers that evolve differently over a yearly cycle of seasons (e.g. in agriculture, different cropping practices exhibit a different dynamic in their radiometric signal over a growing season). SITS are nowadays the standard input to any land cover classification task [6] where the goal is to combine remote sensing data with limited ground truth labels on a study area by means of supervised machine learning methods in order to provide a classification (also referenced as land cover map) of the whole study area.

Despite the high performances achieved by recent deep learning frameworks on this task, they remain black-box models with limited understanding on their internal behavior. Due to this limitation, there is a growing need for improving the interpretability of deep learning models in remote sensing with the objective to raise up their acceptability and usefulness, as their decision-making processes are often not transparent [7–9]. Counterfactual explanation methods have recently received increasing attention as a means to provide some level of interpretability [10–12] to these black-box models. Such methods aim to describe the behaviour of a model by providing minimal changes (or perturbations) to the input data that would result in a realistic counterfactual that is predicted by the model as a different class. Recent works on counterfactual explanations have demonstrated great applicability in different prediction tasks, such as classification of tabular data [13,14], images [15] and time series [16,17]. Generally, to be more easily interpretable it is desirable that these perturbations be minimal, sparse, associated to some semantic element of the input data and plausible (representative of the underlying data distribution). These different points can be seen as requirements that a counterfactual sample should meet [12]. In the case of time series data, the first two requirements can be implemented by forcing the perturbation to cover a short and contiguous section of the timeline [17].

Most of the approaches for time series counterfactual explanation [16,17] make, at least, one of the two following assumptions. Firstly, they require to manually associate each sample to an alternative/different class label. Secondly, they systematically generate a counterfactual for each input sample resulting in new counterfactuals that can be unrealistic or not plausible according to the underlying application domain. These assumptions can hardly fit real domain applications in which the underlying classification problem is multi-class and the application domain is strongly influenced by physical process and natural laws, as land cover classification from remote sensing data. In this context, the problem is generally multi-class, the classifier needs to distinguish among several land cover classes, making it challenging to define a priori the class transition (the alternative class) for each sample to obtain the corresponding counterfactual. In addition, due to the fact that satellite image time series describe biophysical processes, the underlying structure is governed by natural and physical laws that constrain the possible shape of the signal. As a consequence, available counterfactual explanation methods can be inadequate to characterize and explain the behaviour of a land cover classifier.

To tackle this challenging problem, we propose a counterfactual generation approach for land cover classification from satellite image time series data, namely *CFE4SITS* (CounterFactual Explanation for Satellite Image Time Series). The proposed approach generates counterfactual explanations that are close to the original data (modifying only a limited set of time entries by a small amount), sparse (localized over a short and contiguous section of the timeline) and plausible (i.e. belong as much as possible to the underlying data distribution). Two distinctive features separate *CFE4SITS* from existing strategies: (1) there is no need for prior assumption on which class to target when producing a counterfactual explanation; (2) explanation plausibility is explicitly enforced via adversarial learning with an additional optimization term. While the former feature allows for the automatic discovery of relationship between classes, the latter forces our method to provide realistic/plausible counterfactual explanations.

The rest of this manuscript is organized as follows. In Sect. 3 we describe the considered study case with the associated remote sensing data. After detailing the proposed method in Sect. 4, we present the experimental results in Sect. 5. Concluding remarks and future works are outlined in Sect. 6.

2   Related Work

Interest in counterfactual explanations for time series data has surged in the last few years in several high-stake applications as underlined in the recent literature survey proposed in [18].

In [16], the authors propose two approaches that try to find the minimum amount of changes to a time series that forces a classifier into changing its output prediction. The two approaches are respectively built upon a k-Nearest Neighbors and a Random Shapelet Forest classifier. Although they are explicitly constructed for these particular classifiers, nothing prevents them to be used with different ones. Additionally, both approaches systematically generate a counterfactual explanation for each input sample besides requiring to manually provide the alternative class for each counterfactual. The counterfactual explanation is directly chosen by the set of training sample.

In [17], the authors have introduced the Native Guided (NG) method for CNN-based time series classification that exploits Class Activation Map (CAM)[1] feature-weight vectors to select a sub-sequence of the original time series to perturb in order to generate the counterfactual explanation. The perturbation in this case consists of replacing the selected sub-sequence by a corresponding section of another sample (called the Native Guide) taken from the training data. Similarly to previous approaches, also this strategy systematically generates a counterfactual explanation given an input sample without any control about its

---

[1] For other types of classifiers, the CAM approach can be replaced by other techniques like weighted dynamic barycentre averaging to define the final perturbation.

quality in term of plausibility. All the previous approaches require access to the training data in order to create a counterfactual explanation for a given test sample. This extra constraint can limit their applicability in scenarios where training data are not available at inference time or the computational burden to access them, for each test sample, is too high.

A different approach has been proposed in [19] where a perturbation is applied in a learned latent space using an auto-encoder. Despite its promising performance, one intrinsic limitation of this approach is that the perturbations affect the entire time series, without any constraints on covering a short and contiguous section of the original sample. This could result in perturbations that are not meaningful to the underlying application domain, hence compromising the interpretability of the generated counterfactuals.

All the approaches for time series counterfactual explanation [16,17,19] either require manually associating an alternative class label to each sample, and/or they systematically generate a counterfactual which might not be compliant nor plausible for the underlying application domain. These assumptions can be too restrictive for the case of land cover classification from remote sensing data as previously discussed in Sect. 1.

3 Study Area and Land Cover Classification

3.1 Study Area

The study site covers an area around the town of *Koumbia*, in the Province of Tuy, *Hauts-Bassins* region, in the south-west of Burkina Faso. This area has a surface of about 2338 km^2, and is situated in the sub-humid sudanian zone. The surface is covered mainly by natural savannah (herbaceous and shrubby) and forests, interleaved with a large portion of land (around 35%) used for rainfed agricultural production (mostly smallholder farming). The main crops are cereals (maize, sorghum and millet) and cotton, followed by oleaginous and leguminous crops. Several temporary watercourses constitute the hydrographic network around the city of Koumbia. Figure 1 presents the study site with the reference data (ground truth) superposed on a Sentinel-2 image.

The satellite data consists of a time series of Sentinel-2 images spanning the year 2020 from January to December [20]. All images were provided by the THEIA Pole platform[2] at level-2A, which consist of atmospherically-corrected surface reflectances (cf. MAJA processing chain [21]) and relative cloud/shadow masks. A standard pre-processing was performed over each band to replace cloudy pixel values as detected by the available cloud masks based on the method proposed in [22]. Figure 2 depicts the acquisition dates of the Sentinel-2 satellite image time series.

From the spectral raw bands at 10-m of spatial resolution, the NDVI (Normalized Differential Vegetation Index) was derived. It is defined as follows:

$$NDVI = \frac{NIR - Red}{NIR + Red} \tag{1}$$

---

[2] http://theia.cnes.fr.

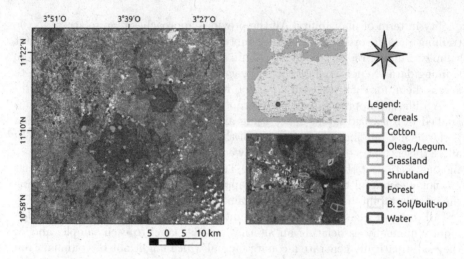

Fig. 1. Location of the *Koumbia* study site. The corresponding ground truth is shown on the right.

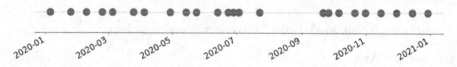

Fig. 2. Acquisition dates of the Sentinel-2 Satellite Image Time Series on the year 2020.

where NIR is the near-infrared band and Red is the red band of the Sentinel-2 imagery. The NDVI index is by far the most widely used biophysical indicator in the field of remote sensing to identify vegetated/non vegetated areas and their "condition" as well as characterize live green plant canopies from multispectral remote sensing data [23]. This is why we adopt it in our case study.

The ground truth (GT) data for the study site is a collection of (i) digitized plots from a GPS field mission performed in October 2020 and mostly covering classes within cropland and (ii) additional reference plots on non-crop classes obtained by photo-interpretation by an expert. Finally, the polygons have been rasterized at the S2 spatial resolution (10-m), resulting in 79961 labeled pixels. The statistics related to the GT are reported in Table 1.

3.2 Land Cover Classification

To tackle the land cover classification task, a supervised machine learning model is trained to classify each time series (the NDVI profile of a pixel) from a set of labelled pixels. In this paper, we adopt the TempCNN [24] model due to its confirmed ability to cope with the task of SITS-based land cover mapping. This approach leverages a 1D convolutional neural network model in order to explicitly take into account the temporal dynamic associated to each pixel time series.

Table 1. *Koumbia* study site Ground Truth statistics.

Class	Label	Pixels
1	*Cereals*	9 731
2	*Cotton*	6 971
3	*Oleaginous*	7 950
4	*Grassland*	12 998
5	*Shrubland*	22 546
6	*Forest*	17 435
7	*Bare Soil*	1 125
8	*Water*	1 205
Total		79 961

The TempCNN model has an encoder composed of three identical blocks followed by a flattening operation and, finally, a fully-connected output layer to perform classification. Each of the encoder blocks is composed by a one-dimensional convolutional operator with 64 filters and a 5×1 kernel, a Batch Normalization layer, a nonlinear activation function (ReLU) and a Dropout layer.

To train the TempCNN classification model, we split the whole data set in two parts. The first one is employed as training/validation set while the second part is used as test set. We imposed that pixels belonging to the same ground truth polygon were assigned exclusively to one of the data partition (training, validation or test) with the aim to avoid possible spatial bias in the evaluation procedure. We consider 1/3 of the original data as test set and the remaining 2/3 as training/validation set (of which 1/4 is used for validation).

The TempCNN classification model was trained over 1000 epochs with batch size 32 and Adam optimizer with learning rate and weight decay equal to 10^{-4}. The model weights corresponding to the best obtained F1-score on the validation set were kept. This model is the classifier that will be considered in the rest of this research work as the classifier for which explanations are supplied.

4   Proposed Method

4.1   Architecture Overview

For the counterfactual generation, we propose a GAN (generative adversarial network) inspired architecture which is summarized in Fig. 3.

A counterfactual explanation x_{CF} is derived for each input sample x by adding a perturbation δ to the original signal:

$$x_{CF} = x + \delta \tag{2}$$

The perturbation δ is generated by a *Noiser* module which is learned with the goal to swap the prediction of the *Classifier*. Finally, a *Discriminator* module is leveraged to ensure the generation of realistic counterfactual examples.

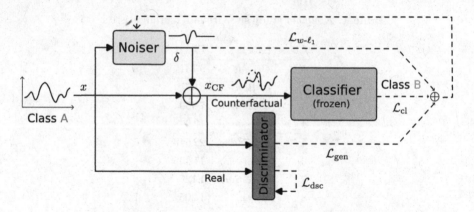

Fig. 3. Schematic representation of the proposed approach.

4.2   Networks Implementation and Training

Regarding the different components of our architecture, we take inspiration from state-of-the-art literature in the field of satellite image time series land cover mapping. For the *Classifier* network we leverage the Temporal Convolutional Neural Network (TempCNN) model [24] described in Sect. 3.2. For the *Discriminator* network we adopt the same architecture as the *Classifier* network and we replace the output layer with a single neuron with sigmoid activation function as commonly done for discriminator networks in adversarial learning [25]. Concerning the *Noiser* module, it is implemented as a multi-layer perceptron network with two hidden layers (each with 128 neurons) and an output layer with the same dimensionality of the time series data. For each of the hidden layers, batch normalization, tangent activation function and a drop-out regularization are employed in this order while for the output layer only the tangent activation function is used. The tangent activation function allows us to restrict the output domain between -1 and $+1$ thus, facilitating the learning process of the different networks. The *Classifier* model is pre-trained on the training set and, successively, frozen during the adversarial learning stage since this stage is devoted to learn the model weights associated to the *Noiser* and the *Discriminator* (see Sect. 4.4).

The *Noiser* module is updated with respect to a composite loss made of three parts detailed in Sects. 4.3 to 4.5.

$$\mathcal{L}_{\text{noiser}} = \mathcal{L}_{\text{cl}} + \lambda_{\text{gen}}\mathcal{L}_{\text{gen}} + \lambda_{w\text{-}\ell_1}\mathcal{L}_{w\text{-}\ell_1} \tag{3}$$

4.3   Class-Swapping Loss

To generate counterfactuals that effectively change the predicted class for a given input we use the following loss:

$$\mathcal{L}_{\text{cl}} = -\frac{1}{n}\sum_{i=1}^{n}\log(1 - p(y^{(i)})) \tag{4}$$

It enforces the reduction of the classifier's softmax output $p(y^{(i)})$ for the initially predicted label $y^{(i)}$, eventually leading to a change on the predicted class.

Note that, conversely to standard literature [26, 27] in which a target class for the counterfactual example is chosen a priori, here we purposely do not enforce the prediction of a predefined target class. Instead, we let the *Noiser* free to generate a perturbation δ that will change the classifier output to any other class different from $y^{(i)}$.

4.4 GAN-Based Regularization for Plausibility

Counterfactual plausibility is enforced via a GAN-inspired architecture, where a discriminator is trained to identify unrealistic counterfactuals while, simultaneously, the *Noiser* module acts as a generator with the goal to fool the discriminator in a two-player game.

The *Discriminator* is updated with respect to a standard GAN loss classifying real versus fake (counterfactual) samples:

$$\mathcal{L}_{\text{dsc}} = -\frac{1}{n} \sum_{i=1}^{n} \left[\log D(x^{(i)}) + \log \left(1 - D(x_{\text{CF}}^{(i)}) \right) \right] \tag{5}$$

where $D(x^{(i)})$ denotes the discriminator's output for a real input $x^{(i)}$ (with expected output 1) and $D(x_{\text{CF}}^{(i)})$ its output for a fake input $x_{\text{CF}}^{(i)}$ (with expected output 0).

The following non-saturating generator loss is used in the *Noiser* update:

$$\mathcal{L}_{\text{gen}} = -\frac{1}{n} \sum_{i=1}^{n} \log \left(D(x_{\text{CF}}^{(i)}) \right) \tag{6}$$

$\mathcal{L}_{\text{gen}}$ is minimized when the discriminator wrongly identifies the counterfactuals as real inputs.

4.5 Unimodal Regularization for Time-Contiguity

To generate perturbations concentrated around a contiguous time frame we employ a weighted L1-norm penalization, with weights growing quadratically around a central time $\tilde{t}^{(i)}$ chosen independently for each sample $i \in \{1, \ldots, n\}$:

$$\mathcal{L}_{w\text{-}\ell_1} = \frac{1}{n} \sum_{i=1}^{n} \sum_{t=1}^{T} d(t, \tilde{t}^{(i)})^2 |\delta_t^{(i)}| \tag{7}$$

where, for the i-th sample, $\tilde{t}^{(i)}$ is chosen as the time step with the highest absolute value perturbation $\tilde{t}^{(i)} = \text{argmax}_t |\delta_t^{(i)}|$.

To avoid biasing $\tilde{t}$ towards the center, we use the modulo distance $d(t, \tilde{t}) = \min \left((t - \tilde{t})\%T, (\tilde{t} - t)\%T \right)$ which treats the time samples as a circular list.

This regularization also brings a degree of sparsity to the generated perturbation δ, since its entries will tend to vanish when getting far away from $\tilde{t}$. Finally, penalizing the entries of δ enforces the proximity between x_{CF} and x.

5 Results

In this section we assess the behaviour of *CFE4SITS* considering the study case introduced in Sect. 3. More precisely, we first compare our approach to recent strategies in the field of time series counterfactual explanation by means of commonly used metrics and then, we investigate how the information provided by *CFE4SITS* can be leveraged to advance the understanding and interpretability of the underlying supervised machine learning classifier.

For the comparative analysis, we consider two recent time series counterfactual explanation approaches referred as k-NN Counterfactual[3] (k-NNC) [16] and Native-guide[4] (NG) [17]. Since the k-NN Counterfactual approach requires the target class for each counterfactual explanation to be defined a priori, given a sample and its predicted class, we generate all the possible counterfactual explanations for the land cover classes different from the predicted one. In this way, we extend this method to the multi-class setting without requiring to arbitrarily input for each sample the target class.

To assess the behaviour of the different competing approaches, we leverage a set of standard metrics from the recent literature on time series counterfactual explanation. More precisely, the following four metrics are considered:

- *Proximity* [12,17]: this metric evaluates how close the generated counterfactual explanations are to the original time series. To implement this metric, we compute the ℓ_2 distance between the original sample and its corresponding counterfactual explanation. Lower values are preferred.
- *Compactness* [16]: this metric estimates the sparsity of the generated perturbations. More precisely, it evaluates the ratio of timestamps which are kept unchanged[5] between the original signal and the corresponding counterfactual explanation. Higher values are preferred.
- *Stability* [28]: this metric quantifies the coherence of a counterfactual generation approach to provide similar explanations for similar input samples. To do so, we compute estimates of a *local Lipschitz constant* as done in [28] and take the average over all samples. Lower values are preferred.
- *Plausibility* [17]: this metric uses an anomaly detection algorithm to detect out-of-distribution (OOD) explanations. More precisely, we use the Isolation Forest [29] approach as surrogate algorithm to evaluate if a generated counterfactual sample belong or not to the original data distribution. The reported metric corresponds to the ratio of counterfactuals identified as inliers. Higher values are preferred.

---

[3] In our experiments we set $k = 1$, as it led to the best results in the original paper.

[4] In the code provided by the authors, a counterfactual explanation is returned as soon as the probability of the originally predicted class falls bellow 0.5, which is insufficient to modify the predicted class in a multiclass setting. Instead, we verify whether any other class probability surpasses that of the initial class.

[5] Any timestamp t with a perturbation δ_t falling below a threshold of $\tau = 10^{-2}$ in absolute value, i.e. $|\delta_t| < 10^{-2}$, is considered as an unchanged.

For all the evaluation metrics, we report the average results over the set of generated counterfactual samples per-method. Finally, note that some of the metrics are not consistent with their denomination. Specifically, the metrics used for proximity and stability actually quantify the inverse of these concepts, but we keep the usual names as a list of desirable properties for the counterfactual generation approach.

For the in-depth analysis of our proposed *CFE4SITS* in Sect. 5.3, we firstly discuss the class transitions induced by the counterfactual explanations, secondly we introduce some examples of average perturbation profiles as well as representative counterfactual explanations. Finally, we provide an ablation study of the different components on which *CFE4SITS* is built. All the analyses are conducted on the test set introduced in Sect. 3.

5.1 Experimental Settings

Regarding *CFE4SITS*, with the classifier weights frozen, the *Noiser* and *Discriminator* modules are simultaneously trained over 100 epochs with batch size 128 and Adam optimizer. We set $\lambda_{\text{gen}} = 5 \cdot 10^{-1}$ and $\lambda_{w\text{-}\ell_1} = 5 \cdot 10^{-2}$ on the reported results. In practice, increasing these weights implies in further constraining the set of admissible perturbations which, in turn, leads to a smaller rate of class-swapping counterfactual samples –i.e., those that actually change the classifier's prediction. The chosen values lead to the generation of class-swapping counterfactual explanations for 46.2% of the samples belonging to the test set.

5.2 Comparative Analysis

Table 2. Performance measures comparison for the proposed approach and two competitors. The measures are defined in Sect. 5. The down arrows indicate that lower values are preferred and best results are bolded.

	Proximity ↓	Compactness ↑	Stability ↓	Plausibility ↑
k-NNC [16]	0.76	10.1%	**1.21**	79.3%
NG [17]	0.31	**53.8%**	2.47	87.0%
CFE4SITS	**0.24**	46.7%	1.64	**89.0%**

The results of the comparative evaluation are reported in Table 2. The proposed approach obtains better performance on both proximity and plausibility measures. This is clearly enforced by the $\mathcal{L}_{w\text{-}\ell_1}$ and $\mathcal{L}_{\text{gen}}$ terms that were explicitly designed to inject these two properties respectively. However, it is interesting to observe that *CFE4SITS* manages to perform better in terms of plausibility, while generating completely *new* data instead of reusing training samples (if even partially) like the competitors. The weighted-ℓ_1 penalization also enforces compactness and, indeed, we obtain comparable results to the NG approach on this measure, while both perform considerably better than k-NNC. Finally, when it comes to counterfactual stability, although k-NNC obtains the best results, we still perform better than NG. Overall, the proposed approach seems to provide a good compromise regarding the results in Table 2, either beating its competitors or coming close second in most measures.

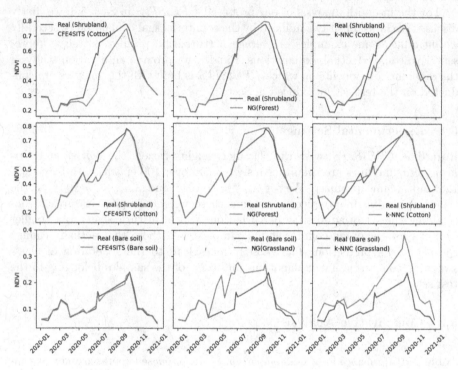

Fig. 4. Some examples of counterfactual explanations from the three compared methods. Left column: *CFE4SITS*. Midddle: Native Guide (NG). Right: k-NNC.

In Fig. 4 we show some examples of counterfactual explanations generated by each of the three compared approaches. On the two first examples (top two rows), we can see that the k-NNC approach modifies the input sample over its entire time span, failing to provide a more compact (and therefore interpretable) explanation. Both *CFE4SITS* and NG approaches do a better job in terms of compactness of the induced perturbation (especially on the second example), but notice that each of the two approaches chooses to modify different time windows, besides leading to different target classes. Yet, the fact that the competitors systematically generate a counterfactual for every input sample ends up penalizing them on the overall metrics. That is because some samples are much harder to provide a counterfactual for than others, thus requiring higher perturbations and potentially resulting in unrealistic/not plausible explanations. In such cases, our method simply refrains from providing a counterfactual explanation, as shown in the third example in Fig. 4.

Execution Times. Differently from its competitors, the proposed technique requires prior training of the noiser module. However, this can be done in a reasonable time (around 20 min). Once learned, the model can be quickly deployed at inference time. The NG method, on the other hand, requires computing both the Class Activation Map (CAM) and a k-nearest neighbors with Dynamic Time Warping (DTW) distance for the inference of each input sample, which can become quite time-consuming. The total inference time for the entire test set (∼26k samples) came down to only 0.25 and 0.6 s for *CFE4SITS* and k-NNC respectively, while it exceeded 16 h for NG[6].

5.3   *CFE4SITS* In-depth Analysis

The class transitions induced by the counterfactual samples derived by *CFE4SITS* are summarized in Fig. 5. The graph was generated from the counterfactual samples obtained by feeding the learned network with the test data. We recall that the class transitions are to no extent pre-defined on our approach, conversely to other counterfactual explanation strategies for time series (e.g. k-NNC) where the target class is fixed a priori. Our method allows input samples from the same class to freely split-up into multiple target classes.

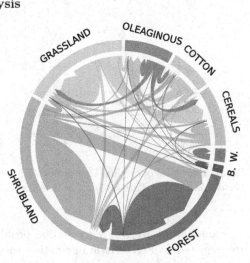

Fig. 5. Summary of class transitions induced by *CFE4SITS*. B. stands for *Bare Soil* and W. for *Water* classes.

The obtained transitions are very much in line with the intuitive relation between the different classes. For instance, the three crop-related classes (*Cereals, Cotton* and *Oleaginous*) form a very coherent cluster, with almost all transitions staying within the sub-group. The vegetation classes *Shrubland* and *Forest* are most often sent to one another, while *Grassland* remains much closer to the crop classes (especially *Cereals*). The *Bare Soil* class is most often transformed into a crop class. Finally, the *Water* class is very rarely modified by the counterfactual learning process, which is somewhat expected due to its very distinct characteristic (NDVI signature) compared to the other classes.

---

[6] All the reported times were measured on an Intel Xeon Gold 6226R, 2.90GHz CPU, 64 cores, 400Gb RAM and 4 GPUs NVIDIA GeForce RTX 3090.

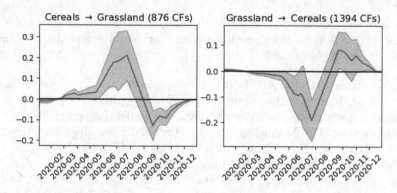

Fig. 6. Examples of average counterfactual perturbations between classes *Cereals* and *Grassland* on both ways. Shaded area corresponds to the standard deviation.

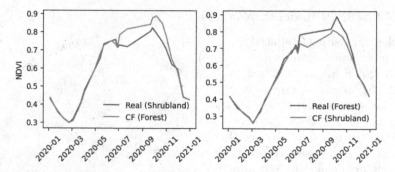

Fig. 7. Examples of original time series with corresponding counterfactual from classes *Shrubland* (4) and *Forest* (5) on both ways.

Examples of average perturbation profiles for two different class transitions are depicted in Fig. 6. It is interesting to notice how the perturbations correspond roughly to the opposite of each other, which is quite suitable since they correspond to opposite transitions between the same two classes. Two illustrative examples of counterfactual explanations are shown in Fig. 7. It is interesting to observe the similarity between the generated counterfactual and a real data example from the same class (shown on the neighboring plot), while being a completely artificially-generated sample not simply drawn from the training set (like done by most competitors).

To transform a *Shrubland* sample into a *Forest* one, NDVI is added between the months of July and October. The opposite is done to obtain the reverse transition, which matches the general knowledge of such land cover classes on the considered study area. Also note that the NDVI peak is slight shifted from one class to another.

From the provided examples, one can verify that the obtained counterfactual do look realistic besides differing from the real signal only on a contiguous time window.

Table 3. Ablation study for *CFE4SITS* ignoring: 1) the generator loss and 2) the weighted-ℓ_1 loss. The down arrows indicate that lower values are preferred. Best results are bolded.

	Proximity ↓	Compactness ↑	Stability ↓	Plausibility ↑	Validity
CFE4SITS	**0.24**	**46.7%**	1.64	**89.0%**	46.2%
No $\mathcal{L}_{gen}$	0.97	81.1%	**1.35**	71.4%	96.5%
No $\mathcal{L}_{w\text{-}\ell_1}$	4.79	0%	1.94	0%	98.9%

Ablation Studies: In Table 3 we compare the proposed model to two ablated variants: 1) ignoring the generator loss ($\mathcal{L}_{gen}$) and 2) removing the weighted-ℓ_1 loss ($\mathcal{L}_{w\text{-}\ell_1}$). We use the same metrics as previously plus the rate of class-swapping counterfactuals, i.e. those that effectively modify the predicted class, among all generated explanations. This additional measure is referred to as *validity* [12]. One can see that the removal of the auxiliary losses significantly bumps up the class-swapping rate (validity), but it comes at the expense of: i) counterfactual plausibility, which is considerably worsened on both considered variants and ii) counterfactual proximity, as demonstrated by the dramatic increase on the norm of the generated perturbations (i.e., the distance between x and x_{CF}) upon removal of $\mathcal{L}_{gen}$ and especially of $\mathcal{L}_{w\text{-}\ell_1}$. Finally, counterfactual compactness is also severely damaged upon removal of the weighted-ℓ_1 loss (giving the worst possible value for this measure). Although the removal of generator loss allows the model to further minimize the compactness (by fully concentrating on the $\mathcal{L}_{w\text{-}\ell_1}$ loss), this is a compromise that we are willing to take in the proposed model to keep both proximity and plausibility on more acceptable levels.

6   Conclusion

In this work we have presented *CFE4SITS*, a new framework to generate counterfactual explanations for the land cover classification task. The proposed method overcomes the restriction of a priori defining the source and the target classes for the counterfactual generation process while exploiting adversarial learning to ensure plausibility. The comparative analysis with recent methods from the literature underlines the quality of *CFE4SITS* according to standard evaluation measures while the in-depth analysis discusses how to exploit the proposed framework to characterize the behaviour of the underlying land cover classifier at global (class transitions) and local (counterfactual explanations) levels.

Unlike neighborhood-based alternatives, a distinctive feature of the proposed approach is the ability to generate plausible counterfactual explanations without disclosing any part of the training data. This feature can be decisive in applications where strict privacy constraints exist (like medicine or finance).

As possible future work, we would extend the framework to the case of multivariate time series satellite data as well as leverage the feedback provided by the generated counterfactual samples to improve the robustness of the land cover classifier regarding the most frequent class confusions.

Ethical statement

This research paper proposes a counterfactual explanation approach for land cover classification from remote sensing time-series data, aiming to enhance the interpretability of AI techniques used for landcover classification. We present hereafter some ethical aspects related to this study:

Satellite Data Licensing: The satellite data used in this study is publicly available and licensed appropriately[7].

Ground Truth Data: The field survey data has been collected in a collaboration between researchers and local farmers, as part of the international project JECAM (http://jecam.org/). Farmers have wilfully consented to the data collection as well as to its sharing with the scientific community. No personal data nor sensitive information has been compromised by this work.

Transparency: This paper seeks to provide clear explanations of our methodology, including assumptions and limitations. Data and code used to produce the paper's results have been made publicly available, further increasing its reproducibility and transparency.

Social and Environmental Impacts: Landcover maps get used to support decision making and deployment of public policies. To increase spatial coverage and time resolution, these maps have increasingly often been done using AI-tools, particularly deep learning classification models. These models consequently may have social and environmental impacts, increasing the need for explainable predictions, which is precisely the topic addressed by interpretability methods such as ours.

References

1. Toth, C., Jóźków, G.: Remote sensing platforms and sensors: a survey. ISPRS J. Photogramm. Remote. Sens. **115**, 22–36 (2016)
2. Pouyanfar, S., et al.: A survey on deep learning: algorithms, techniques, and applications. ACM Comput. Surv. **51**(5), 92:1–92:36 (2019)
3. Yuan, Q., et al.: Deep learning in environmental remote sensing: achievements and challenges. Remote Sens. Environ. **241**, 111716 (2020)
4. Inglada, J., Vincent, A., Arias, M., Tardy, B., Morin, D., Rodes, I.: Operational high resolution land cover map production at the country scale using satellite image time series. Remote. Sens. **9**(1), 95 (2017)
5. Berger, M., Moreno, J., Johannessen, J.A., Levelt, P.F., Hanssen, R.F.: ESA's sentinel missions in support of earth system science. Remote Sens. Environ. **120**, 84–90 (2012)

---

[7] Sentinel-2 level 2A data distributed by THEIA is subject to the open ETA-LAB V2.0 license available here: https://theia.cnes.fr/atdistrib/documents/Licence-Theia-CNES-Sentinel-ETALAB-v2.0-en.pdf.

6. Pelletier, C., Webb, G.I., Petitjean, F.: Temporal convolutional neural network for the classification of satellite image time series. Rem. Sens. **11**(5), 523 (2019)
7. Adadi, A., Berrada, M.: Peeking inside the black-box: a survey on explainable artificial intelligence (XAI). IEEE Access **6**, 52138–52160 (2018)
8. Guidotti, R., Monreale, A., Ruggieri, S., Turini, F., Giannotti, F., Pedreschi, D.: A survey of methods for explaining black box models. ACM Comput. Surv. **51**(5), 1–42 (2019)
9. Arrieta, A.B., et al.: Explainable Artificial Intelligence (XAI): concepts, taxonomies, opportunities and challenges toward responsible AI. Inf. Fusion **58**, 82–115 (2020)
10. Wachter, S., Mittelstadt, B., Russell, C.: Counterfactual explanations without opening the black box: automated decisions and the GDPR. Harv. JL Tech. **31**, 841 (2017)
11. Verma, S., Dickerson, J., Hines, K.: Counterfactual explanations for machine learning: a review, arXiv preprint arXiv:2010.10596 (2020)
12. Guidotti, R.: Counterfactual explanations and how to find them: literature review and benchmarking. Data Mining Knowl. Discov. 1–55 (2022)
13. Karimi, A., Barthe, G., Balle, B., Valera, I.: Model-agnostic counterfactual explanations for consequential decisions. In: AISTATS, vol. 108, pp. 895–905. PMLR (2020)
14. Pawelczyk, M., Broelemann, K., Kasneci, G.: Learning model-agnostic counterfactual explanations for tabular data. In: WWW, pp. 3126–3132. ACM/IW3C2 (2020)
15. Van Looveren, A., Klaise, J.: Interpretable counterfactual explanations guided by prototypes. In: Oliver, N., Pérez-Cruz, F., Kramer, S., Read, J., Lozano, J.A. (eds.) ECML PKDD 2021. LNCS (LNAI), vol. 12976, pp. 650–665. Springer, Cham (2021). https://doi.org/10.1007/978-3-030-86520-7_40
16. Karlsson, I., Rebane, J., Papapetrou, P., Gionis, A.: Locally and globally explainable time series tweaking. Knowl. Inf. Syst. **62**(5), 1671–1700 (2020)
17. Delaney, E., Greene, D., Keane, M.T.: Instance-based counterfactual explanations for time series classification. In: Sánchez-Ruiz, A.A., Floyd, M.W. (eds.) ICCBR 2021. LNCS (LNAI), vol. 12877, pp. 32–47. Springer, Cham (2021). https://doi.org/10.1007/978-3-030-86957-1_3
18. Theissler, A., Spinnato, F., Schlegel, U., Guidotti, R.: Explainable AI for time series classification: a review, taxonomy and research directions. IEEE Access **10**, 100700–100724 (2022)
19. Wang, Z., Samsten, I., Mochaourab, R., Papapetrou, P.: Learning time series counterfactuals via latent space representations. In: Soares, C., Torgo, L. (eds.) DS 2021. LNCS (LNAI), vol. 12986, pp. 369–384. Springer, Cham (2021). https://doi.org/10.1007/978-3-030-88942-5_29
20. Jolivot, A., et al.: Harmonized in situ datasets for agricultural land use mapping and monitoring in tropical countries. Earth Syst. Sci. Data **13**(12), 5951–5967 (2021)
21. Hagolle, O., Huc, M., Pascual, D.V., Dedieu, G.: A multi-temporal and multi-spectral method to estimate aerosol optical thickness over land, for the atmospheric correction of FormoSat-2, LandSat, VENμs and Sentinel-2 images. Remote Sens. **7**(3), 2668–2691 (2015)
22. Inglada, J., Vincent, A., Arias, M., Tardy, B.: iota2-a25386 (2016). https://doi.org/10.5281/zenodo.58150

23. Julien, Y., Sobrino, J.A.: The yearly land cover dynamics (YLCD) method: an analysis of global vegetation from NDVI and LST parameters. Remote Sens. Environ. **113**(2), 329–334 (2009)

24. Pelletier, C., Webb, G.I., Petitjean, F.: Temporal convolutional neural network for the classification of satellite image time series. Remote. Sens. **11**(5), 523 (2019)

25. Creswell, A., White, T., Dumoulin, V., Arulkumaran, K., Sengupta, B., Bharath, A.A.: Generative adversarial networks: an overview. IEEE Signal Process. Mag. **35**(1), 53–65 (2018)

26. Filali Boubrahimi, S., Hamdi, S.M.: On the mining of time series data counterfactual explanations using barycenters. In: ACM CIKM, pp. 3943–3947. ACM (2022)

27. Lang, J., Giese, M., Ilg, W., Otte, S.: Generating sparse counterfactual explanations for multivariate time series, arXiv preprint arXiv:2206.00931 (2022)

28. Ates, E., Aksar, B., Leung, V.J., Coskun, A.K.: Counterfactual explanations for multivariate time series. In: International Conference on Applied Artificial Intelligence (ICAPAI), pp. 1–8 (2021)

29. Liu, F.T., Ting, K.M., Zhou, Z.: Isolation forest. In: ICDM, pp. 413–422. IEEE Computer Society (2008)

Cloud Imputation for Multi-sensor Remote Sensing Imagery with Style Transfer

Yifan Zhao, Xian Yang, and Ranga Raju Vatsavai[✉]

Computer Science Department, North Carolina State University, Raleigh, USA
{yzhao48,xyang45,rrvatsav}@ncsu.edu

Abstract. Widely used optical remote sensing images are often contaminated by clouds. The missing or cloud-contaminated data leads to incorrect predictions by the downstream machine learning tasks. However, the availability of multi-sensor remote sensing imagery has great potential for improving imputation under clouds. Existing cloud imputation methods could generally preserve the spatial structure in the imputed regions, however, the spectral distribution does not match the target image due to differences in sensor characteristics and temporal differences. In this paper, we present a novel deep learning-based multi-sensor imputation technique inspired by the computer vision-based style transfer. The proposed deep learning framework consists of two modules: (i) cluster-based attentional instance normalization (CAIN), and (ii) adaptive instance normalization (AdaIN). The combined module, CAINA, exploits the style information from cloud-free regions. These regions (land cover) were obtained through clustering to reduce the style differences between the target and predicted image patches. We have conducted extensive experiments and made comparisons against the state-of-the-art methods using a benchmark dataset with images from Landsat-8 and Sentinel-2 satellites. Our experiments show that the proposed CAINA is at least 24.49% better on MSE and 18.38% better on cloud MSE as compared to state-of-the-art methods.

Keywords: Cloud imputation · Multi-sensor · Deep learning · Style transfer

1 Introduction

Remote sensing imagery has been widely used as an important research material and information source in many applications ranging from crop monitoring, disaster mapping, nuclear proliferation, and urban planning since 1950's. However, since more than 50% of Earth's surface is covered by clouds [10] at any time, the performance of various downstream tasks such as segmentation, recognition, and classification on remote sensing images could be seriously affected because of the cloud-contaminated pixels. Fortunately, the advancing remote sensing technology and increasing number of satellite collections have significantly increased the spatial and temporal density of multi-sensor images.

© The Author(s), under exclusive license to Springer Nature Switzerland AG 2023
G. De Francisci Morales et al. (Eds.): ECML PKDD 2023, LNAI 14175, pp. 37–53, 2023.
https://doi.org/10.1007/978-3-031-43430-3_3

Given the limitations of cloud-contaminated remote sensing images in the downstream applications (e.g., classification, change detection), a large number of techniques have been developed for imputation under clouds by exploiting multi-sensor imagery collections [1, 2, 4, 14, 34]. Multi-sensor imagery is preferred for cloud imputation as the large revisit cycle of a single satellite (more than 15 days) makes it hard to find temporally close-by images. In contrast, the chance of finding temporally close-by (less than a week) cloud-free images significantly increases if images from several satellites (that is, multi-sensor) are used [14]. Multi-sensor cloud imputation problem is often formulated as an image restoration task with a triplet consisting of the target, and before and after images [2, 14, 34]. Additionally, it is assumed that necessary cloud masks are often given beforehand, as these masks help focus the imputation to cloudy regions [17, 34]. Given the computation and memory limitations, deep learning approaches often work with small images (e.g., 384×384). However, the typical size of a remote sensing image is more than 7000×7000 for Landsat and 10000×10000 for Sentinel satellites. In order to use these large images in training deep learning models, we often split them into smaller patches. For convenience, we call these input patches as images. Any subpart of this image is called as a patch (for example, the cloudy portion of an image is called a patch, and any small portion of the background (non-cloudy image) is also referred to as a patch). Usually, an image with a cloudy patch is treated as the target, and two temporally nearby geo-registered cloud-free images as input. These nearby images may come from the same sensor as the target image or a different sensor.

Though recent advances in deep learning-based multi-sensor cloud imputation methods have improved imputation performance significantly against single-sensor cloud imputation methods, they still have limitations. In particular, these methods can preserve the spatial structure of the imputed patches close to the input images. However, to the best of our knowledge, the existing multi-sensor cloud imputation models can't preserve the pixel-level spectral properties of the target image. As a result, the imputed patches are not close to the target images in terms of color style (spectral values). To address this issue, we propose a novel deep learning framework that harmonizes the imputed cloudy patches to the target image. The multi-sensor component of the network preserves the structure of the imputed patch and the harmonization component learns to transfer the color style by utilizing the cloud-free background and the land cover information of the target image.

From computer vision literature, earlier methods of style transfer between images can be attributed to the work of [6]. They used VGG-based deep learning architecture with a goal of style transfer to synthesize a texture from a source image, called "style," while preserving the semantic content of a target image called "content." Later works by [3, 8, 24] found that the feature statistics such as mean and standard deviation are highly effective in controlling the "style" of the output images. In particular, the adaptive instance normalization (AdaIN) method proposed by [8] can accommodate arbitrary style images without pre-training using adaptive affine transformations learned from the style inputs. This AdaIN approach gave us the idea of adopting it to the multi-sensor cloud imputation problem by transferring the style of cloud-free background to imputed patches. In the multi-sensor cloud imputation problem, the cloud-free background of the target image will be the style and the input images from which the imputed patches are derived will be the content.

(1) Cloud mask   (2) Ground truth   (3) MDRN   (1) Cloud mask   (2) Ground truth   (3) MDRN

Fig. 1. Figure shows the spectral (color style) differences (red circles) in the imputed regions. From left to right: (1) the cloud-masked image, (2) the ground truth, (3) the imputed image by a state-of-the-art method called MDRN [34] (Color figure online).

However, the existing AdaIN only takes the mean and standard deviation of the whole style feature as the transferring style information. Remote sensing images often contain multiple types of land covers (e.g., forests, crops, buildings) and thus multiple and complicated styles in a single image. Therefore, AdaIN could only provide limited improvement for the multi-sensor cloud imputation task. To address this limitation, we propose a novel extension to the AdaIN that exploits the land cover information of the target image and transfers style information from targeted patches called cluster-based attentional instance normalization (CAIN). Without requiring extra land cover data, the land cover information can be extracted with an unsupervised clustering method such as K-means [30]. Recall that a patch is a small portion of the image, these smaller patches can effectively capture the individual land cover types. CAIN first splits both the cloud-free style and imputed content portions of the image into smaller patches and matches each of the style and content patches according to their land cover clustering results. For each imputed content patch, the cloud-free background patches with the same land cover cluster are selected for transferring the feature statistics, that is, the mean and standard deviation of the cloud-free patches. This way, each patch of the imputed feature will be transferred to the style of the patches with the same land cover cluster and, thus, to the style closer to the target image. However, CAIN could be prone to the noise and bias contained by a single land cover cluster. Therefore to overcome the limitations of both AdaIN and CAIN, we combine them using a weighted combination scheme called CAINA (CAIN + AdaIN). Thorough experimentation showed that both the bias (via MSE) and variance (via box-plots) have significantly reduced as the CAINA captures both general global and particular land cover style information.

Another advantage of the style transfer modules described above is that they can be easily plugged into various deep learning architectures. In this paper, we incorporated CAIN and CAINA modules in the deep learning networks inspired by MDRN [34] and $MSOP_{unet}$ [2] and named the resulting architecture as MDRN_{unet}. While MDRN_{unet} has the same multi-stream-fusion structure and composite upsampling structure as of MDRN, it also has U-Net [18] components inspired by MSOP_{unet} [2].

Overall, the contributions of this paper are two-fold. First, a novel style transfer module, CAINA, is designed to exploit the remote sensing feature statistics for harmonizing the imputed cloudy patches using the cloud-free background. Second, a new deep learning network architecture was proposed by combining the merits of two state-of-the-art multi-sensor cloud imputation models (MDRN and MSOP_{unet}) for testing our proposed style transfer module. Finally, extensive experiments are conducted on a multi-sensor cloud imputation benchmark dataset for evaluating the performance of our proposed style transfer module. Experimental results showed that our proposed CAINA outperformed the state-of-art methods by at least 18.38% and 24.49% using mean squared error (MSE) in cloudy regions and the entire images, respectively.

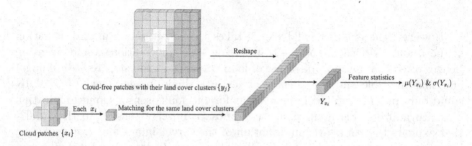

Fig. 2. The illustration for cluster-based attentional instance normalization (CAIN). We split the content feature X and the style feature Y into two sets of patches, $\{x_i\}$ and $\{y_j\}$, respectively. Then a lightweight K-means clustering method is employed to extract each patch's land cover type (Illustrated with different colors in $\{x_i\}$ and $\{y_j\}$). Then for each x_i, all the patches with the same land cover type in $\{y_j\}$ are selected and denoted as Y_{x_i}. Then Y_{x_i} can be aggregated for transferring the mean $\mu(Y_{x_i})$ and standard deviation $\sigma(Y_{x_i})$ to x_i.

2   Related Work

2.1   Multi-sensor Cloud Imputation

The remote sensing cloud imputation problem has been primarily considered in single-sensor or single-image settings previously in [9, 21, 22, 29, 31, 33]. Although these works made significant improvements on the cloud imputation task, single-sensor settings can only be adopted to limited practical situations as it has more restrictions for input compared to multi-sensor settings. In contrast, cloud imputation with multi-sensor data was considered in [1, 4, 14, 19]. [2, 4, 14] used optical and SAR channels for cloud imputation tasks. However, they did not explicitly address the multi-resolution issue between SAR and optical images.

Instead, they artificially down-sampled the SAR images to the same lower resolution as optical images and thus caused a loss of spectral and spatial information. The multi-resolution settings in remote sensing imagery were tackled while other problems such as land cover classification and segmentation were addressed in [13, 16, 20, 23, 25–27, 36]. Recently, the multi-resolution issue in the cloud imputation problem was tackled by a multi-stream deep residual network (MDRN) [34]. MDRN used a multi-stream-fusion structure to process inputs with different resolutions separately and achieved state-of-the-art performance. However, MDRN could not effectively harmonize the imputed patches to the same color style as the target image. Therefore, in this paper, we attempt to improve the harmonization of imputed patches with our proposed style transfer modules, CAIN and CAINA while keeping the effective components of MDRN in our deep learning network, MDRN$_{unet}$.

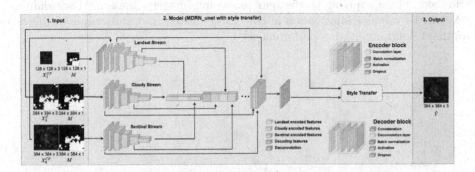

Fig. 3. The architecture and data flow of our testing deep learning network. The detailed structures of the encoder and decoder blocks are shown in the right-hand side. X_1^{CF} (CF stands for cloud-free) is the cloud-free Landsat-8 input, X_2^C is the cloudy Sentinel-2 input, and X_3^{CF} is the cloud-free Sentinel-2 input. $\hat{Y}$ is the predicted target cloud-free image.

2.2 Style Transfer

Style transfer between images was tackled with deep learning networks first in [6]. The goal of style transfer is to synthesize a texture from a source image, called "style," while preserving the semantic content of a target image called "content." Later works done by [3, 8, 24] discovered that the feature statistics such as mean and standard deviation in a deep learning network can be effective in controlling the style of the output images. In particular, adaptive instance normalization (AdaIN) was proposed by [8] for arbitrary style transfer. AdaIN has no learnable affine parameters. Each content could be paired with a style in every data instance. AdaIN's adaptiveness enabled the possibility of improving multi-sensor cloud imputation with style transfer ideas, as the cloud-free background could be the style and the imputed patches could be the content. However, AdaIN computed the statistics over the entire style feature and could contain tangent information in the feature statistics. The tangent information could compromise the performance as it is not expected in the cloud patch. In contrast, our proposed CAINA extracts feature statistics more accurately from the semantically similar cloud-free regions with the same land cover cluster as the cloud patch so that the cloud patch could be transferred with reduced tangent style information.

In addition to the instance normalization methods that directly inspired our work, style transfer has also been tackled with other works focusing on the innovation of deep learning architectures [12,15]. Multi-level interactive Siamese filtering (MISF) [12] aims at the high-fidelity transformation of background in image inpainting by exploiting the semantic information with a kernel prediction branch and filling details with an image filtering branch. Whereas contrastive unpaired translation (CUT) [15] proposed a patchwise contrastive loss based on the famous Cycle-consistent GAN [37] to overcome the restriction of bijective assumption with more accurate contrastive translation in the style transfer task. However, while applying to the remote sensing imagery, these methods didn't exploit the valuable information in land cover clusters and, thus, cannot achieve optimal cloud imputation performance.

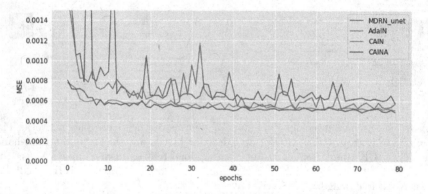

Fig. 4. The validation MSE loss curves of the same deep learning architecture without style transfer, with AdaIN, with CAIN, with CAINA.

The idea and methods of style transfer were considered to be helpful for cloud imputation in remote sensing imagery only starting from recent years [32,35]. AdaIN was adopted and applied to a cloud imputation model in [35] for controlling the global information of the images. Two parameters generated by a pre-trained MLP network were used to replace the feature statistics used in [8]. Another example of employing AdaIN for cloud imputation is presented by [32]. AdaIN enabled incorporating physical attributes such as cloud reflection, ground atmospheric estimation, and cloud light transmission to the deep learning networks in [32]. However, the usages of AdaIN in [32,35] relied on the reinforcement of pre-trained models and external physical information. Additionally, they still applied identical style information for all cloud patches. In contrast, our proposed

CAINA applied the style of the corresponding land cover type by clustering techniques to each cloud patch and do not rely on any pre-trained models or external physical information.

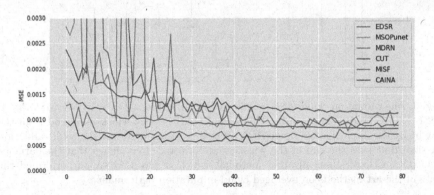

Fig. 5. The validation MSE loss curves of the state-of-the-art deep learning cloud imputation model, EDSR, MSOP$_{unet}$, MDRN, CUT, MISF comparing with CAINA.

3   Methodology

Existing multi-sensor cloud imputation methods could generally detect the missing values and derive the spectral content from the temporally-nearby cloud-free images reasonably well. Though the spatial structure under the cloud patches is close to the target image, the existing models do not effectively preserve the pixel-level spectral properties of the target image due to spectral and temporal differences. Figure 1 shows some examples of the cloud patches imputed by an existing cloud imputation method (MDRN). As can be seen from the images, the imputed patches do not match the spectral distribution (color style) of the target image.

As the pixel-level spectral properties of remote sensing images tend to depend on time and the sensor collection, the patches imputed by existing deep learning networks often do not match the surrounding regions in the target image. Thus, to make the imputed patches consistent with the target image, we need to transfer the style of the cloud-free background to the imputed patches. Therefore, the style transfer techniques in the computer vision (CV) area were considered and evaluated. In this section, we demonstrate our attempts to bridge the style transfer area to the multi-sensor cloud imputation problem and propose new style transfer modules that serve the multi-sensor cloud imputation problem better.

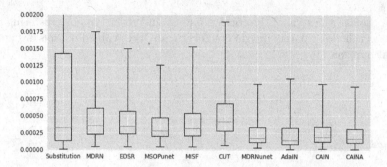

Fig. 6. The validation cloud MSE boxplots of Substitution, MDRN, EDSR, MSOP$_{unet}$, MISF, CUT, MDRN$_{unet}$, AdaIN, CAIN, and CAINA. The whiskers extend from the box by 3x the inter-quartile range (IQR). Outliers (around 10% of the total validation set size) that pass the end of the whiskers are omitted. It is shown that the variance of CAINA is lower than all other methods, which is why CAINA outperformed the state-of-the-art methods on averaged cloud imputation performance.

3.1 Adaptive Instance Normalization (AdaIN)

AdaIN [8] is an arbitrary style transfer technique that could take an arbitrary style image as input without pre-training. The goal of style transfer is to synthesize a texture from a source image, called "style," while preserving the semantic content of a target image called "content." The intuition of AdaIN is to make the content image aligned with the mean and standard deviation of the "style" image. More formally, suppose X and Y are content and style features, respectively, then AdaIN aligns the feature-wise mean (μ) and standard deviation (σ) of X to those of Y.

$$\mathbf{AdaIN}(X, Y) = \sigma(Y)\left(\frac{X - \mu(X)}{\sigma(X)}\right) + \mu(Y) \tag{1}$$

In the case of cloud imputation, we are dealing with the following image triplets similar to [31,34], X_1^{CF}, $Y^C = X_2^C$, and X_3^{CF} (CF stands for cloud-free and C stands for cloudy), where Y^C is the target image containing the cloud patches, and X_1^{CF} and X_3^{CF} are nearby cloud-free images which could be from a different sensor than the target image Y^C. From the perspective of style transfer notation, the content feature X comes from $X_{\{1,3\}}^{CF}$, and the style feature Y comes from the cloud-free region of the target image Y^C.

3.2 Cluster-Based Attentional Instance Normalization (CAIN)

Although experiments show that transferring the global mean and standard deviation of the cloud-free background to cloud patches could improve the cloud imputation performance, the improvement is still limited since remote sensing images often contain multiple types of land covers (e.g., forests, crops, buildings). Thus more focused and accurate style information for the cloudy patches

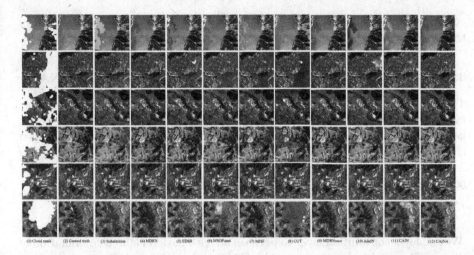

(1) Cloud mask   (2) Ground truth   (3) Substitution   (4) MDRN   (5) EDSR   (6) MSOPunet   (7) MISF   (8) CUT   (9) MDRNunet   (10) AdaIN   (11) CAIN   (12) CAINA

Fig. 7. Few examples of cloud imputed images showing the comparison across the state-of-the-art deep learning cloud imputation models and our testing methods, MDRN$_{unet}$, AdaIN, CAIN, and CAINA. From the left to the right: (1) the cloud-masked images; (2) the ground truths; the restored images by: (3) Substitution, (4) MDRN, (5) EDSR, (6) MSOP$_{unet}$, (7) MISF, (8) CUT, (9) MDRN$_{unet}$, (10) AdaIN, (11) CAIN, (12) CAINA.

is expected to further reduce the style inconsistency between predicted images and the target images.

Therefore, we propose a new module called cluster-based attentional instance normalization (CAIN). Instead of simply normalizing all pixels in the content feature X with the global mean and standard deviation of the style feature Y, we only transfer the feature statistics of the pixels with the same land cover type as the cloudy pixels. Specifically, we first employ a lightweight clustering model such as K-means [30] on a temporally close cloud-free image, X_3^{CF}, for obtaining the land cover information. Then we split X and Y into two sets of patches $\{x_i\}$ and $\{y_j\}$ as shown in Fig. 2.

Then for each x_i, we extract all the cloud-free patches in the same land cover cluster, Y_{x_i},

$$Y_{x_i} = \tau_{\{y_j\}}\Big(C(y_j) = C(x_i)\Big) \tag{2}$$

where $\tau(\cdot)$ is the choice function. $C(y_j)$ and $C(x_i)$ are y_j and x_i's land cover clusters, respectively. Then x_i is aligned to the mean and standard deviation, Y_{x_i}, as given by CAIN(,):

$$\mathbf{CAIN}(x_i, Y) = \sigma(Y_{x_i})\left(\frac{x_i - \mu(x_i)}{\sigma(x_i)}\right) + \mu(Y_{x_i}) \tag{3}$$

This way, the content patches $\{x_i\}$ are transferred to the mean and standard deviation of the style patches in the same land cover cluster, $\{Y_{x_i}\}$. And the content feature X could be more consistent with the cloud-free background of the target image Y.

3.3   Composite Style Transfer Module, CAIN + AdaIN (CAINA)

Though experiments show that CAIN could provide more accurate style information, the mean and standard deviation of the same land cover type are aggregated from a subset of cloud-free patches and could be prone to the employed clustering method's limitations. Therefore, a weighted combination of CAIN and AdaIN (CAINA) is proposed to overcome their disadvantages and utilize their advantages simultaneously,

$$\mathbf{CAINA}(X, Y) = \mathbf{Convolution}(\mathbf{CAIN}(X, Y) \oplus \mathbf{AdaIN}(X, Y)) \qquad (4)$$

We employ a convolution layer to perform an automatic weighted combination of the concatenated features returned by CAIN and AdaIN. In this setup, the style information from the same land cover type is focused, while the style information from the entire image could also contribute to the predictions. Experiments show that the variance of the predictions is reduced with CAINA and the average error of cloud imputation is further reduced as well.

3.4   The Deep Learning Network Architecture

Since the style transfer modules demonstrated above are independent from any particular deep learning networks, they can be easily plugged into various deep learning architectures. In this paper, we incorporate AdaIN, CAIN, and CAINA in a deep learning architecture (MDRN$_{unet}$), inspired by MDRN [34] and MSOP$_{unet}$ [2]. As the multi-sensor, multi-resolution cloud imputation problem is considered in this paper, the architecture has the same multi-stream-fusion structure and composite upsampling structure as MDRN. On the other hand, inspired by MSOP$_{unet}$ [2], more U-Net [18] components were employed. Figure 3 shows the architecture and dataflow of our deep learning network.

4   Experiments

4.1   Dataset and Environmental Configuration

We test and compare all the methods on the benchmark dataset introduced in [34] with remote sensing images from Landsat-8[1] and Sentinel-2[2]. This collection includes the temporally closest image triplets, thus ideal for testing our proposed methods. Another recent cloud imputation benchmark dataset, Sen12MS-CR-TS [5], also includes temporally close-by multi-sensor image collections. However, Sen12MS-CR-TS uses SAR channels, two airborne microwave channels that

---

[1] https://landsat.gsfc.nasa.gov/satellites/landsat-8/.
[2] https://sentinel.esa.int/web/sentinel/missions/sentinel-2.

can penetrate clouds but contain non-negligible noises. Thus, Sen12MS-CR-TS is not an ideal benchmark dataset for evaluating the proposed methods here.

The most widely used RGB channels are used for training our model. However, the proposed architecture does not depend on any specific channel combination and it could be readily trained on any number of channels and their combinations as long as the system permits (memory and compute power). The dataset is split into independent training (consisting of 4,003 instances) and validation (1,000 instances). All the models are trained with the following parameters: batch-size = 16, epochs = 80, mean squared error (MSE) loss, ADAM optimizer, and a step learning rate scheduler starting from 0.01 and every 10 epochs decreases at the rate of 0.75. The source code is implemented with PyTorch[3] and has been deployed to our sponsor's system.

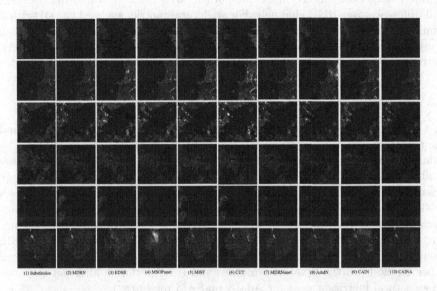

Fig. 8. The cloud residual maps of the same examples in Fig. 7 showing the comparison across the state-of-the-art deep learning cloud imputation models and our proposed CAINA. From the left to right: the cloud residual maps by: (1) Substitution, (2) MDRN, (3) EDSR, (4) MSOP$_{unet}$, (5) MISF, (6) CUT, (7) MDRN$_{unet}$, (8) AdaIN, (9) CAIN, (10) CAINA. The darker residual maps implies better cloud imputation results.

4.2   Experiment Settings

We perform two sets of experiments. In the first set of experiments, we compare the cloud imputation performance of the baseline method MDRN$_{unet}$ and the style transfer extensions: MDRN$_{unet}$ + AdaIN, MDRN$_{unet}$ + CAIN, and MDRN$_{unet}$ + CAINA. In the second set of experiments, we compare our best-performing cloud imputation model with the style transfer module, MDRN$_{unet}$

---

[3] https://github.com/YifanZhao0822/CAINA.

+ CAINA, with other state-of-the-art deep learning cloud imputation methods, namely, MDRN [34], MSOP$_{unet}$ [2], EDSR [14], MISF [12], and CUT [15]. Besides, we also compare with the imputation results by simply substituting the cloud region of the target image with the corresponding area from the temporally closest Sentinel-2 image and call this baseline method as "Substitution."

We report the quantitative comparison results using two types of error metrics: pixel-wise metrics and structural metrics. For pixel-wise metrics, we are using three well-known measures. These include Mean Square Error (MSE) for the entire image and the cloud area separately, whereas peak-signal-to-noise ratio (PSNR) [7] and spectral angle mapper (SAM) [11] on full images. The MSE shows how close the predicted pixels are with respect to the ground truth; the peak-signal-to-noise ratio (PSNR) approximates the human perception of the restored image; the spectral angle mapper (SAM) is used for evaluating the spectral difference over RGB channels. For structural metric, we used the structural similarity index (SSIM) [28] for measuring the image restoration quality from a visual perception standpoint. For the hyperparameters in CAIN and CAINA, we tuned the patch size$= 3 \times 3$ and the K-means # clusters $k = 4$.

4.3   Quantitative Results of the First Set of Experiments

In this section, we present the experimental results of various extension and their relative performance over the baseline method: MDRN$_{unet}$, MDRN$_{unet}$ + AdaIN, MDRN$_{unet}$ + CAIN, and MDRN$_{unet}$ + CAINA. For simplicity, we are omitting the prefix of MDRN$_{unet}$, for example MDRN$_{unet}$ + CAINA is simply referred to as CAINA. Figure 4 shows the validation MSE loss curve of each model at the end of each epoch. We observe that both CAIN and AdaIN outperform MDRN$_{unet}$ in a significant way. CAINA further improves the performance on the basis of CAIN and AdaIN. Table 1 shows the comparison using MSE, cloud MSE, PSNR, SSIM, and SAM. As can be seen, CAINA outperforms all other methods on the pixel-wise metrics and it outperforms all other methods on structural metrics except for AdaIN on SAM measure.

Table 1. The comparison on MSE, cloud MSE, PSNR, and SSIM for MDRN$_{unet}$, AdaIN, CAIN, and CAINA. The best result of each metric is bolded.

Methods	MSE (10^{-4})	Cloud MSE (10^{-4})	PSNR	SSIM	SAM (10^{-2})
MDRN$_{unet}$	5.7871	16.2712	42.0875	0.9876	4.6549
AdaIN	5.0939	15.1207	42.6586	0.9878	**3.9988**
CAIN	5.1214	15.0891	42.2273	0.9871	4.3729
CAINA	**4.8222**	**14.3214**	**42.9390**	**0.9881**	4.1365

4.4   Quantitative Results of the Second Set of Experiments

In this section, we further compare our best-performing CAINA with the baseline method, Substitution, and the state-of-the-art deep learning cloud imputation models, namely MDRN [34], MSOP$_{unet}$ [2], EDSR [14], MISF [12], and CUT [15]. We used the same quantitative metrics as in Sect. 4.3, namely MSE, cloud MSE, PSNR, SSIM, and SAM for comparing the performance of each model. Figure 5 shows the validation MSE loss curves of each model except Substitution at the end of each training epoch. EDSR has the most stable convergence among the state-of-the-art models. However, its best MSE is still suboptimal. We observe that MSOP$_{unet}$ outperforms EDSR significantly, however, its validation loss is not stable. MDRN outperforms the other state-of-the-art methods on MSE but its validation MSE loss is still higher than CAINA. CAINA outperforms all methods significantly and has also reached a stable convergence after 40 epochs. Table 2 shows the comparison using MSE, cloud MSE, PSNR, SSIM, and SAM. As can be seen, CAINA outperforms all other methods on both the pixel-wise and structural metrics. Compared to the state-of-the-art cloud imputation models in Table 2, using the primary measure of MSE, CAINA shows at least 18.38% and 24.49% improvement in cloudy regions and the entire image, respectively. Additionally, MISF achieved the second-best cloud MSE although its performance on other metrics is limited. In our understanding, it could be the significant contribution of the novel kernel prediction module in MISF, which could be an inspiring point that leads to future innovations.

Table 2. The comparison on MSE, cloud MSE, PSNR, SSIM, and SAM for Substitution, MDRN, EDSR, MSOP$_{unet}$, CAINA. The best result of each metric is bolded.

Methods	MSE (10^{-4})	Cloud MSE (10^{-4})	PSNR	SSIM	SAM (10^{-2})
Substitution	25.6594	83.2660	38.6478	0.9704	4.6629
MDRN	6.3895	19.0507	39.5097	0.9810	5.1440
EDSR	8.1018	22.8269	39.3500	0.9805	4.9847
MSOP$_{unet}$	7.6326	21.4471	39.1222	0.9803	5.2841
CUT	10.9325	28.5818	36.1848	0.9701	8.6621
MISF	8.1022	17.5454	35.3311	0.9573	9.6810
CAINA	**4.8222**	**14.3214**	**42.9390**	**0.9881**	**4.1365**

4.5   Analysis on Variances Among the Compared Methods

We further analyze the results using boxplots to understand the performance gains of the CAINA better. Figure 6 shows the boxplot for Substitution, MDRN, EDSR, MSOP$_{unet}$, MISF, CUT, MDRN$_{unet}$, AdaIN, CAIN, and CAINA on the cloud MSE. Both CAIN and CAINA have the lowest third quartile (the upper bound of the boxes). In addition, CAINA has the lowest median among the boxplots. Therefore, the variance of CAINA is lower than all other methods, which is why CAINA outperformed the state-of-the-art methods on averaged cloud imputation performance.

4.6   Qualitative Results and Residual Maps

Figure 7 and 8 shows a few examples of the restored RGB images and cloud residual maps for comparing across the state-of-the-art deep learning cloud imputation models and the testing methods in the same order as in Sect. 4.5. Images in Fig. 8 are residual maps generated by subtracting the predicted image from the ground truth in Fig. 7. The darker residual maps implies better cloud imputation results. Our proposed CAINA outperformed the state-of-the-art models consistently by achieving the darkest residual maps.

5   Conclusions

In this paper, we presented an effective cloud imputation model with a novel style transfer function (CAINA) that harmonizes imputed patches by exploiting image style information from the cloud-free region of the image to reduce the style differences between the target and predicted image patches. We have experimentally shown that our method not only brings improvements as an add-on module to the $MDRN_{unet}$, but also provides an improved cloud imputation performance in comparison to the several state-of-the-art deep learning models on a benchmark dataset. In particular, CAINA is at least 24.49% better on MSE as compared to the state-of-the-art models, and 18.38% better on cloud MSE. However, the current proposed CAINA relies on the results of K-means clustering and cloud-free regions of the target image. In the future, we will work on introducing land cover segmentation maps to replace K-means clustering for improving the reliability of the cloud imputation method. Additionally, our future work will also try to reduce the dependence on cloud-free regions of the target image by possibly exploiting sensor-level metadata.

Acknowledgments. This research is based upon work supported in part by the Office of the Director of National Intelligence (ODNI), Intelligence Advanced Research Projects Activity (IARPA), via Contract #2021-21040700001. The views and conclusions contained herein are those of the authors and should not be interpreted as necessarily representing the official policies, either expressed or implied, of ODNI, IARPA, or the U.S. Government. The U.S. Government is authorized to reproduce and distribute reprints for governmental purposes notwithstanding any copyright annotation therein. We would like to thank Benjamin Raskob at ARA for useful feedback on this project.

Ethical Statement

Our proposed method improves cloud imputation performance. Remote sensing imagery has been widely used in applications ranging from land-use land-cover mapping to national security. By improving the imputation performance, we are directly improving the downstream applications such as assessing damages due to natural disasters, forest fires, and climate impacts. Our work does not have direct ethical implications or adverse impacts on humans.

References

1. Cresson, R., Ienco, D., Gaetano, R., Ose, K., Minh, D.H.T.: Optical image gap filling using deep convolutional autoencoder from optical and radar images. In: IGARSS 2019–2019 IEEE International Geoscience and Remote Sensing Symposium, pp. 218–221. IEEE (2019)
2. Cresson, R., et al.: Comparison of convolutional neural networks for cloudy optical images reconstruction from single or multitemporal joint SAR and optical images. arXiv preprint arXiv:2204.00424 (2022)
3. Dumoulin, V., Shlens, J., Kudlur, M.: A learned representation for artistic style. arXiv preprint arXiv:1610.07629 (2016)
4. Ebel, P., Meraner, A., Schmitt, M., Zhu, X.X.: Multisensor data fusion for cloud removal in global and all-season sentinel-2 imagery. IEEE Trans. Geosci. Remote Sens. **59**(7), 5866–5878 (2020)
5. Ebel, P., Xu, Y., Schmitt, M., Zhu, X.X.: SEN12MS-CR-TS: a remote-sensing data set for multimodal multitemporal cloud removal. IEEE Trans. Geosci. Remote Sens. **60**, 1–14 (2022)
6. Gatys, L.A., Ecker, A.S., Bethge, M.: Image style transfer using convolutional neural networks. In: Proceedings of the IEEE Conference on Computer Vision and Pattern Recognition, pp. 2414–2423 (2016)
7. Hore, A., Ziou, D.: Image quality metrics: PSNR vs. SSIM. In: 2010 20th International Conference on Pattern Recognition, pp. 2366–2369. IEEE (2010)
8. Huang, X., Belongie, S.: Arbitrary style transfer in real-time with adaptive instance normalization. In: Proceedings of the IEEE International Conference on Computer Vision, pp. 1501–1510 (2017)
9. Kang, S.H., Choi, Y., Choi, J.Y.: Restoration of missing patterns on satellite infrared sea surface temperature images due to cloud coverage using deep generative inpainting network. J. Mar. Sci. Eng. **9**(3), 310 (2021)
10. King, M.D., Platnick, S., Menzel, W.P., Ackerman, S.A., Hubanks, P.A.: Spatial and temporal distribution of clouds observed by MODIS onboard the terra and aqua satellites. IEEE Trans. Geosci. Remote Sens. **51**(7), 3826–3852 (2013)
11. Kruse, F.A., et al.: The spectral image processing system (SIPS)–interactive visualization and analysis of imaging spectrometer data. Remote Sens. Environ. **44**(2–3), 145–163 (1993)
12. Li, X., Guo, Q., Lin, D., Li, P., Feng, W., Wang, S.: MISF: multi-level interactive siamese filtering for high-fidelity image inpainting. In: Proceedings of the IEEE/CVF Conference on Computer Vision and Pattern Recognition, pp. 1869–1878 (2022)
13. Ma, W., et al.: A novel adaptive hybrid fusion network for multiresolution remote sensing images classification. IEEE Trans. Geosci. Remote Sens. **60**, 1–17 (2021)
14. Meraner, A., Ebel, P., Zhu, X.X., Schmitt, M.: Cloud removal in sentinel-2 imagery using a deep residual neural network and SAR-optical data fusion. ISPRS J. Photogramm. Remote. Sens. **166**, 333–346 (2020)

15. Park, T., Efros, A.A., Zhang, R., Zhu, J.-Y.: Contrastive learning for unpaired image-to-image translation. In: Vedaldi, A., Bischof, H., Brox, T., Frahm, J.-M. (eds.) ECCV 2020. LNCS, vol. 12354, pp. 319–345. Springer, Cham (2020). https://doi.org/10.1007/978-3-030-58545-7_19

16. Qu, J., Shi, Y., Xie, W., Li, Y., Wu, X., Du, Q.: MSSL: hyperspectral and panchromatic images fusion via multiresolution spatial-spectral feature learning networks. IEEE Trans. Geosci. Remote Sens. 60, 1–13 (2021)

17. Requena-Mesa, C., Benson, V., Reichstein, M., Runge, J., Denzler, J.: Earthnet 2021: a large-scale dataset and challenge for earth surface forecasting as a guided video prediction task. In: Proceedings of the IEEE/CVF Conference on Computer Vision and Pattern Recognition, pp. 1132–1142 (2021)

18. Ronneberger, O., Fischer, P., Brox, T.: U-Net: convolutional networks for biomedical image segmentation. In: Navab, N., Hornegger, J., Wells, W.M., Frangi, A.F. (eds.) MICCAI 2015. LNCS, vol. 9351, pp. 234–241. Springer, Cham (2015). https://doi.org/10.1007/978-3-319-24574-4_28

19. Roy, D.P., et al.: Multi-temporal MODIS-Landsat data fusion for relative radiometric normalization, gap filling, and prediction of landsat data. Remote Sens. Environ. 112(6), 3112–3130 (2008)

20. Rudner, T.G., et al.: Multi3Net: segmenting flooded buildings via fusion of multiresolution, multisensor, and multitemporal satellite imagery. In: Proceedings of the AAAI Conference on Artificial Intelligence, vol. 33, pp. 702–709 (2019)

21. Singh, P., Komodakis, N.: Cloud-Gan: cloud removal for sentinel-2 imagery using a cyclic consistent generative adversarial networks. In: IGARSS 2018–2018 IEEE International Geoscience and Remote Sensing Symposium, pp. 1772–1775. IEEE (2018)

22. Stock, A., et al.: Comparison of cloud-filling algorithms for marine satellite data. Remote Sens. 12(20), 3313 (2020)

23. Sun, Z., Zhou, W., Ding, C., Xia, M.: Multi-resolution transformer network for building and road segmentation of remote sensing image. ISPRS Int. J. Geo Inf. 11(3), 165 (2022)

24. Ulyanov, D., Vedaldi, A., Lempitsky, V.: Improved texture networks: maximizing quality and diversity in feed-forward stylization and texture synthesis. In: Proceedings of the IEEE Conference on Computer Vision and Pattern Recognition, pp. 6924–6932 (2017)

25. Varshney, D., Persello, C., Gupta, P.K., Nikam, B.R.: Multiresolution fully convolutional networks to detect clouds and snow through optical satellite images. arXiv preprint arXiv:2201.02350 (2022)

26. Wang, L., Weng, L., Xia, M., Liu, J., Lin, H.: Multi-resolution supervision network with an adaptive weighted loss for desert segmentation. Remote Sens. 13(11), 2054 (2021)

27. Wang, L., Zhang, C., Li, R., Duan, C., Meng, X., Atkinson, P.M.: Scale-aware neural network for semantic segmentation of multi-resolution remote sensing images. Remote Sens. 13(24), 5015 (2021)

28. Wang, Z., Bovik, A.C., Sheikh, H.R., Simoncelli, E.P.: Image quality assessment: from error visibility to structural similarity. IEEE Trans. Image Process. 13(4), 600–612 (2004)

29. Weiss, D.J., Atkinson, P.M., Bhatt, S., Mappin, B., Hay, S.I., Gething, P.W.: An effective approach for gap-filling continental scale remotely sensed time-series. ISPRS J. Photogramm. Remote. Sens. 98, 106–118 (2014)

30. Yadav, J., Sharma, M.: A review of k-mean algorithm. Int. J. Eng. Trends Technol. 4(7), 2972–2976 (2013)

31. Yang, X., Zhao, Y., Vatsavai, R.R.: Deep residual network with multi-image attention for imputing under clouds in satellite imagery. In: 2022 27th International Conference on Pattern Recognition (ICPR). IEEE (2022)

32. Yu, W., Zhang, X., Pun, M.O., Liu, M.: A hybrid model-based and data-driven approach for cloud removal in satellite imagery using multi-scale distortion-aware networks. In: 2021 IEEE International Geoscience and Remote Sensing Symposium IGARSS, pp. 7160–7163. IEEE (2021)

33. Zhang, Q., Yuan, Q., Zeng, C., Li, X., Wei, Y.: Missing data reconstruction in remote sensing image with a unified spatial-temporal-spectral deep convolutional neural network. IEEE Trans. Geosci. Remote Sens. **56**(8), 4274–4288 (2018)

34. Zhao, Y., Yang, X., Vatsavai, R.R.: Multi-stream deep residual network for cloud imputation using multi-resolution remote sensing imagery. In: 2022 21st IEEE International Conference on Machine Learning and Applications (ICMLA), pp. 97–104. IEEE (2022)

35. Zhao, Y., Shen, S., Hu, J., Li, Y., Pan, J.: Cloud removal using multimodal GAN with adversarial consistency loss. IEEE Geosci. Remote Sens. Lett. **19**, 1–5 (2021)

36. Zhu, H., Ma, W., Li, L., Jiao, L., Yang, S., Hou, B.: A dual-branch attention fusion deep network for multiresolution remote-sensing image classification. Inf. Fusion **58**, 116–131 (2020)

37. Zhu, J.Y., Park, T., Isola, P., Efros, A.A.: Unpaired image-to-image translation using cycle-consistent adversarial networks. In: Proceedings of the IEEE International Conference on Computer Vision, pp. 2223–2232 (2017)

Comprehensive Transformer-Based Model Architecture for Real-World Storm Prediction

Fudong Lin[1], Xu Yuan[1(✉)], Yihe Zhang[1], Purushottam Sigdel[2], Li Chen[1], Lu Peng[3], and Nian-Feng Tzeng[1]

[1] University of Louisiana at Lafayette, Lafayette, LA 70504, USA
xu.yuan@louisiana.edu
[2] Intel Corporation, Santa Clara, CA 95054, USA
[3] Tulane University, New Orleans, LA 70118, USA

Abstract. Storm prediction provides the early alert for preparation, avoiding potential damage to property and human safety. However, a traditional storm prediction model usually incurs excessive computational overhead due to employing atmosphere physical equations and complicated data assimilation. In this work, we strive to develop a lightweight and portable Transformer-based model architecture, which takes satellite and radar images as its input, for real-world storm prediction. However, deep learning-based storm prediction models commonly have to address various challenges, including limited observational samples, intangible patterns, multi-scale resolutions of sensor images, *etc.* To tackle aforementioned challenges for efficacious learning, we separate our model architecture into two stages, *i.e.*, "representation learning" and "prediction", respectively for extracting the high-quality feature representation and for predicting weather events. Specifically, the representation learning stage employs (1) multiple masked autoencoders (MAE)-based encoders with different scalability degrees for extracting multi-scale image patterns and (2) the Word2vec tool to enact their temporal representation. In the prediction stage, a vision transformer (ViT)-based encoder receives the input sequence derived from packing the image patterns and their temporal representation together for storm prediction. Extensive experiments have been carried out, with their results exhibiting that our comprehensive transformer-based model can achieve the overall accuracy of 94.4% for predicting the occurrence of storm events, substantially outperforming its compared baselines.

Keywords: Storm Predictions · Vision Transformers · AI for Science

1 Introduction

Storms can cause areal catastrophes resulting from property damage, injuries, and even deaths. It has long been a critical and essential task for prompt and accurate storm occurrence prediction to facilitate emergency alert broadcasting in advance for early preparation actions. However, conventional physical

G. De Francisci Morales et al. (Eds.): ECML PKDD 2023, LNAI 14175, pp. 54–71, 2023.
https://doi.org/10.1007/978-3-031-43430-3_4

models for storm predictions tend to suffer from excessive computational overhead caused by vast climate data simulation and complicated data assimilation from different sources. Meanwhile, deep learning (DL) has enjoyed impressive advances in various applications [3,7,9,12,15,17,18,22,27,31,34,38,46,49], including those [1,23,33,40–42,59] for weather forecasting.

A few attempts have been made to develop DL-based models for storm prediction [8,20,58,60] with unsatisfactory outcomes. Their main obstacles are multifold, including limited observational storm samples in real-world scenarios, complicated and intangible patterns existing in typical storm data, which are usually multi-modal and multi-scalar, among others. Known prediction models often failed to address one or multiple such obstacles with inflexible and coupled structures, thus hindering their generalization to the real scenarios. To date, it remains open and challenging to harness DL-based models by effectively dealing with those obstacles for accurately predicting the occurrence of storm events.

To tackle the aforementioned obstacles, we endeavor to develop a comprehensive model architecture able to flexibly admit the satellite and radar images for real-world storm prediction, resorting to the vision transformer (ViT) [12] and masked autoencoders (MAE) [15]. In particular, we separate our model architecture into two stages, *i.e.*, "representation learning" and "prediction", respectively for learning high-quality representations of data and predicting weather events of interest. In the representation learning stage, three MAE-based encoders with different scalability degrees corresponding to multi-scale sensor images are utilized for extracting affluent image patterns. Meanwhile, the Word2vec [36] tool is employed to learn the temporal representations of weather events, with such representations viewed as the critical features of storm events. A pooling layer and a linear projection layer are designed to bridge the two stages for matching the length of the input sequence and the hidden vector size, respectively, able to significantly reduce the memory utilization and computation cost of self-attention as well. In the prediction stage, a ViT-based encoder is employed to receive latent representations constructed by packing image and temporal representations together. Similar to the original ViT, a multi-layer perceptron (MLP) is used to serve for predicting the occurrence of storm events, based on the learnable classification token. Inspired by the segment embedding in BERT [9], we also propose a novel content embedding for MAE-based and ViT-based encoders, able to differentiate the memberships of various sources of representations.

We have conducted extensive experiments on the real SEVIR dataset [47], which includes a collection of real-world satellite and radar images with different resolutions, as well as detailed weather event descriptions (*e.g.*, times and locations). The experimental results demonstrate that our Transformer-based architecture achieves 94.4% overall accuracy in predicting the occurrence of storm events. In addition, we conduct comprehensive ablation studies, whose results exhibit the significance and necessity of our novel designs on the ViT and MAE encoders for real-world storm predictions. These empirical results demonstrate the practical impact of our solution for precisely predicting storm events to avoid potential catastrophic loss and damage.

2   Related Work

This section presents prior work on vision transformers and deep learning-based weather forecasting.

Vision Transformers. Popularized by ViT [12], vision transformers have been a powerful surrogate to conventional neural networks (CNNs) for vision tasks. It splits an image into a set of patches and relies on its encoder to receive the input constructed by summing up a linear projection of patches and positional embeddings. Then, an extra learnable classification token is used for performing classification tasks. Subsequent work built upon the ViT abounds. For example, DEiT [45] addresses the original ViT's overfitting issue by appending a novel distillation token. Swin [35] tackles high-resolution inputs by adopting the hierarchical structure from CNNs. TiT-ViT [55] aggregates structure information by recursively merging neighboring tokens into one token, and MAE [15] introduces self-supervised learning to the vision domain built upon ViT backbones. Some studies, including MViT [13,30], PiT [50], PVT [19], among many others [5,11,28,29,53,54,56,57], also address the limitations of original ViT for better performance on vision tasks. Despite effectiveness in theoretical deep learning, prior studies all focus on image data with very similar resolutions only, thereby difficult to make it adapt the rich real-world satellite and radar images with varying resolutions. Although our comprehensive model architecture builds on ViT and MAE, several novel designs (*e.g.*, content embedding) are tailored to address such real-world challenges as limited observational samples, intangible patterns, multi-modality data, and multi-scale input images.

Deep Learning for Weather Predictions. Deep learning (DL) has been popularly adopted for addressing critical and challenging meteorological issues in recent years. [42] has proposed a convolutional LSTM (ConvLSTM) network, based on the fully connected LSTM (FC-LSTM) to construct an encoding-forecasting structure by concatenating several ConvLSTM layers, arriving at an end-to-end trainable model for short-term weather predictions. Motivated by ConvLSTM, subsequent studies employ various deep neural network structures, such as Autoencoders [21,32], DLWP models [1,44], LSTM [4,43,48,51,52], and others [23,40,41], for weather predictions. A few studies [8,20,58,60] also started to tackle storm predictions from the DL perspective. However, their proposed architectures are often coupled and inflexible, thereby difficult to be generalized to the real scenario. In sharp contrast, we separate our comprehensive model architecture into two loosely coupled stages, permitting multiple MAE encoders to be flexibly incorporated into or detached from our proposed architecture. Such a design approach can be flexible to tackle multi-resolution image data from different sources, capturing rich intangible patterns for accurate storm prediction.

3   Problem Statement, Challenge, and Idea

3.1   Problem Statement

In this work, we aim to develop a deep learning (DL)-based model, for effectively capturing the complex weather data patterns, to predict the occurrence

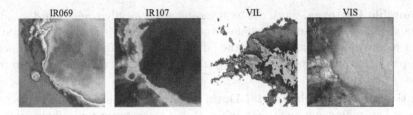

Fig. 1. Illustration of four types of sensor data for storm predictions.

Table 1. Description of the SEVIR dataset

Type	Satellite/Radar	Resolution	Description
IR069	GOES-16 C09 6.9 µm	192 × 192	Infrared Satellite imagery (Water Vapor)
IR107	GOES-16 C13 10.7 µm	192 × 192	Infrared Satellite imagery (Window)
VIL	Vertically Integrated Liquid (VIL)	384 × 384	NEXRAD radar mosaic of VIL
VIS	GOES-16 C02 0.64 µm	768 × 768	Visible satellite imagery

of storm events. Despite massive storm data available publicly (*e.g.*, the NOAA Storm Events database [39]), their tremendous sizes and extraordinary complexity usually hinder the training process of DL models. To guide our model design for storm event predictions, we employ a storm dataset downsampled from NOAA called SEVIR [47], which contains a collection of sensor images captured by satellite and radar, characterizing weather events during 2017–2019. Those sensor images can be grouped into four categories, *i.e.*, IR069, IR107, VIL, and VIS, captured respectively by GOES-16 C09 6.9 µm, GOES-16 C13 10.7 µm, Vertically Integrated Liquid, and GOES-16 C02 0.64 µm. Figure 1 depicts a set of sensor images for a weather event and Table 1 presents the details of the SEVIR dataset. This dataset also contains abundant numerical and statistical description for weather events, *e.g.*, time widow, location, *etc.* In particular, it contains 10, 180 normal and 2, 559 storm events.

The primary aim of our model is to predict whether storms will occur, deemed as a binary storm prediction, *i.e.*, either storm or normal events. Following prior studies [10,20], we frame the storm prediction as the binary classification problem.

3.2 Challenges

Limited Observational Samples. In real-world scenarios, storms belong to rare events, having fewer observational data samples than normal, non-storm events. This poses grant challenges to DL models for learning sufficient patterns, whereas the normal events' patterns dominate the data. For example, in the preprocessed SEVIR dataset, the overall storm events only include 2, 559 samples, accounting for just 20% of total events. How to develop an effective model to learn from the limited observational samples for achieving satisfactory performance remains open and challenging.

Intangible Patterns. Since the weather images typically come from the satellite and radar, they usually include erratic and intangible shapes compared to other real-world objects. This lifts the difficulty in designing the model for accurate prediction, requiring to deeply capture the hidden and common storm patterns.

Multi-scale and Multi-modal Data. The conventional DL models are only designed for taking one small-scale input. But, a storm event typically has images from different sources with multi-scale resolutions. For example, there are four types of sensor images (*i.e.*, IR069, IR107, VIL, and VIS) in the SEVIR dataset with three different resolutions, *i.e.*, 192×192, 384×384, and 768×768, as listed in Table 1. We aim to take all types of images into account to increase the data sample amounts for use. So far, how to effectively align the features from multiple types of sensor images with multi-scale resolutions remains open. Beyond sensor images, the language data (*e.g.*, time description) is also closely correlated to storm occurrences. Our model is expected to feed both image and language data concurrently, deemed as multi-modal data, whose effective processing by the DL approach is still a big challenge.

3.3   Our Idea

To tackle the aforementioned challenges, we develop a comprehensive transformer-based model architecture for storm predictions, where the predictions are made under the simultaneous consideration of all types of sensor images as well as language-based prior knowledge (*i.e.*, time description).

Our design is driven by the following three observations. *First,* as shown in Fig. 1, different types of sensor images for a weather event contain very similar high-level patterns (*e.g.*, the shape). Based on this observation, for each weather event, we can construct its comprehensive image representation by concatenating the feature embedding extracted from all types of sensor images, arriving at a higher-quality representation. *Second,* thank to vision transformer (ViT) [12], the gap between natural language processing (NLP) and computer vision (CV) has been significantly mitigated [15]. Besides, vision transformer can benefit from task-specific domain knowledge [29]. Hence, it is feasible to explore some mechanisms to incorporate language-based prior knowledge into the vision transformer, thus in turn augmenting its efficacious DL from limited observational samples. *Third,* to handle the multi-scale resolutions problem, we can tailor multi-scale transformer encoders for embedding different types of sensor images, as shown in Fig. 2 (Bottom). Meanwhile, a novel content embedding (see Figs. 3a, 3b, and 3c) can be included for differentiating the membership of various sources of representations, motivated by the segment embedding in BERT [9].

4   Method

Figure 2 illustrates the overview of our proposed model architecture for storm predictions, consisting of two stages, *i.e.*, *representation learning* and *prediction*. The representation learning stage (*i.e.*, Fig. 2 Bottom) involves three different

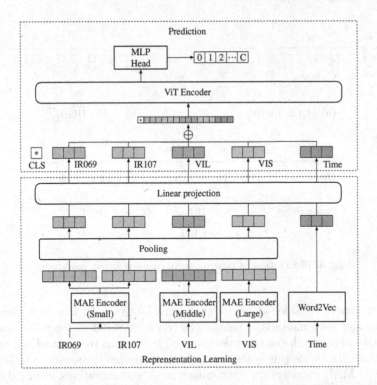

Fig. 2. Overview of our transformer-based comprehensive model architecture.

scales of transformer encoders trained by Masked Autoencoders (MAE)-denoted as MAE encoders-for extracting image representation from IR069 (or IR107), VIL, and VIS, respectively. The Word2vec tool is used to extract the temporal representation of weather events. The pooling layer and the linear projection layer serve to bridge the two stages by matching the input sequence length and the hidden vector dimension, respectively, making it possible for our model architecture to decouple the two stages to some extent.

The prediction stage (*i.e.*, Fig. 2 Top) derives the input sequence from a weather event by concatenating its comprehensive image representation extracted from four types of sensor images and its temporal representation extracted from the time description of that event. A learnable classification token is fed to the multi-layer perceptron (MLP) for storm predictions.

4.1   Representation Learning

This stage attains both the image representation and the temporal representation, respectively for the sensor data and the descriptive time data.

Image Representation. MAE encoders are applied for extracting the image representation here. To tackle input images with different resolutions, prior studies [15, 25, 26, 29] often randomly scale up or crop input images to a fixed resolution (*e.g.*, 224 × 224). This simple solution is effective in conventional vision tasks

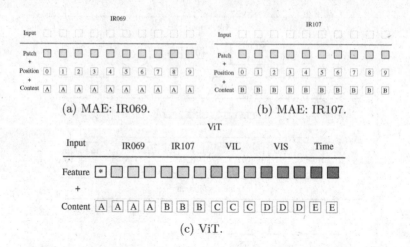

(a) MAE: IR069.   (b) MAE: IR107.

(c) ViT.

Fig. 3. Illustration of how we construct the input sequence.

as they typically consider identical small-scale images only. However, given our sensor images have multi-scale resolutions (*e.g.*, 192 × 192 vs 768 × 768), scaling up (or cropping) to the same scale may add redundant (or discard important) information. To tackle this issue, we respectively design the small-, middle-, and large-scale MAE encoders for extracting image representations from IR069 (or IR107), VIL, and VIS, based on their resolutions listed in Table 1 (the 3rd column). Notably, each MAE encoder in our design can be fed with several types of sensor images with similar resolutions. Meanwhile, inspired by the segment embedding in BERT [9], we devise a learnable content embedding to differentiate the membership of various sources of images fed into the same MAE encoder for high-quality feature embeddings. Similar to MAE, we divide an image into a set of image patches and construct the patch embeddings by a linear projection of image patches. The position embedding is used to indicate positional informa-tion of image patches. The input sequence for MAE is constructed by adding the patch embedding, position embedding, and our novel content embedding. Figures 3a and 3b show examples of the input sequence for IR069 and IR107, respectively. Notably, content embeddings in the middle- or large-scale MAE encoders are removed as only one type of sensor image is fed into them.

Temporal Representation. This part is inspired by the prior study [29], which has reported that vision transformer can benefit from task-specific prior knowl-edge. So, we incorporate the temporal representation into the input representa-tion sequence of the ViT encoder. The temporal representation for a storm event is extracted from its beginning date in a month interval manner. Specifically, for a given weather event, we use Word2vec [36] to embed three dates relevant to its beginning date (*i.e.*, two weeks before its beginning date, its beginning date, and two weeks after its beginning date). The temporal representation is constructed by packing together the three date embeddings to form a monthly interval. The intuition underlying this month interval manner is that using the month to capture a storm's occurrence is more informative than its specific day. That is, a storm event is more likely to happen within a specific month interval rather than a specific date.

If constructing the input representation sequence for the prediction stage naively by concatenating the image and temporal representations directly, the self-attention in our ViT encoder will incur considerable memory and computation burden. Instead, we employ a pooling layer to shrink the length of the image representation by consolidating the latent representation outputted via MAE encoders. Notably, regarding the temporal representation, which is already of small length (*i.e.*, 3), it is unnecessary to apply the pooling to it. After that, a linear projection layer is utilized to match the hidden vector sizes between the two stages. This way decouples our representation learning and prediction stages to some extent. Note that the hidden vector sizes in our two stages are different.

4.2   Prediction

In this stage, the feature embedding for a weather event is constructed by concatenating a learnable "classification token" (*i.e.*, CLS token) and its image and temporal representations, as shown in Fig. 1. Similar to the small-scale MAE encoder, the content embeddings are used for differentiating the membership of various sources of the feature embedding (*i.e.*, IR069, IR107, VIL, VIS, or event time). We remove the positional embedding here as no valuable position information exists among various sources of representation. Hence, the input for our ViT encoder is derived by summing up the feature embedding and the content embedding, as illustrated in Fig. 3c. A multi-layer perceptron (MLP) receives the CLS token output by the ViT decoder (*i.e.*, the head of the output sequence) to predict whether a storm (or a specific storm type) will occur.

Our technical contributions are summarized as follows. First, to tackle the issue of scarce observational samples for storm predictions, we enrich the latent representations of weather events by concatenating image representations extracted from different types of sensor images. As such, our ViT encoder can benefit from higher-quality representations. Second, we leverage language-based prior knowledge for storm predictions by appending temporal representations extracted from the descriptive time data of weather events. To the best of our knowledge, this is the very first work on DL-based storm predictions that addresses multi-modality data. Third, we devise a novel content embedding for both MAE and ViT encoders, benefiting Transformer-based models by indicating the membership of various input types. This can greatly improve the performance of Transformers when handling multiple types of inputs simultaneously. Fourth, although we use the SEVIR dataset to demonstrate the feasibility of our model architecture, it in effect can be generalized to deal with any type of satellite/radar image with various resolutions from NOAA for real-world storm predictions.

Table 2. Details of MAE and ViT encoders used in our design

Model	Scale	Layers	Hidden size	Heads	Patch size	Input Size	MLP Ratio
MAE encoder	Small	12	192	6	16×16	224×224	4
	Middle	12	384	12	32×32	448×448	4
	Large	12	768	16	48×48	672×672	4
ViT encoder	ViT-Base	12	768	12	–	–	4

5   Experiments and Results

We implement our proposed model architecture and conduct extensive experiments to evaluate its performance in storm prediction. We follow the 80/20 training/test to split on the SEVIR dataset, whose event counts for normal and storm events are $10,180$ and $2,559$, respectively.

5.1   Experimental Setting

Baselines. We take the convolutional neural networks (CNN) and vision transformer (ViT) as our baselines for comparison. Specifically, the models of ResNet-50 [16] and ViT-Base [12] are used for the two baselines. The hyperparameters are set as reported in their original studies. Since the baselines cannot take input with multiple resolutions, we consider two cases for comparison: 1) each type of sensor image is regarded as a single dataset, and 2) scaling up or cropping four types of sensor images to the same size (*i.e.*, 224×224).

Parameter Settings. We build our MAE and ViT encoders on the top of MAE's official code[1]. But due to the computational limitations, we prune their models to the relevant small models for use, with detailed parameters listed in Table 2. They in effect can be easily scaled up to large model sizes for real-world storm predictions.

We employ the AdamW with $\beta_1 = 0.9$, $\beta_2 = 0.999$, the weight decay of 0.05, and a batch size of 128 (or 64) for MAE encoder (or ViT encoder). Following [2, 14,15,24,37], we employ the layer-wise learning rate decay [6] of 0.75. We train MAE encoder (or ViT encoder) for 50 (or 100) epochs, with the base learning rate of $1e-3$, the linear warmup epochs of 5, and the cosine decay schedule. We train small-, middle-, and large-scale MAEs, including encoders and decoders, respectively on IR069 (and IR107), VIL, and VIS, with a masking ratio of 75%. After training, we only use the encoders to extract image representation without any masking.

For the *Word2vec*, we use its implementation by Gensim[2], with sg = 0 (*i.e.*, CBOW), vector size = 768, min count = 1, window = 3, and the training epoch of $1,000$. Note that the training data for Word2vec is pre-processed by the days through the years 2017–2019.

---

[1] https://github.com/facebookresearch/mae.
[2] https://github.com/RaRe-Technologies/gensim.

Table 3. Storm predictions on the SEVIR dataset. *All* in the two baselines denotes the scenario that scales up or crops multi-scale images to a fixed resolution. The best results are shown in bold

Method	Image Types	Normal			Storm			Accuracy
		Precision	Recall	F1 Score	Precision	Recall	F1 Score	
Resnet-50	IR069	90.1	87.2	88.6	53.4	60.4	56.7	82.0
	IR107	88.6	94.8	91.6	69.9	49.5	58.0	86.0
	VIL	90.8	85.2	87.9	51.3	64.2	57.0	81.1
	VIS	87.7	96.2	91.8	74.1	44.3	55.4	86.1
	All	86.1	93.5	89.6	58.3	37.6	45.7	82.5
ViT-Base	IR069	90.5	91.7	91.1	63.7	60.4	62.0	85.5
	IR107	88.0	92.5	90.2	60.9	47.9	53.6	83.8
	VIL	91.9	93.9	92.9	72.2	66.0	69.0	88.4
	VIS	87.7	92.0	89.8	58.7	46.9	52.1	83.2
	All	87.9	97.1	92.3	78.9	45.1	57.4	86.9
Ours	–	**95.5**	**97.7**	**96.6**	**89.4**	**81.1**	**85.0**	**94.4**

5.2   Overall Performance Under Storm Event Predictions

We take precision, recall, and F1 score as our evaluation metrics to exhibit the performance in predicting the occurrence of storm events (*i.e.*, binary storm prediction). Table 3 presents the values of three metrics of our model architectures as well as the comparative results to the CNN (*i.e.*, ResNet-50) and vision transformer (*i.e.*, ViT-Base) baselines. For two baselines, we consider both scenarios: 1) taking each type of sensor image as the individual input and 2) scaling up or cropping all sensor images to the 224×224 for inputting as a whole dataset, denoted as *All*. We observe that our approach can always beat all baselines in predicting both normal and storm events, achieving the precision, recall, and F1 score values of $95.5\%, 97.7\%, 96.6\%$ and of $89.4\%, 81.1\%, 85.0\%$, respectively. Our overall accuracy is 94.4%, exceeding 8.3% and 6.0%, respectively, to the best results of ResNet-50 (86.1% on VIS) and of ViT-Base (88.4% on VIL). In terms of predicting normal events, both our approach and the baselines can achieve promising prediction results, with most values of three metrics more than 90%. The reason is that the normal events belong to the majority in the dataset (10180 of 12667), so their patterns are easy to be learned by both our approach and the baselines. But when predicting the storm events, the performance of two baselines degrades largely, with most values below 70%. In particular, among three metrics, the recall corresponding to the column under Storm in Table 3 is the most difficult but very important. We observe that our approach can still achieve the value of 81.1%. Regarding the ResNet-50 and ViT-Base, their best values are only 64.2% and 66.0%, respectively, largely underperforming our approach, demonstrating their limited learning ability from the storm samples. This also signifies the importance of our approach, which has novel designs of representation learning, temporal representation, and content embedding, which

Table 4. Ablation studies for different components on our comprehensive model

Method	Normal			Storm			Accuracy
	Precision	Recall	F1 Score	Precision	Recall	F1 Score	
MAE encoder⁻	93.0	92.7	92.8	70.3	71.0	70.7	88.5
Temporal⁻	94.9	92.2	93.5	71.2	79.5	75.1	89.7
Content⁻	94.0	96.5	95.2	83.7	74.4	78.8	92.2
Ours	**95.5**	**97.7**	**96.6**	**89.4**	**81.1**	**85.0**	**94.4**

can better learn storm patterns with limited observational samples. Besides, we observe that naively scaling up or cropping multi-scale images to a fixed resolution results in the lowest recall on both baselines, *i.e.*, 37.6% on ResNet-50 (the 7th row) and 45.1% on ViT-based (the 12th row). The reason is that this naive solution may add redundant or discard valuable information.

5.3 Significance of Our Design Components for Storm Predictions

We next conduct ablation studies to show the necessity and significance of each design component in our comprehensive model, in contributing to the storm prediction. In particular, the representation learning, temporal representation, and content embedding are removed in turn, as our design variants to evaluate the performance of the remaining system. The three corresponding variants are denoted as MAE encoder⁻, Temporal⁻, and Content⁻, respectively. Notably, in MAE encoder⁻, image representations are constructed by a linear projection of image patches, similar to the original ViT. Table 4 presents our experimental results. We have three observations. First, all three variants perform worse than our original model architecture, especially for predicting storm events. Second, MAE encoder⁻ performs worst among three variants, with its respective precision, recall, and F1 score values of 19.1%, 10.1%, and 14.3% less than ours, in terms of predicting storm events. This demonstrates the necessity of using MAE encoders to learn high-quality image representation in our design. Third, although Content⁻ and Temporal⁻ can achieve better performance than MAE encoder⁻, they still perform much inferior to ours for predicting storm events. Specifically, for Content⁻, its recall and F1 score values are respectively 6.7% and 6.2% worse than ours. For Temporal⁻, its precision and F1 score values are respectively 18.2% and 9.9% worse than ours. This validates that both temporal representation and content embedding are also important to our design. Hence, we can conclude that all design components are necessary and important in contributing to our model architecture's prediction performance.

5.4 Necessity of Content Embedding in Our MAE Encoder

Here, we show the importance and necessity of novel content embedding in our MAE encoder (See Figs. 3a and 3b) when addressing multiple types of sensor

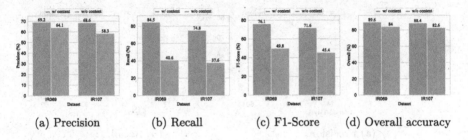

(a) Precision   (b) Recall   (c) F1-Score   (d) Overall accuracy

Fig. 4. Comparative results of our MAE encoder with/without the proposed content embedding.

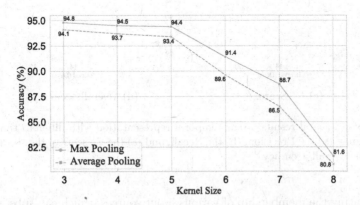

Fig. 5. Results under two pooling methods with various kernel sizes.

images with similar resolutions. The experiments were conducted on our small-scale MAE encoder only, as content embedding is not applied on our middle- and large-scale MAE encoders. Similar to our experiments on ViT-Base, we regard IR069 and IR107 as two datasets. The experimental settings are the same as "end-to-end fine-tuning" in the original MAE [15]. Notably, the experimental results in this section are obtained by removing content embedding in our MAE encoder, different from those in Sect. 5.3 whose results are obtained by removing content embedding on our ViT encoder.

Figure 4 depicts comparative results of our MAE encoder with/without the content embedding. In particular, we focus on the precision, the recall, and the F1-score of the storm event, as well as the overall accuracy, as shown in Figs. 4a, 4b, 4c and 4d, respectively. We have two observations. First, our MAE encoder with the content embedding achieves better performance under all scenarios, with overall accuracy improvements of 5.6% and of 5.8% on IR069 and IR107, respectively. Second, regarding the recall, our MAE encoder with the content embedding achieves the best improvement, with respective 43.9% and 37.2% improvements on IR069 and IR107. This statistical evidence exhibits the necessity and importance of the proposed content embedding in our MAE encoder for

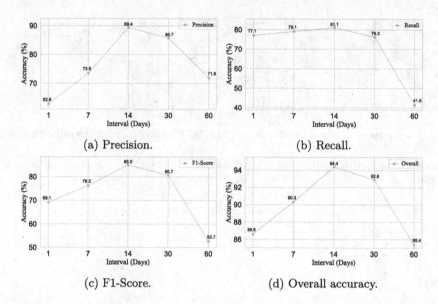

Fig. 6. Experimental results of our temporal representation with different time intervals, including (a) the Precision, (b) the Recall, and (c) the F1-score of the storm event, and (d) the overall accuracy.

differentiating the membership of various input sources, which can substantially elevate our model performance.

5.5 Detailed Design Underlying Our Pooling Layer

We present the detailed design underlying our pooling layer to support our architecture mentioned in Sect. 4.1. Two common pooling methods (*i.e.*, the max and the average pooling) with different sizes of the sliding window (*i.e.*, the kernel size) are taken into account. The kernel size varies from 3 to 8^3. The stride of the sliding window is set to the same as the kernel size. As such, a larger kernel size can reduce the memory and computation cost of self-attention. Figure 5 presents experimental results in terms of overall accuracy. We observe that the max pooling outperforms the average pooling under all scenarios. Besides, when the kernel size is greater than 5, increasing the kernel size will quickly degrade our model performance under both pooling methods. Hence, to balance the trade-off between computational efficiency and overall accuracy, we employ the max pooling with the kernel size of 5 in our pooling layer.

---

[3] Notably, when the kernel size equals 2, our computational resources cannot afford the computational overhead incurred by self-attention.

Table 5. Comparative results of our ViT encoder with/without the positional embedding. The best results are bold

Case	Normal			Storm			Accuracy
	Precision	Recall	F1-Score	Precision	Recall	F1-Score	
w/ position	95.4	97.2	96.3	87.5	80.5	83.9	94.0
w/o position	**95.5**	**97.7**	**96.6**	**89.4**	**81.1**	**85.0**	**94.4**

5.6 Constructing Temporal Representations

In this section, we conduct experiments to support our design in Sect. 4.1, where we construct the temporal representation for a weather event by embedding three dates relevant to its beginning date in a month-interval manner (*i.e.*, two weeks before its beginning date, its beginning date, and two weeks after its beginning date). We conduct experiments to exhibit the impact of various time intervals on our model performance. In particular, if the time interval is set to T days, we construct its temporal representation by embedding T days before its beginning date, its beginning date, and T days after its beginning date. Figure 6 presents our experimental results in terms of precision, recall, and F1-score of predicting storm events as well as the overall accuracy, when varying T from 1 to 60. We discover that when the time interval T equals 14 (*i.e.*, two weeks), our proposed model architecture achieves the best performance under all metrics. The reason may be due to: (i) compared to a small time interval (*i.e.*, ≤ 7 days), the month interval manner (*i.e.*, time interval = 14 days) is more informative; and (ii) if the time interval is too large (*i.e.*, ≥ 30 days), the relevance between weather events and temporal information is hard to learn.

5.7 Impact of Positional Embedding on Our ViT Encoder

This section conducts experiments to support our design in Sect. 4.2, where we drop the positional embedding in our ViT encoder. Hence, two cases are taken into account, *i.e.*, our ViT encoder with or without the positional embedding. Table 5 presents our experimental results with and without the positional embedding. We observe that our ViT encoder with positional embedding actually hurts the prediction performance, with a performance degradation of 0.4% in terms of the overall accuracy (*i.e.*, 94.0% with the positional embedding versus 94.4% without the positional embedding). The reason is that no valuable positional information exists among the input sequences of our ViT encoder as they come from various sources of representation. To reduce the redundancy, we remove the positional embedding in our ViT encoder.

6   Conclusion

This work has developed a comprehensive Transformer-based model architecture for real-world storm prediction. Our model architecture separates its "representation learning" and "prediction" stages to effectively extract the high-quality representations and accurately predict the occurrence of storm events, respectively. Multiple MAE-based encoders, the Word2vec tool, and a ViT-based encoder, with a collection of novel designs (such as image representation concatenation, temporal representation, and content embedding) are incorporated into our comprehensive model architecture to tackle practical challenges associated with real-world storm prediction. Experimental results exhibit the excellent learning capability of our model architecture. Although we conduct experiments on the SEVIR dataset, our model architecture can be generalized to effectively handle any type of real-world satellite and radar image data.

Acknowledgments. This work was supported in part by NSF under Grants 1763620, 2019511, 2146447, and in part by the BoRSF under Grants LEQSF(2019-22)-RD-A-21 and LEQSF(2021-22)-RD-D-07. Any opinion and findings expressed in the paper are those of the authors and do not necessarily reflect the view of funding agencies.

References

1. Agrawal, S., Barrington, L., Bromberg, C., Burge, J., Gazen, C., Hickey, J.: Machine learning for precipitation nowcasting from radar images. arXiv preprint arXiv:1912.12132 (2019)
2. Bao, H., Dong, L., Wei, F.: BEiT: BERT pre-training of image transformers. arXiv preprint arXiv:2106.08254 (2021)
3. Chen, L., Wang, W., Mordohai, P.: Learning the distribution of errors in stereo matching for joint disparity and uncertainty estimation. In: Computer Vision and Pattern Recognition (CVPR) (2023)
4. Chen, R., Wang, X., Zhang, W., Zhu, X., Li, A., Yang, C.: A hybrid CNN-LSTM model for typhoon formation forecasting. GeoInformatica **23**, 375–396 (2019)
5. Chen, W., et al.: A simple single-scale vision transformer for object localization and instance segmentation. arXiv preprint arXiv:2112.09747 (2021)
6. Clark, K., Luong, M., Le, Q.V., Manning, C.D.: ELECTRA: pre-training text encoders as discriminators rather than generators. In: International Conference on Learning Representations (ICLR) (2020)
7. Cui, Y., Yan, L., Cao, Z., Liu, D.: TF-blender: temporal feature blender for video object detection. In: Proceedings of the IEEE/CVF International Conference on Computer Vision (2021)
8. Cuomo, J., Chandrasekar, V.: Developing deep learning models for storm nowcasting. IEEE Trans. Geosci. Remote Sens. **60**, 1–13 (2021)
9. Devlin, J., Chang, M., Lee, K., Toutanova, K.: BERT: pre-training of deep bidirectional transformers for language understanding. In: Conference of the North American Chapter of the Association for Computational Linguistics: Human Language Technologies (NAACL-HLT) (2019)
10. Domico, K., Sheatsley, R., Beugin, Y., Burke, Q., McDaniel, P.: A machine learning and computer vision approach to geomagnetic storm forecasting. arXiv preprint arXiv:2204.05780 (2022)
11. Dong, G., Tang, M., Cai, L., Barnes, L.E., Boukhechba, M.: Semi-supervised graph instance transformer for mental health inference. In: IEEE International Conference on Machine Learning and Applications (ICMLA) (2021)

12. Dosovitskiy, A., et al.: An image is worth 16×16 words: transformers for image recognition at scale. In: International Conference on Learning Representations (ICLR) (2021)
13. Fan, H., et al.: Multiscale vision transformers. In: International Conference on Computer Vision (ICCV) (2021)
14. He, J., Wang, T., Min, Y., Gu, Q.: A simple and provably efficient algorithm for asynchronous federated contextual linear bandits (2022)
15. He, K., Chen, X., Xie, S., Li, Y., Dollár, P., Girshick, R.B.: Masked autoencoders are scalable vision learners. CoRR (2021)
16. He, K., Zhang, X., Ren, S., Sun, J.: Deep residual learning for image recognition. In: IEEE Conference on Computer Vision and Pattern Recognition (CVPR) (2016)
17. He, Y., Lin, F., Yuan, X., Tzeng, N.: Interpretable minority synthesis for imbalanced classification. In: International Joint Conference on Artificial Intelligence (IJCAI) (2021)
18. He, Y., et al.: HierCat: hierarchical query categorization from weakly supervised data at Facebook marketplace. In: ACM Web Conference (WWW) (2023)
19. Heo, B., Yun, S., Han, D., Chun, S., Choe, J., Oh, S.J.: Rethinking spatial dimensions of vision transformers. In: International Conference on Computer Vision (ICCV) (2021)
20. Hinz, R., et al.: Towards very-low latency storm nowcasting through AI-based onboard satellite data processing. In: International Conference on Information and Knowledge Management Workshop (CIKM Workshop) (2021)
21. Hossain, M., Rekabdar, B., Louis, S.J., Dascalu, S.: Forecasting the weather of Nevada: a deep learning approach. In: International Joint conference on Neural Networks (IJCNN) (2015)
22. Jumper, J., et al.: Highly accurate protein structure prediction with AlphaFold. Nature **596**, 583–589 (2021)
23. Klocek, S., et al.: MS-nowcasting: Operational precipitation nowcasting with convolutional LSTMs at microsoft weather. arXiv preprint arXiv:2111.09954 (2021)
24. Kong, R., et al.: Getting the most from eye-tracking: user-interaction based reading region estimation dataset and models. In: Symposium on Eye Tracking Research and Applications (2023)
25. Lai, Z., Wang, C., Cheung, S.c., Chuah, C.N.: SAR: self-adaptive refinement on pseudo labels for multiclass-imbalanced semi-supervised learning. In: Computer Vision and Pattern Recognition (CVPR) (2022)
26. Lai, Z., Wang, C., Gunawan, H., Cheung, S.C.S., Chuah, C.N.: Smoothed adaptive weighting for imbalanced semi-supervised learning: improve reliability against unknown distribution data. In: International Conference on Machine Learning (ICML), pp. 11828–11843 (2022)
27. Li, J., Wang, W., Abbas, W., Koutsoukos, X.: Distributed clustering for cooperative multi-task learning networks. IEEE Trans. Netw. Sci. Eng. **596**, 583–589 (2023)
28. Li, X., Metsis, V., Wang, H., Ngu, A.H.H.: TTS-GAN: a transformer-based time-series generative adversarial network. In: Michalowski, M., Abidi, S.S.R., Abidi, S. (eds.) Artificial Intelligence in Medicine (AIME) (2022)
29. Li, Y., Mao, H., Girshick, R., He, K.: Exploring plain vision transformer backbones for object detection. arXiv preprint arXiv:2203.16527 (2022)
30. Li, Y., et al.: Improved multiscale vision transformers for classification and detection. arXiv preprint arXiv:2112.01526 (2021)

31. Lin, F., Yuan, X., Peng, L., Tzeng, N.: Cascade variational auto-encoder for hierarchical disentanglement. In: International Conference on Information & Knowledge Management (CIKM) (2022)
32. Lin, S.Y., Chiang, C.C., Li, J.B., Hung, Z.S., Chao, K.M.: Dynamic fine-tuning stacked auto-encoder neural network for weather forecast. Futur. Gener. Comput. Syst. **89**, 446–454 (2018)
33. Liu, D., Cui, Y., Cao, Z., Chen, Y.: A large-scale simulation dataset: Boost the detection accuracy for special weather conditions. In: 2020 International Joint Conference on Neural Networks (IJCNN) (2020)
34. Liu, D., Cui, Y., Tan, W., Chen, Y.: SG-Net: spatial granularity network for one-stage video instance segmentation. In: Proceedings of the IEEE/CVF Conference on Computer Vision and Pattern Recognition (2021)
35. Liu, Z., et al.: Swin transformer: hierarchical vision transformer using shifted windows. In: International Conference on Computer Vision (ICCV) (2021)
36. Mikolov, T., Chen, K., Corrado, G., Dean, J.: Efficient estimation of word representations in vector space. In: International Conference on Learning Representations (ICLR), Workshop Track Proceedings (2013)
37. Min, Y., He, J., Wang, T., Gu, Q.: Learning stochastic shortest path with linear function approximation. In: International Conference on Machine Learning (ICML) (2022)
38. Min, Y., Wang, T., Zhou, D., Gu, Q.: Variance-aware off-policy evaluation with linear function approximation (2021)
39. NOAA: The NOAA storm events database. https://www.ncdc.noaa.gov/stormevents/
40. Ravuri, S., et al.: Skillful precipitation nowcasting using deep generative models of radar. Nature **597**, 672–677 (2021)
41. Samsi, S., Mattioli, C.J., Veillette, M.S.: Distributed deep learning for precipitation nowcasting. In: High Performance Extreme Computing Conference (HPEC) (2019)
42. Shi, X., Chen, Z., Wang, H., Yeung, D., Wong, W., Woo, W.: Convolutional LSTM network: a machine learning approach for precipitation nowcasting. In: Advances in Neural Information Processing Systems (NeurIPS) (2015)
43. Shi, X., et al.: Deep learning for precipitation nowcasting: a benchmark and a new model. In: Advances in Neural Information Processing Systems, vol. 30 (2017)
44. Sønderby, C.K., et al.: MetNet: a neural weather model for precipitation forecasting. arXiv preprint arXiv:2003.12140 (2020)
45. Touvron, H., Cord, M., Douze, M., Massa, F., Sablayrolles, A., Jégou, H.: Training data-efficient image transformers & distillation through attention. In: International Conference on Machine Learning (ICML) (2021)
46. Vaswani, A., et al.: Attention is all you need. In: Advances in Neural Information Processing Systems (NeurIPS) (2017)
47. Veillette, M.S., Samsi, S., Mattioli, C.J.: SEVIR: a storm event imagery dataset for deep learning applications in radar and satellite meteorology. In: Advances in Neural Information Processing Systems (NeurIPS) (2020)
48. Wang, B., et al.: Deep uncertainty quantification: a machine learning approach for weather forecasting. In: ACM SIGKDD International Conference on Knowledge Discovery & Data Mining (2019)
49. Wang, W., et al.: Real-time dense 3d mapping of underwater environments. arXiv preprint arXiv:2304.02704 (2023)
50. Wang, W., et al.: Pyramid vision transformer: a versatile backbone for dense prediction without convolutions. In: International Conference on Computer Vision (ICCV) (2021)

51. Wang, Y., Gao, Z., Long, M., Wang, J., Philip, S.Y.: PredRNN++: towards a resolution of the deep-in-time dilemma in spatiotemporal predictive learning. In: International Conference on Machine Learning (2018)

52. Wang, Y., Long, M., Wang, J., Gao, Z., Yu, P.S.: PredRNN: recurrent neural networks for predictive learning using spatiotemporal LSTMs. In: Advances in Neural Information Processing Systems, vol. 30 (2017)

53. Wang, Z., Li, T., Zheng, J., Huang, B.: When CNN meet with VIT: towards semi-supervised learning for multi-class medical image semantic segmentation. In: Karlinsky, L., Michaeli, T., Nishino, K. (eds.) ECCV 2022. LNCS, vol. 13807, pp. 424–441. Springer, Cham (2022). https://doi.org/10.1007/978-3-031-25082-8_28

54. Wang, Z., Zhao, W., Ni, Z., Zheng, Y.: Adversarial vision transformer for medical image semantic segmentation with limited annotations. In: British Machine Vision Conference 2022 (2022)

55. Yuan, L., et al.: Tokens-to-token VIT: training vision transformers from scratch on ImageNet. In: International Conference on Computer Vision (ICCV) (2021)

56. Zhang, D., Zhou, F.: Self-supervised image denoising for real-world images with context-aware transformer. IEEE Access **11**, 14340–14349 (2023)

57. Zhang, D., Zhou, F., Jiang, Y., Fu, Z.: MM-BSN: self-supervised image denoising for real-world with multi-mask based on blind-spot network. In: Computer Vision and Pattern Recognition Workshop (CVPRW) (2023)

58. Zhang, W., Zhang, R., Chen, H., He, G., Ge, Y., Han, L.: A multi-channel 3D convolutional-recurrent neural network for convective storm nowcasting. In: 2021 IEEE International Geoscience and Remote Sensing Symposium IGARSS, pp. 363–366. IEEE (2021)

59. Zhang, Y., et al.: Precise weather parameter predictions for target regions via neural networks. In: Machine Learning and Knowledge Discovery in Databases (ECML-PKDD) (2021)

60. Zhang, Z., He, Z., Yang, J., Liu, Y., Bao, R., Gao, S.: A 3D storm motion estimation method based on point cloud learning and doppler weather radar data. IEEE Trans. Geosci. Remote Sens. **60**, 1–5 (2021)

Explaining Full-Disk Deep Learning Model for Solar Flare Prediction Using Attribution Methods

Chetraj Pandey(✉) [iD], Rafal A. Angryk[iD], and Berkay Aydin[iD]

Georgia State University, Atlanta, GA 30303, USA
{cpandey1,rangryk,baydin2}@gsu.edu

Abstract. Solar flares are transient space weather events that pose a significant threat to space and ground-based technological systems, making their precise and reliable prediction crucial for mitigating potential impacts. This paper contributes to the growing body of research on deep learning methods for solar flare prediction, primarily focusing on highly overlooked near-limb flares and utilizing the attribution methods to provide a post hoc qualitative explanation of the model's predictions. We present a solar flare prediction model, which is trained using hourly full-disk line-of-sight magnetogram images and employs a binary prediction mode to forecast ≥M-class flares that may occur within the following 24-h period. To address the class imbalance, we employ a fusion of data augmentation and class weighting techniques; and evaluate the overall performance of our model using the true skill statistic (TSS) and Heidke skill score (HSS). Moreover, we applied three attribution methods, namely Guided Gradient-weighted Class Activation Mapping, Integrated Gradients, and Deep Shapley Additive Explanations, to interpret and cross-validate our model's predictions with the explanations. Our analysis revealed that full-disk prediction of solar flares aligns with characteristics related to active regions (ARs). In particular, the key findings of this study are: (1) our deep learning models achieved an average TSS~0.51 and HSS~0.35, and the results further demonstrate a competent capability to predict near-limb solar flares and (2) the qualitative analysis of the model's explanation indicates that our model identifies and uses features associated with ARs in central and near-limb locations from full-disk magnetograms to make corresponding predictions. In other words, our models learn the shape and texture-based characteristics of flaring ARs even when they are at near-limb areas, which is a novel and critical capability that has significant implications for operational forecasting.

Keywords: Solar flares · Deep learning · Explainable AI

1 Introduction

Solar flares are temporary occurrences on the Sun that can generate abrupt and massive eruptions of electromagnetic radiation in its outermost atmosphere.

ⓒ The Author(s), under exclusive license to Springer Nature Switzerland AG 2023
G. De Francisci Morales et al. (Eds.): ECML PKDD 2023, LNAI 14175, pp. 72–89, 2023.
https://doi.org/10.1007/978-3-031-43430-3_5

These events happen when magnetic energy, accumulated in the solar atmosphere, is suddenly discharged, leading to a surge of energy that spans a wide range of wavelengths, from radio waves to X-rays. They are considered critical phenomena in space weather forecasting, and predicting solar flares is essential to understanding and preparing for their effects on Earth's infrastructure and technological systems. The National Oceanic and Atmospheric Administration (NOAA) classifies solar flares into five groups based on their peak X-ray flux level, namely A, B, C, M, and X, which represent the order of the flares from weakest to strongest [8] and are commonly referred to as NOAA/GOES flare classes, where GOES stands for Geostationary Operational Environmental Satellite. M- and X-class flares, which are rare but significant, are the strongest flares that can potentially cause near-Earth impacts, including disruptions in electricity supply chains, airline traffic, satellite communications, and radiation hazards to astronauts in space. This makes them of particular interest to researchers studying space weather. Therefore, developing better methods to predict solar flares is necessary to prepare for the effects of space weather on Earth.

Active regions (ARs) are typically characterized by strong magnetic fields that are concentrated in sunspots. These magnetic fields can become highly distorted and unstable, leading to the formation of plasma instabilities and the release of energy in the form of flares and other events [41]. Most operational flare forecasts target these regions of interest and issue predictions for individual ARs, which are the main initiators of space weather events. In order to produce a comprehensive forecast for the entire solar disk using an AR-based model, a heuristic function is used to combine the output flare probabilities ($P_{FL}(AR_i)$) for each active region (AR) [29]. The resulting probability, $P_{aggregated} = 1 - \prod_i [1 - P_{FL}(AR_i)]$, represents the likelihood of at least one AR producing a flare, assuming that the flaring events from different ARs are independent. However, there are two main issues with this approach for operational systems. Firstly, magnetic field measurements, which are the primary feature used by AR-based models, are subject to projection effects that distort measurements when ARs are closer to the limb. As a result, the aggregated full-disk flare probability is restricted to ARs in central locations, typically within $\pm30°$ [11], $\pm45°$ [20] to $\pm70°$ of the disk center [12]. Secondly, the heuristic function assumes that all ARs are equally important and independent of one another, which limits the accuracy of full-disk flare prediction probability. In contrast, full-disk models use complete magnetograms covering the entire solar disk, which are used to determine shape-based parameters such as size, directionality, borders, and inversion lines [13]. Although projection effects still exist in these images, full-disk models can learn from the near-limb areas and provide a complementary element to AR-based models by predicting flares that occur in these regions [27].

Machine learning and deep learning methods are currently being applied to predict solar flares, with experimental success and interdisciplinary collaboration from researchers in various fields [11,14,20,25–27,42]. Although these approaches have improved image classification and computer vision, they learn complex data representations, resulting in so-called black-box models. The decision-making process of these models is obscured, which is crucial for operational forecasting communities. To address this issue, several attribution methods, or post hoc analysis methods, have been developed to explain and interpret the decisions made by deep neural networks. These methods focus on analyzing trained models and do not contribute to the model's parameters during training. In this study, we develop a convolutional neural network (CNN) based full-disk model for predicting solar flares with a magnitude of $\geq$M-class flares. We evaluate and explain the model's performance using three attribution methods: Guided Gradient-weighted Class Activation Mapping (Guided Grad-CAM) [32], Integrated Gradients [39], and Deep Shapley Additive Explanations (Deep SHAP) [22]. Our analysis reveals that our model's decisions are based on the characteristics corresponding to ARs, and it successfully predicts flares appearing on near-limb regions of the Sun.

The rest of this paper is organized as follows. In Sect. 2, we present the related work on flare forecasting. In Sect. 3, we present our methodology with data preparation and model architecture. In Sect. 4, we provide a detailed description of all three attribution methods used as methods of explanation. In Sect. 5, we present our experimental evaluation. In Sect. 6, we discuss the interpretation of our models, and in Sect. 7, we present our conclusion and future work.

2   Related Work

Currently, there are four main types of methods in use for predicting solar flares, which include (i) human-based prediction techniques based on empirical observations [6,7] (ii) statistical approaches [18,19] (iii) numerical simulations based on physics-based models [15,17], and (iv) data-driven models which made use of machine·learning and deep learning techniques [2,4,11,20,27,28]. The application of machine learning in predicting solar flares has seen significant progress due to recent advances. In one such application of machine learning, a multilayer perceptron model based on machine learning was employed for predicting $\geq$C- and $\geq$M-class flares in [25] using 79 manually selected physical precursors derived from multi-modal solar observations.

Later, a CNN-based model was developed for predicting $\geq$C-, $\geq$M-, and $\geq$X-class flares using solar AR patches extracted from line-of-sight (LoS) magnetograms within $\pm 30°$ of the central meridian in [11], taking advantage of the increasing popularity of deep learning models. [20] also used a CNN-based model to predict $\geq$C- and $\geq$M-class flares within 24 h using AR patches located within $\pm 45°$ of the central meridian. To address the class imbalance issue, they employed undersampling and data augmentation techniques. However, while undersampling led to higher experimental accuracy scores, it often failed to deliver similar real-time performance [1]. It is worth noting that both of these models have limited operational capability as they are restricted to a small portion of the observable disk in central locations ($\pm 30°$ and $\pm 45°$).

In addition, in [30], a CNN-based hybrid model was introduced which combined GoogleLeNet [40] and DenseNet [10]. The model was trained using a large volume of data from both the Helioseismic and Magnetic Imager (HMI) instrument onboard Solar Dynamics Observatory (SDO) and magnetograms from the Michelson Doppler Imager (MDI) onboard the Solar and Heliospheric Observatory (SOHO). The aim of this model was to predict the occurrence of $\geq$C-class flares within the next 24 h. However, it is important to note that these two instruments are not currently cross-calibrated for forecasting purposes, which may result in spurious or incomplete patterns being identified. More recently, an AlexNet-based [16] full-disk flare prediction model was presented in [27]. The authors provided a black-box model, but training and validation were limited due to a lower temporal resolution.

To interpret a CNN-based solar flare prediction model trained with AR patches, [3] used an occlusion-based method, and [43] presented visual explanation methods using daily observations of solar full-disk LoS magnetograms at 00:00 UT. They applied Grad-CAM [32] and Guided Backpropagation [36] to explore the relationship between physical parameters and the occurrence of C-, M-, and X-class flares. However, these methods had limitations in predicting near-limb flares. Recently, [38] evaluated two additional attribution methods, DeepLIFT [34] and Integrated Gradients [39], for interpreting CNNs trained on AR patches from central locations, i.e., within $\pm 70°$ for predicting solar flares.

In this paper, a CNN-based model is presented for predicting $\geq$M-class flares, which was trained using full-disk LoS magnetogram images. The contributions of this study are threefold: (i) demonstrating an overall improvement in the performance of a full-disk solar flare prediction model, (ii) utilizing recent attribution methods to provide explanations of our model's decisions, and (iii) for the first time, demonstrating the capability of predicting flares in near-limb regions of the Sun, which are traditionally difficult to predict with AR-based models.

3   Data and Model

We used compressed images of full-disk LoS solar magnetograms obtained from the HMI/SDO available in near real-time publicly via Helioviewer[1] [23]. We sampled the magnetogram images every hour of the day, starting at 00:00 and ending at 23:00, from December 2010 to December 2018. We collected a total of 63,649 magnetogram images and labeled them using a 24-h prediction window based on the maximum peak X-ray flux (converted to NOAA/GOES flare classes) within the next 24 h, as illustrated in Fig. 1. To elaborate, if the maximum X-ray intensity of a flare was weaker than M (i.e., $< 10^{-5} W m^{-2}$), we labeled the observation as "No Flare" (NF: <M), and if it was $\geq$M, we labeled it as "Flare" (FL: $\geq$M). This resulted in 54,649 instances for the NF class and 9,000 instances for the FL class. The detailed class-wise distribution of our data is shown in Fig. 2(a). Finally, we created a non-chronological split of our data into four temporally non-overlapping tri-monthly partitions for our cross-validation experiments. We created this partitioning by dividing the data timeline from December 2010 to December 2018 into four partitions. Partition-1 contained data from January

---

[1] Helioviewer API V2: https://api.helioviewer.org/docs/v2/.

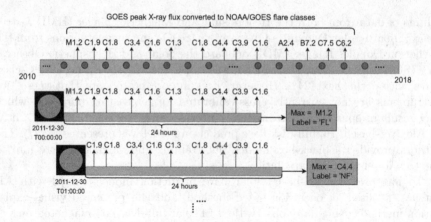

Fig. 1. A visual representation of the data labeling process using hourly observations of full-disk LoS magnetograms with a prediction window of 24 h. Here, 'FL' and 'NF' indicates Flare and No Flare for binary prediction (≥M-class flares). The gray-filled circles indicate hourly spaced timestamps for magnetogram instances.

to March, Partition-2 contained data from April to June, Partition-3 contained data from July to September, and Partition-4 contained data from October to December, as shown in Fig. 2(b). Due to the scarcity of ≥M-class flares, the overall distribution of the data is highly imbalanced, with FL:NF ∼1:6.

In our study, we employed transfer learning with a pre-trained VGG-16 model [35] for solar flare prediction. To use the pre-trained weights for our 1-channel input magnetogram images, we duplicated the channels twice, as the pre-trained model requires a 3-channel image for input. Additionally, we used the 7 × 7 adaptive average pooling after feature extraction using the convolutional layer and prior to the fully-connected layer to match the dimension of our 1-channel, 512×512 image. This ensures efficient utilization of the pre-trained weights, irrespective of the architecture of the VGG-16 model, which is designed to receive

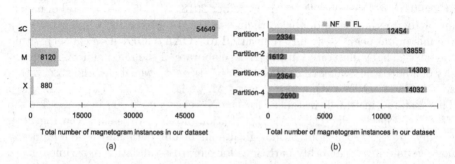

Fig. 2. (a) The total number of hourly sampled magnetograms images per flare classes. (b) Label distribution into four tri-monthly partitions for predicting ≥M-class flares.

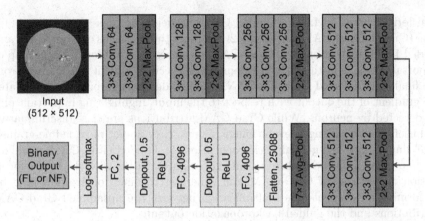

Fig. 3. The architecture of our full-disk solar flare prediction model.

224×224, 3-channel images. Our model comprises 13 convolutional layers, each followed by a rectified linear unit (ReLU) activation, five max pool layers, one average pool layer, and three fully connected layers, as illustrated in Fig. 3.

4   Attribution Methods

Deep learning models are often seen as black boxes due to their intricate data representations, making them difficult to understand, leading to issues of inconsistency in the discovered patterns [21]. The attribution methods are post hoc approaches for model interpretation that provides insights into the decision-making process of the trained CNN models without influencing the training process. These methods generate an attribution vector, or heat map, of the same size as the input, where each element in the vector represents the contribution of the corresponding input element to the model's decision. Attribution methods can be broadly classified into two main categories: perturbation-based and gradient-based [9]. Perturbation-based methods modify the parts of the input to create new inputs and compute the attribution by measuring the difference between the output of the original and modified inputs. However, this approach can lead to inconsistent interpretations due to the creation of Out-of-Distribution (OoD) data caused by random perturbations [31]. In contrast, gradient-based methods calculate the gradients of the output with respect to the extracted features or input using backpropagation, enabling attribution scores to be estimated more efficiently and robustly to input perturbations [24].

Therefore, in this study, we employed three recent gradient-based methods to evaluate our models due to their reliability and computational efficiency. Our primary objective is to provide a visual analysis of the decisions made by our model and identify the characteristics of magnetogram images that trigger specific decisions by cross-validating the generated explanations from all three methods, which can clarify the predictive output of the models and help with operational forecasting under critical conditions.

Guided Grad-CAM: The Guided Gradient-weighted Class Activation Mapping (Guided Grad-CAM) method [32] combines the strengths of Grad-CAM and guided backpropagation [36]. Grad-CAM produces a coarse localization map of important regions in the image by using class-specific gradient information from the final convolutional layer of a CNN, while guided backpropagation calculates the gradient of the output with respect to the input, highlighting important pixels detected by neurons. While Grad-CAM attributions are class-discriminative and useful for localizing relevant image regions, they do not provide fine-grained pixel importance like guided backpropagation [5]. Guided Grad-CAM combines the fine-grained pixel details from guided backpropagation with the coarse localization advantages of Grad-CAM and generates its final localization map by performing an element-wise multiplication between the upsampled Grad-CAM attributions and the guided backpropagation output.

Integrated Gradients: Integrated Gradients (IG) [39] is an attribution method that explains a model's output by analyzing its features. To be more specific, IG calculates the path integral of gradients along a straight line connecting the baseline feature to the input feature in question. A baseline reference is required for this method, which represents the absence of a feature in the original image and can be a zero vector or noise; we used a zero vector of the size of the input as a baseline for our computation. IG is preferred for its completeness property, which states that the sum of integrated gradients for all features equals the difference between the model's output with the given input and the baseline input values. This property allows for attributions to be assigned to each individual feature and, when added together, should yield the output value itself [37].

Deep SHAP: SHAP values, short for SHapley Additive exPlanations [22], utilize cooperative game theory [33] to enhance the transparency and interpretability of machine learning models. This method quantifies the contribution or importance of each feature on the model's prediction rather than evaluating the quality of the prediction itself. In the case of deep-learning models, Deep SHAP [22] improves upon the DeepLIFT algorithm [34] by estimating the conditional expectations of SHAP values using a set of background samples. For each input sample, the DeepLIFT attribution is computed with respect to each baseline, and the resulting attributions are averaged. This method assumes feature independence and explains the model's output through the additive composition of feature effects. Although it assumes a linear model for each explanation, the overall model across multiple explanations can be complex and non-linear. Similar to IG, Deep SHAP also satisfies the completeness property [37].

5   Experimental Evaluation

5.1   Experimental Settings

We trained a full-disk flare prediction model using Stochastic Gradient Descent (SGD) as an optimizer and Negative Log-Likelihood (NLL) as the objective function. To apply NLL loss, we used logarithmic-softmax activation on the raw logits from the output layer. Our model was initialized with pre-trained weights from the VGG-16 model [35]. We further trained the model for 50 epochs with a batch size of 64 using dynamic learning rates (initialized at 0.001 and halved every 5 epochs). To address the class imbalance issue, we used data augmentation and class weights in the loss function. Specifically, we applied three augmentation techniques (vertical flipping, horizontal flipping, and rotations of $+5°$ to $-5°$) during the training phase to explicitly augment the minority FL-class three times. However, this still left the dataset imbalanced, so we adjusted the class weights inversely proportional to the class frequencies after augmentations and penalized misclassifications made in the minority class. To improve the generalization of our model without introducing bias in the test set, we applied data augmentation exclusively during the training phase, and we opted for augmentation over oversampling and undersampling as the latter two may lead to overfitting of the model [2]. Finally, we conducted 4-fold cross-validation experiments using tri-monthly partitions to train our models.

We assess the overall performance of our models using two forecast skills scores: True Skill Statistics (TSS, in Eq. 1) and Heidke Skill Score (HSS, in Eq. 2), derived from the elements of confusion matrix: True Positive (TP), True Negative (TN), False Positive (FP), and False Negative (FN). In this context, FL and NF represent positive and negative classes respectively.

$$TSS = \frac{TP}{TP + FN} - \frac{FP}{FP + TN} \tag{1}$$

$$HSS = 2 \times \frac{TP \times TN - FN \times FP}{((P \times (FN + TN) + (TP + FP) \times N))} \tag{2}$$

where $N = TN + FP$ and $P = TP + FN$. TSS and HSS values range from -1 to 1, where 1 indicates all correct predictions, -1 represents all incorrect predictions, and 0 represents no skill. In contrast to TSS, HSS is an imbalance-aware metric, and it is common practice to use HSS for the solar flare prediction models due to the high class-imbalance ratio present in the datasets and for a balanced dataset, these metrics are equivalent as discussed in [1]. Lastly, we report the subclass and overall recall for flaring instances (M- and X-class), which is calculated as ($\frac{TP}{TP+FN}$), to demonstrate the prediction sensitivity. To reproduce this work, the source code and detailed experimental results can be accessed from our open source repository[2].

---

[2] explainFDvgg16: https://bitbucket.org/gsudmlab/explainfdvgg16/src/main/.

5.2   Evaluation

We performed 4-fold cross-validation using the tri-monthly dataset for evaluating our models. Our models have on average TSS~0.51 and HSS~0.35, which improves over the performance of [27] by ~4% in terms of TSS (reported ~0.47) and competing results in terms of HSS (reported ~0.35). In addition, we evaluate our results for correctly predicted and missed flare counts for class-specific flares (X-class and M-class) in central locations (within ±70°) and near-limb locations (beyond ±70°) of the Sun as shown in Table 1. We observe that our models made correct predictions for ~89% of the X-class flares and ~77% of the M-class flares in central locations. Similarly, our models show a compelling performance for flares appearing on near-limb locations of the Sun, where ~77% of the X-class and ~52% of the M-class flares are predicted correctly. This is important because, to our knowledge, the prediction of near-limb flares is often overlooked. More false positives in M-class are expected because of the model's inability to distinguish bordering class [C4+ to C9.9] flares from ≥M-class flares, which we have observed empirically in our prior work [28] as well. Overall, we observed that ~86% and ~70% of the X-class and M-class flares, respectively, are predicted correctly by our models.

We also quantitatively and qualitatively evaluated our models' effectiveness by spatially analyzing their performance with respect to the locations of M- and X-class flares responsible for the labels. To conduct our analysis, we have spatially binned the responsible flares (maximum X-ray flux within the next 24 h) and analyzed whether these instances were correctly (TP) or incorrectly predicted (FN). For this, we used the predictions of our models in the validation set from the 4-fold cross-validation experiments. Here, each bin represents a 5° by 5° spatial cell in Heliographic Stonyhurst (HGS) coordinate system (i.e., latitude and longitude). For each subgroup, represented in a spatial cell, we calculate the recall for M-class, X-class, and M- and X-class flares, separately to assess the models' sensitivity at a fine-grained level. The heatmaps demonstrating the spatial distribution of recall scores of our models can be seen in Fig. 4. This allows us to pinpoint the locations where our models were more effective in making accurate predictions and vice versa. We observed that our models demonstrated reasonable performance overall, particularly for X-class flares, in both near-limb

Table 1. Counts of correctly (TP) and incorrectly (FN) classified X- and M-class flares in central ($|longitude| \leq \pm 70°$) and near-limb locations. The recall across different location groups is also presented. Counts are aggregated across folds.

Flare-Class	Within ±70°			Beyond ±70°		
	TP	FN	Recall	TP	FN	Recall
X-Class	597	71	0.89	164	48	0.77
M-Class	4,464	1,366	0.77	1,197	1,093	0.52
Total (X&M)	5,061	1,437	0.78	1,361	1,141	0.54

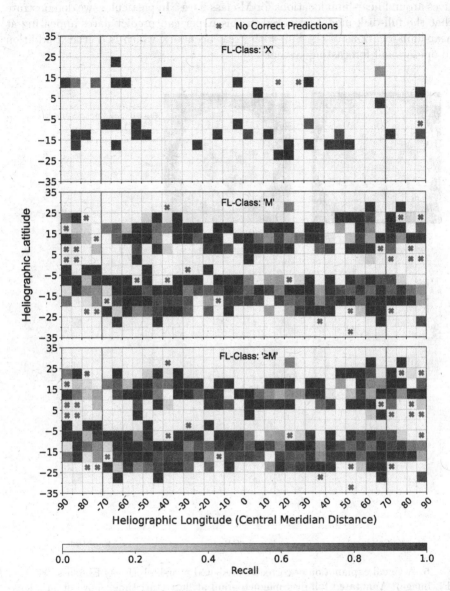

Fig. 4. A heat map showcasing recall for individual FL-Class (X- and M-class flares) and when combined (≥M-class flares) binned into 5° × 5° flare locations used as the label. The flare events beyond ±70° longitude (separated by a vertical red line) represent near-limb events. Note: Red cross in white grids represents locations with zero correct predictions while white cells without red cross represent unavailable instances. (Color figure online)

and central locations. However, we also observed a higher number of false negatives around near-limb locations for M-class flares. In particular, we demonstrate that the full-disk model proposed in this paper can predict flares appearing at near-limb locations of the Sun with great accuracy, which is a crucial addition to operational forecasting systems.

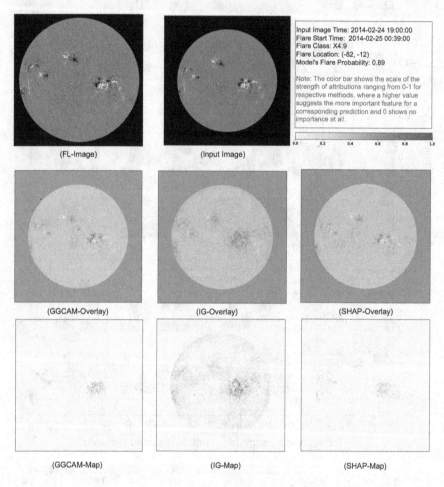

Fig. 5. A visual explanation of correctly predicted near-limb (East) FL-class instance. (FL-Image): Annotated full-disk magnetogram at flare start time, showing flare location (green flag) and NOAA ARs (red flags). (Input Image): Actual magnetogram from the dataset. Overlays (GGCAM, IG, SHAP) depict the input image overlayed with attributions, and Maps (GGCAM, IG, SHAP) showcase the attribution maps obtained from Guided Grad-CAM, Integrated Gradients, and Deep SHAP, respectively. (Color figure online)

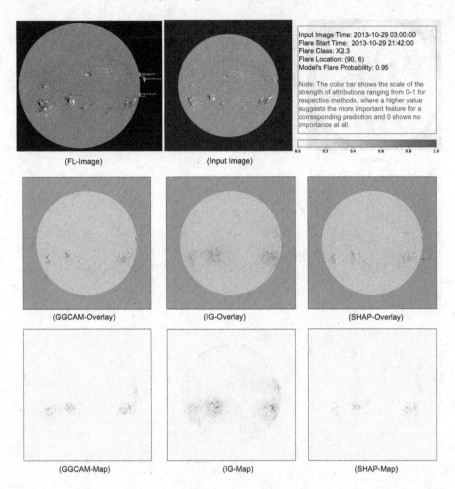

Fig. 6. A visual explanation of incorrectly predicted NF-class instance. (FL-Image): Annotated full-disk magnetogram at flare start time, showing flare location (green flag) and NOAA ARs (red flags). (Input Image): Actual magnetogram from the dataset. Overlays (GGCAM, IG, SHAP) depict the input image overlayed with attributions, and Maps (GGCAM, IG, SHAP)) showcase the attribution maps obtained from Guided Grad-CAM, Integrated Gradients, and Deep SHAP, respectively. (Color figure online)

6   Discussion

In this section, we interpret the visual explanations generated using the attribution methods mentioned earlier for correctly predicted near-limb flares and the model's high confidence in an incorrect prediction. As the major focus of this study is on the near-limb flares, we interpret the predictions of our model for an east-limb X4.9-class (note that East and West are reversed in solar coordinates) flare observed on 2014-02-25 at 00:39:00 UTC with a visual explanation generated using all three attribution methods. For this, we used an input

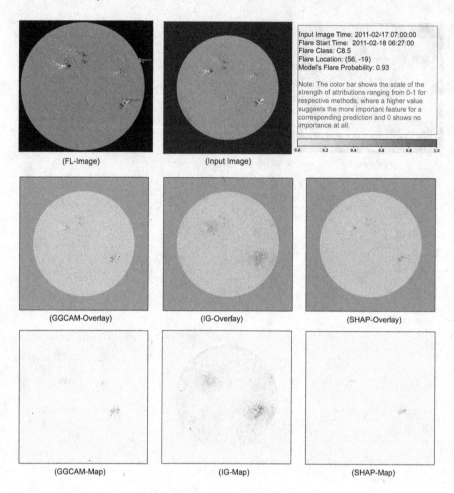

Fig. 7. A visual explanation of correctly predicted near-limb (West) FL-class instance. (FL-Image): Annotated full-disk magnetogram at flare start time, showing flare location (green flag) and NOAA ARs (red flags). (Input Image): Actual magnetogram from the dataset. Overlays (GGCAM, IG, SHAP) depict the input image overlayed with attributions, and Maps (GGCAM, IG, SHAP) showcase the attribution maps obtained from Guided Grad-CAM, Integrated Gradients, and Deep SHAP, respectively. (Color figure online)

image at 2014-02-24 19:00:00 UTC ($\sim$6 h prior to the flare event), where the sunspot for the corresponding flare becomes visible in the magnetogram image. We observed while all three methods highlight features corresponding to an AR in the magnetogram, Guided Grad-CAM and Deep SHAP provide finer details by suppressing noise compared to IG as shown in Fig. 5. Furthermore, the visualization of attribution maps suggests that for this particular prediction, although barely visible, the region responsible for the flare event is considered important and hence contributes to the consequent decision. The explanation shows that as soon as a region becomes visible, the pixels covering the AR on the east-limb are activated. Similarly, we analyze another case of correctly predicted near-limb flare (West-limb) of the Sun. For this, we provide a case of X2.3-class flare observed on 2013-10-29T21:42:00 UTC where we used an input image at 2013-10-29T03:00:00 UTC (~19 h prior to the flare event) shown in Fig. 6. We observed that the model focuses on specific ARs including the relatively smaller AR on the west limb, even though other ARs are present in the magnetogram image. This shows that our models are capable of identifying the relevant AR even when there is a severe projection effect.

Similarly, to analyze a case of false positive, we present an example of a C8.5 flare observed on 2011-02-18 at 06:27:00 UTC, and to explain the result, we used an input magnetogram instance at 2014-02-17 07:00:00 UTC (~23.5 h prior to the event). We observed that the model's flaring probability for this particular instance is about 0.93. Therefore, we seek a visual explanation of this prediction using all three interpretation methods. Similar to the observations from our positive prediction, the visualization rendered using Guided Grad-CAM and Deep SHAP provides smoothed details and reveals that out of three ARs present in the magnetogram, only two of them are activated while the AR on the west-limb is not considered important for this prediction as shown in Fig. 7. Although an incorrect prediction, the visual explanation shows that the model's decision is based on an AR which is, in fact, responsible for the eventual C8.5 flare event. This incorrect prediction can be attributed to the interference of these bordering class flares, which is problematic for binary flare prediction models.

7   Conclusion and Future Work

In this paper, we employed three recent gradient-based attribution methods to interpret the predictions made by our binary flare prediction model based on VGG-16, which was trained to predict ≥M-class flares. We addressed the issue of flares occurring in near-limb regions of the Sun, which has been widely ignored, and our model demonstrated competent performance for such events. Additionally, we assessed the model's predictions with visual explanations, indicating that the decisions were primarily based on characteristics related to ARs in the magnetogram instance. Despite the model's enhanced ability, it still suffers from a high false positive rate due to high C-class flares. In an effort to address this problem, we plan to examine the unique features of each flare class to create a more effective method for segregating these classes based on background flux and generate a new set of labels that better handle border class flares. Moreover, our models currently only examine spatial patterns in our data, but we intend to broaden this work to include spatiotemporal models to improve performance.

Acknowledgements. This work is supported in part under two NSF awards #2104004 and #1931555, jointly by the Office of Advanced Cyberinfrastructure within the Directorate for Computer and Information Science and Engineering, the Division of Astronomical Sciences within the Directorate for Mathematical and Physical Sciences, and the Solar Terrestrial Physics Program and the Division of Integrative and Collaborative Education and Research within the Directorate for Geosciences. This work is also partially supported by the National Aeronautics and Space Administration (NASA) grant award #80NSSC22K0272.

Ethical Statement

Space weather forecasting research raises several ethical implications that must be considered. It is important to note that the data used for the full-disk deep learning model for solar flare prediction is publicly available as a courtesy of NASA/SDO and the AIA, EVE, and HMI science teams – and not subject to data privacy and security concerns. The use of SDO images for non-commercial purposes and public education and information efforts is strongly encouraged and requires no expressed authorization. However, it is still essential to consider the ethical implications associated with developing and using a full-disk deep learning model for solar flare prediction, particularly in terms of fairness, interpretability, and transparency. It is crucial to ensure that the model is developed and used ethically and responsibly to avoid any potential biases or negative impacts on individuals or communities. Moreover, post hoc analysis for full-disk deep learning models for solar flare prediction should avoid giving wrongful assumptions of causality and false trust. While these models may have robust and novel forecast skills, it is crucial to understand the scarcity of extreme solar events and the skill scores used to assess model performance. We note that these models are not perfect and have limitations that should be considered when interpreting their predictions. Therefore, it is important to use these models with caution and to consider multiple sources of information when making decisions, especially when in operations, related to space weather events. By being transparent about the limitations and uncertainties associated with these models, we can ensure that they are used ethically and responsibly to mitigate any potential harm to individuals or communities.

Furthermore, the impact of space weather events can range from minor disruptions to significant damage to critical infrastructure, such as power grids, communication systems, and navigation systems, with the potential to cause significant economic losses. Therefore, it is crucial to ensure public safety, particularly for astronauts and airline crew members, by providing information about potential dangers associated with space weather events. Finally, it is imperative to ensure that space weather forecasting research is used for peaceful purposes, i.e., early detection and in part avoiding vulnerabilities that may be caused by extreme space weather events.

References

1. Ahmadzadeh, A., Aydin, B., Georgoulis, M., Kempton, D., Mahajan, S., Angryk, R.: How to train your flare prediction model: revisiting robust sampling of rare events. Astrophys. J. Suppl. Ser. **254**(2), 23 (2021)
2. Ahmadzadeh, A., et al.: Challenges with extreme class-imbalance and temporal coherence: a study on solar flare data. In: 2019 IEEE International Conference on Big Data. IEEE (2019)
3. Bhattacharjee, S., Alshehhi, R., Dhuri, D.B., Hanasoge, S.M.: Supervised convolutional neural networks for classification of flaring and nonflaring active regions using line-of-sight magnetograms. Astrophys. J. **898**(2), 98 (2020)
4. Bobra, M.G., Couvidat, S.: Solar flare prediction using SDO/HMI vector magnetic field data with a machine-learning algorithm. Astrophys. J. **798**(2), 135 (2015)
5. Chattopadhay, A., Sarkar, A., Howlader, P., Balasubramanian, V.N.: Grad-CAM++: generalized gradient-based visual explanations for deep convolutional networks. In: Winter Conference on Applications of Computer Vision. IEEE (2018)
6. Crown, M.D.: Validation of the NOAA space weather prediction center's solar flare forecasting look-up table and forecaster-issued probabilities. Space Weather **10**(6) (2012)
7. Devos, A., Verbeeck, C., Robbrecht, E.: Verification of space weather forecasting at the regional warning center in Belgium. J. Space Weather. Space Clim. **4**, A29 (2014)
8. Fletcher, L., et al.: An observational overview of solar flares. Space Sci. Rev. **159**(1–4), 19–106 (2011)
9. Holzinger, A., Saranti, A., Molnar, C., Biecek, P., Samek, W.: Explainable AI methods - a brief overview. In: Holzinger, A., Goebel, R., Fong, R., Moon, T., Müller, KR., Samek, W. (eds.) xxAI - Beyond Explainable AI. LNCS, vol. 13200, pp. 13–38. Springer, Cham (2022). https://doi.org/10.1007/978-3-031-04083-2_2
10. Huang, G., Liu, Z., Maaten, L., Weinberger, K.: Densely connected convolutional networks. In: Conference on Computer Vision and Pattern Recognition. IEEE, July 2017
11. Huang, X., Wang, H., Xu, L., Liu, J., Li, R., Dai, X.: Deep learning based solar flare forecasting model. Astrophys. J. **856**(1), 7 (2018)
12. Ji, A., Aydin, B., Georgoulis, M.K., Angryk, R.: All-clear flare prediction using interval-based time series classifiers. In: 2021 IEEE International Conference on Big Data, pp. 4218–4225. IEEE, December 2020
13. Ji, A., et al.: A systematic magnetic polarity inversion line data set from SDO/HMI magnetograms. Astrophys. J. Suppl. Ser. **265**(1), 28 (2023)
14. Ji, A., Wen, J., Angryk, R., Aydin, B.: Solar flare forecasting with deep learning-based time series classifiers. In: 2022 26th International Conference on Pattern Recognition (ICPR). IEEE, August 2022
15. Korsós, M.B., et al.: Solar flare prediction using magnetic field diagnostics above the photosphere. Astrophys. J. **896**(2), 119 (2020)
16. Krizhevsky, A.: One weird trick for parallelizing convolutional neural networks (2014)
17. Kusano, K., Iju, T., Bamba, Y., Inoue, S.: A physics-based method that can predict imminent large solar flares. Science **369**(6503), 587–591 (2020)
18. Lee, K., Moon, Y.J., Lee, J.Y., Lee, K.S., Na, H.: Solar flare occurrence rate and probability in terms of the sunspot classification supplemented with sunspot area and its changes. Solar Phys. **281**(2), 639–650 (2012)

19. Leka, K., Barnes, G., Wagner, E.: The NWRA classification infrastructure: description and extension to the discriminant analysis flare forecasting system (DAFFS). J. Space Weather Space Clim. **8**, A25 (2018)

20. Li, X., Zheng, Y., Wang, X., Wang, L.: Predicting solar flares using a novel deep convolutional neural network. Astrophys. J. **891**(1), 10 (2020)

21. Linardatos, P., Papastefanopoulos, V., Kotsiantis, S.: Explainable AI: a review of machine learning interpretability methods. Entropy **23**(1), 18 (2021)

22. Lundberg, S.M., Lee, S.I.: A unified approach to interpreting model predictions. In: Proceedings of the 31st International Conference on Neural Information Processing Systems, NIPS 2017, pp. 4768–4777. Curran Associates Inc., Red Hook (2017)

23. Muller, D., et al.: JHelioviewer: visualizing large sets of solar images using JPEG 2000. Comput. Sci. Eng. **11**(5), 38–47 (2009)

24. Nielsen, I.E., Dera, D., Rasool, G., Ramachandran, R.P., Bouaynaya, N.C.: Robust explainability: a tutorial on gradient-based attribution methods for deep neural networks. IEEE Signal Process. Mag. **39**(4), 73–84 (2022)

25. Nishizuka, N., Sugiura, K., Kubo, Y., Den, M., Ishii, M.: Deep flare net (DeFN) model for solar flare prediction. Astrophys. J. **858**(2), 113 (2018)

26. Nishizuka, N., Sugiura, K., Kubo, Y., Den, M., Watari, S., Ishii, M.: Solar flare prediction model with three machine-learning algorithms using ultraviolet brightening and vector magnetograms. Astrophys. J. **835**(2), 156 (2017)

27. Pandey, C., Angryk, R., Aydin, B.: Solar flare forecasting with deep neural networks using compressed full-disk HMI magnetograms. In: 2021 IEEE International Conference on Big Data (Big Data), pp. 1725–1730. IEEE, December 2021

28. Pandey, C., Angryk, R.A., Aydin, B.: Deep neural networks based solar flare prediction using compressed full-disk line-of-sight magnetograms. In: Lossio-Ventura, J.A., et al. (eds.) Information Management and Big Data. CCIS, vol. 1577, pp. 380–396. Springer, Cham (2022). https://doi.org/10.1007/978-3-031-04447-2_26

29. Pandey, C., Ji, A., Angryk, R., Georgoulis, M., Aydin, B.: Towards coupling full-disk and active region-based flare prediction for operational space weather forecasting. Front. Astron. Space Sci. **9**, 897301 (2022)

30. Park, E., et al.: Application of the deep convolutional neural network to the forecast of solar flare occurrence using full-disk solar magnetograms. Astrophys. J. **869**(2), 91 (2018)

31. Qiu, L., et al.: Generating perturbation-based explanations with robustness to out-of-distribution data. In: Proceedings of the ACM Web Conference 2022. ACM, April 2022

32. Selvaraju, R.R., Cogswell, M., Das, A., Vedantam, R., Parikh, D., Batra, D.: Grad-CAM: visual explanations from deep networks via gradient-based localization. In: 2017 IEEE International Conference on Computer Vision (ICCV). IEEE, October 2017

33. Shapley, L.: A Value for N-Person Games. RAND Corporation (1952)

34. Shrikumar, A., Greenside, P., Kundaje, A.: Learning important features through propagating activation differences (2019)

35. Simonyan, K., Zisserman, A.: Very deep convolutional networks for large-scale image recognition (2014)

36. Springenberg, J.T., Dosovitskiy, A., Brox, T., Riedmiller, M.: Striving for simplicity: the all convolutional net (2014)

37. Sturmfels, P., Lundberg, S., Lee, S.I.: Visualizing the impact of feature attribution baselines. Distill **5**(1), e22 (2020)

38. Sun, Z., et al.: Predicting solar flares using CNN and LSTM on two solar cycles of active region data. Astrophys. J. **931**(2), 163 (2022)

39. Sundararajan, M., Taly, A., Yan, Q.: Axiomatic attribution for deep networks (2017)
40. Szegedy, C., et al.: Going deeper with convolutions. In: 2015 IEEE Conference on Computer Vision and Pattern Recognition (CVPR). IEEE, June 2015
41. Toriumi, S., Wang, H.: Flare-productive active regions. Living Rev. Sol. Phys. **16**(1), 3 (2019)
42. Whitman, K., et al.: Review of solar energetic particle models. Advances in Space Research, August 2022
43. Yi, K., Moon, Y., Lim, D., Park, E., Lee, H.: Visual explanation of a deep learning solar flare forecast model and its relationship to physical parameters. Astrophys. J. **910**(1), 8 (2021)

Deep Spatiotemporal Clustering: A Temporal Clustering Approach for Multi-dimensional Climate Data

Omar Faruque[1] , Francis Ndikum Nji[1], Mostafa Cham[1],
Rohan Mandar Salvi[1], Xue Zheng[2], and Jianwu Wang[1](✉)

[1] Department of Information Systems, University of Maryland, Baltimore County,
Baltimore, MD, USA
{omarfaruque,fnji1,mcham2,rsalvi2,jianwu}@umbc.edu
[2] Climate Science Section, Lawrence Livermore National Laboratory,
Livermore, CA, USA
zheng7@llnl.gov
https://bdal.umbc.edu

Abstract. Clustering high-dimensional spatiotemporal data using an unsupervised approach is a challenging problem for many data-driven applications. Existing state-of-the-art methods for unsupervised clustering use different similarity and distance functions but focus on either spatial or temporal features of the data. Concentrating on joint deep representation learning of spatial and temporal features, we propose Deep Spatiotemporal Clustering (DSC), a novel algorithm for the temporal clustering of high-dimensional spatiotemporal data using an unsupervised deep learning method. Inspired by the U-net architecture, DSC utilizes an autoencoder integrating CNN-RNN layers to learn latent representations of the spatiotemporal data. DSC also includes a unique layer for cluster assignment on latent representations that uses the Student's t-distribution. By optimizing the clustering loss and data reconstruction loss simultaneously, the algorithm gradually improves clustering assignments and the nonlinear mapping between low-dimensional latent feature space and high-dimensional original data space. A multivariate spatiotemporal climate dataset is used to evaluate the efficacy of the proposed method. Our extensive experiments show our approach outperforms both conventional and deep learning-based unsupervised clustering algorithms. Additionally, we compared the proposed model with its various variants (CNN encoder, CNN autoencoder, CNN-RNN encoder, CNN-RNN autoencoder, etc.) to get insight into using both the CNN and RNN layers in the autoencoder, and our proposed technique outperforms these variants in terms of clustering results.

Keywords: Temporal clustering · Multivariate spatiotemporal climate data · Deep neural network · U-net

© The Author(s), under exclusive license to Springer Nature Switzerland AG 2023
G. De Francisci Morales et al. (Eds.): ECML PKDD 2023, LNAI 14175, pp. 90–105, 2023.
https://doi.org/10.1007/978-3-031-43430-3_6

1   Introduction

Spatiotemporal data is commonly available in many disciplines such as Earth sciences, atmospheric science, and environmental science. Such data is often generated by monitoring a certain area over a period of time, which results in datasets in four dimensions (4D): time, longitude, latitude, and measured variables such as temperature and humidity. One important way to study such spatiotemporal data is to categorize the records into smaller groups by conducting unsupervised data clustering along the temporal dimension.

There are several challenges in clustering such 4D spatiotemporal data. First, most traditional clustering algorithms like k-means [20] only work on 2D tabular data and face challenges to work with 4D spatiotemporal data. Converting 4D spatiotemporal data directly into 2D tabular data will not only end up with very high dimensional data but also lose spatial and temporal patterns in the original data. Second, common dimension reduction approaches such as PCA [12] can reduce data dimensionality before applying clustering algorithms, but such efforts [2,12] fail to preserve the dataset's nonlinear relationship, which leads to subpar clustering accuracy. Third, recently developed deep learning-based clustering algorithms [6,10,16,24] are able to learn nonlinear characteristics of the dataset. But these techniques only focused on the spatial or temporal features of the dataset, not spatiotemporal features jointly.

To address the above challenges of high-dimensional spatiotemporal clustering, we propose a novel spatiotemporal autoencoder model drawing inspiration from the recent success of the U-net architecture [15] in representation learning. Our model is applied to a popular climate data called ECMWF ERA5 global reanalysis product [3] to evaluate its performance. The proposed model nonlinearly maps the input dataset with the lower dimensional hidden feature space. To make this latent feature generation more robust, we evaluated both the spatial and temporal properties of the dataset by combining CNN and LSTM layers in the encoder module. A custom clustering layer is applied to the latent features to generate clustering results. The clustering layer uses the inherent logic of the Student's t-distribution and iteratively improves the result. At the same time, the decoder module adjusts its weights to reduce the disparity between the input and reconstructed data while learning to reconstruct the high-dimensional input data from lower-dimensional latent features. From our experimental analysis, it is evident that the proposed model achieved significant improvement in cluster accuracy and holds the ability to capture the generic properties of different time series. In summary, our contributions are i) end-to-end learning of both spatial and temporal features in the same model, ii) significant improvement in clustering accuracy, and iii) iterative joint optimization of latent features and clustering assignment. Our implementation source code can be accessed at the Big Data Analytics Lab GitHub repository: https://github.com/big-data-lab-umbc/multivariate-weather-data-clustering/tree/DSC.

The remainder of the paper is structured as follows. Section 2 explains the background and definition of our clustering task. State-of-the-art related works are summarized in Sect. 3. Section 4 gives a detailed description of the proposed procedure. The experimental details of the proposed model are provided in Sect. 5 along with the results and an ablation study of the proposed model. Finally, we conclude and summarize in Sect. 6.

2   Background and Problem Definition

2.1   Clustering Multi-dimensional Climate Data

Earth's climate system is a highly complicated and interconnected global system formed with a large number of dynamic components such as global temperature, ocean temperature, arctic sea ice, precipitation, wind pattern, pressure, aerosol, cloud, etc. Climate change is one of the most threatening issues because it has diverse effects on the global ecosystem and will make the weather more hazardous [20]. Due to its high importance, many researchers focused on studying the interactions of constituent components of the climate system and the changes caused by each other. In Earth's climate system, one of the significant components is the air-sea-cloud and their inherent interactions. The dynamic, thermodynamic, and anthropogenic processes that connect the atmosphere and oceans through clouds are referred to as air-sea-cloud interaction. Specifically, marine boundary layer clouds play an important role in air-sea-cloud interactions, as it has a strong influence to lower the sea surface and earth's temperature, and also the microphysical and dynamical characteristics of marine boundary layer clouds are sensitive to the sea surface situation [21].

Observations of air-sea-cloud interactions show the tendency of high variability for a wider range of temporal and spatial scales. This is caused by different interacting atmospheric components that fuse various uncertainties in the Earth system. To untangle the effect of different components on atmospheric interactions as a function of synoptic-scale (approximately 1000 km) changes requires quantification of their interaction patterns [14]. To achieve this goal, it is required to study different atmospheric properties of synoptic-scale regions covering a wide range of longitude and latitude over a longer period. Studying this large volume of spatial and temporal data is very complex and time-consuming for domain experts. The inherent complexity of atmospheric system study can be reduced by grouping environmental contexts based on spatial and temporal similarity, as each sub-group will demonstrate a higher small-scale perturbation and will minimize the boundary of the global atmospheric effects.

To study the atmospheric properties over a synaptic regime we need to consider the measurements of different variables over a range of longitude and latitude. To untangle the interaction and relative effect of these components we need to quantify these atmospheric properties for a longer period. Hence, the problem size can be represented by a dataset of four dimensions: time, longitude, latitude, and variables. We can consider the task as an unsupervised spatiotemporal clustering problem of the multidimensional data, as the observations contain both the location and time-varying features. Also, the absence of the labeled dataset makes the problem an unsupervised learning task.

2.2   Problem Definition

The goal of the proposed model is to assign observation records of the dataset into different clusters based on the latent spatial and temporal features learned by the deep autoencoder model. Let us assume, n atmospheric variables (v_i) are measured over a grid region covering L longitudes and W latitudes and stored in a vector $V = \{v_1, v_2, v_3, ..., v_n\}$. So for each time step, every grid location has n values for all variables. Also, these variables are measured for T different time steps, $V_i = \{v_1, v_2, v_3, ..., v_n\}$, $i \in \{1, ..., T\}$.

Input

$$Dataset = \{V_1, V_2, V_3, ..., V_T\}$$

$$V_i = \left\{ \begin{bmatrix} v_1(1,1) & v_1(1,2) & \cdots & v_1(1,W) \\ v_1(2,1) & v_1(2,2) & \cdots & v_1(2,W) \\ \vdots & \vdots & \ddots & \vdots \\ v_1(L,1) & v_1(L,2) & \cdots & v_1(L,W) \end{bmatrix} \begin{bmatrix} v_2(1,1) & v_2(1,2) & \cdots & v_2(1,W) \\ v_2(2,1) & v_2(2,2) & \cdots & v_2(2,W) \\ \vdots & \vdots & \ddots & \vdots \\ v_2(L,1) & v_2(L,2) & \cdots & v_2(L,W) \end{bmatrix} \vdots \begin{bmatrix} v_n(1,1) & v_n(1,2) & \cdots & v_n(1,W) \\ v_n(2,1) & v_n(2,2) & \cdots & v_n(2,W) \\ \vdots & \vdots & \ddots & \vdots \\ v_n(L,1) & v_n(L,2) & \cdots & v_n(L,W) \end{bmatrix} \right\}$$

Here, V_i represents one observation, v means one variable of an observation, $i \in \{1, ..., T\}$, T is the number of time steps, n is the number of atmospheric variables, L is the longitude and W is the latitude.

Output

In particular, the proposed model will categorize the dataset $\{V_1, V_2, V_3, ..., V_T\}$ into k clusters: C_1, C_2, C_3, ..., C_k, where $k < T$, so that the members of a cluster are more similar to each other and dissimilar from the members of all other clusters. Formally:

$$C_1 = \{V_{C_1}^1, V_{C_1}^2, ..., V_{C_1}^{n_1}\}, C_2 = \{V_{C_2}^1, V_{C_2}^2, ..., V_{C_2}^{n_2}\}, ..., C_k = \{V_{C_k}^1, V_{C_k}^2, ..., V_{C_k}^{n_k}\}$$

$$V_{C_j}^i \in V, i \in \{1, ..., n_j\}, j \in \{1, ..., k\}$$

$n_j=$ number of observations of cluster j.

$$\bigcup_{j=1}^{k} C_j = V \text{ and } C_j \cap C_l = \varnothing$$

Here, $j \neq l$ and $(j, l) \in \{1, ..., k\}$.

3   Related Works

Traditional Clustering Algorithms. Unsupervised clustering is an extensively explored branch of machine learning. A large number of clustering algorithms have been developed by focusing on feature selection, similarity measure, grouping process, and cluster validation strategies. The k-means algorithm [13] is one of the most popular clustering methods. This method is very effective for a large number of unsupervised clustering problems and computationally very efficient. However, the k-means algorithm performs better for low dimensional data than for high dimensional data. Density-based spatial clustering of applications with noise (DBSCAN) [5] is another popular unsupervised clustering technique that works mainly focusing on the number of neighboring data points. This method can work with any shape of the cluster and it automatically identifies a suitable number of clusters for the dataset. But the DBSCAN performs poorly if the dataset's density varies by a large margin. The agglomerative hierarchical clustering technique [4] is a bottom-up approach, which initially considers each data point as a separate cluster and iteratively reduces the number of clusters by aggregating two similar clusters into a new cluster until the desired number of clusters is found. The time and space complexity of this method is high and also does not perform well for high-dimensional datasets. To apply the k-means, DBSCAN, and hierarchical clustering algorithms on a high dimensional dataset, several variations were proposed in [23,25] using dimensionality reduction. But these dimensionality reduction methods create a linear mapping between the input data space to the low-dimensional embeddings and fail to address nonlinear complex data.

Deep Learning based Clustering. In recent years, deep learning models have been applied dominantly to learn the nonlinear and complex patterns of the input data [1,9,17]. Deep Embedded Clustering (DEC) [24] is an unsupervised clustering method that maps the input data into a low-dimensional embedding space using a deep neural network. Starting with an initial representation and cluster assignment DEC iteratively optimizes both by using Kullback-Leibler (KL) divergence loss. Although DEC generates better classification results but loses the spatial details of the image. To solve this problem the Clustering-Augmented Segmentation (CAS) [6] model proposed an autoencoder-based representation learning method using U-net architecture. CAS model generates the land segmentation using clustering loss and data reconstruction loss. Deep Temporal Clustering Representation (DTCR) [10] is a novel unsupervised clustering model for time series data that used the bidirectional recurrent neural network to learn temporal representation. In this model data reconstruction and k-means loss are combined into the seq2seq model to generate cluster-specific representations. To cluster the time series data, the Deep Temporal Clustering (DTC) [16] model utilizes an autoencoder to reduce the input data in a lower dimensional space and then optimizes the clustering objective. The DTC model used temporal reconstruction loss and clustering loss to optimize the model parameters and clustering results. The authors in [7] also used autoencoder to generate latent representations from sentence embeddings of short text and then performed clustering using latent features. One limitation of these models is that they either concentrate on temporal features or pixel-level similarities. So these approaches lack a general methodology for learning effective latent representation and unsupervised clustering of spatiotemporal data.

4 Proposed Methodology

In this paper, we propose a novel autoencoder model for clustering unlabeled spatiotemporal datasets. To capture the hidden spatial and sequential features from the dataset, we integrate the Convolution Neural Network (CNN) and Long Short Term Memory (LSTM) in the model. The proposed model is illustrated in Fig. 1. The encoder module transforms the input data into a latent representation ignoring any cluster-specific features. Then, using that latent representation, the decoder reconstructs the input data. The clustering objective is also incorporated into the model to train it for better outcomes in representation learning and clustering.

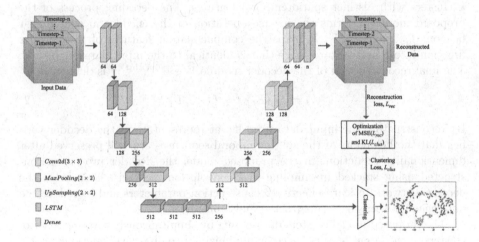

Fig. 1. Illustration of the proposed deep spatiotemporal clustering model architecture (best viewed in color). The number at the bottom of each block means the number of feature layers. (Color figure online)

4.1 Overview of Our Deep Spatiotemporal Clustering (DSC) Approach

Given the spatiotemporal dataset V such that $V_t \in \mathbb{R}^{lon \times lat \times n}$, where n is the number of the time series variables and $t \in \{1, ..., T\}$. To sub-group T timesteps into $k < T$ clusters the encoder module transforms the input data V into a high-level latent representation E with reduced data dimension. The mapping from the input data space to the latent feature space is a nonlinear function $f_{en} := V \rightarrow E$. Here $E \in \mathbb{R}^m$ is an m-dimensional high-level representation of all the variables at each timestep.

$$E_t = f_{en}(V_t), t = \{1, ..., T\} \tag{1}$$

For unsupervised clustering of the high dimensional data, it is very crucial to learn a latent representation that well represents the input data. To achieve this requirement in the nonlinear encoder, we used 2D convolution, which extracts the hidden spatial features from the dataset. To extract latent features at different scales and reduce the dimensionality, we used several stacks of 2D convolution and max pooling layers. For further processing, dimensionality reduction is essential to prevent extremely long sequences, which might result in weak performance, and to overcome the curse of dimensionality. The activations of the convolution layers are then applied to the LSTM layers to learn temporal changes. LSTM layers cast the latent representation into a more compact space in the temporal direction. Finally, using the latent features of the encoder model, the clustering layer assigns the set of data points V_i, $i = \{1, ..., T\}$, into k clusters with distinct spatiotemporal features. The decoding process of the proposed model performs the inverse operation of the encoder in a nonlinear fashion, $f_{de} := E \rightarrow \widehat{V}$. It maps the compact latent features of the encoder function into a new feature space that is identical to the input dataset, $\widehat{V} \approx V$. The final reconstruction of the decoder module $\widehat{V} \in \mathbb{R}^{lon \times lat \times n}$ is defined as

$$\widehat{V}_t = f_{dc}(E_t), t = \{1, ..., T\} \tag{2}$$

By reconstructing the input data from latent representations the decoder verifies that the behaviors of the spatiotemporal sequences are well preserved after dimensionality reduction. In the proposed model the decoder process is constructed using stacked upsampling and convolution methods. This helps the decoder network to learn effective reconstruction parameters and to reduce the difference between the reconstructed and input data.

The proposed model clusters data points by simultaneously learning a set of clusters in the latent feature space by minimizing two objective functions jointly (more at Sect. 4.3). The first objective function emphasizes generating well-separated groups in the latent space by reducing the clustering loss. The second objective function tries to reduce the mean square error of the reconstructed data from the input dataset, called reconstruction loss. The collective optimization of both objective functions guides the autoencoder to extract efficient spatiotemporal features that are best suited to distribute the input data into k categories. The property of learning spatial and temporal features through end-to-end optimization establishes our autoencoder model prominent from the state-of-the-art unsupervised clustering algorithms. The traditional models either emphasize the clustering loss or the reconstruction. Some models optimize both the clustering and reconstruction loss but loosely concentrate on the temporal and spatial features together. The experiments in Sect. 5 will show the improvement of our proposed model over these related unsupervised clustering algorithms.

4.2   Clustering Assignment

At the beginning of the model training process, the input data V_i is applied to the freshly initialized autoencoder to obtain the first generation latent representation E_i which is a vector of 256 dimensions. To estimate the initial cluster centroids $C_j, j = \{1, ..., k\}$ the k-means algorithm applied on these latent features E_i. Then the proposed unsupervised clustering layer iteratively improves the clustering by a two-step procedure inspired by the previous work [24]. In the first step, a soft assignment of each data point V_i to all clusters is computed based on the similarity between the cluster centroid C_j and latent representation E_i. In the second step, the nonlinear mapping E_i and the cluster centroids C_j are refined by using the clustering loss function, which learns from high-confidence cluster assignment of the current target distribution. Each data point's soft assignment is computed using the Student's t-distribution [11], which measures the similarity between the embedded representation E_i and the cluster centroids C_j. The soft assignment of data point i to cluster j is given by:

$$q_{ij} = \frac{(1 + ||E_i - C_j||^2/\alpha)^{-\frac{\alpha+1}{2}}}{\sum_{l=1}^{k}(1 + ||E_i - C_l||^2/\alpha)^{-\frac{\alpha+1}{2}}} \tag{3}$$

Here q_{ij} represents the probability of assigning the i'th data point to the j'th cluster and α is the degree of the freedom of the Student's t-distribution which is set as 1 in our proposed model. At each iteration, the value of q_{ij} is computed based on the previous iteration's cluster centroids. As q_{ij} are soft assignments, the predictions are strengthened using a target distribution of data points. The target distribution puts more attention on data points with the high-confidence cluster assignment and normalizes the loss contribution of each centroid to prevent the distortion of the latent feature space. The target assignment p_{ij} is given by:

$$p_{ij} = \frac{q_{ij}^2/\sum_{i=1}^{n} q_{ij}}{\sum_{l=1}^{k}(q_{il}^2/\sum_{i=1}^{n} q_{il})} \tag{4}$$

Once the values of q_{ij} and p_{ij} are computed for all data points, the cluster centroids C_j are refined using gradient descent. Each data point's cluster assignment gets recalculated following the change of the cluster centroids, and it is then compared to the previous cluster assignment. If there is no change in the cluster assignment of any data point for several consecutive iterations, the model terminates the optimization process and returns the cluster assignment from that iteration.

4.3   Joint Optimization

In the proposed unsupervised clustering process, we used the autoencoder model to reconstruct the input data V and the clustering layer for cluster assignment from latent features E_i of the input data V_i. During the learning process, we jointly optimized the autoencoder weights and the clustering by minimizing the mean squared error and the Kullback-Leibler (KL) divergence loss respectively. This optimization task is implemented using the Stochastic Gradient Descent (SGD) method with momentum. SGD guides the autoencoder model to learn efficient latent embeddings to capture distinctive and representative features of the input dataset. The reconstruction loss of the model is computed by the mean squared error, which is given by

$$L_{rec} = min(\frac{1}{T} \sum_{i=1}^{T} \left\| V_i - \widehat{V_i} \right\|_2^2) \tag{5}$$

Here $V_i \in \mathbb{R}^{lon \times lat \times n}$ is the input data and $\widehat{V_i} \in \mathbb{R}^{lon \times lat \times n}$ is the output of the autoencoder model. The cluster centroids and eventually the cluster assignment is iteratively refined in the model by minimizing the clustering loss. The KL divergence is used to compute the clustering loss between the soft assignment q_{ij} and the target distribution p_{ij} of each data point to clusters. The formula of the KL divergence loss is

$$L_{clus} = min(KL(P \parallel Q)) = min(\frac{1}{T} \sum_{i=1}^{T} \sum_{j=1}^{k} p_{ij} log \frac{p_{ij}}{q_{ij}}) \tag{6}$$

Here T is the number of timestamp/data points and k is the number of clusters, $k < T$. Finally, the combined loss for training the proposed unsupervised clustering models is defined by:

$$L = L_{clus} + L_{rec}$$
$$= \frac{1}{T} \sum_{i=1}^{T} \left(\left\| V_i - \widehat{V_i} \right\|_2^2 + \sum_{j=1}^{k} p_{ij} log \frac{p_{ij}}{q_{ij}} \right) \tag{7}$$

5 Experiments

Our proposed model was implemented using the Python deep-learning libraries Keras 2.11 and TensorFlow 2. All the baseline models and proposed models were tested in the Google Colab notebook with 12 GB GPU memory support. For a fair comparison, we used the same Keras library for all baseline models. We executed each model 20 times with random initialization and reported the best evaluation result.

5.1 Dataset and Data Preprocessing

For this study, we use the open-access atmospheric reanalysis data from European Centre for Medium-Range Weather Forecasts (ECMWF) ERA-5 global reanalysis product [3]. The ERA5 atmospheric dataset contains 31 km high-resolution reanalysis and a reduced resolution ten-member ensemble [8]. The ensemble is required for the data assimilation procedure. Seven atmospheric reanalysis variables from the ERA5 dataset were selected for this study. These are Sea Surface Temperature (unit: k, and range: 285 to 300), Surface Pressure (unit: Pa, and range: 98260 to 103788), Surface Sensible Heat Flux (unit: J/m^2, and range: -674528 to 200024), Surface Latent Heat Flux (unit: J/m^2, and range: -1840906 to 90131), 2-meter Air Temperature (unit: k, and range: 281 to 299), 10-meter U-component of Wind (unit: m/s, and range: -16 to 19), and 10-meter V-component of Wind (unit: m/s, and range: -15 to 16). These variables are included in the dataset based on their impact on the air-sea-cloud interaction system and were measured in a latitude-longitude grid of (41×41). Temporally, the dataset covers one year period and one observation per day. If we directly convert the data into a 2D tabular data frame, the total feature count for each record would be 11,767 $(41 \times 41 \times 7)$, which is clearly a high-dimensional dataset.

After exploring the dataset we found the presence of null values. These null values may occur due to the sensor malfunction or any physical conditions. The null values are replaced by the overall mean of the dataset because the replacement with any neighboring values may create a different pattern in the data, which obviously will change the actual behavior of the variable. From the description of the dataset, it is clear that the value ranges of the variables are different. It is also necessary to make the features of the dataset into the same scale for better feature learning through a deep neural network [19]. For this dataset, we utilized the standard Min-Max Normalization (MMN) normalization to rescale all features within the range of 0 to 1. Each variable V_i rescaled using the following formula:

$$V_i = \frac{V_i - min(V_i)}{max(V_i) - min(V_i)} \tag{8}$$

5.2 Baseline Methods

We compared the result of the proposed model with the k-means algorithm and the hierarchical clustering algorithm. These methods are the most popular methods for unsupervised clustering. The original 4D input dataset is transformed into a 2D matrix with one row per timestep to apply these algorithms. To contrast with our suggested approach, we additionally used the DEC [24], DTC [16], and DTCR [10] algorithms from the deep-learning family and these algorithms employed a deep neural network for dimensionality reduction after transforming each observation's data from a multi-dimension matrix to a one-dimensional row. The low-dimensional latent features produced by the deep neural network were then subjected to the clustering algorithm. The comparison between baseline models and the proposed model is depicted in Table 1.

5.3 Evaluation Metrics

We used Average Intercluster Distance, Average Variance, $RMSE_{mean}$, Silhouette coefficient, and Davies-Bouldin score evaluation metric to measure the per-

Table 1. Comparison among baseline methods.

Method	Input Shape	Technology	Pretraining
k-means	2D Matrix	Traditional distance/similarity-based model	Not required
Hierarchical Clustering	2D Matrix	Traditional distance/similarity-based model	Not required
DEC	2D Matrix	Deep learning model with dense layers	Required
DTC	2D Matrix	Deep learning model with LSTM layers	Required
DTCR	2D Matrix	Deep learning model with GRU layers	Required
DSC (ours)	4D Matrix	Deep learning model with CNN and LSTM layers	Not required

formance of our experiments. As the dataset does not have any ground truth cluster values, intercluster distance will give a reasonable estimation of the quality of the clustering by representing the proximity of generated clusters. Intercluster distance is measured as the minimum distance between any two data points belonging to two different clusters.

$$\Delta_{inter}(C_a, C_b) = min_{C_a \neq C_b, X \in C_a, Y \in C_b} d(X, Y) \tag{9}$$

Here C_a and C_b are two different clusters, $X \in C_a$ means every observation of cluster C_a, and similarly $Y \in C_b$ means every observation of cluster C_b.

By measuring the variance of the clusters it is possible to evaluate the homogeneity and compactness of the clusters. Also, the distribution of time series over clusters should be carried out to minimize intracluster variance. The variance of each cluster will be computed as an evaluation criterion of the proposed method using the following equation

$$Var_{C_j} = \frac{1}{n_{C_j}} \sum_{X \in C_j} \left\| X - \mu_{C_j} \right\|^2 \tag{10}$$

Here n_{C_j} is the total number of observations in the cluster C_i and μ_{C_j} is mean of the cluster.

The root-mean-squared error (RMSE) is another common measure of clustering quality evaluation. For each observation, the error is the distance between every observation and its associated cluster centroid. The total clustering error is therefore the sum of the errors associated with each data point. Then we take root over the average of the total error.

$$RMSE_{mean} = \sqrt{\frac{1}{n} \sum_{j=1}^{k} \sum_{X \in C_j} \left\| X - \mu_{C_j} \right\|^2} \tag{11}$$

Here n is the length of the dataset, k is the number of clusters, X is the member of cluster C_j, and μ_{C_j} is the mean of the cluster C_j. The lower $RMSE_{mean}$ score means the members of each cluster are very similar and close to the cluster centroid. On the other hand, the higher $RMSE_{mean}$ means the opposite and is not desired from a clustering algorithm.

Besides the above metrics, we also used the Silhouette coefficient and Davies-Bouldin score as additional metrics. The silhouette coefficient [22] is applied to measure the cohesion and separation of the generated clusters. This is defined in the range $[-1, 1]$, where positive numbers denote a significant degree of cluster separation. Moreover, negative values show that the clusters are jumbled together (i.e., an indication of overlapping clusters). The data are said to be evenly dispersed when the silhouette coefficient is zero. The Davies-Bouldin score [18] measures the similarity of various formed clusters and a lower value indicates better clustering, with zero being the lowest attainable value.

5.4   Experiment Results

The comparison of the proposed method with baseline algorithms is presented in Table 2. The best results for each metric are in bold. We initialized the cluster number hyperparameter as 7 for clustering the dataset. To compute these evaluation results we trained each model 20 times and picked the best result from them. The results of DEC and DTC methods are generated by running their published codes. The hyperparameters of these models like batch size, learning rate, maximum iteration, etc. are finetuned to get better results on the applied dataset. The k-means and hierarchical clustering method are taken from sklearn python library and applied to preprocessed data without any dimension reduction. As shown in Table 2, the proposed DSC algorithm outperforms all the baseline methods except that the DEC algorithm [24] has a lower $RMSE_{mean}$ score. Note that the DEC method does not consider spatial features and uses a greedy pretraining process. In contrast, our proposed method achieved $RMSE_{mean}$ close to DEC without any preprocessing step and significant improvement for the other four evaluation metrics.

Table 2. Evaluation result comparison of the proposed DSC method with baseline methods.

Method	Silhouette Coefficient	Davies-Bouldin Score	$RMSE_{mean}$	Avg Inter Cluster Distance	Average Variance
k-means	0.25	1.6867	13.66	7.00	0.0451
Hierarchical Clustering	0.23	1.5669	13.99	7.78	0.0453
DEC	0.26	1.6080	**13.62**	6.75	0.0448
DTC	0.28	1.6850	14.70	6.52	0.0457
DTCR	−0.10	7.2765	21.14	4.79	0.0504
DSC (ours)	**0.37**	**1.4348**	13.79	**8.16**	**0.0430**

In Fig. 2, we visualize the clusters generated by the DEC and the proposed DSC method. As the latent feature space is not suitable for visualization we use t-SNE [11] to reduce the dimension of the feature space. The cluster plot of the DEC method shows some clear overlap between the three clusters represented by red, orange, and cyan, even though the DEC method achieved a better $RMSE_{mean}$ score. On the other hand, in the plot of our proposed model (DSC), all clusters are reasonably separated from each other except for some data points located far distant from the original cluster centroids. There may be one possible argument that due to the application of t-SNE dimensionality reduction, the clusters are overlapped in the DEC plot. To scrutinize that possibility, the visualization is generated multiple times, and the resultant cluster plotting reveals similar overlapping each time.

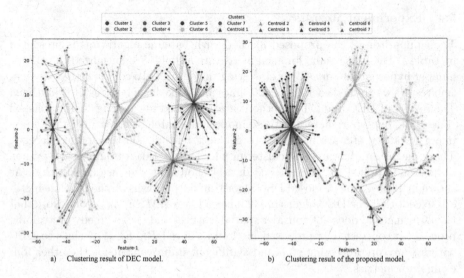

| a)   Clustering result of DEC model. | b)   Clustering result of the proposed model. |

Fig. 2. Visualization of the clusters formed by DEC and our proposed model (DSC). The generated latent features are subjected to the t-SNE method to decrease dimension for visualization. The colors indicate the cluster label and centroid of each cluster pointed by the triangle.

5.5   Ablation Study

To verify the impact of the spatiotemporal autoencoder of the proposed model on clustering, a comparative study of this model with its different variants is shown here. The quantitative results of these models are illustrated in Table 3. In the CNN models, we only utilized convolutional neural network layers available in the Keras library and the same custom clustering layer as the proposed model. On the other hand, the CNN-LSTM Encoder model only uses the encoder part of the proposed DSC model while other functionality and parameters remain the same in both models. To gain the best performance from these models we tuned some hyperparameters like batch size, activation function, learning rate, and initial weight initialization so that we can get the actual impact of the autoencoder and custom clustering layer. The ablation study results show that the integration of LSTM layers with the CNN layers in the encoder module improves the average cluster distance and Davies-Boulding score for a significant magnitude, but the CNN encoder model achieves a little lower $RMSE_{mean}$. Out of these four variations, the proposed CNN-LSTM autoencoder model generated a better Silhouette Coefficient, Davies-Bouldin Score, average cluster distance, and variance. In summary, the proposed model increases the similarity of the observations in the formed clusters with better cluster separation.

Table 3. Ablation results of the proposed DSC method.

Method	Silhouette Coefficient	Davies-Bouldin Score	$RMSE_{mean}$	Avg Inter Cluster Distance	Average Variance
CNN Encoder	0.35	1.4769	**13.74**	7.31	0.0449
CNN Autoencoder	0.31	1.6404	13.96	7.58	0.0458
CNN-LSTM Encoder	0.36	1.4382	13.82	8.10	0.0450
CNN-LSTM Autoencoder (DSC)	**0.37**	**1.4348**	13.79	**8.16**	**0.0430**

6   Conclusions

In this paper, we proposed a novel deep learning-based model, called Deep Spatiotemporal Clustering (DSC) model, to cluster high-dimensional spatiotemporal data without any supervision from previous knowledge. This model is able to learn a fine-level latent representation of the data using both spatial and temporal features, and extracting better cluster structure from the complex dataset. The joint optimization of the clustering and representation objectives using the custom clustering layer helps the model to gain better performance. The comparison with baseline unsupervised models clearly illustrates the superior clustering quality and effectiveness of the DSC model. Also, the impact of the proposed model can be perceived from the quantitative analysis of the ablation study.

For future work, we plan to apply this model to additional high-dimensional datasets including ones from other domains. We also plan to study whether incorporating domain knowledge into the end-to-end training process could improve the results further and/or make the proposed model more robust to the domain-specific application.

Acknowledgment. This work was supported by the DOE Office of Science Early Career Research Program. This work was performed under the auspices of the U.S. Department of Energy (DOE) by LLNL under contract DE-AC52-07NA27344. LLNL-CONF-846980. Faruque and Wang were also partially supported by grant OAC-1942714 from the U.S. National Science Foundation (NSF) and grant 80NSSC21M0027 from the U.S. National Aeronautics and Space Administration (NASA).

References

1. Athmaja, S., Hanumanthappa, M., Kavitha, V.: A survey of machine learning algorithms for big data analytics. In: 2017 International conference on Innovations in Information, Embedded and Communication Systems (ICIIECS), pp. 1–4. IEEE (2017)
2. Choi, S.W., Lee, C., Lee, J.M., Park, J.H., Lee, I.B.: Fault detection and identification of nonlinear processes based on kernel PCA. Chemom. Intell. Lab. Syst. **75**(1), 55–67 (2005)
3. Dataset: Era-5 global reanalysis data (2021), from European Centre for Medium-Range Weather Forecasts. Copernicus Climate Change Service (C3S)
4. Day, W.H., Edelsbrunner, H.: Efficient algorithms for agglomerative hierarchical clustering methods. J. Classif. **1**(1), 7–24 (1984)
5. Ester, M., Kriegel, H.P., Sander, J., Xu, X.: A density-based algorithm for discovering clusters in large spatial databases with noise. In: KDD 1996, pp. 226–231. AAAI Press (1996)
6. Ghosh, R., Jia, X., Yin, L., Lin, C., Jin, Z., Kumar, V.: Clustering augmented self-supervised learning: an application to land cover mapping. In: Proceedings of the 30th International Conference on Advances in Geographic Information Systems, pp. 1–10 (2022)
7. Hadifar, A., Sterckx, L., Demeester, T., Develder, C.: A self-training approach for short text clustering. In: Proceedings of the 4th Workshop on Representation Learning for NLP (RepL4NLP-2019), pp. 194–199 (2019)
8. Hersbach, H., et al.: The era5 global reanalysis. Quart. J. Roy. Meteorol. Soc. **146**(730), 1999–2049 (2020)
9. LeCun, Y., Bengio, Y., Hinton, G.: Deep learning. Nature **521**(7553), 436–444 (2015)
10. Ma, Q., Zheng, J., Li, S., Cottrell, G.W.: Learning representations for time series clustering. In: Advances in Neural Information Processing Systems, vol. 32 (2019)
11. Van der Maaten, L., Hinton, G.: Visualizing data using t-SNE. J. Mach. Learn. Res. **9**(11), 2579–2605 (2008)
12. Maćkiewicz, A., Ratajczak, W.: Principal components analysis (PCA). Comput. Geosci. **19**(3), 303–342 (1993)
13. MacQueen, J.: Classification and analysis of multivariate observations. In: 5th Berkeley Symposium Mathmetical Statistics Probability, pp. 281–297. University of California Los Angeles LA USA (1967)
14. Mechem, D.B., Wittman, C.S., Miller, M.A., Yuter, S.E., De Szoeke, S.P.: Joint synoptic and cloud variability over the northeast Atlantic near the Azores. J. Appl. Meteorol. Climatol. **57**(6), 1273–1290 (2018)
15. Ronneberger, O., Fischer, P., Brox, T.: U-Net: convolutional networks for biomedical image segmentation. In: Navab, N., Hornegger, J., Wells, W.M., Frangi, A.F. (eds.) MICCAI 2015. LNCS, vol. 9351, pp. 234–241. Springer, Cham (2015). https://doi.org/10.1007/978-3-319-24574-4_28
16. Sai Madiraju, N., Sadat, S.M., Fisher, D., Karimabadi, H.: Deep temporal clustering: Fully unsupervised learning of time-domain features. arXiv e-prints pp. arXiv-1802 (2018)
17. Schmidhuber, J.: Deep learning in neural networks: an overview. Neural Netw. **61**, 85–117 (2015)

18. Singh, A.K., Mittal, S., Malhotra, P., Srivastava, Y.V.: Clustering evaluation by Davies-Bouldin index (DBI) in cereal data using k-means. In: 2020 Fourth International Conference on Computing Methodologies and Communication (ICCMC), pp. 306–310. IEEE (2020)
19. Singh, D., Singh, B.: Investigating the impact of data normalization on classification performance. Appl. Soft Comput. **97**, 105524 (2020)
20. Solomon, S., et al.: Climate Change 2007-the Physical Science Basis: Working Group I Contribution to the Fourth Assessment Report of the IPCC, vol. 4. Cambridge University Press, Cambridge (2007)
21. Takahashi, N., Hayasaka, T.: Air-sea interactions among oceanic low-level cloud, sea surface temperature, and atmospheric circulation on an intraseasonal time scale in the summertime north pacific based on satellite data analysis. J. Clim. **33**(21), 9195–9212 (2020)
22. Tan, P.N., Steinbach, M., Kumar, V.: Introduction to Data Mining (2005)
23. De la Torre, F., Kanade, T.: Discriminative cluster analysis. In: Proceedings of the 23rd International Conference on Machine Learning, pp. 241–248 (2006)
24. Xie, J., Girshick, R., Farhadi, A.: Unsupervised deep embedding for clustering analysis. In: International Conference on Machine Learning, pp. 478–487. PMLR (2016)
25. Ye, J., Zhao, Z., Wu, M.: Discriminative k-means for clustering. In: Advances in Neural Information Processing Systems, vol. 20 (2007)

Circle Attention: Forecasting Network Traffic by Learning Interpretable Spatial Relationships from Intersecting Circles

Espen Haugsdal[1]([⊠])(ID), Sara Malacarne[2](ID), and Massimiliano Ruocco[1,3](ID)

[1] Norwegian University of Science and Technology, Trondheim, Norway
{espen.haugsdal,massimiliano.ruocco}@ntnu.no
[2] Telenor Research, Oslo, Norway
sara.malacarne@telenor.com
[3] SINTEF Digital, Trondheim, Norway

Abstract. Accurately forecasting traffic in telecommunication networks is essential for operators to efficiently allocate resources, provide better services, and save energy. We propose Circle Attention, a novel spatial attention mechanism for telecom traffic forecasting, which directly models the area of effect of neighboring cell towers. Cell towers typically point in three different geographical directions, called sectors. Circle Attention models the relationships between sectors of neighboring cell towers by assigning a circle with learnable parameters to each sector, which are: the *azimuth* of the sector, the *distance* from the cell tower to the center of the circle, and the *radius* of the circle. To model the effects of neighboring time series, we compute attention weights based on the intersection of circles relative to their area. These attention weights serve as multiplicative gating parameters for the neighboring time series, allowing our model to focus on the most important time series when making predictions. The circle parameters are learned automatically through back-propagation, with the only signal available being the errors made in the traffic forecasting of each sector. To validate the effectiveness of our approach, we train a Transformer to forecast the number of attempted calls to sectors in the Copenhagen area, and show that Circle Attention outperforms the baseline methods of including either all or none of the neighboring time series. Furthermore, we perform an ablation study to investigate the importance of the three learnable parameters of the circles, and show that performance deteriorates if any of the parameters are kept fixed. Our method has practical implications for telecommunication operators, as it can provide more accurate and interpretable models for forecasting network traffic, allowing for better resource allocation and improved service provision.

Keywords: Forecasting · Telecommunications Networks · Attention

1 Introduction

Accurately predicting mobile traffic is crucial for effective network management, resource allocation, and to optimize energy consumption. Nonetheless, it is a

G. De Francisci Morales et al. (Eds.): ECML PKDD 2023, LNAI 14175, pp. 106–121, 2023.
https://doi.org/10.1007/978-3-031-43430-3_7

challenging task to achieve precise traffic predictions due to the complex spatial-temporal correlations involved. Telecommunication networks are designed to handle a massive number of users concurrently. Whenever required, additional capacity is provided by constructing more radio towers or upgrading existing ones. However, maintaining continuous power supply to these towers is inefficient due to the fluctuating traffic load. Hence, precise prediction of future traffic can significantly reduce costs and improve energy efficiency. Telecommunications towers typically have antennas pointing in three different geographical directions, which are called *sectors*. Each sector has multiple *cells* that correspond to different frequencies and communication technologies (i.e., 2G, 3G, 4G). These cells can be divided into two groups: those belonging to the *coverage layer* and those belonging to the *capacity layer*. Cells in the coverage layer must remain powered on at all times to meet critical infrastructure requirements, such as for emergency service calls. In contrast, cells within the capacity layer can be switched off during periods of low demand, which is desirable from an energy savings perspective. However, turning off cells during periods of high demand can lead to service disruptions for customers, which is undesirable from the perspective of customer satisfaction. Accurately forecasting the traffic can allow the telecom operator to switch off cells in the capacity layer during periods of low demand. It is thus essential to be able to capture the spatial relations between the towers in order to understand beforehand how power saving on one tower would affect the neighboring ones.

Several previous attempts have been made to concurrently model the intricate spatial and temporal interdependencies between multiple radio towers. Deep learning methods have also been utilized, primarily employing Recurrent Neural Networks (RNNs) to model the temporal relationships and Convolutional Neural Networks (CNNs) or Graph Convolutional Networks (GCNs) [7] to capture the spatial relationships [1,2,6,13]. However, all of these techniques depend on constructing graphs manually, by using certain measures of correlation between the time series of various towers. We propose a method that models the spatial relationship between sectors of towers automatically and end-to-end, as part of the training process of a neural network. To the best of our knowledge, our approach is the first to learn spatial relationships in this way instead of predefining them.

Our method, called Circle Attention, first assigns a circle with learnable parameters to each sector. Then, the spatial relationship between sectors is modeled by the area of intersection between circles. The method does not depend on any specific network architecture, rather it is a general method for modeling spatial relationships. Circle Attention has several desirable properties. First, by employing a geometric design, our approach provides an interpretable way for experts to verify the plausibility of the modeled effects by plotting the learned circles on a map. Second, circular areas of effects are also somewhat plausible from a physical perspective. Consequently, it might be possible to infer *true* physical properties of the world, given a strong enough learning signal. Third, the area of intersection between two circles is relatively easy to compute, compared to other plausible geometric shapes. Each step of the computation is differentiable, which allows for end-to-end learning with back-propagation.

To evaluate the usefulness of our method, we learn to forecast the number of attempted cell phone calls to telecommunication towers in the Copenhagen area. We use a Transformer [10] as the baseline model for our experiments, and investigate whether the use of Circle Attention improves the model's forecasting performance. However, Circle Attention is not a replacement for regular attention over time, as it works exclusively in the spatial domain, and not in the temporal domain.

Overall, the proposed method offers a customizable, interpretable, and computationally efficient way to model the spatial relationships between towers, and has the potential to infer physical properties of the world. The major contributions of this work can be summarized as follows. Firstly, the proposed Circle Attention method is a novel approach that models the spatial relationships between telecommunication towers using the area of intersecting circles. The method offers a customizable and interpretable way to model these relationships, which is important for understanding the complex spatial dependencies in cell phone traffic. Secondly, we show that Circle Attention improves accuracy on the task of forecasting cell phone traffic. Lastly, we perform ablation studies to investigate the importance of the different components of the proposed method. Understanding the importance of these components is important for potential further improvements of Circle Attention and other similar methods in the future.

The contributions of this paper provide insights into the effectiveness of modeling spatial relationships in cell phone traffic data and offer a novel approach that can be applied to other spatial data prediction tasks. The proposed method has the potential to infer physical properties of the world and can be utilized in various applications in the telecommunication industry.

The work in this paper was done using proprietary data, which cannot be made publicly available. We also cannot share code related to processing of data or other data specific details. However, we have made a public implementation of our proposed method available online[1].

2   Related Work

Network traffic prediction has been an active research topic for quite some time. Traditional approaches for modeling traffic patterns involve either statistical time series methods [9,16], or statistical learning methods [5,14]. However, these approaches either treat base stations independently or rely on manually designed features to capture spatio-temporal correlations, and therefore do not fully account for the spatial dependencies and interrelationships between base stations.

Recent advances in deep learning have opened up promising avenues for modeling spatial relations using both grid-based and tower/cell-based approaches [2,4,6,13,15]. For modeling spatial relations, both GCNs [2,6] and CNNs [1,13]

---

[1] A public implementation is available at https://github.com/EspenHa/Circle-Attention.

have been adopted, while RNNs have been used primarily for capturing temporal connections. A popular approach has consisted in combining the "spatial" models with the "temporal" models by constructing a graph capturing spatial relationships, and then replacing matrix multiplications in RNN-based models with matrix convolutions with respect to this graph. Many studies have utilized static graphs, constructed based on topological information or overall correlations between time series patterns [1,2,4,6]. However, recent research has explored the use of dynamic graphs [6,8]. GRUs and LSTMs have been widely adopted for mobile traffic forecasting, but their inability to capture long temporal relationships has led researchers to augment hourly input windows with corresponding daily and/or weekly patterns [2]. Another approach involves training hourly, daily, and weekly models in parallel, and then concatenating their outputs [15]. To address the limitations of RNNs, researchers have explored alternative approaches such as Transformer [10] architectures. Liu et al. [8] were the first to use a Transformer to forecast mobile network traffic, incorporating the spatial component to achieve superior results compared to state-of-the-art methods. The authors' approach models spatial relations using a dynamic correlation matrix between time series windows of grids, similar to graph-based techniques. In contrast, our method focuses on learning the interactions between neighboring sectors directly during model training, which allows us to capture more fine-grained spatial dependencies.

3 Method

3.1 Problem Definition

In this work we focus on forecasting the Key Performance Indicator (KPI) associated with the number of attempted calls to cell towers in the Copenhagen area. A *tower* is a critical part of telecommunication networks, providing wireless communication services to millions of people. Their performance is essential for ensuring reliable service to end-users. Each tower has up to three *sectors*, which can be thought of as a grouping of antennas and cells pointing in the same direction. Different sectors are associated with different geographical areas around the towers. Figure 1 illustrates the concepts of sectors and towers.

For each sector, a number of KPIs are measured and recorded as time series data. The KPIs include measurements such as the number of attempted calls, the number of successful calls, the call duration, and data usage. The main focus of this work is to forecast the KPI that counts the number of attempted calls to a sector of a tower. Forecasting this KPI is crucial for understanding the performance of the telecommunication network, as it provides insights into the traffic demand and usage patterns for different sectors. This task is important for ensuring that the telecommunication network is operating efficiently and providing reliable service to users.

We have a total of $N_{towers} = 510$ towers in our dataset, each with its antennas assigned to one of three sectors. (In reality some towers have less than three sectors, but for ease of explanation, and without loss of generality, we

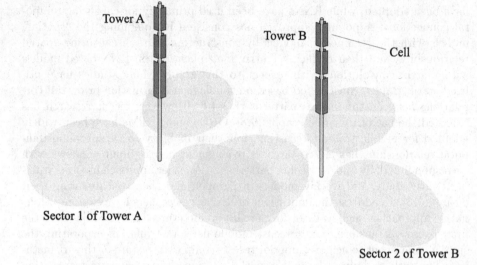

Tower A

Tower B

Cell

Sector 1 of Tower A

Sector 2 of Tower B

Fig. 1. Two telecommunication towers, each with three associated sectors. The cells with red coloring belong to the capacity layer, and the cells with blue coloring belong to the coverage layer. (Color figure online)

will consider all towers to have three sectors.) We will use the index variable $a \in \{1, \ldots, 3 \cdot N_{\text{towers}}\}$ to refer to sector number a. Each sector a originates from a tower at a geographical location given by a coordinate pair $(x_a^{\text{TOWER}}, y_a^{\text{TOWER}})$. Moreover, each sector a points in an azimuth direction $\alpha_a \in [0, 2\pi)$, measuring the clockwise angle from north.

The dataset contains time series that are sampled at hourly frequency. A time step t is defined as $t \in \{1, \ldots, T\}$, where T is the total number of hours in the dataset. We use a dataset consisting of 410 days, so T is $410 \cdot 24 = 9840$. We denote by z_a the time series associated with sector a. Another subscript is used to denote a time index, such that $z_{a,t}$ is the number of attempted calls within hour t for sector a.

The *neighborhood* of a sector a is chosen to be the $N_{\text{neighbors}} = 16$ sectors with the smallest Euclidean distance between their associated towers, including the sector a itself. In the next section we specify a method for modeling relationship between neighboring sectors, by associating each sector with a circle.

3.2 Circle Attention

Circle Attention models the relationship between neighboring sectors by associating a circle with each sector. The strength of the relationship between two sectors is given by the intersection of the areas of the circles, relative to the area of the circles. Figure 2 provides a graphical illustration of the formula for the intersection of two circles.

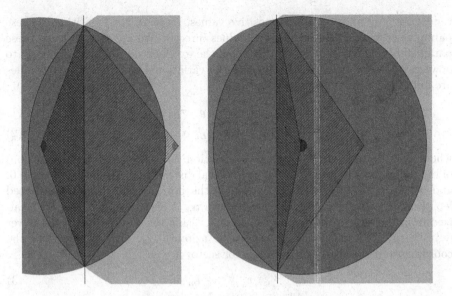

Fig. 2. Left: The intersection between two circles is given by the sum of two *circular segments*, shown here as the two purple areas to either side of the vertical line. The area of a circular segment is equal to the area of a *circular sector* (not shown), minus the area of an *isosceles triangle* (shown with hatched filling). The area of a circular sector is a proportion of the total area of the circle, which is given by the angles indicated in dark blue and dark red. **Right:** The line of intersection is "behind" the center of the blue circle, but the same method applies, except that the area of the blue triangle is instead *added* to the area of the circular sector (of the blue angle). (Color figure online)

The area of intersection between two circles can be found adding two *circular segments*, which are defined by the line going through the two points of intersection of the circles. These are the purple areas of Fig. 2. The area of a circular segment can be found by first finding the areas of two associated geometrical objects. First, find the area of the isosceles triangle formed by the center of the circle and the two intersection points. These triangles are shown in Fig. 2 with hatched filling. Second, find the area of the associated *circular sector*, which is exactly identical to the area covered by both the circular segment and the isosceles triangle. This area is easily computed by using the inverse cosine function on the vertex angle of the triangle. Now we can define the area of the circular segment as the area of the circular sector, minus the area of the isosceles triangle. Note that this approach generalizes to the case where the line of intersection is "behind" the center of the circle (i.e. the right sub-figure of Fig. 2), by instead adding the area of the isosceles triangle to the area of the sector.

We model the relationships between sectors by associating a circle with each sector. Each sector a has a parameter $R_a \in \mathbb{R}^+$ determining the radius of the circle, a length $L_a \in \mathbb{R}^+$ determining the distance between the coordinates of the tower and the center of the circle, and an azimuth angle α_a. As the length and radius are only allowed to take positive values, we learn the logarithm of these parameters instead of modeling the values directly. We are able to learn these parameters by back-propagation by using the exponential function, similarly to how variances are typically parametrized in variational methods. The log-values are initialized from normal distributions:

$$\log(R_a) \sim \mathcal{N}(\mu_R,\ \sigma_R^2) \tag{1}$$

$$\log(L_a) \sim \mathcal{N}(\mu_L,\ \sigma_L^2), \tag{2}$$

where $\mathcal{N}(\cdot, \cdot)$ represents the normal distribution. Consequently, the initial values of the radius and the length form a log-normal distribution. We set $\mu_R = \mu_L = 0$, and $\sigma_R^2 = \sigma_L^2 = 0.1^2$, which means that the initial circles have an expected length and radius of ca. 1 km. The azimuth α_a is also learnable, but is initialized from the value recorded in the dataset. Using the coordinates of the tower $(x_a^{\text{TOWER}}, y_a^{\text{TOWER}})$, the length L_a, and the azimuth α_a, we can determine the coordinates of the center of the circle for sector a:

$$x_a^{\text{CIRCLE}} = x_a^{\text{TOWER}} + L_a \sin \alpha_a \tag{3}$$

$$y_a^{\text{CIRCLE}} = y_a^{\text{TOWER}} + L_a \cos \alpha_a \tag{4}$$

We now describe the steps to find the area of intersection between two circles, each associated with a sector. Let a be the index of the first sector, and b be the index of the second sector. The first step is to compute the Euclidean distance between the centers of the circles. Additionally, a small ϵ is added to avoid numerical issues due to divisions by zero in later computations.

$$D_{a,b} = \sqrt{(x_a^{\text{CIRCLE}} - x_b^{\text{CIRCLE}})^2 + (y_a^{\text{CIRCLE}} - y_b^{\text{CIRCLE}})^2 + \epsilon} \tag{5}$$

Second, compute the triangle segment lengths V:

$$V_{a,b} = \frac{D_{a,b}^2 + R_a^2 - R_b^2}{2D_{a,b}} \tag{6}$$

To avoid numerical issues when the circles for a and b do not intersect, we have to ensure that each segment length is bounded by the radius of its circle. Next, we ensure that the absolute value of the segment length is bounded by the radius of its circle, minus a small ϵ', such that the gradients of later computations stay well-defined.

$$\tilde{V}_{a,b} = \begin{cases} -R_a + \epsilon' & \text{if } V_{a,b} \leq -R_a + \epsilon', \\ R_a - \epsilon' & \text{if } V_{a,b} \geq R_a - \epsilon', \\ V_{a,b} & \text{otherwise} \end{cases} \tag{7}$$

Now we can safely compute circular sectors S and signed triangle areas T:

$$S_{a,b} = R_a^2 \arccos\left(\frac{\tilde{V}_{a,b}}{R_a}\right) \tag{8}$$

$$T_{a,b} = \tilde{V}_{a,b}\sqrt{R_a^2 - \tilde{V}_{a,b}^2} \tag{9}$$

Finally, we compute the intersection by adding the areas of the two circular segments. The areas of the circular segments are found by subtracting the area of a signed triangle from the area of a circular sector:

$$I_{a,b} = (S_{a,b} - T_{a,b}) + (S_{b,a} - T_{b,a}) \tag{10}$$

In order to ensure numerical stability, we do an additional masking step to cover the case where circle a is completely inside circle b. In this case the intersection is equal to the area of the circle:

$$\widetilde{I}_{a,b} = \begin{cases} A_a = \pi R_a^2 & \text{if } D_{a,b} + R_a \leq R_b, \\ I_{a,b} & \text{otherwise} \end{cases} \tag{11}$$

While $\widetilde{I}_{a,b}$ should equal $I_{a,b}$ also in the case when the circles overlap due to the masking performed in Eq. 7, we consistently find that using $\widetilde{I}_{a,b}$ leads to better performance. We hypothesize that this is due to numerical instabilities during training resulting from small numerical values of the distance $D_{a,b}$ between overlapping circles. Alternatively, this might be due to differences in the gradient computations between the case when the boundaries of the circles meet at a tangent point, and the case when the boundaries of the circles are overlapping but not tangent.

We can now define the *intersection score* or *Intersection over Area* (IoA) for a circle a relative to circle b:

$$\text{IoA}_{a,b} = \frac{\widetilde{I}_{a,b}}{A_a} \tag{12}$$

The intersection scores are used to create an input matrix X, with shape $T_{\text{window}} \times N_{\text{features}} = 64 \times 40$. The matrix consists of four stacked sub-matrices, corresponding to different types of input features, such that:

$$X = \left[X^{(\text{NEIGHBORS})} \mid X^{(\text{IoA})} \mid X^{(\text{LOCATION})} \mid X^{(\text{TIME})} \right] \tag{13}$$

The first type of feature is the neighboring time series, masked by intersection scores. The neighborhood of a sector a is defined by the function $\text{NEIGHBOR}(a, i)$, which returns the sector index of the ith closest sector, as measured by the Euclidean distance between the towers of the sectors. A sector a is its own first neighbor, i.e. $\text{NEIGHBOR}(a, 1) = a$. The size of the neighborhood is defined by a fixed hyper-parameter $N_{\text{neighbors}} = 16$. The circle intersection attention mechanism is implemented by multiplying the time series of the neighboring sectors by their intersection score. In other words, for a sector to be forecasted a, column number $i \in \{1, \ldots, N_{\text{neighbors}}\}$ of the matrix $X^{(\text{NEIGHBORS})}$ is the time series for sector $b = \text{NEIGHBOR}(a, i)$, multiplied by the intersection score between a and b:

$$X_i^{(\text{NEIGHBORS})} = \tilde{z}_b \cdot \text{IoA}_{a,b} \tag{14}$$

Here, $\tilde{z}_b$ is defined as the time series z_b divided by its maximum value in the training set. Second, we include the intersection scores directly, without multiplying with its associated time series. The primary motivation for this choice was to give the model a more reliable way to update the parameters of the circle, regardless of the values of the time series $\tilde{z}_b$. The intersection scores do not depend on time, so we extend the scores such that they form a constant sequence. Using the same notation as previously, this is:

$$X_i^{(\text{IoA})} = \text{IoA}_{a,b} \tag{15}$$

Third, we include a location feature based on the coordinates of the cell tower. The location feature is the coordinate pair $(x_a^{\text{TOWER}}, y_a^{\text{TOWER}})$, with a suitable normalization applied to ensure an approx. standard normal distribution of values:

$$X^{(\text{LOCATION})} = \begin{bmatrix} (x_a^{\text{TOWER}} - m_x)/s_x \\ (y_a^{\text{TOWER}} - m_y)/s_y \end{bmatrix}^T, \tag{16}$$

where m_x, m_y, s_x, s_y are fixed scaling parameters. Because the location does not vary in time, we extend these values such that they are constant for all time steps. Fourth, we include seasonal encodings of time, which consists of 3 pairs of sine/cosine encoded seasonal features: hour of day, day of the week, and day of the year:

$$X^{(\text{TIME})} = \begin{bmatrix} \sin(2\pi \cdot \text{HourOfDay} / 24) \\ \cos(2\pi \cdot \text{HourOfDay} / 24) \\ \sin(2\pi \cdot \text{DayOfWeek} / 7) \\ \cos(2\pi \cdot \text{DayOfWeek} / 7) \\ \sin(2\pi \cdot \text{DayOfYear} / 365) \\ \cos(2\pi \cdot \text{DayOfYear} / 365) \end{bmatrix}^T \tag{17}$$

3.3 Transformer Model

As our forecasting model, we use an autoregressive decoder-only Transformer [10]. More specifically, we use a recently proposed Transformer variant, called the PI-Transformer [3]. The main benefit of the PI-Transformer is the use of *Persistence Initialization*, which ensures that the initial forecasts are equal to that of a simple persistence model. This is done by adding a skip connection and a gating parameter γ. Because the PI-Transformer assumes time series with only one feature (i.e. univariate inputs), we need to modify the definition of the inputs to the first layer of the PI-Transformer. In order to transform our input matrix X to the required shape for the Transformer model, we use a weight matrix W_{in} of shape $N_{\text{features}} \times d_{\text{model}}$:

$$X_0 = XW_{\text{in}} \tag{18}$$

X_0 is then used as the input to the first Transformer layer, which produces an output X_1, and so on, until the output of the final layer; X_N. The output of the final layer is projected to a univariate series by a weight matrix W_{out} of shape $d_{\text{model}} \times 1$. This output is then multiplied by the gating parameter γ and added to the value for the previous time step, such that the (max-scaled) forecast for $z_{b,t+1}$ becomes:

$$\hat{\tilde{z}}_{b,t+1} = \tilde{z}_{b,t} + \gamma \cdot (X_N W_{\text{out}}) \tag{19}$$

4   Experimental Settings

This section describes our approach to windowing, sampling of windows, validation and test sets, optimization, and model hyperparameters. We consider telecom data from multiple cell tower antennas in the area of Copenhagen, where
some towers and/or sectors may not be operational at time $t = 1$. For those
sectors, we consider the time series to start at the first non-zero value. Time
series with more than 50% missing or zero values are excluded from the dataset.
The data is sampled on an hourly frequency, and we chose to set the forecasting
horizon size to be 24 h. To evaluate the performance of our proposed model, we
split the data into training, validation, and test sets in time. The test and validation sets each cover a period of 7 days. In other words, values of the test set are
given by time indices in the range $t \in \{T_{\text{val}} + 1, \ldots, T\}$, where $T_{\text{val}} = T - 7 \cdot 24$.
Similarly, the values of the validation set are given by time indices in the range
$t \in \{T_{\text{train}} + 1, \ldots, T_{\text{val}}\}$, where $T_{\text{train}} = T_{\text{val}} - 7 \cdot 24$. Finally, the values of the
training set are given by indices in the range $t \in \{1, \ldots, T_{\text{train}}\}$. To handle the
large amount of data in our dataset, we use a windowing technique where we
split the time series into windows of total size $T_{\text{window}} = 64$. For the training set,
we use a stride of 1 to generate training windows, while for the validation and
test set, a stride of 24 is used. The model is trained using teacher forcing [11].
The last 24 entries of each window are used as both inputs and targets to be
learned with teacher forcing, while the first 40 entries serve only as inputs. For
the test set, forecasts within a 24-h window are generated autoregressively. This
means that it is necessary to forecast the values of all sectors for a single time
step, before the next time step can be generated.

To ensure that the training data is representative of the overall population of
sectors, we first sample sectors from the training data with uniform probability,
and then sample a window within that sector's time series with conditional uniform probability. This is done in order to balance the dataset, by compensating
for the fact that some sectors have fewer valid windows (because they started
recording data at a later time than the initial time $t = 1$).

We use the Mean Absolute Error (MAE) in the max-scaled space as the loss
function. However, we report performance metrics in the original scale. Optimization was done using the Lamb [12] optimizer, with bias correction, gradient
clipping for norms greater than 10, and otherwise default parameters. A training
epoch is defined to consist of 128 training batches, with each batch containing
1024 randomly sampled windows. We use an early stopping strategy to dynamically stop training if the validation loss does not improve within 8 training
epochs.

Our Transformer model consists of 4 layers, each with 4 attention heads. We
set $d_{\text{model}} = 64$ and $d_{\text{feedforward}} = 256$, which results in a total of around 200,000
learnable parameters within the Transformer model.

Table 1. Median MAE test set scores of 101 repeated experiments. We also include the naïve predictor as a simple baseline to give some context regarding the magnitude of the numbers provided. S refers to the seasonality of the naïve predictor, such that $S = 24$ is the model that always predicts the value from the current hour of the previous day, and $S = 1$ is the model that always predicts the value from the previous hour. Note that Naïve with $S = 1$ has access to more information than the Transformer models, as these generate forecasts of the entire horizon autoregressively, and therefore cannot similarly use the true previous values in their forecast.

	Naïve $S = 24$	Naïve $S = 1$	All neighbors	Self only	CA w/o feat.	CA w/feat.
Median MAE	23.68	19.48	15.59	15.14	15.04	**14.49**

5 Results and Discussion

5.1 Experiment 1: Baseline Comparison

In this section we present a comparison of Transformer models with Circle Attention (CA) relative to two baseline Transformer models, on the task of network traffic forecasting. The two baseline Transformer models are called "All neighbors", which has $X_i^{(\text{NEIGHBORS})} = 1$ for all neighbors, and "Self only", which has $X_i^{(\text{NEIGHBORS})} = 0$ for all neighbors except the sector to be forecasted (i.e. itself). In addition, we also compare against a Transformer which uses Circle Attention, but without using the intersection scores directly as features, i.e. with Eq. 15 replaced by $X_i^{(\text{IOA})} = 0$. We perform 101 repeated experiments for each of the four model types. Table 1 contains the median MAE scores on the test set for each model type. We also include the scores of simple naïve predictors to give additional context. Figure 3 shows box-plots of MAE scores on the test set, and Fig. 4 shows loss curves for the training and validation sets.

The models using the Circle Attention (CA) with intersection scores as features clearly outperform the three other methods on the test set. However, models using CA without the intersection scores as features only perform marginally better than the "Self only" baseline. We hypothesize that having access to the intersection scores directly as features results in more stable gradients for the circle parameters. This might be due to the amount of variation within the time series of our dataset. (The gating of the time series by the intersection scores means that the circle parameter gradients are proportional on the values of the time series in the case where the intersection scores are not included as features.)

Interestingly, the loss curves in Fig. 4 show a clear difference in both training and validation loss for the four methods. The models with Circle Attention achieve lower loss values than the two baselines, and having access to the intersection scores as features is also clearly beneficial for training. Interestingly, the "All neighbors" baseline achieves lower loss values than "Self only" baseline, while performing worse on the test set. This can likely be explained by the differences in how the forecasts are generated for the training and validation sets,

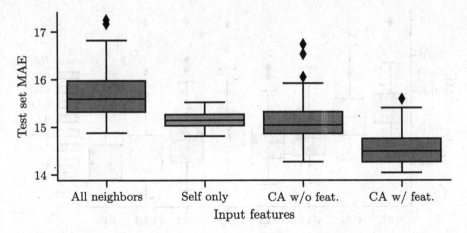

Fig. 3. Box-plot of MAE scores on the test set for the four model types of Experiment 1. Each box represents 101 repeated experiments.

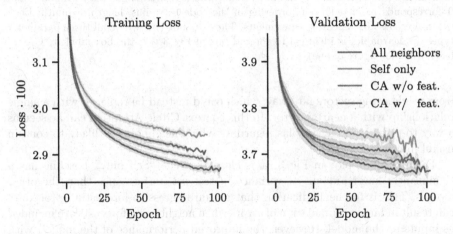

Fig. 4. Loss curves for the four model types of Experiment 1. Each curve represents the average loss of 101 repeated experiments, and the shaded regions represent the standard deviation. Please note that the plot has a survivorship bias due to the training process being stopped if the validation loss does not decrease for 8 consecutive epochs.

versus the test set. For the validation set, teacher forcing is used to generate a full horizon of one-step predictions in one model evaluation. In contrast, the forecasts on the test set are generated autoregressively, by iteratively feeding the previous forecasts as inputs, including forecasts of neighboring sectors. It is well known that such autoregressive forecasts typically accumulate errors as the forecasting horizon increases. Consequently, it seems likely that the "All neighbors" baseline accumulates errors to a greater degree than the other models, which do not rely as heavily on the neighboring forecasts. This can be seen as a form of overfitting, as the model might learn multiple spurious relationships

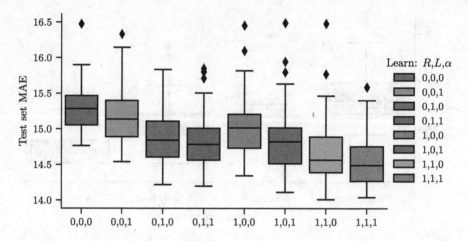

Fig. 5. Box-plot of MAE scores on the test set for the 8 ablation settings of Experiment 2. We label the boxes by a binary code, where 1 corresponds to "learnable", and 0 corresponds to "fixed". The ordering of the code is: radius, length, azimuth. Each box represents 101 repeated experiments. The gray box (i.e. where all three parameter types are learnable) is identical to the red box of Fig. 3 (i.e. the box labeled "CA w/ feat."). (Color figure online)

from neighboring sectors far away, which could instead be replaced with a single relationship with a nearby sector. In this context Circle Attention can be seen as a way to provide inductive bias regarding which neighbors are likely to contain useful information.

From the box-plot in Fig. 3, it is clear that the "Self only" baseline has a significantly lower amount of variance in test set performance than the other models. This is further indication that an autoregressive forecasting procedure can result in large accumulation of errors when neighboring forecasts are included as inputs to the model. However, the improved performance of the models with CA shows that having access to neighboring sectors also has the potential to improve autoregressive forecasts, despite the additional error accumulated. In other words, there seems to be trade-off between access to additional information at training time, and increased accumulation of errors at test time.

5.2   Experiment 2: Ablation Study of Circle Parameters

In this section we present an ablation study on the effect of the three circle parameter types; the azimuth α, the length L, and the radius R. We perform the ablation by keeping the values of each of parameter type fixed (i.e. not learned). While we showed in the previous experiment that CA performs better than baselines which include all or none of the neighboring sectors, it is not clear that learning of all the circle parameters is required. The baselines of the previous experiment represent the extremes of possible *effective* neighborhood sizes, and models with CA fall somewhere in between these two extremes (one way to mathematically define the effective neighborhood size could be by the sum of the intersection scores of each neighborhood). Hence, it is not clear from the previous experiment that learning of the parameters is necessary, as it might be the case that simply having an effective neighborhood between the extremes would be enough. Furthermore, as the azimuth values are initialized directly from values recorded in the dataset, the model should be able to perform at a similar level regardless of whether this parameter is learned or not.

To investigate the importance of learning of the parameters, we test all the $2^3 = 8$ combinations of learned and fixed parameters, by performing 101 repeated experiments for each combination. Figure 5 shows the box-plots of the test scores of this experiment. As can be seen from the figure, learning of the parameters appears to be critical for good forecasting performance, as learning improves performance for each of the three parameter types. However, as expected, the radius and the length are of greater importance than the azimuth, which was already initialized to the value recorded in the dataset. Interestingly, the model which has all circle parameters fixed performs better than the "All neighbors" baseline of the previous experiment, which indicates that simply reducing the effective neighborhood size is beneficial.

6   Conclusion

In this paper, we propose Circle Attention (CA), a general method to model the spatial relationships between telecommunication towers, and for improving forecasting accuracy on the task of cell phone traffic prediction. The proposed method uses the area of intersecting circles to model spatial relationships and learns the circle parameters end-to-end through back-propagation. We compare the performance of two versions of the CA method with two strong baseline Transformer models and conduct ablation studies to investigate the importance of the circle parameters. The experiments show that the models using Circle Attention outperform the other models on the test set. Additionally, the ablation studies demonstrate that learning of the circle parameters is critical for good forecasting performance, with radius and length being of greater importance than azimuth. Overall, our paper presents a novel approach to forecasting cell phone traffic, and contributes to advancing the understanding of how spatial relationships can be effectively modeled for improved forecasting accuracy in the domain of telecommunication data. We suggest several potential directions for further work. First, the concept could be extended to three dimensions by modeling the height of towers and pitch of cell antennas. Second, the idea could be extended to include variations due to temporal dynamics. Third, regularization terms could be added to constrain the circles to realistic ranges of values. Finally, a variational probabilistic approach could be used to improve interpretability and estimate uncertainty.

7   Ethical Statement

This research project focuses on forecasting telecom network traffic by analyzing one key performance indicator (KPI) aggregated per sector. Specifically, we examine the *number of attempted calls* made in each sector. To protect the privacy, security, and confidentiality of the data and the individuals whose data were used, we conducted this research project in compliance with ethical guidelines and standards.

The data we used for this project were collected at the radio tower level and do not include any personal information about the users. Instead, the data only represent the current load of the tower. We collected data in accordance with the legal and regulatory requirements of the relevant data protection agencies. We obtained informed and written consent from the telecommunications provider to use the data for this research project, ensuring that our use of the data was aligned with their terms of service and privacy policy.

Our proposed method aims to restrict the use of radio towers whenever they are underused, thereby reducing energy emissions. This method has no ethical impact apart from giving the telecommunications provider guidance on how to reduce their environmental impact.

We also emphasize the importance of ethical considerations in machine learning research. By conducting research in an ethical and responsible manner, researchers can ensure that the use of data and machine learning methods is beneficial to societal progress.

References

1. Andreoletti, D., Troia, S., Musumeci, F., Giordano, S., Maier, G., Tornatore, M.: Network traffic prediction based on diffusion convolutional recurrent neural networks. In: IEEE INFOCOM 2019-IEEE Conference on Computer Communications Workshops (INFOCOM WKSHPS), pp. 246–251. IEEE (2019). https://doi.org/10.1109/INFCOMW.2019.8845132
2. Fang, L., Cheng, X., Wang, H., Yang, L.: Mobile demand forecasting via deep graph-sequence spatiotemporal modeling in cellular networks. IEEE Internet Things J. **5**(4), 3091–3101 (2018). https://doi.org/10.1109/JIOT.2018.2832071
3. Haugsdal, E., Aune, E., Ruocco, M.: Persistence initialization: a novel adaptation of the transformer architecture for time series forecasting. Appl. Intell. 1–16 (2023). https://doi.org/10.1007/s10489-023-04927-4
4. He, K., Chen, X., Wu, Q., Yu, S., Zhou, Z.: Graph attention spatial-temporal network with collaborative global-local learning for citywide mobile traffic prediction. IEEE Trans. Mob. Comput. **21**(4), 1244–1256 (2020). https://doi.org/10.1109/TMC.2020.3020582
5. Hong, W.C.: Application of seasonal SVR with chaotic immune algorithm in traffic flow forecasting. Neural Comput. Appl. **21**, 583–593 (2012). https://doi.org/10.1007/s00521-010-0456-7
6. Kalander, M., Zhou, M., Zhang, C., Yi, H., Pan, L.: Spatio-temporal hybrid graph convolutional network for traffic forecasting in telecommunication networks. arXiv preprint arXiv:2009.09849 (2020). 10.48550/arXiv. 2009.09849

7. Kipf, T.N., Welling, M.: Semi-supervised classification with graph convolutional networks. In: International Conference on Learning Representations (2017)

8. Liu, Q., Li, J., Lu, Z.: ST-Tran: spatial-temporal transformer for cellular traffic prediction. IEEE Commun. Lett. **25**(10), 3325–3329 (2021). https://doi.org/10.1109/LCOMM.2021.3098557

9. Taylor, S.J., Letham, B.: Forecasting at scale. Am. Stat. **72**(1), 37–45 (2018). https://doi.org/10.1080/00031305.2017.1380080

10. Vaswani, A., et al.: Attention is all you need. In: Advances in Neural Information Processing Systems, pp. 5998–6008 (2017)

11. Williams, R.J., Zipser, D.: A learning algorithm for continually running fully recurrent neural networks. Neural Comput. **1**(2), 270–280 (1989). https://doi.org/10.1162/neco.1989.1.2.270

12. You, Y., et al.: Large batch optimization for deep learning: training BERT in 76 minutes. In: International Conference on Learning Representations (2020)

13. Zhang, K., Chuai, G., Gao, W., Liu, X., Maimaiti, S., Si, Z.: A new method for traffic forecasting in urban wireless communication network. EURASIP J. Wirel. Commun. Netw. **2019**, 1–12 (2019). https://doi.org/10.1186/s13638-019-1392-6

14. Zhang, S., et al.: Traffic prediction based power saving in cellular networks: a machine learning method. In: Proceedings of the 25th ACM SIGSPATIAL International Conference on Advances in Geographic Information Systems, pp. 1–10 (2017). https://doi.org/10.1145/3139958.3140053

15. Zhao, N., Ye, Z., Pei, Y., Liang, Y.C., Niyato, D.: Spatial-temporal attention-convolution network for citywide cellular traffic prediction. IEEE Commun. Lett. **24**(11), 2532–2536 (2020). https://doi.org/10.1109/LCOMM.2020.3012279

16. Zhou, B., He, D., Sun, Z.: Traffic modeling and prediction using ARIMA/GARCH model. In: Nejat Ince, A., Topuz, E. (eds.) Modeling and Simulation Tools for Emerging Telecommunication Networks, pp. 101–121. Springer, Boston (2006). https://doi.org/10.1007/0-387-34167-6_5

Transportation and Urban Planning

Pre-training Contextual Location Embeddings in Personal Trajectories via Efficient Hierarchical Location Representations

Chung Park[1,2], Taesan Kim[1], Junui Hong[1,2], Minsung Choi[1], and Jaegul Choo[2(✉)]

[1] SK Telecom, Seoul, Republic of Korea
{skt.cpark,ktmountain,skt.juhong,ms.choi}@sk.com
[2] Kim Jaechul Graduate School of AI, KAIST, Daejeon, Republic of Korea
{cpark88kr,secondrun3,jchoo}@kaist.ac.kr

Abstract. Pre-training the embedding of a location generated from human mobility data has become a popular method for location based services. In practice, modeling the location embedding is too expensive, due to the large number of locations to be trained in situations with fine-grained resolution or extensive target regions. Previous studies have handled less than ten thousand distinct locations, which is insufficient in the real-world applications. To tackle this problem, we propose a Geo-Tokenizer, designed to efficiently reduce the number of locations to be trained by representing a location as a combination of several grids at different scales. In the Geo-Tokenizer, a grid at a larger scale shares the common set of grids at smaller scales, which is a key factor in reducing the size of the location vocabulary. The sequences of locations preprocessed with the Geo-Tokenizer are utilized by a causal location embedding model to capture the temporal dependencies of locations. This model dynamically calculates the embedding vector of a target location, which varies depending on its trajectory. In addition, to efficiently pre-train the location embedding model, we propose the Hierarchical Auto-regressive Location Model objective to effectively train decomposed locations in the Geo-Tokenizer. We conducted experiments on two real-world user trajectory datasets using our pre-trained location model. The experimental results show that our model significantly improves the performance of downstream tasks with fewer model parameters compared to existing location embedding methods.

Keywords: Pre-trained Causal Location Embedding · Hierarchical Auto-regressive Location Model · Spatial Hierarchy

1 Introduction

For modeling human mobility patterns using large-scale mobility data, pre-training location embeddings using a self-supervised objective has advantages,

© The Author(s), under exclusive license to Springer Nature Switzerland AG 2023
G. De Francisci Morales et al. (Eds.): ECML PKDD 2023, LNAI 14175, pp. 125–140, 2023.
https://doi.org/10.1007/978-3-031-43430-3_8

because it allows comprehensive information about locations to be incorporated [6]. The pre-trained location embedding models can also be shared by a wide range of downstream models, such as those used for next location prediction or transportation mode classification, to improve the prediction performance as well as enhance computation efficiency [14].

Many previous studies have applied language-modeling-based approaches to spatial-temporal datasets [6,22]. For example, in DeepMove [22], the latent representations of places are trained by applying the skip-gram of word2vec [7] to user trajectories. CTLE [6] is a self-attention based location embedding model that considers a target location's contexts. However, these previous studies still have limitations, as follows: First, the approaches are not scalable to real-world applications, which require numerous locations to be trained. With the fine-grained resolution or extensive target regions, the number of distinct locations, the so-called **location vocabulary**, increases. This deteriorates the quality and efficiency of the pre-trained embedding model because of the heavy embedding layer to be trained. However, previous studies including Geo-Teaser [18], TrajFormer [5], and CTLE [6] train the location embedding model with less than ten thousand locations. Second, locations in a trajectory are often dependent on previously visited locations, meaning that the likelihood of visiting a specific location might be influenced by the locations stayed before [6,21]. These dependencies can be short-term (e.g., dependencies between consecutive locations) or long-term (e.g., dependencies spanning multiple locations), and they are crucial factors for modeling the context-aware location embedding model. However, previous studies have had difficulty capturing this sequential dependence between locations in their models.

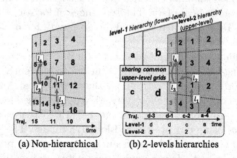

(a) Non-hierarchical   (b) 2-levels hierarchies

Fig. 1. An illustration of spatial hierarchies at different scales ($H = 2$). (a) A trajectory with a non-hierarchical case is described. (b) In our hierarchical case, each grid in the level-1 hierarchy shares the common grids set of $1, 2, 3, 4$ in the level-2 hierarchy. For instance, *Grid* 6 in the non-hierarchical case can be represented as (*Grid a*+*Grid* 4) in the hierarchical case.

In order to tackle the discussed problems, we suggest a pre-trained location embedding model to efficiently handle numerous location vocabularies in various real-world applications. First, we devised the **geo-tokenizer embedding layer**, which represents a particular location as a combination of multiple grids at different scales to reduce the number of locations to be trained. In this scheme, a specific location is represented as the combination of the H tokens. For example, as the location is composed of two hierarchies' grids in Fig. 1, its final representation is calculated by an element-wise sum of two hierarchies' grid embeddings. Note that in our model, a grid in a lower (i.e., coarser-grained) hierarchy shares the common set of grids in upper (i.e., finer-grained) hierarchies, which is a key factor in reducing the location vocabulary size.

Second, we designed a **causal location embedding model** consisting of the stack of the transformer decoder [12]. The transformer decoder inherently models temporal relationships due to its auto-regressive nature. This allows the model to capture the sequential patterns in the trajectory. Therefore, we dynamically calculate the embedding of a target location considering its temporal order, which varies depending on its trajectory.

Lastly, to pre-train our location embedding model, we modified the Auto-regressive Language Model (ALM) objective introduced in the transformer [12]. Since a grid in the lower hierarchy shares the those of the upper hierarchies in our model, specific two locations with far distance would have same lower-level (e.g., coarser-grained) embeddings despite that they may have different semantics or functionalities. To solve this problem, we devised a **Hierarchical Auto-regressive Location Model (HALM)**. This incorporated information from the lower-level hierarchies into the upper-level hierarchies when implementing ALM tasks to propagate the predicted output of lower-level hierarchies to the upper-level hierarchies. These components are incorporated in our model, as shown in Fig. 2. As a result, our location embedding model has relatively fewer parameters to learn and less computational cost than other competitive baselines. In addition, it allows downstream task performance, such as next location prediction or transportation mode classification, to be improved with faster training and inference speed.

2   Preliminaries

A supplementary material (Appendix) with more details about the model, datasets and experiments is available at Github[1].

Definition 1. Trajectory: A trajectory is a sequence of locations where a person stays for a predefined time period [11, 20]. We set each location as a grid shape and l_t as the t-th grid-shaped location. Then, the sequence of visiting locations, denoted as a trajectory, can be defined as follows,

$$s = \{l_0, l_1, \ldots, l_T\} \tag{1}$$

where T is the length of the trajectory s and l_0 is the special token SOS which indicates the start of the trajectory. We also denote S as a set of trajectories. We

---

[1] https://github.com/cpark88/ECML-PKDD2023

define the **location vocabulary** as the set of locations appearing in the train dataset, and denote it as L. The size of L is the vocabulary size of locations, denoted as $|L|$.

Definition 2. Spatial Hierarchy: Suppose that we set H-levels of **spatial hierarchies** $\{1, 2, ..., H\}$, where the level-h hierarchy consists of grids with sizes of r_h meters. The uppermost hierarchy level H has the smallest scale of r_H, thus the upper-level hierarchy has finer-grained grids than the lower-level.

Each grid in the level-$(h\text{-}1)$ hierarchy is divided into a common grid set in the level-h hierarchy, and the t-th location l_t can be represented with a combination of H grids at different scales. From this spatial hierarchy, the location l_t can be decomposed into the tuple of grids $(l_t^1, l_t^2, ..., l_t^H)$. Therefore, trajectory s consisting of decomposed locations from different hierarchies can be re-defined as follows,

$$s = \{(l_0^1, l_0^2, ..., l_0^H), (l_1^1, l_1^2, ..., l_1^H), ..., (l_T^1, l_T^2, ..., l_T^H)\} \tag{2}$$

where l_t^h is a level-h grid at the t-th step and l_0^h is the SOS token of the level-h hierarchy. We define the set of all level-h grids appearing in the train dataset as the location vocabulary of level-h hierarchy, and denote it as L^h. The size of L^h is denoted as $|L^h|$. Since $|L| \geq \sum_{h=1}^{H} |L^h|$, using the trajectories of decomposed locations is significantly efficient.

Problem Statement. Pre-training Location Embedding Model for Hierarchically Decomposed Locations: Our goal is to pre-train a location embedding model u to calculate a contextual embedding vector $k(l_t)$ by predicting a next location $l_{t+1} = (l_{t+1}^1, l_{t+1}^2, ..., l_{t+1}^H)$ given its context $s_{<t+1} = \{(l_0^1, l_0^2, ..., l_0^H), (l_1^1, l_1^2, ..., l_1^H), ..., (l_t^1, l_t^2, ..., l_t^H)\}$ with H hierarchies. We pre-train our model in a self-supervised manner as shown in Fig. 2.

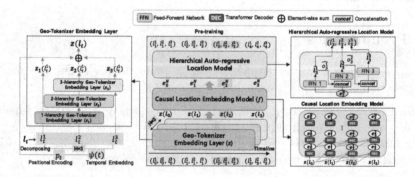

Fig. 2. We display the pre-training process of our model. The model with three level hierarchies(H) case is illustrated. Note that $k(l_2) = f(z(l_0), z(l_1), z(l_2)) = u(s_{<3}) = e_2^N$ as described in Eqs. 5 and 7.

3   Model

3.1   Geo-Tokenizer Embedding Layer

We propose the geo-tokenizer embedding layer, which allows the location embeddings to be trained efficiently with a reduced number of location tokens. By employing spatial hierarchies with different grid sizes, we can potentially capture varying levels of spatial patterns. We first transform the input sequence into an embedding vector sequence. As shown in Fig. 2, we fetch an input latent representation $z(l_t)$ for t-th location l_t from the embedding layer z. We call the embedding layer z the geo-tokenizer embedding layer. The embedding vector $z(l_t)$ can be described as follows,

$$z(l_t) = (\sum_{h=1}^{H} z_h(l_t^h)) + p_t + \psi(t) \tag{3}$$

where z_h is a fully-connected embedding layer of the level-h hierarchy, l_t^h is a grid of the level-h hierarchy at the t-th step, and p_t is the t-th item of the positional encoding (PE) introduced in Transformer [12]. The PE has an important role to capture the relative temporal position in the sequence. In addition, inspired by the previous study [4], we devised the temporal embedding $\psi(t)$. For trajectories, the visiting records have temporal information which may significantly determine predicted locations. $\psi(t)$ is calculated as follows,

$$\psi(t) = \phi(log(r_t)W_d + b_d), \tag{4}$$

where ϕ is a nonlinear activation function (e.g., ReLU), and r_t is an absolute timestamp at the t-th time step such as the real number in Unix Time. W_d is the trainable parameters for linearly transforming $log(r_t)$ and b_d is the bias term. The log transformation is conducted with r_t to effectively cover the wide numerical range of temporal value [4]. The dimension of $\psi(t)$ is equal to that of $z_h(l_t^h)$ and p_t. This procedure generates an input sequence embedding $\{z(l_0), z(l_2), ..., z(l_t)\}$ for the causal location embedding model we will discuss in the next section. Therefore, each embedding layer is represented by a matrix $z_h \in \mathbb{R}^{|L^h| \times W}$, where $|L^h|$ is the size of the vocabulary in the level-h hierarchy, and W is the embedding dimension.

3.2   Causal Location Embedding Model

The context of a target location can be obtained by the sequence of other locations before the target location in a trajectory. From this perspective, we propose a causal location embedding model, which calculates a location's latent representation by considering its contextual neighbors. As shown in Fig. 2, given a $(t+1)$-th target location l_{t+1} and its context $s_{<t+1}$, we generate t-th location's final embedding vector $k(l_t)$ by using the casual location embedding model f and the geo-tokenizer embedding layer z, denoted as follows:

$$k(l_t) = f(z(l_0), z(l_1), ..., z(l_t))$$
$$= u(l_0, l_1, ..., l_t), \tag{5}$$
$$= u(s_{<t+1}),$$

where u is our total location embedding model. The embedding vector $k(l_t)$ is t-th item in output vectors' sequence of u. Therefore, the embedding vector of l_t is dynamically generated depending on the context $s_{<t+1}$.

The causal location embedding model f consists of the stack of the transformer decoder [12]. Due to the sequential nature of a trajectory, the model should take into account only the first t items when predicting the $(t+1)$-th item. This can consider the causal correlations of a target location and its contexts. In addition, compared to the traditional sequential models such as LSTM [3], it has the advantage of the long-term dependency and the parallelization with sequential datasets such as trajectories. Also, unlike previous studies using the transformer encoder structure [6,8], our model processes location information sequentially and can better handle both short-term and long-term dependencies in the trajectory (See the Appendix A.5).

Specifically, the input sequence embedding $\{z(l_0), z(l_2), ..., z(l_t)\}$ calculated in the geo-tokenizer embedding layer, is then fed into the causal location embedding model f, which is the stack of the transformer decoder. A multi-head self-attention module with a causality mask and a feed-forward network are inherent in each transformer decoder [12]. This process is described as:

$$\{\mathbf{e}_0^{(k)}, \mathbf{e}_1^{(k)}, ..., \mathbf{e}_t^{(k)}\}$$
$$= \mathbf{Decoder}(\{\mathbf{e}_0^{(k-1)}, \mathbf{e}_1^{(k-1)}, ..., \mathbf{e}_t^{(k-1)}\}), \tag{6}$$
$$\{\mathbf{e}_0^{(0)}, \mathbf{e}_1^{(0)}, ..., \mathbf{e}_t^{(0)}\} = \{z(l_0), z(l_1), ..., z(l_t)\},$$

where the **Decoder** represents the transformer decoder. The output sequence of the k-th layer and the input sequence of the $(k+1)$-th layer are the same as $\{\mathbf{e}_0^{(k)}, \mathbf{e}_1^{(k)}, ..., \mathbf{e}_t^{(k)}\}$. We stack the N transformer decoders in our causal location embedding module f. The t-th item of the N-th transformer decoder is denoted as $\mathbf{e}_t^N$, which is the causal embedding vector of the location l_t. In short, the final output vector of the location l_t in the N stack of the Decoder can be represented as:

$$k(l_t) = \mathbf{e}_t^N. \tag{7}$$

3.3   Pre-training Hierarchical Auto-Regressive Location Model

The relationship between target locations and their corresponding contexts should be considered in the location embedding model. For this purpose, we propose the novel variant of the Auto-regressive Language Model (ALM) objective introduced in the transformer [9,10,12]. In this paper, since we predict the next location in our pre-trained model, the ALM is rewritten as the Auto-regressive Location Model. The ALM objective encourages the model to predict the next token with its context uni-directionally. In this way, the correlation between the target token and its contexts can be captured in a self-supervised manner. However, since a grid in the lower hierarchy shares the those of the upper hierarchies in our model, specific two locations with far distance would have same upper-level embeddings despite that they may have different semantics. For this reason, we incorporated information from the lower-level hierarchies into the upper-level hierarchies when implementing ALM tasks to propagate the information of lower-level hierarchies to the upper-level hierarchies. In short, the predictions of upper-level hierarchies are contingent upon the predicted outcomes of lower-level hierarchies.

As shown in Fig. 2, we utilized a decomposed trajectory $s = \{l_0, l_1, \ldots, l_t\} = \{(l_0^1, l_0^2, \ldots, l_0^H), (l_1^1, l_1^2, \ldots, l_1^H), \ldots, (l_t^1, l_t^2, \ldots, l_t^H)\}$ as the input of our location embedding model, and predicted the *shifted* version of the input sequence s. We train our model with multiple training objectives. The ALM objectives of all hierarchies are trained simultaneously. However, each ALM objective has a different task complexity. Actually, since the grid size of the lower-level hierarchies is larger than that of the upper-level hierarchies, the trajectories of the lower-level hierarchies have monotonic patterns. Therefore, the ALM objectives of lower hierarchies are much less demanding to train than the ALM objectives of upper hierarchies, which causes a learning imbalance between tasks. In a multi-task architecture, the learning imbalance between tasks leads to causes the model to memorize a specific task instead of generalizing a pattern of data [1]. To solve this problem, in the ALM objectives, we sequentially incorporate the information from the lower hierarchy into the upper hierarchy. We denote this multi-task objective as Hierarchical ALM (HALM). The next location $l_{t+1} = (l_{t+1}^1, l_{t+1}^2, \ldots, l_{t+1}^H)$ to be predicted in the model consist of the H tokens. For this, we design H fully-connected feed-forward networks to predict the H next tokens using the causal location embedding model's output $\mathbf{e}_t^{(N)}$. First, we predict l_{t+1}^1, the token of level-1 (i.e., the coarsest-grained) hierarchy in the $(t+1)$-step, as follows:

$$\widehat{l_{t+1}^1} = FFN_{HLM}^1(\mathbf{e}_t^{(N)}), \tag{8}$$

where FFN_{HLM}^1 is the fully-connected feed-forward network of the level-1 hierarchy and $\widehat{l_{t+1}^1}$ is the prediction output for the next location token l_{t+1}^1. In general, the prediction of the token of the level-h hierarchy (i.e., $h > 1$) in the $(t+1)$-step, is sequentially implemented as follows:

$$\widehat{l_{t+1}^h} = FFN_{HLM}^h(\mathbf{e}_t^{(N)} \parallel \widehat{o_{t+1}^{h-1}}),$$
$$\widehat{o_{t+1}^0} = \mathbf{0}, \tag{9}$$

where $\parallel$ is the concatenation operation and $\widehat{o_{t+1}^{h-1}}$ is the one-hot encoding vector from prediction result $\widehat{l_{t+1}^{h-1}}$. FFN_{HLM}^h is composed of two fully-connected layers in this paper. We construct the HALM objective to maximize the prediction accuracy of all of the hierarchies in the next location l_{t+1}. The pre-training objective of the HALM can be described as:

$$O_{HALM} = \underset{\theta}{\arg\max} \sum_{h=1}^{H} \sum_{t=0}^{T} log(p(l_{t+1}^h | \widehat{l_{t+1}^h})), \tag{10}$$

where θ denotes the set of all trainable parameters in our model, T is the length of the trajectory, and H is the uppermost level of the hierarchy (i.e., the finest-grained).

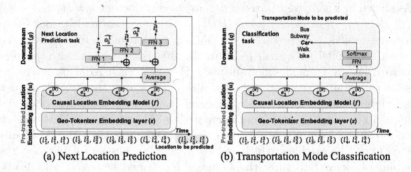

(a) Next Location Prediction (b) Transportation Mode Classification

Fig. 3. Illustration of the downstream tasks. (a) Model architecture of the next location prediction task using an FFN layer stacked on the pre-trained location embedding model. (b) Model architecture of transportation mode classification task using one FFN layer stacked on the pre-trained location embedding model.

3.4   Fine-Tuning Downstream Tasks

Next Location Prediction Task. We implemented a next location prediction as a downstream task widely used in the location-based service in the real world [6,17]. The trajectory up to T is used as an input in the downstream model, and the ground-truth is the three decomposed location records in $T + 1$ (Fig. 3a).

Classification Task. The model architecture for the transportation mode classification using a fully connected layer stacked on top of the pre-trained location embedding model is described in Fig. 3b. A whole trajectory is used as an input in the downstream model, and the output is the transportation mode of the trajectory. See Appendix A.4 for details of above two downstream models.

4   Experiments

Our experiments are designed to answer the following research questions:
(RQ1): How effective is our pre-trained location embedding model compared to the state-of-the-art models in the various downstream tasks?

(RQ2): How do the different components affect the downstream tasks' performance?

(RQ3): What is the effect of the level of hierarchies in our pre-trained model?

(RQ4): How effective is the pre-training of the location embedding model in the self-supervised manner on the downstream tasks?

Table 1. Statistics of datasets

Dataset	Data Type	#Users	#Original Locations (100m)	#Tokenized Locations (100m)				#Traj	Time span
				Total	#Locations level-1 (100km)	#Locations level-2 (1km)	#Locations level-3 (100m)		
Mobile-T	Mobile Signal	0.4M	**79,812**	**6,740**	24	6,616	100	1.3M	7/1,2021-7/31,2021
Geo-Life	GPS	182	**50,003**	**8,476**	183	8,193	100	17,621	4/1,2007-8/31,2012

4.1 Datasets

Mobile-T: This data is a set of user trajectories collected by the base stations of the major cellular network operator, denoted as Mobile-T. As shown in Table 1, the size of location vocabularies at a 100m scale is 79812, which is too large to train for location embeddings. However, using the Geo-tokenizer, the sizes of the location vocabularies in each hierarchy, 100 km, 1 km, and 100 m scale, are 24, 6616, and 100, respectively. This means that the total summation of the size of location vocabularies is 6740, which is less than 79812. Meanwhile, Mobile-T contains the land usage of the last location of a trajectory, associated with the purpose of the trajectory. There are 15 unique land usages of a trajectory, such as Apartment House or Business Facilities.

Geo-Life [19]: We also used the public GPS trajectory dataset, Geo-Life, which was collected with 182 users over a period of five years in Microsoft Research Asia. In the Geo-Life dataset, the trajectories are described as sequences of locations represented as GPS coordinates. Like the Mobile-T, the location record in this dataset was converted into a grid at a 100m scale. In this dataset, the number of distinct decomposed locations with three hierarchies (8476) was less than the number of original locations (50003), as shown in Table 1. The Geo-life dataset contains five unique transportation modes of a trajectory. See Appendix A.1 for details of two datasaets.

4.2 Settings

For both datasets, we assigned pre-train and fine-tune datasets of 80% and 20% of the total dataset. Then, we assigned train, validation, and test datasets of 80%, 10%, and 10% of the fine-tune datasets. We trained fine-tuning (i.e., downstream) models with the train datasets and chose the optimal hyper-parameters with the validation datasets. We set the hierarchy level H as three, and the scales of the level-1, level-2, and level-3 hierarchies were 100 km, 1 km, and 100 m, respectively. We demonstrated the superiority of our pre-trained location model by comparing six location embedding models: (1) SERM [15], (2) HIER [11], (3) DeepMove [22], (4) TALE [13], (5) CTLE [6], and (6) TrajFormer [5]. Including our model, the dimension of the embedding layer and final location embedding vector was set to 256 in all models. We described the model details in Appendix A.2 and the pre-training setting in Appendix A.3.

Table 2. Comparison of Next Location Prediction performance and efficiency with those of previous studies. The top two methods are highlighted in bold and underlined.

Downstream Model		FFN		LSTM		#Params	#FLOPs	TR-time	Inf-time
Metric		Top-1 Acc(%)	Top-5 Acc(%)	Top-1 Acc(%)	Top-5 Acc(%)				
Dataset	Pre-trained Model								
	SERM [15]	8.41±0.11	26.77±0.32	8.23±0.09	25.08±0.35	12.68M	1.31B	647.25	56.00
	HIER [11]	10.09±0.05	30.37±0.15	8.99±0.12	28.75±0.34	18.47M	1.42B	837.39	71.47
	DeepMove [22]	9.05±0.15	30.81±0.19	9.38±0.30	31.75±0.54	49.92M	2.62B	1338.47	116.55
Mobile-T	TALE [13]	9.02±0.14	30.28±0.48	9.43±0.14	29.12±0.42	49.92M	7.85B	3493.91	285.57
	CTLE [6]	10.71±0.24	32.39±1.09	9.31±0.14	25.77±0.46	43.72M	1.71B	642.61	56.60
	TrajFormer [5]	10.45±0.02	30.48±0.06	8.88±0.10	21.47±0.26	40.31M	1.55B	693.37	56.20
	Ours	11.47±0.13	38.41±0.11	11.20±0.05	40.21±0.08	6.90M	0.44B	400.63	43.37
	SERM [15]	18.35±0.11	29.02±0.18	18.58±0.31	36.46±0.44	12.60M	0.82B	187.12	15.20
	HIER [11]	18.80±0.13	31.33±0.19	18.09±0.16	38.34±0.13	13.67M	0.96B	207.43	16.37
	DeepMove [22]	17.46±0.11	35.72±0.12	18.68±0.19	38.03±0.22	25.60M	1.64B	345.66	30.38
Geo-Life	TALE [13]	17.58±0.13	31.17±0.18	19.04±0.12	38.15±0.14	25.60M	4.92B	678.68	59.59
	CTLE [6]	24.69±0.25	45.12±0.15	21.53±0.38	43.49±0.36	30.39M	1.18B	192.10	16.48
	TrajFormer [5]	27.71 ± 0.97	50.51 ± 0.93	26.34 ± 0.19	51.53 ± 0.30	28.91M	1.06B	223.44	16.97
	Ours	28.58±0.21	60.07±0.31	26.99±0.28	53.68±0.61	7.71M	0.48B	179.92	14.74

The number of parameters and FLOPs are derived from only location embedding models, except downstream task models (FFN and LSTM). M and B denote million and billion, respectively. We executed each baseline ten times and recorded the mean and standard deviation of each baseline. TR-time and Inf-time indicate the training time (seconds) per epoch and inference time (seconds) per epoch in the FFN case of the next location prediction model respectively. The training and inference speed were calculated by averaging those of FFN and LSTM with each pre-trained model, using one V100 GPU.

4.3   Experimental Results (RQ1)

Next Location Prediction Task. The performance of the next location prediction task was assessed using the accuracy of the test dataset. The rate at cutoff k, denoted as **Acc@k**, counts the fraction of cases where the target location is among the top k. We reported this metric as $k=1$ and $k=5$. We also evaluated the efficiency of the pre-trained location embedding model by measuring the number of model parameters and operations (FLOPs). A performance comparison for the next location prediction task is shown in Table 2. SERM [15] with the randomly initialized embedding layers did not perform well because this method has difficulty incorporating the context of a trajectory. DeepMove [22] and TALE [13] adopting Skip-gram and CBOW utilize the co-occurrence probabilities of target locations and their contexts, but the contexts they consider were restricted to specific window size. More importantly, these methods train the heavy embedding layers due to the large size of the location vocabulary, which was over 50,000 in both datasets.

Unlike the above previous studies, CTLE [6] and TrajFormer [5] incorporate the multi-functionality of a location via a self-attention module to consider the contexts of trajectories. As a result, they showed significantly better performance than the other baselines. However, they also had difficulty dealing with the large size of the location vocabulary and needed to train the heavy embedding layers. Our model consistently outperformed other methods, even with fewer parameters and the number of FLOPs. This can be attributed to the efficient processing of large amounts of location vocabulary using the Geo-tokenizer embedding layer and HALM objective. In addition, our model was faster than other baselines in the training and inference for both datasets (Table 2).

Classification Task. The performance of the land usage and transportation mode classification task was assessed using the accuracy, macro-precision, and macro-recall of the test dataset. A performance comparison for these tasks is shown in Table 3. With the fewest parameters, our pre-trained location embedding model showed the best performances among other location embedding models for both tasks, and was faster than other baselines in the training and inference. This indicates the superior quality of our pre-trained location embeddings.

Table 3. Comparison of Land Usage and Transportation Mode Classification task with those of previous studies. The top two methods are highlighted in bold and underlined.

Dataset	Downstream Task	Metric Pre-trained Model	Accuracy(%)	Precision(%)	Recall(%)	F-1(%)	TR-time	Inf-time
Mobile-T	Land Usage Classification	SERM [15]	79.12±0.02	73.83±0.03	70.35±0.02	70.65±0.02	58.23	5.42
		HIER [11]	79.39±0.05	76.70±0.03	73.31±0.03	74.42±0.02	121.28	6.94
		DeepMove [22]	81.05±0.09	77.95 ± 0.02	73.43 ± 0.03	75.38±0.02	129.09	10.99
		TALE [13]	83.02±0.06	77.09±0.07	73.33±0.10	76.47 ± 0.11	310.95	26.33
		CTLE [6]	87.44 ± 1.29	75.42±2.97	73.31±2.37	73.22±2.04	58.36	4.98
		TrajFormer [5]	73.65±0.83	67.37±4.90	56.24±1.36	59.42±2.08	66.86	6.68
		Ours	89.47±0.29	82.27±1.65	84.19±0.94	82.80±0.95	41.72	4.51
Geo-Life	Transportation Mode Classification	SERM [15]	68.19±0.02	69.13±0.03	69.21±0.03	69.19±0.03	5.26	0.58
		HIER [11]	64.45±0.17	60.56±0.12	64.52±0.21	64.44±0.14	6.44	0.74
		DeepMove [22]	69.81±0.09	71.46±0.02	69.96±0.07	69.95±0.08	9.58	1.28
		TALE [13]	62.88±0.08	70.32±0.09	65.86±0.11	66.53±0.11	18.78	2.51
		CTLE [6]	68.15±1.10	71.36±1.10	73.21±0.84	71.01±1.06	5.30	0.72
		TrajFormer [5]	73.68 ± 1.88	77.37 ± 1.33	76.49 ± 1.95	76.10 ± 1.68	5.88	0.59
		Ours	81.17±0.40	81.58±0.74	82.70±0.75	81.81±0.32	4.34	0.46

The number of parameters and FLOPs in each pre-trained embedding model is equal to the case of the next location prediction task, as shown in Table 2. We executed each baseline ten times and recorded the mean and standard deviation of each baseline.

4.4   Ablation Study

Study on the Components (RQ2). We investigated the effectiveness of each component of our pre-trained location embedding model by designing three variants as follows:

(1) Baseline: This model utilizes the original transformer decoder using the ALM objective for pre-training without the Geo-tokenizer embedding layer. This is a simple auto-regressive pre-trained model.

(2) +Geo-tokenizer(GT): This model replaces the embedding layers in the baseline with the Geo-tokenizer embedding layer, which decomposes each location record into the three hierarchical components (100 km, 1 km, 100 m). The pre-trained model's objective is the basic ALM proposed in the transformer [12]. Therefore, the ALM objectives of the three hierarchies are independent.

(3) +Geo-tokenizer(GT)+HALM: This model uses the Geo-tokenizer fused on the baseline and employs the HALM objective. This is our proposed model.

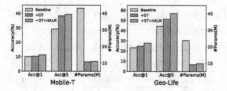 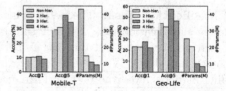

Fig. 4. Comparison of next location prediction performance and efficiency for different combinations of components.

Fig. 5. Next location prediction performance and efficiency comparison of different hierarchy levels.

The comparison of these three variants was conducted with our pre-trained location embedding model on the next location prediction task, shown in Fig. 4. The performance was calculated by averaging two downstream models (FFN and LSTM). Compared to the baseline model, the model with the Geo-tokenizer embedding layer showed higher performance in both datasets. In addition, the model combining the HALM objective with the Geo-tokenizer embedding layer outperformed other variants. This means that the learning imbalance caused by location decomposition into multiple hierarchies by the Geo-tokenizer embedding layer was resolved through HALM. The comparison of these three variants was conducted with our pre-trained location embedding model on the classification tasks shown in Fig. 6. In the land usage and transportation mode classification tasks, both the Geo-tokenizer embedding layer and HALM can improve the prediction performance over the baseline.

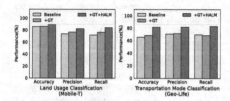 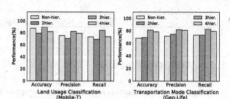

Fig. 6. Comparison of classification performance and efficiency for different combinations of components.

Fig. 7. Comparison of classification performance and efficiency for different hierarchy levels.

Study on the Level of Hierarchies (RQ3). We studied the effectiveness of the level of hierarchies by comparing three variants in terms of the degree of hierarchies: **(1) Four** (100 km,10 km, 1 km, and 100 m), **(2) Three** (100 km, 1 km, and 100 m), and **(3) Two hierarchies case** (10 km and 100 m).

The performance was calculated by averaging those of FFN and LSTM. As shown in Fig. 5, the three hierarchies case showed the best Acc@*1* and Acc@*5* with relatively few parameters for both datasets on the next location prediction task. In addition, we determined that increasing the hierarchy level did not necessarily improve the next location prediction performance. The larger the hierarchy level(H), the smaller the location vocabulary size, resulting in a smaller model size. If the model size is too small, the performance deteriorates, so it can be seen that setting an appropriate H is essential. We also compared these three variants with the non-hierarchies model on the two classification tasks, as shown in Fig. 7. In the both classification tasks, the three hierarchies case showed the best performance with the fewest parameters. It can be seen that the performance of the hierarchical case above a certain level is better than that of the non-hierarchical case with fewer model parameters.

Study on the Pre-training (RQ4). Pre-training significantly improved the performance of downstream tasks. We compared the performance of our model in two cases: with pre-training (w/PT) and without pre-training (wo/PT). As shown in Fig. 8, the model with the pre-trained backbone showed higher performance in both datasets for the next location prediction task than the wo/PT. In the Geo-Life dataset, the performance gap between the w/PT and wo/PT was relatively small compared to that of Mobile-T. This is because the number of trajectories of Mobile-T is larger than Geo-Life's. In other words, the larger the data, the greater the performance improvement of the downstream task due to pre-training. In the classification task, the w/PT performed significantly better than the wo/PT in terms of accuracy, precision, and recall in both datasets, as shown in Fig. 9.

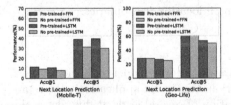 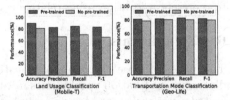

Fig. 8. Effect on the pre-training for the next location prediction task.   **Fig. 9.** Effect on the pre-training for the classification task.

4.5   Deployed Solution

Our pre-trained model has been implemented in an inter-company marketing tool, designed to predict individuals likely to visit a particular area for location-based marketing purposes. The deployed solution effectively encompasses entire regions within the author's country by utilizing the next-location prediction model built upon our pre-trained model. More details, including a screenshot of our graphical user interface (GUI) tool, can be found in the Appendix A.6.

5   Related Work

In recent years, pre-training an embedding model with self-supervised objectives has become a common practice in spatial-temporal data mining. For example, DeepMove [22] and TALE [13] implemented skip-gram and CBOW [7], respectively, to model human mobility, and an N-gram model is adopted to learn latent representations of a location [11,16]. SERM [15] jointly trained the embeddings of user, location, time, and keyword. These location embedding models generated a single latent representation for each location, which indicates they can not discriminate among variable functionalities of a location. To address this problem, previous studies have employed a transformer encoder architecture [12] with Masked Language Model [2] to generate the dynamic embeddings derived along the dissimilar trajectories [6,8]. Specifically, TrajFormer [5], CTLE [6] and BERTLoc [8] proposed a transformer encoder based location embedding model that dynamically assigns the embedding vector of a target location, varying with the location's trajectory. Nevertheless, previous studies are difficult to be applied in the real world, where the number of locations can be considerably large, or a fine-grained resolution is needed [11]. Previous studies have dealt with at most ten thousand locations to train their representations [6,11,18]. This problem can be addressed by reconstructing a location with several grids at different scales and making each grid at a large scale share the grids at a small scale. HIER [11] decomposed a location at several spatial scales to consider the spatial hierarchy in the location embeddings. However, in their approaches, locations in each level of the hierarchy are independently trained, and therefore the number of locations to be embedded is still large. For this reason, we encourage grids in the lower-level hierarchies to share the grid set in the upper-level hierarchy in order to represent a location using relatively small location vocabularies.

6   Conclusions

This paper proposed a contextual location embedding model to efficiently handle numerous location vocabularies in various real-world applications. We represented a particular location as a combination of several grids at different scales to reduce the number of locations to be trained. In addition, to incorporate various location functionalities, our model dynamically calculated the embedding vector of a target location, which varies depending on its trajectory. We employed a variant of the ALM objective, which trains the model with several ALM objectives sequentially. The experimental results demonstrated that our model significantly improved the performance of downstream models with fewer model parameters, compared to the existing location embedding methods.

Acknowledgment. This work was supported by the institute of Information & communications Technology Planning & Evaluation (IITP) grant funded by the Korea government (MSIT) (No. 2019-0-00075, Artificial Intelligence Graduate School Program (KAIST)) and the National Research Foundation of Korea (NRF) grant funded by the Korea government (MSIT) (No. NRF-2022R1A2B5B0 2001913). The authors would like to thank the AI Service Business Division of SK Telecom for providing GPU cluster support to conduct massive experiments.

Ethical Statement

There are no ethical issues.

References

1. Aksoy, Ç., Ahmetoğlu, A., Güngör, T.: Hierarchical multitask learning approach for BERT. arXiv preprint arXiv:2011.04451 (2020)
2. Devlin, J., Chang, M.W., Lee, K., Toutanova, K.: BERT: pre-training of deep bidirectional transformers for language understanding. In: Proceedings of the 2019 Conference of the North American Chapter of the Association for Computational Linguistics: Human Language Technologies, pp. 4171–4186 (2019)
3. Hochreiter, S., Schmidhuber, J.: Long short-term memory. Neural Comput. **9**(8), 1735–1780 (1997)
4. Li, Y., Du, N., Bengio, S.: Time-dependent representation for neural event sequence prediction. arXiv preprint arXiv:1708.00065 (2017)
5. Liang, Y., et al.: Trajformer: efficient trajectory classification with transformers. In: Proceedings of the 31st ACM International Conference on Information & Knowledge Management, pp. 1229–1237 (2022)
6. Lin, Y., Wan, H., Guo, S., Lin, Y.: Pre-training context and time aware location embeddings from spatial-temporal trajectories for user next location prediction. In: Proceedings of the AAAI Conference on Artificial Intelligence (2020)
7. Mikolov, T., Chen, K., Corrado, G., Dean, J.: Efficient estimation of word representations in vector space. arXiv preprint arXiv:1301.3781 (2013)
8. Park, S., Lee, S., Woo, S.S.: BERTloc: duplicate location record detection in a large-scale location dataset. In: Proceedings of the 36th Annual ACM Symposium on Applied Computing, pp. 942–951 (2021)
9. Radford, A., Narasimhan, K., Salimans, T., Sutskever, I., et al.: Improving language understanding by generative pre-training (2018)
10. Radford, A., Wu, J., Child, R., Luan, D., Amodei, D., Sutskever, I., et al.: Language models are unsupervised multitask learners. OpenAI blog **1**(8), 9 (2019)
11. Shimizu, T., Yabe, T., Tsubouchi, K.: Learning fine grained place embeddings with spatial hierarchy from human mobility trajectories. arXiv preprint arXiv:2002.02058 (2020)
12. Vaswani, A., et al.: Attention is all you need. In: Advances in neural information processing systems, pp. 5998–6008 (2017)
13. Wan, H., Li, F., Guo, S., Cao, Z., Lin, Y.: Learning time-aware distributed representations of locations from spatio-temporal trajectories. In: Li, G., Yang, J., Gama, J., Natwichai, J., Tong, Y. (eds.) DASFAA 2019. LNCS, vol. 11448, pp. 268–272. Springer, Cham (2019). https://doi.org/10.1007/978-3-030-18590-9_26

14. Wan, H., Lin, Y., Guo, S., Lin, Y.: Pre-training time-aware location embeddings from spatial-temporal trajectories. IEEE Trans. Knowl. Data Eng. (2021)
15. Yao, D., Zhang, C., Huang, J., Bi, J.: SERM: a recurrent model for next location prediction in semantic trajectories. In: Proceedings of the 2017 ACM on Conference on Information and Knowledge Management, pp. 2411–2414 (2017)
16. Yao, Z., Fu, Y., Liu, B., Hu, W., Xiong, H.: Representing urban functions through zone embedding with human mobility patterns. In: IJCAI, pp. 3919–3925 (2018)
17. Zhao, P., et al.: Where to go next: a spatio-temporal gated network for next poi recommendation. IEEE Trans. Knowl. Data Eng. **34**, 2512–2524 (2020)
18. Zhao, S., Zhao, T., King, I., Lyu, M.R.: Geo-teaser: geo-temporal sequential embedding rank for point-of-interest recommendation. In: Proceedings of the 26th International Conference on World Wide Web Companion, pp. 153–162 (2017)
19. Zheng, Y., Xie, X., Ma, W.Y., et al.: GeoLife: a collaborative social networking service among user, location and trajectory. IEEE Data Eng. Bull. **33**(2), 32–39 (2010)
20. Zhou, F., Gao, Q., Trajcevski, G., Zhang, K., Zhong, T., Zhang, F.: Trajectory-user linking via variational autoencoder. In: IJCAI, pp. 3212–3218 (2018)
21. Zhou, F., Yue, X., Trajcevski, G., Zhong, T., Zhang, K.: Context-aware variational trajectory encoding and human mobility inference. In: The World Wide Web Conference, pp. 3469–3475 (2019)
22. Zhou, Y., Huang, Y.: DeepMove: learning place representations through large scale movement data. In: 2018 IEEE International Conference on Big Data (Big Data), pp. 2403–2412. IEEE (2018)

Leveraging Queue Length and Attention Mechanisms for Enhanced Traffic Signal Control Optimization

Liang Zhang[iD], Shubin Xie[iD], and Jianming Deng[✉][iD]

State Key Laboratory of Herbage Improvement and Grassland Agro-ecosystems,
College of Ecology, Lanzhou University, Lanzhou 730000, China
{liangzhang21,xieshb20,dengjm}@lzu.edu.cn

Abstract. Reinforcement learning (RL) techniques for traffic signal control (TSC) have gained increasing popularity in recent years. However, most existing RL-based TSC methods tend to focus primarily on the RL model structure while neglecting the significance of proper traffic state representation. Furthermore, some RL-based methods heavily rely on expert-designed traffic signal phase competition. In this paper, we present a novel approach to TSC that utilizes queue length as an efficient state representation. We propose two new methods: (1) Max Queue-Length (M-QL), an optimization-based traditional method designed based on the property of queue length; and (2) Attention-Light, an RL model that employs the self-attention mechanism to capture the signal phase correlation without requiring human knowledge of phase relationships. Comprehensive experiments on multiple real-world datasets demonstrate the effectiveness of our approach: (1) the M-QL method outperforms the latest RL-based methods; (2) AttentionLight achieves a new state-of-the-art performance; and (3) our results highlight the significance of proper state representation, which is as crucial as neural network design in TSC methods. Our findings have important implications for advancing the development of more effective and efficient TSC methods. Our code is released on Github (https://github.com/LiangZhang1996/AttentionLight).

Keywords: traffic signal control · reinforcement learning · state representation · attention mechanism

1 Introduction

With the growth of population and economy, the number of vehicles on the road has surged, leading to widespread traffic congestion. This congestion causes fuel waste, environmental pollution, and economic losses. Enhancing transportation efficiency and alleviating traffic congestion has become crucial. Signalized intersections are common bottlenecks in urban areas, and traffic signal control (TSC) is critical for effective traffic management. Common TSC systems in modern cities include FixedTime [8], GreenWave [19], SCOOT [6], and SCATS [11].

© The Author(s), under exclusive license to Springer Nature Switzerland AG 2023
G. De Francisci Morales et al. (Eds.): ECML PKDD 2023, LNAI 14175, pp. 141–156, 2023.
https://doi.org/10.1007/978-3-031-43430-3_9

These systems predominantly rely on expert-designed traffic signal plans, making them unsuitable for dynamic traffic and various intersections.

Reinforcement learning (RL) [17], a branch of machine learning, focuses on how intelligent agents should take action within an environment to maximize cumulative rewards. RL has attracted increasing attention for TSC, with researchers applying RL to address the TSC problem [1,14,15,18,23–25,30]. Unlike traditional TSC methods, RL models can directly learn from the environment through trial and reward without requiring strict assumptions. Furthermore, deep neural networks [13] powered RL models can learn to manage complex and dynamic traffic environments. RL-based TSC methods [1,23,24] become a promising solution for adapting the dynamic traffic. RL-based methods such as PressLight [23], FRAP [29], MPLight [1], and CoLight [24] have emerged as promising solutions for adapting to dynamic traffic.

The performance in RL-based approaches can be influenced by the model framework, state representation, and reward function design. FRAP [29] develops a specific network that constructs phase features and models phase competition correlations to obtain the score of each phase, yielding excellent performance for TSC. CoLight [24] uses graph attention network [22] to facilitate intersection cooperation, achieving state-of-the-art performance. LIT [30] leverages the network from IntelliLight [25] with a simple state scheme and reward function, significantly outperforming IntelliLight. PressLight [23] further optimizes the state and reward using pressure, considerably surpassing LIT. MPLight [1] improves the state representation from PressLight and adopts a more efficient framework FRAP [29], significantly improving PressLight.

Various traffic state representations are employed, but the most effective state representation remains unknown. State representations for RL-based TSC differ considerably compared to RL approaches in Atari games [12]. In the TSC field, state representation mainly varies in terms of the number of vehicles [23–27,27,29,30], vehicle image [15,25], traffic movement pressure [1], queue length [14,25], average velocity [14], current phase [23–27,27,29,30], and next phase [25,26]; reward representation varies in: queue length [23,24,26,29], pressure [1,23], total wait time [14,15,25,26], and delay [15,25,26]. Some methods such as LIT [30] and PressLight [23], employ a simple state and reward and outperform IntelliLight [25], even with the same neural network. Although traffic state representation plays an essential role in RL models, most research focuses on developing new network structures to improve TSC performance. Consequently, state design for TSC merits further consideration.

Recent studies, such as MPLight [1] and MetaLight [27], have adopted FRAP as their base model. However, FRAP necessitates manually designed phase correlations, such as competing, partial competing, and no competing relationships in a standard four-way and eight-phase (Fig. 1) intersection [29]. While the analysis of phase and traffic movements can aid in determining phase correlations, this approach may be impractical for more complex intersections, such as five-way intersections.

To tackle the aforementioned challenges, this article presents the following key contributions: (1) we propose an optimization-based TSC method called Max Queue-Length (M-QL), and (2) develop a novel RL model, Attention-Light, which leverages self-attention to learn phase correlations without requiring human knowledge of phase relationships. Extensive numerical experiments demonstrate that our proposed methods outperform previous state-of-the-art approaches, with AttentionLight achieving the best performance. Additionally, our experiments highlight the significance of state representation alongside neural network design for RL.

2 Related Work

2.1 Traditional Methods

Traditional methods for traffic signal control (TSC) can be broadly categorized into four types: fixed-time control [8], actuated control [3,4], adaptive control [6,11], and optimization-based control [10,16,20]. Fixed-time control [8] utilizes pre-timed cycle length, fixed cycle-based phase sequence, and phase split, assuming uniform traffic flow during specific periods. Actuated control [3] decides whether to maintain or change the current phase based on the pre-defined rules and real-time traffic data, such as setting a green signal for a phase if the number of approaching vehicles exceeds a threshold. Self-organizing traffic lights (SOTL) [3] is one typical actuated control method. Adaptive control [6,11] selects an optimal traffic plan for the current situation from a set of traffic plans based on traffic volume data from loop sensors. Each plan includes cycle length, phase split, and offsets. SCOOT [6] and SCATS [11] are widely used adaptive control methods in modern cities. Optimization-based control [10,16,20] formulates TSC as an optimization problem under a specific traffic flow model, using observed traffic data to make decisions. Max Pressure [20] is a typical optimization-based control method that often requires turn ratio (the proportion of turning vehicles at an intersection).

2.2 RL-Based Methods

Reinforcement learning (RL)-based methods have been employed to improve traffic signal control (TSC) performance, with several studies concentrating on optimizing state and reward design. A trend has emerged favoring simpler yet more efficient state representations and reward functions. For example, IntelliLight [25] employed six state representations and six features to compute the reward function, resulting in moderate performance. In contrast, LIT [30] used the current phase and the number of vehicles as the state, and queue length as the reward, significantly outperforming IntelliLight. PressLight [23] further improved upon LIT and IntelliLight by incorporating 'pressure' into the state and reward function design. MPLight [1] enhanced FRAP [29] by adopting traffic movement pressure in the state and reward function design.

Other studies have focused on improving control performance by employing more powerful networks or RL techniques. For instance, FRAP [29] developed a unique network structure to construct phase features and capture phase competition relations, resulting in invariance to symmetrical cases such as flipping and rotation in traffic flow. GCN [14] utilized graph convolution networks [7] with queue length and average velocity as the state and total wait time as the reward. CoLight [24] introduced graph attention network [22] to facilitate intersection cooperation, using the number of vehicles and current phase as the state and queue length as the reward. HiLight [26] incorporated the concept of hierarchical RL [9], using the current phase, next phase, and the number of vehicles as state, while employing queue length, delay, and waiting time as the reward.

Although numerous studies strive to develop complex network structures for TSC, few focus on appropriate traffic state representation design. LIT [30] demonstrated that queue length serves as a more effective reward function than delay, and the number of vehicles surpasses waiting time and traffic image as the state representation. PressLight [23] discovered that pressure outperforms queue length as the reward function. MPLight [1] integrated pressure into state design, resulting in improvements to the model. These findings indicate that further research on state representation is required to enhance TSC methods. Moreover, the exploration of novel network structures within RL techniques for TSC should be considered.

3   Preliminary

In this study, our primary focus is on conventional and representative 4-way, 12-lane, 4-phase intersections (Fig. 1). In this section, we provide a comprehensive summary of the definitions that are integral to TSC methods.

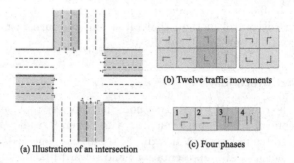

(a) Illustration of an intersection

(b) Twelve traffic movements

(c) Four phases

Fig. 1. The illustration of an intersection. In case (a), phase #2 is activated.

Definition 1 (Traffic network). The traffic network is described as a directed graph where each node represents an intersection, and each edge represents a road. One road consists of several lanes with vehicles running on it. We denote the set of incoming lanes and outgoing lanes of intersection i as $\mathcal{L}_i^{in}$ and $\mathcal{L}_i^{out}$ respectively. The lanes are denoted with l, m, k. As is shown in Fig. 1 (a), there are one intersection, four incoming roads, four outgoing roads, twelve incoming lanes, and twelve outgoing lanes.

Definition 2 (Traffic movement). A traffic movement is defined as the traffic traveling across an intersection towards a specific direction, i.e., left turn, go straight, and right turn. According to the traffic rules in some countries, vehicles that turn right can pass regardless of the signal but must yield at red lights. As shown in Fig. 1 (b), there are twelve traffic movements.

Definition 3 (Signal phase). Each signal phase is a set of permitted traffic movements, denoted by d, and $\mathcal{D}_i$ denotes the set of all the phases at intersection i. As shown in Fig. 1, twelve traffic movements can be organized into four-phase (c), and phase #2 is activated in case (a).

Definition 4 (Phase queue length). The queue length of each phase is the sum queue length of the incoming lanes of that phase, denoted by

$$q(p) = \sum q(l), l \in p \tag{1}$$

in which $q(l)$ is the queue length of lane l.

Definition 5 (Intersection queue length). The queue length of each intersection is defined as the total queue length of the incoming lanes of the intersection, denoted by

$$Q_i = \sum q(l), l \in \mathcal{L}_i^{in} \tag{2}$$

in which $q(l)$ represents the queue length of lane l.

Definition 6 (Action duration). The action duration of our TSC models is denoted by $t_{duration}$. It can also represent the minimum duration of each phase.

Problem (Multi-intersection TSC). We consider multi-intersection TSC, in which each intersection is controlled by one RL agent. Every $t_{duration}$, agent i views the environment as its observation o_i^t, takes the action a_i^t to control the signal of intersection i, and obtains reward r_i^t. Each agent can learn a control policy by interacting with the environment. The goal of all the agents is to learn an optimal policy (i.e. which phase to actuate) to maximize their cumulative reward, denoted as:

$$\sum_{t=1}^{T} \sum_{i=1}^{n} r_i^t \tag{3}$$

where n is the number of RL agents and T is the timestep. The well-trained RL agents will be evaluated with multiple real-world datasets.

4   Method

In this section, we first propose a TSC method, Max-QueueLength(M-QL), based on the property of queue length. Next, we present a novel RL model called AttentionLight, which employs multi-head self-attention [21] to model phase correlation and utilizes queue length both as the state and reward.

4.1 Introduce Queue Length for TSC Methods

Property of Queue Length. In TSC, vehicles within the traffic network can be in one of two states: moving or queuing. Queuing vehicles can lead to congestion and are essential for representing the traffic condition. The phase signal can directly change the state of the queuing vehicles in the traffic network. A deterministic change transpires when each phase is activated, causing the queue length of that phase to decrease to zero. In contrast, subsequent changes, such as the number of vehicles, vehicle position, and vehicle speed, exhibit greater uncertainty compared to queue length.

RL agents learn the state-action values from the environment through trial and reward. The feedback on actions significantly influences the learning effect. Suppose the state representation omits critical contents of traffic movement. In such cases, agents may become confused about the state and fail to learn an appropriate policy for TSC. For example, consider a scenario where one case has only queuing vehicles and another has only moving vehicles, and the state representation is based solely on the number of vehicles. Under the same state representation, there could be different optimal policies, which may confuse the RL agents. Furthermore, the state space of queue length is larger than that of the number of vehicles. As a result, the queue length is considered an effective state representation. Using queue length as both the reward and the state can support reward optimization. Consequently, we employ queue length as a traffic state representation and reward function.

While previous studies have incorporated queue length in state and reward design, our work is the first to use it as both. IntelliLight [25], GCN [14], and Tan et al. [18] employ more complex state representations. In contrast, our approach uniquely emphasizes simplicity and efficiency by focusing solely on queue length.

Max-QueueLength Control. Based on Max Pressure (MP) [20] and the property of queue length, we introduce a new TSC method called Max Queue-Length (M-QL), which directly optimizes intersection queue length. The M-QL control chooses the phase that has the maximum queue length in a greedy manner. At intersection i, the queue length of each phase is calculated using equation (1). During each action duration, M-QL activates the phase that has the maximum queue length, denoted by

$$\hat{p} = \operatorname{argmax}\left(q(p) p \in \mathcal{P}_i\right) \tag{4}$$

where $q(p)$ is calculated according to Eq. (1), and $\mathcal{P}_i$ denotes the phases. Our approach is straightforward and efficient, and we believe it has the potential to improve traffic conditions significantly.

M-QL Can Stabilize the Network. We present proof of the stability of M-QL control for TSC.

Definition 7 (Queue length process stability) [20]. The queue length process $Q(t) = \{q(l)\}$ is stable in the mean (and u^* is a stabilizing control policy) if for some $M < \infty$:

$$\frac{1}{T} \sum_{t=1}^{T} \sum_{l} E[q(l)] < M, \forall T. \tag{5}$$

where E denotes expectation. Stability in the mean implies that the chain is positively recurrent and has a unique steady-state probability distribution.

Theorem 1. *The M-QL control u^* is stabilizing whenever the average demand is admissible[1].*

Proof. We use $x(l)$ and $x_{max}(l)$ to denote the number of vehicles and the maximum permissible vehicle number on lane l, respectively. Based on the property of queue length, we have $q(l) \leqslant x(l)$. Moreover, as the average demand is admissible, $x(l) \leqslant x_{max}(l)$. For a rough estimation, we obtain $M \leqslant \frac{1}{T} \sum_{t=1}^{T} \sum_{l} E[x_{max}(l)]$.

For the traffic conditions in this study, such as shown in Fig. 1 (a), there are four phases and twelve lanes. Vehicles that turn right can pass regardless of the signal. Additionally, M-QL always actuates one phase, and there are no queuing vehicles on the lane of that corresponding phase. Hence, there are no queuing vehicles on half of the lanes. For a more precise estimation, we can get $M \leqslant \frac{1}{T} \sum_{t=1}^{2T} \sum_{l} E[x_{max}(l)]$.

Therefore, based on the stability criterion defined in Eq. (5), we prove that the M-QL control policy is stabilizing, and the queue length process is stable in the mean whenever the average demand is admissible.

Comparison of M-QL and MP. The MP control selects the phase with the maximum pressure, which is the difference in queue length between upstream and downstream, indicating the balance of the queue length. Similarly, the M-QL control opts for the phase with the maximum queue length in a greedy manner. These two methods are identical for single intersection control, where the outgoing lanes are infinite, and the calculated pressure equals the queue length.

However, MP also considers the neighboring influences and stabilizes the queue length by ensuring that vehicles are not stopped by upstream queuing vehicles. Consequently, a phase with higher pressure would result in a larger queue length. MP is effective for short traffic road lengths, where the influence of adjacent intersections is felt rapidly. Nevertheless, for long road lengths, pressure may not be as effective since the impact can be several $t_{duration}$ (action duration) away. For example, for a road length of 300m, with a $t_{duration}$ of 15 s and a vehicle maximum velocity of $10m/s$, it would take at least 30 s to reach the neighbor,

---

[1] An admissible demand means the traffic demand can be accommodated by traffic signal control policies, not including situations like long-lasting over-saturated traffic that requires perimeter control to stop traffic getting in the system.

rendering the neighbor condition ineffective. In contrast, M-QL might perform better on longer traffic roads, as it directly optimizes queue length. Experiments will be conducted later to verify this assumption.

4.2 AttentionLight Agent Design

Prior to delving into the network architecture of AttenditonLight, it is essential to elucidate the state, action, and reward for each RL agent. Considering queue length's role in M-QL, we suggest incorporating it in both state and reward design, expected to boost our model's performance and efficiency.

- **State.** The current phase and queue length are used as the state representation (agent observations). The state at time t is denoted as s_t.
- **Action.** At the time t, each agent chooses a phase $\hat{p}$ according to the observations, and the traffic signal will be changed to $\hat{p}$. The action thus influences traffic flow by modifying the traffic signal.
- **Reward.** The negative intersection queue length is used as the reward. The reward for the agent that is controlling intersection i is denoted by

$$r_i = -\sum q(l), l \in \mathcal{L}_i^{in} \tag{6}$$

in which $q(l)$ is the queue length at lane l. By maximizing the reward, the agent is trying to maximize the throughput in the system. In this study, we update our agent based on the average reward (r_i) over the action duration, taking into account the reward delay.

Advanced RL framework The DQN [13] is used as the function approximator to estimate the Q-value function, and the RL agents are updated by the Bellman Equation. We also employ a decentralized RL paradigm, including ApeX-DQN [5], for scalability. This approach shares parameters and replay memory among all agents, enabling intersections to learn from each other's experiences, a technique proven to enhance model performance [1].

4.3 Network Design of AttentionLight

Though some RL-related methods [1,27,29] using FRAP [29] have achieved impressive performance, they rely on human-designed phase correlations. To overcome this limitation, we propose AttentionLight, an RL model based on FRAP that utilizes self-attention [21] to automatically model phase correlations.

The core idea of AttentionLight is to apply self-attention [21] to learn phase correlations and predict the Q-value of each phase through the phase feature constructed by the self-attention mechanism. This approach enables the Q-value of each phase to fully consider its correlation with others. We divide the prediction of Q-values (i.e. the score of each phase) into three stages: phase feature construction, phase correlation learning with multi-head self-attention, and Q-value prediction.

Phase Feature Construction. AttentionLight utilizes queue length and current phase as inputs. Initially, AttentionLight embeds the feature of each lane from l-dimensional into a m-dimensional latent space via a layer of multi-layer perceptron:

$$h_1 = \text{Embed}(o) = \sigma(oW_e + b_e) \tag{7}$$

where $o \in \mathbb{R}^l$ is the observation at time t, $W_e \in \mathbb{R}^{l \times m}$ and $b_e \in \mathbb{R}^m$ are weight matrix and bias vector to learn, σ is the sigmoid function. Subsequently, the feature of each phase is constructed through feature fusion of the participating lanes:

$$h_2 = \text{Fusion}(h_1) \tag{8}$$

in this case, the fusion function is a direct addition.

Phase Correlation Learning. In this stage, our model takes the phase feature as input and uses multi-head self-attention(MHA) [21] to learn the phase correlation:

$$h_3 = \text{MHA}(h_2) \tag{9}$$

we find that the head number does not have a significant influence on the model performance, and we finally adopt four attention heads as default.

Q-Value Prediction. In this stage, our model takes the correlated phase feature as input to get the Q-value for each phase:

$$\widetilde{q} = \text{Embed}(h_3) = h_3 W_p + b_p \tag{10}$$

where $W_p \in \mathbb{R}^{c \times 1}$ and $b_p \in \mathbb{R}^1$ are parameters to be learned, p denotes the number of phases (action space), $\widetilde{q}$ refers to the predicted q-values. The agent selects the phase that has the maximum Q-value.

AttentionLight and FRAP. AttentionLight is a novel RL model that uses self-attention to automatically model phase correlation for TSC. Unlike FRAP [29], which requires human-designed phase correlation, AttentionLight does not rely on human knowledge of the complex competing relationships between phases. For instance, in a typical 4-way and 8-phase intersection, phases can have competing, partial competing, or no competing relationships. Although the competing relationships of the 8 phases in such an intersection can be easily acquired through analysis of phase and traffic movements, this task becomes considerably more challenging for more complex intersections or phases.

AttentionLight is better suited for real-world deployment than FRAP, as it significantly reduces the complexity of phase relation design. By learning the phase correlation through a neural network, our model enables scalability and eliminates the need for human intervention.

5 Experiment

Settings. We conduct comprehensive numerical experiments on CityFlow [28], where each green signal is followed by a five-second red time to prepare for the signal phase transition. Within this simulator, vehicles navigate toward their respective destination following pre-defined routes, adhering strictly to traffic regulations. Control methods are deployed to control the signals at each intersection to optimize the traffic flow. We evaluate our proposed methods using seven real-world traffic datasets [24][2] sourced from JiNan, HangZhou, and New York. These datasets have been extensively utilized by various methods, such as CoLight [24], HiLight [26], and PRGLight [2]. The traffic networks under JiNan, HangZhou, and New York each exhibit unique topologies. In JiNan, the road network comprises 12 intersections (3 × 4), each linking two 400-meter East-West and two 800-meter South-North road segments; in HangZhou, the road network consists of 16 intersections (3 × 4), each connecting two 800-meter East-West and two 600-meter South-North road segments; in New York, the road network has 196 intersections (28 × 7), each connecting four 300-meter (two East-West and two South-North) road segments. The average arrival rate (vehicles/second) of the seven datasets is 1.75, 1.21, 1.53, 0.83, 1.94, 2.97, and 4.41 respectively. These traffic flow datasets not only vary in terms of arrival rate but also in travel patterns, thereby demonstrating the diversity and validity of our experiments.

Drawing upon prior research [24,26,29], we select the average travel time as the evaluation metric and compare our methods with various traditional and RL approaches. To ensure a fair comparison, we set the phase number as four(Figure 1 (c)), and the action duration as 15 s. All RL methods are trained using the same hyper-parameters, such as optimizer (Adam), learning rate (0.001), batch size (20), sample size (3000), memory size (12000), epochs number (100), discount factor γ (0.8), etc. In order to derive definitive results for all the RL methods, a total of 80 episodes are utilized. Each episode, both in training and testing, executes a simulation lasting 60 min. The mean value is then calculated based on the final ten testing episodes. To bolster the reliability of our findings, we conducted three independent experiments and reported the average outcome. This rigorous approach ensures the robustness and reproducibility of our results.

Compared Methods. The traditional methods include: **FixedTime** [8], a policy that uses a fixed cycle length with a pre-defined phase split among all the phases; **Max Pressure (MP)** [20]: a policy that selects the phase with the maximum pressure. The RL-based methods include: **FRAP** [29], which uses a modified network structure to capture phase competition relation between signal phases; **MPLight** [1], which uses FRAP as the base model, incorporates pressure in the state and reward design, and has shown superior performance in city-level TSC; **PRGLight** [2], which employs a graph neural network to predict traffic state and adjusts the phase duration according to the current observed traffic state and predicted state; **CoLight** [24], which uses a graph attention network [22] to facilitate intersection cooperation and has shown superior performance in large-scale TSC, making it a state-of-the-art method.

---

[2] https://traffic-signal-control.github.io.

5.1 Overall Performance

Table 1 reports the performance of all the methods under JiNan, HangZhou, and New York real-world datasets in terms of average travel time. Traditional TSC methods, such as MP [20] and M-QL, continue to demonstrate competitive results. Specifically, MP [20] outperforms FRAP [29], MPLight [1], PRGLight [2], and CoLight [24] under JiNan and HangZhou datasets. Our proposed M-QL consistently outperforms all other previous methods under JiNan and HangZhou datasets, with an improvement of up to 4.21% (averaging 2.47%), while MP surpasses M-QL under New York datasets. We hypothesize that the length of traffic roads influences the performance of TSC methods, with M-QL potentially excelling on longer roads and MP on shorter roads. These results can validate this hypothesis.

Table 1. Overall performance. For average travel time, the smaller the better.

Method	JiNan			HangZhou		New York	
	1	2	3	1	2	1	2
FixedTime	429.27	370.34	384.89	497.87	408.31	1507.12	1733.30
MP	274.99	**246.41**	**244.63**	**289.54**	349.85	1179.55	1536.17
FRAP	299.56	268.57	269.20	308.73	355.80	1192.23	1470.51
MPLight	297.68	274.32	268.00	313.16	355.35	1321.40	1642.05
PRGLight	291.27	257.52	261.74	301.06	369.98	1283.37	1472.73
CoLight	**271.17**	251.22	248.87	300.07	**339.76**	**1065.64**	**1367.54**
M-QL	**268.87**	**240.02**	**238.51**	**284.32**	**325.44**	1197.59	1551.46
AttentionLight	**254.82**	**239.68**	**236.62**	**283.64**	**316.38**	**1013.78**	1401.32

Additionally, our proposed AttentionLight achieves new state-of-the-art performance and outperforms all other previous methods over JiNan and HangZhou datasets, with an improvement of up to 6.88% (averaging 4.34%). Attention-Light exclusively utilizes queue length information of a specific intersection, thus requiring less computation and offering deployment advantages over CoLight, MPLight, and FRAP. Finally, we reemphasize the importance of parameter sharing for RL-based models in TSC. MPLight [1] has demonstrated superior performance than FRAP and addressed the importance of parameter sharing. When FRAP is trained and tested with parameter sharing in the same manner as MPLight, it slightly outperforms MPLight.

5.2 Queue Length Effectiveness Analysis

To further illustrate the effectiveness of queue length as a state representation, we incorporate queue length as both the state and reward for additional RL

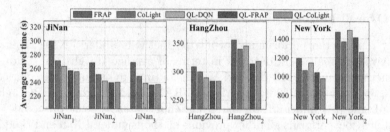

Fig. 2. Model performance comparison.

methods, including FRAP [29] and CoLight [24], which are referred to as QL-FRAP and QL-CoLight, respectively. Additionally, we introduce a simple DQN containing two multiple-layer perceptrons as QL-DQN.

Figure 2 demonstrates the model performance of QL-DQN, QL-FRAP, and QL-CoLight. The results show that QL-FRAP significantly outperforms FRAP, and QL-CoLight significantly outperforms CoLight. These improvements highlight the importance of state representation for RL-based TSC. Moreover, QL-DQN outperforms FRAP and CoLight, further emphasizing the critical role of state representation in RL. Efficient state representation is also essential as the neural network structure for TSC. QL-DQN employs a simple neural network structure, but efficient state representation. In contrast, FRAP and CoLight use well-designed neural network structures but have less efficient state representation. Furthermore, FRAP, CoLight, and QL-DQN use the same reward function. When comparing the performance of QL-DQN with FRAP and CoLight, QL-DQN consistently performs better under JiNan and HangZhou datasets. These experimental results suggest that queue length serves as an efficient state representation.

5.3 Reward Function Investigation

Previous studies, such as PressLight [23] and MPLight [1], have demonstrated the superior performance of RL approaches under pressure compared to queue length in the context of reward functions. This study revisits these findings, focusing on the impact of reward settings when queue length is used as the state representation. We utilize two base models for our investigation: AttentionLight (**Model 1**) and CoLight (**Model 2**). Our experiments are structured around two configurations: **Config1**: uses queue length and current phase as the state, with negative queue length as the reward function; and **Config2**: uses the same state representations but with negative absolute pressure as the reward function.

Experiments are conducted over JiNan and HangZhou, and the results are reported in Fig. 3. Our findings show that AttentionLight performs slightly better under queue length than pressure. Conversely, CoLight-based models demonstrate significantly better performance under queue length compared to pressure. In terms of state and reward calculation, queue length, which can be directly obtained from the traffic environment, is simpler to acquire than pressure, which

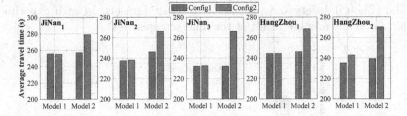

Fig. 3. Model performance under different rewards w.r.t average travel time, the smaller the better.

necessitates complex calculation and neighbor information. Therefore, using queue length as both the state and reward is a more favorable choice over pressure. In conclusion, our experiments highlight the significance of selecting suitable reward functions in RL-based TSC approaches. Utilizing queue length as both state and reward can enhance performance, especially in the case of CoLight-based models.

5.4 Action Duration Study

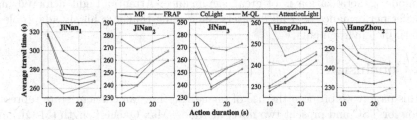

Fig. 4. Model performance under different action duration.

To evaluate the impact of action duration on model performance, we conduct extensive experiments using our proposed methods. Figure 4 illustrates the model performance under different action duration. Our proposed AttentionLight consistently outperforms other methods over JiNan and HangZhou datasets. Notably, M-QL exhibits better performance than FRAP and CoLight in most cases, suggesting that the traditional TSC methods remain powerful and essential. The results highlight the crucial role action duration plays in the effectiveness of TSC models, and indicate that our proposed methods are robust and efficient under various action durations.

5.5 Model Generalization

Model generalization is a critical property of RL models, as an ideal RL model should be resilient to different traffic conditions after training in one traffic situation. To evaluate the transferability of AttentionLight, We train it on JiNan and HangZhou datasets and transfer it to other datasets. In each experiment, we calculated the average result of the final ten episodes.

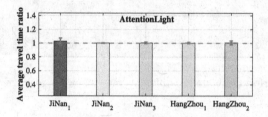

Fig. 5. The average travel time of transfer divided by the average travel time of direct training. The error bars represent the 95% confidence interval for the average travel time ratio.

The transfer performance is denoted as the average travel time ratio: $\frac{t_{transfer}}{t_{train}}$, where $t_{transfer}$ and t_{train} represent the average travel time of transfer and direct training, respectively. The closer the average travel time ratio is to one, the less degradation is caused when facing a new environment. Figure 5 demonstrates the transferability of AttentionLight on JiNan and HangZhou, indicating that its model generalization is of great significance. AttentionLight achieved high transfer performance over all datasets, suggesting that it is highly adaptable to new traffic environments.

6   Conclusion

In this paper, we propose the use of queue length as an efficient state representation for TSC and present two novel methods: Max Queue-Length (M-QL) and AttentionLight. M-QL is an optimization-based method that is built on queue length, and AttentionLight uses self-attention to learn the phase correlation without requiring human knowledge. Our proposed methods outperform previous state-of-the-art methods, with AttentionLight achieving the best performance. Furthermore, our experiments highlight the importance of state representation in addition to neural network design for RL.

However, we acknowledge that queue length alone may not be sufficient for complex traffic conditions, and additional information should be incorporated into the state representation. In future research, we aim to explore the inclusion of more information about the traffic conditions in the RL agent observations. Additionally, we aim to investigate the use of more complex reward functions and network structures to further improve the performance of TSC.

Acknowledgements. This work was supported by grants from the National Natural Science Foundation of China (32225032, 32001192, 31322010, 32271597, 42201041), the Innovation Base Project of Gansu Province (20190323), the Top Leading Talents in Gansu Province to JMD, the National Scientific and Technological Program on Basic Resources Investigation (2019FY102002).

References

1. Chen, C., et al.: Toward a thousand lights: Decentralized deep reinforcement learning for large-scale traffic signal control. In: Proceedings of the AAAI Conference on Artificial Intelligence, vol. 34, pp. 3414–3421 (2020)
2. Chenguang, Z., Xiaorong, H., Gang, W.: PRGLight: a novel traffic light control framework with pressure-based-reinforcement learning and graph neural network. In: IJCAI 2021 Reinforcement Learning for Intelligent Transportation Systems (RL4ITS) Workshop (2021)
3. Cools, S.B., Gershenson, C., D'Hooghe, B.: Self-organizing traffic lights: a realistic simulation. In: Prokopenko, M. (eds.) Advances in Applied Self-Organizing Systems. Advanced Information and Knowledge Processing, pp. 45–55. Springer, London (2013). https://doi.org/10.1007/978-1-4471-5113-5_3
4. Gershenson, C.: Self-organizing traffic lights. arXiv preprint nlin/0411066 (2004)
5. Horgan, D., et al.: Distributed prioritized experience replay. arXiv preprint arXiv:1803.00933 (2018)
6. Hunt, P., Robertson, D., Bretherton, R., Royle, M.C.: The scoot on-line traffic signal optimisation technique. Traffic Eng. Control. $23(4)$, 190–192 (1982)
7. Kipf, T.N., Welling, M.: Semi-supervised classification with graph convolutional networks. arXiv preprint arXiv:1609.02907 (2016)
8. Koonce, P., Rodegerdts, L.: Traffic signal timing manual. Technical report, United States. Federal Highway Administration (2008)
9. Kulkarni, T.D., Narasimhan, K., Saeedi, A., Tenenbaum, J.: Hierarchical deep reinforcement learning: integrating temporal abstraction and intrinsic motivation. In: Advances in Neural Information Processing Systems, vol. 29 (2016)
10. Le, T., Kovács, P., Walton, N., Vu, H.L., Andrew, L.L., Hoogendoorn, S.S.: Decentralized signal control for urban road networks. Transp. Res. Part C Emerg. Technol. 58, 431–450 (2015)
11. Lowrie, P.: Scats: A traffic responsive method of controlling urban traffic control. Roads and Traffic Authority (1992)
12. Mnih, V., et al.: Playing Atari with deep reinforcement learning. arXiv preprint arXiv:1312.5602 (2013)
13. Mnih, V., et al.: Human-level control through deep reinforcement learning. Nature $518(7540)$, 529–533 (2015)
14. Nishi, T., Otaki, K., Hayakawa, K., Yoshimura, T.: Traffic signal control based on reinforcement learning with graph convolutional neural nets. In: 2018 21st International Conference on Intelligent Transportation Systems (ITSC), pp. 877–883. IEEE (2018)
15. Van der Pol, E., Oliehoek, F.A.: Coordinated deep reinforcement learners for traffic light control. In: Proceedings of Learning, Inference and Control of Multi-Agent Systems (at NIPS 2016) (2016)
16. Sun, X., Yin, Y.: A simulation study on max pressure control of signalized intersections. Transp. Res. Rec. $2672(18)$, 117–127 (2018)
17. Sutton, R.S., Barto, A.G.: Reinforcement Learning: An Introduction. MIT Press, Cambridge (2018)
18. Tan, T., Bao, F., Deng, Y., Jin, A., Dai, Q., Wang, J.: Cooperative deep reinforcement learning for large-scale traffic grid signal control. IEEE Trans. Cybern. $50(6)$, 2687–2700 (2019)
19. Török, J., Kertész, J.: The green wave model of two-dimensional traffic: transitions in the flow properties and in the geometry of the traffic jam. Physica A $231(4)$, 515–533 (1996)

20. Varaiya, P.: Max pressure control of a network of signalized intersections. Transp. Res. Part C Emerg. Technol. **36**, 177–195 (2013). https://doi.org/10.1016/j.trc.2013.08.014

21. Vaswani, A., et al.: Attention is all you need. In: Advances in Neural Information Processing Systems, vol. 30 (2017)

22. Veličković, P., Cucurull, G., Casanova, A., Romero, A., Lio, P., Bengio, Y.: Graph attention networks. arXiv preprint arXiv:1710.10903 (2017)

23. Wei, H., et al.: PressLight: learning max pressure control to coordinate traffic signals in arterial network. In: Proceedings of the 25th ACM SIGKDD International Conference on Knowledge Discovery & Data Mining, pp. 1290–1298 (2019)

24. Wei, H., et al.: Colight: learning network-level cooperation for traffic signal control. In: Proceedings of the 28th ACM International Conference on Information and Knowledge Management, pp. 1913–1922 (2019)

25. Wei, H., Zheng, G., Yao, H., Li, Z.: IntelliLight: a reinforcement learning approach for intelligent traffic light control. In: Proceedings of the 24th ACM SIGKDD International Conference on Knowledge Discovery & Data Mining, pp. 2496–2505 (2018)

26. Xu, B., Wang, Y., Wang, Z., Jia, H., Lu, Z.: Hierarchically and cooperatively learning traffic signal control. In: Proceedings of the AAAI Conference on Artificial Intelligence, vol. 35, pp. 669–677 (2021)

27. Zang, X., Yao, H., Zheng, G., Xu, N., Xu, K., Li, Z.: MetaLight: value-based meta-reinforcement learning for traffic signal control. In: Proceedings of the AAAI Conference on Artificial Intelligence, vol. 34, pp. 1153–1160 (2020)

28. Zhang, H., et al.: CityFlow: a multi-agent reinforcement learning environment for large scale city traffic scenario. In: The World Wide Web Conference, pp. 3620–3624 (2019)

29. Zheng, G., et al.: Learning phase competition for traffic signal control. In: Proceedings of the 28th ACM International Conference on Information and Knowledge Management, pp. 1963–1972 (2019)

30. Zheng, G., et al.: Diagnosing reinforcement learning for traffic signal control. arXiv preprint arXiv:1905.04716 (2019)

PICT: Precision-enhanced Road Intersection Recognition Using Cycling Trajectories

Wenyu Wu[1], Wenyi Shen[1], Jiali Mao[1,3(✉)], Lisheng Zhao[2],
Shaosheng Cao[2(✉)], Aoying Zhou[1,3], and Lin Zhou[2]

[1] East China Normal University, Shanghai, China
{51215903025,51215903053}@stu.ecnu.edu.cn,
{jlmao,ayzhou}@dase.ecnu.edu.cn
[2] DiDi Chuxing, Beijing, China
{zhaolisheng,shelsoncao,realzhoulin}@didiglobal.com
[3] Shanghai Engineering Research Center of Big Data Management, Shanghai, China

Abstract. To recognize road intersections using cycling trajectories accurately is vital to the quality of the digital map that cycling navigation apps use. However, the existing approaches mainly identify road intersections based on motor vehicles' trajectories, and they fail to tackle unique challenges posed by cycling trajectories: (i) Cycling trajectories of minor intersections and their adjacent road segments are quite sparse. (ii) Turning behaviors occur at different areas in intersections of various sizes. To address the above challenges, in this paper, we propose a precision-enhanced road intersection recognition method using cycling trajectories, called *PICT*. Initially, to enhance the representations of minor intersections, a grid topology representation module is designed to extract intersection topology. Then an intersection inference module based on multi-scale feature learning is put forward to identify the intersections of different scales correctly. Finally, extensive comparative experiments on two real-world datasets demonstrate that *PICT* significantly outperforms the state-of-the-art methods by 52.13% in the F1-score of intersection recognition.

Keywords: Cycling trajectories · Intersection recognition · Topology · Multi-scale feature learning

1 Introduction

Cycling has gradually become a popular travel mode for residents to reduce carbon emissions and traffic congestion in the city, which requires the demand for high-quality digital maps to support accurate cycling navigation services. As road intersection in a road network determines the connectivity of the road segments and turning rules among the roads, to identify them accurately is most critical for improving the quality of a digital map. Owing to the properties such as high coverage and low cost of trajectory data generated by the vehicles, the issue of road intersection recognition using trajectories has gained attention from

© The Author(s), under exclusive license to Springer Nature Switzerland AG 2023
G. De Francisci Morales et al. (Eds.): ECML PKDD 2023, LNAI 14175, pp. 157–173, 2023.
https://doi.org/10.1007/978-3-031-43430-3_10

(a) Sparse trajectories at (b) Turning behavior at (c) Turning behavior at
minor intersection   major intersection   minor intersection

Fig. 1. Illustrations of challenges for recognizing intersections using cycling trajectories

academics and industry, and hence quite a few works have emerged [1–3]. Most
of them utilize motor vehicles' trajectories to identify central positions and then
the coverage of intersections, according to the property of high-frequency turning
and speed-shifting behaviors of motor vehicles at intersections.

Distinct from the route planning of motor vehicles, a small number of cyclists
prefer to ride through minor intersections instead of major intersections to reach
their destinations quickly. But such minor intersections and their adjacent road
segments have highly sparse trajectories due to only a few bicycles passing by. As
shown in Fig. 1(a), a minor intersection v_1 and its two adjacent road segments
(denoted as e_1 and e_2) have more sparse trajectories (marked by green dots)
compared with its neighboring intersection v_2. Additionally, as compared to
traveling of motor vehicles, turning behaviors of cyclists are more complex and
disorganized at intersections of different sizes. As illustrated in Fig. 1(b) and 1(c),
it can be observed that turning behaviors usually occur at the margins of major
intersections (e.g., v_3) or in the central area of minor intersections (e.g., v_8). As
a result, the existing recognition methods have faced the following challenges in
precisely recognizing road intersections using cycling trajectories.

- **Trajectories of minor intersections and their adjacent road segments are sparse.** The recognition accuracy of the existing methods heavily
  depends on the number of motor vehicles' trajectories. That is, the more the
  number of trajectories, the higher the accuracy of detecting road intersections.
  Therefore, the existing methods cannot tackle the issue of cycling trajectory
  sparsity of road intersections and their neighboring road segments, resulting
  in miss recognition of minor intersections.
- **Turning behaviors occur in different regions within the range of
  intersections at different scales.** The existing methods consider that
  high-frequency turning behaviors of motor vehicles often occur at the central area of intersections, and determine the central positions of intersections
  by searching areas with the highest turning density through using clustering algorithm (e.g., Mean-Shift) [1,3]. So they are unfit for detecting major
  intersections where turning cycling trajectories occur on the margins of intersections (marked by blue dotted circles), and may misidentify a major intersection (e.g., v_3) into several minor ones (e.g., v_4, v_5, v_6 and v_7).

To tackle the trajectory sparsity issue of minor intersections, we introduce the concept of intersection topology to represent the linking relationship between intersections and their adjacent road segments. On the basis of that, we design a grid topology representation module, which first constructs a hierarchical trajectory transition graph to build the intersection topology using limited amounts of trajectories, then leverages a hierarchical graph attention network to integrate that topology into the representations of intersections. Additionally, to tackle the second challenge, inspired by the idea of identifying objects of different sizes through exploiting multi-scale features in the computer vision field [4], we cast intersection recognition as an object detection task and instance segmentation task. Further, we design a deformable transformer-based intersection inference strategy to infer intersections in a multi-scale paradigm. In summary, we make the following contributions:

- We present a *deep learning-based* intersection recognition method using cycling trajectories, called *PICT*, consisting of geometry feature extraction, grid topology representation and intersection inference.
- To identify the intersections having sparse trajectories correctly, we incorporate intersection topology into intersection representations by constructing a hierarchical trajectory transition graph.
- To discover the intersections of various scales accurately, we provide a solution based on *multi-scale learning* based technique, which casts intersection recognition as an object detection task and instance segmentation task.
- A detailed experimental and comparative evaluation is conducted on two real-world datasets, and experimental results show that *PICT* significantly outperforms the state-of-the-art intersection recognition methods.

2   Related Work

In past decades, the issue of map inference using motor vehicles' trajectories has garnered attention from academia and industry that many approaches were proposed to address it [5–9]. The existing approaches employed such techniques as clustering, trace merging and kernel density estimation to infer the digital map. In the latest work, the deep neural network was introduced into the map inference solution to distinguish between parallel roads, which did not need multiple empirical parameters tuning [10]. Considering that the intersection is the convergence of several adjacent road segments, the above approaches attempted to infer the road segments using trajectories first and then to treat the convergence points among the road segments as the centers of the intersections. However, they easily misidentified the endpoints on the road segments as the road intersections.

To improve the recognition precision of road intersections, some works tried to identify the intersection according to unique behaviors of motor vehicles occurring at the intersections [2,11–15]. To be specific, they identified the central positions of road intersections according to the fact that high-frequency turning and speed-shifting behaviors of motor vehicles often occur at the central area of intersections. Recently, a few works also identified the coverage of a road intersection and the turning rules within it [1,3]. Nevertheless, the aforementioned methods did not concentrate on the trajectory sparsity issue existing in road intersections and their adjacent road segments. What's more, they did not consider that turning behaviors may occur at different areas in intersections of different sizes. Therefore, all of them cannot be used for detecting road intersections in the cycling map.

3   Methods

3.1   Problem Formulation

Definition 1 (Cycling Trajectory). *A cycling trajectory tr refers to a GPS positional point sequence generated from cycling of cyclists, denoted as $tr = \{p_1, p_2, ..., \cdots, p_n\}$, where $p_i = (l_i, t_i)$, here l_i denotes the longitude and latitude coordinate of one point p_i at timestamp t_i, i.e. $l_i = (lng_i, lat_i)$, and $\forall i < j$, p_i arrives earlier than p_j. Two adjacent points are connected into a trajectory segment, denoted as (p_i, p_{i+1}).*

Definition 2 (Cycling Road Network). *A cycling road network is represented as a directional graph $G = (V, E)$, where the set of vertexes (denoted as V) refers to the road intersections, and the set of edges (denoted as E) refers to the road segments among the vertexes.*

As mentioned earlier, we cast the intersection recognition issue as an object detection task and instance segmentation task. To this end, we partition the whole cycling road network into $M \times N$ fine-grained grids Gr. Here a grid (denoted as g) corresponds to a pixel of the image, which is represented by a square space with a side length $g.size$.

Definition 3 (Intersection). *An intersection in G, denoted as $v_i \in V$, is represented as a tuple $(v_i.cp, v_i.cr)$, where $v_i.cp = (lng, lat)$ denotes the central position of v_i, and $v_i.cr = \{g | g \in Gr\}$ denotes the coverage of v_i which consists of a set of grids.*

Problem Definition. Given a set of cycling trajectories TR, our task is to infer the central positions and coverages of all intersections V for a cycling road network G using TR.

3.2   Framework Overview

Figure 2 shows the architecture of *PICT*, which consists of three modules: (i) *Geometry Feature Extraction* that partitions the region of the road network into grids and extracts features of grids based on trajectories, then employs the sliding window model to generate the tile samples composed of grids (a tile corresponds to an image in computer vision); (ii) *Grid Topology Representation* that incorporates the intersection topology into grid representations through a

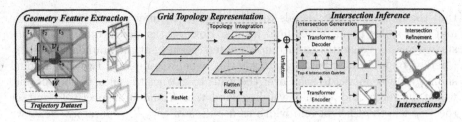

Fig. 2. Overview of *PICT*

convolutional neural network and a hierarchical graph attention network; (iii) *Intersection Inference* that infers the central positions and coverage of intersections from the grid representations based on a multi-scale learning paradigm through a deformable transformer-based strategy.

3.3   Geometry Feature Extraction

In view of that partitioning spatial region into grids is helpful to model cyclists' behaviors of trajectories and can easily align each grid with a pixel of the image, we first partition the region of the whole road network into $M \times N$ regular square grids Gr according to a preset grid size $g.size$. Then we extract the geometry features of grids based on the trajectories passing through them, including (i) *Point Frequency*, which denotes the number of trajectory points in each grid. As the convergence of road segments, the number of trajectory points in an intersection is always greater than that on its linked road segments; (ii) *Turning Frequency*, which indicates the number of turning points in each grid. Here a turning point refers to a point whose angle difference between its previous point and itself is beyond $40°$. Turning behaviors of cyclists always occur in intersections. (iii) *Segment Frequency*, which indicates the number of trajectory segments passing through each grid; Segment feature can effectively alleviate the point sparsity problem [6]; (iv) *Direction Distribution*, which indicates the direction distribution of each grid, here the direction of each trajectory point is mapped into 8 normalized equal-size direction histogram (e.g., $0°-45°$, $45°-90°$, etc.) to obtain an 8-direction distribution. The direction of each point is the direction of the line segment connecting that point and its next one; (v) *Average Speed*, which indicates the average speed of trajectory points in each grid, where the speed of each point is calculated by dividing the distance between two consecutive points by their time gap. Usually, the speed of trajectory points in any intersection is lower than that of its linked road segments.

After that, we construct a 12-dimensional vector with the above features for each grid, denoted as $\boldsymbol{GF} \in \mathbb{R}^{12 \times M \times N}$ (here the dimension of direction distribution equals to 8). Consider that the region of a road network is too large to perform tasks like roadway segmentation based on $\boldsymbol{GF}$ directly [16], the existing methods often adopt a strategy consisting of the following two steps: (i) crop $M \times N$ grids into a series of tiles, each of which consists of $H \times W$ grids, thus the number of tiles equals to $\lfloor \frac{M}{H} \rfloor \times \lfloor \frac{N}{W} \rfloor$; (ii) infer results from each tile and then splice them to get final results. However, as shown in Fig. 2, such a strategy easily generates an incomplete intersection v_i at the boundary of tile t_1 (marked by an orange part). To tackle this issue, we employ a two-dimensional sliding window model to scan over the grids to extract the tiles. To be specific, we set the height and width of a sliding window as H and W respectively, and set the step length of height and width as $h = \frac{H}{2}$ and $w = \frac{W}{2}$ separately. Next, we extract a few tiles (denoted as $\boldsymbol{TF} \in \mathbb{R}^{12 \times H \times W}$) to ensure that each intersection locates in the non-boundary area of at least one tile, e.g., v_i in t_5. Then tiles are viewed as data samples and fed into subsequent grid topology representation.

3.4   Grid Topology Representation

Considering that the differences in turning density and speed between intersections and their neighboring regions are beneficial to detect intersections [3], we adopt CNN to encode the grid features into dense representations. The reason for employing CNN is its convolution operation can efficiently model the feature differences between the grids and their neighbors. Specifically, we employ the most commonly adopted feature extraction backbone ResNet50 [17] to encode the grid features, and feed the tile features $\boldsymbol{TF} \in \mathbb{R}^{12 \times H \times W}$ into ResNet50 and 1×1 convolution. Then we extract the grid features at different scales $\{\mathbf{X}_s^l \in \mathbb{R}^{C \times \frac{H}{2^{l+1}} \times \frac{W}{2^{l+1}}}\}_{l=1}^4$ from the stages C2 through C5 in ResNet50, where C is the size of the embedded dimension.

However, the geometry features of regions with trajectory sparsity, present highly sparse as well, which makes it difficult to detect intersections in these regions. Inspired by the idea that combining context information can reduce the influences of the feature sparsity problem [18], we introduce the concept of intersection topology to indicate the linking relationship between the intersections and their adjacent road segments. Then we attempt to incorporate the intersection topology into grid representations. However, there is no information about the road network in advance. Therefore we face the challenge of using limited amounts of trajectories to effectively represent the intersection topology.

Transition Graph Construction. In view of that cyclists always turn at intersections, we represent intersection topology by constructing a hierarchical transition graph, where each grid forms a node, as shown in Fig. 3. Specifically, we extract all turning points and their previous point and next point to get turning triads, each turning triad is represented by (p_{i-1}, p_i, p_{i+1}). Here p_i can be viewed as the point sampled from the intersection, p_{i-1} and p_{i+1} can be viewed as the points sampled from the linked road segments. Then we construct an edge between the corresponding grids of p_{i-1} and p_i, as well as between the corresponding grids of p_{i+1} and p_i. Considering that constructing the transition graph under the fine-grained grids limits the context information of intersections, we construct the transition graph in a hierarchical way to capture more global topology information of intersections(e.g., higher-hop adjacent road segments of

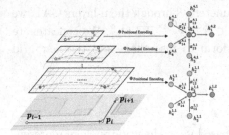
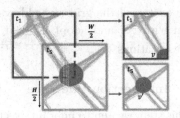

Fig. 3. Illustration of Transition Graph Construction and Topology Integration

Fig. 4. Illustration of Intersection RefinementThe bigraph B_2

an intersection), denoted as $\{TG^l\}_{l=1}^4$. In each layer l of it, a node's corresponding grid size is $2^{l+1} \times g.size$ which is aligned with the grid size of $\mathbf{X}_s^l$ at layer l. Through the above process, the hierarchical transition graph can capture the intersection topology at different scales.

Topology Integration. Considering that Graph neural networks like GAT [19] are suitable for learning topology features, we utilize GAT to integrate intersection topology into grid representations. It can adaptively assign weights to the grids on linked road segments to represent the intersection grids by computing the attention scores between them. However, the classical GAT model can only model the interaction of grid features that is unable to perceive the position differences of different road segments. The latter is crucial for distinguishing adjacent intersections since they are linked with road segments by different positions. To this end, we interact with their features and positions simultaneously when computing the attention scores of node pairs. Specifically, we map grid features output from ResNet $\{\mathbf{X}_s^l \in \mathbb{R}^{C \times \frac{H}{2^{l+1}} \times \frac{W}{2^{l+1}}}\}_{l=1}^4$ to the initialized node features by a 1×1 convolution with ReLU. Then we employ n-layers graph attention network to learn node representations at each scale. Note that the learning at each scale is parameter non-sharing. The attention weight α_{ij} between the grid g_i and g_j of each layer is computed as (the layer is ignored here for simplicity):

$$e_{ij} = ((\mathbf{h}_i + pe_i)\mathbf{W}_1 + (\mathbf{h}_j + pe_j)\mathbf{W}_1)\mathbf{W}_2 \tag{1}$$

$$\alpha_{ij} = \frac{exp(LeakyReLU(e_{ij}))}{\sum_{k \in N_i} exp(LeakyReLU(e_{ik}))} \tag{2}$$

where $\mathbf{h}_i$, $\mathbf{h}_j \in \mathbb{R}^C$ are node representations of g_i and g_j, $\mathbf{W}_1 \in \mathbb{R}^{C \times C}$ and $\mathbf{W}_2 \in \mathbb{R}^{C \times 1}$ are learnable parameters. pe_i and pe_j mean the positional encoding of g_i and g_j in the feature matrix [20].

Then we obtain the output feature $\mathbf{h}_i$ of the grid g_i through integrating the features of its neighborhood nodes (denoted as $N(i)$):

$$\mathbf{h}_i = \sum_{j \in N(i)} \alpha_{ij}\mathbf{W}_3\mathbf{h}_j \tag{3}$$

where $\mathbf{W}_3 \in \mathbb{R}^{C \times C}$ are the learnable parameters. Through the n-layers GAT, we have extracted the grid embeddings $\{\mathbf{X}_t^l \in \mathbb{R}^{C \times \frac{H}{2^{l+1}} \times \frac{W}{2^{l+1}}}\}_{l=1}^4$. We concatenate them with $\mathbf{X}_s^l$ and adopt a linear transform to fuse them into the new grid representations $\{\mathbf{X}_{st}^l \in \mathbb{R}^{C \times \frac{H}{2^{l+1}} \times \frac{W}{2^{l+1}}}\}_{l=1}^4$.

3.5   Intersection Inference

In this step, we aim to infer intersections based upon the grid topology representation. Trajectories in intersections of different sizes show significant differences, which makes it hard to effectively detect intersections of variable sizes. Additionally, the number of intersections in each tile is not a fixed constant, making it difficult to infer the intersections through classical classification and regression models. To overcome these challenges, we borrow the idea from the computer vision field and take advantage of multi-scale feature learning [4], then cast intersection recognition as an object detection task and instance segmentation task.

Preliminaries. Object detection and instance segmentation are important subfields of computer vision research [21]. Their common goal is to locate and identify all instances of a particular object class within an image. Object detection involves drawing a bounding box around each object instance, while instance segmentation goes further by aligning each pixel in the image with a specific object instance. One of the main challenges in the above two fields is to identify objects at different scales. To tackle it, multi-scale learning provides a solution by first exploiting multi-scale features and then modeling the interaction between features in different scales [4]. In our scenario, we encode geometry features and intersection topology into grid representations, with each grid aligning with a pixel and each tile aligning with an image. In this way, inferring the central positions and coverage of intersections are redefined as regressing the center coordinates of the bounding box in the object detection task and predicting the instance mask in instance segmentation task, respectively.

Intersection Generation. To be specific, we adopt the transformer architecture of MaskDINO [21] to detect intersections, the reasons for choosing which include : (i) the deformable attention in MaskDINO allows it to execute in a multi-scale paradigm [4]; and (ii) MaskDINO is a unified framework to perform object detection and instance segmentation, which is in line with our purpose for detecting the central positions and coverage of intersections. As shown in Fig. 2, the transformer architecture of MaskDINO contains an encoder and a decoder. The encoder builds multi-scale correlation of grid representations through layers of deformable attention module. Based on this, the decoder obtains intersection queries from the encoder and adopts deformable attention to probe features from the grid representations, then infers the central positions $v.cp$ and the coverage $v.cr$ of candidate intersections (aligning with the center coordinates of bounding box and the instance mask respectively). Besides, each candidate intersection v_i

is associated with a predicted probability pr_{v_i} that is output simultaneously with the central positions and coverage. Due to the space limitation, we recommend readers visit MaskDINO [21] for a more detailed description.

Intersection Refinement. Recall that we adopt a sliding window model to ensure that each intersection is located in the non-boundary area of at least one tile. Further, we design an intersection refinement strategy that aims to replace incomplete candidate intersections in the current tile with the optimal complete candidate intersections from neighboring tiles. Specifically, we first traverse the candidate intersections of the tiles. As shown in Fig. 4, if an incomplete candidate intersection v is located at the boundary in tile t_1, we search its corresponding complete one v' in the non-boundary area of its neighboring tile t_5, where the position of the neighboring tile must be equal to the position of the current tile t_1 after moving one step of the sliding window towards the overlapping boundaries of the intersection v (down to the right). After determining the neighboring tile, the next step is to select the highest confidence candidate intersection v' to replace incomplete intersection v. We follow the approach described in [22], and define the confidence as $pr_{v'} \times IOU(v'.cr, v.cr)$, where $pr_{v'}$ denotes the prediction probability of v' output from the intersection generation and $IOU(v'.cr, v.cr)$ denotes the intersection over union between the coverage of v' and v.

Training and Inference. During the training process, only the grid topology representation module and the intersection generation module participate in the model optimization. We adopt the same optimization procedure as MaskDINO including a bipartite matching between inferred intersections and the ground truth and the same loss function. The intersection refinement module is specially designed for detecting intersections in test regions under a trained model.

4 Experiment

4.1 Experiment Settings

Datasets. We evaluate *PICT* on two real-world cycling trajectory datasets, including WH21 and WB20, both of which contain a lot of alleys and minor intersections. WH21 is a real-world cycling trajectory dataset in the area near WuHou Avenue of a major Chinese city over 2 months, provided by a leading location-based service company. WB20[1] is a publicly available sharing-bikes' trajectory dataset in the area near Wuyuan Bay, Xiamen City. The detailed statistics of the dataset are given in Table 1, where the statistics of the test region are given in the parentheses.

---

[1] https://data.xm.gov.cn/contest-series/digit-china-2021/index.html#/3/
competition_data.

Table 1. Description of experimental datasets

Dataset	WH21	WB20
Sampling Rate (s)	10	15
Size (km^2)	15×15 (3×3)	15×16 (4×4)
Point Count	227M	175M
Trajectory Count	92165	147,722
Intersection Count	5264(301)	4217(365)

Baselines. To evaluate the benefits of our proposed method, we compare *PICT* with five state-of-the-art intersection recognition approaches.

- **Huang** [2] clusters the convergence points and constrained convergence points respectively using DBSCAN to get major and minor intersections.
- **CITT** [3] discovers the intersection grids based on speed and direction analysis, then identifies intersections from all turning points in intersection grids using Mean-Shift.
- **Wang** [13] generates the central positions of intersections by hierarchical clustering for high directional-entropy grids.
- **Qing** [14] builds a binary classification model to determine whether a trajectory point is around the intersection, then clusters the positive samples to generate the intersections by Mean-Shift.
- **Hu** [15] designs a two-trajectory intersect angle-based strategy to extract the candidate intersection centers, then clusters them using DBSCAN.

To further evaluate the grid topology representation module and intersection generation module fairly, we expand our framework by replacing our grid topology representation and intersection generation with four instance segmentation models, including MaskRCNN [23], Solov2 [24], Mask2former [25], MaskDINO [21], respectively denoted as PICT-MR, PICT-SL, PICT-MF, PICT-MD, which can be viewed as the variants of PICT. We regard the barycenter of their inferred instances as the central position of intersections.

Evaluation Criteria. The ground truth central positions and coverage of the intersections are generated by volunteers' manual labeling according to *Open-StreetMap* and the trajectory data set. Here the procedure of labeling intersection coverage is similar to the procedure of labeling the instance mask in computer vision [26]. Let L_{tru} denote the amount of the ground truth intersections, L_{det} denote the number of detected intersections, and L_{match} denote the number of matching intersections. We define a successful match between a detected intersection and a ground truth intersection if the distance between them is less than a preset matching distance d. The matching process is one-to-one which means each ground truth intersection is only aligned with its nearest detected intersection. Specifically, *Precision*, *Recall*, *F1-score* can be calculated as follows:

$$Precision = \frac{L_{match}}{L_{det}}, Recall = \frac{L_{match}}{L_{tru}}, F1\text{-}score = 2 * \frac{Precision * Recall}{Precision + Recall}.$$

(4)

Implement Details. All the experimental codes are written in Python 3.8. Our experiments run on a GPU server with 64 GB memory and RTX-5000 GPU. Before extracting features for each grid, we applied several preprocessing algorithms on raw trajectories, including trajectory segmentation and simplification in [3]. We take the trajectories outside the test region as the training data and employ the same sliding window to extract the tile samples for training. The number of tile samples for training, validation and testing is 3069, 351, 169 for WH21, 3171, 362 and 289 for WB20. Besides, considering the diversity of road orientation distribution, we adopt random horizontal flipping, vertical flipping and horizontal then vertical flipping for data augmentation of the training set and the probability for each flipping type is set to 0.75, notice the direction distribution of each grid will change after flipping. The training strategy mainly follows the MaskDINO.

Parameter Settings. We set the value of H and W to 256, and the grid size $g.size$ is set to 2 meters. The number of GAT layers is set to 3. In intersection generation, we keep all hyperparameters the same as MaskDINO, except for the number of intersection queries, we set it to 150 which is significantly larger than the number of intersections in a tile. We train *PICT* with AdamW [21] with

Table 2. Quantitative Results of Central Position Recognition

Dataset	Type	Methods	Evaluation Criteria								
			d = 10 m			d = 20 m			d = 30 m		
			Precision	Recall	F1-score	Precision	Recall	F1-score	Precision	Recall	F1-score
WH21	Unsupervised	Huang2019	0.4582	0.4405	0.4492	0.5920	0.5691	0.5803	0.7023	0.5702	0.6885
		CITT2020	0.4513	0.5659	0.5021	0.5590	0.7010	0.6220	0.6411	0.7749	0.7017
		Wang2020	0.2295	0.2691	0.2477	0.4079	0.4784	0.4404	0.5184	0.6080	0.5596
		Qing2021	0.3968	0.3256	0.3577	0.6680	0.5482	0.6022	0.7166	0.5880	0.6460
		Hu2022	0.3657	0.2734	0.3218	0.4829	0.5528	0.5176	0.7054	0.5760	0.6325
	Supervised	PICT-MR	0.7597	0.7143	0.7363	0.8339	0.7841	0.8082	**0.8834**	0.8306	0.8562
		PICT-SL	0.7081	0.7010	0.7045	0.7953	0.7874	0.7913	0.8154	0.8073	0.8114
		PICT-MF	0.7574	0.7331	0.7451	**0.8439**	0.8167	0.8301	0.8424	0.8562	0.8715
		PICT-MD	0.7627	0.7749	0.7687	0.8322	0.8457	0.8389	0.8513	0.8650	0.8581
		PICT	**0.7962**	**0.8306**	**0.8130**	0.8378	**0.8738**	**0.8553**	0.8790	**0.9169**	**0.8976**
WB20	Unsupervised	Huang2019	0.3247	0.2444	0.2789	0.6199	0.4667	0.5325	0.7232	0.5444	0.6212
		CITT2020	0.3462	0.5178	0.3457	0.5192	0.5178	0.5185	0.6456	0.6438	0.6447
		Wang2020	0.1835	0.1589	0.1703	0.3861	0.3342	0.3583	0.5348	0.4630	0.4963
		Qing2021	0.2311	0.2849	0.2552	0.3822	0.4712	0.4221	0.4933	0.6082	0.5448
		Hu2022	0.3262	0.3025	0.3142	0.5047	0.4785	0.4923	0.6653	0.5738	0.6235
	Supervised	PICT-MR	0.6064	0.5697	0.5876	0.7464	0.7014	0.7232	0.7988	0.7507	0.7740
		PICT-SL	0.5914	0.5671	0.5769	0.6943	0.6658	0.6797	0.7486	0.7178	0.7329
		PICT-MF	0.5851	0.6027	0.5938	0.6941	0.7151	0.7045	0.7660	0.7890	0.7773
		PICT-MD	0.6122	0.6055	0.6088	0.7729	0.7644	0.7686	0.8087	0.8000	0.8044
		PICT	**0.6965**	**0.6602**	**0.6779**	**0.8324**	**0.7890**	**0.8101**	**0.8699**	**0.8247**	**0.8467**

the learning rate 1e-4 and weight decay 1e-4 under a learning rate schedule by multiplying the learning rate by 0.1 every 10 epochs.

Please add the following required packages to your document preamble:

4.2   Main Results

Quantitative Comparison. As shown in Table 2, we observe that *PICT* is significantly superior to the existing methods, outperforming the best baseline algorithm by 37.51%, 52.13% on WH21 and WB20 in F1-score, respectively. Comparing the existing methods with *PICT* and variants of *PICT*, the existing methods do not perform well on both datasets, as they are all clustering-based methods without any supervised learning procedure. Additionally, they ignore modeling the intersection topology and do not detect intersections in a multi-scale paradigm. Variants of *PICT* perform better than the existing approaches since they can model the multi-scale interaction of the grids. Meanwhile, they are supervised-based methods, which proves the potential of introducing deep learning into intersection recognition. However, they still attain a lower F1-score than *PICT* on both datasets. This is due to that *PICT* leverages intersection topology into intersection recognition. It proliferates the accuracy of intersection recognition, especially for identifying intersections with sparse trajectories.

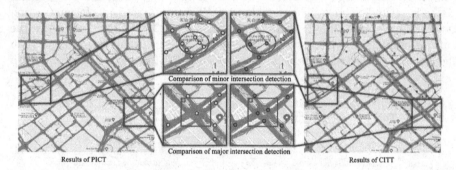

Fig. 5. Visualization Comparison

Visualization Comparison. We visualize the intersection recognition results of a typical region on WH21. Due to the space limitation, we choose CITT as the comparison approach because it performs best in Recall and F1-score (The following experiments are also the same). As shown in Fig. 5, the trajectories are highlighted with green lines and the detected locations of intersections are represented by different colors of marbles. It can be seen that the performance of *PICT* is significantly superior to CITT. Specifically, while meeting a region with trajectory sparsity (highlighted with red circles), CITT misses detecting a few intersections. Meanwhile, CITT wrongly generates redundant intersections

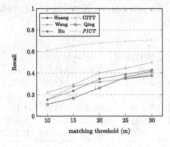

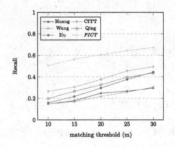

Fig. 6. Performance on *WH21*.   **Fig. 7.** Performance on *WB20*.

around a major intersection (highlighted with red rectangles). In comparison, *PICT* can precisely detect intersections of different sizes and in regions with trajectory sparsity due to that *PICT* takes intersection topology into consideration and detects intersections in a multi-scale paradigm.

Comparison of Minor Intersection Recognition. To further assess the ability of *PICT* for detecting minor intersections, we report the experimental results of detecting the central positions of minor intersections. Considering that minor intersections only link multiple single-lane road segments, we regard intersections with a radius of less than 5 m as minor intersections as 5 m is slightly wider than the lane width. Figure 6 and Fig. 7 show *Recall* rates of minor intersection recognition of *PICT* and other approaches. Due to that *PICT* considers the intersection topology, *PICT* outperforms CITT by 68.97% and 60.55% in Recall on WH21 and WB20 under $d = 20$ meters, respectively.

Evaluation of Coverage Recognition. To evaluate the effectiveness of *PICT* on intersection coverage recognition, we compare *PICT* with CITT, PICT-MR, PICT-SL, PICT-MF and PICT-MD. We adopt average precision (AP) as our metric which is widely adopted in the instance segmentation field, it is calculated by the mean of the IOU threshold of 0.25 and 0.5. To keep fairness, CITT would not participate in the quantitative evaluation due to that it utilizes the circle geometry to represent the coverage, and we design an extra visualization evaluation to compare *PICT* with CITT.

From Table 3, we find that PICT-MR and PICT-SL have low precision as they adopt the *nms*-based strategy that cannot build the correlation between adjacent intersections. Therefore they easily generate redundancy results. PICT-MF and PICT-MD performs better due to that the attention mechanism can build the correlation between the intersections. *PICT* achieves the best performance which proves that intersection topology is vital for detecting intersections.

For visualization evaluation, we use several central positions detected by *PICT* as the input of the coverage recognition algorithm in CITT, and visualize the coverage results generated by *PICT* and CITT in Fig. 8(a) and Fig. 8(b). It can be seen that CITT generates some overlaps when meeting the adjacent

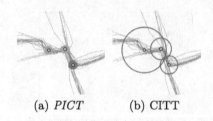

(a) *PICT*   (b) CITT

Fig. 8. Coverage Recognition of *PICT* and CITT.

Table 3. Quantitative Results of Coverage Recognition

Methods	WH21		WB20	
	AP_{25}	AP_{50}	AP_{25}	AP_{50}
PICT-MR	0.7592	0.4573	0.6538	0.4027
PICT-SL	0.7028	0.3764	0.6145	0.3563
PICT-MF	0.7895	0.4835	0.7128	0.4276
PICT-MD	0.8027	0.5013	0.7459	0.4729
PICT	**0.8256**	**0.5472**	**0.7839**	**0.4957**

Table 4. Quantitative Results of Map Inference

Methods	WH21			WB20		
	Preci.	Recall	F1	Preci.	Recall	F1
Huang	0.6339	0.5717	0.6012	0.4498	0.4686	0.4590
CITT	0.5823	0.5905	0.5864	0.4194	0.4687	0.4423
Wang	0.4814	0.3922	0.4323	0.4701	0.2767	0.3484
Qing	0.6189	0.6020	0.6103	0.4212	0.4432	0.4319
Hu	0.6630	0.5686	0.6122	0.4307	0.4399	0.4353
PICT	**0.7474**	**0.6629**	**0.7026**	**0.5466**	**0.5717**	**0.5589**

Table 5. Quantitative Results of Ablation Study

Methods	WH21			WB20		
	Preci.	Recall	F1	Preci.	Recall	F1
PICT-RP	0.7571	**0.8904**	0.8183	0.8160	0.7534	0.7835
PICT-RL	**0.8885**	0.7940	0.8386	**0.8408**	0.7238	0.7706
PICT-RO	0.8104	0.8521	0.8307	0.8029	0.7699	0.7860
GTR-1	0.8538	0.8264	0.8399	0.7989	0.7837	0.7911
GTR-5	0.8269	0.8299	0.8283	0.7606	0.7836	0.7719
GTR-RP	0.8382	0.8328	0.8355	0.8155	0.7507	0.7817
PICT-RG	0.8322	0.8457	0.8329	0.7729	0.7644	0.7686
PICT	0.8396	0.8870	**0.8627**	0.8324	**0.7890**	**0.8101**

intersections. In comparison, *PICT* can avoid this drawback well, which further proves the ability of *PICT* in coverage recognition.

Evaluation of the Impact on Map Inference. We evaluate *PICT* and existing methods on map inference task to illustrate the practicality of *PICT*. Specifically, we adopt the intersection detected by *PICT* and the existing methods as the input of the road network construction method in [2], then use the de-facto standard proposed in [8] to measure the quality of the constructed map. The parameter settings in this evaluation method are consistent with [2]. As shown in Table 4, *PICT* achieves better performance than existing methods in both datasets. On the one hand, as *PICT* discovers more minor intersections than the existing methods, *PICT* can infer more road segments with trajectory sparsity. Therefore *PICT* attains a higher Recall score. On the other hand, as *PICT* accurately detects intersections of various sizes, the inferred road segments are more in line with the actual shape than the existing methods. Therefore *PICT* attains a higher Precision score. Overall, the above experiments show the significant meaning of *PICT* for map inference.

4.3 Ablation Study

Effect of Different Features. We evaluate the importance of different features in Table 5 under $d = 20$ meters, where PICT-RP and PICT-RL denote removing point or segment feature, PICT-RO denotes removing turning, direction and speed features. If the point feature is removed, the precision in each dataset decreases a few. And if the segment feature is removed, the recall decreases a lot. We attribute these phenomena to 2 reasons: 1) While meeting adjacent intersections, there are several consecutive points directly passing them due to the low sampling rate of cycling trajectories. Therefore the segment feature is not convincing. In comparison, the point feature can provide more accurate information. 2) While meeting region with trajectory sparsity, the point feature is sparse as well. Segment feature can provide the passing grids generated by the consecutive points which helps to alleviate the feature sparsity. Besides, if the turning, direction and speed features are removed, the F1-score decreases a lot. It shows the importance of considering the property of multiple directions and frequent speed-shifting behaviors at intersections.

Effect of Grid Topology Representation. To determine the effect of grid topology representation (GTR), we evaluate GTR in the following settings:

- GTR-1, 5: We set the number of GAT layers as 1, 5.
- GTR-RP: We remove the position encoding in GTR.
- PICT-RG: We remove GTR in *PICT*.

As shown in Table 5, PICT-RG achieves the best F1-score compared to GTR-1 and GTR-5. On the one hand, if the number of GAT layers is set too small, GAT has limited respective fields resulting in a low F1-score. On the other hand, if the number is set too large, the problem of feature over-smoothing arises which is detrimental to detecting minor intersections. Further, if the position encoding is removed, the F1-score in both datasets decreases a lot. It proves that the positions of adjacent road segments are crucial to model the intersection topology. PICT-RG achieves inferior performance than *PICT* which shows the importance of considering intersection topology.

5 Conclusion

To improve the recognition accuracy of the road intersections in the cycling map, we present a deep learning-based intersection recognition framework based upon cycling trajectories, called *PICT*, to infer the central positions and coverage of the intersections. Not only does it identify minor intersections having sparse trajectories, but it can also effectively distinguish intersections of different sizes. Experiments on two real-world datasets demonstrate *PICT* outperforms the existing approaches significantly. In the future, we plan to infer more accurate road links between detected intersections to obtain a cycling map that is consistent with the real road network topology.

Acknowledgments. This work is supported by NSFC (Nos.62072180 and U191 1203), and CCF-DiDi GAIA Collaborative Research Funds for Young Scholars.

Ethical Statement. This paper involves the development and evaluation of a road intersection recognition method using cycling trajectories, which has meaningful implications in cycling navigation. We value the importance of ethical considerations in the field of data mining and guarantee that our research does not involve the collection and inference of personal data, and will not cause adverse effects on society.

References

1. Wang, J., Wang, C., Song, X., Raghavan, V.: Automatic intersection and traffic rule detection by mining motor-vehicle gps trajectories. Comput. Environ. Urban Syst. **64**, 19–29 (2017)
2. Huang, Y., Xiao, Z., Xiaoyou, Yu., Wang, D., Havyarimana, V., Bai, J.: Road network construction with complex intersections based on sparsely sampled private car trajectory data. TKDD **13**(3), 1–28 (2019)
3. Zhao, L., et al.: Automatic calibration of road intersection topology using trajectories. In: ICDE, pp. 1633–1644 (2020)
4. Zhu, X., Su, W., Lu, L., Li, B., Wang, X., Dai, J.: Deformable DETR: deformable transformers for end-to-end object detection. In: ICLR (2020)
5. Chao, P., Hua, W., Mao, R., Jiajie, X., Zhou, X.: A survey and quantitative study on map inference algorithms from GPS trajectories. IEEE Trans. Knowl. Data Eng. **34**(1), 15–28 (2020)
6. Wang, T., Mao, J., Jin, C.: HyMU: a hybrid map updating framework. In: DASFAA, pp. 19–33 (2017)
7. He, S., et al.: Roadrunner: improving the precision of road network inference from GPS trajectories. In: SIGSPATIAL, pp. 3–12 (2018)
8. Biagioni, J., Eriksson, J.: Map inference in the face of noise and disparity. In: SIGSPATIAL, pp. 79–88 (2012)
9. Li, L., Li, D., Xing, X., Yang, F., Rong, W., Zhu, H.: Extraction of road intersections from GPS traces based on the dominant orientations of roads. ISPRS Int. J. Geo Inf. **6**(12), 403 (2017)
10. Ruan, S., et al.: Learning to generate maps from trajectories. In: AAAI vol. 34, pp. 890–897 (2020)
11. Karagiorgou, S., Pfoser, D.: On vehicle tracking data-based road network generation. In: SIGSPATIAL, pp. 89–98 (2012)
12. Pu, M., Mao, J., Du, Y., Shen, Y., Jin, C.: Road intersection detection based on direction ratio statistics analysis. In: MDM, pp. 288–297 (2019)
13. Wang, C., Hao, P., Wu, G., Qi, X., Barth, M.J.: Intersection and stop bar position extraction from vehicle positioning data. IEEE Trans. Intell. Transp. Syst. (2020)
14. Qing, R., Liu, Y., Zhao, Y., Liao, Z., Liu, Y.X.: Using feature interaction among GPS data for road intersection detection. In: HUMA @ ACM Multimedia, pp. 31–37 (2021)
15. Rong, H., Yong, X., Chen, H., Zou, F.: A novel method for the detection of road intersections and traffic rules using big floating car data. IET Intel. Transp. Syst. **16**(8), 983–997 (2022)
16. Máttyus, G., Luo, W., Urtasun, R.: Deeproadmapper: extracting road topology from aerial images. In ICCV, pp. 3438–3446 (2017)
17. He, K., Zhang, X., Ren, S., Sun, J.: Deep residual learning for image recognition. In: CVPR, pp. 770–778 (2016)

18. Dai, Y., Wu, Y., Zhou, F., Barnard, K.: Asymmetric contextual modulation for infrared small target detection. In: WACV, pp. 950–959 (2021)
19. Veličković, P., et al.: Graph attention networks. In: ICLR (2017)
20. Parmar, N., et al.: Image transformer. In: ICML, pp. 4055–4064. PMLR (2018)
21. Li, F., Zhang, H., Liu, S., Zhang, L., Ni, L.M., Shum, H.-Y., et al.: Mask DINO: lards a unified transformer-based framework for object detection and segmentation. arXiv preprint arXiv:2206.02777 (2022)
22. Redmon, J., Divvala, S., Girshick, R., Farhadi, A.: You only look once: Unified, real-time object detection. In: CVPR, pp. 779–788 (2016)
23. He, K., Gkioxari, G., Dollár, P., Girshick, R.: Mask R-CNN. In: ICCV, pp. 2961–2969 (2017)
24. Wang, X., Zhang, R., Kong, T., Li, L., Shen, C.: Solov2: dynamic and fast instance segmentation. NeurIPS **33**, 17721–17732 (2020)
25. Cheng, B., Misra, I., Schwing, A.G., Kirillov, A., Girdhar, R.: Masked-attention mask transformer for universal image segmentation. In: CVPR, pp. 1290–1299 (2022)
26. Deng, J., Dong, W., Socher, R., Li, L.-J., Li, K., Fei-Fei, L.: ImageNet: a large-scale hierarchical image database. In 2009 IEEE Conference on Computer Vision and Pattern Recognition, pp. 248–255. IEEE (2009)

FDTI: Fine-Grained Deep Traffic Inference with Roadnet-Enriched Graph

Zhanyu Liu[1], Chumeng Liang[1], Guanjie Zheng[1(✉)], and Hua Wei[2]

[1] Shanghai Jiao Tong University, Shanghai, China
{zhyliu00,gjzheng}@sjtu.edu.cn
[2] Arizona State University, Tempe, USA
hua.wei@asu.edu

Abstract. This paper proposes the fine-grained traffic prediction task (e.g. interval between data points is 1 min), which is essential to traffic-related downstream applications. Under this setting, traffic flow is highly influenced by traffic signals and the correlation between traffic nodes is dynamic. As a result, the traffic data is non-smooth between nodes, and hard to utilize previous methods which focus on smooth traffic data. To address this problem, we propose **F**ine-grained **D**eep **T**raffic **I**nference, termed as **FDTI**. Specifically, we construct a fine-grained traffic graph based on traffic signals to model the inter-road relations. Then, a physically-interpretable dynamic mobility convolution module is proposed to capture vehicle moving dynamics controlled by the traffic signals. Furthermore, traffic flow conservation is introduced to accurately infer future volume. Extensive experiments demonstrate that our method achieves state-of-the-art performance and learned traffic dynamics with good properties. To the best of our knowledge, we are the first to conduct the city-level fine-grained traffic prediction.

Keywords: Spatio-Temporal Data · Traffic Forecasting

1 Introduction

Traffic prediction is an important part of an intelligent traffic system and benefits downstream tasks. Some downstream tasks are sensitive to the granularity of prediction results, such as traffic signal control, congestion discovery, and route planning. Taking traffic signal control as an example, predictions on the 1-minute level could timely evaluate the impact of the incoming traffic signal and improve traffic policy because the interval of traffic signal change is approximately 1 min [22]. Previous deep methods [8,9,38] focus on the coarse-grained traffic data. However, it remains unexplored that utilizes deep methods to solve traffic prediction tasks under the fine-grained setting.

Under the fine-grained setting, the traffic flow is determined by traffic signals [25]. When the signal turns green, the vehicles could flow into downstream roads. As a result, the correlations between these roads are strong under the traffic prediction context, which is shown in Fig. 1(a). However, previous research

G. De Francisci Morales et al. (Eds.): ECML PKDD 2023, LNAI 14175, pp. 174–191, 2023.
https://doi.org/10.1007/978-3-031-43430-3_11

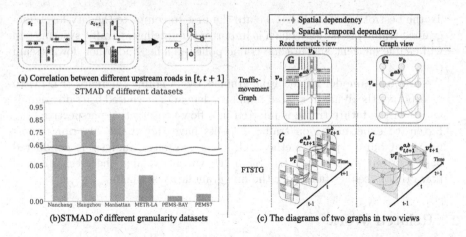

Fig. 1. (a) The traffic signal determines the traffic flow, thereby determining the correlation between roads. (b) Our fine-grained data is much more unsmooth than previous datasets. (Low STMAD indicates smoother and the wavy line indicates the omitted space). (c) Diagrams of Traffic-movement graph and FTSTG.

ignores the explicit highly dynamic correlation between nodes under the fine-grained settings and utilizes static graphs [28,46] or data-driven graphs [2,36,37] to aggregate the knowledge of nodes.

Due to the highly dynamic correlations resulting from the traffic signals, spatial neighbors do not have similar traffic volumes. Therefore, as shown in Fig. 1(b), the fine-grained traffic data is non-smooth, which is evaluated by Spatial Temporal Mean Average Distance (STMAD) defined in this paper. Previous methods have satisfying results on coarse-grained smooth datasets. However, since smoothing is the essential nature of the GCN design [4], experiments show previous methods still make smooth predictions on the nonsmooth fine-grained data which leads to big errors.

To better model the dynamic correlations and tackle the non-smoothness of the data under the fine-grained setting, we propose a model called **F**ine-grained **D**eep **T**raffic **I**nference (**FDTI**). First, to adapt the characteristic that traffic signal controls traffic flow in fine-grained traffic inference, we construct a **Fine-grained Traffic Spatial-Temporal Graph (FTSTG)**. Specifically, we build a road network feature enriched multi-layer traffic graph, in which each layer represents a time frame as shown in Fig. 1(c). Edges inside the graph represent traffic flow links between two nodes at adjacent time frames, which are controlled by traffic signals. Then, we propose a **Dynamic Mobility Convolution Network** to induce consistency with the traffic policy on FTSTG. People can make a metaphor between a traffic network and a water flow network, in which the traffic signal is similar to the tap controlling the flow. Based on the previous two modules, we further infer the traffic volume of each node following **Flow Conservative Traffic State Transition**. Our contribution can be summarized as follows.

- To the best of our knowledge, we are the first to complete the city-level fine-grained traffic prediction, which is important in intelligent traffic systems and will enable efficient and in-time traffic policy-making and other downstream tasks.
- We propose a model named Fine-grained Deep Traffic Inference (FDTI) to incorporate the dynamic spatial temporal dependency caused by traffic signals and then the future traffic is inferred in a flow-conservative perspective.
- Extensive experiments on traffic datasets have shown the superior performance of our proposed method. Graph smoothness analysis is conducted based on our proposed metric STMAD, which explains the mechanism of how other baselines fail under the fine granularity setting.

2   Related Work

Conventional Traffic Prediction. Traffic prediction research draws lots of attention [44], while conventional methods focus on statistical methods. Kalman filter based methods [30,32] show good results for short-term traffic volume prediction. ML methods such as SVM [31] built on non-linear relationships achieve better performance. The spatial dependency is modeled by methods such as Bayesian Network [49], and probabilistic model [1]. However, they have not exploited the rich spatial information enough.

Deep Spatial-Temporal Traffic Prediction. The utilization of graph convolutional networks (GCNs) [21,39] contributes significantly to the advancement of spatial-temporal traffic prediction. DCRNN [28], STGCN [46], GSTNet [10], STDN [45], STFGNN [27], LSGCN [19] combines modules such as diffusion, GCN and GRU to model the spatial and temporal relations. Recently many adaptive methods for spatial-temporal data have been proposed. Methodologies such as Graph Wavenet [43], AGCRN [2], GMAN [47], FC-GAGA [33], D2STGNN [37], HGCN [13], ST-WA [8], DSTAGNN [23] utilize techniques such as node embedding and attention to reconstruct the adaptive adjacent matrix and fuse the temporal long term relation. MDTP [12], MTGNN [42], and DMSTGCN [16] utilize multimodal data to help forecast the traffic. Z-GCNET [6] introduces time-aware persistent homology. STGODE [11], STG-NCDE [7], STDEN [20] use differential equations to model the traffic. However, most of those methods would utilize enormous parameters on learning graphs with node embeddings which ignores the influence of traffic signals between different nodes. [34,35] researches the fine-grained volume inference. However, they focus on spatial-fine-grained grid-based data and utilize CNN-based methods, which can not be applied to our temporal-fine-grained graph-based data. A recent work [25] focuses on fine-grained graph-based traffic prediction, which incorporates a similar state transition function but uses a different setting of missing data.

3   Preliminaries

Definition 1 (Traffic-Movements Grap). *We model the traffic system as a traffic-movement graph* $\mathbb{G} = (\mathbb{V}, \mathbb{E})$ *where* $\mathbb{V}$ *is the set of* N *traffic-movements [48] and* $\mathbb{E}$ *is the set of connections between traffic movements. Each traffic-movement* v^i *is a set of lanes with the same moving direction* $d^i \in \{Left, Straight, Right\}$. *Each directed edge* e^{ij} *denotes the link from traffic movement* v^i *to traffic movement* v^j. *Figure 1(c) shows a sample traffic-movement graph* $\mathbb{G}$ *generated from the real traffic system.*

Definition 2 (Traffic State). *The traffic state* x_t^i *of a traffic-movement* v^i *at timestamp* t *includes various measurements such as speed and volume. Thus, the traffic state of the whole system is represented as* $X_t = \{x_t^1, x_t^2, \cdots, x_t^N\}$. *In this paper, we mainly focus on traffic volume, defined as the number of vehicles on the traffic-movement* v^i *at timestamp* t. *The time granularity of the traffic volume is 1 min.*

Definition 3 (Roadnet-enriched Feature). *Roadnet is an abbreviation for road network. The roadnet-enriched feature indicates the road-network-related feature that helps infer future traffic states. It contains the traffic signal (described as green signal time* p_i) *and the static information of traffic-movements (e.g., length* l^i *and direction* d^i). *Foramally, the system-wise roadnet-enriched feature is represented as* $S_t = \{s_t^1, s_t^2, \cdots, s_t^N\}$ *where* $s_t^i = \{p_t^i, l^i, d^i\}$ *is the features of traffic-movement* v^i *at time* t.

3.1   Problem Definition

Problem 1 (One-step inference). Given a city-level traffic system $\mathbb{G} = (\mathbb{V}, \mathbb{E})$, the goal is to learn a model f to perform traffic inference of next time step X_{t+1} based on traffic state observations $X_{t-T+1:t}$ and roadnet-enriched feature $S_{t-T+1:t}$ of previous T time steps. Formally, the problem is defined as

$$\hat{X}_{t+1} = f(X_{t-T+1:t}, S_{t-T+1:t}). \tag{1}$$

Problem 2 (Q-step inference). Based on one-step state inference, Q-step state inference can be achieved by performing one-step inference Q times. Formally, this problem could be denoted as

$$\hat{X}_{t'+1} = f(\hat{X}_{t'-T+1:t'}, S_{t'-T+1:t'}), t' = t + 1, \cdots, t + Q \tag{2}$$

Here $\hat{X}_{t'-T+1:t'}$ is the input of function f and it could include both predicted value and ground truth value.

4   Method

To solve the defined problem, we propose **F**ine-grained **D**eep **T**raffic **I**nference (**FDTI**) as illustrated in Fig. 2(a). Firstly, traffic states and roadnet-enriched

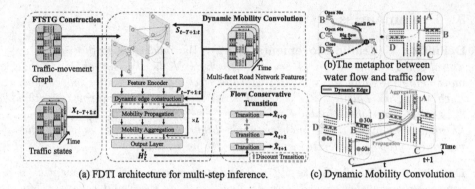

Fig. 2. Diagrams of Fine-grained Deep Traffic Inference (FDTI). (Color figure online)

features are organized to construct FTSTG, which represents the traffic node in a graph with multiple time layers. Then, a dynamic mobility convolution is conducted to model the traffic flow transition via dynamic edges. Lastly, the model predicted the traffic flow, and the future traffic volume of each node is inferred on considering the conservation of the traffic system.

4.1   Fine-Grained Traffic Spatial-Temporal Graph

Graph Construction. In this section, we introduce the construction of Fine-grained Traffic Spatial-Temporal Graph as shown in Fig. 1(c). For the sake of understanding, we make an analogy between a traffic flow network controlled by traffic signals and a water network controlled by taps (as shown in Fig. 2(b)). For the simple water network, the water volume of A (denoted as x_t^A at step t) can be inferred based on the flow-in volume ι_t^A and flow-out volume o_t^A as

$$x_{t+1}^A = x_t^A + \iota_t^A - o_t^A. \tag{3}$$

By considering the spatial dependency, ι_t^A and o_t^A can be calculated with the data B, C, and D, as shown below.

$$\iota_t^A = \sigma(x_t^B, \tau_t^B, x_t^C, \tau_t^C, x_t^D, \tau_t^D) \tag{4}$$

$$o_t^A = \phi(x_t^A, \tau_t^A) \tag{5}$$

where σ and ϕ calculate the flow-in volume and flow-out volume based on x and the turn-on time of the water tap τ.

A traffic system can be represented similarly. Traffic signals can naturally substitute the role of taps in the water network. Equations (3), (4) and (5) show that the states of spatial neighbors of A at timestamp t (x_t^B, x_t^C, x_t^D) are highly related to the state of A at timestamp $t + 1$ (x_{t+1}^A), which inspires us how to construct Fine-grained Traffic Spatial-Temporal Graph (FTSTG). Formally, FTSTG is denoted as $\mathcal{G} = \{\mathcal{V}, \mathcal{E}\}$, where each vertex $v_t^i \in \mathcal{V}$ denotes the node i at timestamp t. Here the size of $\mathcal{V}$ is calculated as $|\mathcal{V}| = N \times T$ where N is the number of traffic movements and T is the total number of timestamps. We model the spatial-temporal dependency by the edges.

$$< v_t^i, v_{t+1}^j >= \begin{cases} 1 & <i,j> \in \mathbb{E} \ or \ i = j \\ 0 & otherwise \end{cases} \quad (6)$$

where $\mathbb{E}$ is the edge set of the graph $\mathbb{G}$. (1) We add the edge between spatial neighbors of different time layers. (2) We add edges between the same node of the adjacent time layer. (3) There is no edge inside the same time layer, which is the key difference between FTSTG and STSGCN [38].

The roadnet-enriched features $\mathbf{S}_t = \{P_t, l, d\}$ along with the historical traffic states $\mathbf{X}_t$ serve as the input of each node. There are two reasons why the features $\mathbf{S}_t$ help forecast future traffic. Firstly, The green signal time P_t controls the traffic flow according to Eqs. (4) and (5) and thus significantly influence the future traffic volume. Secondly, the length l and the turning direction d influence the volume distribution of the traffic node since longer roads tend to have more traffic volume, and right-turning lanes tend to have less traffic volume.

4.2 Dynamic Mobility Convolution

To capture the spatial temporal dependencies, we propose Dynamic Mobility Convolution on FTSTG, which is shown in Fig. 2(c). This builds a model that approximates the function σ and ϕ in Eqs. (4) and (5).

Dynamic Edge Construction. To utilize the spatial temporal dependency, a traditional methodology is to apply graph convolution operation on the FTSTG. However, as shown in Fig. 2(b), the traffic flow between different nodes is highly related to the green signal time. Inspired by this fact, we add Dynamic Edge Construction on FTSTG as shown in Fig. 2(c). The dynamic edges are related to the green signal time of each vertex and could represent the traffic flow mobility. A higher weight of dynamic edges indicates higher mobility of traffic flow. Thus, by denoting the edge weight of $< v_t^i, v_{t'}^j >$ as $w_{t,t'}^{i,j}$, and the green signal time of v_t^i as p_t^i, we build the edge of FTSTG as follow.

$$w_{t,t'}^{i,j} = \begin{cases} \frac{p_t^i}{t'-t} & if \ < v_t^i, v_{t'}^j > \in \mathcal{E} \\ 0 & otherwise \end{cases} \quad (7)$$

Mobility Propagation and Mobility Aggregation. After the Dynamic Edge Construction, we conduct Mobility Propagation and Mobility Aggregation based on the idea of GraphSAGE [15], which is a representative inductive graph learning method. The key idea of Mobility Propagation and Mobility Aggregation is that the hidden states of FTSTG represent the traffic flow and the dynamic edge represents the traffic flow mobility. Then one propagation-aggregation operation layer is simulating the process that vehicles flow into downstream nodes once, which is also an inductive operation. The output of the l-th layer can be derived as follows.

$$H_{t,i}^l = Agg(H_{t,i}^{l-1}, Prop(\{H_{t-1,j}^{l-1}|j\}))$$ (8)

Here $j \in \{k| < v_{t-1}^k, v_t^i >\in \mathcal{E}\}$, which are the spatial neighbors of i and i itself at previous adjacent timestamp. For Mobility Propagation, we take the dynamic edge into the operation. Formally we can write.

$$\hat{H}_{t,i}^l = f(\{H_{t-1,j}^{l-1} \cdot w_{t-1,t}^{j,i}|j\}).$$ (9)

Then Mobility Aggregation is conducted to aggregate the result of Mobility Propagation and hidden states, which could be formulated as.

$$H_{t,i}^l = g(H_{t,i}^{l-1}, \hat{H}_{t,i}^l).$$ (10)

For f and g, multiple functions such as $MEAN(\cdot)$, $POOL(\cdot)$, $Concat(\cdot)$, $FC(\cdot)$ could be chosen. Furthermore, we add residual links [17] between adjacent blocks

A key observation is that one layer of propagation and aggregation feeds all the required input contained in Eqs. (3),(4), and (5) to state x_{t+1}^i. This means the number of layers of propagation and aggregation is equal to the number of historical horizons that are aggregated to $H_{t+1,i}^l$. Typically, the model only needs to consider several adjacent horizons and get good results, which keeps consistent with the fact that only traffic states of adjacent time stamps are useful in the fine-grained traffic inference scenario.

4.3 Flow Conservative Traffic State Transition

Traffic Flow Prediction. The Dynamic Mobility Convolution learns representations $\mathbf{H}_t^L$ that capture the fine-grained spatial temporal dynamics. Based on that, we can predict the flow features, i.e., the out number $\hat{\mathbf{O}}_t$ and in number $\hat{\mathbf{I}}_t$ by using two fully connected layers.

$$\hat{\mathbf{O}}_t = FC(\mathbf{H}_t^L), \hat{\mathbf{I}}_t = FC(\mathbf{H}_t^L)$$ (11)

One-Step Traffic Inference. After the out number $\hat{\mathbf{O}}_t$ and in number $\hat{\mathbf{I}}_t$ is predicted, the future traffic could be inferred in a flow conservative perspective. Equation (12) shows the transition from current observation $\mathbf{X}_t$ to the inference of next timestamp $\hat{\mathbf{X}}_{t+1}$ based on the out number $\hat{\mathbf{O}}_t$ and in number $\hat{\mathbf{I}}_t$.

$$\hat{\mathbf{X}}_{t+1} = \mathbf{X}_t + \hat{\mathbf{I}}_t - \hat{\mathbf{O}}_t$$ (12)

This shows a flow-conservative perspective for traffic inference. Intuitively, the volume of a node would stay conserved if there are no vehicles driving in or driving out. Hence, by considering each node as a closed traffic system, we only need to focus on the number of the drive-in and drive-out vehicles for future volume inference. This is a key difference between FDTI and other conventional

(a) Nanchang   (b)Hangzhou   (c) Manhattan

Fig. 3. The running screenshots of the traffic simulator.

approaches to traffic prediction. Conventional approaches focus on capturing the numerical pattern based on mechanisms such as convolution and ignore the conservative traffic state transition which is the intrinsic dynamics.

Multi-step Traffic Inference. For multi-step traffic volume inference, the future multi-faceted features $S_{t+1:t+P}$ is predefined since the traffic signal policy is set in advance. Thus, we can simply apply traffic state transition Eq. (12) multiple times. However, multi-step inference still suffers from error accumulation [3] when a vertex takes inaccurate information from the previous one. Thus, we propose a discounting mechanism to reduce the accumulated error. The discounted multi-step traffic volume inference could be formulated as Eq. (13) where λ denotes the discounting factor.

$$\hat{\mathbf{X}}_{t+Q} = \mathbf{X}_t + \sum_{q=0}^{Q-1} \lambda^q (\hat{\mathbf{I}}_{t+q} - \hat{\mathbf{O}}_{t+q}) \tag{13}$$

We choose MSE loss as the objective function for the one-step flow feature inference to train the model. Thus the loss function of FDTI for flow prediction can be formulated as

$$\mathcal{L} = \frac{1}{NT} \sum_{i=1}^{N} \sum_{t=1}^{T} (\iota_t^i - \hat{\iota}_t^i)^2 + \frac{1}{NT} \sum_{i=1}^{N} \sum_{t=1}^{T} (o_t^i - \hat{o}_t^i)^2. \tag{14}$$

5 Experiment

5.1 Experiment Settings

Datasets. We evaluate our model on three city-wide large-scale datasets of Nanchang, Manhattan, Hangzhou, and one small dataset Hangzhou-Small. Current city traffic data is sparse, coarse-grained, and lacks traffic signal information. Hence, utilizing real roadnet data and vehicle trajectory data as input, we collect 1-h fine-grained data from the wildly-used traffic simulator of KDD-CUP2021 [29]. The roadnet data of these three cities is extracted from OpenStreetMap[1]. The vehicle trajectory of Manhattan is processed real data from [40].

---

[1] https://www.openstreetmap.org/.

Table 1. Details of datasets

City	Intersections	Nodes	Connections between nodes
Nanchang	2,048	18,072	73,170
Hangzhou	3,819	32,772	76,788
Manhattan	3,938	40,026	107,442
Hangzhou-Small	211	1,944	4,770

The vehicle trajectories of Hangzhou and Nanchang are from the real information reported by the traffic police. The details of the four datasets are shown in Table 1. The running traffic screenshots of Nanchang, Hangzhou, and Manhattan in the traffic simulator are shown in Fig. 3. Code and data are released in https://github.com/zhyliu00/FDTI.

Setup of Experiments

- *Data preprocessing:* The first 10 min are used to initialize the road network with sufficient vehicles. The remaining part of the data is split by the ratio of 6:2:2 in chronological order for training, validation, and testing.
- *Network Structure:* In mobility propagation, we use max-pooling as the function f. For the function g in mobility aggregation, we concatenate $H_{t,i}^{l-1}$ and $\hat{H}_{t,i}^{l}$ and feed them into a fully-connected layer. $tanh$ is used as the activation function. we set the hidden dimension of graph convolution as 256 and the graph convolution layers L as 4.
- *Training & Evaluating:* The model is optimized by Adam optimizer for at most 500 epochs. The learning rate is set to 0.0005. We evaluate the performance of related models by RMSE and MAPE.

$$RMSE = \sqrt{\frac{1}{s}\sum_{i=1}^{s}(y_i - \hat{y}_i)^2}, \quad MAPE = \frac{1}{s}\sum_{i=1}^{s}|\frac{y_i - \hat{y}_i}{y_i}|$$

Compared Methods. We compare FDTI with the following baselines. For the sake of fairness, all of the baselines except HA and ARIMA take the same node feature ($[v_t^i, p_t^i, l^i,$ one hot coding for $d^i]$) and all of them are fine-tuned. Four types of baselines are compared.

- *Traditional methods:* **HA** is historical average method, and **ARIMA** [41] is a statistical time series analysis method.
- *Basic Machine Learning models:* **LSTM** [18] is a classic RNN-based model for series analysis. **LR** exploits the linear correlations between data. **XGBoost** [5] is a competitive method based on boosting-tree.
- *Convolution-Kernel-based STGNN:* **DCRNN** [28] and **STGCN** [46] use GCN, GRU, and diffusion techniques to model the spatial and temporal

Table 2. Performance comparison between FDTI and baselines on three large datasets. All adaptive methods can not run on these large-scale datasets due to the huge memory consumption. The lower the RMSE and MAPE are, the better. Horizon means the number of forecasting steps and one horizon means one minute. FDTI achieves the best performance

	Nanchang						Manhattan						Hangzhou					
	Horizon 1		Horizon 3		Horizon 5		Horizon 1		Horizon 3		Horizon 5		Horizon 1		Horizon 3		Horizon 5	
	RMSE	MAPE	RMSE	MAPE	RMSE	MAPE	RMSE	MAPE	RMSE	MAPE	RMSE	MAPE	RMSE	MAPE	RMSE	MAPE	RMSE	MAPE
HA	4.91	23.18	7.79	25.73	10.41	29.97	3.86	13.80	5.45	15.25	6.76	17.96	4.72	21.41	7.47	23.36	10.06	27.21
ARIMA	4.42	24.30	6.90	26.00	9.58	30.77	3.78	14.02	5.26	15.23	6.47	17.95	4.36	22.76	6.62	23.95	9.07	27.75
LSTM	3.71	17.17	5.45	22.40	7.20	28.10	3.68	12.30	5.04	16.81	5.41	18.60	3.55	16.52	5.07	22.00	6.79	27.83
LR	3.19	18.78	5.02	24.70	6.80	30.07	2.68	12.93	4.43	18.56	5.70	22.61	3.24	19.31	4.91	25.45	6.73	32.40
XGBoost	2.85	14.74	4.91	20.70	6.86	26.23	2.53	9.87	4.31	15.17	5.45	19.33	2.94	14.92	4.84	20.95	6.79	27.48
DCRNN	3.98	18.91	5.48	26.42	7.38	31.94	3.92	14.31	5.42	21.48	7.01	29.56	3.85	20.19	5.44	27.27	7.49	35.14
STGCN	11.35	33.35	12.59	37.18	13.71	38.90	8.51	25.40	9.29	27.85	9.94	30.03	10.78	33.30	12.00	36.52	13.22	39.94
STDEN	15.05	37.43	16.11	39.18	17.34	40.37	7.38	25.97	12.26	35.32	15.79	43.21	9.06	28.92	10.14	32.14	11.78	35.01
FDTI	**1.30**	**6.55**	**4.17**	**19.18**	**6.50**	**25.34**	**1.20**	**4.84**	**3.62**	**13.63**	**5.22**	**17.75**	**1.46**	**7.20**	**4.40**	**20.44**	**6.65**	**25.95**

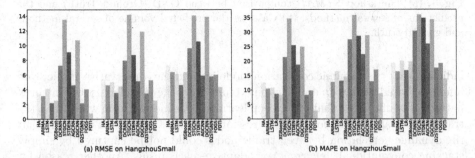

(a) RMSE on HangzhouSmall   (b) MAPE on HangzhouSmall

Fig. 4. The performance of different methods w.r.t. RMSE and MAPE on Hangzhou-Small under horizon 1, 3 and 5. Horizon means the number of forecasting steps and one horizon means one minute. The lower the RMSE and MAPE are, the better. FDTI achieves the best performance.

dependencies. **STDEN** [20] is a physics-based ODE method that models the traffic flow.

- *Adaptive-based STGNN:* **AGCRN** [2], **DGCRN** [26], **D2STGNN** [37] focuses on learning the dynamic graph by various methods such as node embeddings and learnable traffic pattern matrix. **FOGS** [36] utilize node2vec-based methods to learn the graph. However, these methods could not run on three large-scale datasets due to the out-of-memory error. They are only evaluated on the HangzhouSmall dataset.

5.2   Overall Performance

The results of the comparison between FDTI and baselines are shown in Table 2 and Fig. 4, where Table 2 shows the performance on three large-scale traffic datasets and Fig. 4 shows the performance on a small traffic dataset. On all four datasets with different scales, our proposed model outperforms all baseline methods in both single-step inference and multi-step inference. The good performance

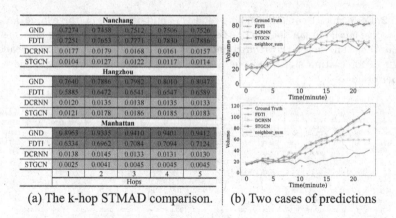

	Nanchang				
GND	0.7274	0.7458	0.7512	0.7506	0.7526
FDTI	0.7251	0.7653	0.7771	0.7830	0.7886
DCRNN	0.0177	0.0179	0.0168	0.0161	0.0157
STGCN	0.0104	0.0127	0.0122	0.0117	0.0114
	Hangzhou				
GND	0.7640	0.7886	0.7982	0.8010	0.8047
FDTI	0.5885	0.6472	0.6541	0.6547	0.6589
DCRNN	0.0120	0.0135	0.0138	0.0135	0.0133
STGCN	0.0121	0.0178	0.0186	0.0185	0.0183
	Manhattan				
GND	0.8963	0.9335	0.9410	0.9401	0.9412
FDTI	0.6334	0.6962	0.7084	0.7094	0.7124
DCRNN	0.0138	0.0145	0.0133	0.0131	0.0130
STGCN	0.0025	0.0041	0.0045	0.0045	0.0045
	1	2	3	4	5
	Hops				

(a) The k-hop STMAD comparison.　(b) Two cases of predictions

Fig. 5. (a) The k-hop *STMAD* comparison between GND (Ground Truth) and the predictions of several methods. (b) Cases of the predicted volume of several methods and ground truth.

indicates that the dynamic correlation modeling and the conservative traffic state inference based on flow-in and flow-out volume help the model grasp the intrinsic pattern of traffic. Note that other deep learning baselines perform worse than the traditional statistic methods and regression-based methods. This indicates that the dynamic correlation between traffic nodes could not be captured by simply stacking convolutional, recurrent, or adaptive mechanisms. Another reason for the bad performance is that these GNN-based methods tend to yield smooth predictions on the nonsmooth dataset. We will discuss the smoothness in detail later. Besides, all of the adaptive methods are not able to run on large-scale datasets for their huge cost. Hence, they are only evaluated on Hangzhou-Small.

5.3　Graph Smooth Analysis

In this part, we explain the reason why previous GCN-based methods yield unsatisfying results by analyzing the smoothness of datasets and prediction results.

To quantitatively measure the smoothness over spatial temporal graphs, we leverage the *STMAD* (Spatial-Temporal Mean Average Distance) based on MAD [4]. The MAD evaluates the smoothness of a given static graph with node features, and lower MAD indicates the graph is smoother. Formally, given a spatial temporal graph in which each node contains a long time series data with length $\mathcal{T}$, we cut the time series data over a sliding window with length $\mathcal{P}$. After that, the spatial temporal graph is cut into $\frac{\mathcal{T}}{\mathcal{P}}$ subgraphs. The feature H of each subgraph is the aligned partial time series data with length $\mathcal{P}$, i.e., $H \in \mathbb{R}^{N \times \mathcal{P}}$. Then, we define the k-hop *STMAD* as follows.

$$STMAD^k = \frac{1}{\frac{\mathcal{T}}{\mathcal{P}}} \sum_{m=1}^{\frac{\mathcal{T}}{\mathcal{P}}} MAD_m^k \tag{15}$$

$$MAD_m^k = \frac{1}{N} \sum_{i=1}^{N} \frac{\sum_{j \in \mathcal{N}_k(i)} \left(1 - \frac{H_m^i \cdot H_m^j}{|H_m^i| \cdot |H_m^j|}\right)}{|\mathcal{N}_k(i)|} \tag{16}$$

Here $STMAD^k$ means k-hop $STMAD$ and it is the average of the k-hop MAD of all subgraphs. MAD_m^k is the k-hop MAD of m-th subgraph and it is essentially the average cosine distance between nodes and their k-hop neighbors. The k-hop neighbors set of node i of m-th subgraph and its corresponding time series are denoted as $\mathcal{N}_k(i)$ and H_m^i respectively.

We show the comparison of $STMAD$ between the ground truth data and the prediction result yielded by several methods in Fig. 5(a). Among all the three datasets, We can observe that the $STMAD$ of ground truth is large due to its non-smoothness. The non-smoothness could also be observed in the prediction result of FDTI, indicating that FDTI preserves the original traffic pattern of the ground truth data, thus making accurate predictions. On the contrary, the $STMAD$ of STGCN and DCRNN is much smaller than the $STMAD$ of ground truth data. Furthermore, the $STMAD$ of STGCN and DCRNN is similar to the previous smooth datasets (METR-LA, PEMS-BAY, PEMSD7) as shown in Fig. 1(b). This result explains that previous methodologies such as STGCN and DCRNN could yield satisfying results on the previous smooth datasets since these methodologies have a high tendency to make smooth predictions despite the smoothness of the input data. However, when it comes to unsmooth datasets, they make predictions with high errors.

Two examples of the smoothness of STGCN and DCRNN are shown in Fig. 5(b). It shows the ground truth and prediction volume of a node along with the sum volume of its neighbors. We could observe that STGCN and DCRNN make relatively reasonable predictions at the beginning since the ground truth volume is similar to the sum volume of neighbors. As the traffic flow goes on, the gap between Ground Truth and the sum volume of neighbors increases, while STGCN and DCRNN fail to follow the Ground Truth. Being consistent with the fact that smoothing is the essential nature of the GCN design [4], this phenomenon indicates that STGCN and DCRNN tend to average the volume of a node and its neighbors and use the result as the prediction. As a result, the prediction is smooth and a big error exists. On the contrary, FDTI keeps consistent with the ground truth value, which is similar to the STMAD comparison.

To sum up, these two comparisons show FDTI performs admirably in the non-smooth situation. We owe this excellent property to the conservative traffic transitions as shown in Eq. (13). This equation shows that FDTI predicts the first-order derivative of the ground truth and is hence resistant to oversmoothness.

5.4   Ablation Study

For FDTI, there are four main designs including FTSTG that models the traffic dynamics, roadnet-enriched features (denoted as R) that help model capture traffic dynamics, the discount mechanism (denoted as D) that reduces the accumulated error of volume inference, and dynamic mobility convolution (denoted as C) that simulates the flow of vehicles. To validate these components, we design four variants by adding blocks sequentially: FTSTG, FTSTG+R, FTSTG+R+D, and FTSTG+R+D+C. Specifically, FTSTG+R+D+C equals FDTI because it has all of these four components.

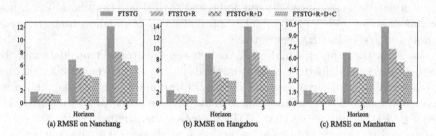

Fig. 6. Performance on the multi-step inference of different variants of FDTI on three datasets. Horizon means the number of forecasting steps.

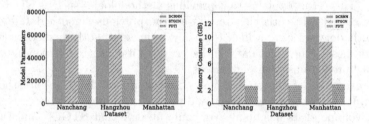

Fig. 7. Model parameter size and memory cost.

Results are shown in Fig. 6 from which we could observe that adding each module can induce further improvement. The improvement induced by adding the roadnet-enriched features (R) is due to that adding traffic-dynamic-related features helps the model aggregate richer information. The performance of multi-step inference is improved by adding the discount mechanism (D), which indicates that the cumulative error could not be neglected and the discount mechanism tackles this error well. Adding dynamic mobility convolution (C) also brings notable performance gain. This demonstrates that considering the dynamic edges contributes to the fine-grained traffic dynamics between nodes.

5.5   Scalability

In this part, we explore the scalability of datasets and models. Then, we explain why previous adaptive methods fail to run on our datasets.

City-scale Datasets and Experiments. To the best of our knowledge, we are the first to complete the city-level traffic state inference. These three city-level traffic datasets Nanchang, Hangzhou, and Manhattan cover more than 2,000 intersections and 18,000 nodes as shown in Table 1. In comparison, we have summarized the datasets used in previous literature as in Table 3. It is easy to observe that our datasets are at least 10 times larger than previously wildly-used datasets in terms of the number of nodes.

Table 3. The scale of datasets. The upper 8 datasets are wildly used by previous research. The lower 4 datasets downside are the datasets of this paper.

Dataset	# of nodes	Dataset	# of nodes
PeMSD7(M) [46]	228	METR-LA [28]	207
PeMSD7(L) [46]	1,026	PEMS-BAY [28]	325
PeMSD4 [14]	307	Xiamen [47]	95
PeMSD8 [14]	170	PeMS3 [38]	358
Nanchang	18,072	Manhattan	40,026
Hangzhou	32,772	Hangzhou-Small	1,944

Model Scalability. The space complexity of FDTI is $O(d \times d)$ and thus the model size is independent of the input graph scale. Furthermore, FDTI is an inductive graph learning method due to the special construction of FTSTG that limited hops of neighbors are required for predicting future traffic. Benefiting from this, our model could deal with large-scale graphs with decent parameter efficiency.

Most of the previous deep spatial temporal methods [13,24,33,36,37] based on adaptive mechanism fail to run on large-scale datasets. Firstly, they have at least $O(N \times d)$ parameters as node embeddings, which is not parameter-efficient. Secondly, the space complexity of calculating the similarity matrix of these methods is $O(N^2)$, which is unacceptable for a large graph. To validate their performance in the fine-grained setting, we extract Hangzhou-Small dataset and implement some of them as baselines.

For the rest deep learning based methods, we select DCRNN (best performance), STGCN (most efficient), and FDTI (this paper) and compare the model efficiency on the large-scale datasets with the same number of hidden states and layers as shown in Fig. 7. We can observe that FDTI has a similar number of parameters while FDTI consumes much less memory.

6 Conclusion

In this paper, we have worked on a brand-new fine-grained traffic volume prediction problem. We demonstrate that the traffic signal significantly influences the correlation between neighboring roads. To address the problems, We propose a novel method FDTI that models the influence of traffic signal and capture the fine-grained traffic dynamics. Extensive experiments are conducted on large-scale traffic datasets, where FDTI outperforms other baselines and shows good properties such as resistance to oversmoothness. We believe that FDTI can better support real-world downstream applications such as traffic policy making.

Acknowledgement. This work was sponsored by National Key Research and Development Program of China under Grant No.2022YFB3904204, National Natural Science Foundation of China under Grant No. 62102246, 62272301, and Provincial Key Research and Development Program of Zhejiang under Grant No. 2021C01034.

Ethical Statement. The data used in this paper is collected from the wildly-used traffic simulator of KDDCUP2021 and does not contain any personal or sensitive data. The authors ensured that the data was collected in an ethical and legal manner. Hence, no personally identifiable information was obtained and people can not infer personal information through the data. The potential use of this work is accurate traffic prediction and better support of downstream tasks such as traffic signal control. This work is not potentially a part of policing or military work. The authors of this paper are committed to ethical principles and guidelines in conducting research and have taken measures to ensure the integrity and validity of the data. The use of the data in this study is in accordance with ethical standards and is intended to advance knowledge in the field of traffic prediction.

References

1. Akagi, Y., Nishimura, T., Kurashima, T., Toda, H.: A fast and accurate method for estimating people flow from spatiotemporal population data. In: IJCAI, pp. 3293–3300 (2018)
2. Bai, L., Yao, L., Li, C., Wang, X., Wang, C.: Adaptive graph convolutional recurrent network for traffic forecasting. arXiv preprint arXiv:2007.02842 (2020)
3. Bengio, S., Vinyals, O., Jaitly, N., Shazeer, N.: Scheduled sampling for sequence prediction with recurrent neural networks. arXiv preprint arXiv:1506.03099 (2015)
4. Chen, D., Lin, Y., Li, W., Li, P., Zhou, J., Sun, X.: Measuring and relieving the over-smoothing problem for graph neural networks from the topological view. In: Proceedings of the AAAI Conference on Artificial Intelligence, vol. 34, pp. 3438–3445 (2020)
5. Chen, T., Guestrin, C.: XGBoost: a scalable tree boosting system. In: Proceedings of the 22nd ACM SIGKDD International Conference on Knowledge Discovery and Data Mining, pp. 785–794 (2016)
6. Chen, Y., Segovia, I., Gel, Y.R.: Z-GCNets: time zigzags at graph convolutional networks for time series forecasting. In: International Conference on Machine Learning, pp. 1684–1694. PMLR (2021)
7. Choi, J., Choi, H., Hwang, J., Park, N.: Graph neural controlled differential equations for traffic forecasting. In: Proceedings of the AAAI Conference on Artificial Intelligence, vol. 36, pp. 6367–6374 (2022)
8. Cirstea, R.G., Yang, B., Guo, C., Kieu, T., Pan, S.: Towards spatio-temporal aware traffic time series forecasting. In: 2022 IEEE 38th International Conference on Data Engineering (ICDE), pp. 2900–2913. IEEE (2022)

9. Diao, Z., Wang, X., Zhang, D., Liu, Y., Xie, K., He, S.: Dynamic spatial-temporal graph convolutional neural networks for traffic forecasting. In: Proceedings of the AAAI Conference on Artificial Intelligence, vol. 33, pp. 890–897 (2019)

10. Fang, S., Zhang, Q., Meng, G., Xiang, S., Pan, C.: GSTNet: global spatial-temporal network for traffic flow prediction. In: IJCAI, pp. 2286–2293 (2019)

11. Fang, Z., Long, Q., Song, G., Xie, K.: Spatial-temporal graph ode networks for traffic flow forecasting. In: Proceedings of the 27th ACM SIGKDD Conference on Knowledge Discovery and Data Mining, pp. 364–373 (2021)

12. Fang, Z., Pan, L., Chen, L., Du, Y., Gao, Y.: MDTP: a multi-source deep traffic prediction framework over spatio-temporal trajectory data. Proc. VLDB Endow. **14**(8), 1289–1297 (2021)

13. Guo, K., Hu, Y., Sun, Y., Qian, S., Gao, J., Yin, B.: Hierarchical graph convolution network for traffic forecasting. In: Proceedings of the AAAI Conference on Artificial Intelligence, vol. 35, pp. 151–159 (2021)

14. Guo, S., Lin, Y., Feng, N., Song, C., Wan, H.: Attention based spatial-temporal graph convolutional networks for traffic flow forecasting. In: Proceedings of the AAAI Conference on Artificial Intelligence, vol. 33, pp. 922–929 (2019)

15. Hamilton, W.L., Ying, R., Leskovec, J.: Inductive representation learning on large graphs. In: Proceedings of the 31st International Conference on Neural Information Processing Systems, pp. 1025–1035 (2017)

16. Han, L., Du, B., Sun, L., Fu, Y., Lv, Y., Xiong, H.: Dynamic and multi-faceted spatio-temporal deep learning for traffic speed forecasting. In: Proceedings of the 27th ACM SIGKDD Conference on Knowledge Discovery and Data Mining, pp. 547–555 (2021)

17. He, K., Zhang, X., Ren, S., Sun, J.: Deep residual learning for image recognition. In: Proceedings of the IEEE Conference on Computer Vision and Pattern Recognition, pp. 770–778 (2016)

18. Hochreiter, S., Schmidhuber, J.: Long short-term memory. Neural Comput. **9**(8), 1735–1780 (1997)

19. Huang, R., Huang, C., Liu, Y., Dai, G., Kong, W.: LSGCN: long short-term traffic prediction with graph convolutional networks. In: IJCAI, pp. 2355–2361 (2020)

20. Ji, J., Wang, J., Jiang, Z., Jiang, J., Zhang, H.: STDEN: towards physics-guided neural networks for traffic flow prediction (2022)

21. Kipf, T.N., Welling, M.: Semi-supervised classification with graph convolutional networks. arXiv preprint arXiv:1609.02907 (2016)

22. Koonce, P., Rodegerdts, L.: Traffic signal timing manual. Technical report, United States. Federal Highway Administration (2008)

23. Lan, S., Ma, Y., Huang, W., Wang, W., Yang, H., Li, P.: DSTAGNN: dynamic spatial-temporal aware graph neural network for traffic flow forecasting. In: International Conference on Machine Learning, pp. 11906–11917. PMLR (2022)

24. Lee, H., Jin, S., Chu, H., Lim, H., Ko, S.: Learning to remember patterns: pattern matching memory networks for traffic forecasting. arXiv preprint arXiv:2110.10380 (2021)

25. Lei, X., Mei, H., Shi, B., Wei, H.: Modeling network-level traffic flow transitions on sparse data. In: Proceedings of the 28th ACM SIGKDD Conference on Knowledge Discovery and Data Mining, pp. 835–845 (2022)

26. Li, F., et al.: Dynamic graph convolutional recurrent network for traffic prediction: benchmark and solution. ACM Trans. Knowl. Discov. Data (TKDD) (2021)

27. Li, M., Zhu, Z.: Spatial-temporal fusion graph neural networks for traffic flow forecasting. In: Proceedings of the AAAI Conference on Artificial Intelligence, vol. 35, pp. 4189–4196 (2021)

28. Li, Y., Yu, R., Shahabi, C., Liu, Y.: Diffusion convolutional recurrent neural network: data-driven traffic forecasting. arXiv preprint arXiv:1707.01926 (2017)
29. Liang, C., et al.: CBLAB: scalable traffic simulation with enriched data supporting. arXiv preprint arXiv:2210.00896 (2022)
30. Lippi, M., Bertini, M., Frasconi, P.: Short-term traffic flow forecasting: an experimental comparison of time-series analysis and supervised learning. IEEE Trans. Intell. Transp. Syst. **14**(2), 871–882 (2013)
31. Nikravesh, A.Y., Ajila, S.A., Lung, C.H., Ding, W.: Mobile network traffic prediction using MLP, MLPWD, and SVM. In: 2016 IEEE International Congress on Big Data (BigData Congress), pp. 402–409. IEEE (2016)
32. Okutani, I., Stephanedes, Y.J.: Dynamic prediction of traffic volume through Kalman filtering theory. Transport. Res. Part B: Methodol. **18**(1), 1–11 (1984)
33. Oreshkin, B.N., Amini, A., Coyle, L., Coates, M.: FC-GAGA: fully connected gated graph architecture for spatio-temporal traffic forecasting. In: Proceedings of the AAAI Conference on Artificial Intelligence, vol. 35, pp. 9233–9241 (2021)
34. Ouyang, K., et al.: Fine-grained urban flow inference. IEEE Trans. Knowl. Data Eng. **34**(6), 2755–2770 (2020)
35. Qu, H., Gong, Y., Chen, M., Zhang, J., Zheng, Y., Yin, Y.: Forecasting fine-grained urban flows via spatio-temporal contrastive self-supervision. IEEE Trans. Knowl. Data Eng. (2022)
36. Rao, X., Wang, H., Zhang, L., Li, J., Shang, S., Han, P.: Fogs: first-order gradient supervision with learning-based graph for traffic flow forecasting. In: Proceedings of International Joint Conference on Artificial Intelligence, IJCAI. ijcai. org (2022)
37. Shao, Z., et al.: Decoupled dynamic spatial-temporal graph neural network for traffic forecasting. arXiv preprint arXiv:2206.09112 (2022)
38. Song, C., Lin, Y., Guo, S., Wan, H.: Spatial-temporal synchronous graph convolutional networks: a new framework for spatial-temporal network data forecasting. In: Proceedings of the AAAI Conference on Artificial Intelligence, vol. 34, pp. 914–921 (2020)
39. Veličković, P., Cucurull, G., Casanova, A., Romero, A., Lio, P., Bengio, Y.: Graph attention networks. arXiv preprint arXiv:1710.10903 (2017)
40. Wei, H., Zheng, G., Gayah, V., Li, Z.: A survey on traffic signal control methods. arXiv preprint arXiv:1904.08117 (2019)
41. Williams, B.M., Hoel, L.A.: Modeling and forecasting vehicular traffic flow as a seasonal Arima process: theoretical basis and empirical results. J. Transp. Eng. **129**(6), 664–672 (2003)
42. Wu, Z., Pan, S., Long, G., Jiang, J., Chang, X., Zhang, C.: Connecting the dots: multivariate time series forecasting with graph neural networks. In: Proceedings of the 26th ACM SIGKDD International Conference on Knowledge Discovery and Data Mining, pp. 753–763 (2020)
43. Wu, Z., Pan, S., Long, G., Jiang, J., Zhang, C.: Graph wavenet for deep spatial-temporal graph modeling. arXiv preprint arXiv:1906.00121 (2019)
44. Xie, P., Li, T., Liu, J., Du, S., Yang, X., Zhang, J.: Urban flow prediction from spatiotemporal data using machine learning: A survey. Inf. Fusion **59**, 1–12 (2020)
45. Yao, H., Tang, X., Wei, H., Zheng, G., Li, Z.: Revisiting spatial-temporal similarity: a deep learning framework for traffic prediction. In: Proceedings of the AAAI Conference on Artificial Intelligence, vol. 33, pp. 5668–5675 (2019)
46. Yu, B., Yin, H., Zhu, Z.: Spatio-temporal graph convolutional networks: a deep learning framework for traffic forecasting. arXiv preprint arXiv:1709.04875 (2017)

47. Zheng, C., Fan, X., Wang, C., Qi, J.: GMAN: a graph multi-attention network for traffic prediction. In: Proceedings of the AAAI Conference on Artificial Intelligence, vol. 34, pp. 1234–1241 (2020)
48. Zheng, G., et al.: Learning phase competition for traffic signal control. In: Proceedings of the 28th ACM International Conference on Information and Knowledge Management, pp. 1963–1972 (2019)
49. Zhu, Z., Peng, B., Xiong, C., Zhang, L.: Short-term traffic flow prediction with linear conditional gaussian Bayesian network. J. Adv. Transp. **50**(6), 1111–1123 (2016)

RulEth: Genetic Programming-Driven Derivation of Security Rules for Automotive Ethernet

Felix Clemens Gail[1], Roland Rieke[2], and Florian Fenzl[1(✉)]

[1] Fraunhofer Institute for Secure Information Technology, Darmstadt, Germany
{Florian.Fenzl,Felix.Gail}@sit.fraunhofer.de
[2] Griesheim, Germany
Roland.Rieke@gmx.de

Abstract. Handcrafted rule-based intrusion detection systems tend to overlook sophisticated intrusions due to unexpected cyberattacker behaviors or human error in analyzing complex control flows. Current machine learning systems, mostly based on artificial neural networks, have the inherent problem that models cannot be verified since the decisions depend on probabilities. To bridge the gap between handcrafted rule systems and probability-based systems, our approach uses genetic programming to generate rules that are verifiable, in the sense that one can confirm that the extracted pattern matches a known attack. The RulEth rules language is designed to be predictive of a packet window, which allows the system to detect anomalies in message flow. Alerts are enriched to include the root cause about the characterization as an anomalous event, which in turn supports decisions to trigger countermeasures. Although the attacks examined in this work are far more complex than those considered in most other works in the automotive domain, our results show that most of the attacks examined can be well identified. By being able to evaluate each rule generated separately, the rules that are not working effectively can be sorted out, which improves the robustness of the system. Furthermore, using design flaws found in a public dataset, we demonstrate the importance of verifiable models for reliable systems.

1 Introduction

Enhanced connectivity needed for driver assistance systems and autonomous driving expands the attack surface. A recent analysis by Upstream [1] shows that almost all 2022 attacks on vehicles were remote and that more than two-thirds of the remote attacks in 2022 were long-range attacks. Therefore, traditional security measures such as data encryption and firewalls must be supplemented with systems that monitor network activity to filter out and prevent intruders. However, despite a lot of quite successful research efforts, machine learning is as of now rarely employed in operational, safety critical real-world settings [2].

R. Rieke—Independent researcher.

G. De Francisci Morales et al. (Eds.): ECML PKDD 2023, LNAI 14175, pp. 192–209, 2023.
https://doi.org/10.1007/978-3-031-43430-3_12

While many machine learning methods such as Artificial Neural Network (ANN) improve the chances of detecting attacks, the use of such a model is accompanied by reduced interpretability [3]. For example, experts cannot directly correlate the weights assigned to the sensor signals with the classification results, which is very important for implementation in cyber threat response [4]. The approval of the detection rules and planned mitigation actions should be done under human supervision to preserve human autonomy. Human agency and oversight is an important requirement in the EU ethical guidelines for trustworthy Artificial Intelligence (AI) [5].

In this work, our goal is to create a system capable of detecting single- and multi-packet attacks in Automotive Ethernet (AE). In order to achieve system reliability, it is important to be able to analyze the output of the algorithm. Therefore, one needs explainable AI algorithms, especially in this context. One option to get explainable results is to use Genetic Programming (GP). We have developed a GP-based tool chain in which we store the GP results as rules, allowing a human-in-the-loop to validate all algorithm results before authorizing them for use in a vehicle. The derived rules are written in RulEth, a Domain Specific Language (DSL) that we defined for this purpose. This DSL addresses the challenge that experts are interested in understandable models in a language that reflects the specific domain, by allowing to formulate rules related to the elements of the protocol. This approach avoids problems when mapping characteristics to e.g. SNORT rules that don't support it or require complex assignments that don't make sense to experts. The main benefit of this human-supervised rule development is that the resulting classification model is transparent and understandable, all rules are auditable, and decisions can be logged and traced. Approved rules are compiled prior to their use, which improves evaluation speed and makes them resource efficient in constrained vehicle settings. Raised alerts are actionable through the identification of anomaly types and detailed reports. The system has been implemented and evaluated using attacks on the Scalable Service-Oriented Middleware Over IP (SOME/IP) protocol.

The remainder of the work is structured as follows. Background and related work is presented in Sect. 2. Section 3 describes our threat model, while Sect. 4 describes the DSL used to define the rules. Section 5 presents the devised Intrusion Detection System (IDS) design, which is evaluated in Sect. 6. Section 7 concludes with a summary.

2   Background and Related Work

Because regular Ethernet does not meet requirements on electromagnetic compatibility, low latency and bandwidth allocation for time- and safety-critical automotive applications, AE [6] has been introduced for the automotive domain. SOME/IP [7] is a middleware proposed by the *AUTOSAR partnership* [8] for onboard communication on top of AE. In SOME/IP, Electronic Control Units (ECUs) can provide or access information through services which are identified by a *Service-ID*. Multiple instances of a service are uniquely identified by

Instance-IDs. Connections between clients and services can be either fixed or dynamically discovered using the SOME/IP Service Discovery (SOME/IP-SD) protocol.

SOME/IP is vulnerable to attacks, since messages are not authenticated and neither the integrity nor confidentiality are secured. Its vulnerability has been addressed several times. Iorio et al. [9] propose fine-grained security control by using a randomly generated symmetric key to encrypt multicast communication. However, this allows malicious users to impersonate the sender. Kreissl [10] makes use of the TESLA [11] protocol for SOME/IP broadcast communication, thus solving the authentication problem. Zelle et al. [12] present an extensive analysis of attacks and a formally verified extension to vanilla SOME/IP that supports both encrypted broadcast and unicast communications.

While much research has been conducted in in-vehicle IDSs, Yu et al. [13] found that only two out of 95 papers target IP based communication. IDSs for SOME/IP have been proposed by Herold [14] and Gehrmann [15]. Herold [14] presents an IDS based on Complex Event Processing (CEP) using SQL-like rules. A major drawback of this approach is the computing power needed for CEP. Gehrmann [15] proposes security policies for security-critical SOME/IP functions. Both, Gehrmann's and Herold's solutions have the problem that the IDS rules have to be defined manually. This is time-consuming and only allows detection of known attacks. Several approaches apply evolutionary rule derivation techniques to address these challenges. Most of these are not directly applicable to AE applications since the attack datasets used such as KDD99 and NSL-KDD are two decades old or rules are only generated for single packets, which does not reveal protocol flow attacks. Li [16] proposes to use Genetic Algorithms (GAs) to generate rule sets and Gong et al. [17] suggest improvements to Li's work, while Song [18] trained a linear GP algorithm that can access a sliding window of two seconds to detect attacks in the KDD99 dataset. Gómez et al. [19] develop a multi-objective evolutionary algorithm using Pareto-optimization in rule generation, and, Rastegari et al. [20] compare GA generated detection rules with those generated by Decision Trees (DTs) and other methods. However, both approaches focus exclusively on attacks that consist of individual packets and do not consider attacks on the packet flow. Buschlinger et al. [21] uses Decision Trees (DTs) to generate a rule set that can be integrated into the well known SNORT [22] Network-based Intrusion Detection System (NIDS). The increased specificity allows detecting attacks that previously went unnoticed. In GA and DT approaches, the resource-intensive generation phase can be decoupled from the lightweight rule application phase, making these approaches ideal for resource-constrained vehicle environments. However, in most approaches, Man-in-the-Middle (MitM) attacks that can only be identified through the traffic flow will not be found. Moreover, the methods target generic TCP/IP traffic, therefore protocol-specific attacks are less likely to be identified correctly.

Alkhatib et al. [23] propose an IDS based on a Recurrent Neural Network (RNN) and evaluate it on labeled SOME/IP data. This IDS provides very good results, but due to the structure of RNNs, it is not possible to verify its decisions.

To avoid this problem, we use GP to generate rules that are verifiable, in the sense that one can confirm that the extracted pattern matches a known attack.

3 Threat Model

As in the model by Dolev-Yao [24], the attacker in our threat model can read, trace, modify, delete, or create new messages. Attacks can occur sequential, or in parallel, and can be coordinated. The adversary is not able to break cryptographic assumptions, but this hardly matters since SOME/IP is not encrypted and extensions [9–12] are not considered here.

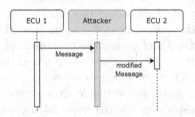

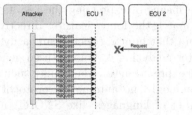

(a) The *Wrong Interface* attack replaces the interface version field of SOME/IP packets with higher values. This field is matched at the receiver. This interference can interrupt communications.

(b) In *Denial of Service* attacks, adversaries flood a victim with many requests, exhausting its resources and aiming to make the victim unavailable [25].

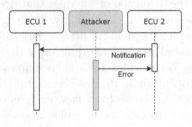

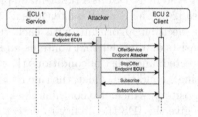

(c) The *Error-On-Event* attack is a more complicated protocol violation attack devised by Herold [14], consisting of two valid messages, which are in itself not distinguishable from benign traffic. The adversary responds with a return code of 0x81 (error) to a preceding event notification. This violates the specification, which does not expect any response to event notifications [7].

(d) In the *De-association* attack [12], a benign server *(ECU1)* broadcasts a service offer for its own endpoint. The adversary follows with a service offer with the same options, but replaces the endpoint with its own. Afterwards, an unicast stop offer in the name of server *ECU1* sent by the attacker makes the client *(ECU2)* believe, the original service is no longer available. This MitM attack will lead to the client connecting to the attacker instead of the real service.

Fig. 1. Attacks considered in this work.

Each attack in Fig. 1 represents a different type of attack. The *Wrong-Interface* attack in Fig. 1a uses a single packet that is independent of the surrounding traffic. The *Distributed Denial of Service (DDoS)* attack in Fig. 1b consisting of multiple packets, but there are no dependencies between the different messages in the attack. The *Error-On-Event* attack in Fig. 1c consists of two interdependent messages that only constitute an attack if they occur together, while the *De-Association* attack in Fig. 1d is a complicated five-stage attack.

4   RulEth Language

In order to close the gap between Machine Learning (ML) output and human understanding of the results, we believe it is of paramount importance that the means of expressing the results on the one hand allow the rule generator to match the found features directly with the rules language and on the other hand that human experts can easily understand and review the proposed rules. After analyzing commonly used general-purpose IDS languages, we found that the expressiveness of languages such as SNORT is not sufficient for our purpose. Commonly, no automotive protocol specific fields are available as features. A subset of languages, like SNORT, allows inspecting specific bytes of the payload, but dynamically placed fields can not be interpreted. Additionally, prior approaches allow only for the inspection of a single packet, which makes the detection of attacks on the protocol flow impossible.

That's why we decided to develop a new Domain Specific Language (DSL) for our system. A DSL is a tailor-made programming language for a specific problem area [26]. The RulEth language is a DSL for the definition of the rules that drive the decision algorithm, with each rule detecting a single anomaly. Each rule consists of a header that contains an identifier for the rule, the attack class to be detected, and a list of conditions that is evaluated as a logical or, meaning that if a single condition is met, the rule returns true. We provide additional resources as repository, which also contains the language definition in Backus-Naur form [27]. To give the IDS the ability to detect anomalies in the protocol flow, such as the presented Error-On-Event and De-Association attacks, the classifier receives a window of the latest packets instead of a single packet at each time. The size of the window configured in the rule header. The condition consists of operators and numerical parameters. The numeric parameters can be any value up to 32 bits in length or characteristics that can be extracted from the different layers of a packet. Selecting a feature that is not present in the examined sample should return false for the rule as a whole. As operators the language offers *and, or*, and *not* logical operators, *less than (lt)* and *equal (eq)* as relational operators, *if* as a conditional operation and *difference* as an arithmetical operation. We plan to expand the available operators in the future. In this paper, the developed DSL is evaluated using the SOME/IP protocol, it is however easily expanded to be compatible to other protocols. Language operators can be split into a general purpose and protocol specific subset. Extending the RulEth language to another protocol, requires only to specify the protocol features and equipping

```
1  rule rule_name class 1 window 100:
2  {
3    lt(1, packet[0].someip.proto_ver),
4    eq(packet[0].sd.entry[ANY].ttl, 0),
5    and(
6      eq(packet[0].someip.service_id, packet[A].someip.service_id),
7      eq(packet[A].someip.message_type, 2),
8    )
9  }
```

Listing 1.1. An examplary rule displaying the DSL concepts.

the interpreter with the ability to retrieve the feature values from a packet. Listing 1.1 displays an exemplary rule written in RulEth. Line 1 contains the rule header, containing the name, anomaly class and window size of the rule.

Array Access. Several places in the DSL require to select an element from a collection. For this purpose, the language contains an access operator. As with many other programming languages, this is expressed by the desired position between square brackets and zero-based. Line 3 of Listing 1.1 illustrates an array access, by checking if 1 is less than the SOME/IP protocol version of the packet at index 0.

Quantifiers. Since traffic flows might be interrupted by other packets and the SOME/IP-SD layer can contain an arbitrary number of entries and options, we introduce the notions of ANY and ALL quantifiers, which can be used instead of a number in an access operator. With the keyword ANY, the surrounding relational operation must hold true for at least one extracted feature. If features are not present for part of the collection, they are ignored. With the keyword ALL, the condition has to be met for each extracted feature value. The use of such a quantifier is shown in line 4 of Listing 1.1, checking if any SOME/IP-SD entry of the packet at index 0 has a TTL of 0.

Variables. Certain attacks might require that multiple features of a packet are compared against multiple features of another packet, while the position of the packets in the packet window is not important. Quantifiers alone are not able to accurately model this behavior. Thus, the language was additionally equipped with the semantics for variables. Syntactically, a variable is a single case-sensitive letter that can replace a positional identifier in an array access. Semantically, the variable is iteratively replaced with every possible positional value until the rule matches, otherwise the rule returns false. Lines 5–8 of Listing 1.1 display the application of variables by checking if a packet at a variable index A has the same SOME/IP service ID as the packet at index 0 and if that same packet has a SOME/IP message type equal to 2.

Internal Handling of Quantifiers. The introduction of quantifiers results in an increased complexity for the operators, as statements have to be evaluated for multiple values. The following paragraphs will therefore discuss, how this complexity is handled internally. We consider a single value as a collection containing one element annotated with the quantifier ANY and only consider operations with an arity of two. This results in four combinations of quantifiers that have to be considered during evaluation, which are all permutations of the two quantifiers ANY and ALL. When matching two quantifiers of the same type, the quantifier is inherited for the result, while the collection now includes all unique combinations of the two sets. The combination of two different quantifiers leads to a list of results. Each result is annotated with an ANY quantifier and consists of all combinations of an element from the ALL set with each element from the ANY set. Relational operations (*i.e. less than, equality*) additionally append a *reduce* operation to the procedure. The return type of each relational operation will be of type boolean. As such, the already discussed procedure will return collections of boolean values bonded with a qualifier. Afterwards, during the reduce procedure, the operation assesses each collection with its bonded quantifier and returns *true* if the semantics of all contained quantifiers holds true. The conditional operator, *if*, simply returns one of the presented collections, depending on the value of the condition. Logical operations are not affected by this feature, as parameters must have already been reduced by a relational operation.

5   RulEth System Architecture

The IDS presented in this work comprises a set of tools that make it possible to describe, generate, optimize and execute a set of rules that forms the basis for decisions about possible security breaches. Since some tools like the rules generator and attack detector can be placed on different devices, a portable representation of the generated model is needed. To represent the rules, we use the RulEth language described in the previous section. Using a human-readable representation has several key advantages. Firstly, the system allows for human-in-the-loop interaction in the detection process, allowing experts to inspect, verify and possibly optimize rules generated by the GP algorithm. Secondly, it is possible to insert rules in the model generated by a GP run, without altering the performance of the existing rule model. These can be either rules from a rule database built prior, or even rules handcrafted by experts. This stands in opposition to ANN-based approaches, where a model has to be trained on all available data and introducing new data can worsen the performance of the model as a whole. Lastly, but most importantly, the human-in-the-loop approach promotes interpretability because rules can be uniquely identified and the system's decision can be traced, supporting planning of counteractions and forensic inspections.

The main components of the system are the rule generator, the rule compiler and the rule-based detector. The rule generator uses GP to uncover attack patterns in datasets labeled as benign or with an appropriate attack class. Uncovered patterns are stored in our custom DSL called RulEth. Rules from the rule generator can be supplemented with handcrafted rules from a database, to improve the IDS performance for known attacks, before passing them into the compiler. The compiler translates the rules in DSL-format into compiled C++-code, which

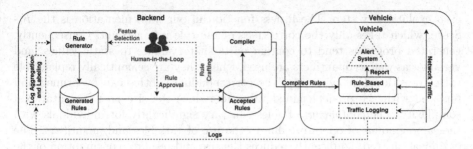

Fig. 2. High level architecture and data flow of the IDS when only the detector is placed within a vehicle. The deployment of new rules has to be authorized by a human expert. Human interaction can further control the feature selection step or by adding handcrafted rules to the database of accepted rules.

is transferred to the vehicles of the fleet and therein used by the rule-based detector. The detector then captures network traffic inside the vehicle and triggers an alert if it detects a rule violation. Additionally, we envision that traffic recorded in vehicles of the fleet can be transferred to a backend, where the logs are aggregated and labeled. In order to maintain the confidentiality and safety of the system, adherence to UN regulation R156 [28] is required for uploading logs to the backend and provisioning new rules. The traffic logging module within the vehicle must be secured using trusted computing and authenticated with the backend. Furthermore, the backend must operate within a secure environment. In a prominent use case [21] depicted in Fig. 2 due to limited resources only the detector is placed in a vehicle to parse the arising traffic, while the rule generation is outsourced. We will now discuss the three main components, i.e. the rule generator, the rule compiler and the rule-based detector.

Rule Generator. The goal of the generator is to evolve rules to detect anomalous behavior. These rules are specified in the RulEth language.

We choose Genetic Programming (GP) as ML algorithm, as it creates interpretable results, has temporal linkage capabilities and can differentiate between multiple attack classes. A major downside of the approach is the large required training time. GP uses the Darwinian principle of reproduction to evolve problem-solving computer programs [29]. The algorithm tries to find a good solution to a problem by creating an initial population with random traits. Each individual represents a possible solution to the problem, and receives a *fitness value* upon evaluation. Then the best performing individuals are selected and transformed into a new generation using the principles of *crossover* and *mutation*. This loop of evaluation, selecting the best performing individuals and breeding a new population is repeated until the *optimization criteria* are met. At this point, the algorithm returns the single best performing individual found.

The rule generator is written in Python3 [30] using the DEAP framework [31] as basis for its GP functionality. Our adapted version of the GP algorithm, differs from the original design by Koza [32] in an additional optimization step within each evolutionary step. The fitness function in our implementation is the F_1-Score, which takes only the correctness of the rule into account. Consequently, generated programs tend to contain parts that evaluate to static values, and variables as well as quantifiers are used, where they are semantically replaceable with a positional array access. The corresponding subtree can be pruned and replaced with the predetermined value to reduce the size and computational complexity. The complexity of rules can vary significantly for individuals with the same amount of operators due to the use of variables and quantifiers. The optimization step significantly reduces the size and resource consumption of the generated rules. This minimization technique was applied by Fenzl [33] to reduce the size of individuals in an GP implementation with a comparable primitive set. In our work, the minimization algorithm is extended, not only to take terminal parameters, but also identical subtrees into account.

Additionally, during the generation and mutation of individuals, random quantifiers and indices inside the allowed package window are chosen as parameter for a feature selection node. It therefore often happens that an individual selects features at one or more indices, without using the complete allowed packet window. In case only a slice of the packet window, which does not start at index zero, is accessed, the rule can be optimized. Moving the selected slice to the beginning of the packet window, will in this situation not change the behavior of the rule, other than that the rule is triggered earlier in the packet stream.

To generate a final rule, the largest array access is assumed as the window size if there is no variable in the generated rule. If a variable is used, the maximum allowed window size is set instead. The nature of the GP algorithm ensures that if the current window size is not sufficient and the rule therefore does not fully recognize the attack, there is a great chance that the window size will be increased in the coming evolutionary steps. Since each rule should detect a single anomaly, the fitness value assigned to a rule during the evolution is dependent on the considered anomaly. Our GP algorithm therefore has to run once per analyzed anomaly, to select the best performing individuals in each step.

Rule Compiler. In order for the interpreter to use the rules calculated by the generator, they must be compiled. At this point, additional rules in the format of the DSL can be added from a database. All rules that should be available to the detector are collected and compiled into executable C++ code using Xtend [34]. Each rule is compiled into a subclass of *Rule*, which is a class provided by the detector implementation.Important attributes stay the same, consequently each rule contains a parameter for the size of the packet window, the name of the rule and the conditions to check. Conditions are compiled as an array of lambda functions that each accept a view of the packet window and return a Boolean. Common functions, such as the logic for the *ANY* and *ALL* quantifiers, and the methods to extract features are made available by the detector framework to reduce duplications in the implementation. The generated C++ source files are transferred and linked to the detector.

Rule Interpreter. The rule interpreter uses the generated rules to identify attacks in the communication traffic. Since performance is an important metric, the prototypical implementation is written in C++ and uses the PcapPlus-Plus [35] framework with added SOME/IP and SOME/IP-SD layers to interpret the traffic. It uses the compiled rules to detect attacks. Upon arrival of a new packet, each rule can be evaluated independently, which offers the possibility for multithreading. Thus, a thread pool handles the asynchronous evaluation. When a rule is triggered, an *Alert* object is created and added to the *Report*. An alert consists of the rule activated and the packets involved. The report implements the observer pattern, providing an interface for future work to react to incidents. In this way, a database containing the necessary prevention steps, proposed for example in the work of Herold [14], could react to the alerts, forming an Intrusion Detection and Response System (IDRS).

6 Evaluation

The evaluation of the project was carried out in three steps. Firstly, we evaluated the meaningfulness of the rule language by trying to map the attacks we used into the rule language. Then we examined the performance of the interpreter and lastly the accuracy of the rule generator. There are very few known research papers that are thematically close enough to be directly comparable to this work. As discussed in Sect. 2, only two approaches can be discussed in the evaluation, namely the approaches of Herold [14] and Alkhatib et al. [23], as both approaches investigate attacks also flow of packets.

Herold discusses only hand-crafted results in their CEP-based approach, and thus can only be compared based on classification speed and resource consumption. Alkhatib et al. [23] focus on classification accuracy with their RNN-based approach without mentioning resource consumption and are therefore only compared based on prediction accuracy.

RulEth Feature Set. We were able to model each attack behavior presented in Sect. 3, leveraging the quantifier and variable feature of the DSL. However, we have also identified opportunities to optimize the current DSL implementation. We found that for both attacks consisting of a series of packets (*i.e., Error-On-Error and De-Association*), a request/response relationship between the messages had to be identified to detect the anomaly. This relationship currently requires assessing that the IP addresses, Ports, and MAC addresses of the sender and receiver have swapped positions with each other, and that the SOME/IP fields for the *ServiceID, ClientID, MethodID* and *SessionID* are equal. Completing a complex syntax tree, similar to this, requires an unnecessary amount of nodes, and therefore reduces the chance for an ML algorithm to find this solution. Improvements for users and the rule generator can therefore be expected when experimenting with additional operators, that combine common checks, like the abovementioned, into a single operation.

Interpreter Performance. The evaluation was carried out on a desktop PC, equipped with a 6-core Intel I5-8600k processor. The test trace used for this contains 272,027 packets, 115,270 of which are malicious, with representatives of all attack classes examined. To achieve comparable results, each configuration was rated five times. Table 1 contains the results for our implementation. Evaluating the dataset without the rules activated, and therefore without the overhead of checking the rules and creating alerts, took on average 106.2 milliseconds. This means that without rules enabled, 2,561,000 packets can be processed per second.

Table 1. Benchmark of the detector with no and with all rules activated, comparing execution speeds and memory consumption with available results from the CEP-IDS [14]. Compared are the average measured run time in milliseconds *(Duration)*, standard deviation over 5 runs (δ), the resulting approximate maximum packet rate per second *(p/s)*, as well as the memory usage (Mem.).

Dataset	Rules	Duration	δ	p/s	Mem.
RulEth	**None**	106.2	2.6	2561k	210kB
	All	4436.2	46.75	61k	240kB
	Error-On-Event	1892.2	80.1	144k	216kB
CEP-IDS [14]	**None**			257k	130MB
	All			26k	1.5GB
	Error-On-Event			276k	650MB

When enabling all rules at the same time, the interpreter required 4436.2 ms on average, to check the packet trace. These are acceptable values for an IDS. An evaluation of the performance of SNORT [22], found that the program was able to process around 46,000 p/s [36]. The preliminary implementation of the security policy based IDS, proposed by Gehrmann [15], processed incoming packets at a speed of 166,600 p/s. Herold's CEP based IDS was able to handle 26,000 p/s with all of its seven rules enabled [14]. However, a closer look at the performance, when inspecting the directly comparable *Error-On-Event* attack, revealed that on this particular rule the CEP-IDS performed at 276,000 p/s, which is considerable faster than the 144,000 p/s our implementation was able to handle. One reason for this is the clever use of sub queries in the SQL-like language used to define rules. With this, the rule was evaluated only once for most inspected packets. Something we plan to integrate in our approach through static analysis of rules.

In turn, our solution performs much better than the CEP-IDS when considering the memory required. The 210 kB required by our solution is much smaller than the approximately 130 MB allocated by the CEP solution. Owing to the use of views that avoid copying collections, adding rules has little impact on the amount of memory required. With all rules enabled, our solution requires only 240 kB, while the CEP solution in this case requires over 1.5 GB of memory.

Datasets. Two different recordings of real SOME/IP traffic in a vehicle were used as the basis of the training and test datasets. The training dataset is based on the recording of a stationary vehicle, while the test dataset is based on a slow moving vehicle. Subsequently, all four considered attacks were injected synthetically into the recordings. This is a significant improvement over earlier publications on SOME/IP IDS, since the evaluations there were carried out on purely synthetic data sets [14,23]. The training dataset consists of 24087 packets, 11323 of which are benign, while the testing datasets consists of 26670 packets, with 11329 benign packets. The differences in size and composition are rooted in the differing source traces and configuration parameters, as additional values and edge cases are added to the test dataset to reveal overfitting of rules.

Table 2. Performance comparison of the generator on different attacks. Performance for each attack class is evaluated with a single rule.

Attack-Class	Training Set			Testing Set		
	F_1	Prec.	Rec.	F_1	Prec.	Rec.
Wrong Interface	**.9933**	1	.9866	**.9924**	1	.9850
DDoS	**1**	1	1	**1**	1	1
Error-On-Event	**.9981**	.9961	1	**.9974**	.9949	1
De-Association	**.7850**	.6461	1	**.7726**	.6294	1

Rule Generation. On the training dataset, the generator was trained for 500 generations, with a population of 500 individuals. Fitness values for individuals were calculated using, the F_1-*Score*, with the formula $F_1 = \frac{2 \cdot TP}{2 \cdot TP + FN + FP}$, which can be interpreted as the harmonic mean of precision and recall. Its components, *True Positive (TP)*, *False Positive (FP)*, and *False Negative (FN)*, denote classes correctly and incorrectly classified as positive and classes incorrectly classified as negative. In each generation, the best individuals were selected using tournament selection, with a tournament size of 50. During creation of the next generation, individuals had a 20% chance to mutate, a 50% chance of crossover and a 20% chance to have a subtree replaced with a matching leaf.

The program was run on a 72-core Intel Xeon Gold 6154 processor, taking around 20 min to generate a single rule. The performance of the GP-based rule generator for both the training and the testing dataset is presented in Table 2. Out of the inspected attacks, all except the multistep *De-Association* attack are identified with good accuracy on the training and testing dataset, reaching F_1-Scores of 0.992, 0.997 and 1 for the *WrongInterface, Error-On-Event* and *DDoS* attacks, respectively. During evaluation of a rule, an alert is only counted as true positive, if the newest seen packet is tagged as malicious packet for the attack class of the rule. A closer inspection and the interpretability of the generated rules allows us to check if the generated rules actually cover the desired attack pattern or if they have found some other association between packets marked as an attack, which is explained below.

As can be seen on the left in Fig. 3, the GP algorithm is able to find a good solution for the *Interface Version* attack, comparing if the field is larger than

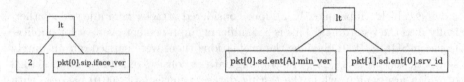

Fig. 3. Graphical representations of the syntax trees deduced by the GP algorithm to detect anomalies for the *Interface Version (left)* and *Deassociation (right)* attacks.

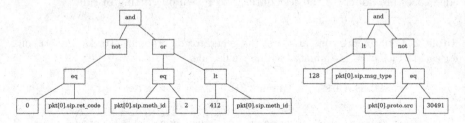

Fig. 4. (left) Rule detecting *Error-On-Event* attacks with perfect accuracy in the training and testing datasets published by Alkhatib et al. [23]. However, this rule does not model the attack pattern and is therefore revealing a flaw in the datasets in the form of an undesirable correlation between all attack packets. (right) Rule detecting *Error-On-Error* attacks in the dataset published by Alkhatib et al., implicating the same flaw in the dataset.

2. The *De-Association* attack by Zelle [12] on the other hand receives a F_1-Score of only 0.77 on the testing set, indicating that the attack pattern was not grasped by the GP algorithm. The rule generated for this attack can be seen on the right in Fig. 3. It classifies a sample as malicious if the *MinorVersion* field of every SOME/IP-SD entry of the first packet in the packet window is smaller than the *Service ID* field of the first SOME/IP-SD entry of the previous packet. This suggests that the algorithm was able to find a connection between an attack and two consecutive service discovery messages, but was unable to identify the complete nature of the attack. It remains to be tested whether using advanced operators that make it easier to detect whether two messages are part of a message sequence can improve the generator. Due to the human-in-the-loop approach used in this work, this rule would not pass the quality control by an expert and therefore would either be revised or deleted. Additionally, knowledge of this shortcoming in the dataset can be used to improve the next iteration of datasets. This is an advantage of the rule-based model over ANN-based solutions, where the only option is to either reject or accept a trained model as a whole.

ML based IDS on SOME/IP to compare the results of our GP approach against is scarce to find. One such work is the RNN based approach by Alkhatib et al. [23], who evaluated their model against a synthetic dataset created using Herold's [14] dataset generator. On this dataset, which was made publicly available, their models achieved F_1-scores on the testing set of up to 0.98 for the *Error-On-Event* attack and 0.86 for the *Error-On-Error* attack. The *Error-On-Error* attack works analogously to the in this work presented *Error-On-Event* attack, and violates the specification by replying with an error message to an error message. However, since the RNN-based models are inexplicable, a fundamental flaw in the data is not apparent. The problem becomes clear when one looks at the rules that describe the anomalies.

The *ErrorOnError* rule, shown on the right in Fig. 4, strikes if the message type is greater than 128 and the source port is different from 30491. The, on the left in Fig. 4 illustrated, *ErrorOnEvent* rule is triggered if the return code is greater than 0 and the *MethodId* is 2 or larger than 412. Both rules achieve a perfect F_1-score on the training and test dataset published, but do not grasp the attack. The packet flow based attack is attempted to be detected on a single packet and are therefore overfitting to the presented datasets. Whether the yielded RNN model has found this connection or has indeed modeled the attack is not discernible from the provided model.

7   Conclusion

This work proposes a ML-based approach capable of detecting various attacks on AE protocols in an explainable and verifiable manner. The tool chain developed uses the RulEth language we defined to represent the rules in a human-verifiable style. The selected GP algorithm was found to be suitable for the rule generation task in this concept. An intermediate step in the proposed tool chain allows a human-in-the-loop to validate all results of the GP algorithm before approval for use in vehicles. If non-optimal rules occur, experts can optimize the GP feature selection or remove these rules from the deployed set. This step is a key benefit for considering this technique in safety-critical systems, as it provides technical robustness, transparency and accountability, while complying with ethical guidelines for trustworthy AI, particularly human action and oversight. To detect MitM attacks, the algorithm can select features from a sliding window containing the most recent packets. The RulEth language comprises quantifiers and variables that can require conditions for any or all packets in the window. An evaluation of the proof-of-concept implementation on recordings of real SOME/IP traffic enriched by various attack types shows that the approach is able to detect such attacks. The variables and quantifier features of the DSL contribute significantly to the detection. The approved rules can be compiled into C++ code and used for resource-efficient, real-time attack detection.

Most of the attacks on the SOME/IP protocol examined in this work were well detected by our approach despite their complexity. With the ability to evaluate each generated rule separately, it is now possible to weed out some rules that do not work effectively, such as those generated to detect the *De-Association* attack, thereby improving the reliability of the system.

The approach is unique in that other authors either don't evaluate their work using real automotive data or don't generate any rules at all. Most GP approaches use outdated KDD99 data, while other works using synthetic SOME/IP data rely on handwritten rules or black box ANN models.

In future work, we plan to extend the RulEth approach to other AE protocols, such as Diagnostics over IP (DoIP), to develop advanced operators that improve the IDS performance and to integrate mitigation rules.

Acknowledgements. This work has been partly funded by the German Federal Ministry of Education and Research and the Hessen State Ministry for Higher Education, Research and the Arts within their joint support of the National Research Center for Applied Cybersecurity ATHENE and by the BMBF project FINESSE (ID 16KIS1586) and has received funding from the European Union's Horizon 2020 research and innovation programme under grant agreement No. 883135 (E-CORRIDOR).

Ethical Discussion. In this paper we present RulEth, a Genetic Programming based solution to generate security rules with the ability to detect attacks based on the packet flow. During the design process, we followed the seven key requirements derived by the European ethics guidelines for trustworthy AI [37], namely (1) human agency and oversight, (2) technical robustness and safety, (3) privacy and data governance, (4) transparency, (5) diversity, non-discrimination and fairness, (6) environmental and societal well-being and (7) accountability. In fact, one major research goal was to improve the current state of human agency, transparency, and accountability in intrusion detection systems.

Human Agency and Oversight. Human Agency is coupled tightly with the developed architecture, as a human-in-the-loop can interact with each step of the rule generation process, and hold back, improve or generate self-written rules as measures of quality control for the generated model.

Technical Robustness and Safety. In order to maintain the confidentiality and safety of the system, adherence to UN regulation R156 [28] is required for uploading logs to the backend and provisioning new rules. The traffic logging module within the vehicle must be secured using trusted computing and authenticated with the backend. Furthermore, the backend must operate within a secure environment.

Privacy and Data Governance. In order to ensure data governance, we envision the sharing of logs from a users vehicle to be optional, verifying informed consent. Additionally, the privacy of shared data is reached during the aggregation phase. Attacks should not depend on personal information like GPS coordinates, therefore the data can be anonymized.

Transparency. The design focuses around transparency, as rules are explainable and easy to understand through the use of a Domain Specific Language. Alerts generated by the system contain the rule and packets responsible for the decision, ensuring traceability.

Diversity, Non-Discrimination and Fairness. We try to mitigate unfair bias by using a blacklist approach, denying only communications that exactly match an anomaly pattern.

Environmental and Societal Well-Being. The goal of the system is to detect anomalies in the packet flow, we do not see the risk of a negative impact on the society. The detection of anomalies using rules is lightweight, minimizing a negative environmental impact.

Accountability. The proposed rule-generation mechanism together with the human approval of the rules facilitate the system's auditability and traceability, as well as logging and documentation of the AI system's processes and outcomes.

References

1. Upstream: 2023 global automotive cybersecurity report (2023). https://upstream. auto/reports/global-automotive-cybersecurity-report/. Accessed 19 June 2023
2. Sommer, R., Paxson, V.: Outside the closed world: on using machine learning for network intrusion detection. In: IEEE Symposium on Security and Privacy 2010, pp. 305–316 (2010)
3. Lundberg, H.: Increasing the trustworthiness of AI-based in-vehicle ids using explainable AI. Master's thesis, Mid Sweden University (2022)
4. Rastogi, N., Rampazzi, S., Clifford, M., Heller, M., Bishop, M., Levitt, K.: Explaining radar features for detecting spoofing attacks in connected autonomous vehicles (2022). https://arxiv.org/abs/2203.00150
5. European Commission: Directorate-General for Communications Networks, Content and Technology, Ethics guidelines for trustworthy AI. Publications Office (2019)
6. Matheus, K., Königseder, T.: Automotive Ethernet. Cambridge University Press, Cambridge (2021)
7. AUTOSAR: Some/IP protocol specification (2016). https://www.autosar.org/ fileadmin/standards/foundation/1-4/AUTOSAR_PRS_SOMEIPProtocol.pdf. Accessed 31 Mar 2023
8. AUTOSAR: Autosar partnership (2022). https://www.autosar.org/. Accessed 31 Mar 2023
9. Iorio, M., Buttiglieri, A., Reineri, M., Risso, F., Sisto, R., Valenza, F.: Protecting in-vehicle services: security-enabled some/IP middleware. IEEE Veh. Technol. Mag. **15**(3), 77–85 (2020)
10. Kreissl, J.: Absicherung der some/IP kommunikation bei adaptive autosar. Master's thesis, University of Stuttgart (2017)
11. Perrig, A., Canetti, R., Tygar, J.D., Song, D.: The tesla broadcast authentication protocol. RSA Cryptobytes **5**(2), 2–13 (2002)
12. Zelle, D., Kern, D., Lauser, T., Kraus, C.: Analyzing and securing some/IP automotive services with formal and practical methods. In: 4th International Conference on Availability, Reliability and Security (ARES). ACM (2021)
13. Yu, J., Wagner, S., Wang, B., Luo, F.: A systematic mapping study on security countermeasures of in-vehicle communication systems, arXiv preprint arXiv:2105.00183 (2021)
14. Herold, N.: Incident handling systems with automated intrusion response. Ph.D. dissertation, Technische Universität München (2017)
15. Gehrmann, T., Duplys, P.: Intrusion detection for some/IP: challenges and opportunities. In: 2020 23rd Euromicro Conference on Digital System Design (DSD), pp. 583–587. IEEE (2020)
16. Li, W.: Using genetic algorithm for network intrusion detection. In: Proceedings of the United States Department of Energy Cyber Security Group, vol. 1, pp. 1–8 (2004)

17. Gong, R.H., Zulkernine, M., Abolmaesumi, P.: A software implementation of a genetic algorithm based approach to network intrusion detection. In: Sixth International Conference on Software Engineering, Artificial Intelligence, Networking and Parallel/Distributed Computing and First ACIS International Workshop on Self-Assembling Wireless Network, pp. 246–253 (2005)

18. Song, D., Heywood, M.I., Zincir-Heywood, A.N.: A linear genetic programming approach to intrusion detection. In: Cantú-Paz, E., et al. (eds.) GECCO 2003. LNCS, vol. 2724, pp. 2325–2336. Springer, Heidelberg (2003). https://doi.org/10.1007/3-540-45110-2_125

19. Gómez, J., Gil, C., Baños, R., Márquez, A.L., Montoya, F.G., Montoya, M.G.: A pareto-based multi-objective evolutionary algorithm for automatic rule generation in network intrusion detection systems. Soft Comput. **17**(2), 255–263 (2013)

20. Rastegari, S., Hingston, P., Lam, C.-P.: Evolving statistical rulesets for network intrusion detection. Appl. Soft Comput. **33**, 348–359 (2015)

21. Buschlinger, L., Rieke, R., Sarda, S., Krauß, C.: Decision tree-based rule derivation for intrusion detection in safety-critical automotive systems. In: 2022 30th Euromicro International Conference on Parallel, Distributed and Network-Based Processing (PDP), pp. 246–254 (2022)

22. Roesch, M., et al.: Snort: lightweight intrusion detection for networks. Lisa **99**(1), 229–238 (1999)

23. Alkhatib, N., Ghauch, H., Danger, J.-L.: Some, IP intrusion detection using deep learning-based sequential models in automotive ethernet networks. In: IEEE 12th Annual Information Technology, Electronics and Mobile Communication Conference (IEMCON) 2021, pp. 0954–0962 (2021)

24. Dolev, D., Yao, A.: On the security of public key protocols. IEEE Trans. Inf. Theory **29**(2), 198–208 (1983)

25. Hussain, A., Heidemann, J., Papadopoulos, C.: A framework for classifying denial of service attacks. In: Proceedings of the 2003 Conference on Applications, Technologies, Architectures, and Protocols for Computer Communications, pp. 99–110 (2003)

26. Zdun, U., Strembeck, M.: Reusable architectural decisions for DSL design: foundational decisions in DSL development. In: 14th European Conference on Pattern Languages of Programs (EuroPLoP) (2009)

27. Anonimized: Additional paper resources (2023). https://anonymous.4open.science/r/ruleth-paper-resources-8D62. Accessed 30 Mar 2023

28. UN Regulation No. 156: Uniform provisions concerning the approval of vehicles with regards to software update and software updates management system. United Nations (2021). https://unece.org/sites/default/files/2021-03/R156e.pdf. Accessed 31 Mar 2023

29. Koza, J.R.: Non-linear genetic algorithms for solving problems. United States Patent 4935877, 19 June 1990, filed may 20, 1988, issued June 19, 1990, 4,935,877. Australian patent 611,350 issued 21 September 1991. Canadian patent 1,311,561 issued 15 December 1992

30. Python Software Foundation: Python3 (2022). https://www.python.org/. Accessed 31 Mar 2023

31. De Rainville, F.-M., Fortin, F.-A., Gardner, M.-A., Parizeau, M., Gagné, C.: Deap: a python framework for evolutionary algorithms. In: Proceedings of the 14th Annual Conference Companion on Genetic and Evolutionary Computation, pp. 85–92 (2012)

32. Koza, J.R.: Genetic Programming: On the Programming of Computers by Means of Natural Selection, vol. 1. MIT Press, Cambridge (1992)

33. Fenzl, F., Rieke, R., Dominik, A.: In-vehicle detection of targeted can bus attacks. In: The 16th International Conference on Availability, Reliability and Security, pp. 1–7 (2021)
34. Eclipse: Xtend (2022). https://www.eclipse.org/xtend. Accessed 31 Mar 2023
35. seladb. Pcapplusplus (2022). https://pcapplusplus.github.io/. Accessed 31 Mar 2023
36. Granberg, N.: Evaluating the effectiveness of free rule sets for snort. Master's thesis, Linköping University, Department of Computer and Information Science, Database and Information Techniques (2022)
37. Independent High-Level Expert Group on Artificial Intelligence: Ethics guidelines for trustworthy AI. European Commission (2019). https://ec.europa.eu/newsroom/dae/document.cfm?doc_id=60419. Accessed 31 Mar 2023

Spatial-Temporal Graph Sandwich Transformer for Traffic Flow Forecasting

Yujie Fan$^{(\boxtimes)}$, Chin-Chia Michael Yeh, Huiyuan Chen, Liang Wang,
Zhongfang Zhuang, Junpeng Wang, Xin Dai, Yan Zheng, and Wei Zhang

Visa Research, Palo Alto, CA, USA
{yufan,miyeh,hchen,liawang,zzhuang,junpenwa,xidai,yazheng,wzhan}@visa.com

Abstract. Traffic flow forecasting has primarily relied on the spatial-temporal models. However, yielding accurate traffic prediction is still challenging due to that the dynamic temporal pattern, intricate spatial dependency and their affluent interaction are difficult to depict. Existing models are often restricted since they can only capture limited-range temporal dependency, shallow spatial dependency, or faint spatial-temporal interaction. In this work, to overcome these limitations, we propose a novel *spatial-temporal graph sandwich Transformer* (STGST) for traffic flow forecasting. In STGST, we design two temporal Transformers equipped with time encoding and a spatial Transformer equipped with structure and spatial encoding to characterize long-range temporal and deep spatial dependencies, respectively. These two types of Transformers are further structured in a sandwich manner with two temporal Transformers as buns and a spatial Transformer as sliced meat to capture prosperous spatial-temporal interactions. We also assemble a set of such sandwich Transformers together to strengthen the correlations between spatial and temporal domains. Extensive experimental studies are performed on public traffic benchmarks. Promising results demonstrate that the proposed STGST outperforms state-of-the-art baselines.

Keywords: Spatial-temporal graph · Transformer · Traffic forecasting

1 Introduction

Traffic forecasting plays an essential role in modern intelligent transportation system. Efficient and accurate flow forecasting allows better traffic management and planning. Generally, traffic flow forecasting aims to predict future traffic conditions by leveraging the historical time-series traffic input and the underlying traffic network. Classic statistic models [20,25] and sequence models [7,18] primarily emphasize the time-series input but overlook the spatial correlations of the traffic network, leaving huge room for improvements.

Through modeling the traffic network as a graph with nodes and edges representing traffic sensors and their spatial connectivity, spatial-temporal graph models have been studied intensively and have achieved state-of-the-art performance in traffic flow forecasting. To be specific, current works explore graph

© The Author(s), under exclusive license to Springer Nature Switzerland AG 2023
G. De Francisci Morales et al. (Eds.): ECML PKDD 2023, LNAI 14175, pp. 210–225, 2023.
https://doi.org/10.1007/978-3-031-43430-3_13

neural networks (GNNs) [10,12,17,23], such as graph convolutional networks (GCNs) and graph attention networks (GATs), to characterize the spatial dependency by introducing the inherent structural information of the traffic network. While in the temporal dimension, they apply either recurrent neural networks (RNNs) [2,15], such as gated recurrent units (GRUs) and long-short term memory (LSTM), or convolution-based sequence learning models [9,13], such as temporal convolutional networks (TCNs), to depict the temporal dependency of the time-series traffic data. By integrating the outputs of the spatial and temporal domains, they are able to jointly capture the spatial-temporal correlations. Although existing spatial-temporal models have demonstrated superior performance than sequence model-based forecasting, they are still restricted in the following three aspects: limited-range temporal dependency, shallow spatial dependency, and faint spatial-temporal interaction.

Concretely, RNNs used in the temporal domain process the time-series inputs step-by-step and retain the past information in hidden states. However, RNNs are faced with the long-term dependency problem when handling long sequences [19]. The same problem of RNNs that happens in the natural language processing (NLP) domain generally happens in the traffic forecasting scenario. Such a limitation leads to *limited-range temporal dependency* described, restricting its use when long-range historical time-series data is needed. On the other hand, GNNs applied in the spatial domain mainly follow a message-passing scheme that iteratively propagates and aggregates neighbor information. However, GNNs have been proven to suffer from the over-smoothing problem [5,14] (i.e., node representations become indistinguishable with increased model depth) due to repeated local aggregation, leading to inferior performance in practice. Such inherent drawbacks limit its ability to learn deep and global spatial features, resulting in *shallow spatial dependency* captured in current methods. Furthermore, most studies characterize the temporal dependency and spatial dependency separately and combine them either in serial [10,21,23] or in parallel [13,24]. These designs weaken the connection between spatial and temporal domains, resulting in *faint spatial-temporal interaction*.

To address these limitations, we propose a novel *spatial-temporal graph sandwich Transformer*, namely STGST, for traffic flow forecasting. The key component of STGST is a sandwich Transformer set consisting of several spatial-temporal sandwich Transformers. Each sandwich Transformer contains a top temporal Transformer, a bottom temporal Transformer as buns, and a spatial Transformer as sliced meat. The two temporal Transformers equipped with time encoding are designed to alleviate the first limitation. The time-series input is processed as a whole rather than step-by-step in the temporal Transformer, allowing it to capture long-range temporal dependency. The spatial Transformer is proposed to accommodate the second limitation. We equip it with structure encoding and spatial encoding to incorporate graph structural information into the Transformer architecture. Applying such a spatial Transformer enables us to capture deep and global spatial dependency. To cope with the third limitation, the temporal and spatial Transformers are structured in a sandwich manner, which help depict prosperous spatial-temporal interactions. Additionally, assembling several sandwich Transformers into a set allows diverse but complementary spatial-temporal interactions to be captured. Comprehensive experiments are conducted on public traffic benchmarks. Promising results demonstrate the superior performance of STGST by comparison with 12 state-of-the-art baselines. In sum, our work makes the following contributions:

- We design a temporal Transformer and a spatial Transformer to characterize long-range temporal and deep spatial dependencies, respectively.
- We propose STGST by structuring the temporal and spatial Transformers in a sandwich manner to capture prosperous spatial-temporal interactions.
- We empirically evaluate the proposed model on real-world traffic benchmarks, and the experimental results confirm the efficacy of our model.

2   Related Work

Traffic flow forecasting has gained significant attention due to its critical importance in modern intelligent transportation systems. Classic statistical models, such as autoregressive integrated moving average (ARIMA) [20] and vector auto-regression (VAR) [25], have been widely studied to predict future traffic conditions using time-series data collected from various traffic sensors. However, these models have limitations in capturing intricate spatial-temporal correlations. To address this issue, a large number of spatial-temporal forecasting models have been proposed to jointly consider the spatial and temporal dependencies for traffic forecasting. Existing works mainly apply sequence models to capture the temporal dependency and use graph learning models to characterize the spatial dependency. STG2Seq [1] uses a graph convolution-based sequence-to-sequence model with an attention mechanism for multi-step prediction. DCRNN [15] integrates graph convolution with GRUs in an encoder-decoder manner to depict the spatial and temporal dependencies. STGCN [23] combines graph convolution with gated temporal convolution to characterize the spatial-temporal correlations. STSGCN [17] leverages a spatial-temporal synchronous modeling mechanism to capture the localized spatial-temporal correlations. ASTGCN [10] utilizes a spatial-temporal attention mechanism with convolution to describe the spatial-temporal dynamics. AGCRN [2] designs a node adaptive parameter learning module and a data adaptive graph generation module to capture fine-grained spatial and temporal correlations. STFGNN [13] uses a spatial-temporal fusion operation to depict the hidden spatial-temporal dependencies. STGODE [9] applies a tensor-based ordinary differential equation to capture the spatial-temporal dynamics. Z-GCNETs [6] integrates time-aware zigzag persistence into time-conditioned GCNs for time-series prediction. DSTAGNN [12] designs a spatial-temporal attention module to capture dynamic spatial-temporal dependency from a dynamic spatial-temporal aware graph. Unlike most existing works that simply combine the spatial and temporal dependencies in a serial or parallel fashion, our proposed STGST explores a sandwich structure to capture the spatial-temporal connections. We will empirically compare these works with STGST in the experiment section.

Table 1. Notations

Symbols	Definitions
$\mathcal{G}, \mathcal{V}, \mathcal{E}$	the traffic network, a set of nodes, a set of edges
$\mathbf{A}, \mathbf{X}^{(t)}$	adjacency matrix, traffic condition at time step t
N, D	the number of nodes, the number of traffic measurements
$\mathcal{X}, \mathcal{X}'$	historical and predicted traffic conditions
$\mathcal{Y}$	actual traffic conditions
S, T	the number of historical and predicted time steps
$\mathcal{F}$	the forecasting model to be learned
H, d	attention head, hidden dimension
K, L	the number of sandwich Transformers and Transformer layers
$\parallel$	concatenation operation
ϕ_{in}, ϕ_{out}	input transformation, muli-step prediction function
XFMR_{top}	top temporal Transformer
XFMR_{spa}	spatial Transformer
XFMR_{bot}	bottom temporal Transformer

3 Preliminaries

Throughout this paper, we use lowercase letters (e.g., x), boldface lowercase letters (e.g., $\mathbf{x}$), boldface uppercase letters (e.g., $\mathbf{X}$), and calligraphic letters (e.g., $\mathcal{X}$) to denote scalars, vectors, matrices, and tensors, respectively. The notations used in this work are described in Table 1.

3.1 Problem Formulation

A traffic network can be represented as a graph $\mathcal{G} = (\mathcal{V}, \mathcal{E})$, where $\mathcal{V}$ denotes a set of N nodes (i.e., sensors) and $\mathcal{E}$ is a set of edges, indicating nodes' connectivity. The adjacency matrix derived from the graph is denoted by $\mathbf{A} \in \mathbb{R}^{N \times N}$, where $\mathbf{A}_{ij} = 1$ if $(v_i, v_j) \in \mathcal{E}$, 0 otherwise. The traffic condition at time step t can be formulated as $\mathbf{X}^{(t)} \in \mathbb{R}^{N \times D}$, where D is the number of traffic measurements (e.g., volume, speed). Given S step historical traffic conditions $[\mathbf{X}^{(t-S+1)}, \cdots, \mathbf{X}^{(t)}]$ and a traffic network $\mathcal{G}$, a forecasting model $\mathcal{F}$ can be learned to predict the traffic conditions of the future T steps $[\mathbf{X}'^{(t+1)}, \cdots, \mathbf{X}'^{(t+T)}]$, as follows:

$$[\mathbf{X}^{(t-S+1)}, \cdots, \mathbf{X}^{(t)}; \mathcal{G}] \xrightarrow{\mathcal{F}} [\mathbf{X}'^{(t+1)}, \cdots, \mathbf{X}'^{(t+T)}]. \tag{1}$$

For simplicity, we use $\mathcal{X}^{(t-S+1):(t)} \in \mathbb{R}^{S \times N \times D}$ and $\mathcal{X}'^{(t+1):(t+T)} \in \mathbb{R}^{T \times N \times D}$ to denote the input and output, respectively.

3.2   Transformer Architecture

The Transformer architecture is composed of a set of Transformer layers [19]. Each Transformer layer consists of a multi-head attention (MHA) block followed by a point-wise feed-forward network (FFN) block, with residual connections and layer normalization (LN) around each. Let $\mathbf{X} \in \mathbb{R}^{N \times D}$ be the input of Transformer, the MHA block is calculated as:

$$\text{MHA}(\mathbf{X}) = \|_{h=1}^{H} \left(\text{Attention}(\mathbf{Q}_h, \mathbf{K}_h, \mathbf{V}_h) \right) \mathbf{W}^O, \tag{2}$$

$$\text{Attention}(\mathbf{Q}_h, \mathbf{K}_h, \mathbf{V}_h) = \text{softmax}\left(\frac{\mathbf{Q}_h \mathbf{K}_h^\top}{\sqrt{D}} \right) \mathbf{V}_h. \tag{3}$$

where $\mathbf{Q}_h = \mathbf{X}\mathbf{W}_h^Q, \mathbf{K}_h = \mathbf{X}\mathbf{W}_h^K, \mathbf{V}_h = \mathbf{X}\mathbf{W}_h^V$, and $\mathbf{W}_h^Q, \mathbf{W}_h^K$ and $\mathbf{W}_h^V$ are the query, key and value weight matrices that linearly project the input $\mathbf{X}$ in h-th attention head, $\|$ denotes the concatenation operation, and $\mathbf{W}^O$ is the output transformation. Residual connection and LN are further applied to the output of MHA, denoted as $\hat{\mathbf{X}} = \text{LN}(\text{MHA}(\mathbf{X}) + \mathbf{X})$. Then, the FFN block is calculated as:

$$\text{FFN}(\hat{\mathbf{X}}) = \sigma(\hat{\mathbf{X}}\mathbf{W}_1 + \mathbf{b}_1)\mathbf{W}_2 + \mathbf{b}_2, \tag{4}$$

where σ denotes the activation function, $\mathbf{W}_1, \mathbf{W}_2, \mathbf{b}_1$ and $\mathbf{b}_2$ are weight matrices and bias. The final output of a Transformer layer is $\tilde{\mathbf{X}} = \text{LN}(\text{FFN}(\hat{\mathbf{X}}) + \hat{\mathbf{X}})$.

4   Proposed Method

4.1   Overall Design

Figure 1(a) shows the architecture of STGST, which takes S step historical time-series traffic data $\mathcal{X}^{(t-S+1):(t)} \in \mathbb{R}^{S \times N \times D}$ and the traffic network $\mathcal{G}$ as inputs and outputs the prediction for the next T steps $\mathcal{X}'^{(t+1):(t+T)} \in \mathbb{R}^{T \times N \times D}$. STGST consists of three modules: input transformation, sandwich Transformer set, and multi-step prediction. The *input transformation* is a fully-connected layer projecting low-dimensional traffic data into a high-dimensional informative space. The *sandwich Transformer set* is the key component of STGST. It is composed of a set of spatial-temporal sandwich Transformers, each of which contains two temporal Transformers as buns and a spatial Transformer as sliced meat. The temporal and spatial Transformers characterize long-range temporal and deep spatial dependencies individually, and their sandwich combination captures prosperous spatial-temporal interactions. Additionally, putting several sandwich Transformers into a set helps the model learn diverse but complementary interactions between spatial and temporal domains. It is worth noting that these spatial-temporal sandwich Transformers can be executed in parallel to speed up the training process. In the *multi-step prediction*, the outputs of sandwich Transformer set are first concatenated and then fed into two fully-connected layers to generate the forecasting results.

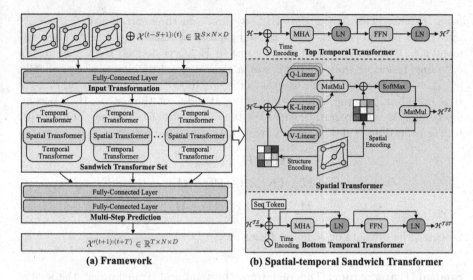

(a) Framework   (b) Spatial-temporal Sandwich Transformer

Fig. 1. (a) The overall design of STGST, which consists of an input transformation module, a sandwich Transformer set with several spatial-temporal sandwich Transformers, and a multi-step prediction module. (b) The architecture of the spatial-temporal sandwich Transformer, which includes two temporal Transformers as buns and a spatial Transformer as sliced meat.

4.2 Spatial-Temporal Sandwich Transformer

The input to the sandwich Transformer set is $\mathcal{H} = \phi_{in}(\mathcal{X})$, where $\phi_{in}(\cdot)$ denotes the input transformation, $\mathcal{H} \in \mathbb{R}^{S \times N \times d}$ with S, N and d as the sequence length, the number of nodes, and the hidden dimension, respectively. Each spatial-temporal sandwich Transformer in the sandwich Transformer set combines a top temporal Transformer, a spatial Transformer, and a bottom temporal Transformer in a sandwich manner. As illustrated in Fig. 1(b), the top temporal Transformer, spatial Transformer, and bottom temporal Transformer are sequentially performed, each of which takes the inputs from the last Transformer and generates outputs for the next one.

Top Temporal Transformer. The top temporal Transformer is performed on each node in the traffic network, aiming to characterize the long-range temporal dependency of the time-series input in the temporal dimension. It is denoted as $\text{XFMR}_{top}(\cdot)$, which can be formulated as follow:

$$\mathcal{H}^{\mathcal{T}} = \text{XFMR}_{top}(\mathcal{H}; \boldsymbol{\Theta}_{top}) \tag{5}$$

where $\mathcal{H}^{\mathcal{T}}$ is the outputs having the same size of $\mathcal{H}$, and $\boldsymbol{\Theta}_{top}$ is the trainable parameters. Note that we treat the dimension N as batchsize in this module.

The design of $\text{XFMR}_{top}(\cdot)$ is built upon the classic Transformer architecture [19]. Given a node with its hidden time-series embedding $\mathbf{H} \in \mathbb{R}^{S \times d}$ fetched from $\mathcal{H}$, before calculating the MHA, we first add time encoding $\mathbf{E}_{time} \in \mathbb{R}^{S \times d}$ into $\mathbf{H}$ to incorporate the time-related factors of time-series input. Each element $p(t, i)$ ($1 \leq t \leq S$ and $1 \leq i \leq d$) in $\mathbf{E}_{time}$ is derived from a frequency encoding function that characterizes a time-dependent sinusoid. Specifically, $p(t, i) = \sin(t/10000^{2i/d})$ if i is even, or $\cos(t/10000^{2i/d})$ if odd. By adding the time encoding into the hidden embedding at different time steps, they become discriminative with regard to time. We then follow the Transformer architecture to learn the temporal dependency, which is formulated as:

$$\mathbf{H}' = \mathbf{H} + \mathbf{E}_{time},$$
$$\hat{\mathbf{H}} = \mathrm{LN}\big(\mathrm{MHA}(\mathbf{H}') + \mathbf{H}'\big), \tag{6}$$
$$\mathbf{H}^{\mathcal{T}} = \mathrm{LN}\big(\mathrm{FFN}(\hat{\mathbf{H}}) + \hat{\mathbf{H}}\big).$$

Stacking the outputs of N nodes forms $\mathcal{H}^{\mathcal{T}}$.

Spatial Transformer. Different from the temporal Transformer, the spatial Transformer is conducted on each time step, aiming to describe the global spatial dependency across all nodes in the traffic network at this time step. Given the traffic network $\mathcal{G}$ and the output from last component $\mathcal{H}^{\mathcal{T}} \in \mathbb{R}^{S \times N \times d}$, the spatial Transformer $\mathrm{XFMR}_{spa}(\cdot)$ is defined as:

$$\mathcal{H}^{\mathcal{TS}} = \mathrm{XFMR}_{spa}(\mathcal{H}^{\mathcal{T}}, \mathcal{G}; \Theta_{spa}), \tag{7}$$

where the output $\mathcal{H}^{\mathcal{TS}}$ has the same size as $\mathcal{H}^{\mathcal{T}}$, and Θ_{spa} is the learnable parameters. It is worth noting that dimension S is regarded as batchsize in this part as we focus on describing the spatial dependency of N nodes.

Inspired by [16,22], we introduce two strategies to encode the graph structural information into the traditional Transformer architecture. Particularly, we add structure encoding, including degree-based and singular value decomposition (SVD)-based encoding, to the node input and add spatial encoding, which is based on nodes' shortest path, as a bias term in the MHA module. By performing these two structure-preserving strategies, we expect the Transformer layer to adaptively adjust the attention coefficient according to the graph structural information. Specifically, the structure encoding $\mathbf{H}_{struc}$ added in the input is formulated as:

$$\mathbf{H}_{struc} = \mathbf{H}_{deg} + \mathbf{H}_{svd}, \tag{8}$$

where $\mathbf{H}_{deg}, \mathbf{H}_{svd} \in \mathbb{R}^{D \times d}$ denote the degree-based and SVD-based encoding. Degree-based encoding assigns each node two real-valued embedding vectors according to its indegree and outdegree. As such, each row in $\mathbf{H}_{deg}$ can be represented as:

$$\mathbf{h}_{v_i} = \mathbf{h}^{-}_{\phi(v_i)} + \mathbf{h}^{+}_{\varphi(v_i)}, \tag{9}$$

where $\phi(v_i)$, $\varphi(v_i)$ are used to compute the indegree and outdegree of node v_i, $\mathbf{h}^{-}$, $\mathbf{h}^{+}$ are learnable vectors identified by these two functions, respectively. SVD-based encoding $\mathbf{H}_{svd}$ is added to further distinguish two nodes with same degree and is formed using the largest r singular values and corresponding left and right singular vectors:

$$\mathbf{A} \overset{\text{SVD}}{\approx} \mathbf{U}\boldsymbol{\Sigma}\mathbf{V}^\top = (\mathbf{U}\sqrt{\boldsymbol{\Sigma}}) \cdot (\mathbf{V}\sqrt{\boldsymbol{\Sigma}})^\top = \hat{\mathbf{U}}\hat{\mathbf{V}}^\top,$$
$$\mathbf{H}_{svd} = \hat{\mathbf{U}}\|\hat{\mathbf{V}}, \tag{10}$$

where $\mathbf{A}$ is the adjacency matrix, $\mathbf{U}, \mathbf{V} \in \mathbb{R}^{N \times r}$ contains r left and right singular vectors, respectively, corresponding to top r singular values in the diagonal matrix $\boldsymbol{\Sigma} \in \mathbb{R}^{r \times r}$, $\|$ denotes concatenation operator along column.

The spatial encoding, denoted as $\mathbf{B}_{spa}$, is defined based on the concept of shortest path. Each element $b_{\psi(v_i,v_j)}$ in $\mathbf{B}_{spa}$ is a learnable scalar indexed by $\psi(v_i, v_j)$ which specfies the distance of the shortest path (SPD) between nodes v_i and v_j. The spatial encoding serves as a bias term in MHA module, guiding the graph structure-aware attention calculation. This process is formulated as:

$$\text{Attention}(\mathbf{Q}, \mathbf{K}, \mathbf{V}) = \text{softmax}\left(\frac{\mathbf{Q}\mathbf{K}^\top}{\sqrt{d}} + \mathbf{B}_{spa}\right)\mathbf{V}. \tag{11}$$

Note that the indegree and outdegree of each node, the SVD vectors, and the SPD between two connected nodes can be pre-computed before model training, which would not largely impact the training time. The design of spatial Transformer is also built upon the traditional Transformer architecture. Given a time step with the hidden embedding $\mathbf{H}^{\mathcal{T}} \in \mathbb{R}^{D \times d}$ for all nodes, we have:

$$\mathbf{H}'^{\mathcal{T}} = \mathbf{H}^{\mathcal{T}} + \mathbf{H}_{struc},$$
$$\hat{\mathbf{H}}^{\mathcal{T}} = \text{LN}\left(\text{MHA}(\mathbf{H}'^{\mathcal{T}}, \mathbf{B}_{spa}) + \mathbf{H}'^{\mathcal{T}}\right), \tag{12}$$
$$\mathbf{H}^{\mathcal{TS}} = \text{LN}\left(\text{FFN}(\hat{\mathbf{H}}^{\mathcal{T}}) + \hat{\mathbf{H}}^{\mathcal{T}}\right).$$

Stacking the outputs of S time steps results in $\mathcal{H}^{\mathcal{TS}}$.

Bottom Temporal Transformer. We connect another temporal Transformer to capture the spatial-temporal interactions. Taking $\mathcal{H}^{\mathcal{TS}} \in \mathbb{R}^{S \times N \times d}$ as input, the bottom temporal Transformer $\text{XFMR}_{bot}(\cdot)$ can be defined as:

$$\mathcal{H}^{\mathcal{TST}} = \text{XFMR}_{bot}(\mathcal{H}^{\mathcal{TS}}; \boldsymbol{\Theta}_{bot}), \tag{13}$$

where $\mathcal{H}^{\mathcal{TST}} \in \mathbb{R}^{(S+1) \times N \times d}$, and $\boldsymbol{\Theta}_{bot}$ is the trainable parameters for this module. The general design of this module is similar with the top temporal Transformer, including time encoding, MHA and FFN. Differently, inspired by the [CLS] token in BERT [8], we append a special token [SEQ] to the beginning of each time-series sequence, summarizing the sequence-level representation.

4.3   Multi-step Prediction

We fetch the embedding of [SEQ] token from $\mathcal{H}^{\mathcal{TST}}$, denoted as $\mathbf{H}^{SEQ}$, as the output of each sandwich Transformer. By concatenating the outputs of K sandwich Transformers, we have $\mathbf{H}^O = \|_{k=1}^K [\mathbf{H}^{SEQ}]_k$, where $\mathbf{H}^O \in \mathbb{R}^{N \times Kd}$. Finally, two fully-connected layers $\phi_{out}(\cdot)$ are applied to map the hidden embeddings to the prediction space $\mathcal{X}' = \phi_{out}(\mathbf{H}^O)$. Huber loss [11] is chose as the loss function since it is less sensitive to outliers than the squared error loss. It is defined as:

$$\mathcal{L} = \begin{cases} \frac{1}{2}(\mathcal{X}' - \mathcal{Y})^2, & \text{if } |\mathcal{X}' - \mathcal{Y}| < \delta \\ \delta(|\mathcal{X}' - \mathcal{Y}| - \frac{1}{2}\delta), & \text{otherwise} \end{cases} \tag{14}$$

where $\mathcal{Y}$ is the actual traffic flow, δ controls the sensitivity to outliers.

Algorithm 1: STGST training procedure

Input: Traffic network $\mathcal{G}$, historical traffic conditions $\mathcal{X}$, actual traffic conditions $\mathcal{Y}$, the number of sandwich Transformers K
Output: Model $\mathcal{F}$

1 Project input temporal signals $\mathcal{H} \leftarrow \phi_{in}(\mathcal{X})$;
2 **for** $k = 1$ **to** K **do**
3   Apply top temporal Transformer $[\mathcal{H}^T]_k \leftarrow$ Eq.(5);
4   Perform spatial Transformer $[\mathcal{H}^{TS}]_k \leftarrow$ Eq.(7);
5   Apply bottom temporal Transformer $[\mathcal{H}^{TST}]_k \leftarrow$ Eq.(13);
6   Fetch [SEQ] embedding $[\mathbf{H}^{SEQ}]_k$ from $[\mathcal{H}^{TST}]_k$;
7 **end**
8 Concatenate output from all sandwich Transformers $\mathbf{H}^O \leftarrow \|_{k=1}^{K} [\mathbf{H}^{SEQ}]_k$;
9 Map to output space $\mathcal{X}' \leftarrow \phi_{out}(\mathbf{H}^O)$;
10 Backpropagation with Eq.(14);

4.4   Training Procedure and Complexity

Algorithm 1 shows the training procedure of the proposed STGST. Line 1 performs input transformation. Line 2–7 execute K sandwich Transformers, in which Line 3, 4, 5 refer to the top temporal Transformer, spatial Transformer, and bottom temporal Transformer, respectively. Line 8 integrates the outputs from all sandwich Transformers. Line 9 conducts multi-step prediction, and Line 10 updates model parameters. In terms of the computation complexity, the top temporal Transformer has a complexity of $O(LN(S^2d + Sd^2))$, where MHA and FFN in each Transformer layer require $O(S^2d)$ and $O(Sd^2)$ time, respectively, L, N, S, d are the Transformer layers, the number of nodes, the number of steps, and the hidden dimension. Similarly, the spatial Transformer and the bottom temporal Transformer have a complexity of $O(LS(N^2d + Nd^2))$ and $O(LN((S+1)^2d + (S+1)d^2))$, respectively. Thus, the overall computational complexity of one spatial-temporal sandwich Transformer is $O(LN(S^2d + Sd^2) + LS(N^2d + Nd^2) + LN((S+1)^2d + (S+1)d^2))$.

Table 2. Dataset Statistics

Datasets	Sensors	Edges	Timesteps	Time Range
PeMS03	358	547	26,208	09/01/2018–11/30/2018
PeMS04	307	340	16,992	01/01/2018–02/28/2018
PeMS07	883	866	28,224	05/01/2017–08/31/2017
PeMS08	170	295	17,856	07/01/2016–08/31/2016

5   Experiments

In this section, we evaluate the performance of our proposed STGST by comparison with state-of-the-art baselines on public traffic network benchmarks. We aim to answer the following research questions:

– **RQ1.** How does STGST perform in traffic flow prediction tasks?
– **RQ2.** How does each component of STGST contribute to the prediction?
– **RQ3.** How is the learning stability of STGST?
– **RQ4.** How do key hyperparameters impact the model performance?

5.1   Experimental Setup

This section introduces the public datasets for evaluation, baselines for comparison, benchmark settings, and implementation details.

Datasets. We evaluate our model using real-world highway traffic data initially collected by the Caltrans Performance Measurement System (PeMS) [4] in real-time every 30 s. We select four traffic datasets, i.e., PeMS03, PeMS04, PeMS07, and PeMS08, which are released by [17] and have been widely studied in the traffic flow forecasting domain [6,9,10,12,13]. The traffic data, including flow, speed, and occupancy, is aggregated every 5 min, and the Z-score normalization is adopted to standardize the data inputs. The spatial relations are constructed according to the actual road network. Table 2 shows the detailed statistics of each dataset.

Baselines. We evaluate the performance of STGST against three types of state-of-the-art baselines: RNN-based models, convolution-based models, and spatial-temporal graph-based models. These baselines represent different approaches commonly used for traffic flow forecasting. As representatives of the first two categories, we select LSTM [18] and TCN [3], respectively. For the third category, we choose 10 competitive models, i.e., STG2Seq [1], DCRNN [15], STGCN [23], STSGCN [17], ASTGCN [10], AGCRN [2], STFGNN [13], STGODE [9], Z-GCNET [6], and DSTAGNN [12], which have been introduced in the related work section.

Table 3. Performance comparison of STGST and baselines on PeMS datasets. The best and second best results are highlighted in **bold** and underlined, respectively.

Model	PeMS03			PeMS04			PeMS07			PeMS08		
	MAE	MAPE	RMSE	MAE	MAPE	RMSE	MAE	MAPE	RMSE	MAE	MAPE	RMSE
LSTM	21.33	23.33%	35.11	26.77	18.23%	40.65	29.98	13.20%	45.94	23.09	14.99%	35.17
TCN	19.32	19.93%	33.55	23.22	15.59%	37.26	32.72	14.26%	42.23	22.72	14.03%	35.79
STG2Seq	19.03	21.55%	29.73	25.20	18.77%	38.48	32.77	20.16%	47.16	20.17	17.32%	30.71
DCRNN	18.18	18.91%	30.31	24.70	17.12%	38.12	25.30	11.66%	38.58	17.86	11.45%	27.83
STGCN	17.49	17.15%	30.12	22.70	14.59%	35.55	25.38	11.08%	38.78	18.02	11.40%	27.83
STSGCN	17.48	16.78%	29.21	21.19	13.90%	33.65	24.26	10.21%	39.03	17.13	10.96%	26.80
ASTGCN	17.69	19.40%	29.66	22.93	16.56%	35.22	28.05	13.92%	42.57	18.61	13.08%	28.16
AGCRN	15.98	15.23%	28.25	19.83	12.97%	32.26	22.37	9.12%	36.55	15.95	10.09%	25.22
STFGNN	16.77	16.30%	28.34	19.83	13.02%	31.88	22.07	9.21%	35.80	16.64	10.60%	26.22
STGODE	16.50	16.69%	27.84	20.84	13.77%	32.82	22.99	10.14%	37.65	16.81	10.62%	25.97
Z-GCNET	16.64	16.39%	28.15	19.50	12.78%	31.61	21.77	9.25%	35.17	15.76	10.01%	25.11
DSTAGNN	<u>15.57</u>	<u>14.68%</u>	<u>27.21</u>	<u>19.30</u>	<u>12.70%</u>	<u>31.46</u>	<u>21.42</u>	<u>9.01%</u>	<u>34.51</u>	<u>15.67</u>	<u>9.94%</u>	<u>24.77</u>
STGST	**15.22**	**14.44%**	**26.54**	**19.22**	**12.59%**	**31.04**	**20.81**	**8.84%**	**34.33**	**15.25**	**9.78%**	**24.60**
Improv.	2.30%	1.66%	2.52%	0.42%	0.87%	1.35%	2.93%	1.92%	0.52%	2.75%	1.64%	0.69%

Benchmark Settings. To facilitate a fair comparison, we follow the standard benchmark setting in this domain and split each dataset into training, validation, and testing sets with a ratio of 6:2:2 in chronological order. We utilize one-hour historical traffic flow data to perform next-hour flow forecasting, which means leveraging the previous 12 consecutive time steps to predict the subsequent 12 consecutive time steps. To assess the performance, we employ metrics such as the mean absolute error (MAE), mean absolute percentage error (MAPE), and root mean squared error (RMSE).

Implementation Details. STGST is implemented using Python 3.9.13, PyTorch 1.12.1 and DGL (Deep Graph Library) 0.9.1. All experiments are conducted on a Linux server equipped with AMD EPYC 7713 64-Core Processor and NVIDIA Tesla A100 GPU. We set the hidden dimension to 128, the number of attention heads to 8, the dropout rate to 0.1, the number of Transformer layers to 4, and the number of sandwich Transformers to 2. We train STGST for 100 epochs using Adam optimizer with a batch size of 32, a learning rate of 3e-4 and a weight decay of 5e-4. We also set the random seed to 0 for reproducibility.

5.2   Performance Comparison and Analysis (RQ1)

Tables 3 illustrates the averaged forecasting errors of STGST and the 12 baselines over 12 future time steps on PeMS03, PeMS04, PeMS07, and PeMS08 datasets. We observe that spatial-temporal graph models considering both time and space dependencies achieve better performance than sequence models that only capture temporal information, as demonstrated by the comparison between LSTM, TCN and other baselines. This observation confirms the benefit of incorporating spatial dependency in traffic flow forecasting. Additionally, we also

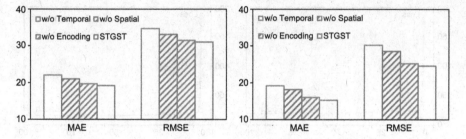

Fig. 2. General comparison of STGST's variants on PeMS04 (left) and PeMS08 (right).

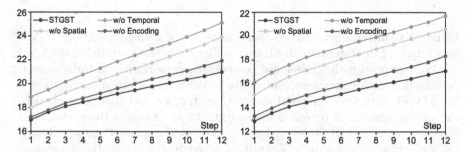

Fig. 3. Per step comparison of STGST's variants on PeMS04 (left) and PeMS08 (right).

find that STGST consistently outperforms all baselines on all datasets in terms of three evaluation metrics. The last row of Table 3 shows the improvement of STGST over the most competitive baseline, i.e., DSTAGNN. On average, STGST has a 2.10%, 1.52%, and 1.27% performance gain over DSTAGNN for MAE, MAPE, and RMSE, respectively. The superior performance of STGST can be attributed to three main factors: the temporal Transformer for capturing long-range temporal dependency, the spatial Transformer for depicting deep spatial dependency, and their sandwich combination for capturing prosperous spatial-temporal interactions.

5.3   Ablation Study (RQ2)

In this section, to verify the contribution of each module of STGST in the prediction task, we prepare three STGST variants as below and conduct ablation studies on PeMS04 and PeMS08 datasets.

- **w/o Temporal** removes two temporal Transformers and adds a average pooling layer to the output of spatial Transformer.
- **w/o Spatial** removes the spatial Transformer module and connects two temporal Transformers directly.
- **w/o Encoding** removes the structure encoding module, i.e., degree encoding and SVD encoding, from spatial Transformer.

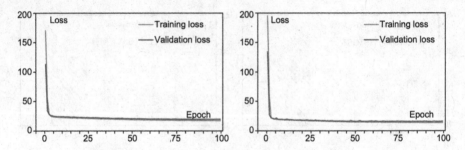

Fig. 4. Training and validation loss of STGST on PeMS04 (left) and PeMS08 (right).

General Comparison. The comparison results of averaged MAE and RMSE over future 12 time steps are illustrated in Fig. 2. As demonstrated in the figure, STGST equipped with all designed components outperforms its three variants, proving that each component contributes to the final performance. By comparing STGST with w/o Temporal and w/o Spatial, we find that ignoring either the spatial domain or temporal domain greatly deteriorates the performance. Moreover, w/o Spatial achieves slightly better performance than w/o Temporal, indicating the advantage of temporal dependency over spatial dependency in traffic flow prediction. In addition, structure encoding in the spatial Transformer helps capture the graph structural information, which can be observed from the results of w/o Encoding and STGST.

Per Step Comparison. Figure 2 provides a summary of the quantitative results obtained from 12 forecasting steps. In order to gain a better understanding of the predictive capability of STGST, this section demonstrates how STGST and its variants perform at each time step. Figure 3 displays the MAE yielded by different models at each forecasting step. It is evident that the prediction error is positively correlated with the forecasting step, with the MAE increasing as the forecasting step increases. We also observe that STGST consistently outperforms its variants at all steps. Moreover, the gap between STGST and its variants progressively widens with increased forecasting step, which proves that STGST is less affected by the forecasting step than other models.

5.4 Learning Stability (RQ3)

This section focuses on investigating the learning stability of STGST on PeMS04 and PeMS08. We plot the training and validation loss curves of STGST on both datasets in Fig. 4. We notice that STGST achieves rapid convergence on both datasets, with the loss steadily decreasing in each epoch after convergence. These findings strongly indicate the stability of STGST's learning process. Furthermore, we observe that the validation loss curve slightly surpasses the training loss curve. This observation suggests that the trained model generalizes well to

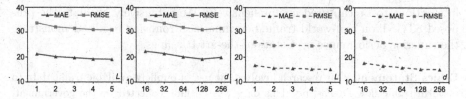

Fig. 5. The effect of model depth L and hidden dimension d on PeMS04 (left two figures with solid lines) and PeMS08 (right two figures with dotted lines).

the validation set, and the learning process avoids encountering overfitting or underfitting phenomena. The consistency between the training and validation loss curves further confirms the stability and reliability of STGST.

5.5 Parameter Sensitivity (RQ4)

We further examine how different choices of hyper-parameters affect the model performance. We vary model depth L (i.e., the number of Transformer layers) from 1 to 5 and hidden embedding dimension d from 16 to 256 to investigate their influence on STGST's performance. The experimental results are shown in Fig. 5, where the left two figures with solid lines and the right two ones with dotted lines are results for PeMS04 and PeMS08, respectively. We observe that STGST is less sensitive with regard to model depth compared to hidden dimension by analyzing the slope of their corresponding curves. With the increased model depth, the performance continually improves, and the best results are achieved on both datasets when model depth equals to 5. However, we set this hyper-parameter to 4 in our experiments since increasing model depth from 4 to 5 only has marginal performance gain but will increase model complexity. In terms of hidden dimension, STGST yields the best performance when it is set to 256 on PeMS08 but 128 on PeMS04. The worse result of 256 dimension on PeMS04 might be because that STGST gets stuck into a local minimum.

6   Conclusion

Traffic flow forecasting has become an essential element in traffic controlling and planning. This paper proposes *spatial-temporal graph sandwich Transformer* (STGST) for traffic flow forecasting. STGST is composed of three modules. The input transformation module projects the time-series input into a high-dimensional feature space. The sandwich Transformer set processes the temporal and spatial dependencies and captures the spatial-temporal interactions. The multi-step prediction module finally maps the hidden representations to the output space. The sandwich Transformer set is the key to STGST. It consists of several spatial-temporal sandwich Transformers, each containing a top temporal Transformer, a bottom temporal Transformer as buns, and a spatial Transformer as meat. Structuring them in a sandwich manner enables the spatial-temporal interactions to be captured comprehensively. We extensively evaluate the proposed STGST on real-world traffic benchmarks. Promising results demonstrate the superior performance over state-of-the-art baselines.

Ethics Statement. Our research involves the use of publicly available traffic data to perform traffic flow forecasting. This data was initially collected by the government. We confirm that all data used in our research is obtained in accordance with relevant laws and regulations, and the data does not contain any personal information, such as identifiable information about individuals or vehicles, and therefore the privacy and confidentiality concerns are minimized. Although the data we are using is already publicly available online, we acknowledge the potential for bias to be introduced into research through a variety of factors, including the location and distribution of traffic sensors.

References

1. Bai, L., Yao, L., Kanhere, S.S., Wang, X., Sheng, Q.Z.: STG2Seq: spatial-temporal graph to sequence model for multi-step passenger demand forecasting. In: International Joint Conference on Artificial Intelligence, pp. 1981–1987 (2019)
2. Bai, L., Yao, L., Li, C., Wang, X., Wang, C.: Adaptive graph convolutional recurrent network for traffic forecasting. In: Advances in Neural Information Processing Systems, vol. 33, pp. 17804–17815 (2020)
3. Bai, S., Kolter, J.Z., Koltun, V.: An empirical evaluation of generic convolutional and recurrent networks for sequence modeling. arXiv preprint arXiv:1803.01271 (2018)
4. Chen, C., Petty, K., Skabardonis, A., Varaiya, P., Jia, Z.: Freeway performance measurement system: mining loop detector data. Transp. Res. Rec. **1748**(1), 96–102 (2001)
5. Chen, M., Wei, Z., Huang, Z., Ding, B., Li, Y.: Simple and deep graph convolutional networks. In: International Conference on Machine Learning, pp. 1725–1735 (2020)
6. Chen, Y., Segovia, I., Gel, Y.R.: Z-gcnets: time zigzags at graph convolutional networks for time series forecasting. In: International Conference on Machine Learning, pp. 1684–1694 (2021)
7. Chung, J., Gulcehre, C., Cho, K., Bengio, Y.: Empirical evaluation of gated recurrent neural networks on sequence modeling. arXiv preprint arXiv:1412.3555 (2014)
8. Devlin, J., Chang, M.W., Lee, K., Toutanova, K.: Bert: pre-training of deep bidirectional transformers for language understanding. arXiv preprint arXiv:1810.04805 (2018)
9. Fang, Z., Long, Q., Song, G., Xie, K.: Spatial-temporal graph ode networks for traffic flow forecasting. In: SIGKDD Conference on Knowledge Discovery and Data Mining, pp. 364–373 (2021)
10. Guo, S., Lin, Y., Feng, N., Song, C., Wan, H.: Attention based spatial-temporal graph convolutional networks for traffic flow forecasting. In: AAAI Conference on Artificial Intelligence, vol. 33, pp. 922–929 (2019)
11. Huber, P.J.: Robust estimation of a location parameter. In: Breakthroughs in Statistics: Methodology and Distribution, pp. 492–518 (1992)
12. Lan, S., Ma, Y., Huang, W., Wang, W., Yang, H., Li, P.: DSTAGNN: dynamic spatial-temporal aware graph neural network for traffic flow forecasting. In: International Conference on Machine Learning, pp. 11906–11917 (2022)

13. Li, M., Zhu, Z.: Spatial-temporal fusion graph neural networks for traffic flow forecasting. In: AAAI Conference on Artificial Intelligence, vol. 35, pp. 4189–4196 (2021)
14. Li, Q., Han, Z., Wu, X.M.: Deeper insights into graph convolutional networks for semi-supervised learning. In: AAAI Conference on Artificial Intelligence, vol. 32, pp. 3538–3545 (2018)
15. Li, Y., Yu, R., Shahabi, C., Liu, Y.: Diffusion convolutional recurrent neural network: data-driven traffic forecasting. In: International Conference on Learning Representations (2018)
16. Min, E., et al.: Transformer for graphs: an overview from architecture perspective. arXiv preprint arXiv:2202.08455 (2022)
17. Song, C., Lin, Y., Guo, S., Wan, H.: Spatial-temporal synchronous graph convolutional networks: a new framework for spatial-temporal network data forecasting. In: AAAI Conference on Artificial Intelligence, vol. 34, pp. 914–921 (2020)
18. Sutskever, I., Vinyals, O., Le, Q.V.: Sequence to sequence learning with neural networks. In: Advances in Neural Information Processing Systems, vol. 27, pp. 3104–3112 (2014)
19. Vaswani, A., et al.: Attention is all you need. In: Advances in Neural Information Processing Systems, vol. 30, pp. 5998–6008 (2017)
20. Williams, B.M., Hoel, L.A.: Modeling and forecasting vehicular traffic flow as a seasonal arima process: theoretical basis and empirical results. J. Transp. Eng. **129**(6), 664–672 (2003)
21. Xu, M., et al.: Spatial-temporal transformer networks for traffic flow forecasting. arXiv preprint arXiv:2001.02908 (2020)
22. Ying, C., et al.: Do transformers really perform badly for graph representation? In: Advances in Neural Information Processing Systems, vol. 34, pp. 28877–28888 (2021)
23. Yu, B., Yin, H., Zhu, Z.: Spatio-temporal graph convolutional networks: a deep learning framework for traffic forecasting. In: International Joint Conference on Artificial Intelligence, pp. 3634–3640 (2018)
24. Zheng, C., Fan, X., Wang, C., Qi, J.: GMAN: a graph multi-attention network for traffic prediction. In: AAAI Conference on Artificial Intelligence, vol. 34, pp. 1234–1241 (2020)
25. Zivot, E., Wang, J.: Vector autoregressive models for multivariate time series. In: Zivot, E., Wang, J. (eds.) Modeling Financial Time Series with S-PLUS®, pp. 385–429. Springer, New York (2006). https://doi.org/10.1007/978-0-387-32348-0_11

Data-Driven Explainable Artificial Intelligence for Energy Efficiency in Short-Sea Shipping

Mohamed Abuella[1]([✉]), M. Amine Atoui[1], Slawomir Nowaczyk[1],
Simon Johansson[2], and Ethan Faghani[2]

[1] Center for Applied Intelligent Systems Research (CAISR), Halmstad University,
30118 Halmstad, Sweden
{mohamed.abuella, amine.atoui,slawomir.nowaczyk}@hh.se
[2] CetaSol AB, 41251 Gothenburg, Sweden
{simon.johansson, ethan.faghani}@cetasol.com

Abstract. The maritime industry is under pressure to increase energy efficiency for climate change mitigation. Navigational data, combining vessel operational and environmental measurements from onboard instruments and external sources, are critical for achieving this goal. Short-sea shipping presents a unique challenge due to the significant influence of surrounding landscape characteristics. With high-resolution onboard data increasingly accessible through IoT devices, appropriate data representations and AI/ML analytical tools are needed for effective decision support. The aim of this study is to investigate the fuel consumption estimation model's role in developing an energy efficiency decision support tool. ML models that lacking explainability may neglect important factors and essential constraints, such as the need to meet arrival time requirements. Onboard weather measurements are compared to external forecasts, and our findings demonstrate the necessity of eXplainable Artificial Intelligence (XAI) techniques for effective decision support. Real-world data from a short-sea passenger vessel in southern Sweden, consisting of 1754 voyages over 15 months (More of data description and code sources of this study can be found in the GitHub repository at https://github.com/MohamedAbuella/ST4EESSS), are used to support our conclusions.

Keywords: Short-sea shipping · Energy efficiency · Explainability · Spatio-temporal aggregation

1 Introduction

Maritime transport of commercial freight is widely considered as one of the most environmentally friendly modes of transportation due to its low emissions of greenhouse gases (GHGs) per unit of capacity and distance traveled. This can result in a reduced carbon footprint and a smaller impact on the global climate, as illustrated in Fig. 1a. Short-Sea Shipping (SSS) represents a mode of commercial transportation that does not involve intercontinental cross-ocean

G. De Francisci Morales et al. (Eds.): ECML PKDD 2023, LNAI 14175, pp. 226–241, 2023.
https://doi.org/10.1007/978-3-031-43430-3_14

travel. SSS provides a cost-effective and eco-friendly alternative by leveraging inland and coastal waterways to transport commercial freight. The statistics presented in Fig. 1b demonstrate the vital role SSS plays in Europe [11].

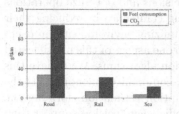
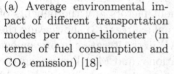

(a) Average environmental impact of different transportation modes per tonne-kilometer (in terms of fuel consumption and CO_2 emission) [18].

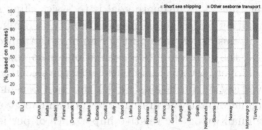

(b) European short-sea shipping of freight versus total sea transport, in 2021 [11].

Fig. 1. The importance of short-sea shipping for Europe.

Despite the advantages of sea transportation for the environment, there remains a significant need to improve the energy efficiency of sea vessels. The SSS continues to produce negative effects on natural habitats and contributes to air pollution along the coasts of populated cities [10]. Therefore, the International Maritime Organization (IMO) has conducted numerous studies, recommended standards, and imposed policies for the maritime sector aimed at reducing carbon dioxide (CO_2) emissions by 40% by 2030 and cut overall GHG emissions by 50% by 2050, compared to the levels from 2008 [6].

Furthermore, the COVID-19 pandemic has accelerated the digitalization of the global shipping industry, drawing significant attention to data collection and preparation stages [8]. Information on select operational and environmental conditions can be obtained from Automatic Identification System (AIS) messages, a service established by the IMO in 2002. AIS was designed to record the sensor measurement data and transmit vessel position information for communication between ships and neighboring shores [13].

While sea transportation boasts a lower carbon footprint compared to other modes of transportation, there is still improvement potential. However, it requires a significant effort to understand and enhance the energy efficiency of sea vessels and how to reduce their negative impact on the environment. One potential approach to achieving this objective is through employing data analytics and Machine Learning (ML) techniques to study vessel operations and quantify the influence of various factors, such as weather and sea conditions, on fuel consumption. This work is a result of collaboration between academia and a Swedish startup company CetaSol AB[1]. CetaSol has developed iHelm, an intelligent digital analytical platform for energy optimization tailored toward small

---

[1] https://cetasol.com/.

and medium-sized vessels. The platform features a data logging and processing unit installed on board and a user interface that provides the captain with relevant visual information and real-time actionable insights for optimal operation. Land-based personnel can access an analytical cloud platform with statistics and reports, enabling them to make informed decisions and optimize operations over time. The ultimate goal is to assist shipping companies in reducing their operating costs, increasing profitability, and minimizing environmental impact.

In this paper, we report our findings related to one aspect of this multifaceted issue: the creation of fuel estimation and prediction algorithms. We believe this work offers several contributions to the scientific community, including: (1) the investigation of various models for fuel consumption estimation, forming the foundation and the first step toward an energy efficiency decision support tool; (2) quantifying the relative importance of pertinent factors and the benefits of data aggregation from various onboard and external sources; (3) showcasing the practical application of eXplainable Artificial (XAI) in the iterative improvement of the ML model, based on real-world considerations; and (4), illustrating the potential to enhance short-sea vessel energy efficiency by employing real-world data from a passenger vessel operating in southern Sweden over a period of 15 months.

With these contributions, our study lays the groundwork for future research in the area. Also, shipping companies can leverage the insights and recommendations presented in this paper. The lessons learned from our experiments will contribute to the optimization of shipping operations and the reduction of adverse environmental effects. Moreover, integrating these innovative insights into upcoming fleet management systems will empower SSS companies to gain a deeper understanding of vessel operations and make well-informed, data-driven decisions to reduce costs. The remainder of the paper is organized as follows: related work is described in Sect. 2. Section 3 introduces the case study and the challenges linked to short-sea shipping. The outcomes of modeling and energy efficiency analysis are covered in Sect. 4. Finally, conclusions and future work are addressed in Sect. 5.

2   Related Work

As digitalization and automation become increasingly prevalent in the maritime sector, the research addressing new challenges has been growing rapidly, particularly with regard to developing frameworks for energy efficiency and Maritime Situational Awareness (MSA) in cross-ocean shipping. On the other hand, the research progress has not kept pace for vessels operating in coastal areas. Thus, this literature review will focus on our primary area of interest, which is research that is related to short-sea shipping.

Recent research studies [9,14] have explored energy-efficient routing for an electric ferry in Western Norway. They rely on operational data from onboard measurements and environmental conditions from the Norwegian Meteorological Institute, interpolated to the nearest temporal and spatial resolutions of the vessel's onboard data. Similarly, the researchers from Napa Ltd. in Finland conducted several studies on voyage optimization, including two cases [12, 20] where environmental conditions were collected from the weather forecasts. Other studies in the literature have also processed environmental data from different weather providers to match the vessel's operational onboard data, as reviewed in [22]. However, such approaches do not account for weather factors that influence both fuel consumption and the Estimated Time of Arrival (ETA), which is a crucial constraint when optimizing the vessel's voyage, especially in SSS.

The maritime industry increasingly adopts digitization and Machine Learning (ML) techniques; however, their black-box nature remains a significant challenge. While ML can provide valuable insights, the reasoning behind the predictions made by such models is often difficult to comprehend due to their lack of explainability. To address this issue, Shapley additive explanations (SHAP) [17] were developed, providing a way to determine the contribution of each input feature toward the model's output. SHAP is commonly used as a solution to the explainability issue in ML. A recent study [16] analyzed feature importance for the power consumption of a chemical tanker. The results indicate that the ship's speed through the water is the most influential feature, while ship heading and other weather features have relatively minor influences. Kim et al. [15] utilized SHAP in combination with an anomaly detection algorithm to detect and interpret anomalies in onboard data from a cargo vessel. It allowed the identification of the specific sensor variable responsible for an anomaly, and SHAP-based clustering was used to interpret and group common anomaly patterns. A validation study for explainability in the maritime time-series data [21] compared two common model-agnostic XAI approaches, SHAP for a global method and LIME as a local method. A literature review on XAI [7] discusses the importance of XAI as a key component in modern AI techniques. The authors present a taxonomy of existing contributions related to the explainability of different machine learning models. Overall, the use and development of ML techniques in the maritime industry requires a careful balance between performance gain and explainability.

3   Case Study Description

Throughout this paper, we will focus on a specific use case of a passenger ferry operating in southern Sweden. The ship's name is Buro, built in 1985, with a carrying capacity of 68 Gross Tonnage, a length of 19 m, and a breadth of 6.41 m. It operates daily passenger traffic between Swedish islands Öckerö, Kalvsund, Framnäs, and Grötö in the Gothenburg archipelago. A single voyage takes approximately 30 min, with an average speed of 8.2 knots (4.2 m/s). The picture of the vessel is provided as in Fig. 2. Additional information about the ship and its voyages can be found on Marine Traffic website [5].

The ship's onboard data have been received using an IoT system designed and developed by CetaSol in Gothenburg, Sweden. The data has been gathered over a period of 15 months, between January 2020 and March 2021. The majority of signals are collected at 3 Hz frequency and record key navigational parameters

Fig. 2. The passenger ship Buro (photo by Owe Johansson [5]) and her diesel engine from Volvo Penta [2].

such as the ship's position, course (direction), and speed; operational parameters such as fuel rate, engine speed, torque, and acceleration; and meteorological data such as apparent and real wind speed and direction.

Additionally, external weather variables such as wave height and speed and direction of both wind and sea current have been collected from external APIs, Copernicus Marine Service [1] and Stormglass [4]. The complete list of available signals is included in the supplementary material[2].

Onboard signals have been resampled from the original 3 Hz frequency to a 1-min time resolution. The external weather data are past forecasts (hindcasts), which have been interpolated from an hourly temporal resolution to a 1-min temporal and a 0.25 to 0.5° spatial resolution. Trilinear interpolation has been applied in time and space dimensions.

3.1   Problem Formulation

From a broad perspective, improving the vessel's energy efficiency for fuel savings and lowering GHG emissions can be done in two stages. The first is during the design, where the shape, materials, and equipment are decided – which is out of the scope of this paper. The second stage is during the ship's operation, both on the water and at ports. The latter, however, is heavily influenced by the former; it is, therefore, challenging to design optimal operation upfront, before fully understanding how each individual vessel behaves [23].

ML-based solutions present an opportunity to leverage domain knowledge and customize it to specific usage patterns and design choices. Our study embraces this approach specifically for short-sea shipping, which exhibits distinct challenges from those encountered in deep-sea shipping.

Continuing with the illustrative case of the Buno passenger ferry, the actual profiles of fuel consumption are illustrated in Fig. 3. In the middle, we showcase (sorted) fuel consumption per voyage on one day, 1st of April 2020. On the left and right, respectively, we show on the map the best and worst voyages, with

---

[2] Due to the limited length of the paper, the complete supplementary material is provided in the GitHub repository at:https://github.com/MohamedAbuella/ST4EESSS.

color-coded speed (upper) and fuel rate (lower). Finally, at the bottom, we show environmental conditions: wind, current, and waves.

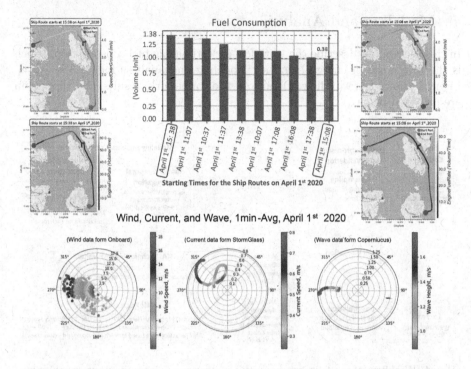

Fig. 3. Vessel's fuel consumption and some navigational data on April 1st, 2020

Notably, the highest fuel consumption voyage started at 15:38; in the final part of the route, Buro is traveling toward the west, against the wind, current and wave directions. This can be compared to the previous voyage, at 15:08, going in the opposite direction – which also happens to be the most fuel-efficient. At the same time, the vessel's speed was also relatively high when traveling westward; in such harsh conditions, the captains tend to overcompensate, unsure about the exact speed profile needed to keep the timetable, and knowing that "catching up" may not be possible due to physical limitations. Thus, at this combination of vessel speed, direction, and weather conditions, the vessel's resistance has increased, leading to 38% higher fuel usage. One can clearly see that the weather impacts fuel consumption significantly, and that there is room for improvement using ML-powered decision support.

In particular, we envision a decision support system that provides a vessel captain with, in real-time, suggestions on the most efficient operation, including vessel trajectory and speed profile. Such a system requires an accurate fuel estimation model capable of counterfactual reasoning, i.e., analyzing the effect a change in speed or direction would have on the overall fuel consumption. By adapting the operation to varying external conditions, the decision support system can thus improve the overall energy efficiency of the vessel.

4   Modeling and Analysis

In this section, we describe the workflow for estimating fuel consumption, which is the first stage of energy efficiency modeling and analysis for an SSS vessel. Figure 4 shows the workflow. Details on the framework, results, and discussion are provided below.

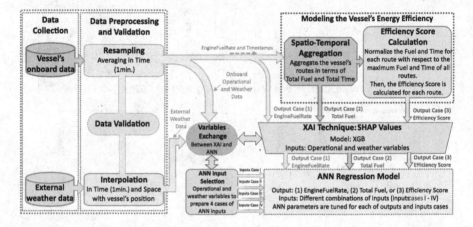

Fig. 4. Workflow of modeling and analysis of energy efficiency in short-sea shipping

4.1   Exploratory Analysis

As a starting point, an Extreme Gradient Boosting (XGBoost) model is initially deployed as a regression model for estimating fuel consumption. The XGBoost model is chosen for its ease of use and minimal need for parameter tuning, making it ideal for exploratory analysis. The navigational variables, as listed in Table 1, are used as inputs to the model. The first model created uses EngineFuelRate directly from onboard data as the regression output, which is the most intuitive case. The initial performance of the model, even without any additional tuning, is relatively good, with an R^2 value of 0.7615.

In the next step, the Shapley additive explanations (SHAP) [17] technique was used, employing the SHAP package, which is publicly available in Python [3]. These SHAP values were used to determine the importance value of each feature to the overall regression accuracy. This highlights the strengths of the XGBoost algorithm since calculating SHAP values for tree-based models is relatively fast compared to many other regression approaches. However, during this stage, a

Table 1. The navigational variables and their data sources.

Variable	Name	Source	Variable	Name	Source
Vo_1	Latitude	Onboard	Vc_1	WindSpeed_cps	Copernicus
Vo_2	Longitude	Onboard	Vc_2	WindDirection_cps	Copernicus
Vo_3	SpeedOverGround	Onboard	Vc_3	WaveHeight	Copernicus
Vo_4	HeadingMagnetic	Onboard	Vc_4	WaveDirection	Copernicus
Vo_5	Pitch	Onboard	Vs_1	WindSpeed_sg	Stormglass
Vo_6	Roll	Onboard	Vs_2	WindDirection_sg	Stormglass
Vo_7	WindSpeed_onb	Onboard	Vs_3	CurrentSpeed	Stormglass
Vo_8	WindDirection_onb	Onboard	Vs_4	CurrentDirection	Stormglass

significant issue was observed with the initial model. The vessel's motion (kinematics) variables such as SpeedOverGround, Pitch, and HeadingMagnetic (direction), were found to be more significant in determining fuel consumption compared to factors such as weather variability.

Figure 5 depicts Beeswarm plots for Shapley values for the XGBoost model, considering the three output cases investigated in this section. The SHAP values are used to determine the contribution of features to the regression model and are often visualized using such beeswarm plots. Ranking features based on their SHAP values allows interpreting how the changes in feature values affect the model estimations.

In the case of the first model, predicting EngineFuelRate, depicted in the top-left of Fig. 5, vessel kinematics were found to be the primary drivers. While such a model may be suitable for explanatory analysis, it cannot be used for optimization and counterfactual estimations.

Therefore, the insights gained from XAI and SHAP values indicate the need to change our approach. Relying solely on the R^2 score is not sufficient in evaluating the usefulness of a regression model. We require a model that is less dependent on kinematics and considers weather variables as more impactful. SHAP values, as an explainable AI tool, enable us to gain more insights into the weaknesses of the developed fuel consumption model and guide future improvements.

To address the limitations of the initial model, and based on the insights obtained, the second model uses an aggregated output of Total Fuel for the entire voyage, instead of instantaneous EngineFuelRate. The performance of the Total Fuel model is similar and also relatively good, with an R^2 value of 0.8400. on the other hand, the SHAP values reveal that weather variables, particularly the waves and the wind from external sources, are much more important. This model is much better at capturing their causal relationships with fuel consumption.

The SHAP values reveal that the second model is more suitable for energy efficiency analysis since it captures known causes for high or low fuel consumption, making it more useful for counterfactual reasoning. This model can answer

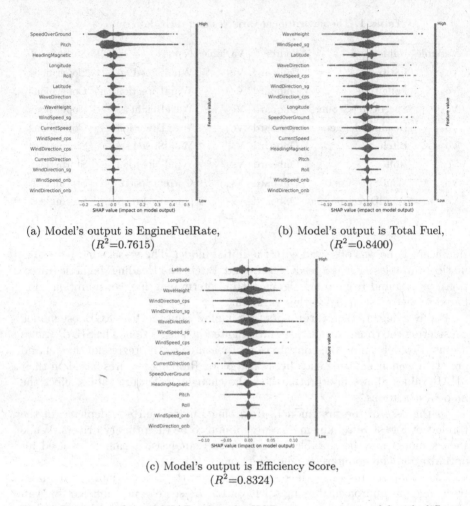

(a) Model's output is EngineFuelRate,
(R^2=0.7615)

(b) Model's output is Total Fuel,
(R^2=0.8400)

(c) Model's output is Efficiency Score,
(R^2=0.8324)

Fig. 5. Beeswarm plots of SHAP values for XGBoost regression model with different outputs

questions like "what would be the effect of changing the speed profile on a particular voyage," which the first model cannot. At the same time, an issue remains that prevents it from being practical as a part of an energy efficiency decision support tool. This issue arises from the strong relationship between fuel consumption and vessel speed, as illustrated in Fig. 6. The trend indicates that higher cruising speeds result in higher fuel consumption. As a result, if this model is used as part of a speed profile optimization tool, it will likely recommend only one solution: to lower the speed. While a correct decision from a pure fuel perspective, it is not practical since the ferry must keep its timetable.

To address the practical limitations of the second model, we introduce a new metric called the Efficiency Score. This metric aims to balance fuel consumption

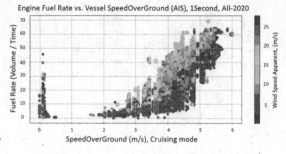

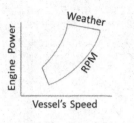

(a) Theoretical analysis of sea vessel's engine operation.

(b) Vessel Buro's actual engine performance.

Fig. 6. A fuel efficiency curve: how the fuel consumption varies as a function of speed.

and time of arrival, two critical factors in determining energy efficiency for SSS vessels. Only by considering both factors together, can we represent the vessel's overall energy efficiency. The efficiency Score is defined as follows:

$$\text{Eff}_{\text{Score}} = 1 - \frac{2 \times Fuel \times Time}{Fuel + Time}, \tag{1}$$

where $Fuel$ and $Time$ are the normalized total fuel and time, respectively, for each route of the vessel. The accumulated fuel is derived from the raw onboard EngineFuelRate data, while the accumulated time is based on the SpeedOver-Ground measurements and the distance traveled. The distance between two points is calculated using the Haversine formula [19], which takes into account the Earth's spherical shape.

Figure 7 illustrates the spatio-temporal aggregation for the vessel's routes. First, in Fig. 7a, we show the routes in spatial dimensions (latitude and longitude). Next, we project these routes as aggregated Efficiency Scores onto new dimensions of fuel and time Fig. 7b. The plot confirms the Efficiency Score correctly captures the original intuition, with voyages that have lower fuel and shorter time having higher Efficiency Scores, and vice versa.

As a result, in our final regression model, we use the Efficiency Score as the output variable, reaching R^2 score of 0.8324. The corresponding SHAP values plot, shown at the bottom of Fig. 5, indicated that spatial variables, namely latitude and longitude, are the most important factors in estimating fuel consumption over time. The model also suggests a causal relationship between fuel consumption and weather variables, with external weather variables being more significant than vessel motion.

4.2   Optimizing the Model

After completing the exploratory analysis, we aim to optimize the performance of the model by switching from XGBoost to Artificial Neural Networks (ANN).

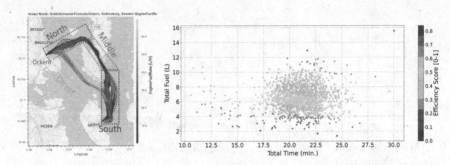

(a) The vessel routes are (b) The routes are projected by aggregated Efficiency mapped by latitude and lon- Score in dimensions of fuel and time. gitude.

Fig. 7. The vessel routes and their projections as Efficiency Scores.

Table 2. Description of the four input cases of ANN.

Inputs Case	Operational Variables	Weather Variables	
		onboard data	external sources
I	Vessel's location, speed, and direction are used for all cases	wind	—
II		—	wind, wave, and current
III		wind	wave and current
IV		wind	wind, wave, and current

Through several experiments involving the various relevant combinations of navigational variables, as depicted in the workflow diagram in Fig. 4, we obtain models with higher performance than XGBoost, albeit at the cost of increased computational complexity.

The first step in optimizing the model is to identify the best set of input parameters. We consider four cases of ANN inputs, where each case consists of different combinations of operational and weather variables. Further details about these ANN input cases are provided in Tables 2 and 3. It is worth noting that some operational variables, such as pitch and roll, are highly correlated and primarily depend on the vessel's speed and weather conditions. Therefore, we have excluded such inputs from our ANN models. In general, the vessel's speed and direction are the most important control variables used to improve energy efficiency.

According to the workflow in Fig. 4, we consider the same output cases for the ANN models as we did for XGBoost: EngineFuelRate, Total Fuel, and Efficiency Score. We optimize the structure of the ANN models using a grid search approach, considering the four different input cases and three output cases, resulting

Table 3. Combinations of variables that are used in the four input cases of ANN. The names and sources of these variables can be found in Table 1.

Inputs Case	# Inputs	List of Inputs
I	6	Vo_1, Vo_2, Vo_3, Vo_4, Vo_7, Vo_8
II	12	Vo_1, Vo_2, Vo_3, Vo_4, Vc_1, Vc_2, Vc_3, Vc_4, Vs_1, Vs_2, Vs_3, Vs_4
III	10	Vo_1, Vo_2, Vo_3, Vo_4, Vo_7, Vo_8, Vc_3, Vc_4, Vs_3, Vs_4
IV	14	Vo_1, Vo_2, Vo_3, Vo_4, Vo_7, Vo_8, Vc_1, Vc_2, Vc_3, Vc_4, Vs_1, Vs_2, Vs_3, Vs_4

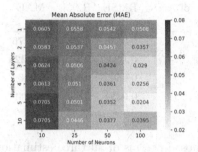
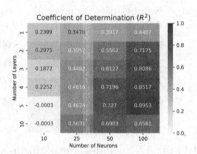

(a) Results in MAE for ANN Structure Search (b) Results in R^2 for ANN Structure Search

Fig. 8. Grid search results for the best ANN structure, with Efficiency Score output.

in twelve ANN models being tuned separately. To measure the estimation accuracy of the different ANN models, we adopt three metrics: root mean squared error (RMSE), mean absolute error (MAE), and the coefficient of determination (R^2).

The heatmaps in Fig. 8 show that the best ANN structure for the Efficiency Score model is achieved with 100 neurons and 5 layers, as it results in the lowest value of MAE and the highest value of R^2. These heatmaps also show that the model's performance is sensitive to changes in the hyperparameters, indicating the importance of carefully tuning the ANN model to achieve optimal results.

Tables 4, 5, and 6 present the results of all twelve ANN regression models. The fourth case of inputs (IV), which considers operational and weather variables from onboard and external sources, led to the best performance (i.e., $R^2 = 0.8088$ and $MAE = 0.0516$) for estimating EngineFuelRate, as shown in Table 4.

On the other hand, for estimating both Total Fuel and Efficiency Score, the best is the combination of inputs for case (II), including the weather variables only from external sources. The former achieves $R^2 = 0.9170$ and $MAE = 0.0221$, as shown in Table 5, and the latter $R^2 = 0.8953$ and $MAE = 0.0204$ (Table 6).

Table 4. Results of ANN with EngineFuelRate output, for different input cases.

Input Cases	Number of ANN Inputs	Number of ANN Layers	Number of ANN Neurons	RMSE	R2	MAE
I	6	10	100	0.0852	0.7153	0.0631
II	12	4	100	0.0730	0.7909	0.0544
III	10	5	100	0.0714	0.8001	0.0531
IV	14	4	100	**0.0698**	**0.8088**	**0.0516**

Table 5. Results of ANN with Total Fuel output, for different input cases.

Input Cases	Number of ANN Inputs	Number of ANN Layers	Number of ANN Neurons	RMSE	R2	MAE
I	6	4	100	0.0980	0.2074	0.0776
II	12	5	100	**0.0317**	**0.9170**	**0.0221**
III	10	5	100	0.0562	0.7398	0.0409
IV	14	5	100	0.0351	0.8986	0.0249

Overall, ANN models outperform XGBoost in terms of all three estimation metrics across all three outputs. At the same time, the results clearly demonstrate the importance of incorporating external weather forecasting sources – the onboard weather information is not sufficient.

The accuracy of the Total Fuel and Efficiency Score models is higher compared to the EngineFuelRate model's estimation. The Total Fuel model yields the highest accuracy, whereas the Efficiency Score model, which takes into account the total time of the vessel's routes, only shows a slight difference.

4.3 Exploiting the Model

The Beeswarm plot in Fig. 5c indicates that the vessel's location has the most significant impact on the Efficiency Score. Therefore, a spatial analysis was conducted to identify the impact of various combinations of operational and weather variables on the Efficiency Score concerning the vessel's location.

As shown in Fig. 7a, we partitioned the vessel's typical route into four distinct sections, namely North, Middle, South, and Direct. The impact of operational and weather combinations on fuel consumption varies in these sections.

The results are shown as heatmaps in Fig. 9, revealing that the direct route from south to north or vice versa, located on the open sea, is particularly susceptible to the impact of weather conditions. Thus, for this direct section of vessel routes, the estimation of Efficiency Score, as shown in Fig. 9b, has the highest accuracy with different inputs combinations.

Meanwhile, in the north section, where strong either head or tail wind is more frequent (in this area, west winds dominate) with respect to the vessel route, the Efficiency Score estimation has the second highest accuracy, as in Fig. 9b.

Table 6. Results of ANN with Efficiency Score output, for different input cases.

Input Cases	Number of ANN Inputs	Number of ANN Layers	Number of ANN Neurons	RMSE	R2	MAE
I	6	3	50	0.0807	0.1886	0.0634
II	12	5	100	**0.0290**	**0.8953**	**0.0204**
III	10	4	100	0.0564	0.6037	0.0431
IV	14	5	100	•	0.0363	0.8361	0.0267

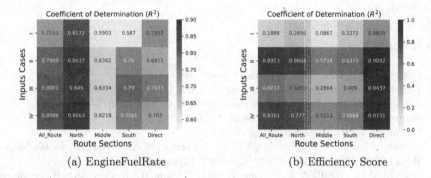

(a) EngineFuelRate   (b) Efficiency Score

Fig. 9. Results (R^2) for ANN regression with EngineFuelRate and Efficiency Score as outputs across different input cases in relation to varying vessel's route sections.

In the other case, when it comes to estimating EngineFuelRate, as shown in Fig. 9a, the results are not accurate. For instance, the direct sections of the route are not achieving the highest accuracy, even though they are supposed to experience more weather conditions than other sections due to these sections being the most similar to an open sea.

5   Conclusion

By using a practical real-world example of a small passenger vessel, this paper showcases how XAI with ML techniques can facilitate decision-making. In this case, we analyze the process of developing a fuel estimation module, which is a crucial component of the vessel's energy efficiency decision support tool. The outcomes presented in this paper have the potential to enhance operation and energy management in short-sea shipping.

Based on the discussed results, it is evident that the proposed approach of aggregating data and estimating the Efficiency Score, instead of directly working with the EngineFuelRate onboard signal, is more effective in facilitating decision-making. The resulting model is based on a more comprehensive understanding of the critical factors that impact fuel consumption, both temporally and spatially, resulting in more dependable counterfactual predictions. Moreover, the quantitative evaluation indicates that estimating the Efficiency Score produces more precise and less biased outcomes than estimating the measured EngineFuelRate.

Moving forward, the developed model will be integrated with the vessel's energy optimization framework to provide decision support to captains on suitable trajectories and speed profiles based on current and forecasted weather conditions, thereby enhancing energy efficiency. Real-world implementation and the evaluation of its value for short-sea shipping are planned in the near future.

Acknowledgments. This research project is funded by Sweden's innovation agency (Vinnova).

References

1. Copernicus Marine Service. https://marine.copernicus.eu
2. Engine Volvo Penta tier13 A2022 8398. https://www.volvopenta.com/about-us/news-page/2022/jun/imo-tier-iii-range-expands-with-new-d13-solutions/
3. Shap package. https://github.com/slundberg/shap
4. StormGlass API. https://stormglass.io
5. Marine Traffic (2022). https://www.marinetraffic.com/en/ais/details/ships/shipid:1088282/mmsi:265513810/imo:8602713/vessel:BURO
6. Ampah, J.D., Yusuf, A.A., Afrane, S., Jin, C., Liu, H.: Reviewing two decades of cleaner alternative marine fuels: towards IMO's decarbonization of the maritime transport sector. J. Clean. Prod. **320**, 128871 (2021)
7. Arrieta, A.B., et al.: Explainable artificial intelligence (XAI): concepts, taxonomies, opportunities and challenges toward responsible AI. Inf. Fusion **58**, 82–115 (2020)
8. Bank, W.: Accelerating Digitalization: Critical Actions to Strengthen the Resilience of the Maritime Supply Chain. World Bank, Washington (2020)
9. Bellingmo, P.R., Pobitzer, A., Jørgensen, U., Berge, S.P.: Energy efficient and safe ship routing using machine learning techniques on operational and weather data. In: 20th International Conference on Computer Applications and Information Technology in the Maritime Industries (2021)
10. Donner, P., Johansson, T.: Sulphur directive, short sea shipping and corporate social responsibility in a EU context. In: Corporate Social Responsibility in the Maritime Industry, pp. 149–166 (2018)
11. Eurostat: Short sea shipping - country level - gross weight of goods transported to/from main ports (2023). https://ec.europa.eu/eurostat/databrowser/view/mar_sg_am_cw/default/table?lang=en
12. Haranen, M., Myöhänen, S., Cristea, D.S.: The role of accurate now-cast data in shi p efficiency analysis. In: 2nd Hull Performance & Insight Conference, pp. 25–38 (2017)
13. Fourth IMO GHG study 2020 (2020)
14. Jørgensen, U., Belingmo, P.R., Murray, B., Berge, S.P., Pobitzer, A.: Ship route optimization using hybrid physics-guided machine learning. In: Journal of Physics: Conference Series, vol. 2311, p. 012037. IOP Publishing (2022)
15. Kim, D., Antariksa, G., Handayani, M.P., Lee, S., Lee, J.: Explainable anomaly detection framework for maritime main engine sensor data. Sensors **21**(15), 5200 (2021)
16. Lang, X., Wu, D., Mao, W.: Comparison of supervised machine learning methods to predict ship propulsion power at sea. Ocean Eng. **245**, 110387 (2022)

17. Lundberg, S.M., Lee, S.I.: A unified approach to interpreting model predictions. In: Advances in Neural Information Processing Systems, vol. 30 (2017)
18. Medda, F., Trujillo, L.: Short-sea shipping: an analysis of its determinants. Maritime Policy Manag. **37**(3), 285–303 (2010)
19. Sinnott, R.W.: Virtues of the haversine. Sky Telescope **68**(2), 158 (1984)
20. Sugimoto, K.: Digital twin for monitoring remaining fatigue life of critical hull structures
21. Veerappa, M., Anneken, M., Burkart, N., Huber, M.F.: Validation of XAI explanations for multivariate time series classification in the maritime domain. J. Comput. Sci. **58**, 101539 (2022)
22. Zakaria, A., Md Arof, A., Khabir, A.: Instruments utilized in short sea shipping research: a review. In: Ismail, A., Dahalan, W.M., Öchsner, A. (eds.) Design in Maritime Engineering, pp. 83–108. Springer, Cham (2022). https://doi.org/10.1007/978-3-030-89988-2_7
23. Zis, T.P., Psaraftis, H.N., Ding, L.: Ship weather routing: a taxonomy and survey. Ocean Eng. **213**, 107697 (2020)

Multivariate Time-Series Anomaly Detection with Temporal Self-supervision and Graphs: Application to Vehicle Failure Prediction

Hadi Hojjati[1,2]([✉]), Mohammadreza Sadeghi[1,2], and Narges Armanfard[1,2]

[1] Department of Electrical and Computer Engineering, McGill University, Montreal, Canada
{hadi.hojjati,mohammadreza.sadeghi,narges.armanfard}@mcgill.ca
[2] MILA - Quebec AI Institute, Montreal, Canada

Abstract. Failure prediction is key to ensuring the reliable operation of vehicles, especially for organizations that depend on a fleet of vehicles. However, traditional approaches often rely on rule-based or heuristic methods that may not be effective in detecting subtle anomalies, rare events, or in more modern vehicles containing a complex sensory network. This paper presents a novel approach to vehicle failure prediction, called mVSG-VFP, which employs self-supervised learning and graph-based techniques. The proposed method realizes the failure prediction task by exploring information hidden in the time-series data recorded through the sensors embedded in the vehicle. mVSG-VFP includes two main components: a graph-based autoencoder that learns representations of normal data while considering the relationship between different sensors and a self-supervised component that maps temporally-adjacent data to similar representations. We propose a novel approach to define the notion of adjacency in vehicle temporal data.

To evaluate mVSG-VFP, we apply it to a dataset comprised of vehicle sensor recordings to identify the abnormal data samples that signal a potential future failure. We performed a flurry of experiments to verify the accuracy of our model and demonstrate it outperforms state-of-the-art models in this task. Overall, the method is robust and intuitive, making it a useful tool for real-world applications.

Keywords: Self-Supervised Learning · Failure Prediction · Time-Series Anomaly Detection · Graph Neural Networks · Predictive Maintenance

1 Introduction

Failure prediction is a crucial aspect of modern predictive maintenance systems in transportation, as it helps to prevent unexpected breakdowns and costly repairs [1, 36]. Modern vehicles are equipped with complex sensory networks,

G. De Francisci Morales et al. (Eds.): ECML PKDD 2023, LNAI 14175, pp. 242–259, 2023.
https://doi.org/10.1007/978-3-031-43430-3_15

which are helpful for the early detection of malfunctioning subsystems before they harm other parts of the vehicle. However, analyzing the sheer volume of sensor data is not feasible for a technician. Therefore, an automated framework is needed to extract relevant information from the data efficiently and objectively. One promising approach to achieving this goal is through deep anomaly detection, a family of machine learning algorithms tailored to detect irregular data patterns [30].

1.1 Problem Statement

Vehicles' sensors commonly output the data as multivariate time series, i.e. a set of sequentially recorded points from different sources. Detecting anomalies in such data is highly challenging for several reasons: First, time-series data can be complex, non-stationary and high-dimensional, making it difficult to identify meaningful patterns [9]. Additionally, distinguishing anomalies from variations in driving patterns or weather and road conditions is an arduous task in time series. Furthermore, capturing the temporal relationship in the data is a complex job, particularly since the length of the recordings is variable, and that they are not continuously recorded. Machine learning models, particularly deep learning algorithms, have helped design efficient algorithms that can address part of these challenges. However, most existing methods suffer from four crucial drawbacks [10]: I) they do not consider the inter-relationship between different sensors; therefore, their application is limited to cases in which anomalies can be easily identified by analyzing the data of individual sensors, which is not the case in complex systems such as a vehicle; II) since the time series recording are commonly very long, the models need to split the data into smaller partitions hence losing the long-term temporal relationships; III) most of the existing methods are not capable of identifying the abnormal sensor and they can only perform system-level anomaly detection; IV) most state-of-the-art algorithms define their anomaly score based on a single data point in the time series. However, time series are commonly contaminated with noise, making the sample-based anomaly scores unreliable, causing performance underestimation. To handle this matter, rather than defining a proper anomaly score, they use a biased evaluation protocol – more specifically, they label the whole data points within a segment of time series as abnormal even if only one data point is abnormal. Such relabeling causes a performance overestimation [23].

1.2 Addressing the Challenges: Our Methodology

Very recently, several studies have revisited the existing deep time-series anomaly detection models more closely and concluded that most of them cannot perform better than simple baselines [11, 23]. According to these papers, confirmed by our own experiments, a combination of simple benchmark datasets and biased evaluation metrics has led to the illusion of progress in this field, and the majority of existing algorithms fail in more challenging datasets if an unbiased evaluation protocol is used [11]. One of the very few exceptions was graph-based methods, which could outperform other baselines in these scenarios [10,23]. Inspired by these findings, in this paper, we develop a graph-based model for tackling the problem of vehicle failure prediction. By representing the data as a graph, we can capture the complex relationships between components, allowing us to detect subtle changes that existing anomaly detection methods may miss [8,40].

To develop a system that can better identify abnormal sensors, we utilize a generative approach wherein we mask one sensor at a time and encourage the model to reconstruct it. In a model trained in this fashion, if it faces a normal sample during inference, we expect it to still have a small reconstruction error. Thus, we can leverage the reconstruction error to detect abnormal sensors [16].

Similar to other machine learning algorithms, graph-based models cannot process long sequences due to memory and computational constraints [10]. Therefore, it is a common practice in the literature to split the data into smaller windows and treat each partition as a single sample when feeding them to the network [28]. As a result of such partitioning, the model ignores the long-term dependencies between adjacent partitions as the partitions are treated as independent and identically distributed (IID) samples during training. This is an undesirable property which limits the performance of models. To overcome this barrier, we leverage the recent progress in self-supervised learning and the unique properties of our dataset to propose a novel and ground-breaking solution. Our idea is based on the notion of contrastive learning – more specifically the proposed maps the adjacent partitions into similar representations. By doing so, the model learns to extract meaningful and discriminative features that can be used for a wide range of downstream tasks [6,15]. Contrastive learning has gained popularity in recent years, particularly in the field of computer vision, where it has achieved state-of-the-art results in tasks such as image recognition and object detection [6]. However, its application in time-series analysis is underexplored mainly because of the fact that it is extremely difficult to define positive and negative pairs in time series [20]. Our method leverages a unique characteristic of vehicle data to overcome this challenge; the data that are recorded during one trip[1] of the vehicle are more similar compared to those that are produced during another trip; e.g. the driver, weather, road, and load conditions are more probably the same during one vehicle trip. Our model uses this unique vehicle data property to learn a better representation of the data. In this paper, we refer to the data recorded in one vehicle trip as *Block*. The Block size varies with the trip duration. We partition each Block into fixed-length time series; these sub-Blocks are referred to as *Segment* throughout this paper. In general, a Block is usually comprised of several data Segments.

Contribution: We can summarize the main contributions of our work as follows:

1. This is the first study that proposes an effective deep learning framework designed based on the unique properties of the vehicle failure prediction task.

---

[1] We define a trip as a continuous recording of sensors in which the engine is not turned off for more than 5 min.

2. This is the first study on multivariate time-series analysis that can effectively capture the long-term dependencies within and across time series.
3. We realized the proposed idea through the concepts of graphs, contrastive, and generative learnings.
4. In addition to the vehicle-level failure prediction, the proposed method is capable of identifying faulty sensors. This makes the model more interpretable and helps technicians fix the vehicle.
5. As opposed to the other time-series anomaly detection methods that provide an anomaly score based on individual timestamps and a biased protocol, our proposed method directly outputs the segment anomaly score, and we use them to determine if the whole block is anomalous.
6. We demonstrate the effectiveness of the proposed method on a real-world dataset for early engine failure prediction. The proposed method significantly outperforms all existing and SOTA time-series anomaly detection methods in Precision, Recall, and F1 score on average by 11.2%, 0.8% and 7.4%.

2 Related Works

2.1 Vehicle Predictive Maintenance with Machine Learning

Machine learning (ML) has been applied to predictive vehicle maintenance to improve the accuracy of detecting potential vehicle failures and reduce maintenance costs [36]. However, there are still challenges to overcome, such as data quality and availability, the interpretability of the machine learning models, and the need for collaboration between domain experts and data scientists. Machine learning algorithms can analyze sensor data from vehicles to detect anomalies and diagnose faults. In an early attempt, Wang et al. [37] leveraged the vibration signals and a neural network to detect engine and fuel injection system failure. A similar study by Wong et al. [39] proposed a supervised method based on the ensemble of Bayesian extreme learning machines (BELMs) [32] to detect engine faults. In another recent work, Wolf et al. [38] used the data of electric control units (ECU) as the input to a customized deep learning model comprised of Convolutional Neural Networks (CNNs) [25] and Long short-term memory (LSTM) [17] to detect faults in turbocharged engines. Besides engine fault detection, machine learning has been extensively used for failure prediction and diagnosis in other vehicle subsystems. For instance, Rengasamy et al. [29] used CNNs to detect faults in the air pressure system of heavy trucks. Recent progress in the design of autonomous vehicles has also led to the development of innovative failure prediction frameworks. Jeong et al. [21] leveraged the IoT infrastructure of autonomous vehicles to design a predictive maintenance model using neural networks. In another work, van Wyk et al. [41] leveraged CNN and anomaly detection methods to identify anomalies in automated vehicles.

2.2 Time-Series Anomaly Detection

Time-series anomaly detection is a longstanding problem in various fields, such as finance [2], healthcare [14], cybersecurity [3], and industrial maintenance [4].

Before the introduction of machine learning algorithms, linear models such as the autoregressive integrated moving average (ARIMA) [42] were used for modelling and anomaly detection in time series. These models could identify linear patterns in the stationary data but failed to generalize to more complex data.

Following the unprecedented success of machine learning and deep learning algorithms, researchers have started to leverage them for designing effective anomaly detection frameworks for time series. In early attempts, generic anomaly detection algorithms such as Autoencoders (AEs) were applied to time series, ignoring their temporal and spatial relationships [13,18]. With the introduction of RNNs and their variants for handling temporal data, methods such as LSTM-AE [33] and OmniAnomaly [34] were developed. Recently, transformers became state-of-the-art in analyzing sequential data, and successful methods such as Anomaly Transformers were designed based on them [28]. All mentioned models have shown promising results on common time-series anomaly detection benchmarks. However, recent studies have cast a shadow of doubt over their generalizability power. They have shown that the performance of deep time-series models is not necessarily better than traditional or, in some cases, random baselines, and the superior performance that some papers have reported can be attributed to other factors, such as incorrect evaluation procedures and inappropriate benchmark detests. Thus, most of the recent progress in deep time-series anomaly detection is not practical for many real-life applications [11,23,26].

Recently, graph-based models became the new research trend for anomaly detection. Graph-based models can effectively handle these relationships and dependencies by modelling the data as a graph, where the nodes represent the different sensors and the edges represent the relationships between them. Based on this idea, several graph-based time series anomaly detection methods have been proposed [10,43,44]. MTAD-GAT, proposed by Zhao et al. [44], was one of the early methods that used two Graph Attention Networks (GAT) [?] to model the relationship between sensors as well as the temporal data. They trained the model to reconstruct and forecast the normal data simultaneously and defined the anomaly score based on reconstruction and prediction errors. In another similar work, Deng and Hooi [10] proposed GDN, which learns the relationship between different sensors and employs GAT for fitting a forecasting model on normal data. In a recent work, DVGCRN [7], authors used Variational AEs [24] to improve the performance of their model. They jointly modelled the stochastic relationship between different sensors and the multi-level temporal dependencies in each sensor. Generative adversarial networks (GANs) [12] have also shown remarkable improvements when combined with graph-based algorithms. For instance, HAD-MDGAT [45] combines GAN with graph attention networks to simultaneously learn the temporal and spatial relationship between sensors. Another popular direction in the field is modelling the density of normal data using normalizing flows and graph neural networks. Graph-augmented Normalizing Flow (GANF) [8] is proposed based on this idea and learns the density of normal data via factorizing its density and a graph encoder. Anomalies can then be detected as points that lie in low-probability regions.

Parallel to the graph-based models, research in developing contrastive learning methods for anomaly detection also gained momentum [20]. Lately, researchers such as Tack et al. [35], and Li et al. [27] have shown that self-supervision can significantly boost anomaly detection performance on images. Since then, most research has been focused on visual anomaly detection [20]. Recently, a few studies attempted to apply these methods to other data types, such as audio [19] and brain signals [16] Ho and Armanfard [16] proposed a method for anomaly detection in brain signals using graphs and self-supervision. However, the method is based on the spatial distance between the sensors, which is not applicable to vehicle data since the spatial configuration of the vehicle sensor does not bear meaningful information about their relationship.

Both Graph-based and self-supervised anomaly detection is a relatively young research field, and there is no surprise that the aforementioned algorithms are not thoroughly investigated in the context of real-world applications. In this paper, we aim to take a step toward filling this research gap by proposing a self-supervised graph-based method which is suitable for vehicle failure prediction applications.

3 Proposed Model

Our model aims to detect anomalies in a multivariate time series at entity and sensor levels after training on normal data. The data is commonly a very long time series. To be able to process it, we use a sliding window of size L and stride length m to generate fixed-size Segments. After windowing, the input to our model is a Segmented multivariate time series dataset denoted by $X \in \mathbb{R}^{N \times L \times (K+1)}$, where N is the number of Segments in a mini-batch, L is the window size, and K is the number of sensors. One additional column also denotes the Block ID of the data points. The algorithm produces a vector $y \in \mathbb{R}^N$ where $y_i \in \{0, 1\}$ denotes the true anomaly score of the ith sample, in which 0 denotes normal condition, and 1 is an abnormality which can signal the failure.

Figure 1 shows an overview of our method. In summary, our method is comprised of the following components:

1. First, we use a sliding window to generate fixed-length Segments from the time series and preprocess them. We then construct a feature vector from each Segment. We build mini-batches from the data and augment them.
2. Several GAT layers then process the data. Each sensor represents a node in the graph and is associated with its feature vector. The GAT layers GNN_e map the features into a lower-dimensional representation, and another stack of GAT layers GNN_d tries to reconstruct them.
3. A contrastive loss is applied to the latent space to pull the Segments with the same Block ID closer and push them away from the rest of the batch.
4. Parallel to the above steps, we stochastically mask the data of one sensor and try to generate the data of the affected sensor. We call this self-supervised task the *generative* task.

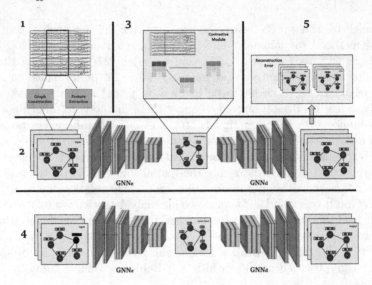

Fig. 1. Overview of the proposed method and its modules.

5. The anomaly score is defined as a combination of the reconstruction error and a score to quantify how accurately the model solves the generative task.

3.1 Data Preprocessing and Feature Construction

As discussed earlier, we Segment the Blocks using a sliding window of size L and stride length of m. To improve the robustness and follow the state-of-the-art literature [10,28], we normalize each Segment with the maximum and minimum values of the training set as follows:

$$\tilde{x}_i = \frac{x_i - \min(X_{\text{train}})}{\max(X_{\text{train}}) - \min(X_{\text{train}})} \tag{1}$$

where x_i is the i-th sample, X_{train} is the set of all training samples and $\min(.)$ and $\max(.)$ represent the minimum and maximum functions, respectively. Then, from each sensor's normalized data, we extract a fixed-length feature vector v_i using a feature extractor $v_i = R(\tilde{x}_i)^2$.

3.2 Graph Autoencoder

We represent the data as a graph structure to consider the relationship between sensors. In this graph, the nodes represent sensors, and the edges denote their relationship. If an edge exists between two sensors, it indicates that they are useful for modelling the behaviour of each other. We represent the edges using

---

[2] Here $R(.)$ can be any feature extraction function, including predefined feature extraction functions as well as trainable neural networks.

an adjacency matrix $\mathcal{A}$, where $\mathcal{A}_{ij} = 1$ if there is an edge between the ith and j^{th} sensors. This adjacency matrix can be built by incorporating prior knowledge about sensor relationships or by using a dependency measure between the sensors. In this work, we use a data-driven approach and build the adjacency matrix based on mutual information (MI). MI is a measure of the statistical dependence between two random variables $\mathcal{X}$ and $\mathcal{Y}$ and can be calculated as:

$$I(\mathcal{X}; \mathcal{Y}) = \sum_{x \in \mathcal{X}} \sum_{y \in \mathcal{Y}} P(x, y) \log(\frac{P(x, y)}{P(x)P(y)}) \tag{2}$$

where $P(x, y)$ is the joint probability between x and y and $P(x)$ and $P(y)$ are marginal probabilities of x and y, respectively. In the context of our work, the MI is used to quantify the amount of information that is shared between two sensors. We digitize the raw time series Segments into bins to calculate the MI. We build the adjacency matrix as follows:

$$\mathcal{A}_{ij} = \begin{cases} 1 & \text{if } \text{MI}(x_i, x_j) > T \\ 0 & \text{otherwise} \end{cases} \tag{3}$$

where T is the connectivity threshold, and MI(.) is the mutual information.

The feature vector of each sensor is used as the node embedding. We then use GAT layers to process the data. GATs are a type of layer used in graph neural networks to perform message passing and feature aggregation on graph-structured data. GATs enhance the ability of GNNs to capture relationships and interactions between nodes in a graph by using attention mechanisms to weight the neighbouring nodes during message passing. This allows the model to focus on the most relevant nodes for a given task, improving its overall performance.

Mathematically, given a set of node features $V = \{v_1; v_2; \ldots; v_K\}$, where $v_i \in \mathbb{R}^F$, we calculate the attention score α_{ij} as follows:

$$e_{ij} = \text{LeakyReLU}(a^T.(\mathbf{W}v_i \oplus \mathbf{W}v_j)) \tag{4}$$

$$\alpha_{ij} = \frac{\exp(e_{ij})}{\sum_{q \in \text{adj}\{i\}} \exp(e_{iq})} \tag{5}$$

where '.' is the standard vector inner product, $\mathbf{W} \in \mathbb{R}^{F \times F'}$ is the weight matrix of a linear transformation that maps feature space F to F', $a \in \mathbb{R}^{2F'}$ is a learnable attention vector, $\oplus$ is the concatenation operation, and adj$\{i\}$ is the set of adjacent nodes of node i. We define a node j to be adjacent to i if $\mathcal{A}_{ij} = 1$. The aggregated representation of node i can then be calculated as:

$$h_i = \text{ReLU}(\alpha_{i,i}\mathbf{W}v_i + \sum_{j \in \text{adj}\{i\}} \alpha_{ij}\mathbf{W}v_j) \tag{6}$$

We stack the GAT layers to encode the node embedding as a low-dimensional representation $\hat{h}_i$, and then use another set of GAT layers to decode them and reconstruct the features:

$$\hat{v}_i = G(v_i, \mathcal{A}) = \text{GNN}_d(\text{GNN}_e(v_i, \mathcal{A}), \mathcal{A}) \tag{7}$$

The loss function of the network is defined as the reconstruction error of the feature embeddings:

$$\mathcal{L}_{rec} = \frac{1}{N} \sum_{n=1}^{N} \frac{1}{K} \sum_{i=1}^{K} \|\hat{v}_i^{(n)} - v_i^{(n)}\| \tag{8}$$

3.3   Graph Generative Learning

We propose a generative task, a self-supervised learning module, to help the model better learn the contextual information and use them in the inference phase for detecting abnormal sensors. It also improves the model generalization.

In this task, we stochastically mask the feature vector of one sensor and use the model and other sensors' data to reconstruct the masked node's embedding. We perform this pretext task during the training on the ζ portion of the mini-batch samples at each epoch. By performing the generative task, the model learns to reconstruct data even in the absence of one sensor embedding. This task operates under the assumption that missing sensor embeddings can be reconstructed by other data points when the data is normal. Consequently, the generative task facilitates anomaly detection by indicating that the sensor data is abnormal or that the other sensors are malfunctioning so that their data is not viable for reconstructing the missing node if the model cannot reconstruct a sensor's embedding. Additionally, the generative task aids in identifying anomalous sensors by concealing their embeddings and evaluating whether the model can successfully reconstruct them.

3.4   Temporal Contrastive Learning

The other notion of self-supervision is Contrastive learning which aims to pull together the Segments with the same Block ID in the latent representation space. Let $X = \{x_1, x_2, \ldots, x_N\}$ represents all Segments of our training dataset, and $\mathcal{B} = \{x_1, x_2, \ldots, x_{\hat{N}}\}$ be a mini-batch of size $\hat{N}$ that we use for training. $\mathcal{B}$ is random subset of X. For every Segment x_i with Block ID b_i in $\mathcal{B}$, we stochastically sample another Segment $\bar{x}_i$ with the same Block ID b_i from X, i.e. $\bar{x}_i \sim \{x_j \in X | b_j = b_i, j \in \{1, \ldots, N\} \backslash i\}$ where '$\backslash$' denotes that j is any number between 1 to N except for i. This makes sure that for every sample in the mini-batch $\mathcal{B}$, we have at least one other sample with the same Block ID.

When we Segment the time series using a sliding window, the information about the temporal dependency between different Segments is lost. To encourage our model to map the Segments from the same Block of operation closer together, we employ the idea of contrastive learning. To this end, we first concatenate the latent embedding of sensors $\hat{h}_i$ and pass them through a projection head $f(.)$:

$$z = f(\hat{h}_1 \oplus \hat{h}_2 \oplus \cdots \oplus \hat{h}_K) \tag{9}$$

As we might have more than one positive sample for some data points of the batch, we use the SupCON loss [22] instead of the normal contrastive loss. If the representation vectors, i.e. the z vectors associated to the mini-batch segments, are normalized, the SupCON loss can be calculated as:

$$\mathcal{L}_{con} = \sum_{i \in I} \frac{-1}{|P(i)|} \sum_{p \in P(i)} \log \frac{\exp\left(z_i.z_p/\tau\right)}{\sum_{a \in A(i)} \exp\left(z_i.z_a/\tau\right)} \tag{10}$$

where $I = \{1, 2, \ldots, 2N\}$ is the set of indices of the augmented batch (each point has an augmentation, so we have $2N$ points in the augmented batch), $A(i) = I \backslash \{i\}$, $P(i) = \{A(i) : b_p = b_i\}$ is the set of indices of Segments that share the same Block IDs, and τ is called the temperature hyperparameter, and determines the strength of repulsion or attraction between representation vectors.

The final loss function of the network is defined as:

$$\mathcal{L}_{\text{total}} = \lambda \mathcal{L}_{rec} + (1 - \lambda)\mathcal{L}_{con} \tag{11}$$

3.5 Anomaly Scoring

To find the anomaly score for a sample x_i during the test phase, we first calculate the reconstruction loss as follows:

$$S_{rec}(x_i) = \|G(x_i, \mathcal{A}) - x_i\| \tag{12}$$

Then, we mask the data of one sensor at a time and re-calculate the average reconstruction error over all masked sensors:

$$S_{gen}(x_i) = \frac{1}{K} \sum_k \|G(M_k(x_i), \mathcal{A}) - x_i\| \tag{13}$$

where $M_k(.)$ is the masking operator which masks out the k-th sensor.

The underlying assumption behind adding the generative loss is that other sensors' information can generate the missing sensor normal data since the model has learned how to leverage the sensors' relationship for data reconstruction. However, for abnormal data, the reconstructed pattern should have a large reconstruction error mainly because the other sensors' data is also abnormal and misses some important structural relationships as well.

4 Experiments

4.1 Dataset

To evaluate the performance of our method, we used a real-world dataset consisting of five trucks. All the trucks are from the same model and same manufacturer and thus have the same set of sensors. The data on the vehicle were recorded

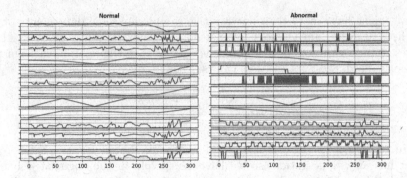

Fig. 2. Visualization of a normal and an abnormal Segment from the dataset. Data are normalized to the range of 0 and 1.

in six months between August 2021 to February 2022. The data also includes information about the operation Blocks of the vehicles, as well as the vehicle's state at each time, both annotated by the company that recorded the data. The vehicle's state is determined by a team of technicians who analyze the data Blocks. The vehicle state identifies if the vehicle is operating in normal condition or if there is a potential defect that may lead to a future failure. Figure 2 shows a visualization of one normal and one abnormal data Segment.

Our work focuses on predicting engine-related failures, and to this end, we picked the data from the same set of sensors that technicians use for engine failure detection and diagnosis. In total, thirteen sensors are used, each monitoring a particular parameter in the engine. The data were recorded with a one-second sampling period. We used a window with length $L = 300$ to partition the data down into 5-minute Segments.

4.2   Evaluation Protocol

We used the labels provided by the company as the ground truth. To evaluate the performance of our algorithm, we used precision (P), recall (R), and F1 score as our metrics. Calculating the F1 score on single timestamps has shown to underestimate the anomaly detector performance [11], mainly because of two reasons: First, even if the data is abnormal, some points might represent normal patterns. Furthermore, for several reasons, one or more normal points might have unexpected values. To alleviate this issue, our proposed algorithm directly outputs the anomaly score for every Segment of the data. Since there are multiple Segments in each Block, we modify the score of different Segments by assigning all of them to abnormal if one anomalous Segment is found in their Block.

More details about the dataset and implementation of the methods can be found in the appendix. We compared our model against several state-of-the-art baselines: One-Class Support Vector Machine (OCSVM) which is a popular traditional anomaly detection method [31], Autoencoder (AE) [13] which is one of the most common tools for anomaly detection [30], LSTM-Autoencoder

Table 1. Precision, Recall, and F1 of Vehicles. Training and test are done on the same vehicle model. V_i is short for the i-th vehicle. The best-performing model is denoted in boldface, and the second best is marked by *.

Algorithm	Metric	V_1	V_2	V_3	V_4	V_5	Average
OCSVM	Prec	0.56	0.48	0.49	0.63	0.46	0.52
	Recall	0.81	0.74	0.71	0.83	0.77	0.77
	F1	0.66	0.58	0.58	0.71	0.57	0.62
AE	Prec	0.58	0.51	0.53	0.67	0.58	0.57
	Recall	0.88	0.83	0.85	0.91	0.81	0.85
	F1	0.69	0.83*	0.65	0.71	0.676	0.68
LSTM-AE	Prec	0.63	0.59	0.63	0.67	0.62	0.62
	Recall	0.93	0.88	0.86	**0.97**	0.91	0.91
	F1	0.75	0.70	0.72	0.79	0.73	0.74
TCN-AE	Prec	0.61	0.52	0.57	0.63	0.59	0.58
	Recall	**0.96**	**0.93**	0.91	0.95	0.93*	0.93
	F1	0.74	0.66	0.70	0.75	0.72	0.71
USAD	Prec	0.68	0.57	0.64*	0.70	0.59	0.63
	Recall	0.92	0.90	0.94*	0.95	0.88	0.91
	F1	0.78	0.69	0.76*	0.80	0.706	0.75
GDN	Prec	0.72*	0.63*	0.61	0.72*	0.68*	0.67*
	Recall	0.94*	0.92*	0.92	0.98	0.93*	0.93*
	F1	0.81	0.74	0.73	0.83*	0.78*	0.78*
mVSG-VFP	Prec	**0.85**	**0.74**	**0.71**	**0.84**	**0.78**	**0.78**
	Recall	0.94*	0.92*	**0.95**	0.96*	**0.96**	**0.94**
	F1	**0.89**	**0.82**	**0.81**	**0.89**	**0.86**	**0.85**

(LSTM-AE), another autoencoder-based method [33] that uses LSTM layers instead of fully-connected ones to capture the temporal relationship, Temporal Convolutional Network Autoencder (TCNAE), which uses TCN instead of fully-connected layers, USAD [5] which uses two adversarial-trained autoencoders to detect anomalies, and Graph Deviation Network (GDN) [10], a graph-based method that detects anomalies based on the prediction error.

4.3   Experimental Results

Vehicle-Specific Training: We compared the performance of our proposed model against several common and state-of-the-art algorithms in Table 1. In this experiment, we train the model on the same vehicle for training and testing. We did the experiments ten times and reported the average.

These results demonstrate the superiority of our method over other baselines in detecting abnormal events which lead to a potential vehicle failure. In terms of F1 and Precision, we can confirm that our model outperforms all the methods in all vehicles and has superior Recall compared to the baselines on average. A remarkable observation is that graph-based methods, such as our algorithm and GDN, outperform other methods. This highlights the key role of capturing sensor relationships in detecting multivariate time-series anomalies. Furthermore, the results show that our proposed model can outperform GDN on all vehicles. This can be attributed to the two main differences between our model and GDN:

1. Our model is reconstruction-based, while GDN is predictive-based and defines the anomaly score based on the deviation from expected future behaviour. Although it showed promising results on benchmarks such as SWAT, the predictive-based nature of GDN limits its performance on data that does not possess predictable temporal patterns. As a result, the GDN model will have a large prediction error even on normal samples of our dataset, which is also suggested by its low precision score in the table.
2. An essential component of our model is the self-supervised module which encourages the network to build a more representative feature space. This module helps capture the long-term dependencies of Segments within a Block, while this relationship is discarded in GDN and other baselines.

Cross-Vehicle Anomaly Detection: A possible vehicle failure prediction system scenario is to train the model using data from a subset of vehicles and deploy it on a new one. To assess the reliability of our framework in this situation, we held one vehicle out for the test and trained the model using the normal samples of the other four. During the test phase, we used the test dataset of the held-out vehicle to measure the performance. The results of this experimental protocol are shown in Table 2.

Table 2. Results of the Cross-vehicle training.

	Metric	V_1	V_2	V_3	V_4	V_5	*Average*
Cross Vehicle	Prec	0.65	0.53	0.51	0.65	0.68	0.60
	Recall	0.74	0.80	0.77	0.77	0.89	0.79
	F1	0.69	0.63	0.61	0.70	0.67	0.66

Comparing these results with Table 1, we can see that the cross-vehicle training has a lower performance than the vehicle-specific training protocol. This can be attributed to the fact that the vehicle operates in different weather and load conditions and has different depreciation levels. Therefore, having access to the recordings of the same vehicle or other vehicles that operate under similar conditions during training can help the model to perform better.

Anamolous Sensor Detection: An interesting aspect of a failure prediction method is its interpretability and the ability to localize the defect location. Therefore, we explore the model's performance for detecting anomalous sensors in this experiment. Since our original dataset did not have the annotation for the abnormal sensors, we devised synthetic data by replacing the embedding of one of the sensors of the normal data with noise. Then we mask one node at a time and reconstruct it. We threshold the reconstruction errors to get the anomaly labels. This experiment yielded a 97.58% F1 score, highlighting the proposed model's application for localizing abnormal channels.

Effect of Hyperparameter λ: Figure 3 shows the average F1 score of our model for different values of λ. The two extreme cases of $\lambda = 0$ and $\lambda = 1$ represent our model if we remove the reconstruction and contrastive losses, respectively. We can confirm that including both losses with $\lambda = 0.8$ yields the best performance. This shows that both loss terms complement each other and can improve the model's efficiency in detecting abnormal patterns.

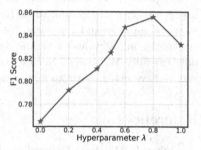

Fig. 3. Effect of Hyperparameter λ

We can still achieve good performance for the case of $\lambda = 1$, which effectively means keeping the reconstruction error alone. However, setting $\lambda = 0$ and removing the construction loss on the other side of the spectrum can significantly degrade the F1 score. This can be attributed to two main causes: I) If we remove the reconstruction loss, the model can trivially minimize the contrastive loss by concentrating the samples of the same Block in one single point [18]. Therefore, the latent space will not represent all data characteristics, II) We defined the anomaly score based on the reconstruction error of the input. If we exclude the reconstruction loss, the model will not be guided to reconstruct the normal samples, and thus, it will have a large reconstruction error on both normal and abnormal samples.

5   Conclusion

Overall, our work presents a significant step forward in predictive vehicle maintenance. By combining the power of graph-based anomaly detection with the unique characteristics of vehicle sensor data, our approach has the potential to improve the reliability and efficiency of transportation systems significantly. Our method identifies defects in the sensor data by modelling the sensor network as a graph and using leveraging self-supervised learning to capture temporal dependency between the features. We evaluated our model on a dataset which includes annotated ground truth and showed that our model achieved promising results for detecting the anomalies that lead to the failure. The results of this work demonstrate the potential of graph-based and contrastive learning in multivariate time-series anomaly detection for solving real-world problems.

Acknowledgement. We would like to express our sincere gratitude to Ken Sills, CTO and Co-Founder of Preteckt Inc. company and his team for their invaluable support in providing us with the data used in this research paper. Their contribution was crucial in enabling us to analyze and draw meaningful conclusions from the dataset. We would also acknowledge Fonds de Recherche du Quebec Nature et technologies (FRQNT), Natural Sciences and Engineering Research Council of Canada (NSERC), and Scale AI for funding this research project.

Ethical Statement. We acknowledge that our research involves collecting and processing potentially sensitive data. We have taken measures to protect the privacy and confidentiality of the organizations represented in the data. We have obtained all necessary permissions and approvals. We recognize that our work has implications for the automotive industry, and we acknowledge our responsibility to consider these implications carefully. We have taken care to report our findings accurately and transparently, and we have made efforts to minimize any potential negative impacts of our research.

References

1. Achouch, M., et al.: On predictive maintenance in industry 4.0: overview, models, and challenges. Appl. Sci. **12**(16) (2022). https://doi.org/10.3390/app12168081. https://www.mdpi.com/2076-3417/12/16/8081

2. Ahmed, M., Mahmood, A.N., Islam, M.R.: A survey of anomaly detection techniques in financial domain. Future Gener. Comput. Syst. **55**, 278–288 (2016). https://doi.org/10.1016/j.future.2015.01.001. https://www.sciencedirect.com/science/article/pii/S0167739X15000023

3. Ahmed, M., Naser Mahmood, A., Hu, J.: A survey of network anomaly detection techniques. J. Netw. Comput. Appl. **60**, 19–31 (2016). https://doi.org/10.1016/j.jnca.2015.11.016. https://www.sciencedirect.com/science/article/pii/S1084804515002891

4. Atha, D.J., Jahanshahi, M.R.: Evaluation of deep learning approaches based on convolutional neural networks for corrosion detection. Struct. Health Monit. **17**(5), 1110–1128 (2018). https://doi.org/10.1177/1475921717737051

5. Audibert, J., Michiardi, P., Guyard, F., Marti, S., Zuluaga, M.A.: USAD: unsupervised anomaly detection on multivariate time series. In: Proceedings of the 26th ACM SIGKDD International Conference on Knowledge Discovery & Data Mining, KDD 2020, pp. 3395–3404. Association for Computing Machinery, New York (2020). https://doi.org/10.1145/3394486.3403392

6. Chen, T., Kornblith, S., Norouzi, M., Hinton, G.: A simple framework for contrastive learning of visual representations. In: International Conference on Machine Learning, pp. 1597–1607. PMLR (2020)

7. Chen, W., Tian, L., Chen, B., Dai, L., Duan, Z., Zhou, M.: Deep variational graph convolutional recurrent network for multivariate time series anomaly detection. In: International Conference on Machine Learning, pp. 3621–3633. PMLR (2022)

8. Dai, E., Chen, J.: Graph-augmented normalizing flows for anomaly detection of multiple time series. In: Proceedings of the Thirty-First International Joint Conference on Artificial Intelligence, IJCAI 2022 (2022)

9. Darban, Z.Z., Webb, G.I., Pan, S., Aggarwal, C.C., Salehi, M.: Deep learning for time series anomaly detection: a survey (2022)

10. Deng, A., Hooi, B.: Graph neural network-based anomaly detection in multivariate time series. In: Proceedings of the AAAI Conference on Artificial Intelligence, AAAI 2021 (2021)

11. Garg, A., Zhang, W., Samaran, J., Savitha, R., Foo, C.S.: An evaluation of anomaly detection and diagnosis in multivariate time series. IEEE Trans. Neural Netw. Learning Syst. **33**(6), 2508–2517 (2022). https://doi.org/10.1109/TNNLS.2021. 3105827

12. Goodfellow, I., et al.: Generative adversarial nets. In: Ghahramani, Z., Welling, M., Cortes, C., Lawrence, N., Weinberger, K. (eds.) Advances in Neural Information Processing Systems, vol. 27. Curran Associates, Inc. (2014)

13. Goodfellow, I.J., Bengio, Y., Courville, A.: Deep Learning. MIT Press, Cambridge (2016). http://www.deeplearningbook.org

14. Gugulothu, N., Malhotra, P., Vig, L., Shroff, G.M.: Sparse neural networks for anomaly detection in high-dimensional time series (2018)

15. Hjelm, R.D., et al.: Learning deep representations by mutual information estimation and maximization. In: International Conference on Learning Representations (2019). https://openreview.net/forum?id=Bklr3j0cKX

16. Ho, T.K.K., Armanfard, N.: Self-supervised learning for anomalous channel detection in EEG graphs: application to seizure analysis. In: Proceedings of the AAAI Conference on Artificial Intelligence, AAAI 2023 (2023)

17. Hochreiter, S., Schmidhuber, J.: Long short-term memory. Neural Comput. **9**(8), 1735–1780 (1997)

18. Hojjati, H., Armanfard, N.: DASVDD: deep autoencoding support vector data descriptor for anomaly detection. In: arXiv (2021)

19. Hojjati, H., Armanfard, N.: Self-supervised acoustic anomaly detection via contrastive learning. In: ICASSP 2022–2022 IEEE International Conference on Acoustics, Speech and Signal Processing (ICASSP), pp. 3253–3257 (2022). https://doi. org/10.1109/ICASSP43922.2022.9746207

20. Hojjati, H., Ho, T.K.K., Armanfard, N.: Self-supervised anomaly detection: a survey and outlook (2022). https://doi.org/10.48550/ARXIV.2205.05173. https:// arxiv.org/abs/2205.05173

21. Jeong, K., Choi, S.B., Choi, H.: Sensor fault detection and isolation using a support vector machine for vehicle suspension systems. IEEE Trans. Veh. Technol. **69**(4), 3852–3863 (2020). https://doi.org/10.1109/TVT.2020.2977353

22. Khosla, P., et al.: Supervised contrastive learning. In: Larochelle, H., Ranzato, M., Hadsell, R., Balcan, M., Lin, H. (eds.) Advances in Neural Information Processing Systems, vol. 33, pp. 18661–18673. Curran Associates, Inc. (2020)

23. Kim, S., Choi, K., Choi, H.S., Lee, B., Yoon, S.: Towards a rigorous evaluation of time-series anomaly detection. In: Proceedings of the AAAI Conference on Artificial Intelligence, vol. 36, no. 7, pp. 7194–7201, June 2022. https://doi.org/10.1609/ aaai.v36i7.20680. https://ojs.aaai.org/index.php/AAAI/article/view/20680

24. Kingma, D.P., Welling, M.: Auto-encoding variational bayes. CoRR abs/1312.6114 (2013)

25. Krizhevsky, A., Sutskever, I., Hinton, G.E.: ImageNet classification with deep convolutional neural networks. In: Pereira, F., Burges, C., Bottou, L., Weinberger, K. (eds.) Advances in Neural Information Processing Systems, vol. 25. Curran Associates, Inc. (2012)

26. Lai, K.H., Zha, D., Xu, J., Zhao, Y., Wang, G., Hu, X.: Revisiting time series outlier detection: definitions and benchmarks. In: Thirty-fifth Conference on Neural Information Processing Systems Datasets and Benchmarks Track (Round 1) (2021). https://openreview.net/forum?id=r8IvOsnHchr

27. Li, C.L., Sohn, K., Yoon, J., Pfister, T.: CutPaste: self-supervised learning for anomaly detection and localization. In: Proceedings of the IEEE/CVF Conference on Computer Vision and Pattern Recognition, pp. 9664–9674 (2021)

28. Li, D., Chen, D., Jin, B., Shi, L., Goh, J., Ng, S.-K.: MAD-GAN: multivariate anomaly detection for time series data with generative adversarial networks. In: Tetko, I.V., Kurková, V., Karpov, P., Theis, F. (eds.) ICANN 2019. LNCS, vol. 11730, pp. 703–716. Springer, Cham (2019). https://doi.org/10.1007/978-3-030-30490-4_56

29. Rengasamy, D., Jafari, M., Rothwell, B., Chen, X., Figueredo, G.P.: Deep learning with dynamically weighted loss function for sensor-based prognostics and health management. Sensors **20**(3) (2020). https://doi.org/10.3390/s20030723. https://www.mdpi.com/1424-8220/20/3/723

30. Ruff, L., et al.: A unifying review of deep and shallow anomaly detection. Proc. IEEE **109**(5), 756–795 (2021). https://doi.org/10.1109/JPROC.2021.3052449

31. Schölkopf, B., Williamson, R., Smola, A., Shawe-Taylor, J., Platt, J.: Support vector method for novelty detection. In: Proceedings of the 12th International Conference on Neural Information Processing Systems, NIPS 1999, pp. 582–588. MIT Press, Cambridge (1999)

32. Soria-Olivas, E., et al.: BELM: Bayesian extreme learning machine. IEEE Trans. Neural Netw. **22**(3), 505–509 (2011). https://doi.org/10.1109/TNN.2010.2103956

33. Srivastava, N., Mansimov, E., Salakhutdinov, R.: Unsupervised learning of video representations using LSTMs. In: ICML (2015)

34. Su, Y., Zhao, Y., Niu, C., Liu, R., Sun, W., Pei, D.: Robust anomaly detection for multivariate time series through stochastic recurrent neural network. In: Proceedings of the 25th ACM SIGKDD International Conference on Knowledge Discovery & Data Mining, KDD 2019, pp. 2828–2837. Association for Computing Machinery, New York (2019). https://doi.org/10.1145/3292500.3330672. https://doi.org/10.1145/3292500.3330672

35. Tack, J., Mo, S., Jeong, J., Shin, J.: CSI: Novelty detection via contrastive learning on distributionally shifted instances. Adv. Neural. Inf. Process. Syst. **33**, 11839–11852 (2020)

36. Theissler, A., Pérez-Velázquez, J., Kettelgerdes, M., Elger, G.: Predictive maintenance enabled by machine learning: use cases and challenges in the automotive industry. Reliab. Eng. Syst. Safety **215**, 107864 (2021). https://doi.org/10.1016/j.ress.2021.107864. https://www.sciencedirect.com/science/article/pii/S0951832021003835

37. Wang, M.H., Chao, K.H., Sung, W.T., Huang, G.J.: Using ENN-1 for fault recognition of automotive engine. Expert Syst. Appl. **37**(4), 2943–2947 (2010). https://doi.org/10.1016/j.eswa.2009.09.041. https://www.sciencedirect.com/science/article/pii/S0957417409008227

38. Wolf, P., Mrowca, A., Nguyen, T.T., Bäker, B., Günnemann, S.: Pre-ignition detection using deep neural networks: a step towards data-driven automotive diagnostics. In: 2018 21st International Conference on Intelligent Transportation Systems (ITSC), pp. 176–183 (2018). https://doi.org/10.1109/ITSC.2018.8569908

39. Wong, P.K., Zhong, J., Yang, Z., Vong, C.M.: Sparse Bayesian extreme learning committee machine for engine simultaneous fault diagnosis. Neurocomputing **174**, 331–343 (2016). https://doi.org/10.1016/j.neucom.2015.02.097. https://www.sciencedirect.com/science/article/pii/S0925231215011765

40. Wu, Z., Pan, S., Chen, F., Long, G., Zhang, C., Philip, S.Y.: A comprehensive survey on graph neural networks. IEEE Trans. Neural Netw. Learn. Syst. **32**(1), 4–24 (2020)

41. van Wyk, F., Wang, Y., Khojandi, A., Masoud, N.: Real-time sensor anomaly detection and identification in automated vehicles. IEEE Trans. Intell. Transp. Syst. **21**(3), 1264–1276 (2020). https://doi.org/10.1109/TITS.2019.2906038
42. Zare Moayedi, H., Masnadi-Shirazi, M.: Arima model for network traffic prediction and anomaly detection. In: 2008 International Symposium on Information Technology, vol. 4, pp. 1–6 (2008). https://doi.org/10.1109/ITSIM.2008.4631947
43. Zhang, W., Zhang, C., Tsung, F.: GRELEN: multivariate time series anomaly detection from the perspective of graph relational learning. In: Proceedings of the Thirty-First International Joint Conference on Artificial Intelligence, IJCAI 2022, pp. 2390–2397 (2022)
44. Zhao, H., et al.: Multivariate time-series anomaly detection via graph attention network. In: 2020 IEEE International Conference on Data Mining (ICDM), pp. 841–850. IEEE (2020)
45. Zhou, L., Zeng, Q., Li, B.: Hybrid anomaly detection via multihead dynamic graph attention networks for multivariate time series. IEEE Access **10**, 40967–40978 (2022). https://doi.org/10.1109/ACCESS.2022.3167640

Predictive Maintenance, Adversarial Autoencoders and Explainability

Miguel E. P. Silva[2]([⊠]) (iD), Bruno Veloso[1,2] (iD), and João Gama[1,2] (iD)

[1] Faculty of Economics - University of Porto, Porto, Portugal
{bveloso,jgama}@fep.up.pt
[2] INESC TEC, Porto, Portugal
miguel.p.silva@inesctec.pt

Abstract. The transition to Industry 4.0 provoked a transformation of industrial manufacturing with a significant leap in automation and intelligent systems. This paradigm shift has brought about a mindset that emphasizes predictive maintenance: detecting future failures when current behaviour of industrial processes and machines is thought to be normal. The constant monitoring of industrial equipment produces massive quantities of data that enables the application of machine learning approaches to this task. This study uses deep learning-based models to build a data-driven predictive maintenance framework for the air production unit (APU), a crucial system for the proper functioning of a *Metro do Porto* train. This public transport system moves thousands of people every day and train failures lead to delays and loss of trust by clients. Therefore, it is essential not only to detect APU failures before they occur to minimize negative impacts, but also to provide explanations for the failure warnings that can aid in decision-making processes. We propose an autoencoder architecture trained with an adversarial loss, known as the Wasserstein Autoencoder with Generative Adversarial Network (WAE-GAN), designed to detect sensor failures in systems connected to the APU. Our model can detect APU failures up to two hours before they occur, allowing timely intervention of the maintenance teams. We further augment our model with an explainability layer, by providing explanations generated by a rule-based model that focuses on rare events. Results show that our model is able to detect APU failures without any false alarms, fulfilling the requisites of *Metro do Porto* for early detection of the failures.

Keywords: Anomaly Detection · Time-series Data Streams · Generative Adversarial Networks

1 Introduction

There are several maintenance techniques applicable in the industrial sector, but the two most commonly employed are preventive and corrective maintenance.

G. De Francisci Morales et al. (Eds.): ECML PKDD 2023, LNAI 14175, pp. 260–275, 2023.
https://doi.org/10.1007/978-3-031-43430-3_16

The key difference between these methods is that, in the case of preventive maintenance, scheduled tasks are performed even if the equipment is functioning correctly, while reactive maintenance involves replacing a specific broken part. The two techniques lead to different types of losses for the company: when using preventive maintenance, a component with good health status may be replaced; on the other hand, a corrective maintenance strategy may lead to losses associated with production line or vehicle shutdowns caused by component failure.

An alternative to these methods that is gaining a lot of traction with the advent of Industry 4.0 is predictive maintenance [19,37]. This strategy employs machine learning algorithms to assess historical and real-time data from various parts of the system to detect anomalies and possible defects in equipment before they lead to system failure, while also often suggesting possible ways to fix the problem. Recent advances have employed deep learning methods for failure prediction, a key part of predictive maintenance [28].

In this work, we focus on a particular predictive maintenance use case: detecting catastrophic failures in metropolitan trains belonging to *Metro do Porto*, the subway system of Porto, Portugal [33]. In this context, catastrophic failure is defined as the train breaking down and having to be towed. This problem is crucial not only for the company to avoid losses in terms of reputation and material damage, but also to minimize mobility issues on the metro network and keep a higher client satisfaction rate. This problem fits the ninth sustainable objective defined by United Nations [25]: it is essential to have sustainable, reliable and resilient infrastructures at a lower cost for all. The metro network infrastructure is a crucial element for sustainable mobility for all citizens living in large cities. Two critical requirements for this problem are the early failure detection and reduced number of false positives, both aiming to increase the metro network uptime. Additionally, the train operator needs to be able to understand why an alarm is being signaled, which requires a low-latency explanatory layer to identify the root causes of a specific alarm.

The metropolitan trains of *Metro do Porto* rely on a vital component, which is the air processing unit (APU). This unit feeds several client systems, such as the pneumatic suspension to keep the train at platform level or the injection of oil onto the tracks to reduce the noise. To collect data from this vital system, the maintenance team installed a set of sensors that collect information from different sub-systems of the APU. The main goal of this work is to detect an upcoming failure before the train operator receives a warning light on the panel indicating that the pressure on the system is below a predetermined level.

We propose data-driven predictive maintenance framework based on deep learning to achieve this goal. In particular, we draw from the rich literature on time series anomaly detection using autoencoders [2,5,6,18]. Our solution uses a Wasserstein Autoencoder regularized with Generative Adversarial Networks [30] (WAE-GAN), based on previous literature that indicates that adversarial training allows the detection of smaller differences in time series [16]. We compare our WAE-GAN architecture against other autoencoder architectures and find supporting evidence for this claim. Our proposed model is able to identify train failures at least two hours before the warning light on the train operator's panel and it does not signal any false alarm, fulfilling the requirements of *Metro do Porto*. We further augment our model with an explainability layer that uses AMRules [24] to provide justifications for the warning signals given as output by the WAE-GAN.

Previous approaches on a similar dataset from *Metro do Porto* [7,8] rely on extracting features by segmenting compressor cycles into bins and computing statistics on these bins for each sensor. We improve on these previous approaches by using raw data from each sensor, a more natural way to use deep learning methods for a predictive maintenance task, grounded on previous literature.

2   Overview of Dataset

Our work uses data from a recently benchmark dataset for predictive maintenance, *MetroPT*, available at [32].

The data is continuously collected from the *Metro do Porto* railway vehicle, containing information about the Air Processing Unit (APU) via sensor data. This data has a sampling rate of 1 Hz and is sent to remote servers for processing every 5 min. For this study, we used a data sample of three months. The data sample was collected between 2022-04-28 and 2022-07-28, containing a total number of 7 116 940 examples. We used 2 659 005 examples for training and the remaining examples 4 457 935 for testing. The dataset is unlabeled, but *Metro do Porto* provided failure reports for evaluation of failure prediction methods. The failure reports are available in Table 1. A short description of sensor behaviour follows.

The APU contains three main sub-systems: the compressor, the air drying, and the pneumatic panel that feeds client systems. These systems include pneumatic suspension, injection of sand to gain traction, injection of oil to reduce noise, and pneumatic connection between trains. To monitor these three sub-systems, the maintenance team installs analogue sensors in the APU that measure air pressure, temperature and energy consumption. There are a total of eight analogue sensors: three in the compressor sub-system, that measure the pressure on the compressor (named *TP2*), the motor oil temperature and the motor electric current consumption; two sensors in the air drying sub-system, that determine the pressure of air escaping in the draining pipes and the air pressure on the pneumatic control valve (named *H1* and *DV-pressure*, respectively); finally, the pneumatic panel contains the last three sensors, these sensors measure the pressure and air flow on the pneumatic panel and the pressure on the air tanks (named *TP3*, *Flowmeter* and *Reservoirs* respectively).

In addition to the analogue sensors, there are also two digital sensors: *COMP* and *LPS*. The latter is a warning signal for the train operator that something

Table 1. Maintenance Report - Failures

#	Start Time	End Time	Failure	LPS Time
1	2022-06-04 10:19:24.300	2022-06-04 14:22:39.188	Air Leak	2022-06-04 11:26:01.422
2	2022-07-11 10:10:18.948	2022-07-14 10:22:08.046	Oil Leak	2022-07-13 19:43:52.593

is wrong with the train. It stands for "Low Pressure Signal" and is active when the system pressure is below 7 bar. This signal is used as ground truth for early detection of failure, according to the instructions provided by *Metro do Porto*, a failure is considered as detected early if produced two hours before this signal is active [33].

The second digital signal, "COMP", is used to identify if the compressor is working or powered off. The APU has two distinct operation modes: charging the pneumatic circuit (COMP has value 0) or consuming air (COMP has value 1). A **compressor cycle** is a full sequence of charging the pneumatic circuit and consuming air, starting from the timestamp when the COMP signal changes to 0 and ending at the timestamp preceding the next change of the COMP signal to 0. These two working modes mark stark differences in the behaviour of some sensors [33].

3   Proposed Solution

3.1   Autoencoder Models for Time Series Anomaly Detection

Let $\mathbf{X} = \{x_1, x_2, \ldots, x_t\}$ denote a multivariate time series with t time steps, where each $x_i \in \mathbb{R}^m$ is a multivariate random variable with m scalar random variables. The objective of anomaly detection is to identify contiguous sequences of data that do not conform with learned patterns of behaviour over time. The scarcity of anomalous data, by the definition of anomaly, gives rise to unsupervised approaches to anomaly detection, where models cannot be trained and optimized with anomaly labels. There is also no simulated normal baseline to determine the expectation of normal behaviour of the system, rather the model learns the time series patterns from the real data itself.

Deep learning methods have enjoyed widespread usage in this task, references [5] and [6] provide comprehensive surveys of the literature in this area. Methods based on autoencoders [2,8,18] are particularly suited for this task. Autoencoders are a category of unsupervised training algorithms applied to artificial neural networks (ANN), where the objective function is recreating the original input. In other words, autoencoders are learning algorithms that attempt to learn an approximation of the identity function, $f(x) \approx x$. This process can also be seen as learning two functions, an encoder $E_\phi : \mathcal{X} \to \mathcal{Z}$ and a decoder $G_\theta : \mathcal{Z} \to \mathcal{X}$, where $\mathcal{X} = \mathbb{R}^n$ and $\mathcal{Z} = \mathbb{R}^m$. We write $E_\phi(x) = z$ to denote the output of the encoder function, where z is called the *latent vector* and $\mathcal{Z}$ the *latent space* learned by the autoencoder. Similarly, we write $G_\theta(z) = \hat{x}$, denoting $\hat{x}$ as the reconstruction of input x. The encoder and decoder functions are trained by minimizing the distance between x and $\hat{x}$, for a distance function $d : \mathcal{X} \times \mathcal{X} \to [0, \infty]$, defining the loss function: $\mathcal{L}(\phi, \theta) = \mathbb{E}_{x \sim P_x} [d(x, G_\theta(E_\phi(x)))]$. In this work, we use the L_2 distance as this distance.

The most common strategy when using autoencoders for anomaly detection is leveraging the distance d between input and autoencoder reconstruction as a metric to identify the outlier time sequences. Models are trained on a dataset that is assumed to have no anomalies, building an expectation of the input distribution. During inference, given a new time series as input, if the autoencoder reconstruction error is above threshold ε informed by the reconstruction errors during training, then the new time series is considered to be anomalous.

To prevent the network from learning a trivial mapping of input to output, constraints are coded into the network structure of the autoencoder. In the original proposal for the autoencoder architecture, this constraint was a limit on the number of hidden units, thus creating a *bottleneck* in the latent space and forcing the autoencoder to learn a compressed representation of the input. An alternative, proposed by Ng [20] and dubbed *sparse autoencoders* (SAE), is adding regularization term on the loss function that enforces sparsity on the activations of the hidden neurons. This constraint encourages neurons to only be active for certain inputs, allowing the network to include a large number of units in the hidden layers, while still discovering hidden structure in the data. This sparsity constraint is imposed in the loss function by minizing the Kullback-Leibler divergence between a neuron's activation and a sparsity parameter.

LSTM Autoencoder. In the context of anomaly detection for time series data, Long Short Term Memory (LSTM) [13] recurrent neural networks (RNN) have been proposed as a natural architecture for the encoder and decoder functions of the autoencoder [10,21,26]. The cyclical connections between neurons of a RNN enable a neuron to carry over its output to affect future inputs, thus have been widely employed to model data with temporal dependencies, such as text or time series. LSTMs were proposed by Hochreiter and Schmidhuber [13] to solve the problem of vanishing gradients with backpropagation through time. This type of network uses a combination of three inputs to determine the output for a single point in time. These three inputs are the input data along with the *cell* and the *hidden state*, which represent the internal memory of the network and the output of the previous time step, respectively. We write $h_t^{(\mathbf{W})}$ to denote the hidden state at time t, computed by a set of parameters $\mathbf{W}$.

To use LSTM networks as the encoder and decoder functions in an autoencoder for a sequence with t time steps, we feed the sequence into the encoder LSTM one time step at a time, and the final hidden state of the LSTM is used as the latent representation $z = h_t^{(E_\phi)}$. To reconstruct the initial sequence, we use the latent representation z as the input variable at each time step for the decoder LSTM. The decoder LSTM takes as input the latent representation z and the previous hidden state $h_{i-1}^{(G_\theta)}$, which starts initialized to 0. The decoder LSTM calculates the current hidden state $h_i^{(G_\theta)}$ using these inputs, and then applies a fully connected linear layer to $h_i^{(G_\theta)}$ to obtain the reconstruction $\hat{x}_i$.

Temporal Convolution Network Autoencoder. Although sequence modelling has traditionally relied heavily on RNNs, convolutional architectures have been shown to outperform recurrent networks on certain tasks [3,22]. Similarly to LSTM, temporal convolutional networks (TCN) have been used for unsupervised anomaly detection in time series using autoencoder architectures [27,29,35]. TCNs use zero padding to ensure that the input and output sequences are the same length and also use causal convolutions to prevent the model from using "future" timesteps to predict the past, that is the output at time t is the result of applying the convolution to elements from time t or earlier of the input. Causal convolutions are only able to perform computation on past time steps and their history (how far into the past they can look to make a prediction) scales linearly with the number of network layers, which are often fewer than the number of time steps of a sequence. To counter this issue, TCNs employ dilated convolutions to enable an exponentially large receptive field [36]. Let k denote the size of the convolution kernel and d the dilation factor per layer, then the receptive field size of the convolution can be described by the expression $d \cdot (k - 1) + 1$. This means that increasing this field can be accomplish by either increasing the kernel size or the dilation factor. By increasing d exponentially per layer ($d = 2^L$ at layer L of the network), the receptive field of a deep network is able to cover all values from the input time series.

We build a TCN autoencoder by having mirrored architectures for the encoder and decoder functions: the encoder runs the input sequence through L layers of temporal convolutions and computes the latent space by applying a fully connected linear layer to the output of the TCN; on the other hand, the decoder network takes the latent space calculated by the encoder, applies a TCN with the same hyperparameters as the encoder and the reconstruction is given by applying a fully connected layer to the output of the temporal convolution.

Wasserstein Autoencoders. Regularization mechanisms [15,34] in autoencoders impose constraints on the latent space $\mathcal{Z}$ to force more interesting structure of the input data to be represented in the latent space. An example of a regularization mechanism is sparsity [20], as we have mentioned previously. In this work, we use the Wasserstein Autoencoder with Generative Adversarial Network (WAE-GAN) [30] as our model to introduce regularization in the latent space encoded by the encoder function.

The encoder function has two objectives: the first, as described before, is to provided latent vectors to the decoder function that are informative enough to reconstruct the initial data point; the second objective is to match the distribution of encoded training examples ($Q_Z = \mathbb{E}_{P_Z} [E_\phi(Z|X)]$) to a prior distribution P_Z, by minimizing a divergence $D_Z(Q_Z, P_Z)$, chosen to be the Jensen-Shannon divergence by Tolstikhin et al. [30]. In practical terms, this leads to the introduction of a discriminator function [12] D_γ, that is trained to separate samples drawn from P_Z from those generated by the encoder function, Q_Z. The discriminator is trained by ascending

$$\frac{\lambda}{n} \sum_i^n log(D_\gamma(z_i)) + log(1 - D_\gamma(E_\phi(x_i))),$$

where λ is a coefficient that regulates the weight of the regularization term of the loss function versus the reconstruction term. The encoder and decoder functions are trained jointly by descending

$$\frac{1}{n}\sum_i^n ||x_i - G_\theta(E_\phi(x_i))||_2^2 - \lambda \cdot log(D_\gamma(E_\phi(x_i))).$$

Note that because we have chosen the Mean Squared Error (MSE) to be the reconstruction loss criterion, this formulation of WAE-GAN is equivalent to the Adversarial autoencoder [17].

Similarly to the encoder and decoder functions, we parameterize the discriminator function using an artificial neural network. The prior distribution chosen is the same as the one used in the experimental setup of Tolstikhin et al. [30], an isotropic Gaussian $P_Z(Z) = \mathcal{N}(Z; 0, \sigma_z^2 \cdot \mathbf{I}_d)$ over $\mathcal{Z}$. Figure 1 summarizes the architecture of the WAE-GAN when the encoder and decoder functions are parametrized by TCNs and the discriminator by a LSTM network.

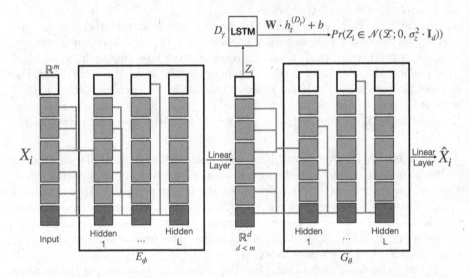

Fig. 1. Wasserstein Autoencoder with Generative Adversarial Network (WAE-GAN) architecture. Encoder E_ϕ and decoder G_θ are Temporal Convolution Networks, the discriminator D_γ is a Long-Short Term Memory network.

3.2   Failure Detection

The compressor cycles of the APU, described in Sect. 2, gives rise to a natural segmentation of the data stream: each cycle becomes an example in our dataset. The problem then shifts to become a classification problem where we want to attribute a label of anomalous or not to each cycle, instead of finding point anomalies in the data. This approach is similar to that of detecting anomalies in electrocardiogram signals [4], where each heartbeat is analyzed individually.

Although this approach is well-founded in the behaviour of the sensors, it has a significant limitation insofar that one must wait for a compressor cycle to end in order to classify it. However, there is no guarantee that a compressor cycle will complete without the train breaking down, for instance if there is a failure and the compressor is working under stress for several hours. To circumvent this limitation, we propose an alternative solution that is based on detecting failures as data from the sensors gets synchronized with our servers. We keep a context of 25 min worth of past data, to which we add the new data packet containing an extra 5 min of data, obtaining data *chunks* of 30 min. We then feed these fixed length *chunks* to our machine learning models to predict failure.

Independently of the deep learning architecture of choice, our models learn to reconstruct the input data, whether it is a compressor cycle or a 30 min data chunk. Using the training dataset, we establish a baseline for the reconstruction error of a normal cycle/chunk by using the boxplot method [31] for detection of outliers: let Q1 and Q3 be the first and third quartiles of the training reconstruction error distribution, then we define a threshold $\varepsilon = Q3 + 3*(Q3 - Q1)$. During the inference step, when the reconstruction error is greater than ε, we consider the input data anomalous. To prevent a high number of false alarms, we use a low pass filter [24] and provide a failure warning when consecutive outputs of the low pass filter exceed 0.5. If there are two failure warnings spaced less than 24 h apart, they are collated and considered part of the same warning.

Inspired by the approach of Geiger et al. [11], we leverage the output of the discriminator network to augment anomaly detection. To achieve this, we compute the Z-score of discriminator outputs and multiply the reconstruction score of the autoencoder by the absolute value of the Z-score.

3.3 Model Explainability

The explainability layer proposed by Ribeiro et al. [23] uses a pipeline of a Chebyshev sampling strategy [1] and the Adaptive Model Rules (AMRules) [9]. AMRules uses a stream-based rule learning algorithm for regression, an approach more suitable for this work as it has the capability to generate rules in real-time without the need for subsequent analysis, unlike Lime or Shap values.

The explainable layer contains a pipeline with two elements: the Chebyshev over-sampling method and the AMRules Regression Model. In the context of predictive maintenance, over-sampling is applied to failures, which are rare events characterized by extreme target values (reconstruction error of the autoencoder). Such rare values are likely to occur far from the mean of the target value, while frequent values are closer to the mean. To determine the rarity of an observation, Chebyshev's inequality can be used with the mean and standard deviation of a random variable. The resulting values are used as weights for each example in the AMRules learning step.

AMRules has the ability to produce both unordered and ordered rules. When using the former all rules that apply to a specific example are shown. On the other hand, when using the ordered rules option, the algorithm behaves like a decision list and shows the first rule that covers the example.

We use the AMRules algorithm to generate ordered rules that fit each sensor reading based on the output of the autoencoder model. When a failure warning is triggered, we send both the sensor data and the autoencoder output to the algorithm, which returns a fitted rule for each example. We pick the rules with highest support, which make up the explanations for the failure warning.

4   Results

We now describe the results of applying the models described in the previous section to the problem of failure detection in *Metro do Porto*. Both when using compressor cycles and data chunks, we approach the problem from an increasing complexity perspective: if a simpler solution is able to achieve good results, then a more complex solution is unnecessary.

The experimental setup designed by *Metro do Porto* [33], indicates that the output of the failure prediction is an interval of time, indicating the period of failure. If the output interval overlaps the failure reported by maintenance teams, then this interval is considered a *true positive* (TP); otherwise, it is a *false alarm* (a false positive, FP). If a failure is reported by maintenance but does not appear in the model output, this interval is a *missed alarm* (a false negative, FN). We report our results using the F_1 metric. The predicted failure is considered *early* if it starts two hours before the LPS signal is active.

Source code for the models, training scripts and failure detection are available at: https://github.com/migueleps/metro-anomaly-ECML2023.

4.1   Failure Detection Based on Compressor Cycles

We start by showing results for our models designed to identify anomalous compressor cycles. Models were trained on one month of data, assumed to be with normal behaviour of sensors. The remaining two months were used as testing data. All models were trained with the Adam optimizer [14]. After hyper parameter tuning, the following models showed best performance:

- *LSTM sparse autoencoder*: both encoder and decoder are composed of 4 layers of stacked LSTMs, each layer with 32 hidden units. Trained for 100 epochs with a learning rate of 1×10^{-3}. The sparsity parameter and weight were set to 0.05 and 1 respectively.
- *TCN autoencoder*: both encoder and decoder are composed of 10 convolution layers, each with 30 hidden units and a kernel size of 5 that leads to receptive field size of $\approx 4 \times 10^3$, a value slightly larger than the majority of compressor cycle lengths. We use a 6-dimensional latent space. Trained for 100 epochs with a learning rate of 1×10^{-4}.
- *WAE-GAN*: both encoder and decoder are composed of 4 layers of stacked LSTMs, each layer with 6 hidden units. The discriminator network has the same structure as the encoder and decoder, 4 LSTM layers with 6 hidden units. Trained for 200 epochs, the encoder and decoder optimizers with a learning rate of 1×10^{-3} and the discriminator optimizer with a learning rate of 1×10^{-4}.

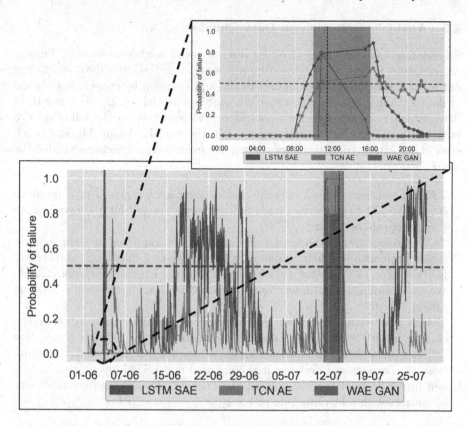

Fig. 2. Probability of APU failure according to three different deep learning models, based on **compressor cycles** as input data. The red horizontal dotted line is the threshold above which two consecutive points are considered a failure. The grey bars represent real failures reported by maintenance teams. The black vertical dotted line indicates when the LPS signal became active in each real failure.

Figure 2 shows the probability of failure outputted by each model over time for the test set. We observe that the LSTM and TCN autoencoders are able to identify the first failure, but only the LSTM achieves early detection. The WAE-GAN model correctly identifies that there is an anomalous cycle within the time frame of the anomaly but because there is only one such cycle, a failure warning is not given. All models correctly identify the second failure early.

In terms of false alarms, the LSTM autoencoder generated two false alarms, both spanning an extensive stretch of time. The TCN autoencoder generated a single false alarm, but the length of the first failure was severely overestimated (40 h instead of 8 h). Finally, the WAE-GAN model did not generate any false alarm. Overall, this means that the TCN autoencoder achieved the highest F_1 score with 0.8, against an F_1 score of 0.67 of the other two models.

4.2   Anomaly Detection on Data Chunks

Considering the challenges faced by our proposed models to identify failures without false alarms when using compressor cycles as the input data, we change our focus towards detecting failures in the input stream by considering chunks of data spanning 30 min. As before, we train our models on the first month of data, which is assumed to be a normal period, and test on the following two months. We use the same optimizer to train the models, Adam [14], and batch sizes of 64. After hyperparameter tuning, the following architectures yielded the top F_1 scores:

- *LSTM autoencoder*: both encoder and decoder are composed of 5 layers of stacked LSTMs, each layer with 4 hidden units. Trained for 150 epochs with a learning rate of 1×10^{-3}.
- *TCN autoencoder*: both encoder and decoder are composed of 8 convolution layers, each with 6 hidden units and a kernel size of 7 that leads to receptive field size of ≈ 1500, a value slightly smaller than the length of each data chunk. We use a 4-dimensional latent space. Trained for 100 epochs with a learning rate of 1×10^{-3}.
- *WAE-GAN*: both encoder and decoder are TCNs with 10 convolution layers, each layer with 30 hidden units and a kernel size of 3 (resulting in a receptive field size of ≈ 2000). The discriminator network has a different architecture from the encoder and decoder, it is composed of 3 LSTM layers with 32 hidden units. Trained for 150 epochs, the encoder, decoder and discriminator optimizers with a learning rate of 1×10^{-3}.

Figure 3 shows the probability of failure outputted by each model over time for the test set. In this case, instead of a data point representing a compressor cycle, it represents an interval 5 min long to simulate the synchronization rate between our servers and the data arriving from the sensors installed in the APU of the train.

We observe that the WAE-GAN model is able to identify the two failures at least two hours before the LPS signal is active and is able to do so without generating any false alarm (achieving a perfect F_1 score). On the other hand, the TCN autoencoder is also able to detect both failures early but generates two false alarms (F_1 of 0.67). The LSTM autoencoder is able to detect both failures without generating a false alarm, but is unable to detect the first failure before the LPS signal.

4.3   Explainability

We generate explainability rules using AMRules and the output of the WAE-GAN model that achieved perfect F_1 with early detection. For the first failure, an air leak with a total of $\approx 31k$ seconds, the model predicted the only 3 different rules with support bigger than the minimum support we defined (5):

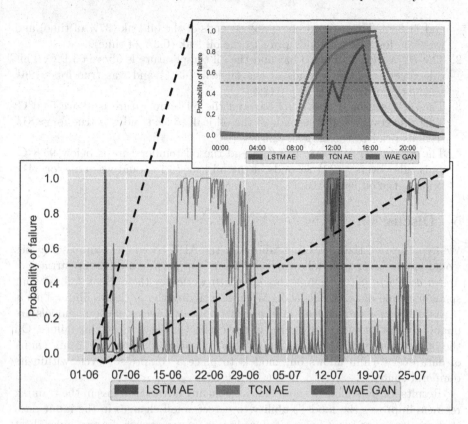

Fig. 3. Probability of APU failure according to three different deep learning models, based on data **chunks** of 30 min as input data. The red horizontal dotted line is the threshold above which two consecutive points are considered a failure. The grey bars represent real failures reported by maintenance teams. The black vertical dotted line indicates when the LPS signal became active in each real failure.

1. *H1* sensor is at or below 8.8 bar and the oil temperature is above 58.5°C. This rule was true for ≈ 21k seconds during the air leak (68% of time) and true for ≈ 15k seconds prior to the air leak (5.6% of time).
2. Oil temperature is above 60.8°C, the *TP2* sensor is above 9.2 bar and the *Reservoirs* sensor is above 9.8 bar. This rule was true for 253 s during the air leak (0.8%) and true for 805 s prior to the air leak (0.3%).
3. Motor current is above 3.8A, the *TP2* sensor is between 7.0 and 7.2 bar and the oil temperature is above 56.7°C. This rule was true for 2264 s seconds during the air leak (7.3%) and true for 28 s before the air leak (0.01%).

For the second failure, an oil leak with a total of ≈ 235k seconds, the model predicted the following top 4 rules with highest support:

1. The *Reservoirs* sensor is above 8.7 bar, the *Flowmeter* is above 0.2 m^3/h, the *H1* sensor is at or below 9.6 bar and the oil temperature is between 65.1°

and 71.5°C. This rule covers $\approx 86k$ seconds of the oil leak (37% of time) and was true for 8982 s seconds prior to the oil leak (0.3% of time).
2. The *H1* sensor is above 0 bar and the oil temperature is above 65.1°C. This rule covers $\approx 113k$ seconds of the oil leak (48%) and was true for $\approx 26k$ seconds prior to the oil leak (0.8%).
3. The *TP2* sensor is above 9.2 bar and the oil temperature is above 54.6°C. This rule covers $\approx 15k$ seconds of the oil leak (6.5%) and was true for $\approx 81k$ seconds prior to the oil leak (2.6%).
4. The *Flowmeter* is above 25 m^3/h and the oil temperature is below 95.8°C. This rule covers $\approx 22k$ seconds of the oil leak (9.1%) and was true for 441 s prior to the oil leak (0.01%).

5   Discussion

We hypothesized that detecting failures in the APU based on compressor cycles would be an easier task, following a previous approach in a different carriage of *Metro do Porto* [8]. Although this approach works for the oil leak failure, that spans multiple days, it falls short when identifying the air leak failure. This is perhaps because the air leak failure spans only two cycles and our models are unable to find anomalous patterns in the cycles that lead up to this failure. On the other hand, smoothing the input data by considering only a 30 min chunk of data every 5 min allows our models to place a compressor cycle within its temporal context.

Results for data chunks show that introducing adversarial loss in the training regimen improves the model's ability to detect small changes in the input data that are crucial to identifying a failure before its occurrence. In particular, best results were achieved when using temporal convolutions as a feature extraction mechanism to learn a descriptive latent space. A key point of this model is the combination of discriminator scores generated by a LSTM network with the reconstruction error. The LSTM discriminator network is particularly suited for identifying anomalous sequences in the latent space generated by the TCN encoder, as the features extracted by the TCN exhibit a temporal pattern that is neither Gaussian nor similar to normal behaviour. On their own, the TCN or LSTM autoencoders show shortcomings (false alarms or inability to detect failures early) that are overcome when joined in an adversarial way.

The combination of reconstruction error with critic score provided as input to AMRules enables the streaming algorithm to find descriptive rules for the failure warnings we detected. Overall, we find that the oil temperature is prevalent in our rules, but the split values are broad enough that cover a lot of time of normal functioning, which indicates that for the oil temperature to be a good predictor of failure, a model needs to take into account the pattern of changes in temperature, rather than the magnitude of temperature values. This is different from, for example, the *Flowmeter* sensor, whose large values are predictive of failures and not how they vary over time.

During the air leak, the rule that describes the majority of the failure time span uses the output of a sensor measuring the pressure of air escaping in the draining pipes (sensor *H1*). The maintenance report provided by *Metro do Porto* for this failure specifies that it was provoked by a malfunction of the pneumatic pilot valve that opens the drain pipes during the operation of the compressor. As for the oil leak, the maintenance report states that the leak led to severe damage to the engine of the compressor, which caused a drop in air pressure. Our explanation rules justify the failure warning by combining outputs of the *Reservoir* sensor, the *Flowmeter*, *H1* and *TP2*, along with the oil temperature. Therefore, the rules we generate to explain our failure warnings have a direct connection to the root cause of the failure as identified by specialists, helping them identify these causes.

6   Conclusion

We developed a solution of predictive maintenance in a train of *Metro do Porto*, the subway system of Porto, Portugal. Avoiding unexpected train breakdowns in the subway system is crucial to increasing customer's trust in the company and therefore reduce the amount of car traffic in the city, as well as avoiding critical breakdowns that can bring losses to a publicly owned company.

Our proposed solution uses a Wasserstein Autoencoder with Generative Adversarial Network to predict the likelihood of failure in data from 8 sensors connected to systems within the air processing unit of the train. By leveraging the strengths of temporal convolutions and Long-Short Term Memory networks, we were able to create a model that, given a 30 min period of data, identifies failures at least 2 h before the failure detection system installed in the train and does so without generating any false alarm. We were also able to generate a set of rules that describe the failure alarms based on sensor data, a necessary output for maintenance teams to restore the train's proper functioning.

Acknowledgements. Miguel E. P. Silva is financed by National Funds through the Portuguese funding agency, FCT - within project UIDP/50014/2020. João Gama is financed by the European Union's Horizon 2020 research and innovation programme under grant agreement No 952026 (HumanE-AI-Net project). We also would like to acknowledge CHIST-ERA-19-XAI-012 and CHIST-ERA/0004/2019.

References

1. Aminian, E., Ribeiro, R.P., Gama, J.: Chebyshev approaches for imbalanced data streams regression models. Data Min. Knowl. Disc. **35**(6), 2389–2466 (2021). https://doi.org/10.1007/s10618-021-00793-1
2. An, J., Cho, S.: Variational autoencoder based anomaly detection using reconstruction probability. Spec. Lect. IE **2**(1), 1–18 (2015)
3. Bai, S., Kolter, J.Z., Koltun, V.: An empirical evaluation of generic convolutional and recurrent networks for sequence modeling. arXiv preprint arXiv:1803.01271 (2018)
4. Chauhan, S., Vig, L.: Anomaly detection in ECG time signals via deep long short-term memory networks. In: 2015 IEEE International Conference on Data Science and Advanced Analytics (DSAA), pp. 1–7. IEEE (2015)

5. Choi, K., Yi, J., Park, C., Yoon, S.: Deep learning for anomaly detection in time-series data: review, analysis, and guidelines. IEEE Access **9**, 120043–120065 (2021). https://doi.org/10.1109/ACCESS.2021.3107975

6. Darban, Z.Z., Webb, G.I., Pan, S., Aggarwal, C.C., Salehi, M.: Deep learning for time series anomaly detection: a survey (2022). https://doi.org/10.48550/arXiv.2211.05244

7. Davari, N., Veloso, B., Ribeiro, R.P., Gama, J.: Fault forecasting using data-driven modeling: a case study for metro do Porto data set. In: Koprinska, I., et al. (eds.) Machine Learning and Principles and Practice of Knowledge Discovery in Databases. ECML PKDD 2022. Communications in Computer and Information Science, vol. 1753, pp. 400–409. Springer, Cham (2023). https://doi.org/10.1007/978-3-031-23633-4_26

8. Davari, N., Veloso, B., Ribeiro, R.P., Pereira, P.M., Gama, J.: Predictive maintenance based on anomaly detection using deep learning for air production unit in the railway industry. In: 2021 IEEE 8th International Conference on Data Science and Advanced Analytics (DSAA), pp. 1–10 (2021). https://doi.org/10.1109/DSAA53316.2021.9564181

9. Duarte, J., Gama, J., Bifet, A.: Adaptive model rules from high-speed data streams. ACM Trans. Knowl. Disc. Data (TKDD) **10**(3), 1–22 (2016)

10. Essien, A., Giannetti, C.: A deep learning model for smart manufacturing using convolutional LSTM neural network autoencoders. IEEE Trans. Industr. Inf. **16**(9), 6069–6078 (2020). https://doi.org/10.1109/TII.2020.2967556

11. Geiger, A., Liu, D., Alnegheimish, S., Cuesta-Infante, A., Veeramachaneni, K.: TadGAN: time series anomaly detection using generative adversarial networks. In: 2020 IEEE International Conference on Big Data (Big Data), pp. 33–43. IEEE (2020)

12. Goodfellow, I., et al.: Generative adversarial networks. Commun. ACM **63**(11), 139–144 (2020)

13. Hochreiter, S., Schmidhuber, J.: Long short-term memory. Neural Comput. **9**(8), 1735–1780 (1997)

14. Kingma, D.P., Ba, J.: Adam: A method for stochastic optimization. arXiv preprint arXiv:1412.6980 (2014)

15. Kingma, D.P., Welling, M.: Auto-encoding variational bayes. arXiv preprint arXiv:1312.6114 (2013)

16. Li, D., Chen, D., Jin, B., Shi, L., Goh, J., Ng, S.-K.: MAD-GAN: multivariate anomaly detection for time series data with generative adversarial networks. In: Tetko, I.V., Kůrková, V., Karpov, P., Theis, F. (eds.) ICANN 2019. LNCS, vol. 11730, pp. 703–716. Springer, Cham (2019). https://doi.org/10.1007/978-3-030-30490-4_56

17. Makhzani, A., Shlens, J., Jaitly, N., Goodfellow, I., Frey, B.: Adversarial autoencoders. arXiv preprint arXiv:1511.05644 (2015)

18. Malhotra, P., Ramakrishnan, A., Anand, G., Vig, L., Agarwal, P., Shroff, G.: Lstm-based encoder-decoder for multi-sensor anomaly detection (2016). https://doi.org/10.48550/arXiv.1607.00148

19. Mobley, R.K.: An introduction to predictive maintenance. Elsevier (2002)

20. Ng, A., et al.: Sparse autoencoder. CS294A Lect. Notes. **72**(2011), 1–19 (2011)

21. Nguyen, H.D., Tran, K.P., Thomassey, S., Hamad, M.: Forecasting and anomaly detection approaches using LSTM and LSTM autoencoder techniques with the applications in supply chain management. Int. J. Inf. Manage. **57**, 102282 (2021). https://doi.org/10.1016/j.ijinfomgt.2020.102282

22. Oord, A., et al.: WaveNet: a generative model for raw audio. arXiv preprint arXiv:1609.03499 (2016)
23. Ribeiro, R.P., Mastelini, S.M., Davari, N., Aminian, E., Veloso, B., Gama, J.: Online anomaly explanation: a case study on predictive maintenance. In: Koprinska, I., et al. (eds.) Machine Learning and Principles and Practice of Knowledge Discovery in Databases. ECML PKDD 2022. Communications in Computer and Information Science, vol. 1753, pp. 383–399. Springer, Cham (2023). https://doi.org/10.1007/978-3-031-23633-4_25
24. Ribeiro, R.P., Pereira, P., Gama, J.: Sequential anomalies: a study in the railway industry. Mach. Learn. **105**, 127–153 (2016)
25. Sachs, J., Kroll, C., Lafortune, G., Fuller, G., Woelm, F.: Sustainable Development Report 2022. Cambridge University Press, Cambridge (2022)
26. Said Elsayed, M., Le-Khac, N.A., Dev, S., Jurcut, A.D.: Network anomaly detection using LSTM based autoencoder. In: Proceedings of the 16th ACM Symposium on QoS and Security for Wireless and Mobile Networks, pp. 37–45 (2020). https://doi.org/10.1145/3416013.3426457
27. Samal, K.K.R., Babu, K.S., Das, S.K.: Temporal convolutional denoising autoencoder network for air pollution prediction with missing values. Urban Clim. **38**, 100872 (2021)
28. Serradilla, O., Zugasti, E., Rodriguez, J., Zurutuza, U.: Deep learning models for predictive maintenance: a survey, comparison, challenges and prospects. Appl. Intell. **52**(10), 10934–10964 (2022)
29. Thill, M., Konen, W., Wang, H., Bäck, T.: Temporal convolutional autoencoder for unsupervised anomaly detection in time series. Appl. Soft Comput. **112**, 107751 (2021)
30. Tolstikhin, I., Bousquet, O., Gelly, S., Schoelkopf, B.: Wasserstein auto-encoders. arXiv preprint arXiv:1711.01558 (2017)
31. Tukey, J.W., et al.: Exploratory Data Analysis, vol. 2. Reading, MA (1977)
32. Veloso, B., Gama, J., Ribeiro, R., Pereira, P.: MetroPT2: A Benchmark dataset for predictive maintenance, July 2022. https://doi.org/10.5281/zenodo.7766691
33. Veloso, B., Ribeiro, R.P., Gama, J., Pereira, P.M.: The metropt dataset for predictive maintenance. Sci. Data **9**(1), 764 (2022). https://doi.org/10.1038/s41597-022-01877-3
34. Vincent, P., Larochelle, H., Bengio, Y., Manzagol, P.A.: Extracting and composing robust features with denoising autoencoders. In: Proceedings of the 25th International Conference on Machine Learning, pp. 1096–1103 (2008)
35. Xu, J., Duraisamy, K.: Multi-level convolutional autoencoder networks for parametric prediction of spatio-temporal dynamics. Comput. Methods Appl. Mech. Eng. **372**, 113379 (2020)
36. Yu, F., Koltun, V.: Multi-scale context aggregation by dilated convolutions. arXiv preprint arXiv:1511.07122 (2015)
37. Zonta, T., Da Costa, C.A., da Rosa Righi, R., de Lima, M.J., da Trindade, E.S., Li, G.P.: Predictive maintenance in the industry 4.0: a systematic literature review. Comput. Indus. Eng. **150**, 106889 (2020)

TDCM: Transport Destination Calibrating Based on Multi-task Learning

Tao Wu[1], Kaixuan Zhu[1], Jiali Mao[1,2(✉)], Miaomiao Yang[1], and Aoying Zhou[1,2]

[1] East China Normal University, Shanghai, China
{52195100007,51215903072,51215903097}@stu.ecnu.edu.cn,
{jlmao,ayzhou}@dase.ecnu.edu.cn
[2] Shanghai Engineering Research Center of Big Data Management, Shanghai, China

Abstract. Accurate location and address of destination are critical for bulk commodity transportation, which determines the service quality of the logistics applications such as transport task dispatching and route planning. But due to manual input errors of the operators and dynamic changes of the destination's location, the address of destination is not always correct and complete. To tackle this issue, we propose Transport Destination Calibration framework based on Multi-task learning, called *TDCM*. To correctly pinpoint the locations of destinations that are close to each other but differ in size, we cluster stay points to get stay areas and then merge them based on *road turn-off location* to obtain stay hotspots. Further, to precisely recognize the transport destination for each waybill, we devise an end-to-end multi-task destination matching model by incorporating with an attention mechanism. It can identify all destinations' instances and meanwhile can match them with the corresponding waybills' addresses respectively. Experimental results on real-world steel logistics data demonstrate the effectiveness and superiority of *TDCM*.

Keywords: Transport destination calibration · Multi-task learning · Attention mechanism · Road turn-off location

1 Introduction

Accurate transport destination is most critical for network freight platforms, as it supports core applications in bulk logistics such as transport task assignment, route planning and freight settlement. But due to manual typing errors of the operators and dynamic changes of destinations' locations, transport destination information maintained by network freight platform may be incorrect or incomplete and even redundant. As illustrated in Fig. 1, the geocoded location (represented as a hollow drop-shaped icon) of the destination "P004359" is 41.2 km away from its real location (represented as a red drop-shaped icon). This heavily affects the transport efficiency of the cargoes and reduces the truck driver's satisfaction with the freight platform. Therefore, it desperately needs a calibration mechanism to update the address and location of destination.

G. De Francisci Morales et al. (Eds.): ECML PKDD 2023, LNAI 14175, pp. 276–292, 2023.
https://doi.org/10.1007/978-3-031-43430-3_17

Recently in the express field, aiming at the issue of imprecise delivery address caused by the couriers' delayed recording, a few researches try to infer real delivery locations based on extracted stay positional points that are not later than the recorded delivery time (or called *delivery point* for short) [5,11,13–15]. But distinct from the express industry, the confirmations of completing transporting (i.e. click on 'Transporting Complete' button) of the truck drivers occur much later than the time of actual finishing transporting due to their busyness. Sometimes the confirmation time may be several hours later than the completion of the transport task because the drivers' confirm clicking when carrying out subsequent task. It leads to that the location of driver's clicking may be far away from that of real destination(marked by the green triangles in Fig. 1). As a result, the solution using delivery points cannot be used to calibrate destination for bulk logistics.

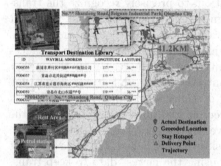

Fig. 1. Illustration of transport destination calibration

Fig. 2. Illustration of transport destination pinpoint

During transportation of commodities, massive positional points (i.e. trajectory) generated by the trucks have been accumulated continuously. It provides us a chance to infer the location of transport destination. In view of that the trucks may stay at the destination for a long time due to unloading the cargoes, we try to recognize the destination using extracted positional points with long-staying duration that generated before the time of truck drivers' confirmation. However, there are also other types of stay hotspots nearby the confirming location of truck drivers, which are very close to transport destinations. As shown in Fig. 2, destinations C and D have their respective stay areas of various sizes, and most of their areas are adjacent to each other. How to discern the location of transport destinations of various sizes from these adjacent places? It becomes the first problem to be solved in calibrating transporting destinations.

Furthermore, to differentiate the transport destination from other types of stay hotspots, one naive solution is to construct a binary classifier based on the features extracted from waybills' trajectories. But for bulk logistics, the transport destinations of different waybills are likely to differ considerably from each other. For instance, to differentiate steel distributor enterprise from logistics park, we need to pay more attention to the feature of truck's *visiting time-of-day* due to the former having a working hour limit. In view of that, a classifier built on equally treating the effect of each feature on classifying result, cannot correctly distinguish different destinations. It is necessary to extract the features and their respective importance for destination identification, based on which to recognize the real transport destination of each waybill.

To correctly identify the locations of transport destinations that are close to each other but differ in size, we put forward a road turn-off location based stay hotspot identification strategy. As illustrated in Fig. 2, when the trucks want to drive to different destinations (e.g., C and D), they often turn off at different locations on the road. Instead, when entering the same destination (e.g., C), the trucks have turning positional points in close proximity. Inspired by this observation, we first merge different stay areas generated by clustering stay points to obtain stay hotspots, and then determine its location based on extracting its corresponding road turn-off location. In addition, to precisely recognize the transport destination for each waybill, we design an end-to-end multi-task transport destination matching method by incorporating with an attention mechanism. To be specific, identifying the destination instances and matching the instances with waybills' addresses are executed simultaneously. The reason for this is that attention mechanism [3] can capture the contribution of each feature to each type of transport destination when identifying destination instance, and multi-task learning technique [7,10,17] can reduce accumulated inference errors during the execution of both tasks. Based on the above, we design a Transport Destination Calibrating framework based on Multi-task learning, called *TDCM*. Note that *TDCM* method is performed periodically using the newest data to keep transport destination up-to-date. In summary, the contributions of this paper are as follows:

- We address the issue of calibrating destination for bulk commodity transporting, and then design a *Multi-task Learning* based calibrating framework consisting of *waybill trajectory pre-processing, stay hotspot detection* and *transport destination matching.*
- Aiming at the issue of adjacent transport destinations having various sizes, we put forward a road turn-off location based stay hotspots identification strategy, including *stay area identification, road turn-off location inference* and *stay area merging.*
- To tackle the variety issue of transport destinations, we present a multi-task matching method by incorporating with an attention mechanism, which can recognize all destination instances and meanwhile match them with corresponding waybills' addresses.
- We conduct extensive experiments on a real steel logistics dataset to evaluate the effectiveness and superiority of *TDCM*.

2   Related Work

Delivery Location Inference. Delivery location inference aims to infer the delivery location of a waybill address from the courier's positional information

[5,11–15,24]. Ruan et al. [11,13] estimate the spatial centroid of *delivery points* as the delivery location. [5,14,15] treat all delivery points that share an address or a similar address group as candidates, and build a model (i.e. UNet [14], ranking learning [5].) to select the most possible as the actual delivery location. The performance of these methods is highly dependent on the accuracy of the delivery point. They are not applicable to the inference of transport destinations because of the significant delays in confirming task completion by truck drivers. Besides, [12] proposed a novel strategy for delivery location inference based on stay points, which first utilized the hierarchical clustering algorithm to cluster stay points to generate candidate locations and model the correlation between these candidates based on Transformer technology to identify delivery locations. It is also not suitable for the calibration of transport destinations with complex stay scenarios. On the one hand, the fact that transport destinations are different in size and close in distance makes it difficult to locate them accurately. On the other hand, the variety of transport destinations and other types of stay hotspots makes it difficult to recognize the transportation for each waybill.

Significant Place Identification. In the past decade, the issues of significant place identification [6,9,18–22,25] have attracted wide attention and interest. Zheng et al. [20–22] tried to infer interesting locations through density-based clustering. Zhu et al. [6,25] first identified candidate locations based on clustering stay points extracted from trucks' trajectories and then detected illegal chemical facilities by determining whether each of them had loading/unloading events. Huang et al. [18] detected intersections by clustering convergence points from trajectories. Mao et al. [9,19] identified road intersections of different scales in terms of heading direction difference and speed variation characteristics of trajectories within various sizes of grid cells. The above approaches usually clustered a number of meaningful trajectory points and intuitively regarded the centers of clusters as the locations of significant places. But they are unsuitable for discovering large-scale places consisting of several different trajectory point gathering areas with a certain distance between them, e.g., a logistics park having multiple companies, a large steel mill with many warehouses, etc.

3   Problem Definition

Definition 1 (Trajectory of a Truck). *A trajectory of a truck j refers to a sequence of positional points that are chronologically sampled during a time period, denoted as $Tr_j = \{p_1, p_2, \cdots, p_n\}$, where $p_i = (lng_i, lat_i, h_i, t_i)$ denotes a trajectory point having the properties of longitude, latitude, heading direction and timestamp, here $1 \leq i < j \leq n$.*

Definition 2 (Waybill). *A waybill refers to the l-th transport task assigned to a truck j, represented by a four-tuple $W_l^j = (DesID, t_s, t_d, C_{type})$, where $DesID$ denotes the identifier of waybill's transport destination, t_s is the start timestamp of transporting, t_f is the timestamp of completing unloading confirmed by a truck driver, and C_{type} denotes the type of cargo to be transported.*

Definition 3 (Destination Set). *A destination set, denoted as S_{Des}, contains all transport destinations of waybills, each of which is represented as $Des_k = (DesID, DesAd, DesL)$, where $DesAd$ and $DesL$ are the address and location for a transport destination separately.*

Problem Definition. Given a destination set S_{Des}, a set of trucks' trajectories and a collection of waybills, our objective is to calibrate S_{Des} with the re-identified locations and addresses of transport destinations.

4   Overview

We proposed a Transport Destination Calibration framework based on Multi-task learning (TDCM). As shown in Fig. 3, TDCM is mainly composed of *waybill trajectory pre-processing* (Sect. 4.1), *stay hotspot detection* (Sect. 4.2) and *transport destination matching* (Sect. 4.3 and 4.4).

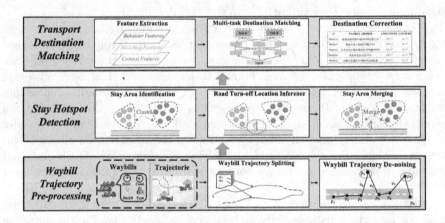

Fig. 3. Overview of TDCM

4.1   Waybill Trajectory Pre-processing

Waybill Trajectory Splitting. Since some drivers do not confirm the completion of the transport task until they move on to the subsequent task, the execution time of multiple consecutive transportation tasks for a truck may be overlapped one another. To tackle this issue, we adjust the completion timestamp of a waybill to be before the start timestamp of its subsequent waybill, and subsequently split the trucks' trajectories into multiple *waybill trajectories* according to the transport start and completion timestamps of different waybills.

Waybill Trajectory De-noising. Due to the weak signal of the GPS device, trucks' trajectories usually contain some noise points. As shown in Fig. 3, the points marked by a red circle are hundreds of meters away from their actual locations. To remove them from *waybill trajectories*, we calculate the speed of each trajectory point in the *waybill trajectory* based on the location of its previous point and itself. We regard the point with speed larger than a preset threshold thr_{sp}(here set as 120 km/h) as a noise point and deleted from the *waybill trajectory*.

4.2   Stay Hotspot Detection

Stay Area Identification. We first extract stay points from *waybill trajectories* to identify stay areas. Given that trucks may stay on road due to waiting for traffic lights or traffic jams, we only focus on the trajectory point sequence that keeps zero velocity for a longer period of time, i.e. stay duration is beyond the preset threshold thr_{dur}(thr_{dur} is empirically set to 8 min). The first point in such a point sequence is regarded as a stay point. Its timestamp is viewed as the start time of one stay behavior of the truck. Then, we cluster the detected stay points, so that each stay area can be uniquely represented as a stay point cluster(as $stay_1$,$stay_2$ shown in Fig. 4(b)). Considering that DBSCAN [4] need not a pre-specifying number of clusters and can find clusters of any shape, we adopt DBSCAN to generate stay areas. To avoid grouping stay points on both sides of the road into the same cluster, we set the cluster radius eps as 5 m based on the minimum road width that trucks can pass. Besides, we set the min_{sample} as 5, ignoring the stay areas with a stay frequency less than 5.

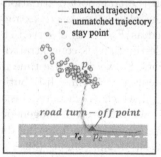   

(a) An example of the road turn-off point extraction   (b) An example of the road turn-off location extraction

Fig. 4. A Case of Road Turn-off Locations Inference.

Road Turn-Off Location Inference. For the waybill trajectory that stay point belongs to, we perform map matching [8] on it to identify the stay point's *turn-off road*. The last matched point on such a road is viewed as corresponding *road turn-off point* of stay point. As shown in Fig. 4(a), p_e is a stay point, and its corresponding road turn-off point is p_c. All *road turn-off point* are clustered using *Mean-shift* method [1] and the centers of clusters with maximum density are extracted. These centers are regarded as *road turn-off location* correspond to stay areas separately, and the centers' turning directions are obtained by calculating the average directions of road turn-off points in their belonged clusters. As shown in Fig. 4(b), the location and direction of the road turn-off location are represented by the arrows with the same color of the corresponding stay area.

Stay Area Merging. Considering that trucks may unload cargo at several warehouses in a logistics park, a *transport hotspot* may contain multiple stay areas. To merge these adjacent stay areas to obtain *transport hotspots*, we put forward a *road turn-off location* based merging strategy using hierarchical clustering method [16]. In specific, we first treat each *road turn-off location* as a cluster, and then search for the cluster pair with distance less than direction threshold thr_{dis} (here set as 10 m) and direction gap less than the threshold thr_{gap} (here set as 15°C) to merge. After that we recalculated the centroid and average direction of the clusters. The above steps are iterated until there are no clusters that can be merged. Subsequently, stay areas corresponding to road turn-off location clusters are merged into a *transport hotspot*, and the centroid of stay areas is treated as the location of *transport hotspot*. As shown in Fig. 4(b), the stay areas *stay$_1$*, *stay$_2$* are merged into one *transport hotspot* as their *road turn-off locations* are clustered into one cluster.

4.3 Hotspot Feature Extraction

Behavior Features. In order to distinguish the transport destinations from the *stay hotspots*, the *behavior features* of the *stay hotspots* are extracted as follows: (1) *Distribution of visit time* (denoted as F_{vt}), it is observed that the distribution of visit time of some transport destinations is concentrated in the daytime because of its working time constraints. So we discretize time interval [00:00, 24:00) into time slots in hour, and calculate visit time distribution. (2) *Distribution of stay duration* (denoted as F_{sd}), which is extracted because of the fact that transport destinations usually have relatively homogeneous stay duration than other types of *stay hotspots*. We generate the following duration intervals as (0,15min], (15min,30min], (30min,1h],(1h,2h], (2h,3h], (3h,+∞], and calculate the proportion of the number of stay points in each stay duration interval. (3) *Distribution of stop frequency* (denoted as F_{sf}). In view of the fact that a truck usually stops at a transport destination several times for unloading cargo at different warehouses, we regard the stop frequency for a single transportation as a contributing feature for identifying transport destinations. Specifically, we express $F_{sf} = [fre_1, fre_2, ..., fre_m]$, and $fre_i (1 \leq i \leq m)$ is the number of waybill trajectories with stop frequency i, here m is set as 5. (4) *Number of cargo types* (denoted as F_{ct}). Intuitively, a larger value of F_{ct} implies a lower possibility of being a transport destination for *stay hotspot*.

Matching Features. In order to further distinguish the transport destinations from different waybill addresses, we extract the matching features of the *stay hotspot* for a waybill address.

- F_{dl} (*Distance from Geocoded location*)- In view of that the transport destination of a waybill address is more likely to be adjacent to its geocoded location, we calculate the distance between the *stay hotspot* and the Geocode location of the given waybill address.
- F_{co} (*Coverage of waybill trajectories*)- Ideally, the transport destination of a waybill address should be passed by all historical *waybill trajectories* it involves, while this may not be the case for other types of *stay hotspots*. Here, given a waybill address $addr_i$ and its involved *waybill trajectories* WT_i^*, the waybill trajectory coverage of a *stay hotspot* hp_j for $addr_i$ is defined as formula (1), which is used to evaluate the proportion of the *waybill trajectories* passing through a *stay hotspot* in WT_i^*.

$$F_{co}^{i,j} = \frac{\sum_{wt \in WT_i^*} \Phi(hp_j \in HP_{wt})}{|WT_i^*|} \tag{1}$$

where HP_{wt} is the set of *stay hotspots* that are passed by the *waybill trajectory* wt, and $\Phi(\cdot)$ is an indicator function that returns 1 if the condition is met, otherwise returns 0. Obviously, the value range of $F_{cwt}^{i,j}$ is between 0 and 1, and a larger $F_{co}^{i,j}$ implies that the *stay hotspot* is more likely to become the transport destination of $addr_i$.

- F_{wa} (*Diversity of waybill addresses*)- It is introduced to evaluate the diversity of a *stay hotspot* involving waybill addresses. Formally, given the *stay hotspot* hp_j and the *waybill trajectories* WT_*^j passing through it, the waybill address commonality of hp_j for waybill address $addr_i$ is defined as follows.

$$F_{wa}^{i,j} = \frac{\sum_{wt \in WT_*^j} sim(addr_i, Addr_{wt})}{|WT_*^j|} \tag{2}$$

$$sim(addr_i, addr_j) = \frac{2 \times len(LCS(addr_i, addr_j))}{len(addr_i) + len(addr_j)} \tag{3}$$

In formula (2), $Addr_{wt}$ represents the waybill address of the *waybill trajectory* wt. $sim()$ is an evaluation function for the similarity between two addresses, which takes two address texts as input and returns a value between 0 and 1. The function $LCS()$ [14] in formula (3) calculates the maximum common subsequence of two address texts, and $len()$ is used to obtain the length of a text string.

Context Features. For each waybill address, We obtain (1) *semantic representation of address text*(denoted as F_{sa}, here Pre-training model [2] is used to encode the address text), (2) *Main categories of cargoes involved* (denoted as F_{mc}) and (3) *Number of waybill trajectories* (denoted as F_{ct}) as contextual features. They are used throughout the training set to learn the contribution of different features of each type of transport destination.

4.4 Transport Destination Calibration

For a waybill address, these *stay hotspots* that are passed by its involved *waybill trajectories* are first extracted as candidates. As a matter of course, this stage aims to perform calibration by building a transport destination matching model to match the most probable *stay hotspot* for waybill addresses.

Identifying the destination instance from *stay hotspots* and then matching the instance with waybill addresses are intuitively considered as two sequential tasks to accurately identify the transport destination of the waybill address. It is easy to transform the destination identification task into a binary classification problem, with the destination instance as positive and the other *stay hotspots* type as negative, and the waybill addresses matching task can be implemented by modeling the matching mode of the transport destination in different waybill address contexts and taking the one with the highest matching degree (score) as its matching transport destination.

The identification task of the destination instance and the matching task of the waybill addresses are not independent but affect each other. For example, accurate identification results of the former can suppress the matching degree of non-destinations in the latter. This motivates us to design a multi-task transport destination matching model. The overall structure of the model is shown in Fig. 5. It takes the context features of waybill addresses and behavior and matching features of candidates as input, treats matching waybill addresses as the main task and treats identifying destination instances as the auxiliary task.

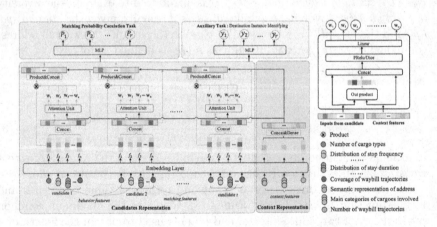

Fig. 5. Overview of multi-task transport destination matching model

As illustrated in Fig. 5, the discrete features (such as the F_{mc} in the context features) are first projected to dense vectors using embedding techniques and then concatenated with the normalized continuous features. Each candidate is represented as a vector $\mathbf{h} = [\mathbf{f}_1, \mathbf{f}_2, \cdots, \mathbf{f}_n]$, where $\mathbf{f}_i \in \mathbb{R}^{K_i}$ is a feature embedding vector. K_i denotes the dimensionality of the feature embedding vector $\mathbf{f}_i$,

$\sum_{i=1}^{n} K_i = K$, K is dimensionality of the entire candidate feature space. Then, the context feature embedding vector is fed into a dense layer of K hidden units to be projected to high-dimension representation $\mathbf{c} \in \mathbb{R}^K$.

Subsequently, the attention mechanism is introduced to apply to candidates, capturing the contribution of each feature value of a *stay hotspot* for the destination instance identification task. Formally, the attention unit [23] is used to calculate candidate representation $\mathbf{v}_h$ given the context representation $\mathbf{c}$, as shown in Eq. (4)

$$\mathbf{v}_h = att\_unit(\mathbf{h}, \mathbf{c}) \odot \mathbf{h} = \mathbf{w} \odot \mathbf{h} = [w_1\mathbf{f}_1, w_2\mathbf{f}_2, \cdots, w_n\mathbf{f}_n] \tag{4}$$

where $att\_unit(\cdot)$ is a feed-forward network with output as the feature weight vector $\mathbf{w} \in \mathbb{R}^n$, $\odot$ is an element-wise operator. The element $w_j(1 \leq j \leq n) \in \mathbf{w}$ denotes the importance of the candidate feature embedding vector f_j for the destination instance task, as illustrated in Fig. 5. Apart from the two input embedding vectors, $att\_unit(\cdot)$ adds the out product of them to feed into the subsequent network, which is an explicit knowledge that helps model the importance of different features for each candidate.

Each new candidate representation $\mathbf{v}_h$ generated by the attention unit is concatenated with the original candidate representation $\mathbf{h}$ and context representation $\mathbf{c}$ to generate a candidate embedding. We use $\{\mathbf{z}_1, \mathbf{z}_2, \ldots, \mathbf{z}_r\}$ to denote a list of candidate embeddings for a waybill address, where r is the number of candidates, $\mathbf{z}_i \in \mathbb{R}^{3K}$. From then on, $\{\mathbf{z}_1, \mathbf{z}_2, \ldots, \mathbf{z}_r\}$ is passed through a one-layer MLP for matching score prediction (main task) and transport destination classification (auxiliary task). The objective function of the MLP for the main task is defined as follows:

$$L_m = -\frac{1}{s} \sum_s \sum_r (y_i^c log(\mathrm{p}(\mathbf{z}_i)) + (1 - y_i^c) log(1 - \mathrm{p}(\mathbf{z}_i))) \tag{5}$$

where s is the number of waybill addresses in the training set, with $y_i^c \in \{0, 1\}$ is the matching label of the candidate embedding $\mathbf{z}_i$ for the context features $\mathbf{c}$, $\mathrm{p}(\mathbf{z}_i)$ is the output of the network after the softmax layer, representing the predicted probability that the candidate $\mathbf{z}_i$ matches the given address context.

Classifying candidates is introduced as the auxiliary task. Considering that the candidate set of a waybill address may contain other transport destinations, there are multiple positives in a candidate list, making the softmax loss work poor because the sum of ground-truth probabilities is larger than 1. Instead, we feed the candidate embedding list into a one-layer MLP followed by sigmoid activations for the auxiliary task, and formulate it as a binary classification problem with the following loss:

$$L_{aux} = -\frac{1}{s} \sum_s \sum_r (y_{aux} log(\hat{y}_{aux}) + (1 - y_{aux}) log(1 - \hat{y}_{aux})) \tag{6}$$

where $y_{aux} \in \{0, 1\}$ indicates whether the candidate is a transport destination, and $\hat{y}_{aux}$ is the predicted probability of the candidate being a transport destination. At last, we combine the two loss functions as multi-task learning:

$$L = (1 - \alpha)L_m + \alpha L_{aux} \tag{7}$$

where α is a hyper-parameter to adjust the effect of L_{aux}.

During calibration, we first replace the original location with the location of the calibrated transport destination by the destination matching model, then correct waybill address with the address text obtained via reverse geocoding service[1], and finally delete those redundant transport destinations with the same waybill address and location.

5 Experiments

5.1 Datasets and Settings

Datasets. we utilize a real dataset of 4 months (Nov. 1st, 2020 to Mar. 1st, 2021) from Steel Logistics Technology Co., Ltd. The Dataset includes the trajectories and waybills of two transportation routes departing from Rizhao City in Shandong, China. They are divided into two datasets according to the cities of transport destinations (hereafter termed *QingDao/LinYi*), whose details are shown in Table 1. The distribution of mileage and stay frequency in Qingdao and Linyi is shown in Fig. 6. As observed, *QingDao* generally exhibits more stay behaviors than *LinYi* in single transportation for longer mileage. Furthermore, the road network with 652,603 vertices and 1,630,544 edges is obtained from *OpenStreetMap*[2]. It is worth noting that the ground-truth locations of the waybill addresses are carefully labeled with driver volunteers.

Table 1. Statistics of dataset

Dataset	# of trajectory points	# of waybills	# of waybill addresses
QingDao	243,528,247	184,144	2,892
LinYi	232,525,232	262,621	2,766

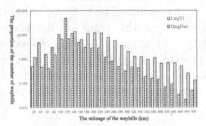
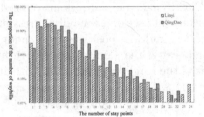

(a) Mileage distribution of waybills   (b) Distribution of stay frequency

Fig. 6. Dataset Descriptions

---
[1] https://docs.mapbox.com/api/search/geocoding/.
[2] https://www.openstreetmap.org/.

We split each dataset into a training set, a validation set and a test set with a splitting ratio of 7:2:1. All experiments are conducted on a GPU-CPU platform with Tesla V100. The program and baselines are implemented in Python 3.8.

Baselines. To evaluate the performance of our proposal, four baselines are presented to compare with $TDCM$

- *DTInf* [13]: It takes the centroid of the annotated delivery points for each address as the delivery location.
- *GeoRank* [5]: This method treats all annotated delivery points sharing the same address as candidates, then introduces a pairwise ranking model to select the one with the most wins as the delivery location.
- *U-Net* [14]: For each address, it creates a fix-sized GeoHash matrix, and each GeoHash grid records the data density of the annotated locations. It then utilizes UNet over the GeoHash matrix to infer the delivery location.
- *DLInfMA* [12]: It employs hierarchical clustering algorithm to cluster stay points to generate candidate locations, and uses an attention-based model to select the one with the highest score as the delivery location.

Variants. To evaluate the effectiveness and necessity of each component of our proposal, we also compare it with the following variants of $TDCM$.

- *TDCM-hClu*: It replaces the *stay hotspot* detection component in $TDCM$ with a hierarchical clustering algorithm as [12] did.
- *TDCM-noAt*: This method removes the attention unit while others remain the same as $TDCM$.
- *TDCM-noMu*: This method removes the auxiliary task, while others remain the same as $TDCM$.

Evaluation Metrics. We utilize MAE, P_{95} and β_k as evaluation criteria. MAE is used to evaluate the mean calibration error of the transport destinations, which is calculated as (8). Given a test dataset of size N, $DesL'_i$ and $DesL_i$ denote the ground truth and the calibrated location of the i_{th} transport destination respectively, and the Euclidean distance between them is *calibration error*. P_{95} is the 0.95 percentile error for the validation dataset. β_k represents the percentage of the evaluation samples with *calibration error* less than a given threshold k meters. Apparently, the model performs better with lower MAE and P_{95} and higher β_k.

$$MAE = \frac{\sum_{i=0}^{N} dist\left(DesL_i, DesL'_i\right)}{N} \tag{8}$$

5.2   Overall Evaluation

Table 2 shows the overall performance of $TDCM$ compared with baselines and its variants, and our proposal outperforms all baselines and variants. First of all, *DTInf*, *GeoRank*, and *U-Net* perform poorly in all metrics. The reason may be that they are highly dependent on the accuracy of the delivery point and cannot be applied directly to infer the destination. Secondly, the performance of *DLInfMA* is weaker than our proposal, we think the reasons are two-fold: 1) *DLInfMA* utilizes a hierarchical clustering algorithm to cluster stay points and regards the centroid of each cluster as the candidate location. It is not suitable for identifying transport destinations with multiple unloading warehouses, as they may generate multiple stay point clusters, which is further verified by variant *TDCM-hClu*. 2) *TDCM* devises a multi-task framework to recognize all destination instances and match them with corresponding waybill addresses. It can reduce accumulated inference errors, which is also validated by the variant *TDCM-noMu*. At last, the weak performance of variant *TDCM-noAt* verifies the effectiveness of attention units.

Table 2. Overall effectiveness evaluation

Dataset		Qingdao				Linyi			
Metric		MAE(m)	P_{95}(m)	β_{500}(%)	β_{1000}(%)	MAE(m)	P_{95}(m)	β_{500}(%)	β_{1000}(%)
Baseline	DTInf	25643.39	102109.11	27.71	30.12	8452.71	32417.51	33.33	37.93
	GeoRank	15485.29	98619.02	74.69	74.69	9756.99	78055.01	68.97	70.11
	U-Net	22803.77	128903.68	72.49	75.91	2563.04	24571.02	79.43	82.75
	DLInfMA	1413.37	3651.49	93.33	93.68	1548.19	2034.71	93.68	94.38
Variant	TDCM-hClu	1833.07	4259.87	92.85	92.85	476.56	1308.31	94.25	94.25
	TDCM-noAt	1403.61	5175.73	90.98	94.04	530.25	2019.38	93.11	93.11
	TDCM-noMu	1295.24	2911.19	91.57	93.97	583.29	1620.77	94.16	94.31
Ours		**545.65**	**1005.07**	**94.25**	**94.25**	**434.78**	**356.31**	**96.38**	**97.59**

5.3   Ablation Analysis of Features

To verify the effectiveness and necessity of each feature for transport destination calibration, we retrained the model with each feature removed in turn and report

Table 3. Features effectiveness evaluation

Dataset		Qingdao				Linyi			
Metric		MAE(m)	P_{95}(m)	β_{500}(%)	β_{1000}(%)	MAE(m)	P_{95}(m)	β_{500}(%)	β_{1000}(%)
Behavior	F_{vt}	+348.76	+3823.28	-3.62	-4.82	+797.88	+3025.96	-3.44	-2.31
	F_{sd}	+214.92	+2495.65	-2.41	-3.61	+1946.78	+17464.07	-4.59	-3.45
	F_{sf}	-78.28	+568.48	-3.62	-2.41	+922.36	+2102.47	-3.44	-3.44
	F_{ct}	+171.88	+2495.65	-2.41	-3.61	+1727.75	+5450.75	-1.14	-1.14
Match	F_{dl}	+472.71	+4242.35	-4.82	-3.61	+928.38	+1931.18	-5.74	-4.59
	F_{co}	+391.8	+3823.28	-3.62	-4.82	**+3595.02**	**+20336.61**	**-6.91**	**-5.74**
	F_{wa}	+356.48	+3823.28	-2.41	-3.61	+1346.14	+3711.35	-2.31	-2.31
Context	F_{sa}	+688.75	+4242.36	-4.82	-3.61	+51.27	+397.48	-1.14	0
	F_{mc}	**+570.39**	**+5811.89**	**-6.03**	**-6.02**	+3252.75	+17464.07	-4.59	-3.45
	F_{nw}	+160.93	+406.51	-1.21	-1.21	-390.97	+1290.42	-2.31	-2.31

the change in metrics of the new model compared to the original model without any feature removal. The results on two datasets are shown in Table 3. We can find that none of the features is redundant, and F_{mc} (*main categories of cargoes involved*) and F_{co} (*coverage of waybill trajectories*) are the two most important features.

5.4 Multi-task Weight α Selection

we varied α vary from 0, 0.2, 0.4, 0.6 and 0.8 to select a proper weight on the two datasets for the multi-task destination matching model. As shown in Fig. 7, the blue and green bars show results of MAE and P_{95} and the red and yellow lines present β_{500} and β_{1000}. We get the best performance when $\alpha = 0.4$, while the performance gets worse as the α increases or decreases.

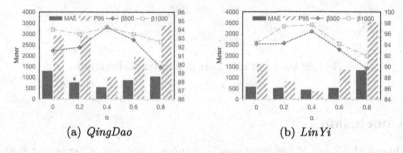

(a) *QingDao*   (b) *LinYi*

Fig. 7. Multi-task weight α tuning

5.5 Case Study

The case of the destination calibration using *TDCM* for "P004359" (as shown in the example in Fig. 1) is illustrated in Fig. 8. The *stay hotspots* are detected by the *stay hotspot detection* component, and 17 of them are fed as candidates to the multi-task destination matching model for destination recognition. The destination instances (A and B) generated by the auxiliary task are shown in the map. Their value for each feature generated by the attention unit is also mapped to the length of the red bar. The "*Distribution of stop frequency*" and "*Coverage of waybill trajectories*" features of A contribute the most. We think the former is caused by the fact that A has multiple unloading locations, i.e. the driver may need to stop several times for unloading. This is also a distinctive feature of being a destination. In addition, A, as the real destination of "P004359", is traversed by most of its waybill trajectories (that is, the value of "*Coverage of waybill trajectories*" of A is high). This is certainly strong evidence that A is a destination instance. Moreover, since B is a steel distributor enterprise with non-24-hour working, it pays more attention to the features of "distribution of visit time", "distribution of stay duration" and "Number of cargo types". This allows B to be correctly recognized by the auxiliary task as positive(destination instance) even if it is a destination instance of another waybill address. A is also output by the main task as the actual destination of "P004359" to perform the calibration. In 2022, *TDCM* has been deployed on a steel logistics platform, serving over 800 transport lines and approximately 69,000 trucks. Up to now, a total of 2,428 transportation destinations have been calibrated.

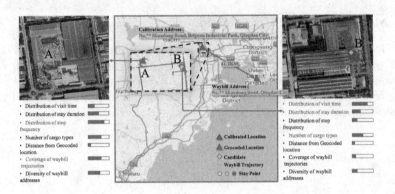

Fig. 8. a case of transport destination calibration

6 Conclusion

To address the issue of incorrectness and incompleteness of transport destinations, we design a Transport Destination Calibration framework based on Multitask learning, called *TDCM*. First, to accurately pinpoint the locations of destinations that are close to each other but differ in size, we put forward a road turn-off location based stay hotspot identification method. Besides, we devise an end-to-end multi-task destination matching model by introducing attention mechanism, to precisely identify each waybill' transport destination. The comparison experiments with the existing methods and the case study validate the effectiveness and superiority of *TDCM*. In the future, we will apply *TDCM* to more application scenarios to verify its rationality and reliability.

Acknowledgments. This work is supported by NSFC (Nos.62072180 and U191 1203).

Ethical Statement. Our submission involves the development and evaluation of a multi-task learning methods for transport destination calibration. we have taken steps to ensure that our research does not infringe upon personal data privacy or contribute to any unethical practices such as those related to policing or military application.

We use trajectory, waybill and other datasets for experimental evaluation. Before the data set is used, some measures are implemented to ensure that any personal data has been anonymized or otherwise rendered non-identifiable. In summary, we recognize the importance of ethical considerations in machine learning and data mining and have taken steps to ensure that our work adheres to ethical principles.

References

1. Comaniciu, D., Meer, P.: Mean shift: a robust approach toward feature space analysis. IEEE Trans. Pattern Anal. Mach. Intell. **24**(5), 603–619 (2002)
2. Cui, Y., Che, W., Liu, T., Qin, B., Yang, Z.: Pre-training with whole word masking for Chinese BERT. IEEE/ACM Trans. Audio, Speech Lang. Process. **29**, 3504–3514 (2021)
3. Dzmitry, B., Yoshua, B.: Neural machine translation by jointly learning to align and translate. In: 3rd International Conference on Learning Representations, ICLR 2015, San Diego, CA, USA, May 7–9, 2015, Conference Track Proceedings (2015)
4. Ester, M., Kriegel, H.P., Sander, J., Xu, X., et al.: A density-based algorithm for discovering clusters in large spatial databases with noise. In: KDD, vol. 96, pp. 226–231 (1996)
5. Forman, G.: Getting your package to the right place: supervised machine learning for geolocation. In: Dong, Y., Kourtellis, N., Hammer, B., Lozano, J.A. (eds.) ECML PKDD 2021. LNCS (LNAI), vol. 12978, pp. 403–419. Springer, Cham (2021). https://doi.org/10.1007/978-3-030-86514-6_25
6. Hu, Y., et al.: Salon: a universal stay point-based location analysis platform. In: Proceedings of the 29th International Conference on Advances in Geographic Information Systems, pp. 407–410 (2021)
7. Li, Y., et al.: Pear: personalized re-ranking with contextualized transformer for recommendation. In: Companion Proceedings of the Web Conference 2022, pp. 62–66 (2022)
8. Newson, P., Krumm, J.: Hidden Markov map matching through noise and sparseness. In: SIGSPATIAL, pp. 336–343 (2009)
9. Pu, M., Mao, J., Du, Y., Shen, Y., Jin, C.: Road intersection detection based on direction ratio statistics analysis. In: 2019 20th IEEE International Conference on Mobile Data Management (MDM), pp. 288–297. IEEE (2019)
10. Ren, H., et al.: Mtrajrec: Map-constrained trajectory recovery via seq2seq multi-task learning. In: Proceedings of the 27th ACM SIGKDD Conference on Knowledge Discovery & Data Mining, pp. 1410–1419 (2021)
11. Ruan, S., et al.: Filling delivery time automatically based on couriers' trajectories. IEEE Trans. Knowl. Data Eng. (2021)
12. Ruan, S., et al.: Discovering actual delivery locations from MIS-annotated couriers' trajectories. In: 2022 IEEE 38th International Conference on Data Engineering (ICDE), pp. 3241–3253. IEEE (2022)
13. Ruan, S., et al.: Doing in one go: delivery time inference based on couriers' trajectories. In: SIGKDD, pp. 2813–2821 (2020)
14. Song, Y., Li, J., Chen, L., Chen, S., He, R., Sun, Z.: A semantic segmentation based poi coordinates generating framework for on-demand food delivery service. In: Proceedings of the 29th International Conference on Advances in Geographic Information Systems, pp. 379–388 (2021)
15. Srivastava, V., Tejaswin, P., Dhakad, L., Kumar, M., Dani, A.: A geocoding framework powered by delivery data. In: Proceedings of the 28th International Conference on Advances in Geographic Information Systems, pp. 568–577 (2020)
16. Ward, J.H., Jr.: Hierarchical grouping to optimize an objective function. J. Am. Stat. Assoc. **58**(301), 236–244 (1963)
17. Yang, S.B., Guo, C., Yang, B.: Context-aware path ranking in road networks. IEEE Trans. Knowl. Data Eng. **34**(7), 3153–3168 (2020)

18. Ye, M., Shou, D., Lee, W.C., Yin, P., Janowicz, K.: On the semantic annotation of places in location-based social networks. In: Proceedings of the 17th ACM SIGKDD International Conference on Knowledge Discovery and Data Mining, pp. 520–528 (2011)

19. Zhao, L., e al.: Automatic calibration of road intersection topology using trajectories. In: 2020 IEEE 36th International Conference on Data Engineering (ICDE), pp. 1633–1644. IEEE (2020)

20. Zheng, Y., Li, Q., Chen, Y., Xie, X., Ma, W.Y.: Understanding mobility based on GPS data. In: Proceedings of the 10th International Conference on Ubiquitous Computing, pp. 312–321 (2008)

21. Zheng, Y., Zhang, L., Xie, X., Ma, W.Y.: Mining correlation between locations using human location history. In: Proceedings of the 17th ACM SIGSPATIAL International Conference on Advances in Geographic Information Systems, pp. 472–475 (2009)

22. Zheng, Y., Zhang, L., Xie, X., Ma, W.Y.: Mining interesting locations and travel sequences from GPS trajectories. In: Proceedings of the 18th International Conference on World Wide Web, pp. 791–800 (2009)

23. Zhou, G., et al.: Deep interest network for click-through rate prediction. In: Proceedings of the 24th ACM SIGKDD International Conference on Knowledge Discovery & Data Mining, pp. 1059–1068 (2018)

24. Zhu, K., Wu, T., Shen, W., Mao, J., Shi, Y.: TDCT: Transport destination calibration based on waybill trajectories of trucks. In: Li, B., Yue, L., Tao, C., Han, X., Calvanese, D., Amagasa, T. (eds.) Web and Big Data. APWeb-WAIM 2022. LNCS, vol. 13423, pp. 435–440. Springer, Cham (2023). https://doi.org/10.1007/978-3-031-25201-3_33

25. Zhu, Z., et al.: ICFinder: a ubiquitous approach to detecting illegal hazardous chemical facilities with truck trajectories. In: Proceedings of the 29th International Conference on Advances in Geographic Information Systems, pp. 37–40 (2021)

Demo

An Interactive Interface for Novel Class Discovery in Tabular Data

Colin Troisemaine[1,2]([✉]), Joachim Flocon-Cholet[1], Stéphane Gosselin[1],
Alexandre Reiffers-Masson[2], Sandrine Vaton[2], and Vincent Lemaire[1]

[1] Orange Innovation, Lannion, France
colin.troisemaine@orange.com
[2] Department of Computer Science, IMT Atlantique, Brest, France

Abstract. Novel Class Discovery (NCD) is the problem of trying to discover novel classes in an unlabeled set, given a labeled set of different but related classes. The majority of NCD methods proposed so far only deal with image data, despite tabular data being among the most widely used type of data in practical applications. To interpret the results of clustering or NCD algorithms, data scientists need to understand the domain- and application-specific attributes of tabular data. This task is difficult and can often only be performed by a domain expert. Therefore, this interface allows a domain expert to easily run state-of-the-art algorithms for NCD in tabular data. With minimal knowledge in data science, interpretable results can be generated.

Keywords: novel class discovery · clustering · transfer learning · open world learning

1 Introduction

Novel Class Discovery (NCD) [5,10] is a new and growing field, where we are given during training a labeled set of known classes and an unlabeled set of different classes that must be discovered. In recent years, many methods have been proposed in the context of computer vision [2–4].

Tabular data refers to data arranged in a table, where each row is an observation and each column is an attribute. It is one of the most common types of data in practical applications such as medical diagnosis, customer churn prediction, cybersecurity, and credit risk assessment [7]. An intuitive example of application of NCD in tabular data would be customer churn prediction: by using a dataset that includes the reasons why customers stopped using a product, we can more accurately identify other causes of churn in an unlabeled set where the reasons have not yet been identified.

While in practice, tabular data is one of the most prevalent data types in the real world, to the best of our knowledge, only one paper has attempted to solve NCD specifically for tabular data [9]. This is partly due to the heterogeneous nature of tabular data, and its lack of spatial and semantic structure,

© The Author(s), under exclusive license to Springer Nature Switzerland AG 2023
G. De Francisci Morales et al. (Eds.): ECML PKDD 2023, LNAI 14175, pp. 295–299, 2023.
https://doi.org/10.1007/978-3-031-43430-3_18

which makes it difficult to apply some computer vision techniques such as data augmentation or Self-Supervised Learning [1]. Furthermore, tabular data contains attributes that are specific to each domain. This means that analyzing and understanding the results of NCD or clustering algorithms can be challenging for a data scientist who is not necessarily familiar with the attributes of the dataset. On the other hand, the domain expert does not necessarily have the knowledge required to write code and run NCD or clustering algorithms.

In an ideal scenario, the domain expert would be included in the training loop to interpret the results produced by the data scientist. But for practical reasons, it can be difficult to dedicate two people to this task, as having a data scientist run an algorithm, present the results to the expert, and update the parameters based on the expert's feedback can be a slow and tedious process.

Hence, the goal of the interface proposed here is to allow a domain expert to visualize his data and run NCD or clustering algorithms without having to write code, as in visual data mining [8]. Given a pre-processed dataset, a user can employ this interface to (i) get a first idea of the separability of the data with T-SNE, (ii) select which features and classes to use, and which classes are considered unknown (iii) parameterize and execute NCD and clustering algorithms and (iv) train decision trees to generate rules and interpret the classes or clusters. Based on theses results, an expert can remove features or classes that have too much influence on the results, re-train a clustering model and re-generate rules. This process can be very tedious through code, but it can be done in only a few clicks with this interface (which even a data scientist could benefit from).

Currently, this interface implements TabularNCD [9], the state-of-the-art for NCD in the context of tabular data. Other clustering methods are implemented: spectral clustering, k-means and a simple baseline method to solve NCD. This baseline trains a classification neural network on the labeled data, and then projects the unlabeled data in its last layer before clustering it with k-means.

As expressed before, this interface cannot replace the domain expert. It only allows him to explore his dataset using machine learning tools without writing code. This interface is also upgradeable, as new NCD or clustering algorithms can be quickly implemented. The application is open source and can be installed locally using the code at https://github.com/ColinTr/InteractiveClustering. The video of the demonstration is available at www.youtube.com/watch?v=W7ru8NHPj-8.

2   Interface Description

As shown in Fig. 1, the interface is composed of 6 different panels that we will describe in this section. For reference, the interface was made in JavaScript with React 18.2.0, and the Python code is executed by a Flask 2.2.2 backend server.

After selecting and loading a dataset with panel (1), the user can select in panel (2) which features to use in the dataset, and indicate which is the class feature. Panel (3) lists the modalities of the class feature picked earlier. Here, the user can choose to remove some classes from the dataset by unchecking them

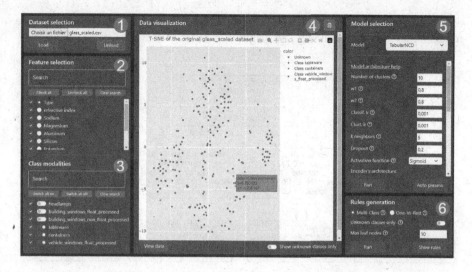

Fig. 1. The interface for interactive clustering and Novel Class Discovery.

and select which classes are considered as known or unknown. In a use-case with a real dataset including both labeled and unlabeled data, a group of observations could be labeled as "unknown", which can thus be selected in this panel.

With panel (4), the data can be visualized in 2 dimensions by running a T-SNE. The user also has the option to view only the unknown classes for easier readability. Clicking on a point displays all its attributes. Note that in an effort of optimization and better responsiveness, if a data plot is requested and has the same coordinates as a previous request, the T-SNE is re-used and only the coloring of the points is updated.

The NCD and clustering models can be selected and configured in panel (5). Currently, 4 models are available: TabularNCD [9] is a NCD method that pre-trains a simple encoder of dense layers with the VIME [11] self-supervised learning method. It adopts an architecture with two "heads": one to classify the known classes and introduce relevant high-level features in the latent space of the encoder, and another classifier for the unlabeled data trained with pseudo-labels defined without supervision in the latent space. Next is k-means, which was implemented for its simplicity and wide adoption in the community. It has the advantage of having a single parameter (the number of clusters). Spectral clustering is also available. It is known for its good results and its ability to discover new patterns across a wide variety of datasets [6]. And finally the baseline method described in Sect. 1 can be selected. Both TabularNCD and the baseline rely on an architecture composed of a combination of dense layers, dropout and activation functions which can all be modified through the interface (even the sizes and number of hidden layers).

Starting the training of TabularNCD or the baseline will produce a pop-up that displays the current progress of the training and the estimated time to completion. It is also possible to visualize a T-SNE of the latent space of these models, instead of visualizing the original features of the data.

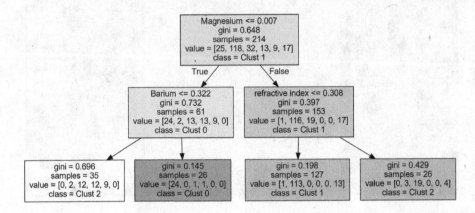

Fig. 2. Example of rules that describe the classes of the *glass identification* dataset.

Finally, in panel (6), the user can get an interpretable description of the results by training a decision tree to classify the known classes and the discovered clusters. Figure 2 is an example of rules in a decision tree obtained for the *glass* dataset. Each box represents a node/leaf of the tree and displays the rule and the majority class. The tree can be multi-class and will give an overview of the relations between all the classes and clusters, but it can be hard to comprehend because of its complexity. For this reason, we can instead use a *one-versus-rest* approach, where for each class or cluster, a decision tree has to predict the class or cluster against all the others. As each individual tree solves a problem of lower complexity, they are shorter compared to the multi-class case and are more easily interpretable.

3   Conclusion

This demo paper introduces an interactive interface for the problem of Novel Class Discovery in tabular data. This interface is mainly targeted to domain experts and data scientists. The user can quickly visualize the data and generate clusters of novel classes along with interpretable decision trees to describe them. Furthermore, the user can easily identify both features and classes to remove from the training process and start a new clustering with different parameters.

In the future, this interface could be improved by adding a function to estimate the number of clusters (i.e. the number of novel classes). New NCD and clustering methods can also be easily integrated. Giving the user the ability to merge or split some clusters and update the decision tree's rules accordingly could also be an interesting addition.

References

1. Borisov, V., Leemann, T., Seßler, K., Haug, J., Pawelczyk, M., Kasneci, G.: Deep neural networks and tabular data: a survey. arXiv preprint: 2110.01889 (2021). https://doi.org/10.48550/ARXIV.2110.01889
2. Chi, H., et al.: Meta discovery: learning to discover novel classes given very limited data. In: International Conference on Learning Representations (2022)
3. Han, K., Rebuffi, S.A., Ehrhardt, S., Vedaldi, A., Zisserman, A.: AutoNovel: automatically discovering and learning novel visual categories. IEEE Trans. Pattern Anal. Mach. Intell. **44**, 6767–6781 (TPAMI) (2021)
4. Han, K., Vedaldi, A., Zisserman, A.: Learning to discover novel visual categories via deep transfer clustering. In: International Conference on Computer Vision (ICCV) (2019)
5. Hsu, Y.C., Lv, Z., Kira, Z.: Learning to cluster in order to transfer across domains and tasks. In: International Conference on Learning Representations (ICLR) (2018)
6. Ng, A., Jordan, M., Weiss, Y.: On spectral clustering: analysis and an algorithm. In: Advances in Neural Information Processing Systems, vol. 14 (2001)
7. Shwartz-Ziv, R., Armon, A.: Tabular data: deep learning is not all you need. Inf. Fusion **81**, 84–90 (2022)
8. Soukup, T., Davidson, I.: Visual data mining: techniques and tools for data visualization and mining (2002)
9. Troisemaine, C., Flocon-Cholet, J., Gosselin, S., Vaton, S., Reiffers-Masson, A., Lemaire, V.: A method for discovering novel classes in tabular data. In: IEEE International Conference on Knowledge Graph (ICKG) (2022)
10. Troisemaine, C., Lemaire, V., Gosselin, S., Reiffers-Masson, A., Flocon-Cholet, J., Vaton, S.: Novel class discovery: an introduction and key concepts (2023). https://doi.org/10.48550/ARXIV.2302.12028
11. Yoon, J., Zhang, Y., Jordon, J., van der Schaar, M.: VIME: extending the success of self- and semi-supervised learning to tabular domain. In: Advances in Neural Information Processing Systems, vol. 33, pp. 11033–11043 (2020)

marl-jax: Multi-agent Reinforcement Leaning Framework for Social Generalization

Kinal Mehta[1]([✉])([iD]), Anuj Mahajan[2]([iD]), and Pawan Kumar[1]([iD])

[1] IIIT Hyderabad, Hyderabad, India
kinal.mehta@research.iiit.ac.in, pawan.kumar@iiit.ac.in
[2] University of Oxford, Oxford, UK
anuj.mahajan@cs.ox.ac.uk

Abstract. Recent advances in Reinforcement Learning (RL) have led to many exciting applications. These advancements have been driven by improvements in both algorithms and engineering, which have resulted in faster training of RL agents. We present marl-jax, a multi-agent reinforcement learning software package for training and evaluating social generalization of the agents. The package is designed for training a population of agents in multi-agent environments and evaluating their ability to generalize to diverse background agents. It is built on top of DeepMind's JAX ecosystem [2] and leverages the RL ecosystem developed by DeepMind. Our framework marl-jax is capable of working in cooperative and competitive, simultaneous-acting environments with multiple agents. The package offers an intuitive and user-friendly command-line interface for training a population and evaluating its generalization capabilities. In conclusion, marl-jax provides a valuable resource for researchers interested in exploring social generalization in the context of MARL. The open-source code for marl-jax is available at: https://github.com/kinalmehta/marl-jax.

Keywords: Multi-agent Reinforcement Learning · Zero-Shot Generalization · General Sum Games

1 Introduction

Multi-agent reinforcement learning (MARL) is an important framework for training autonomous agents that operate in dynamic environments with multiple learning agents. Many potential real-world applications require the trained agents to cooperate with humans or agents not seen during training. That is, they should be able to zero-shot generalize to novel social partners. Most of the existing MARL frameworks are either designed for cooperative MARL research or naively extend existing single-agent RL frameworks to work with multiple agents.

Demo Video: https://youtu.be/WQVQXPIUZxk
Github: https://github.com/kinalmehta/marl-jax.

© The Author(s), under exclusive license to Springer Nature Switzerland AG 2023
G. De Francisci Morales et al. (Eds.): ECML PKDD 2023, LNAI 14175, pp. 300–304, 2023.
https://doi.org/10.1007/978-3-031-43430-3_19

On the contrary, marl-jax is designed specifically for multi-agent research and facilitate the training and assessment of the generalization capacities of multi-agent reinforcement learning (MARL) algorithms when facing new social partners. We utilize the functionalities of JAX [3] including autograd, vectorization through *vmap*, parallel processing through *pmap*, and compilation through *jit*, resulting in highly optimized training for multiple agents.

2   Related Works

The RL community has developed several frameworks targeting various aspects such as implementation simplicity, ease of adaptation and scaling deep RL agents. In marl-jax, we focus on ease of experimentation and adaption for training a population of agents in multi-agent environments.

A number of libraries that concentrate on single-agent reinforcement learning have been created, such as stable-baselines3 [17], dopamine [7], acme [10], RLlib [12], and CleanRL [11]. These libraries prioritize features like modularity by providing useful abstractions, ease of use by requiring minimal code to get started, distributed training and ease of comprehension and reproducibility. Other libraries such as Reverb [6], rlax [2], and launchpad [23] concentrate on specific components of an RL system.

For multi-agent reinforcement learning, several libraries have been developed, including PyMARL [18], epymarl [15], RLlib [12], Mava [16], and PantheonRL [19]. RLlib and PantheonRL enhance existing single-agent RL algorithms to enable multi-agent training, while Mava, PyMARL, and epymarl are specifically designed for MARL but only support cooperative environments.

The advancements of Reinforcement Learning (RL) algorithms have been greatly influenced by libraries providing a range of environments. Single agent RL has been aided by libraries such as OpenAI Gym [4] and dm-env [14], which established the framework for environment interactions. Multi-agent RL has been supported by SMAC [18] and PettingZoo [21]. Recently, DeepMind has contributed to the field by open-sourcing MeltingPot [1], a library for evaluating multi-agent generalization to new social partners at scale. Similarly, efforts for measuring generalization in cooperative multi-agent settings [13] are being supported by libraries like [8].

Several recent works [2,10,11,16] have begun utilizing JAX [3] due to its various benefits. These benefits include auto-vectorization, just-in-time compilation, and easy multi-GPU scaling.

3   marl-jax

Inspired by Acme [10], we share a lot of design philosophies with it. Reverb [6] is used as a data-store server for the replay buffer. Launchpad [23] is used for distributed computing. We use JAX [3] as the numerical computation backend for neural networks. We use *dm-env* API as our environment interaction API and extend it for multi-agent environments (Fig. 1).

3.1   System Architecture

We follow IMPALA-style distributed training architecture. Our system consists of three main components running in parallel as separate processes.

- **Environment Loop:** The environment loop process interacts with the environment using the available policy and adds the collected experience to the replay buffer. Multiple parallel environment loop processes are run, each with its own copy of the environment. We use CPU inference for action selection on each process. To keep the policy parameters in sync with the learner process, the parameters are periodically fetched from the learner process. The action selection step is optimized using *vamp* auto-vectorization to select the action for all agents in the environment.
- **Learner:** The actual policy learning happens in this process. The learner fetches experience from the replay buffer and performs the optimization step on policy and value function parameters. We use *pmap* to auto-scale the optimization step to multiple GPUs and *vmap* based auto-vectorization to perform the optimization step for all agents in parallel.
- **Replay Buffer:** A separate process with reverb [6] server is used as a replay buffer. All the actors add experience to this server, and the learner process samples experience from the server and perform the optimization.

3.2   Supported Environments

We support two multi-agent environment suits, which consist of simultaneous acting homogeneous agents.

- **Overcooked:** Overcooked [5] is a cooperative environment where a team of agents must cook a soup and deliver it as fast as possible. The reward is shared among all agents. A variety of different layouts are available that focus on different learning aspects. The generalization of the trained agents can be tested against human data provided by the suite.
- **MeltingPot:** MeltingPot [1] consists of more than 50 different environments and over 256 unique test scenarios. Once a population of agents is trained in an environment, the generalization to novel partners can be tested on the various test scenarios provided in the suite.

3.3   Algorithms Implemented

We currently support two major algorithms

- **IMPALA:** A standard actor-critic based independent learning algorithm using V-trace [9] for off-policy corrections.
- **OPRE:** Options as Responses [22] follows actor-critic based learning but its objective is specifically designed to generalize to novel partners. It is used as one of the baseline in MeltingPot [1]. We are the first to provide an open-source implementation of OPRE.

Fig. 1. marl-jax supports two major environment surits, Meltingpot [1] and Over-cooked [5]

3.4 Utilities

We provide two major utilities 1) *train.py* and 2) *evaluate.py*

- **train.py:** The entry point for training a population of agents in the given environment
- **evaluate.py:** Used to evaluate the generalization performance on with various partner agents
- **evaluation_results.py:** Aggregates the evaluation results by averaging across multiple seeds and presents a table.

4 Conclusion and Future Works

In this paper, we introduced marl-jax, a highly optimized package for training and evaluation of the generalization of a population of agents to novel partners. The package provides an easy-to-use utility to train and evaluate the trained agents. It also provides an open-source implementation of ORPE [22], a MARL algorithm designed for generalization. This package is targeted for researchers working on generalization in MARL and reduces the entry barrier for new researchers in MARL generalization. As any software package, marl-jax is under continuous development and, in future, aims to implement other population learning algorithms [20].

Acknowledgement. The first author was supported by RIPPLE grant at International institute of information technology, Hyderabad, India. The last author was partially funded by Qualcomm grant. We thank the host institute for providing compute resources for an extended period of time, and for HPC resources funded under the RIPPLE grant.

References

1. Agapiou, J.P., et al.: Melting Pot 2.0 (2022)
2. Babuschkin, I., et al.: The DeepMind JAX ecosystem (2020)
3. Bradbury, J., et al.: JAX: composable transformations of Python+NumPy programs (2018)
4. Brockman, G., et al.: OpenAI Gym (2016)
5. Carroll, M., et al.: On the utility of learning about humans for human-AI coordination. In: Advances in Neural Information Processing Systems, vol. 32. Curran Associates, Inc. (2019)
6. Cassirer, A., et al.: Reverb: a framework for experience replay (2021)
7. Castro, P.S., Moitra, S., Gelada, C., Kumar, S., Bellemare, M.G.: Dopamine: a research framework for deep reinforcement learning (2018)
8. Ellis, B., et al.: SMACv2: an improved benchmark for cooperative multi-agent reinforcement learning. arXiv preprint arXiv:2212.07489 (2022)
9. Espeholt, L., et al.: IMPALA: scalable distributed deep-RL with importance weighted actor-learner architectures. In: Proceedings of the 35th International Conference on Machine Learning. PMLR (2018)
10. Hoffman, M.W., et al.: Acme: a research framework for distributed reinforcement learning (2022)
11. Huang, S., et al.: CleanRL: high-quality single-file implementations of deep reinforcement learning algorithms. J. Mach. Learn. Res. **23**(274) (2022)
12. Liang, E., et al.: RLlib: abstractions for distributed reinforcement learning. In: Proceedings of the 35th International Conference on Machine Learning. PMLR (2018)
13. Mahajan, A., et al.: Generalization in cooperative multi-agent systems. arXiv preprint arXiv:2202.00104 (2022)
14. Muldal, A., Doron, Y., Aslanides, J., Harley, T., Ward, T., Liu, S.: dm_env: a Python interface for reinforcement learning environments (2019)
15. Papoudakis, G., Christianos, F., Schäfer, L., Albrecht, S.V.: Benchmarking multi-agent deep reinforcement learning algorithms in cooperative tasks. In: Proceedings of the Neural Information Processing Systems Track on Datasets and Benchmarks (NeurIPS) (2021)
16. Pretorius, A., et al.: Mava: a research framework for distributed multi-agent reinforcement learning (2021)
17. Raffin, A., Hill, A., Gleave, A., Kanervisto, A., Ernestus, M., Dormann, N.: Stable-Baselines3: reliable reinforcement learning implementations. J. Mach. Learn. Res. **22**(268) (2021)
18. Samvelyan, M., et al.: The StarCraft multi-agent challenge. CoRR abs/1902.04043 (2019)
19. Sarkar, B., Talati, A., Shih, A., Sadigh, D.: PantheonRL: a MARL library for dynamic training interactions. Proc. AAAI Conf. Artif. Intell. **36**(11) (2022)
20. Team, O.E.L., et al.: Open-ended learning leads to generally capable agents (2021)
21. Terry, J., et al.: PettingZoo: gym for multi-agent reinforcement learning. In: Advances in Neural Information Processing Systems (2021)
22. Vezhnevets, A.S., Wu, Y., Leblond, R., Leibo, J.Z.: Options as responses: grounding behavioural hierarchies in multi-agent RL (2020)
23. Yang, F., et al.: Launchpad: a programming model for distributed machine learning research (2021)

Temporal Graph Based Incident Analysis
System for Internet of Things

Peng Yuan[1], Lu-An Tang[1], Haifeng Chen[1(✉)], David S. Chang[2], Moto Sato[1],
and Kevin Woodward[2]

[1] NEC Labs America, Princeton, NJ, USA
haifeng@nec-labs.com
[2] Lockheed Martin Space, Denver, CO, USA

Abstract. Internet-of-things (IoTs) deploy massive number of sensors to monitor the system and environment. Anomaly detection on sensor data is an important task for IoT maintenance and operation. In real applications, the occurrence of a system-level incident usually involves hundreds of abnormal sensors, making it impractical for manual verification. The users require an efficient and effective tool to conduct incident analysis and provide critical information such as: (1) identifying the parts that suffered most damages and (2) finding out the ones that cause the incident. Unfortunately, existing methods are inadequate to fulfill these requirements because of the complex sensor relationship and latent anomaly influences in IoTs. To bridge the gap, we design and develop a Temporal Graph based Incident Analysis System (TGIAS) to help users' diagnosis and reaction on reported anomalies. TGIAS trains a temporal graph to represent the anomaly relationship and computes severity ranking and causality score for each sensor. TGIAS provides the list of top k serious sensors and root-causes as output and illustrates the detailed evidence on a graphical view. The system does not need any incident data for training and delivers high accurate analysis results in online time. TGIAS is equipped with a user-friendly interface, making it an effective tool for a broad range of IoTs.

Keywords: Internet of things · temporal graph · anomaly diagnosis · causality analysis

1 Introduction

With rapid development in recent years, Internet-of-Things (IoTs) are widely used in different fields such as smart city, healthcare, transportation, spacecraft, and environment monitoring [1]. One major task of IoT maintenance is to handle the system failures and incidents. Many algorithms and methods are proposed for effective anomaly detection on IoTs [7–9]. However, the detection of anomalies is just the beginning of incident handling process. To fix the problem and repair IoT, the users need to know the components that suffer most damages and the root causes of the incident. In many cases, a system level incident involves hundreds of abnormal sensors, which needs extensive human analysis and strong domain expertise to check manually. The users require an efficient and effective tool to automatically diagnose IoT incidents and help repair the damages.

© The Author(s), under exclusive license to Springer Nature Switzerland AG 2023
G. De Francisci Morales et al. (Eds.): ECML PKDD 2023, LNAI 14175, pp. 305–309, 2023.
https://doi.org/10.1007/978-3-031-43430-3_20

Unfortunately, many existing IoT monitoring systems [7–9] lack the ability to analyze detected anomalies, mainly due to the following challenges: (1) Complex sensor relationships: An IoT monitoring system may include thousands of sensors, many of them are mutually influenced. The users cannot provide their relationship in advance, instead they want to learn such relations as system output. (2) Latent anomaly influences: Unlike the computer systems (e.g., servers, networks, etc.), the influences on the mechanic systems monitored by IoT are relatively slow, it may take hours or even days for anomalies to expand. Therefore, the analysis tools without considering temporal factors and anomaly propagation patterns [2–5] cannot work on IoT related scenarios. (3) Noisy data: The IoTs are full of noisy data and false alerts caused by the normal dynamics. The analysis system needs to filter them out automatically. (4) Lack of training data: The incidents are very rare in IoTs. It is hard to collect a large dataset of incidents for training. In addition, the users always expect the system to analyze "unseen" incidents that are different from existing ones.

To overcome these challenges, we design and develop a Temporal Graph based Incident Analysis System (TGIAS) to analyze incident data and diagnose the root causes for IoT applications. TGIAS constructs a temporal graph by retrieving sensor relationship from historical data. The system filters out false alerts based on graph patterns, conducts severity ranking and causality analysis along the edges. A major advantage of TGIAS is on the applicability, TGIAS does not need any incident data for training and delivers accurate analysis results in online time. A demo video of TGIAS can be accessed from the project page at: https://github.com/pengyuan0106/Temporal-Graph-based-Incident-Analysis-Tool-for-IoT.

2 System Description

2.1 Overall Framework

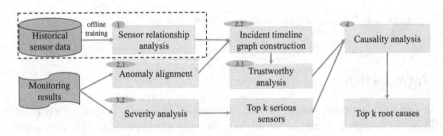

Fig. 1. System Framework of TGIAS

The overall process of TGIAS is shown in Fig. 1: (1) TGIAS first scans historical data to retrieve the sensor relationship. This step is conducted offline. (2) In online analysis, TGIAS takes the anomaly detection results by IoT monitoring systems as inputs and aligns them by time. Then the system integrates the anomalies with sensor relationship to construct an incident timeline graph. The graph nodes are the abnormal sensors, and the edges represent the anomaly propagation effects among sensors. (3) TGIAS conducts trustworthy analysis on the graph and filters out false alerts. The system also carries out severity analysis to find out the top k serious sensors. (4) TGIAS employs a graph reasoning algorithm to trace back the propagation of anomalies by visiting the edges in reverse time order. Finally, the top k root causes are found out and output to end users with detailed evidence.

2.2 Demo Scenario

Figure 2 shows an example of using TGIAS to analyze incident data for an IoT application. There are more than 4000 sensors installed in the system to monitor multiple components. The main dashboard of TGIAS has two parts: a tool panel (left) and views (right).

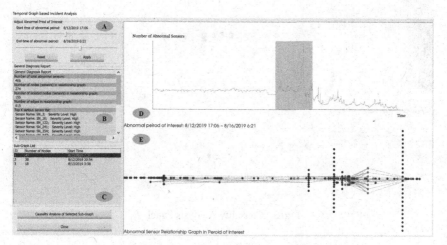

Fig. 2. The Main Dashboard of TGIAS

Tool Panel: Given the input of detected anomalies by monitoring system, TGIAS automatically determines the incident period by the size of abnormal sensors. The user can adjust the start and end timestamps of incidents in Fig. 2.A. TGIAS conducts trustworthiness analysis for detected anomalies and filters out the false alerts. TGIAS reports diagnosis results for each sensor in Fig. 2.B and lists out the trustworthy abnormal sensor groups as sub-graphs in Fig. 2.C.

Views: TGIAS shows the number of abnormal sensors over time in Fig. 2.D. The incident period is highlighted in blue rectangle. The temporal graph constructed from abnormal sensors is shown in Fig. 2.E. The graph nodes are the sensors, they are plotted along the timeline (X-axis) by the first anomaly timestamp. The edges represent the sensor relationship retrieved from historical data. The green nodes belong to the selected anomaly sensor group (sub-graph). They will be used for further analysis.

When user clicks the button of "Causality Analysis", TGIAS pops out a panel to provide detailed analysis results as shown in Fig. 3. The system lists out the sensors ranked by causality scores (Fig. 3.A). The red, orange, and yellow sensors are the top ranked ones that most likely to cause the incident. TGIAS also provides the rankings of sensor severity and alert time. The user can easily switch between different rankings by clicking the measures. A detailed timeline of the anomaly sensor group is plotted in Fig. 3.C. If user would like to zoom into a specific sensor, he just selects a node in Fig. 3.C. TGIAS will highlight the edges linked to that sensor as yellow lines. The system then plots an ego-graph of selected sensor in Fig. 3.D. The user can further select an edge (highlighted as green line) to study the detailed relationship. The system plots the original data of both sensors in Fig. 3. E&F. The red lines indicate the timestamps of the first anomalies. In this example, the sensor in Fig. 3.E likely causes the anomalies of another sensor in Fig. 3.F.

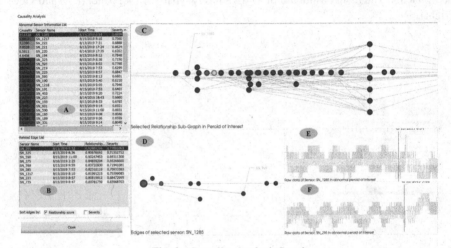

Fig. 3. Causality Analysis Panel

3   Conclusion

In this paper, we present a novel incident analysis tool for IoTs: Temporal Graph based Incident Analysis System (TGIAS). TGIAS represents the incident process by a temporal graph, filters out false alerts, conducts severity ranking and causality reasoning to provide useful information for incident recovery. TGIAS only requires historical normal data for training. It provides analysis results with high accuracy and delivers results in online time. The system is currently deployed to handle incidents for spacecraft and satellites. TGIAS can be extended to a wide variety of IoT applications and help system recover from different types of incidents.

References

1. Tang, S., Shelden, D.R., Eastman, C.M., Pishdad-Bozorgi, P., Gao, X.: A review of building information modeling (BIM) and the internet of things (IoT) devices integration: present status and future trends. Autom. Constr. **101**, 127–139 (2019)

2. Li, Z., et al.: Generic and robust localization of multi-dimensional root causes. In: 2019 IEEE 30th International Symposium on Software Reliability Engineering (ISSRE), pp. 47–57 (2019)
3. Liu, P., et al.: FluxRank: a widely-deployable framework to automatically localizing root cause machines for software service failure mitigation. In: 2019 IEEE 30th International Symposium on Software Reliability Engineering (ISSRE), pp. 35–46 (2019)
4. Meng, Y., et al.: Localizing failure root causes in a microservice through causality inference. In: 2020 IEEE/ACM 28th International Symposium on Quality of Service (IWQoS), pp. 1–10 (2020)
5. Ma, M., et al.: Diagnosing root causes of intermittent slow queries in cloud databases. Proc. VLDB Endowment **13**(8), 1176–1189 (2020)
6. Chen, H., Horak, M., Narayanappa, S., Woodward, K.: Integrating AI into planning, diagnostic, and prescription systems for human & robotic deep space exploration missions. In: AAAI 2018 Fall Symposium Series (2018)
7. Yuan, P., Tang, L.A., Chen, H., Sato, M., Woodward, K.: 3D histogram based anomaly detection for categorical sensor data in internet of things. Open J. Internet Things (OJIOT) **8**(1), 32–43 (2022)
8. Yuan, P., Tang, L.A., Chen, H., Sato, M., Woodward, K.: Explainable anomaly detection system for categorical sensor data in internet of things. In: Amini, M.R., Canu, S., Fischer, A., Guns, T., Kralj Novak, P., Tsoumakas, G. (eds.) Machine Learning and Knowledge Discovery in Databases. ECML PKDD 2022. LNCS (LNAI), vol. 13718, pp. 594–598. Springer, Cham (2023). https://doi.org/10.1007/978-3-031-26422-1_37
9. Behniafar, M., Nowroozi, A., Shahriari, H.A.: A survey of anomaly detection approaches in internet of things. ISC Int. J. Inf. Secur. **10**(2), 79–92 (2018)

MEMENTO: Facilitating Effortless, Efficient, and Reliable ML Experiments

Zac Pullar-Strecker[1], Xinglong Chang[1], Liam Brydon[1], Ioannis Ziogas[1,2],
Katharina Dost[1(✉)], and Jörg Wicker[1]

[1] University of Auckland, Auckland, New Zealand
{zpul156,xcha011,lbry121,izio995}@aucklanduni.ac.nz, {katharina.dost,
j.wicker}@auckland.ac.nz
[2] University of Mississippi, Oxford, MS, USA

Abstract. Running complex sets of machine learning experiments is
challenging and time-consuming due to the lack of a unified framework.
This leaves researchers forced to spend time implementing necessary
features such as parallelization, caching, and checkpointing themselves
instead of focussing on their project. To simplify the process, in this
paper, we introduce MEMENTO, a Python package that is designed to aid
researchers and data scientists in the efficient management and execution
of computationally intensive experiments. MEMENTO has the capacity
to streamline any experimental pipeline by providing a straightforward
configuration matrix and the ability to concurrently run experiments
across multiple threads. A demonstration of MEMENTO is available at:
wickerlab.org/publication/memento.

Keywords: Experimental pipeline · Parallel computing · Reliable ML

1 Introduction

As machine learning (ML) and data science continue to shape decision-making
across a wide range of domains [6], researchers and practitioners are facing
the ever-growing challenge of designing and executing complex experiments efficiently and reliably [8]. This challenge is particularly acute in machine learning,
where the traditional experimental pipeline involves a complex set of intermediate steps, such as data pre-processing, model selection, hyperparameter tuning,
and model evaluation. Benchmarking multiple options for each of these steps
easily results in an overwhelming number of individual experiments, long waiting times when run sequentially, and the need to adjust scripts or restart entire
sets of experiments when errors occur.

Aiming to avoid these challenges in practice, automated machine learning
(AutoML) tools can help choose the best combination of steps in the ML pipeline
automatically [1,3,4,7], but they may not be flexible enough to integrate new
algorithms or match multiple libraries as is necessary for research. In Python,
scikit-learn's pipeline functionality [5] allows users to conveniently choose and

© The Author(s), under exclusive license to Springer Nature Switzerland AG 2023
G. De Francisci Morales et al. (Eds.): ECML PKDD 2023, LNAI 14175, pp. 310–314, 2023.
https://doi.org/10.1007/978-3-031-43430-3_21

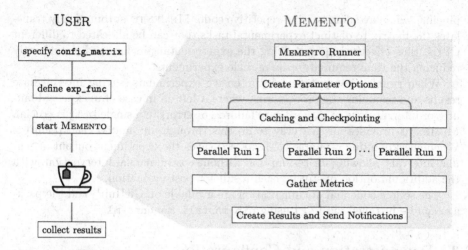

Fig. 1. The roles of the user and MEMENTO when running a complex and large set of experiments with MEMENTO.

chain the steps involved in a single experiment but falls short in handling the setup of entire experiment sets.

To date, there exists no unified framework for the parallelization of experimental setups beyond a narrow range of machine learning applications [2]. Most often, researchers have to manually implement workflow features, such as caching and checkpointing, which introduce an added layer of complexity. Moreover, remedial corrections to potential errors occurring partway through the execution of a series of long experiments require tedious debugging.

To fill this gap, we present MEMENTO (*Marvelous ExperiMENt TOol*), a simple and flexible Python library designed to help researchers, data analysts, and machine learning practitioners streamline the experimental pipeline, parallelize experiments across threads, save and restore results, checkpoint in-progress experiments, and receive notifications when experiments fail or finish. By providing a unified framework for the parallelization of experimental setups, MEMENTO can significantly reduce the amount of time and coding expertise required to structure and execute experimental workflows, as Fig. 1 shows.

In the following sections, we present the main features of MEMENTO, explain how it can streamline any experimental workflow, and conclude the paper.

2   The MEMENTO Package: Features and Strengths

MEMENTO is a modular, flexible, and easily configurable Python library that allows for the parallel execution of multiple experimental setups with the added benefits of automatic checkpoint creation, output caching, and error tracing. At the core of MEMENTO's design lies a user-friendly and customizable configuration matrix outlining the building blocks of the intended experiments within a pipeline, while avoiding writing repetitive code. MEMENTO automatically translates the matrix to distinct experimental tasks that can be allocated to different CPUs, thus effectively parallelizing the experimental pipeline and significantly reducing the time required for large-scale experiments.

When running computationally intensive experiments, saving intermediate results and resuming the process from where it left off in case of unexpected failures or interruptions (e.g., hardware failures, or errors in a single task) is crucial. MEMENTO provides an easy way to do this through automated checkpointing. When checkpointing is enabled, MEMENTO saves the experiment output at regular intervals, allowing for resumption without costly manual intervention, with the additional option of storing each result for post-evaluation.

The source code and documentation are available on GitHub[1], and the package can be installed via PyPI using `pip install memento-ml`.

3   Demonstration and Configuration

To run a set of experiments with MEMENTO, the user only needs to do the steps outlined in Fig. 1 (left). After installing and importing MEMENTO using

```
1  import memento
2  # ...
```

the user needs to define a configuration matrix (`config_matrix`). This matrix is the core of MEMENTO and describes the list of experiments the user wants to run. One example is

```
3   # The configuration matrix conveniently specifies the experiments to be run.
4   config_matrix = {
5       "parameters": {
6           "dataset": [load_digits, load_wine, load_breast_cancer],
7           "feature_engineering": [DummyImputer, SimpleImputer],
8           "preprocessing": [DummyPreprocessor, MinMaxScaler, StandardScaler],
9           "model": [AdaBoost, RandomForest, SVC]
10      },
11      "settings": {"n_fold": 5},
12      "exclude": [{"dataset": load_digits, "feature_engineering": SimpleImputer}]
13  }
```

Note that the parameters are **not predefined but user-configured keywords** the user can customize to their needs, e.g., to add additional experimental steps. MEMENTO automatically constructs tasks using every combination of defined parameters, e.g., for all combinations of datasets, feature engineering methods, preprocessing techniques, and models in Lines 6-9 above resulting in $3 \times 2 \times 3 \times 3 = 54$ tasks. The `settings` keyword (Line 11) stores constants that can be accessed by each task, removing the need to access global constants. The keyword `exclude` (Line 12) is used as a lookup table to skip any unwanted combinations during the task generation allowing for a more fine-grained specification of required experiments. The name and number of parameters can be fully customized,

---

[1] MEMENTO source code and documentation: github.com/wickerlab/memento.

making MEMENTO compatible with any type of machine-learning pipeline. Each task is self-isolated and can be run in parallel.

Once the configuration matrix is defined, MEMENTO passes every individual created task as a parameter set into the user-defined experiment function, e.g.,

```
14  # The experiment function is called for each individual set of parameters.
15  def exp_func(context: memento.Context, config: memento.Config) -> any:
16      if context.checkpoint_exist():  # Based on the hashing value.
17          result = context.restore()  # Recover results from cache.
18      else:
19          # access the parameters for an individual experiment
20          X, y = config.dataset()
21          model = config.model()
22          n_fold = config.settings["n_fold"]
23          # prepare the experimental pipeline and run
24          pipeline = make_pipeline(config.feature_engineering, config.preprocessing, model)
25          result = cross_val_scores(pipeline, X, y, cv=n_fold)
26          context.checkpoint(result)  # Caching results
27      return result
```

MEMENTO is designed with fault tolerance and exception handling in mind. Each parameter is assigned a hash value when generating the tasks. If an error occurs during the execution, we can update the code and rerun it. To avoid running duplicate experiments, we specify in Lines 16-17 to restore checkpoints if available. If not, we access the input parameters for this task (Lines 20-22) and specify the individual experiment that needs to be run (Lines 24-25). Lastly, we specify the outputs that should be checkpointed (Line 26).

Once both the configuration matrix and the experiment function are set up, the user can start MEMENTO:

```
28  # start MEMENTO
29  notif_provider = memento.ConsoleNotificationProvider()
30  results = memento.Memento(exp_func, notif_provider).run(config_matrix)
```

and relax while it runs `exp_func` for each task in parallel based on the number of threads available on the computer, caching results, and creating checkpoints. The notification provider specifies the notification sent to the user once MEMENTO completes the tasks.

4   Conclusion

In this paper, we introduced MEMENTO, a Python library that helps researchers and data scientists run and manage computationally expensive experiments efficiently and reliably. MEMENTO's simple configuration matrix and parallelization capabilities allow for running large numbers of experiments quickly. The ability to checkpoint in-progress experiments adds convenience and reliability to the process, making it easier to manage long-running experiments. While MEMENTO is particularly well-suited to running machine learning experiments, it can be used for any type of laborious and time-consuming experimental pipeline.

References

1. Feurer, M., Klein, A., Eggensperger, K., Springenberg, J.T., Blum, M., Hutter, F.: Auto-sklearn: efficient and robust automated machine learning. In: Hutter, F., Kotthoff, L., Vanschoren, J. (eds.) Automated Machine Learning. TSSCML, pp. 113–134. Springer, Cham (2019). https://doi.org/10.1007/978-3-030-05318-5_6
2. Idowu, S., Strüber, D., Berger, T.: Asset management in machine learning: state-of-research and state-of-practice. ACM Comput. Surv. **55**(7), 1–35 (2022). https://doi.org/10.1145/3543847
3. Karmaker, S.K., Hassan, M.M., Smith, M.J., Xu, L., Zhai, C., Veeramachaneni, K.: AutoML to date and beyond: challenges and opportunities. ACM Comput. Surv. **54**(8), 1–36 (2021). https://doi.org/10.1145/3470918
4. Komer, B., Bergstra, J., Eliasmith, C.: Hyperopt-sklearn: automatic hyperparameter configuration for scikit-learn. In: van der Walt, S., Bergstra, J., (eds.) Proceedings of the 13th Python in Science Conference, pp. 32–37 (2014). https://doi.org/10.25080/Majora-14bd3278-006
5. Pedregosa, F., et al.: Scikit-learn: machine learning in python. J. Mach. Learn. Res. **12**, 2825–2830 (2011)
6. Sarker, I.H.: Machine learning: algorithms, real-world applications and research directions. SN Comput. Sci. **2**(3), 160 (2021). https://doi.org/10.1007/s42979-021-00592-x
7. Thornton, C., Hutter, F., Hoos, H.H., Leyton-Brown, K.: Auto-weka: combined selection and hyperparameter optimization of classification algorithms. In: Proceedings of the 19th ACM SIGKDD International Conference on Knowledge Discovery and Data Mining KDD 2013, pp. 847–855, Association for Computing Machinery, New York, NY, USA (2013). https://doi.org/10.1145/2487575.2487629
8. Zöller, M.A., Huber, M.F.: Benchmark and survey of automated machine learning frameworks. J. Artif. Int. Res. **70**, 409–472 (2021). https://doi.org/10.1613/jair.1.11854

Cad2graph: Automated Extraction of Spatial Graphs from Architectural Drawings

Pratik Maitra[1], Masahiro Kiji[1], Talal Riaz[2], Philip M. Polgreen[1],
Alberto M. Segre[1], Sriram V. Pemmaraju[1], and Bijaya Adhikari[1(✉)]

[1] University of Iowa, Iowa City, USA
{pratik-maitra,masahiro-kiji,philip-polgreen,alberto-segre,
sriram-pemmaraju,bijaya-adhikari}@uiowa.edu
[2] Yelp, San Francisco, USA

Abstract. A significant obstacle to spatial epidemiology in healthcare facilities is the absence of computationally amenable maps of the underlying space. Spatial data for built spaces are typically stored in computer aided design (CAD) architectural files which are difficult to parse, query, and combine with other data sources. To alleviate this difficulty, we design a tool, CAD2GRAPH, which automatically extracts spatial maps from CAD files. To ensure that the spatial map is easily amenable to computation, we represent it as a graph whose vertices represent spatial units of a uniform size and whose edges represent obstacle-free, walkable paths of uniform length connecting adjacent pairs of spatial units. CAD2GRAPH extracts key information such as walls, doors, and room labels from the CAD file and through a series of geometric transformations, extracts a spatial graph.

Keywords: spatial graphs · graph extraction · architectural drawings · epidemiology · healthcare associated infections

1 Introduction

Spatial epidemiology at the scale of healthcare facilities is critical for modelling and combating healthcare associated infections (HAIs). Some example include spatio-temporal clustering of *Clostridioides Difficile* infections (CDI) in hospitals [8], characterizing spatial distribution of healthcare professionals (HCPs) [4,5], optimizing microbial swabbing for disease surveillance [1], and non pharmaceutical interventions to combat CDI and *Methicillin-resistant Staphylococcus Aureus* (MRSA) [3,7]. A major obstacle in spatial epidemiology at the healthcare facility level is the lack of spatial maps of the architectural layout of the facilities. While many healthcare facilities have spatial data, it is often stored as computer aided design (CAD) files. It is non-trivial to analyze these together with other datasets often required for spatial analysis such as healthcare professionals mobility, patient transfers between rooms, and patient-room-doctors interactions [2,6]. On the other hand, if the data present in CAD files

G. De Francisci Morales et al. (Eds.): ECML PKDD 2023, LNAI 14175, pp. 315–319, 2023.
https://doi.org/10.1007/978-3-031-43430-3_22

could be extracted as a spatial graph, it could easily be stored in the same database as other data and be analyzed together. In prior work [5,6], we have used hand-crafted spatial graphs. Generating hand-crafted spatial graphs for the entire University of Iowa Hospitals and Clinics took many months of work by 4-5 undergraduate students, 2-3 masters students, and 3 faculty members. This is a significant effort that not all healthcare facilities can afford.

To address the issues mentioned above, here we develop and demonstrate CAD2GRAPH, a novel tool to automatically generate a spatial graph representing the physical space within a hospital given an input CAD file. CAD2GRAPH carefully reads the outline of the architectural drawing and extracts spatial graph via a series of geometric transformations. Our target audience include data mining researchers who are applying their work towards the understanding and mitigation of HAIs and epidemiologists who are seeking to apply data mining techniques for clinical applications.

2   System Overview

The input to CAD2GRAPH is a CAD file representing a specific floor in a specific building. We first extract the external layout of the floor and structure of the walls and doors. We then construct a two dimensional grid with a pre-defined spacing and overlay the grid on the structure with walls and doors. We then assign a label to each grid node based on whether the given grid node is within a polygon of walls. We then repeat the same process and label the door nodes. We then add edges between the grid nodes in eight directions. Finally, we sparsify the grid and extract spatial graph. To this tool, we added a graphical user interface (in Python). The overview of the system and GUI are presented in Fig. 1.

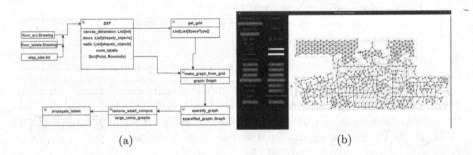

(a)	(b)

Fig. 1. (a) Overview of CAD2GRAPH. (b) The interface of the tool implemented in Python. The left panel consists of interactive elements and the right panel visualizes generated graph on top of the architectural layout.

The system presented here automatically extracts spatial graph $G_L(L, E, W, X)$ from a given CAD file. The graph is defined between the locations L within healthcare facilities including patient rooms, hallways, and so on. Each edge $e(l_1, l_2) \in E$ between two locations l_1 and l_2 indicates that they are in close proximity. The corresponding edge weight depends on whether l_1 and l_2 are within the same closed space or are connected via doors, stairs, and elevators. We provide a high-level summary of the steps involved in CAD2GRAPH next.

1. Canvas construction. We read the CAD file and extract the architectural layout and room labels, positions of walls and doors, and the dimension of the outer most walls. We then construct a 2-d canvass and assign (x, y) co-ordinates to each label read from the CAD file.

2. Grid extraction. We then construct an evenly spaced 2-d grid on the generated canvas. The number of rows and columns on the grid is determined by the size of the canvas and a user-specified parameter ρ. We then assign numeric labels to each point on the grid. Points on walls and doors are labelled 1 and 2 respectively. Others are labelled 0.

3. Graph extraction from the grid. The next step involves creating a spatial graph $G'(L', E', W', X')$ from the grid defined above. First we go over the labels extracted in step 1 and assign them as nodes L' (note: each room has a single label in the underlying CAD graph). We then add edges E' between the newly added nodes L'. Since the nodes were extracted from the grid, they too are organized in a 2-d space. We connect nodes in horizontal, vertical, and diagonal directions and assign weights depending on whether an edge crosses a door.

4. Graph sparsification. $G'(L', E', W', F')$ could be very dense for small values of ρ. This would imply that even a small room could have multiple nodes inside it, which is not ideal. Therefore, we sparsify $G'(L', E', W', F')$ to obtain a sparse spatial graph $G(L, E, W, F)$ using K-nearest neighbor search [9] and finally we remove small disconnected components. We then add edges between disjoint connected components while ensuring that the newly added edges are between the nodes which are geographically close. Note that only very few edges are added in the post processing step.

3   Demonstration

We run CAD2GRAPH on CAD files obtained from the University of Iowa Hospitals and Clinics (UIHC). Here we present a subsection of the visualization of a CAD file for a floor in the Roy Carver building[1] for demonstration. Figure 2 (a) visualizes the input CAD files. The red rectangles represent a subset of labelled rooms. Figure 2 (b) shows spatial graph extracted by CAD2GRAPH on top of the architectural layout. Here, we are only showing some of the labels in a subsection of the floor for legibility; notice that CAD2GRAPH is able to assign the labels to the correct nodes. As observed, the stairs, storage rooms, mechanical rooms, and staff's rooms are all assigned in the right place. Next, we observe that the cross door edges (in brown) and non-cross door edges (in blue) have been correctly identified: none of the blue edges cross any doors and all brown edges cross a door. Finally, we see a reasonable number of nodes within each open spaces,

---

[1] https://www.facilities.uiowa.edu/building/0359.

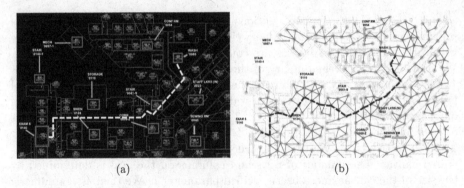

(a)   (b)

Fig. 2. (a) Visualization of a subset of the CAD file showing one of the floors of the Roy Carver building in the University of Iowa Healthcare and Clinics.(b) Spatial graph extracted by CAD2GRAPH from the CAD file shown on the left.

only one node in small rooms, and the hallways are represented by single chain of blue edges. These observations are consistent with our design goal.

The dashed white line in Fig. 2 (a) shows obstacle free walkable path from the room EXAM 6 to the room WASH 0065. The dashed black line in Fig. 2 (b) is drawn over the edges along the shortest paths between the two rooms. As observed in the figure, the spatial graph extracted by CAD2GRAPH is actually able to infer edges which correspond to meaningful obstacle-free walkable paths between physical spaces. For additional validation, we first computed euclidean distances between all pairs of rooms in the same floor as above. We then computed shortest hop distance on extracted spatial graph between the same pairs of rooms. The Pearson's correlation between the two distances was 0.83, further validating that the spatial graphs extracted by CAD2GRAPH do capture the underlying architectural space well. A short demonstration video is available online[2].

4   Conclusion

In this paper, we presented CAD2GRAPH, an automated approach to extracting spatial graphs from CAD files. CAD2GRAPH carefully constructs a sparse graph from the architectural information in the input CAD file. We demonstrated a subsection of spatial graph generated from a CAD file obtained from University of Iowa Hospitals and Clinics. Additional demos along with out source code are publicly available. Our results show that the generated graphs are meaningful. These graphs can be stored in relational databases along with other datasets obtained from hospital operations and can be easily leveraged for spatial analysis of epidemics within healthcare facilitates.

---

[2] https://www.dropbox.com/s/9j6q1l5q11q2uuq/Pr_Final.mp4?dl=0.

References

1. Adhikari, B., Lewis, B., Vullikanti, A., Jiménez, J.M., Prakash, B.A.: Fast and near-optimal monitoring for healthcare acquired infection outbreaks. PLoS Comput. Biol. **15**(9), e1007284 (2019)
2. Cruz-Correia, R., et al.: Integration of hospital data using agent technologies-a case study. Artif. Intell. Commun. **18**(3), 191–200 (2005)
3. Curtis, D.E., Hlady, C.S., Kanade, G., Pemmaraju, S.V., Polgreen, P.M., Segre, A.M.: Healthcare worker contact networks and the prevention of hospital-acquired infections. PLoS ONE **8**(12), e79906 (2013)
4. Curtis, D.E., Hlady, C.S., Pemmaraju, S.V., Polgreen, P.M., Segre, A.M.: Modeling and estimating the spatial distribution of healthcare workers. In: Proceedings of the 1st ACM International Health Informatics Symposium, pp. 287–296 (2010)
5. Hasan, D.H., et al.: Modeling and evaluation of clustering patient care into bubbles. In: 2021 IEEE 9th International Conference on Healthcare Informatics (ICHI), pp. 73–82. IEEE (2021)
6. Jang, H., Pai, S., Adhikari, B., Pemmaraju, S.V.: Risk-aware temporal cascade reconstruction to detect asymptomatic cases: for the CDC mind healthcare network. In: 2021 IEEE International Conference on Data Mining (ICDM), pp. 240–249. IEEE (2021)
7. Monsalve, M.N., Pemmaraju, S.V., Thomas, G.W., Herman, T., Segre, A.M., Polgreen, P.M.: Do peer effects improve hand hygiene adherence among healthcare workers? Infect. Control Hosp. Epidemiol. **35**(10), 1277–1285 (2014)
8. Pai, S., Polgreen, P.M., Segre, A.M., Sewell, D.K., Pemmaraju, S.V., et al.: Spatiotemporal clustering of in-hospital clostridioides difficile infection. Infect. Control Hosp. Epidemiol. **41**(4), 418–424 (2020)
9. Peterson, L.E.: K-nearest neighbor. Scholarpedia **4**(2), 1883 (2009)

PIQARD System for Experimenting and Testing Language Models with Prompting Strategies

Marcin Korcz, Dawid Plaskowski, Mateusz Politycki, Jerzy Stefanowski, and Alex Terentowicz[✉]

Poznan University of Technology, Institute of Computer Science, Poznań, Poland
jstefanowski@cs.put.poznan.pl, alex.terentowicz@gmail.com

Abstract. Large Language Models (LLMs) have seen a surge in popularity due to their impressive results in natural language processing tasks, but there are still challenges to be addressed. Prompting in the question is a solution for some of them. In this paper, we present PIQARD, an open-source Python library that allows researchers to experiment with prompting techniques and information retrieval, and combine them with LLMs. This library includes pre-implemented components and also allows users to integrate their own methods.

Keywords: Large language models · Prompting · Information retrieval

1 Introduction

The rapid development of Large Languages Models (LLMs), such as GPT's, has led to an unprecedented increase in interest also outside the research community. However, despite successes in NLP tasks, important challenges such as *knowledge hallucination* persist. This is a phenomenon in which the model generates a wrong answer with high confidence, which is not justified by any of its training data. Fine-tuning the model could be a solution, but this involves huge costs and the risk of catastrophic forgetting of important information due to new data.

Prompting with the in-context learning technique is an alternative approach. It directs the model response in the right direction by providing a pattern containing instructions on the task along with examples of its solution [1]. Note that it doesn't require additional training or tuning LLM and can be efficiently customized to suit specific tasks or domains. However, the prompting strategies that are being recently introduced are not yet sufficiently well recognized and require further intensive research. This has motivated us to develop specialized software for this purpose, i.e. the open-source PIQARD library[1]. This library empowers users to integrate the custom systems from several components

---

[1] PIQARD is an acronym from Prompted Intelligent Question Answering with Retrieval of Documents.

G. De Francisci Morales et al. (Eds.): ECML PKDD 2023, LNAI 14175, pp. 320–323, 2023.
https://doi.org/10.1007/978-3-031-43430-3_23

responsible for: language models, information retrieval, and several prompting techniques. Furthermore, users can not only exploit techniques provided by us such as, e.g. ReAct prompting, language models e.g. BLOOM, but they can also extend PIQARD by integrating their own methods and testing them. To facilitate immediate access and testing queries by non-programmers, we also provide a web application for PIQARD.

In our opinion, there is still a lack of open systems available for such experiments, with prompting strategies and the extension of the LLM question answering using information retrieval in an external document or knowledge database. In this sense, our proposal may be unique to the research community today. Furthermore, despite the numerous advantages of using prompting, it seems that this should be appropriately adapted not only to the task domain but also to the language models – which just requires experimentation, as we already conducted with PIQARD.

2   Prompt Engineering

Prompting comprises techniques for communicating with Language Model systems in order to guide their behavior toward desired outcomes without the need to tune the model weights. Below we describe the ones currently implemented in PIQARD.

Few-shot prompting involves providing the model with relevant input and output examples, typically accompanied by a task description, to enable the model to generalize to new tasks with minimal supervision. In contrast, the *chain of thought prompting* goes beyond input-output pairs and includes reasoning steps that lead to the final answer. This approach is particularly useful for common-sense reasoning tasks and question answering based on retrieved context. As part of our experimental work, we modified the *self-ask prompting*, which repeatedly prompts the model to ask follow-up questions, to classify whether a given question requires retrieval of information from the web. Additionally, we implemented *ReAct*, a prompting method that iteratively plans and retrieves relevant information from Wikipedia to answer a question.

Prompt engineering is an empirical discipline and the efficacy of varying prompting strategies can vary considerably across models, which requires extensive experimentation and support from software tools.

3   General Overview of PIQARD System

The PIQARD system is designed in the form of a Python library for scientists prototyping new prompting techniques, and additionally, as an Open System web application suited for inexperienced users seeking to utilize available templates. The library is implemented in Python 3 using tools such as YAML, Jinja2.

Following Fig. 1 PIQARD consists of three main modules: *Information Retriever*, *Prompting*, and *Language Model*. In the most basic prompt strategy, the user's query is first passed to the **Information Retriever** module,

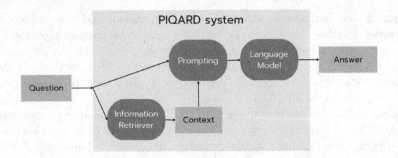

Fig. 1. Modules making up the PIQARD system

which searches the provided text database or the web for contextual information. Semantic search with FAISS and ANNOY packages, or lexical search using BM25 are available for searching in locally stored databases. Semantic search is performed on indexed datasets of text documents encoding using pre-trained language models available in the Sentence-transformers package, like *multi-qa-MiniLM-L6-cos-v1* used in our experiments. In the next step, the context document is passed to the **Prompting** module, which combines the question and retrieved context according to the predetermined fields in the prompt template.

Finally, the completed prompt is sent to the **Language Model** module standing as a proxy for the chosen language model generating an answer. The system can make use of remotely hosted LLM accessed by an API, as well as locally deployed ones. Only models available for public use, such as the open-source *Bloom 176B* and *Cohere xlarge*, were used in the presented experiments, but other, more commercial solutions could also be employed.

Our Web Application is deployed using tools such as *FastAPI* and JavaScript framework *ReactJS*. It builds on top of the library and provides a straightforward way of interacting with the models enriched by prompting techniques. The user interface clearly shows each step taken in order to answer the question using the specific prompt template. For more technical information visit our website[2].

4   An Example of Use

Presented below is an example of using the PIQARD library to answer a question. It uses a basic prompt template to provide the BLOOM model with context obtained by an ANNOY retriever from a custom, locally stored text document database. The BLOOM model was released on July 6th, 2022, but the model can accurately answer questions when provided with the appropriate context and prompt, despite the absence of up-to-date information in the training set.

The presented example is only a brief demonstration of the general use. However, we have experimentally tested several available prompting strategies, and more interesting results can be observed on our website (see footnote 2).

---

[2] More information about the library, examples of its use as well as a video presentation are available at PIQARD GitHub website https://plaskod.github.io/.

```
1  from piqard.PIQARD import PIQARD
2  from piqard.utils.prompt_template import PromptTemplate
3  from piqard.information_retrievers import AnnoyRetriever
4  from piqard.language_models import BLOOM176bAPI
5
6  prompt_template = PromptTemplate(template='context_prompt.txt')
7  llm = BLOOM176bAPI(stop_token="\n", temperature=1, top_k=1)
8  ir = AnnoyRetriever(k=1,
9                      database="custom_database",
10                     database_path="corpus.jsonl",
11                     database_index="custom_database_index.ann")
12
13 piqard = PIQARD(language_model=llm,
14                 information_retriever=ir,
15                 prompt_template=prompt_template)
16 piqard("Who is the Prime Minister of the United Kingdom?")
```

Output: [base_prompt]
Answer the question given the context.
Question: Who is the Prime Minister of the United Kingdom?
Context: The prime minister of the United Kingdom is the head of government
of the United Kingdom. The prime minister advises the sovereign on the exercise
of much of the royal prerogative, chairs the Cabinet and selects its ministers.
Rishi Sunak is the Prime Minister of the United Kingdom
Answer: Rishi Sunak is the Prime Minister of the United Kingdom

5   Conclusions

Recent research indicates that prompting is a very vast and still developing
field, which requires systems such as PIQARD to facilitate experimentation.
We believe that there is potential for proposing new tools that could leverage
prompting to a new level, such as access to video/audio retrievers, or other third-
party systems. This allows not only to enhance question-answering systems, but
also to assess and mitigate the risks associated with the inappropriate use of
models (GPT-4 red teaming [2]). It should be noted that some existing libraries,
such as LangChain [3], are developed alongside, which also provide tailored-
made prompting solutions. However, they put more emphasis on providing a
component for developers to build applications on top of, rather than offering
a system suited for prototyping prompts. Furthermore, we are also willing to
collaborate and extend the capabilities of our system to address the specific needs
of various fields where NLP has significant potential, such as law, or medicine.

Acknowledgements. The research was partially supported by SBAD/0740 grant.

References

1. Reppert, J., et al.: Iterated Decomposition: Improving Science Q&A by Supervising
   Reasoning Processes. arXiv:2301.01751
2. OpenAI GPT-4 Technical Report. arXiv:2303.08774
3. Chase, H.: LangChain (2022). https://github.com/hwchase17/langchain

Using Multiple RDF Knowledge Graphs for Enriching ChatGPT Responses

Michalis Mountantonakis[1,2(✉)] [iD] and Yannis Tzitzikas[1,2] [iD]

[1] Institute of Computer Science - FORTH-ICS, Heraklion, Greece
{mountant,tzitzik}@ics.forth.gr
[2] Computer Science Department, University of Crete, Heraklion, Greece

Abstract. There is a recent trend for using the novel Artificial Intelligence ChatGPT chatbox, which provides detailed responses and articulate answers across many domains of knowledge. However, in many cases it returns plausible-sounding but incorrect or inaccurate responses, whereas it does not provide evidence. Therefore, any user has to further search for checking the accuracy of the answer or/and for finding more information about the entities of the response. At the same time there is a high proliferation of RDF Knowledge Graphs (KGs) over any real domain, that offer high quality structured data. For enabling the combination of ChatGPT and RDF KGs, we present a research prototype, called GPT•LODS, which is able to enrich any ChatGPT response with more information from hundreds of RDF KGs. In particular, it identifies and annotates each entity of the response with statistics and hyperlinks to LODsyndesis KG (which contains integrated data from 400 RDF KGs and over 412 million entities). In this way, it is feasible to enrich the content of entities and to perform fact checking and validation for the facts of the response at real time.
URL: https://demos.isl.ics.forth.gr/GPToLODS/Annot_Enrichment
Demo Video: https://youtu.be/H30bSv9NfUw

Keywords: ChatGPT · LOD · RDF · Knowledge Graphs · Annotation

1 Introduction

ChatGPT is a novel Artificial Intelligence (AI) chatbox (https://chat.openai.com/), which is built on GPT-3.5 and GPT-4 families of large language models (LLMs) [2], and provides detailed responses and human-like answers across many domains of knowledge. However, it has not been designed to store or retrieve facts, e.g., like a relational database or a Knowledge Graph (KG). For this reason, in many cases it returns plausible-sounding but incorrect or inaccurate responses [3]. Thereby, it is hard for the user to check the validity of the answers returned by ChatGPT. Sometimes the responses contain entities that do not exist, URLs that are wrong, facts that cannot be verified, outdated data, and many others.

G. De Francisci Morales et al. (Eds.): ECML PKDD 2023, LNAI 14175, pp. 324–329, 2023.
https://doi.org/10.1007/978-3-031-43430-3_24

On the contrary, there are available numerous RDF KGs [4] (e.g., DBpedia [5], Wikidata [17], YAGO [15], etc.), that provides high quality structured data (that are updated at least periodically), by using Linked Data techniques [1].

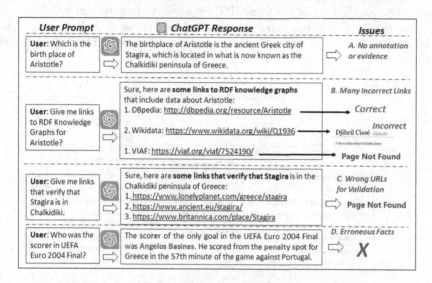

Fig. 1. ChatGPT issues through real conversations (March 27, 2023)

Concerning some key issues of ChatGPT (that can be improved by using KGs), Fig. 1 shows a real conversation with ChatGPT (in March 27, 2023). First, we asked about the birth place of Aristotle (issue A), and the output was a plain text, without evidence or annotations. Afterwards, we desired to find available RDF links for Aristotle (issue B), and only one of them was correct, whereas the URI of Wikidata refers to a completely different entity. Then, we asked about sources verifying that Stagira is located in Chalkidiki, and all the returned URIs were invalid (issue C). In the last case, we asked a question from a different domain, i.e., "Who scored the goal in UEFA Euro 2004 Final?", and we retrieved erroneous facts (issue D); its response was "Angelos Basinas from the penalty", however the correct answer is "Angelos Charisteas with a header".

The objective of this paper is to aid the above issues, however, there are several challenges that should be tackled. Indeed, it is quite difficult to check the validity of entities and URIs, since it requires access to numerous KGs, sources and resources in general. For tacking these challenges, we demonstrate the research prototype GPT•LODS, that enables the user to make a question, and instead of getting the raw answer from ChatGPT, it retrieves the ChatGPT response annotated with the identified entities, and with relevant data about these entities (URIs, facts and KGs). For making this feasible at real time, we exploit LODsyndesis suite of services [9,11] including an Information Extraction (IE) service [12]. These services rely on LODsyndesis KG; a large KG, equipped with special indexes and algorithms, that has integrated 2 billion facts for 412 million entities, from 400 real RDF KGs. In this way, the user is able to speed up the validation of the ChatGPT response and to retrieve more information. Concerning the novelty, to the best of our knowledge it is the first system offering annotation and linking of the ChatGPT responses to hundreds of KGs.

The rest of this demo paper is organized as follows; Sect. 2 describes the related work, Sect. 3 presents the process and the use cases and Sect. 4 concludes the paper.

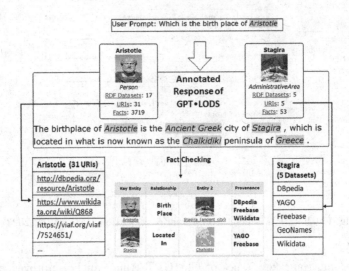

Fig. 2. Screenshots from GPT•LODS research prototype

2   Related Work

First, concerning ChatGPT and KGs, [13] provides a comparison for the Question Answering task and they concluded that ChatGPT can have high precision in general knowledge domains but very low scores in unseen domains, compared to a KG-based approach. Regarding IE tools for Entity Recognition, there are available approaches from several areas, i.e., from Natural Language Processing (NLP) [6], from KGs [7,8,14], and from Neural Networks [16]. However, these tools link the entities to a single KG, and for this reason GPT•LODS uses the machinery of LODsyndesisIE [12], which combines tools from NLP and KGs, and links the entities to 400 RDF KGs. Regarding the novelty, to the best of our knowledge there is no other related system that annotates the response of ChatGPT and provides links and services using hundreds of KGs at real time.

3   The Process of GPT•LODS and Use Cases

First, the name of the prototype GPT•LODS comes from the mathematical notation for function composition, i.e. $(GPT \bullet LODS)(x) = LODS(GPT(x))$, where

LODS comes from LODSyndesis [11]. Concerning the process (see Fig. 2), the user submits through the web application a question (in english), GPT•LODS sends the question to the ChatGPT API and retrieves the response. Afterwards, it applies the machinery of LODsynesisIE (described in [12]), i.e., it combines widely used Entity Recognition tools (i.e., DBpedia Spotlight [7], WAT [14] and Stanford CoreNLP [6]) for recognizing the entities of the ChatGPT response. The next step is to further process the response for creating the annotations and for adding statistics and links to LODsyndesis KG for each recognized entity, and finally it returns the annotated response. Figure 2 shows that by clicking on each entity, one can see its name, image, type and statistics, such as the number of its RDF KGs, URIs and facts that occur in LODsyndesis. By clicking on the links the user can browse (or download) all this data (e.g., the list of all the URIs of an entity). In addition, many other services are offered, including a fact checking service (see Fig. 2) that shows all the relations between any pair of entities of the response (for fact validation). Finally, GPT•LODS can be easily extended for annotating and enriching the response of any LLM (e.g., a new version of ChatGPT or any new LLM) in case of offering an analogous API as ChatGPT.

Scenario and Use Cases. Below, we present a scenario which will be demonstrated in the conference. The target audience can be any researcher of AI area, since GPT•LODS (which is accessible in https://demos.isl.ics.forth.gr/GPToLODS, including a link to github) is a research prototype that combines tools and techniques of several AI components, including LLMs, NLP, and Knowledge Representation and Reasoning (Linked Data and KGs). The scenario is about the user questions (and needs) shown in Fig. 1, i.e., starting with the question "Which is the birth place of Aristotle?". For tackling the needs of this scenario, the results include: the annotated entities, related information (identifiers, facts and datasets) about these entities and fact validation. The scenario can be accessed in a video (https://youtu.be/H30bSv9NfUw), that presents the issues of Fig. 1 and how they can be solved through the following use cases.

Use Case 1. Annotation, Evidence and Linking. This refers to the issues A and B of Fig. 1, i.e., by having the annotation of the entities of the response, we are able to find more information (links, datasets and facts) for each of the entities. Moreover, we can have access to the correct URIs for each entity, e.g., in Fig. 2 we retrieved the correct Wikidata and VIAF URIs for Aristotle (e.g., https://www.wikidata.org/wiki/Q868), and in total 31 URIs.

Use Case 2. Fact Validation and Correct Answer. In Fig. 1 we can see that a ChatGPT response can either provide wrong links for validation or even erroneous facts (issues C, D). In the first case, GPT•LODS can be used for fact validation, e.g., in Fig. 2 it verified 2 facts of the response from popular KGs, like DBpedia and Wikidata. Regarding issue D, GPT•LODS provides links to all the facts for each entity, and the user can further browse these facts (by clicking on the corresponding link), for finding the correct answer to an erroneous fact.

Use Case 3. Dataset Discovery and Enrichment. The user can discover all the datasets of each entity (see the lower right part of Fig. 2), and all (or a part of) the facts of that entity in the KGs that are included in LODsyndesis. This can be useful for enriching the available content of each entity, e.g., for creating an application, a data warehouse [10], for performing an analysis, etc.

4   Concluding Remarks

In this paper, we presented the research prototype GPT•LODS, which enables the real time annotation and linking of a ChatGPT response to hundreds of RDF KGs, the enrichment of its entities and the validation of its facts. As a future work, we plan to improve the GUI, and the fact checking service by performing relation extraction, to offer a REST API and to support multilinguality.

References

1. Bizer, C., Heath, T., Berners-Lee, T.: Linked data: The story so far. In: Semantic Services, Interoperability and Web Applications: Emerging Concepts, pp. 205–227. IGI global (2011)
2. Brown, T., et al.: Language models are few-shot learners. Adv. Neural Inf. Process. Syst. **33**, 1877–1901 (2020)
3. van Dis, E.A., Bollen, J., Zuidema, W., van Rooij, R., Bockting, C.L.: ChatGPT: five priorities for research. Nature **614**(7947), 224–226 (2023)
4. Hogan, A., et al.: Knowledge graphs. ACM Comput. Surv. (CSUR) **54**(4), 1–37 (2021)
5. Lehmann, J., Isele, R., Jakob, M., Jentzsch, A., Kontokostas, D., et al.: DBpedia-a large-scale, multilingual knowledge base extracted from wikipedia. Seman. web **6**(2), 167–195 (2015)
6. Manning, C.D., Surdeanu, M., Bauer, J., Finkel, J.R., Bethard, S., McClosky, D.: The Stanford CoreNLP natural language processing toolkit. In: Proceedings of 52nd Annual Meeting of the Association for Computational Linguistics: System Demonstrations, pp. 55–60 (2014)
7. Mendes, P.N., Jakob, M., García-Silva, A., Bizer, C.: DBpedia spotlight: shedding light on the web of documents. In: Proceedings of the 7th International Conference on Semantic Systems, pp. 1–8 (2011)
8. Moro, A., Cecconi, F., Navigli, R.: Multilingual word sense disambiguation and entity linking for everybody. In: ISWC (Posters & Demos), pp. 25–28. Citeseer (2014)
9. Mountantonakis, M.: Services for Connecting and Integrating Big Numbers of Linked Datasets, vol. 50. IOS Press (2021)
10. Mountantonakis, M., Tzitzikas, Y.: Large-scale semantic integration of linked data: a survey. ACM Comput. Surv. (CSUR) **52**(5), 1–40 (2019)
11. Mountantonakis, M., Tzitzikas, Y.: Content-based union and complement metrics for dataset search over RDF knowledge graphs. ACM JDIQ **12**(2), 1–31 (2020)
12. Mountantonakis, M., Tzitzikas, Y.: Linking entities from text to hundreds of RDF datasets for enabling large scale entity enrichment. Knowledge **2**(1), 1–25 (2022)

13. Omar, R., Mangukiya, O., Kalnis, P., Mansour, E.: ChatGPT versus traditional question answering for knowledge graphs: current status and future directions towards knowledge graph chatbots. arXiv preprint arXiv:2302.06466 (2023)
14. Piccinno, F., Ferragina, P.: From tagme to wat: a new entity annotator. In: Proceedings of the First International Workshop on Entity Recognition & Disambiguation, pp. 55–62 (2014)
15. Rebele, T., Suchanek, F., Hoffart, J., Biega, J., Kuzey, E., Weikum, G.: YAGO: a multilingual knowledge base from wikipedia, wordnet, and Geonames. In: Groth, P., et al. (eds.) ISWC 2016. LNCS, vol. 9982, pp. 177–185. Springer, Cham (2016). https://doi.org/10.1007/978-3-319-46547-0_19
16. Van Hulst, J.M., Hasibi, F., Dercksen, K., Balog, K., de Vries, A.P.: Rel: an entity linker standing on the shoulders of giants. In: Proceedings of the 43rd International ACM SIGIR Conference on Research and Development in Information Retrieval, pp. 2197–2200 (2020)
17. Vrandečić, D., Krötzsch, M.: Wikidata: a free collaborative knowledgebase. Commun. ACM **57**(10), 78–85 (2014)

Interactive Visualization
of Counterfactual Explanations
for Tabular Data

Victor Guyomard[1,2,4(✉)], Françoise Fessant[1,4], Thomas Guyet[3,4],
Tassadit Bouadi[2,4], and Alexandre Termier[2,4]

[1] Orange Innovation, Lannion, France
victor.guyomard@orange.com
[2] Univ Rennes, Inria, CNRS, IRISA, Rennes, France
[3] Inria, AIstroSight, Lyon, France
[4] ENSAI, Rennes, France

Abstract. In this paper we present an interactive visualization tool that
exhibits counterfactual explanations to explain model decisions. Each
individual sample is assessed to identify the set of changes needed to flip
the output of the model. These explanations aim to provide end-users
with personalized actionable insights with which to understand automated decisions. An interactive method is also provided so that users
can explore various solutions. The functionality of the tool is demonstrated by its application to a customer retention dataset. The tool is
compatible with any counterfactual explanation generator and decision
model for tabular data.

Keywords: Counterfactual explanation · Interactive visualisation tool

1 Motivation

A counterfactual explanation is a modified version of an example to be explained
that answers the question: what would have to change to get a different prediction? These explanations are intended to provide users with personalised and
actionable information that allows them to understand, and possibly challenge
or improve, automated decisions [5]. Beyond the generation of this counterfactual explanation, it is necessary that its presentation be understood so that the
user knows how to exploit this information. There is still little work dedicated to
the visualization of individual explanations of the counterfactual type. Gomez et
al. [4] proposed ViCE, a tool that allows the generation of counterfactual explanations and visualise them as part of the credit granting classification. ViCE
deals only with numerical variables. SDA-Vis [3] is another example used in
a context of helping analysis of school drop-out. Bove et al. [2] were able to
identify through a user study that the most interesting visual information for
them were contextualisation, with a description of the variables that are used
for prediction, and the interactivity of the visualisation tool which gives the user

G. De Francisci Morales et al. (Eds.): ECML PKDD 2023, LNAI 14175, pp. 330–334, 2023.
https://doi.org/10.1007/978-3-031-43430-3_25

freedom to explore an explanation. Their study focused on individual explanations by feature importance, in a context of car insurance. We have built on this work to specify the functionalities of our tool in the context of counterfactual explanations.

2   Demonstrator

The tool we propose is intended for users who are not specialists in machine learning algorithms. It can be a business expert or an end user impacted by the decisions of a model. Through the tool, the user has access to explanations and can interact with the decision system. The main objective of the tool is to provide an intuitive visual representation of the counterfactual explanations provided by any algorithm. More precisely, our objective is to show, for a given instance, 1) which features must be modified for the model decision to change, 2) what the magnitude of the change must be and 3) to allow the exploration of alternative solutions.[1]

2.1   Interface Description

Figure 1 displays a counterfactual explanation for a binary classification problem of customer churn (more details in use case study section below).

Various information can be found on the upper part of the interface concerning the example and its prediction. ① gives the predicted class for the individual to explain (labelled churner by the scoring model, with a probability of 69%). ② gives the predicted class for the proposed counterfactual (labelled non churner as with a probability of churn of 21%). A colour code allows the identification of each class (here orange for a churner, and green for a non churner). As expected the class of the counterfactual is different from those of the observed individual. The pie chart ③ shows the proportion of variables in the individual that have been modified to generate the counterfactual. By clicking on it, one can navigate between the modified variables and those that have remained unchanged. A drop-down menu ④ allows you to select the individuals.

The central part of the interface is dedicated to the modified variables between the individual and the counterfactual. Here 7 variables were changed. The direction of the change is specified by an arrow with its magnitude in the case of a numerical variable ⑤. In the case of a categorical variable, the change is indicated by an upward arrow pointing to the new modality ⑥.

Additionally, the variable changes are summarized in textual form in the lower part of the interface ⑧. The text also precises whether the individual had been misclassified by the decision model (if the information is available) by a circle with a hatched pattern ⑨.

By clicking on ⑦, the user accesses another screen (see Fig. 2), where he/she can select another counterfactual depending on whether he/she wants to focus

---

[1] https://drive.google.com/file/d/1yog5J1QVq2zQ9WK4P3ujg4Zxn_NZScJB/view?usp=share_link.

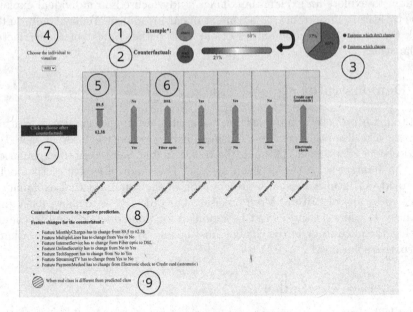

Fig. 1. Interface for presenting an example to be explained and an associated counterfactual.

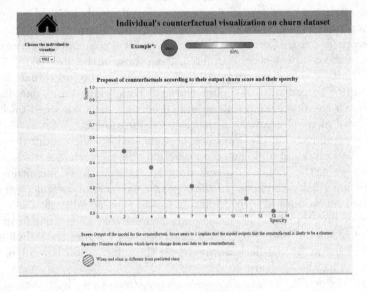

Fig. 2. Interface for alternative counterfactual selection according to the two axes sparsity/classification score.

on sparsity (as few modified variables as possible) or prediction performance (the lowest predicted score for the counterfactual for the individual class). The counterfactual that requires the least number of modified variables is proposed by default. Finally, a home page (not shown here) gives a description of the analyzed data (characteristics and semantic of variables).

2.2 Implementation

The implementation is based on Flask, which is a micro-framework for web development in Python to present data and display web pages. Visualizations and interactions are created using JavaScript and d3js. Flask applications can easily be embedded in website or even in Jupyter Notebooks. In this demo, we use HTML and CSS to create the web pages. We can interface with any prediction model, and any counterfactual explanation generator. The data needed for the visualization is provided via a JSON file which must include the variables names and 2 variable/instance matrices, one with the instances to explain and another with the counterfactuals. The file must also contain some classification results: the prediction probabilities of the model and the predicted classes both for the instances to explain and their counterfactuals.[2]

3 Use Case Study

We illustrate the tool on the Telco Customer Churn dataset [1] which contains 7,043 instances described by 20 input variables. The goal is to predict the churn of a telecom operator's customers (with 2 classes: *churn* vs *no churn*). For our experiments we used VCNet, an architecture that is able to generate at the same time the decision and a counterfactual explanation and is well adapted for processing mixed tabular data [6]. We discuss the analysis of the example shown in Fig. 1. It corresponds to an individual (Id 1682) labelled by the decision model as a churner with a probability of 69%. The displayed counterfactual changes the class of the example from churn to no churn with a 79% probability of no churn (21% probability of churn). The counterfactual was obtained by the modification of 7 variables from the initial example (37% of the input variables). The reader who wants more details about the changes can look at the details in Fig. 1. Figure 2 shows that other counterfactuals with a good compromise on the performance and sparsity objectives are available. A first counterfactual that proposes the modification of 2 variables (decrease of the monthly bill from 89.5\$ to 77.25\$ and modification of the payment method) reduces the probability of churn from 69% to 49%. The other counterfactuals can be discussed in the same way. The business expert is thus able to choose the criterion that seems the best between sparsity and classification score.

---

[2] https://github.com/fwallyn/counterfactualViz.

4   Further Developments

The tool presented will evolve to include new features. For now, interactions with the user are limited to the choice of a counterfactual in a possible set according to criteria of sparsity or classification performance. The user could also be interested in selecting the variables that make up the counterfactual. Another area for improvement concerns the textual formalization of the explanation, which is currently very limited. Work on the ergonomics of the interface would also be of interest, as would a user study.

References

1. https://www.kaggle.com/datasets/blastchar/telco-customer-churn
2. Bove, C., Aigrain, J., Lesot, M.J., Tijus, C., Detyniecki, M.: Contextualization and exploration of local feature importance explanations to improve understanding and satisfaction of non-expert users. In: Proceedings of the 27th International Conference on Intelligent User Interfaces (IUI), pp. 807–819. Association for Computing Machinery (2022)
3. Garcia-Zanabria, G., Gutierrez-Pachas, D.A., Camara-Chavez, G., Poco, J., Gomez-Nieto, E.: SDA-Vis: a visualization system for student dropout analysis based on counterfactual exploration. Appl. Sci. **12**(12), 5785 (2022)
4. Gomez, O., Holter, S., Yuan, J., Bertini, E.: ViCE: visual counterfactual explanations for machine learning models. In: Proceedings of the 25th International Conference on Intelligent User Interfaces (IUI), pp. 531–535. Association for Computing Machinery (2020)
5. Guidotti, R.: Counterfactual explanations and how to find them: literature review and benchmarking. Data Min. Knowl. Discovery, 1–55 (2022)
6. Guyomard, V., Fessant, F., Guyet, T.: VCNet: a self-explaining model for realistic counterfactual generation. In: Proceedings of the European Conference on Machine Learning and Principles and Practice of Knowledge Discovery in Databases (ECML/PKDD), p. 10 (2022)

χiplot: Web-First Visualisation Platform for Multidimensional Data

Akihiro Tanaka[1], Juniper Tyree[1], Anton Björklund[1(✉)],
Jarmo Mäkelä[1,2], and Kai Puolamäki[1]

[1] University of Helsinki, Helsinki, Finland
{akihiro.tanaka,anton.bjorklund,jarmo.makela,kai.puolamaki}@helsinki.fi
[2] CSC – IT Center for Science Ltd., Espoo, Finland
jarmo.makela@csc.fi

Abstract. χiplot is an HTML5-based system for interactive exploration of data and machine learning models. A key aspect is interaction, not only for the interactive plots but also between plots. Even though χiplot is not restricted to any single application domain, we have developed and tested it with domain experts in quantum chemistry to study molecular interactions and regression models. χiplot can be run both locally and online in a web browser (keeping the data local). The plots and data can also easily be exported and shared. A modular structure also makes χiplot optimal for developing machine learning and new interaction methods.

Keywords: Visualisation · Interactive visualisation · Data
visualisation · Python · HTML5 · WASM · HCI

1 Introduction and Related Work

This paper introduces χiplot (|ˈkaɪplɒt|), a modular system for interactive exploration of data and pre-trained machine learning models. χiplot can be run locally on the user's computer or installation-free in a web browser. Our motivation for writing χiplot was three-fold.

(i) First, we want a Python-based system to develop and test machine learning and dimensionality reduction methods, such as [1], a manifold visualisation method for explainable AI. For this purpose, we prefer a *modular* system that is easy to expand and modify to test new machine learning and visualisation methods and interaction ideas.

(ii) Second, we need a tool to facilitate collaboration with primarily domain experts in quantum chemistry but also other domains. Ideally, we want to avoid forcing our collaborators to install additional software. However, we also do not want to set up and maintain server infrastructure to host a web-accessible service.

(iii) Third, the system should be practical and usable for the end user, including physicists and chemists, despite being built for quick prototyping and painless

Supported by the Research Council of Finland (decisions 346376 and 345704) and the Future Makers Funding Programme of Technology Industries of Finland Centennial Foundation and Jane and Aatos Erkko Foundation.

G. De Francisci Morales et al. (Eds.): ECML PKDD 2023, LNAI 14175, pp. 335–339, 2023.
https://doi.org/10.1007/978-3-031-43430-3_26

implementation. We know no prior system satisfies all of these three requirements.

Many interactive visualisation tools are available; see, e.g., [7] for a recent survey and references. Much of our research collaboration targets quantum chemistry; hence the system must also be capable of visualising, e.g., molecular structures from SMILES strings [11]. ChemInformatics Model Explorer [5] (CIME) is another tool that explores explainable AI in small molecule research. However, CIME has only four fixed views, and full functionality requires a server. Another recent example is XSMILES [4], where users can examine individual molecules in 2D diagrams and visualise attribution scores for atoms and non-atom tokens.

2   Usage

The main idea of χiplot is to simultaneously show multiple plots and visualisations to compare and contrast diverse information. Since χiplot also targets non-technical end users, intuitive visual selection and configuration of the plots are required.

χiplot comes with six types of plots out-of-the-box – scatterplots, histograms, heat maps, bar plots, data tables, and SMILES plots, which render molecules in a stick structure from a SMILES string [11] – but more can be added with χiplot's plugin system. Users can add and remove plots to create a layout that is the most optimal for their specific needs. The end users have the capability to generate clusters by running a k-means algorithm or by lasso selection on a scatterplot. Unique colours distinguish the generated clusters. In addition, the end users can generate a 2D embedding through Principal Component Analysis (PCA).

To use χiplot, the user may install it with `pip install xiplot`. The `xiplot` console command is then available to host a local χiplot server. Alternatively, an *installation-free* WebAssembly (WASM)[1] version can be used immediately at https://edahelsinki.fi/xiplot.

We demonstrate the main concepts with the QM9 molecular dataset [8,9], a collection of quantum chemical properties calculated for small organic molecules. Our machine-learning task is to estimate some quantum chemical properties from their structural description. We can use physics simulators with varying fidelity or regression models. In this example, we want to study how the structures in the dataset relate to the estimation task. We have precomputed a 2D Slisemap [1] embedding (revealing the structures relevant to a regression model) and attached the embedding to the dataset file we uploaded to χiplot.

Figure 1 shows a view of the χiplot interface during our exploration. A chemist can explore the Slisemap embedding in a scatter plot on the left. There is a notable cluster structure, so we use χiplot to find the clusters and plot their distribution in the middle. If we compare the two clusters, we notice that the distributions of the functional groups differ. For example, we could manually

---

[1] WASM is supported in most modern browsers; see https://caniuse.com/wasm.

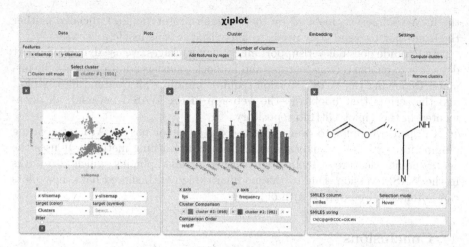

Fig. 1. χiplot interface when studying a regression model on a QM9 dataset.

draw an additional cluster in the scatter plot to further study the two subgroups in the rightmost cluster.

The behaviour of a molecule is not only determined by the functional groups but also by how they are structured. However, finding good summary statistics for structure is much more difficult. Therefore, we add a visualisation of individual molecules on the right of Fig. 1. A chemist can then rapidly inspect multiple molecules inside and between clusters by hovering over the points in the scatter plot; the molecule visualisation is automatically updated.

3   Description of the System

A key aspect of χiplot is interactivity, not just for a single plot but also between plots. For example, selecting a data item in one might show you more information about it in another, as described above. To accomplish this interactivity, the plots of χiplot are implemented as independent modules, communicating through shared data storage. Furthermore, to support collaboration and sharing, the set of active plots, their configuration, and the data can be saved to and restored from a file. Since χiplot is an interactive system, time-consuming computations (e.g., learning the Slisemap embedding) should be done as part of data preprocessing.

χiplot is implemented in **Python** using **Plotly** [6] for the plots and **Dash** for the interactivity. Usually, this would require the users to be able to install **Python** packages (see Sect. 2). However, we also provide a static server-less webpage version of χiplot that runs both the **Dash** backend and the **Plotly** frontend installation-free inside a browser using WebAssembly [10] (WASM). This also means no data leaves the user's computer in the WASM version.

In detail, the WASM version of χiplot uses **Pyodide** [3] to run Python in the browser. The front- and backend communication is intercepted and redirected to the in-WASM server, inspired by the `WebDash` prototype [2]. Crucially, neither the front- nor backend code needs to know that it runs inside a browser.

As Pyodide does not yet support all Python packages, we use dynamic import detection to enable certain features and fallbacks, such as additional data file formats. Deploying the WASM version requires bundling all frontend files, χiplot, and the scripts that bootstrap the web app in the WASM backend, all documented in the χiplot GitHub repository.

To open up χiplot to even more use cases, χiplot has an API for creating plugins for, e.g., new visualisations and machine learning methods. It uses the "entry points" feature of `Python` to discover installed plugins, which also works in the WASM version. Due to the modular design with shared data, new plots can automatically interact with old ones.

4   Conclusions

We have already found χiplot helpful when collaborating with domain experts since it lets them configure interactive plots without programming or installing anything[2]. The online version also enables easy results sharing without exposing the data to any third party. For more technical users χiplot is easy to maintain end expand due to the modular architecture. Finally, χiplot is available under the Open Source MIT license from GitHub[3] (which includes documentation, usage examples, and a demonstration video).

References

1. Björklund, A., Mäkelä, J., Puolamäki, K.: SLISEMAP: supervised dimensionality reduction through local explanations. Mach. Learn. **112**(1), 1–43 (2023). https://doi.org/10.1007/s10994-022-06261-1
2. Dafna, I., Tulop, J., Ivanov, P.: Webdash (2022). https://github.com/ibdafna/webdash
3. Droettboom, M., Chatham, H., Yurchak, R., Choi, G., et al.: Pyodide/pyodide: 21.0, August 2022. https://doi.org/10.5281/ZENODO.6977227
4. Heberle, H., Zhao, L., Schmidt, S., Wolf, T., Heinrich, J.: XSMILES: interactive visualization for molecules, SMILES and XAI attribution scores. J. Cheminformatics **15**(1), 2 (2023). https://doi.org/10.1186/s13321-022-00673-w
5. Humer, C., et al.: ChemInformatics Model Explorer (CIME): exploratory analysis of chemical model explanations. J. Cheminformatics **14**(1), 1–14 (2022). https://doi.org/10.1186/s13321-022-00600-z
6. Plotly: Plotly Open Source Graphing Library for Python (2023). https://plotly.com/python/
7. Qin, X., Luo, Y., Tang, N., Li, G.: Making data visualization more efficient and effective: a survey. VLDB J. **29**(1), 93–117 (2019). https://doi.org/10.1007/s00778-019-00588-3

---

[2] Installation-free version at https://edahelsinki.fi/xiplot.

[3] https://github.com/edahelsinki/xiplot.

8. Ramakrishnan, R., Dral, P.O., Rupp, M., von Lilienfeld, O.A.: Quantum chemistry structures and properties of 134 kilo molecules. Sci. Data **1**(1), 140022 (2014). https://doi.org/10.1038/sdata.2014.22
9. Stuke, A., et al.: Chemical diversity in molecular orbital energy predictions with kernel ridge regression. J. Chem. Phys. **150**(20), 204121 (2019). https://doi.org/10.1063/1.5086105
10. W3C: WebAssembly Core Specification, April 2022. https://www.w3.org/TR/wasm-core-2
11. Weininger, D.: SMILES, a chemical language and information system. 1. Introduction to methodology and encoding rules. J. Chem. Inf. Comput. Sci. **28**(1), 31–36 (1988). https://doi.org/10.1021/ci00057a005

Lumos in the Night Sky: AI-Enabled Visual Tool for Exploring Night-Time Light Patterns

Jakob Hederich[1], Shreya Ghosh[2(✉)] [iD], Zeyu He[2], and Prasenjit Mitra[1,2]

[1] L3S Research Center, Leibniz University, Hannover, Germany
jakob.hederich@stud.uni-hannover.de
[2] College of IST, Pennsylvania State University, State College, USA
{shreya,zeyuhe,pmitra}@psu.edu

Abstract. We introduce NightVIEW, an interactive tool for Night-time light (NTL) data visualization and analytics, which enables researchers and stakeholders to explore and analyze NTL data with a user-friendly platform. Powered by efficient system architecture, NightVIEW supports image segmentation, clustering, and change pattern detection to identify urban development and sprawl patterns. It captures temporal trends of NTL and semantics of cities, answering questions about demographic factors, city boundaries, and unusual differences.

Keywords: Visualization · Night-time light (NTL) · pattern mining

1 Introduction

Night-time light (NTL) data [14], derived from satellite imagery [9], has emerged as a critical resource for understanding human activity [6,7,11], urban development [2,3,11], and animal behavior [1]. NTL data offers numerous advantages over traditional sources, such as consistent and continuous information and applicability in areas with limited data availability [8]. However, the effective analysis and interpretation of NTL data, necessitates overcoming several technical challenges including: (a) Data volume and accessibility: Downloading and managing 140 GB in GeoTiff images of NTL monthly composite data (2015) from the NASA website. (b) Upscaling automated data analysis: Examining spatial patterns, such as urban growth and land use changes, and temporal patterns, such as annual or seasonal trends can be time-consuming. (c) Contextual data fusion: Integrating NTL data with other data, such as road networks, political maps, and population density, is challenging due to discrepancies in spatial and temporal resolutions, data formats, and calibration methods, as well (d) Customized visualization and user queries: **Q1:** How do urban sprawl and land use patterns visually manifest in NTL data over time? Can a visualization tool enable the comparison of NTL data from different regions or cities to assess their relative development, economic activity, or energy efficiency? **Q2:** How can a visualization tool help analyze and display the impact of major events, such as natural disasters, political changes/war, or economic shifts, on NTL data? **Q3:** How do cultural practices and festivities impact NTL data, particularly in regions with distinct religious or

G. De Francisci Morales et al. (Eds.): ECML PKDD 2023, LNAI 14175, pp. 340–344, 2023.
https://doi.org/10.1007/978-3-031-43430-3_27

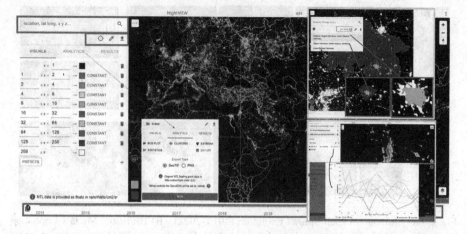

Fig. 1. NightVIEW: Red boxes depict spatial and temporal selection, and features (reverse geocoding, finding extrema, compare), analytics box offers computing features including clustering, temporal trend and export based on any selection of region and time-span. On the top-right, we show the reverse-geocoding feature, where the region (Hannover, Lower Saxonomy) is selected based on zoom level (city, state, etc.). End-users can select/ define any range of NTL values for visualization. In the bottom-right, the user compares the NTL usage in 2020 and finds it to be lower than that in 2016–2019 in Seattle because people stayed home during lockdown. (Color figure online)

cultural events? For instance, a study [12] using NASA-NOAA satellite data showed Middle Eastern cities experienced a 50–100% increase in brightness during Ramadan. This variation in lighting patterns was not solely determined by economic factors, but also reflected social and cultural identities.

We introduce **NightVIEW,** *a semi-automatic, interactive visual analytics toolkit,* which enables real-time NTL data exploration and extraction of insights. NightVIEW surpasses existing tools (Kepler.gl[1], NASA Worldview[2], tool by International Dark Sky association[3], GeoTime [5], TrajAnalytics [15]) in functionality and versatility.

2   NightVIEW: Key Visualization and Computing Features

NightVIEW is a flexible and user-friendly platform with customizable time and region selection, overlays, OSM map layer integration, pipette and extrema features, reverse geocoding, and image segmentation with thresholding (Fig. 1). Users can integrate its output into workflows, precisely analyze NTL data, and identify spatial patterns/trends.

Clustering: NightVIEW deploys the Marching Squares [10] algorithm for generating contours from the NTL map. The algorithm calculates the NTL value for each grid

---

[1] https://kepler.gl/.

[2] NASA Worldview.

[3] https://www.darksky.org/our-work/conservation/idsp/finder/.

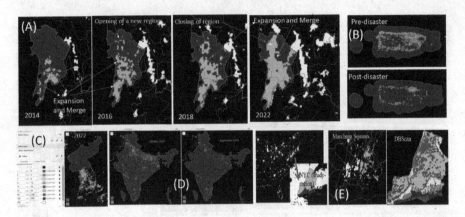

Fig. 2. (A) Mumbai's Urban Sprawl Evolution (2014–2022), (B) Hurricane Maria's Impact on Puerto Rico (2017), (C) North and South Korea's NTL Distribution, (D) Diwali lights up India, and (E) Marching Squares and NightVIEW-DBScan Algorithm applied to NY

cell independently. Subsequently, a cell index is computed by comparing the contour levels with the NTL intensity values at the cell corners. Finally, a pre-constructed lookup table is employed to describe the output geometry for each cell. A variant of DBSCAN [13] algorithm is used augmenting temporal information. By incorporating temporal information and intensity-based filtering, our algorithm enables the discovery of clusters that exhibit both spatial proximity and temporal consistency. Figure 2(E) reveals insights (six major clusters, represented by distinct color boundaries) by deploying the NightVIEW-DBScan algorithm (right image) and Marching squares algorithm (left) on NYC images (2014–2021). The results highlight consistently high night-time light intensity in Manhattan, seasonal variations in areas like the Rockefeller Center, and long-term trends of increasing light intensity in peripheral neighbourhoods (Staten Island or the far reaches of Brooklyn and Queens), indicating urban expansion and infrastructure development.

Urban Sprawl Pattern Detection: NightVIEW uses mathematical morphology [4] to analyze and process images based on their shapes to detect urban sprawl. Urban sprawl patterns, such as shrink, merge, expand, and split, can be measured and quantified by analyzing the regions in the transformed images. Structural changes in urban areas occur due to population dynamics, booming economies, or improved connectivity. Figure 2(A) captures Mumbai's growth pattern through NTL data from 2014 to 2022. NightVIEW helps identify and quantify these different types of changes, which cannot be achieved by simply comparing two images.

Data Interpretation Capacity: *(1) Propaganda and accuracy of government statistics:* Pyongyang and Seoul have vastly different night-time lighting patterns (Fig. 2(C)). North Korea's centrally planned economy, energy shortages, and political isolation have created sparse and dim night-time lighting; South Korea's bustling economy, modern infrastructure, and global integration have created a bright and extensive lighting pattern in Seoul. *(2) Economic Development:* India's NTL data (See Fig. 3) from 2014,

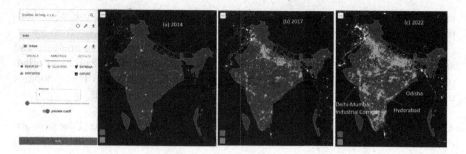

Fig. 3. Urbanization, Infrastructure Development, and Economic Growth. India:'14, '17, and '22

2017, and 2022, shows urban expansion, infrastructure development, and economic growth, e.g., expansion in the Delhi-NCR region, Bengaluru, and Hyderabad metropolitan areas, infrastructure development (such as highways, airports, and industrial zones, development of industrial corridors like the Delhi-Mumbai Industrial Corridor); economic growth (correlated to India's overall economic development and rural electrification); spatial inequality (e.g., Odisha's lagging economic growth and infrastructure development).(3) *Assessing disaster impact:* E.g., power outages and the pace of recovery. Figure 2(B) shows the impact of Hurricane Maria on Puerto Rico after the hurricane made landfall on September 16, 2017. This is valuable for disaster response, resource allocation, and assessing the effectiveness of recovery efforts. We can see the socioeconomic impacts of the Russia-Ukraine war on affected regions, e.g., NTL drop due to disruptions in human activity, infrastructure damage, or population displacement, as well NTL increases due to Diwali across India (Fig. 2(D)).

Demonstration Plan: We will demonstrate the following (and more):

DQ1: Can NightVIEW connect socioeconomic indicators, such as income and population density, and energy consumption patterns? A1: Its GeoJSON upload and overlay features allow users to incorporate additional data layers, like income and population density, on top of the NTL map. Users can correlate NTL and overlaid features, e.g., socioeconomic factors and energy consumption across the world at different times.

DQ2: Can NightVIEW identify natural disasters or monitor recovery efforts? A2: NightVIEW's compare and clustering identify natural disasters like earthquakes, hurricanes, or floods, provide insights into the pace of recovery and infrastructure rebuilding.

DQ3: Identifying City Borders and Green Spaces Thresholding and light contours pinpoint city limits and areas in a city that are greener, either in terms of vegetation or eco-friendly practices or less green such as airports. Parks, urban forests, or neighborhoods have low NTL usage and airports high.

DQ4: Recognizing Specific Map Elements from NTL Data Can NightVIEW distinguish map components like roads, railway networks, and Points of Interest (POIs), such as commercial centers and residential areas? A4: Major highways and other well-traveled routes often appear as bright lines connecting cities and regions. POIs exhibit unique NTL signatures that differentiate between varying types of land use, e.g., shopping malls, office complexes, or distinct residential neighborhoods.

NightVIEW is the first visual analytics toolkit that offers real-time analyses and answers to queries on NTL data, empowering researchers and organizations in urban planning and policy-making to make informed decisions and design better policies using insights on human activity patterns and urban development trends.

Acknowledgements. This research was funded by the Federal Ministry of Education and Research (BMBF), Germany under the project LeibnizKILabor with grant No. 01DD20003.

References

1. Amichai, E., Kronfeld-Schor, N.: Artificial light at night promotes activity throughout the night in nesting common swifts (apus apus). Sci. Rep. **9**(1), 1–8 (2019)
2. Chen, Z., et al.: The potential of nighttime light remote sensing data to evaluate the development of digital economy: a case study of china at the city level. Comput. Environ. Urban Syst. **92**, 101749 (2022)
3. Fang, G., Gao, Z., Tian, L., Fu, M.: What drives urban carbon emission efficiency?-spatial analysis based on nighttime light data. Appl. Energy **312**, 118772 (2022)
4. Haralick, R.M., Sternberg, S.R., Zhuang, X.: Image analysis using mathematical morphology. IEEE Trans. Pattern Anal. Mach. Intell. **4**, 532–550 (1987)
5. Kapler, T.: Geo time information visualization. In: INFOVIS 2004: Proceedings of the IEEE Symposium on Information Visualization, pp. 25–32 (2004)
6. Kyba, C.C., Altıntaş, Y.Ö., Walker, C.E., Newhouse, M.: Citizen scientists report global rapid reductions in the visibility of stars from 2011 to 2022. Science **379**(6629), 265–268 (2023)
7. Li, C., et al.: Study on average housing prices in the inland capital cities of China by nighttime light remote sensing and official statistics data. Sci. Rep. **10**(1), 1–20 (2020)
8. Li, D., Zhao, X., Li, X.: Remote sensing of human beings-a perspective from nighttime light. Geo-Spat. Inf. Sci. **19**(1), 69–79 (2016)
9. Li, X., Zhou, Y., Zhao, M., Zhao, X.: A harmonized global nighttime light dataset 1992–2018. Sci. Data **7**(1), 168 (2020)
10. Maple, C.: Geometric design and space planning using the marching squares and marching cube algorithms. In: 2003 International Conference on Geometric Modeling and Graphics, 2003. Proceedings, pp. 90–95. IEEE (2003)
11. Sánchez de Miguel, A., Bennie, J., Rosenfeld, E., Dzurjak, S., Gaston, K.J.: Environmental risks from artificial nighttime lighting widespread and increasing across Europe. Sci. Adv. **8**(37), eabl6891 (2022)
12. NASA Earth Observatory: The Lights of Ramadan and Eid al-Fitr (2014). https://earthobservatory.nasa.gov/images/84923/the-lights-of-ramadan-and-eid-al-fitr. Accessed 05 Apr 2023
13. Schubert, E., Sander, J., Ester, M., Kriegel, H.P., Xu, X.: DBSCAN revisited, revisited: why and how you should (still) use DBSCAN. ACM Trans. Database Syst. (TODS) **42**(3), 1–21 (2017)
14. Suomi-NPP: Visible Infrared Imaging Radiometer Suite (VIIRS) (2011). https://www.earthdata.nasa.gov/eosdis/daacs/laads. Accessed 05 Nov 2022
15. Zhao, Y., et al.: TrajAnalytics: a web-based visual analytics software of urban trajectory data. In: Proceeding of IEEE Visualization Conference (2016)

Automated Financial Analysis Using GPT-4

Sander Noels[1,2](✉)(iD), Adriaan Merlevede[2](iD), Andrew Fecheyr[2],
Maarten Vanhalst[2], Nick Meerlaen[2], Sébastien Viaene[2](iD), and Tijl De Bie[1](iD)

[1] Department of Electronics and Information Systems, Ghent University, 9000
Ghent, Belgium
{sander.noels,tijl.debie}@ugent.be
[2] Silverfin, Gaston Crommenlaan 12, 9050 Ghent, Belgium
{adriaan.merlevede,andrew.fecheyr,
maarten.vanhalst,nick.meerlaen,sebastien.viaene}@silverfin.com
https://www.silverfin.com/

Abstract. We introduce a novel application employing GPT-4 for automated financial analysis, aiming to improve the evaluation process of
financial performance for businesses and accountants. Our application
interprets financial ratios over a two-year period and generates actionable advice. Through specific design objectives and prompt engineering,
we ensure the generated advice is concise, language-flexible, and informative. Integrated as a proof-of-concept (PoC) into Silverfin's accounting
cloud service, our application showcases the potential of large language
models in the specialized fields of finance and accounting.

Keywords: GPT-4 · Automated Financial Analysis · Prompt
Engineering

1 Introduction

The rapid advancement of large language models (LLMs) has enabled automation in various domains, including finance and accounting [1]. However, due to
the financial domain's complexity, unique terminology, limited data availability,
and privacy regulations, LLMs have had limited success in providing valuable
insights in this area [2].

In this paper, we introduce a novel application that employs GPT-4 for automated financial analysis, interpreting a company's financial ratios over a two-
year period and suggesting future action points. This application aims to transform financial performance evaluation for businesses and accountants, making
financial analysis more accessible and easier to interpret for a wider audience,
including those who are not financial experts. This allows accountants to shift
from traditional compliance-based tasks to value-added advisory services, aligning with the evolving demands of their profession [3].

We have defined specific design objectives for the application, which include
ensuring that the generated advice is actionable, concise, language-flexible, and

G. De Francisci Morales et al. (Eds.): ECML PKDD 2023, LNAI 14175, pp. 345–349, 2023.
https://doi.org/10.1007/978-3-031-43430-3_28

informative. Additionally, the advice should conclude with a summary of the company's current financial situation, offering a comprehensive understanding for both accountants and their clients.

This PoC has been developed for Silverfin, a Belgian scale-up providing a cloud platform for accounting firms. The application has been integrated into the live environment, enabling accountants to efficiently assess the financial situations of their clients.

2   Application Design and Engineering Choices

The primary goal is to generate accurate and useful financial advice based on the provided information while minimizing the need for manual intervention, taking into account the proposed design objectives.

2.1   Naive Implementation

Initially, we considered fine-tuning LLMs with prompt-completion pairs containing financial ratios over a two-year period and an accounting specialist-generated financial analysis. However, this approach was not chosen due to the costly process of labeling financial reports and the need for hundreds of samples. In order to generate financial advice based on table information, we opted for providing structured financial statement information to the prompt, along with a description of the column headers followed by the action statement.

2.2   Prompt Engineering

Prompt engineering is vital for obtaining accurate and useful results from LLMs like GPT-4. Well-designed prompts guide the model's behavior, ensuring that the generated output meets the desired design objectives and reduces manual intervention.

Designing effective prompts for financial analysis presented several challenges such as misinterpretation of financial evolution, inaccurate understanding of financial table information, inability to draw logical conclusions, difficulty in identifying the most important financial ratios, and alignment issues with the specific design objectives.

To address these challenges, we implemented a specialist-in-the-loop approach, which involved accounting specialists actively participating in the prompt engineering process. Secondly, we utilized role-level instructions provided by the ChatGPT API to guide the LLM's behavior throughout the conversation. This was achieved by composing the prompt in two parts, clarifying the role of the system and the user.

The System Role Prompt. System messages serve as crucial tools for establishing the model's behavior prior to initiating a conversation. The inclusion of the specific design objectives within the system message played a pivotal role in steering our model towards the desired direction, along with the incorporation of a language-specific rule mandating the system to respond exclusively in Dutch, French, or English.

Example of the system message prompt.

Assistant is an intelligent accountant designed to help other accountants interpret the financial status of a company:
- The advice should contain a maximum of five bullet point topics.
- Every bullet point should contain financial reasoning and financial values.
- Every bullet point should start with instruction-based advice.
- The advice should start with 'Based on the financial analysis report from the period ending on' and end with a conclusion describing how the company is doing in general.
- The assistant should answer in English.

The User Role Prompt. The user message prompt, which includes the structured financial statement data and the instruction to generate financial advice, has undergone several refinements. Firstly, the financial information was transformed into a textual format, with the relative change in financial ratios categorized into five distinct descriptions such as 'decreased strongly,' 'decreased slightly,' etc., based on the magnitude of the change. This addition of textual descriptions helps to reduce misinterpretations regarding the evolution of financial ratios. Secondly, rule-based comments were integrated to enhance the model's accuracy, with accounting specialists formulating these comments based on financial academic literature. Thirdly, financial ratios were organized by importance, with those exhibiting the most significant relative changes appearing first, forcing the model to talk about the most important financial ratios, since we noticed that the model tends to focus on the first ratios. Lastly, a rule-based approach was used to exclude irrelevant or unimportant financial ratios, namely those whose values were close to the global median and with a negligible relative change. Overall, these refinements significantly improved the user message prompt's accuracy and relevance, leading to enhanced efficacy of the LLM.

Example of the user message prompt.

The first column shows the financial ratios that evolved from the financial period ending on 2021-12-31 to the period ending on 2022-12-31.
The second column contains a comment based on the evolution of the financial values.
Days of client credit decreased strongly from 5.48 to 2.42 | Customers are paying their invoices quickly.
Days of supplier credit increased strongly from 33.65 to 42.58 | The company takes longer to pay its suppliers.
Generate advice based on the financial analysis report:

---

3   Application Overview

To use the new feature, accountants need Silverfin platform access. After logging in and selecting a client file, a banner with "We are exploring what GPT could do for your client files" and a "Prepare financial analysis" button appears. Clicking the button spawns a modal where a set of action points are generated within an editable text field. Accountants can modify the advice and post it as a note in the client file's communication pane, which facilitates the efficient sharing of information with other users within the accounting firm. The following URL leads to an online video that demonstrates the execution of the application: https://vimeo.com/818357457 (Fig. 1).

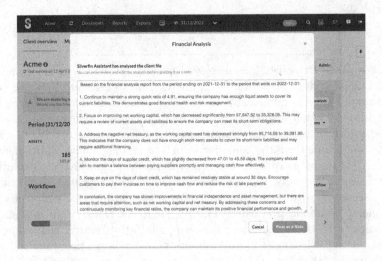

Fig. 1. Editable text field displaying the automated financial analysis and generated action points for a selected client file.

4   Conclusion

Our novel GPT-4-based application for automated financial analysis demonstrates the potential of LLMs in specialized fields like finance and accounting. By making use of specific design objectives and prompt engineering, we have developed a concise, language-flexible, and informative solution. Future research may explore incorporating more granular financial information, such as ledger account data, to provide more client-specific advice.

Acknowledgements. This research received funding from the Flemish Government, through Flanders Innovation & Entrepreneurship (VLAIO, project HBC.2020.2883) and from the Flemish Government under the "Onderzoeksprogramma Artificiële Intelligentie (AI) Vlaanderen" program.

References

1. Brown, T., et al.: Language models are few-shot learners. Adv. Neural. Inf. Process. Syst. **33**, 1877–1901 (2020)
2. Wu, S., et al.: BloombergGPT: A large language model for finance. arXiv preprint arXiv:2303.17564 (2023)
3. Zainuddin, Z.N., Sulaiman, S.: Challenges faced by management accountants in the 21st century. Procedia Econ. Financ. **37**, 466–470 (2016)

Gait-Based Biometrics System

Aleksander Sawicki[1(✉)] [iD] and Khalid Saeed[1,2] [iD]

[1] Faculty of Computer Science, Bialystok University of Technology, Bialystok, Poland
a.sawicki@pb.edu.pl
[2] Department of Computer Science and Electronics, Universidad de La Costa, Barranquilla, Colombia

Abstract. Behavioral biometrics is the field of study related to person identification based on the way an activity is performed. Despite the difficulties of implementation and achieving high recognition metrics, this field has advantages that attract the interest of the scientific community. In the case of gait analysis, active interaction between the user and the acquisition device is not required. This enables signals to be safely assessed remotely, that is important in the times of pandemic. Furthermore, it is not easy to deliberately mimic a person's gait. The work concerns on the development of system that enables identifying individuals based on gait with the use of wearable sensors such as accelerometers or gyroscopes. The work describes the data preprocessing pipeline and the innovative data augmentation mechanism performed with the use of generative models. The validation of the system is carried out using three different datasets collected under laboratory, semi-laboratory and field conditions. This article focuses on presenting a comprehensive solution, with a special authors' aspect of data augmentation.

Keywords: Biometrics · CNN · IMU

1 Introduction

In this work, we aim to present a complex gait-based personal identification system that use wearable sensors. The work presents the construction of a biometric system using the data from a triaxial accelerometer and a triaxial gyroscope. Sensors of this type can be embedded in smartphone or smartwatch devices. The demonstration of the system execution can be found at: https://vimeo.com/818295324. Currently, the gait analysis systems are not reserved for the worlds created by Hollywood directors, but are an actual core of research and implementation. In order to provide credence to the interest, two references can be mentioned [1, 2]. One of them is the Polish research and development project "BIOMETRICS - a biometric system for identifying persons using their gait" [1]. The project is involved in the construction of a corridor in which data acquisition and analysis of human gait could be carried out. It is based on a vision-based manner and maintaining a constant type of substrate and lighting. One of the potential users of the product was declared to be the internal use of the Polish Border Guard.

© The Author(s), under exclusive license to Springer Nature Switzerland AG 2023
G. De Francisci Morales et al. (Eds.): ECML PKDD 2023, LNAI 14175, pp. 350–355, 2023.
https://doi.org/10.1007/978-3-031-43430-3_29

On the other hand, it is worth mentioning the opening of the European competition "Beyond the state-of-the-art biometrics on the move for border checks" [2]. This European grant mainly concerns non-contact gait analysis of persons for the purpose of border controls. However, without granting the official award or even without the opening of the competition, it is difficult to detail the actual use-case. These two references [1, 2] indicate that behavioral biometric systems are of interest not only to academia, but to important institutions at national/international level as well as to private capital.

Classical physiological biometrics systems that for example are based on a fingerprints or an iris photos, require active user interaction - the user must walk up to the data acquisition device. It is not possible to identify a person remotely. In addition, such systems could be susceptible to various types of attacks in which artificial samples are provided instead of the original data. In previous years, researchers have demonstrated that the so-called MasterPrints attack [3] has successfully frauded biometrics systems.

Under such circumstances, it may seem that the use of the additional keys, in the authentication process - in the form of RFID cards, is a more reasonable solution. However, such approach is not ideal. When an unwanted person obtains the key through theft/robbery, it will automatically gain unauthorized access. It should be emphasized that the theft of a carrier such as an RFID card is a relatively simple operation, but the intentional imitation of its owner's gait is much more difficult [4].

The target users of this system may be institutions that aim to increase the security access. The entities that are concerned, for example, about the theft of the access keys and would like to upgrade security systems might use an additional behavioral biometrics module that is resistant to device theft. The final point is that nowadays, solutions based on behavioral biometrics in practice do not exist on their own. They complement the systems based on biometrics of physiological features or key-based authorization systems.

1.1 Dataset Description

The evaluation of the performance of the proposed biometrics system was conducted using three data corpora, in each of which participants took part in two acquisition sessions during two separate days. This approach is quite relative to a real-world scenario in which the biometric system is trained once and then evaluated (even under changed conditions, e.g., footwear, ground surface). The validation of the system was carried out with three datasets: (*I*) Białystok University of Technology; laboratory conditions with constants shoes types and ceramic walking surface; 100 Participants, acquisition performed using Perception Neuron Inertial Motion Capture system [5]. Signals were collected using proprietary software "Axis Neuoron"; (*II*) Signet (University. of Padova [6, 7]); semi-laboratory conditions with varying clothes and constant walking surface; 28 Participants, acquisition performed using Android mobile phone. Data acquisition was carried out using the developed custom application; (*III*) Boston dataset [8]; field conditions with varying clothes and walking surfaces; 29 Participants, acquisition performed using iPhone. Official "SensorLog" app was used for data acquisition.

Data acquisition for each case proceeded differently. For dataset (*I*), participants completed 20 repetitions along a straight distance of about 3 m. For the base (*II*), subjects completed a standard walk for about 5 min, and for base (*III*), participants covered a distance of approximately 640 m. The implemented gait cycle segmentation algorithm recognized a total of 6,697 gait cycles for the base (*I*), 19,262 for base (*II*) and 25,569 for base (*III*). Small intervals between training and testing sessions characterize all selected databases. The case where the period is much longer is much more demanding and is omitted in this study. According to the literature, a period of 9 months is the time when the gait does not change significantly [9], after which it is recommended to collect new samples.

1.2 Preprocessing

Preprocessing was carried out in three steps. The first was detecting the moment when a person's right leg touches the ground. Despite the fact that the IMU sensor was placed in the trouser pocket/right thigh area, it was possible to indicate this moment in time. In the segmentation process, only the accelerometer measurement data were used. For this purpose, the algorithm described in our previous work [10] was applied. The segmentation process made it possible to extract the so-called gait cycles, i.e. (the gait cycle is defined as the time inversion between two successive occurrences of the foot contacting the ground [11]). The second preprocessing step involved assembling the data into a coherent dataset by removing outliers and performing frequency filtering. At the same time, it should be noted that the data processed in this step concerned the IMU measurement values directly read by the sensor. Therefore, they were in the so-called local reference system depending on the mounting method. In Fig. 1 (middle step), it can be seen that there are significant differences between the two days for the X and Y axes. The data in their original form depend on the way the sensor is placed in the trouser pocket.

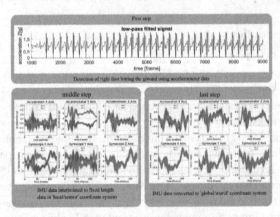

Fig. 1. IMU preprocessing flow diagram

The last step involved converting the data from a local reference system to a global world system. This conversion requires additional information about the phone's orientation at the measurement time (The application uses time series of quaternions). The result of this step is the independence of the measurement data from the way the sensor is mounted.

1.3 Data Augmentation

In our research, we used the technique of data augmentation, which involves the use of distributional models. In the development of the model, we made use of studies such as [12, 13]. In each of these publications, the output of the neural networks was not expected to be a single value, but instead modeled the mean value with variance. For this purpose, a architecture consisting of an LSTM member and a Dense layer was used (Fig. 2). The idea behind this form of augmentation is to use historical samples to train a person's typical gait cycles, which can have a positive effect on identification results. Moreover, a model of this type has an interesting property. With a small computational cost, the variance of the generated time series can be easily multiplied/amplified. This approach is in opposition to the use of VAE-based models (such as RH-VAE [14] aka pyraug [15]). In which the so-called bottleneck connecting the encoder and decoder is modeled by normal distribution parameters.

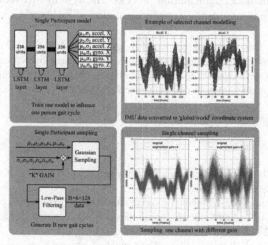

Fig. 2. Data augmentation flow diagram

1.4 Classification Results

The classification was carried out as follows. The data collected during the first day constituted the training set, while the gait cycles collected during the second day entirely constituted the test set. A CNN network with an attentional mechanism [16] was used as a classifier. For augmentation, 50% of the synthetic gait samples were added for each participant. Table 1 shows results in the form of an F1-score metrics.

Table 1. Classification Results

Augmentation Method	Dataset:BUT	Dataset:Signet	Dataset:Boston
BASELINE (NO AUG.)	0.921 ± 0.017	0.815 ± 0.020	0.712 ± 0.019
PURAUG[14]	0.914 ± 0.010	0.697 ± 0.020	0.699 ± 0.014
PROPOSED (NO GAIN)	0.812 ± 0.010	0.812 ± 0.010	0.748 ± 0.015
PROPOSED (GAIN 16)	**0.932 ± 0.007**	**0.831 ± 0.019**	**0.754 ± 0.009**

2 Conclusions

This paper described the authors' biometric system based on the measurement values of sensors such as accelerometers and gyroscope. The paper proposed the use of distributional models in the data augmentation process. The system was validated using three data corpora with different degrees of representation of real-world conditions.

Acknowledgment. This work was supported by grant 2021/41/N/ST6/02505 from Białystok University of Technology and funded with resources for research by National Science Centre, Poland. For the purpose of Open Access, the author has applied a CC-BY public copyright license to any Author Accepted Manuscript (AAM) version arising from this submission.

References

1. "Biometrics - a biometric system for identifying persons using their gait, POIR.01.01.01-00-1942/20. Accessed 16 Mar 2023
2. "Beyond the state-of-the-art biometrics on the move for border checks" project page. https://ec.europa.eu/info/funding-tenders/opportunities/portal/screen/opportunities/topic-details/horizon-cl3-2023-bm-01-03. Accessed 16 Mar 2023
3. Roy, A., Memon, N., Ross, A.: MasterPrint attack resistance: a maximum cover based approach for automatic fingerprint template selection. In: IEEE 10th International Conference on Biometrics Theory, Applications and Systems (BTAS), pp. 1–9 (2019)
4. Wan, C., Wang, L., Phoha. V.V.: A survey on gait recognition. ACM Comput. Surv. **51**, 5, Article 89 (2019). https://doi.org/10.1145/3230633
5. Perception Neuron 32 official website. https://neuronmocap.com/products/perception_neuron/. Accessed 16 Jan 2019
6. SIGNET research, Smartphone gait signals dataset, Department of Information Engineering, University of Padova, Italy. https://signet.dei.unipd.it/research/ Accessed 02 April 2023
7. Gadaleta, M., Rossi, M.: IDNet: Smartphone-based gait recognition with convolutional neural networks. Pattern Recogn. **74**, 25–37 (2018)
8. Vajdi, A., et al.: Human gait database for normal walk collected by smart phone accelerometer. arXiv preprint arXiv:1905.03109 (2019)
9. Matovski, D., et al.: The effect of time on gait recognition performance. Trans. Inf. Forensics Secur. **7**(2), 543–552 (2011)
10. Sawicki, A., Saeed, K.: Application of LSTM networks for human gait-based identification. In: Zamojski, W., Mazurkiewicz, J., Sugier, J., Walkowiak, T., Kacprzyk, J. (eds.) Theory and Engineering of Dependable Computer Systems and Networks. DepCoS-RELCOMEX 2021.

Advances in Intelligent Systems and Computing, vol. 1389, pp. 402–412. Springer, Cham (2021). https://doi.org/10.1007/978-3-030-76773-0_39

11. Whittle, M.: Gait Analysis: an Introduction. Butterworth-Heinemann, Oxford (1991)

12. Graves A.: Generating sequences with recurrent neural networks. arXiv:1308.0850 (2013)

13. Alzantot, M., Chakraborty, S., Srivastava, M.: SenseGen: a deep training architecture for synthetic sensor data generation. In: 2017 IEEE International Conference on Pervasive Computing and Communications Workshops (PerCom Workshops) (2017)

14. Chadebec, C., Thibeau-Sutre, E., Burgos, N., et al.: Data augmentation in high dimensional low sample size setting using a geometry-based variational Autoencoder. arXiv:2105.00026 (2021)

15. Pyraug augmentation framework official reposity. https://github.com/clementchadebec/pyraug. Accessed 16 Mar 2023

16. Huang, H., Zhou, P., Li, Y., Sun, F.: A Lightweight attention-based CNN model for efficient gait recognition with wearable IMU sensors. Sensors 2021, **21**, 2866 (2021)

The Good, The Bad, and The Average: Benchmarking of Reconstruction Based Multivariate Time Series Anomaly Detection

Arn Baudzus[1]([✉]), Bin Li[2], Adnane Jadid[1], and Emmanuel Müller[2]

[1] Federal Institute for Occupational Safety and Health (BAuA), Dortmund, Germany
baudzus.arn@baua.bund.de
[2] Department of Computer Science, TU Dortmund University, Dortmund, Germany

Abstract. Reconstruction-based algorithms offer state-of-the-art performance in multivariate time series anomaly detection. But as always: there is no single best algorithm. To find the optimal solution, one has to compare different methods and tune their hyperparameters. This paper introduces a lightweight modular benchmarking framework for data scientists and researchers in the field. The framework can be easily set up and automatically create a visual summary of the relevant performance indicators and automatically selected examples to give insight into the behavior of the model and aid during the development.

Keywords: Anomaly Detection · Multivariate Time Series · Reconstruction-based Models · Autoencoder · Benchmark · Experiment tracking · MLOps · Visualisation

1 Introduction

Reconstruction-based models offer state-of-the-art performance in anomaly detection. Various approaches have been shown to be successful in different applications. Zong et al. [14] proposed using a Deep Autoencoding Gaussian Mixture Model (DAGMM), which performs joint optimization of the deep autoencoder parameters and the Gaussian Mixture Model to reduce the reconstruction error. Ackay et al. [10] used a conditional generative adversarial network with an extra encoder sub-network and showed how it improved the data distribution estimation. Su et al. in [13] presented *OmniAnomaly* – a stochastic recurrent neural network with stochastic variable connection and planar normalizing flow. Kaminskyi et al. [12] introduced an autoencoder-based concept drift detector – a model which allows tracking the reconstruction error of the encoder – and provided a visualization of the drift in the reconstruction error space. Further potential for anomaly detection lies in ensemble methods like e.g. Böing et al. [11] who propose a robustification method for ensemble methods and apply it to the Deep Ensemble Anomaly detectioN (DEAN) method, showing the vast potential for

G. De Francisci Morales et al. (Eds.): ECML PKDD 2023, LNAI 14175, pp. 356–360, 2023.
https://doi.org/10.1007/978-3-031-43430-3_30

improving the robustness of already trained models as well as verification scalability. These and other works on reconstruction-based models present and showcase novel methods and approaches; however, it is usually practically challenging to compare them with each other. As stated in the no free lunch theorem: to find the best algorithm for a specific task, tests including various algorithms have to be conducted.

Our framework is aimed at data scientists and researchers in the field who:

- are interested in reconstruction-based time series anomaly detection or
- are developing anomaly detection algorithms for their real-world problem,
- require deep insight into model training details.

A good understanding of the system in use is the key to success in data science. This is especially true for researchers who are developing novel algorithms. In order to understand the algorithm under development, it is essential to know how it behaves in different situations. To gain this knowledge, multiple performance metrics, statistics, the input data, and outputs should be assessed. This is a lot of information that usually has to be extracted from the training process. Furthermore, this information needs to be visualized to become interpretable.

The framework presented in this paper assesses these requirements. Not only does it handle the training and testing of the model under test while extracting the performance data for benchmarking. It also extracts and visualizes necessary information to help understand the tested models and data. Our framework provides the necessary information efficiently during training, which enables its usage in an iterative development cycle.

2   Related Software

The framework falls into two categories of software. It is a benchmark environment bundled with experiment tracking and visualisation software.

Standard tools for experiment tracking include e.g. TensorBoard [8], WandB [9], DeepADoTS [2], MLflow [3], CometML [1] and Neptune.ai [5]. Without further configuration, most model tracking tools focus on high-level performance indicators like accuracy averaged over the validation set, whereas our framework provides more detailed insight into the training process by visualizing examples (see Sect. 3).

There are also Benchmark environments like Orion [6], MTAD [4], and pythae [7]. These libraries are mainly focused on giving the user a ranking of different algorithms. Our framework, in comparison, gives an output that provides insights to cultivate an understanding of the model's behavior and data under testing environment.

3   Framework

Our framework[1] consists of different modules for data sets, models, performance indicators, and training algorithms. The interfaces for each group of modules are

---

[1] Code and documetnation of our framework: https://github.com/Arn-BAuA/ TimeSeriesAEBenchmarkSuite.

standardized. Benchmarking, Evaluation, and Visualisation are on the standardized level. This way, modules can be swapped and altered quickly. To conduct a benchmark experiment, the user can use module instances provided by the framework or self-implemented ones to fit a specific area in reconstruction based time series anomaly detection[2]. In addition to that, the user can specify milestone epochs. On milestone epochs, histograms of the performance indicators over the data set, as well as selected example inputs and reconstructions are saved. The evaluation at different epochs is done on the training, validation, and test set, although only training and validation sets are used during training. This procedure gives the user the ability to verify that the validation set behaves like the test set w.r.t. the performance indicators.

The parameters used to generate the experiments, like hyperparameters passed to the modules and the hash of the current Git head, are also logged so that the output can be used as auxiliary documentation. The output is saved as .csv and .json files as they are human-readable and supported by most tools for later evaluation. The outputs can also be evaluated within the framework. The framework automatically generates plots for all saved data, as well as a model analysis report .html-file for convenient evaluation of the results[3].

The model analysis report consists of a first section showing the user-specified performance scores averaged over the data sets during the training procedure. The report also contains a series of histograms showing how the distribution of these performance metrics changed during training. This information is essential since the shape of the error distribution contains information on the effectiveness of the training and the quality of the model for anomaly detection.

To further help the users understand data and models, example inputs and reconstructions are presented. These examples are selected within our framework based on the reconstruction accuracy of the trained model indicated by a user-specified performance indicator.

Example inputs are chosen where the final model generates reconstructions with an exceptionally low error (**The Good**), an exceptionally high error (**The Bad**), and an error that is close to the average error per data point of the data set (**The Average**).

For these selected inputs, four visualisations are created. An example of these four visualisations is depicted in Fig. 1 for a data point with exceptionally high L1-Loss on the validation set. Two of the plots are made to give the user an in-depth understanding of the data, the model, and the effectiveness of the training. One shows just the raw data (Fig. 1a), and the other shows the raw data and reconstructions created by the model at the milestone epochs (Fig. 1b).

To keep these plots from getting crowded in case of high dimensional data, the user can also specify a maximum number of dimensions that shall be displayed. If this number is exceeded, the script will select dimensions to plot after the same principle as the examples where selected. Dimensions with high, low, and average reconstruction errors for that example are selected.

---

[2] Detailed information on the interfaces is provided in the documentation.

[3] Our demo video: https://youtu.be/QPpVbOcZ_xU.

In addition, to gain a better insight into the role of the particular example in the its data set, two other plots are provided. One shows the average reconstruction error of all inputs in that set with epochs and the reconstruction error of the example data point at the milestone (Fig. 1c). The other shows the histogram of the reconstruction error on the final model and the position of the example in this histogram so that the example can be associated with a particular region in the distribution of the errors (Fig. 1d).

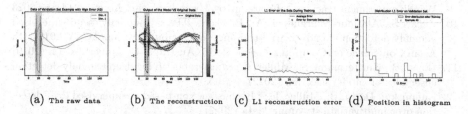

(a) The raw data   (b) The reconstruction   (c) L1 reconstruction error   (d) Position in histogram

Fig. 1. The four plots provided by the framework for one example with a high loss on the validation set. The shown data has been generated by a data generator in the environment.

Comparing multiple examples side by side where the algorithm performed similarly can increase the awareness of the relevant features of the problem. This can be understood from two perspectives: (1) from the data perspective: when working with unknown data, one usually doesn't know what anomalies and relevant features look like. This visualisation aids in the process of data understanding. (2) from the model perspective: inspecting the reconstructions the model creates, especially during different phases of the training, can increase the understanding of the model and the training process.

In conclusion, we proposed a framework providing multiple detailed analysis information for benchmarking reconstruction-based time series anomaly detection models. The automatically generated and summarized information can speed up the iterative process of adjusting or developing a model suited for the studied problem.

Acknowledgements. This work was supported by the Observatory on Artificial Intelligence in Work and Society as part of the Policy Lab Digital, Work & Society of the Federal Ministry for Labour and Social Affairs (BMAS).

This work was supported by the Research Center Trustworthy Data Science and Security, an institution of the University Alliance Ruhr.

References

1. Cometml experiment tracking software. https://www.comet.com/site/. Accessed 14 Apr 2023
2. Mlflow experiment tracking software. https://github.com/KDD-OpenSource/DeepADoTS. Accessed 14 Apr 2023

3. Mlflow experiment tracking software. https://mlflow.org/. Accessed 14 Apr 2023
4. Mtad repository. https://github.com/OpsPAI/MTAD. Accessed 14 Apr 2023
5. Neptune.ai experiment tracking software. https://neptune.ai/. Accessed 14 Apr 2023
6. Orion repository. https://github.com/sintel-dev/Orion. Accessed 14 Apr 2023
7. pythae repository. https://github.com/clementchadebec/benchmark_VAE. Accessed 14 Apr 2023
8. Tensorboard experiment tracking software. https://www.tensorflow.org/tensorboard. Accessed 14 Apr 2023
9. Wandb experiment tracking software. https://wandb.ai/site. Accessed 14 Apr 2023
10. Akcay, S., Atapour-Abarghouei, A., Breckon, T.P.: : Ganomaly: semi-supervised anomaly detection via adversarial training. In: Computer Vision-ACCV 2018:14th Asian Conference on Computer Vision, Perth, Australia, December 2–6 14. (2019)
11. Böing, B., Klüttermann, S., Müller, E.: : Post-robustifying deep anomaly detection ensembles by model selection (2022)
12. Kaminskyi, D., Li, B., Müller, E.: : Reconstruction-based unsupervised drift detection over multivariate streaming data (2022)
13. Su, Y., Zhao, Y., Niu, C., Liu, R., Sun, W., Pei, D.: Robust anomaly detection for multivariate time series through stochastic recurrent neural network (2019)
14. Zong, B., et al.: Deep autoencoding gaussian mixture model for unsupervised anomaly detection (2018)

INCLUSIVELY: An AI-Based Assistant for Inclusive Writing

Moreno La Quatra[1,3]($\boxtimes$)(iD), Salvatore Greco[2](iD), Luca Cagliero[3](iD), and Tania Cerquitelli[3](iD)

[1] Kore University of Enna, Enna, Italy
moreno.laquatra@unikore.it
[2] Politecnico di Torino, Turin, Italy
salvatore_greco@polito.it
[3] Politecnico di Torino, Turin, Italy
{luca.cagliero,tania.cerquitelli}@polito.it

Abstract. Inclusive writing is compulsory in formal communications. However, employees in private organizations, universities, and ministries often lack inclusive writing skills. For example, despite Italian grammar having masculine and feminine declensions of words, many official documents have a disrespectful prevalence of the masculine form. To promote inclusive writing practices, we present INCLUSIVELY, a language support tool that leverages natural language processing techniques to automatically identify instances of non-inclusive language and suggest more inclusive alternatives. The tool can be used as a text proofreader and, at the same time, fosters self-learning of inclusive writing forms. The recorded demo of the tool, available at https://youtu.be/3uiW_ti8wmY, shows how end-users can interact with INCLUSIVELY to feed new data, visualize the non-inclusive pieces of text, explore the list of alternative forms, and provide feedback or human annotations for system fine-tuning.

Keywords: Inclusive language · Natural Language Processing · Human-in-the-analytics-loop

1 Introduction

The language used in official communications is crucial for shaping the community's perception of gender, race, and language-related issues. Inclusive language ensures equal opportunities and respect for all groups, including minorities. However, many official communications, particularly in Romance languages like Italian, still lack inclusivity. Regarding gender, writers struggle to correctly use masculine and feminine declensions of nouns, adjectives, pronouns, and articles. Still, the masculine form is often inappropriately predominant, showing a lack of training and awareness. For example, the Italian form of *"the students"* can be masculine (i.e., *"gli studenti"*) or feminine (i.e., *"le studentesse"*). To promote inclusivity, it would be preferable to use collective nouns *"la componente sudentesca"* (translated in English as *"student community"*) referring to neuter groups of people instead of specifying a gender.

G. De Francisci Morales et al. (Eds.): ECML PKDD 2023, LNAI 14175, pp. 361–365, 2023.
https://doi.org/10.1007/978-3-031-43430-3_31

As part of the E-MIMIC project [1,6], we aim to promote inclusive writing practices by leveraging Natural Language Processing (NLP) techniques. To this end, we propose INCLUSIVELY, a writing assistant tool that comprises (1) a classification model for automatically detecting non-inclusive sentences and (2) a sequence-to-sequence model for generating inclusive reformulations of non-inclusive expressions, acting as an automated text proofreader. INCLUSIVELY also leverages the *human-in-the-analytics-loop* to receive continuous feedback[1] and enhance the quality of the automatically generated text reformulations. We believe that the widespread adoption of deep learning architectures for advanced language analysis and reformulation can promote more respectful communication while safeguarding the rights of linguistic minorities and people with disabilities.

To our best knowledge, INCLUSIVELY is the first inclusive language assistant, designed to be user-friendly and accessible for a wide range of users seeking to improve the inclusivity of their written communication. The platform provides regular users with feedback on the inclusivity of each sentence, along with a reformulated version of the non-inclusive text. Expert users and linguists can provide human feedback, useful for model fine-tuning, whereas data scientists can leverage an explainable AI interface to gain insights into the reasons behind the models' outcomes. INCLUSIVELY currently supports the Italian language, with short-term perspectives of extension to other languages (e.g., French, Spanish)[2]

2   The Inclusively Tool

INCLUSIVELY implements a two-stage AI-based process. In the first stage, a classification model detects non-inclusive sentences. In the second stage, a sequence-to-sequence model provides inclusive reformulations of non-inclusive sentences.

Data Collection and Annotation. Inclusive language experts first defined detailed language criteria for inclusiveness specific to the Italian language. Then, they collected and annotated approximately 10,000 sentences labelled as *inclusive*, *not-inclusive*, and *neutral* (i.e., sentences are neutral when their content is not related to any inclusivity issues), and more than 4,500 non-inclusive sentence pairs with the corresponding inclusive reformulation.

Models' Training. We fine-tuned the classification and the reformulation models integrated into INCLUSIVELY on the collected corpus. The classification model leverages the language understanding capabilities offered by transformer-based architectures to identify whether the sentences include non-inclusive expressions. The classifier achieves 0.88 F1 score in classifying *inclusive*, *not-inclusive*, and *neutral* sentences. The reformulation model leverages language-specific encoder-decoder architectures [4,9]. It takes in a non-inclusive sentence and generates a new, more inclusive sentence as output. The reformulation model achieved 80.1 in the BLEU and 87.47 in the Rouge-2 scores [3]. Linguistic experts validated both models before being integrated into the tool.

---

[1] In compliance with the current privacy regulations.

[2] The code is available at https://github.com/MorenoLaQuatra/inclusively-demo.

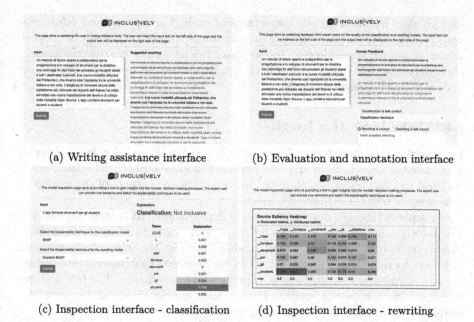

(a) Writing assistance interface

(b) Evaluation and annotation interface

(c) Inspection interface - classification

(d) Inspection interface - rewriting

Fig. 1. Screenshots of the INCLUSIVELY tool, showing the writing assistance interface (a), the evaluation and annotation interface (b), and the model inspection interface (c and d). (Color figure online)

2.1 Writing Assistance Interface

The INCLUSIVELY tool provides end-users with a user-friendly interface for inclusive writing assistance. The interface allows users to input a piece of text into a text box, get feedback on the inclusivity of the input, and, eventually, a reformulated text version annotated at the sentence level. Figure 1a shows a screenshot of the provided interface. It color-codes each sentence in the text as either *non-inclusive* (**red**), *inclusive* (**green**), or *neutral* (**black**) based on the outputs of the classification model. The *non-inclusive* sentences, reported crossed out in red (e.g., ~~gli studenti~~), are also followed by the generated reformulation in green (e.g., la componente studentesca). This color-coded system allows users to easily identify which sentences may need to be rephrased and which ones are already inclusive or neutral to inclusivity issues.

2.2 Evaluation and Annotation Interface

The *evaluation and annotation interface* is designed for expert users to provide feedback on the classification accuracy and reformulation quality of INCLUSIVELY. Figure 1b shows an example of the interface. It reports the model's output divided sentence-per-sentence, with the corresponding classification and suggested reformulation, color-coded to indicate inclusivity. Expert users can then provide feedback on the correctness of each classification and reformulation. If necessary, they can use the dropdown menus and text boxes to propose human-generated annotations. That feedback can be used to improve the models' performance and to integrate feedback in a reinforcement learning with human feedback (RLHF) fashion [12].

2.3   Model Inspection Interface

The model inspection interface included in INCLUSIVELY provides detailed explanations of the classification and reformulation models' outputs. This interface is designed for data scientists interested in inspecting the outputs of the models to gain insights into the AI model decisions.

To achieve this, INCLUSIVELY exploits explainability techniques [5,7,10,11]. It currently employs the `ferret` [2] library, which integrates multiple explainability algorithms for classification models (see Fig. 1c). The interface allows end-users to understand which tokens in the sentence have mainly determined the inclusiveness/non-inclusiveness/neutrality of the sentence. The token scores rate the influence on the predicted class. Such explanations can be useful for double-checking automatic sentence classification.

INCLUSIVELY also integrates the `inseq` [8] library which contains several explainability techniques for sequence-to-sequence models. It generates visualizations of the attribution scores (see Fig. 1d). The interface displays the attribution scores between the tokens of the source and target sentences, allowing the end-user to understand whether the model has focused on the correct portion of the input to produce each part of the sentence reformulation.

3   Conclusions and Future Works

We introduced INCLUSIVELY, a deep learning-based writing assistant tool for creating more inclusive text. The tool relies on a cascade of two deep learning models that classify the inclusiveness of arbitrary sentences and provide alternatives, more inclusive reformulations for non-inclusive ones. INCLUSIVELY exhibits three user-friendly interfaces aimed to facilitate the process of writing inclusive texts and provide feedback to improve the models' performance.

Currently, INCLUSIVELY supports the Italian language, whereas the model for two other Romance languages, i.e., French and Spanish, will be released soon. Beyond offering multilingual writing assistance, we plan to conduct a large-scale evaluation of the model's performance.

Acknowledgement. We thank Prof. Rachele Raus and Prof. Michela Tonti for their valuable work in defining the linguistic criteria for inclusivity and creating the corpus of Italian administrative documents.

References

1. Attanasio, G., et al.: E-MIMIC: empowering multilingual inclusive communication. In: 2021 IEEE International Conference on Big Data (Big Data), pp. 4227–4234 (2021). https://doi.org/10.1109/BigData52589.2021.9671868
2. Attanasio, G., Pastor, E., Di Bonaventura, C., Nozza, D.: ferret: a framework for benchmarking explainers on transformers. In: Proceedings of the 17th Conference of the European Chapter of the Association for Computational Linguistics: System Demonstrations, Dubrovnik, Croatia, pp. 256–266. Association for Computational Linguistics (2023). https://aclanthology.org/2023.eacl-demo.29
3. El-Kassas, W.S., Salama, C.R., Rafea, A.A., Mohamed, H.K.: Automatic text summarization: a comprehensive survey. Expert Syst. Appl. **165**, 113679 (2021). https://doi.org/10.1016/j.eswa.2020.113679. https://www.sciencedirect.com/science/article/pii/S0957417420305030
4. La Quatra, M., Cagliero, L.: BART-IT: an efficient sequence-to-sequence model for Italian text summarization. Future Internet **15**(1) (2023). https://doi.org/10.3390/fi15010015. https://www.mdpi.com/1999-5903/15/1/15
5. Lundberg, S.M., Lee, S.I.: A unified approach to interpreting model predictions. In: Advances in Neural Information Processing Systems, vol. 30 (2017)
6. Raus, R., et al.: L'analyse du discours et l'intelligence artificielle pour réaliser une écriture inclusive: le projet emimic. In: SHS Web Conference, vol. 138, p. 01007 (2022). https://doi.org/10.1051/shsconf/202213801007
7. Ribeiro, M.T., Singh, S., Guestrin, C.: "why should i trust you?": explaining the predictions of any classifier. In: Proceedings of the 2016 Conference of the North American Chapter of the Association for Computational Linguistics: Demonstrations, pp. 97–101 (2016)
8. Sarti, G., Feldhus, N., Sickert, L., van der Wal, O.: Inseq: an interpretability toolkit for sequence generation models. arXiv abs/2302.13942 (2023). https://arxiv.org/abs/2302.13942
9. Sarti, G., Nissim, M.: IT5: large-scale text-to-text pretraining for Italian language understanding and generation. arXiv preprint arXiv:2203.03759 (2022)
10. Sundararajan, M., Taly, A., Yan, Q.: Axiomatic attribution for deep networks. In: International Conference on Machine Learning, pp. 3319–3328. PMLR (2017)
11. Ventura, F., Greco, S., Apiletti, D., Cerquitelli, T.: Trusting deep learning natural-language models via local and global explanations. Knowl. Inf. Syst. **64**(7), 1863–1907 (2022). https://doi.org/10.1007/s10115-022-01690-9
12. Ziegler, D.M., et al.: Fine-tuning language models from human preferences. arXiv preprint arXiv:1909.08593 (2019)

A Risk Prediction Framework to Optimize Remote Patient Monitoring Following Cardiothoracic Surgery

Ricardo Santos[1,2](✉)(iD), Bruno Ribeiro[1], Pedro Dias[3,4], Isabel Curioso[1], Pedro Madeira[1], Federico Guede-Fernández[3,4], Jorge Santos[4,5], Pedro Coelho[4,5], Inês Sousa[1], and Ana Londral[3,4]

[1] Associação Fraunhofer Portugal Research, Porto, Portugal
ricardo.santos@fraunhofer.pt
[2] LIBPhys-UNL, NOVA School of Science and Technology, Caparica, Portugal
[3] Value for Health CoLAB, Lisboa, Portugal
[4] Comprehensive Health Research Center, NOVA Medical School, Lisboa, Portugal
[5] Hospital de Santa Marta, Centro Hospitalar Universitário Lisboa Central, Lisbon, Portugal

Abstract. Remote Patient Monitoring (RPM) in cardiac surgery can become valuable for clinicians to follow patients post-discharge closely. However, these services require additional and frequently limited human and technical resources. We present the CardioFollow.AI Framework, a decision support system to assist doctors in selecting patients to be monitored remotely. Currently supporting a clinical trial, it leverages a Machine Learning model to predict the risk of post-discharge complications. Interpretable assessments are included so that clinicians can evaluate individual predictions. Additionally, the user-friendly interface of the CardioFollow.AI Framework enhances the follow-up of discharged patients by granting access to centralised information. This paper outlines the design and implementation of the CardioFollow.AI Framework and its potential impact on improving personalised patient careq.

Keywords: Machine Learning · Decision Support Systems · Remote Patient Monitoring · Cardiothoracic Surgery

1 Introduction

Despite the technological progress in Cardiothoracic Surgery (CS), post-discharge complications are still common, with readmission rates of 13% to 17% in the first month [10,17], and up to 30% in the first year [4,6] after the intervention. Ergo, economic costs arise and, more importantly, long-term survival decreases [15,18].

Remote Patient Monitoring (RPM) may enhance surgical outcomes by enabling an efficient detection of complications [8,16]. CS risk prediction models can aid clinicians in identifying patients who would benefit most from RPM, and prompt an efficient distribution of limited resources.

© The Author(s), under exclusive license to Springer Nature Switzerland AG 2023
G. De Francisci Morales et al. (Eds.): ECML PKDD 2023, LNAI 14175, pp. 366–371, 2023.
https://doi.org/10.1007/978-3-031-43430-3_32

Several risk prediction models have been proposed. However, most were are limited to specific outcomes within 30 days post-surgery, from the traditional EuroSCORE and STS scores [14, 19, 20], to more recent Machine Learning (ML) approaches [1, 7, 13]. To efficiently allocate RPM resources to higher-risk patients, an extended prediction interval and a broader range of complications are needed.

This work addresses the need for tools to streamline the allocation and unlock the potential of RPM resources, by proposing an innovative ML-powered framework for complication risk evaluation and remote patient management.

2   CardioFollow.AI Framework

This platform is designed to catalyse an efficient allocation of follow-up RPM resources to high-risk patients. Clinicians interact with this system through a web-hosted interface, to visualise patient information, including individual post-discharge ML-based risk predictions. Figure 1 represents the proposed system. A web-hosted platform provides interactive functionalities, including data insertion and results evaluation. The AI framework processes data received through HTTP requests based on representational state transfer (REST) and returns interpretable predictions on the risk of post-surgery complications.

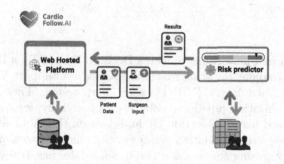

Fig. 1. Overview of the CardioFollow.AI framework.

The video available at https://youtu.be/ob6pqzHmVlw contains a detailed description of the functionalities of the platform, in the context of an ongoing clinical trial designed to clarify the benefits of RPM [2]. In this trial, the system is used in the weekly selection of patients to receive RPM equipment at discharge, including a smartphone, a scale, a sphygmomanometer, and a smartband. These devices continuously collect information on the health status of the patient, which is available to the physicians at all times through CardioFollow.AI's web platform, facilitating patients' follow-up.

2.1   Risk Prediction

Powered by an ML classifier, the risk prediction module receives data associated with an individual patient and returns: (i) a prediction both in a probabilistic (likelihood of a post-discharge complication) and a binary (high or low risk) format, and (ii) estimations of impact for each variable in achieving that prediction.

The predictive model used was trained on a binary classification task, where the positive class refers to patients that suffered a complication up to 90 days post-discharge. This horizon was selected as opposed to the common target of 30 days post-surgery, as the RPM service lasts for three months. The database used consisted of anonymised tabular data with information collected prior to, during, and after CS procedures, occurring from 2008 to 2019 in the CS department of Hospital de Santa Marta (Lisbon, Portugal). Data collection was approved by the hospital's ethical committee (INV 303) in conformity with the Declaration of Helsinki. The dataset was divided into train and test (Test A) through a 70/30% grouped stratified split. Data from the most recent year, 2019, formed a second test set (Test B). Table 1 presents a quick description of these datasets.

Table 1. Sample distributions of the Train, Test A, Test B and complete dataset.

	Train (2008-18)	Test A (2008-18)	Test B (2019)	Total
No. Samples	3 479	667	1 479	5 625
No. Positives	262	49	99	410
% Positives	7.5	7.3	6.7	7.3

To achieve a well-performing model, a Decision Tree (DT), a Random Forest (RF), a Light Gradient Boosting Machine (LGBM), a Support Vector Machine (SVM), and a Naive-Bayes (NB) classifier were tested. These were trained through an optimisation pipeline involving grid search hyperparameter tuning, permutation-based feature selection [3], and decision threshold adjustment [21]. A 5-fold grouped cross-validation strategy was followed, to avoid overfitting. Moreover, in optimising the decision threshold, a false negative was considered to have a two times higher cost than a false positive, according to clinicians.

The best-performing model, an RF, was selected according to the Area Under the Receiver Operating Characteristic Curve (AUROC), achieving an average of **72±2%** across the five training folds. When tested against Test A, the measured performance was **70%** and **66%**, for the AUROC and Sensitivity, respectively. In Test B, the performance dropped to **65%** AUROC and **52%** Sensitivity, which suggests the presence of data drift. Nevertheless, these results were considered satisfactory by the clinical team, given the challenging task (multiple types of complications to capture across a longer time horizon, when compared to the literature [1,7,13,14,19]), and the severe imbalance of the dataset (Table 1).

The impact of each feature is given by the Shapley values [9], computed through the TreeExplainer module [11] of the SHAP library [12]. This information is sent to the web-hosted interface with the prediction it refers to.

2.2   Web Hosted Platform

The second key element is the web platform. Developed using Django [5] and hosted on a cloud server, it was designed to gather and display data at all times. In-hospital patient information can be consulted along with the risk predictions and explanations, to help identify patients who would benefit from receiving RPM technology. Figure 2 shows the information available for a certain patient.

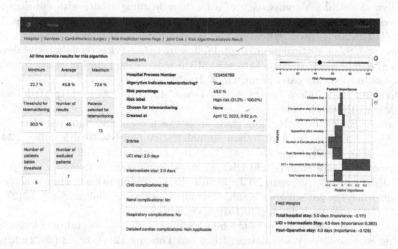

Fig. 2. Interpretable risk prediction information presented to the clinicians.

Additionally, the web platform receives RPM patient data daily, including measures such as heart rate and blood pressure, but also photos of the surgical wound and answers to questionnaires regarding common symptoms. All this data is automatically displayed, analysed, and used to trigger alerts if the values are outside clinically defined thresholds. Beyond this, the platform allows the clinical team to (i) write notes regarding the patient's status, (ii) prescribe and manage patient medication, and (iii) send health literacy messages to the patients.

3   Conclusion

The CardioFollow.AI Framework is a promising solution to optimise the allocation of limited RPM resources in CS. By leveraging an ML predictive model, our framework provides clinicians with interpretable predictions of postoperative complications risk, contributing to an informed decision-making process in selecting patients for RPM. Moreover, the user-friendly interface enables efficient management of remote monitoring data, paving the way to improve patient outcomes and reduce the burden on healthcare institutions. Future research should focus on refining the predictive model, incorporating the final results from the ongoing clinical trial, and scaling this framework to other surgical domains.

Acknowledgements. This work refers to the project "CardioFollow.AI: An intelligent system to improve patients' safety and remote surveillance in follow-up for cardiothoracic surgery", and is supported by 'FCT - Portuguese Foundation for Science and Technology, I.P.', with the reference DSAIPA/AI/0094/2020.

References

1. Allyn, J., et al.: A comparison of a machine learning model with euroscore ii in predicting mortality after elective cardiac surgery: a decision curve analysis. PLoS ONE **12** (2017). https://doi.org/10.1371/journal.pone.0169772

2. Azevedo, S., et al.: Scaling-up digital follow-up care services: collaborative development and implementation of remote patient monitoring pilot initiatives to increase access to follow-up care. Front. Digit. Health **4** (2022)

3. Breiman, L.: Random forests. Mach. Learn. **45**, 5–32 (2001). https://doi.org/10.1023/a:1010933404324

4. Caruso, E., Zadra, A.R.: The trade-off between costs and outcome after cardiac surgery. Evidence from an Italian administrative registry. Health Policy **124**(12), 1345–1353 (2020). https://doi.org/10.1016/j.healthpol.2020.09.005

5. Django Software Foundation: Django. https://djangoproject.com

6. Efthymiou, C.A., O'regan, D.J.: Postdischarge complications: what exactly happens when the patient goes home? Interact. Cardiovasc. Thorac. Surg. **12**(2), 130–134 (2011). https://doi.org/10.1510/icvts.2010.249474

7. Fan, Y., et al. Development of machine learning models for mortality risk prediction after cardiac surgery. Cardiovasc. Diagnosis Therapy **12**(1), 12–23 (2022). https://doi.org/10.21037/cdt-21-648

8. Farias, F.A.C.d., Dagostini, C.M., Bicca, Y.d.A., Falavigna, V.F., Falavigna, A.: Remote patient monitoring: a systematic review. Telemedicine e-Health **26**(5), 576–583 (2020). https://doi.org/10.1089/tmj.2019.0066

9. Hart, S.: Shapley Value, pp. 210–216. Palgrave Macmillan UK, London (1989). https://doi.org/10.1007/978-1-349-20181-5_25

10. Khoury, H., et al.: Readmission following surgical aortic valve replacement in the United States. Ann. Thorac. Surg. **110**(3), 849–855 (2020). https://doi.org/10.1016/j.athoracsur.2019.11.058

11. Lundberg, S.M., et al.: From local explanations to global understanding with explainable AI for trees. Nat. Mach. Intell. **2**(1), 2522–5839 (2020). https://doi.org/10.1038/s42256-019-0138-9

12. Lundberg, S.M., Lee, S.I.: A unified approach to interpreting model predictions. In: Guyon, I., et al. (eds.) Advances in Neural Information Processing Systems, vol. 30, pp. 4765–4774. Curran Associates, Inc. (2017)

13. Mortazavi, B., et al.: Prediction of adverse events in patients undergoing major cardiovascular procedures. IEEE J. Biomed. Health Inform. **21**, 1719–1729 (2017). https://doi.org/10.1109/JBHI.2017.2675340

14. Nashef, S.A.M., et al.: Euroscore ii. Eur. J. Cardio-thoracic Surg. Off. J. Eur. Assoc. Cardio-thoracic Surg. **41**(4), 734–44 (2012). https://doi.org/10.1093/ejcts/ezs043

15. Pahwa, S., et al.: Impact of postoperative complications after cardiac surgery on long-term survival. J. Card. Surg. **36**, 2045–2052 (2021). https://doi.org/10.1111/jocs.15471

16. Park, D.K., et al.: Telecare system for cardiac surgery patients: implementation and effectiveness. Healthc. Inform. Res. **17**, 93–100 (2011). https://doi.org/10. 4258/hir.2011.17.2.93

17. Sanchez, C.E., et al.: Predictors and risk calculator of early unplanned hospital readmission following contemporary self-expanding transcatheter aortic valve replacement from the STS/ACC TVT-registry. Cardiovasc. Revascularization Med. Including Mol. Interventions **21**(3), 263–270 (2020). https://doi.org/10.1016/j. carrev.2019.05.032

18. Seese, L.M., et al.: The impact of major postoperative complications on long-term survival after cardiac surgery. Ann. Thorac. Surg. **110**(1), 128–135 (2019). https:// doi.org/10.1016/j.athoracsur.2019.09.100

19. Shahian, D.M., et al.: The society of thoracic surgeons 2018 adult cardiac surgery risk models: part 1-background, design considerations, and model development. Ann. Thorac. Surg. **105**(5), 1411–1418 (2018). https://doi.org/10.1016/j. athoracsur.2018.03.002

20. Sullivan, P., Wallach, J.D., Ioannidis, J.P.A.: Meta-analysis comparing established risk prediction models (euroscore ii, STS score, and ACEF score) for perioperative mortality during cardiac surgery. Am. J. Cardiol. **118**(10), 1574–1582 (2016). https://doi.org/10.1016/j.amjcard.2016.08.024

21. Zhao, H.: Instance weighting versus threshold adjusting for cost-sensitive classification. Knowl. Inf. Syst. **15**, 321–334 (2008). https://doi.org/10.1007/s10115-007-0079-1

MWPRanker: An Expression Similarity Based Math Word Problem Retriever

Mayank Goel[1], V. Venktesh[2(✉)], and Vikram Goyal[2]

[1] NSUT, Delhi, India
mayank.co19@nsut.ac.in
[2] Indraprastha Institute of Information Technology, Delhi, India
{venkteshv,vikram}@iiitd.ac.in

Abstract. Math Word Problems (MWPs) in online assessments help test the ability of the learner to make critical inferences by interpreting the linguistic information in them. To test the mathematical reasoning capabilities of the learners, sometimes the problem is rephrased or the thematic setting of the original MWP is changed. Since manual identification of MWPs with similar problem models is cumbersome, we propose a tool in this work for MWP retrieval. We propose a hybrid approach to retrieve similar MWPs with the same problem model. In our work, the problem model refers to the sequence of operations to be performed to arrive at the solution. We demonstrate that our tool is useful for the mentioned tasks and better than semantic similarity-based approaches, which fail to capture the arithmetic and logical sequence of the MWPs. A demo of the tool can be found at https://www.youtube.com/watch?v=gSQWP3chFIs.

1 Introduction

Math Word Problems (MWPs) are intriguing as they require one to decipher the problem model and operators from the given problem statement. Studies have shown that users lacking this ability often commit mistakes when presented with new problems [12]. It has been demonstrated that solving paraphrased versions of the original problem might aid in better learning to make critical inferences from varying linguistic information [5]. However, manual curation of such problems is cumbersome. Hence, we design a tool in this work to recommend problems with similar algebraic expressions as the input MWP.

Numerous works have tackled the automated solving of Math Word Problems (MWPs) task [8,9,14]. Recently, large language models (LLMs) have demonstrated multi-step reasoning ability to solve MWPs [13] among other tasks. However, the authors, in their work [1], demonstrate that LLMs fail when problems contain certain linguistic variations. However, very few works have dealt with the retrieval of MWPs. Certain works like *Recall and Learn* [3] leverage the task of retrieving analogous problems to solve MWPs using semantic similarity. However, they may wrongly recommend problems with different algebraic operations. For instance, "John had 5 apples, and Mary had 6 oranges. Find the total number of fruits" would be considered similar to "John had 5 apples, and Mary had twice as many oranges after selling 2 of them.

G. De Francisci Morales et al. (Eds.): ECML PKDD 2023, LNAI 14175, pp. 372–377, 2023.
https://doi.org/10.1007/978-3-031-43430-3_33

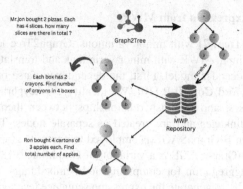

Fig. 1. MWPRanker system pipeline

Find the total number of fruits". Though these MWPs look similar, the second MWP requires additional multiplication and subtraction operation.

An overview of the workflow of the proposed system is shown in Fig. 1. The core contributions of our work are:

- We propose a hybrid approach to retrieve similar Math Word Problems based on expression tree similarity.
- The code and data can be found at https://github.com/goelm08/MWP-ranker

2 System Design

In this section, we describe the proposed system for identifying similar Math Word Problems for a given input. Given a corpus of MWPs $P = \{p_1, p_2....p_n\}$ and a new input MWP sequence $p_{new} = w_1, w_2...w_n$, the goal is to recommend exact duplicate problems p_{dup} based on expression similarity.

In our proposed pipeline, two problems could be similar if they are paraphrased versions of each other but evaluate the same algebraic expression. We propose a hybrid pipeline *MWPRanker* which is efficient for similar MWP retrieval. The pipeline consists of the following stages.

- The input MWP p_{new} is parsed into an algebraic expression a_{new} using the neural expression generator *Graph2Tree*. We derive an expression tree from the resulting expression.
- We devise a tree matching algorithm to match the resulting tree with other expression trees in the repository. The MWPs corresponding to matching expressions are returned to the user. The expressions trees are derived and indexed for efficient retrieval at inference time. This is a one time activity as this is the repository our pipeline performs search on.

2.1   Generating Expression from MWPs

We employ Graph2Tree [7] with minor variations. Graph2Tree leverages the dependency graph of the input MWP with minor variations and translates it to an algebraic expression using a decoder model. First, the dependency parse of the input MWP is obtained using Stanford CoreNLP [10]. We identify the keyphrases in the sentence, such as noun phrases, and establish relationships between them. The relationships indicate important linkages and are created as separate nodes. This yields a heterogeneous graph. Then BiGraphSAGE is employed to compute graph-based contextualized embeddings. BiGraphSAGE is a variation of GraphSAGE [2], including forward and reverse mode aggregation for computing node embeddings. Then a Bi-LSTM is employed as a decoder to generate the expression sequence leveraging the node embeddings from the graph. The decoder at inference time yields an algebraic expression y_{exp} which is sent to the tree generator and matching module for retrieving similar MWPs. We adapt and modify the implementation of Graph2Tree in MWPToolkit [6] with same hyperparameters.

2.2   Tree Matching and Retrieval

We derive a postfix expression and convert it to an expression tree for clear operator precedence. $t_{exp} = f_{tree}(y_{exp})$. We replace numbers that represent variables with variable names. We replace constant values with the expression "<CONSTANT>" The generated expression tree is compared with other expression trees $T_{exp} = \{t_{exp}^1 .... t_{exp}^n\}$ in the MWP repository and the top-k problems are recommended to the user (Fig. 2).

The matching algorithm works as follows:

- The expression trees are matched pairwise through postorder traversal.
- If the node in a tree contains an operator, the other tree must contain the same operator in the same place.
- In the same way, variable nodes must match. If a variable is encountered, the corresponding node in the other tree should also be a variable. When encountering a constant, we just check if the corresponding node in the other tree also contains the same placeholder. When a match is encountered, the corresponding natural language form of the MWP from the repository is returned.

3   Demonstration

We train the models using PyTorch. The models are served through a Flask API as backend, and UI is designed using Streamlit[1]. We employ the MAWPS [4] and ASDIV-a [11] datasets, which contains algebraic word problems of varying complexity curated from various websites. We filter out ungrammatical MWPs, yielding 1873 in MAWPS and 1844 train samples in ASDIV-a.

---

[1] https://streamlit.io/.

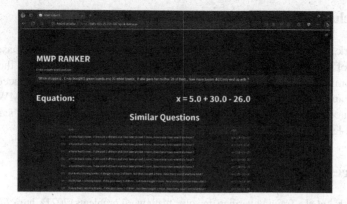

Fig. 2. MScreenshot of MWPRanker

Table 1. Performance Evaluation for MWP Similarity Detection

Dataset	Method	Accuracy (%)
MAWPS [4]	*MWPRanker*	**83.76**
	VectorSim [3]	61.54
ASDIV-a [11]	*MWPRanker*	**85.41**
	VectorSim [3]	42.71

3.1 Qualitative Analysis

We evaluated the tool with 19 graduate level users. The interface and an example are shown in a screenshot in Fig. 2. We can observe from recommended results that all MWPs have the same sequence of algebraic operations. The overall feedback in terms of ease of use and relevance of results was positive. Around **94%** of the users found the tool easy to use and **84%** found the tool to produce relevant results. About **15.8%** of the users found the results to be relevant, with minor errors. Overall, all users rated that they would recommend the tool to the academicians.

3.2 Quantitative Analysis

For quantitative analysis, we collect 40 samples from a test set of MAWPS and ASDIV-a and use them as queries to retrieve top 3 questions from an MWP repository curated from the mentioned data sources. We present them to two independent researchers and asked them to annotate a recommendation as 1 if it is a similar (duplicate) MWP, else 0. We use the vector based semantic similarity based model proposed in [3] as a baseline. We observed a reasonable level of agreement between the annotators, with a Cohen's kappa of **0.629**. From Table 1, we observe that the proposed MWPRanker tool outperforms the semantic similarity based approach by a significant margin.

The quality of retrieval depends on the quality of algebraic expression generated by the neural expression generator. To generate better questions, complexity based attributes are necessary for more fine-grained retrieval, which are not currently supported by MWPRanker.

4   Conclusion

In this work, we propose a new task of retrieving Math Word Problems based on the similarity of the algebraic expression. We develop and deploy a tool for the same to aid in recommending more practice questions. In the future, for ease of access to the tool, we plan to explore automated search completion and the usage of MWPRanker for automated problem-solving. This module can also be used to retrieve samples for In-Context learning in language models.

References

1. Cobbe, K., et al.: Training verifiers to solve math word problems (2021). https://doi.org/10.48550/ARXIV.2110.14168. https://arxiv.org/abs/2110.14168
2. Hamilton, W.L., Ying, R., Leskovec, J.: Inductive representation learning on large graphs (2017). https://doi.org/10.48550/ARXIV.1706.02216. https://arxiv.org/abs/1706.02216
3. Huang, S., Wang, J., Xu, J., Cao, D., Yang, M.: Recall and learn: a memory-augmented solver for math word problems. In: Findings of the Association for Computational Linguistics: EMNLP 2021, pp. 786–796. Association for Computational Linguistics, Punta Cana, Dominican Republic, November 2021. https://doi.org/10.18653/v1/2021.findings-emnlp.68. https://aclanthology.org/2021.findings-emnlp.68
4. Konćel-Kedziorski, R., Roy, S., Amini, A., Kushman, N., Hajishirzi, H.: MAWPS: a math word-problem repository. In: Proceedings of the 2016 Conference of the North American Chapter of the Association for Computational Linguistics: Human Language Technologies, pp. 1152–1157. Association for Computational Linguistics, San Diego, California, June 2016. https://doi.org/10.18653/v1/N16-1136. https://aclanthology.org/N16-1136
5. Kong, J., Swanson, H.: The effects of a paraphrasing intervention on word problem-solving accuracy of English learners at risk of mathematic disabilities. Learn. Disabil. Q. **42**, 073194871880665 (2018). https://doi.org/10.1177/0731948718806659
6. Lan, Y., et al.: MWPToolkit: an open-source framework for deep learning-based math word problem solvers (2021)
7. Li, S., Wu, L., Feng, S., Xu, F., Xu, F., Zhong, S.: Graph-to-tree neural networks for learning structured input-output translation with applications to semantic parsing and math word problem (2020). https://doi.org/10.48550/ARXIV.2004.13781. https://arxiv.org/abs/2004.13781
8. Li, Z., et al.: Seeking patterns, not just memorizing procedures: contrastive learning for solving math word problems (2021). https://doi.org/10.48550/ARXIV.2110.08464. https://arxiv.org/abs/2110.08464
9. Liang, C.C., Wong, Y.S., Lin, Y.C., Su, K.Y.: A meaning-based statistical English math word problem solver. In: Proceedings of the 2018 Conference of the North American Chapter of the Association for Computational Linguistics: Human Language Technologies, Volume 1 (Long Papers), pp. 652–662. Association for Computational Linguistics, New Orleans, Louisiana, June 2018. https://doi.org/10.18653/v1/N18-1060. https://aclanthology.org/N18-1060
10. Manning, C., Surdeanu, M., Bauer, J., Finkel, J., Bethard, S., McClosky, D.: The Stanford CoreNLP natural language processing toolkit. In: Proceedings of 52nd Annual Meeting of the Association for Computational Linguistics: System Demonstrations, pp. 55–60. Association for Computational Linguistics, Baltimore, Maryland, June 2014. https://doi.org/10.3115/v1/P14-5010. https://aclanthology.org/P14-5010

11. Miao, S.Y., Liang, C.C., Su, K.Y.: A diverse corpus for evaluating and developing English math word problem solvers (2021)
12. Nathan, M.J., Kintsch, W., Young, E.: A theory of algebra-word-problem comprehension and its implications for the design of learning environments. Cogn. Instr. **9**(4), 329–389 (1992). https://doi.org/10.1207/s1532690xci0904_2
13. Shridhar, K., Stolfo, A., Sachan, M.: Distilling multi-step reasoning capabilities of large language models into smaller models via semantic decompositions (2022). https://doi.org/10.48550/ARXIV.2212.00193. https://arxiv.org/abs/2212.00193
14. Wu, Q., Zhang, Q., Wei, Z., Huang, X.: Math word problem solving with explicit numerical values. In: Proceedings of the 59th Annual Meeting of the Association for Computational Linguistics and the 11th International Joint Conference on Natural Language Processing (Volume 1: Long Papers), pp. 5859–5869. Association for Computational Linguistics, Online, August 2021. https://doi.org/10.18653/v1/2021.acl-long.455. https://aclanthology.org/2021.acl-long.455

Correction to: Continually Learning Out-of-Distribution Spatiotemporal Data for Robust Energy Forecasting

Arian Prabowo⬤, Kaixuan Chen, Hao Xue⬤,
Subbu Sethuvenkatraman⬤, and Flora D. Salim⬤

Correction to:
Chapter 1 in: G. De Francisci Morales et al. (Eds.): *Machine Learning and Knowledge Discovery in Databases: Applied Data Science and Demo Track,* **LNAI 14175,**
https://doi.org/10.1007/978-3-031-43430-3_1

The originally published version of the chapter 1 contains unintentional errors in the table 3 and a small punctuation error in the section 6.3. These errors have been corrected.

The updated version of this chapter can be found at
https://doi.org/10.1007/978-3-031-43430-3_1

Table 3. Comparing the performance of different algorithm with or without continual learning (CL). The metric used is MAE. Results are average over 10 runs with different random seed. The standard deviation is shown.

	dataset	FSNet (no CL)	FSNet	TCN (no CL)	OGD	ER	DER++
Pre-Lockdown	BC1	0.3703	**0.1583**	0.3668	0.2056	0.1820	0.1696
		±0.0607	±0.0280	±0.0379	±0.0413	±0.0217	±0.0130
	BC2	0.6272	**0.1712**	0.5176	0.2465	0.2322	0.2272
		±0.0914	±0.0063	±0.0607	±0.0105	±0.0056	±0.0062
	BC3	0.6750	**0.2462**	0.6500	0.3308	0.2862	0.2726
		±0.0638	±0.0151	±0.0698	±0.0812	±0.0432	±0.0334
	BC4	1.0018	**0.2802**	1.1236	0.3910	0.3511	0.3408
		±0.1053	±0.0312	±0.1040	±0.0520	±0.0323	±0.0210
Post-Lockdown	BC1	0.4537	**0.1429**	0.4179	0.1797	0.1589	0.1482
		±0.0517	±0.0275	±0.0443	±0.0342	±0.0168	±0.0094
	BC2	0.6506	**0.1628**	0.5209	0.2313	0.2188	0.2148
		±0.0994	±0.0057	±0.0535	±0.0085	±0.0060	±0.0068
	BC3	0.7168	**0.2255**	0.7083	0.3014	0.2636	0.2518
		±0.0632	±0.0145	±0.0793	±0.0709	±0.0373	±0.0286
	BC4	1.8415	**0.3314**	1.8307	0.4496	0.4162	0.4043
		±0.2765	±0.0520	±0.2319	±0.0643	±0.0475	±0.0338

Author Index

G. De Francisci Morales et al. (Eds.): ECML PKDD 2023, LNAI 14175, pp. 379–381, 2023.
https://doi.org/10.1007/978-3-031-43430-3

Printed in the United States
by Baker & Taylor Publisher Services